# SIMPLE, EASY TO UNDERSTAND

Here, in one volume, are the best and newest ideas in modern homemaking to save you time, effort and money in running your household. They tell you how to decorate your home, how to care for your garden, how to paint, make repairs, mend, shop, entertain, take care of medical emergencies and keep your family finances straight.

Prepared simply and concisely, this compact 12-manuals-in-1 library is written in easy-to-understand language, with step-by-step instructions. There are over 1,000 explanatory illustrations and scores of charts and tables. A special index simplifies the finding of solutions to your problems.

With **The Household Encyclopedia** as your guide, you can make your home happier, healthier and more attractive.

*Books by N. H. and S. K. Mager*

The Complete Letter Writer
A Guide to Tropical Fish
The Office Encyclopedia

*Also by Sylvia K. Mager*

A Complete Guide to Home Sewing

*Also by N. H. Mager*

How to Work With Tools and Wood

Published by POCKET BOOKS

**This edition was produced exclusively for Cotter & Company, Chicago, Illinois, through the facilities of the Publishers Special Projects Office, The Benjamin Company, 485 Madison Avenue, New York, N.Y. 10022.**

# THE HOUSEHOLD ENCYCLOPEDIA

### What to Do—
### How to Do It

Twelve Big Manuals in One Big Volume

More Than 1,000 Helpful Hints on
How to Save Time, Effort, Energy and Money

A How-to-Do-It Dictionary on Every Household Subject

NEW REVISED AND ENLARGED EDITION

Compiled and Edited by

## N. H. and S. K. MAGER

PUBLISHED BY POCKET BOOKS NEW YORK

# THE HOUSEHOLD ENCYCLOPEDIA

POCKET BOOK edition published August, 1953
19 printings

Revised and Enlarged edition published October, 1966
16 printings

2nd Revised and Enlarged edition published June, 1973
3rd printing......................December, 1973

This original POCKET BOOK edition is an enlarged, revised and up-dated version of *The Household Encyclopedia*. It is printed from brand-new plates made from completely reset, clear, easy-to-read type. POCKET BOOK editions are published by POCKET BOOKS, a division of Simon & Schuster, Inc., 630 Fifth Avenue, New York, N.Y. 10020. Trademarks registered in the United States and other countries.

L

---

# INTRODUCTION AND ACKNOWLEDGMENTS

*The Pocket Household Encyclopedia* is designed to do two things: to tell you *what to do,* and to tell you *how to do it.* It covers every field of housekeeping and household management except the preparation and preservation of foods.

To cover so large a field in a single handy volume has required an immense amount of condensation. The editors have attempted to cover every common household problem with sufficient detail so that the ordinary homemaker will be able to solve the problems which come up, from the instructions given. What has been eliminated is the glamor and "sell" which usually surrounds such instructions.

A book like this necessarily cannot be the work of one person or two or even of a hundred. It is, essentially, the result of the experiences of thousands of men and women, through the years, in doing the hundreds of things that have to be done in running a house, and the experience of professional people who do the housekeeping chores and repairs for government institutions and establishments.

Much of the material contained in *The Pocket Household Encyclopedia* is the result of special studies made and published by various government agencies, particularly the Departments of Agriculture and Commerce and the Defense Department. These studies, representing, in aggregate, generations of study and compilation, have been culled, digested, and distilled to bring you the latest and most complete information available. A great deal of the material is drawn from the many articles which have appeared in newspapers and magazines. Another large portion is the result of special projects conducted by various trade associations and companies as a public service in the field of their own products.

The editors are particularly indebted to the following organizations for the use of material and for personal assistance:

The American Brass Company; American Dental Association; American Medical Association; American National Retail

Jewelers Association; The American Optometric Association; American Red Cross; Arco Publishing Co., Inc.; Armour and Company; Armstrong Cork Company; Baldwin-Hill Company; Barbara Bernie Associates; The Better Business Bureau of New York; Boy Scouts of America; Bureau of Home Nutrition, Department of Agriculture.

Cannon Mills, Inc.; Celanese Corporation of America; Cereal Institute, Inc.; Consumers' Research, Inc.; Consumers Union of U. S., Inc.; Council on Marriage Relations, Inc.; Dennison Manufacturing Co.; Department Store Economist; Drexel Furniture Co.; E. I. du Pont de Nemours & Company; Florists Telegraph Delivery Association; Frigidaire Division, General Motors Co.; Gemological Institute of America; General Electric Company; Home Life Insurance Company; The Consumer Education Library of the Household Finance Corporation.

Institute of Life Insurance; Jewelry Industry Council; Johns-Manville Sales Corporation; Godfrey Leeman Nurseries; Lennon Wall Paper Company; C. M. McCay, Prof. of Nutrition, Cornell University; Magee Carpet Company; Masback, Incorporated; Men's Tie Foundation; Metropolitan Life Insurance Co.; Milk Industry Foundation.

National-American Wholesale Grocers' Association; National Association of Bedding Manufacturers; National Association of Secondary-School Principals; National Board of Fire Underwriters; National Consumers Retail Council, Inc.; National Live Stock and Meat Board; National Paint, Varnish and Lacquer Association, Inc.; National Retail Furniture Association; *The New York Times;* New York *World-Telegram and Sun.*

Pepperell Manufacturing Co.; Plumbing and Heating Industries Bureau; Portland Cement Association; Poultry and Egg National Board; Wm. V. Schmidt Co., Inc.; F. Schumacher & Co.; The Sherwin-Williams Co.; Simon and Schuster, Inc., publishers (for material from *How to Win Friends and Influence People,* copyright 1936 by Dale Carnegie); Society of American Florists; Switzerland Cheese Association, Inc.

Tanners Council of America; Underwriters' Laboratories, Inc.; Israel Unterman; Wallpaper Institute, Inc.; Waverly Fabrics Division of F. Schumacher & Co.; Western Union Telegraph Co.; Westinghouse Electric Co.; and *The World Almanac.*

# CONTENTS

vii

## BOOK III. Lawn and Garden Guide .................................. 174

## BOOK IV. Home Painting Guide ...................................... 250

# CONTENTS

# BOOK I

# Guide to Good Housekeeping

**The Cleaning Plan:** Every homemaker has a standard of cleanliness for her home. She may not be conscious of her standard, but if it is high she feels uncomfortable when her house is disordered or dirty. The pressure of preparing meals, doing the laundry, caring for children, or working at personal or professional interests outside the home may make it impossible to keep her home up to the standard she wishes to attain. Usually working out a definite but flexible plan and working system and checking on methods and equipment makes cleaning easier and simpler. Frequent light cleaning is the most economical of time, energy, cleaning supplies, and household surfaces. Time spent to experiment with systematic work schedules and better methods will help to increase leisure, relieve the mind of worry caused by the pressure of things to be done, and create a more restful, pleasant home. The homemaker with a schedule and sound methods is better equipped not only to do the work at hand, but to teach and guide her assistants, whether they are members of the family or paid employees. The objective is to make the job more interesting and less fatiguing by controlling it, rather than letting it control her.

Daily cleaning consists chiefly of dusting. In the bedroom, beds, which have been airing while the family is at breakfast, are made first. Then in all rooms, inside sills may be dusted, then furniture, wood floors, and finally rugs are cleaned. If a broom is used, upholstered furniture is brushed first and covered, then rugs swept, and finally floors, woodwork, and furniture dusted.

Weekly cleaning follows the same general procedure but is more thorough. Pictures and mirrors, light bulbs and lighting fixtures, closet floors, backs of furniture, and window shades and venetian blinds are dusted. Baseboards are brushed, and if much dirt has blown in, it may be advisable to wipe the floor and baseboard with a damp cloth. Furniture should be moved so that every inch of the floor is cleaned. Every other week, upholstered furniture is cleaned with a vacuum cleaner if possible. Mattresses are turned side for side one week and end for end the next. Light bulbs, enclosing globes, and diffusing bowls and shades in a few rooms are cleaned each week so that all are included once a month. The brushing of walls, wood trim, and draperies, and washing of windows, mirrors, and pictures may be rotated in the same manner.

Thorough cleaning is more like the old-fashioned housecleaning procedure. Some homemakers may find it easier to do a little along with the weekly cleaning; others may prefer to use the following procedure with one room each month.

Take down the curtains and draperies, brush them if they do not need washing, and lay them in another room. Remove window shades and brush them, or brush Venetian blinds and wipe them when necessary.

Brush the radiator. If there is a register, lift it out and brush it on a newspaper; clean the screen and the pipe. If the register needs washing, wipe it off with kerosene and dry it thoroughly with a clean cloth.

Remove the pictures. Brush the walls with a wall brush, beginning at the bottom and working up toward the ceiling, brushing it last. Dust hangs down and by lifting it up with the brush it will not be rubbed in and smear the walls. The wood trim may be brushed as one comes to it in cleaning the walls.

Clean the closet. Remove everything, brushing the walls and wood trim, and wiping the shelves and floor.

Dust picture frames. Wash the glasses over pictures, the mirrors, and windows. Wipe light bulbs, enclosing and diffusing bowls with damp cloth, and brush lamp shades.

Remove things from drawers and wipe them out; replace, or dust and turn the paper linings.

Dust and polish furniture. If the furniture is very dusty, another cloth should be used for polishing; waxed furniture will need only rubbing unless it is time to wash it and give it the yearly coat of fresh wax.

Turn the rug back and wipe under it. Clean the under side of the rug as well as the upper. Underlays may be cleaned on both sides with a vacuum cleaner, detaching the belt that revolves the brush if the cleaner has a brush; the brush will tear up the loose fibers. After the rug and floors are cleaned, place the furniture in order and hang the curtains and pictures.

In cleaning a bedroom the mattress and box springs should be brushed or vacuum-cleaned, and the bed made before the furniture is dusted. If a broom is used instead of a vacuum cleaner or carpet sweeper, the furniture should be dusted and polished last.

It takes less time and energy to continue one cleaning process as long as possible, such as dusting the rooms on one floor, then cleaning the rugs. Dropping one tool frequently to pick up another causes some nervous adjustment. For this reason, too, it is best to complete the one job and put the tools away before taking up another household task.

## CLEANING TOOLS

In general, well-selected good-quality tools pay for their extra cost in their efficiency and in the time and energy they save.

**Brooms:** Fiber brooms cost more than those of broomcorn, but last several times as long and are more satisfactory to use. A good broom has comparatively few split ends and these splits should be short. When stored, these brooms, like others should be hung or rested on the end of the handle. Tampico fiber brooms have about 4″ of tough vegetable fibers extending from a hardwood block.

The electric broom is a light vacuum device for cleaning carpets, drapes, upholstery, and hard-surface flooring. It is handier than a vacuum cleaner for everyday use.

**Brushes:** Brushes are useful because they tend to gather and hold dust instead of scattering it. To stop old brushes from shedding, apply lacquer to the base, with an oil can, then allow it to harden.

A few simple principles should be followed in the care of brushes. All of them should be washed frequently using warm water and soap, rinsing thoroughly in clear water, and shaking to straighten the bristles or fibers. Brushes twisted in wire should be hung to dry; those set in wood blocks should be dried with the bristle side down so water will not soak into the wood. All brushes should be hung on hooks when not in use.

FLOOR BRUSHES of the best quality for household use are made of grade-A horsehair, with full tufts stapled firmly in a

**BRUSHES FOR SPECIAL CLEANING JOBS:** (1) Bottle brush. (2) Bottle brush. (3) Dish mop. (4) Toilet brush. (5) Window brush. (6) Radiator brush. (7) Shoe dauber. (8) Shoe brush. (9) Clothes brush. (10) Fiber broom. (11) Feather duster. (12) Counter brush. (13) Barn broom. (14) Pot brush. (15) Bath tub brush. (16) Floor broom. (17) Waxer.

hardwood block. In most brushes the handle can be changed from one side of the block to the other each week so the hair will wear down evenly.

RADIATOR BRUSHES that have the greatest usefulness are long-handled, cylindrical in shape, and made of bristles twisted in rustless wire. Those tapered toward the end get into the corners with less manipulation; those with flared ends are somewhat more expensive. Upholstery brushes are made with bristles or hair. Venetian-blind brushes of the best quality are made of gray or white goat hair twisted in rustless wire. Toilet bowl brushes that are easiest to keep sanitary are made of stiff bristles or of Tampico fibers twisted in rustless wire, in either circle or ball shapes. Scrub brushes usually are made of Tampico fiber and are inexpensive. More durable brushes are made of palmetto fibers, but it may be more sanitary to use the Tampico fiber brushes and replace them when the fibers soften and mat.

POLISHING BRUSHES for use on waxed floors are of two types, the electric and the hand operated. Both have stiff vegetable fiber stock for polishing. Hand-polishing brushes have fibers set in heavy blocks weighing about 5 to 15 lbs.

The electric waxer and polisher is used on hard floors, for shampooing rugs, and for similar housecleaning jobs.

WAX APPLICATORS may be cotton yarns twisted in wire or lamb's wool which can be detached from a block for cleaning. The latter absorb less wax.

Mops: Mops should be washed in suds as often as necessary to keep them clean and sanitary, then rinsed and dried in the sun. Dry mops, including those of the "dustless" type, require washing. Mops should be hung by the handle when not in use. Wet mops come in a variety of styles. The cheapest, called yacht mops, have yarns wired around a handle. Some are devised so they may be wrung without putting the hands in water. Others have yarns held in a clamp. If stray ends of yarn are kept trimmed, baseboards are not so easily splashed. Some dry mops have a spring to facilitate dusting and shaking. Triangular mops are popular because they cover as large a floor space as the oval mops and are easier to push into corners.

Dusters, cloths, and sponges: Dusters may be made from old clothing or household fabrics. Pieces of fine, soft wool make the most satisfactory dusting cloths; next in usefulness are soft cotton, especially knitted materials, or cheesecloth and linen. Chamois is excellent for washing windows because it cleans and polishes at the same time. It is made of sheepskin, oil tanned. French chamois costs more than domestic of a like quality and size, but is heavier and more durable. The quality of chamois can be judged by the elasticity. Sponges are better than cloths for washing walls, woodwork, and upholstery. Natural sponges, the most satisfactory type for house cleaning, are available in many grades and sizes. Those called sheep's wool sponges are the best quality for household use, and next in desirability are velvet and yellow sponges. It is cheaper and more satisfactory to buy two small sponges than to buy one large one and cut it. Both chamois and sponges should be washed in lukewarm suds, thoroughly rinsed, as much moisture as possible squeezed out, and dried in the shade. A heavy thread or string run through sponges and tied at the ends makes it possible to hang them on hooks when drying or storing. Artificial sponges are also used for cleaning purposes, but are more expensive than natural sponges.

**Dustpans and pails:** Dustpans with long handles that eliminate stooping are the most desirable. It is desirable to have two pails for use in cleaning, one for water with soap and the other with clear water for rinsing. Small twin pails fastened together at the handle are the most convenient because both may be carried in one hand or set together on a stepladder. Galvanized-iron pails are the most durable.

**Vacuum cleaners:** A vacuum cleaner is one of the most useful household tools because it removes dust and litter without scattering. Suction, sweeping, and agitation are employed in the various types of vacuum cleaners to remove dirt. The straight-air cleaner depends largely on suction for dirt removal. The motor-driven-brush machine uses suction plus sweeping and agitation, and because of these other factors, the suction may be considerably lower than that used by the straight-air cleaner.

Non-electric vacuum cleaners resemble the electric type in appearance, except that there is no motor. The revolving brush in the nozzle and the fan are operated by the action of the wheels as the cleaner is pushed across the floor covering. The dirt is drawn into a bag similar to that of electric cleaners. It combines some of the suction of an electric cleaner with

**Portable Cleaner**

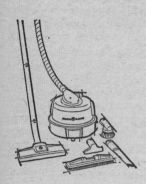

**Vacuum Cleaner**

**Shoe Polishers**

**Electric Toothbrush**

**Electric Floor Polisher**

the sweeping action of a carpet sweeper, and its cost lies between the two. Built-in vacuum systems have outlets in baseboards throughout the house and a tank in the basement.

Carpet sweepers: Carpet sweepers are useful in sweeping the dust and litter from floor coverings. Some are made to adjust automatically to carpet pile of various heights with a minimum of pressure. Unless the brush is kept clean, its efficiency is seriously impaired and the sweeper is harder to push. To remove string, hair, and ravelings without injuring the brush, it is better to clip them first with scissors. The brush should be wiped occasionally with a dry-cleaning fluid when it gets sticky from oil in the dust or wax on floors. The sweeper should be oiled regularly each month.

Carpet beaters: The beating of carpets and rugs is not recommended because it loosens the pile tufts and may injure the backing of the rug. However, in homes without vacuum cleaners where it is impossible to send floor coverings to a good cleaner once a year, it may be necessary to use a beater. Those made of rattan are less injurious to rugs than wire beaters. Rugs should be placed nap down on grass or snow, but should never be beaten while hung over a clothesline.

Pads: Nylon reinforced with abrasive mineral impregnated into the pad shows up as an aggressive, long-lasting cleaning and finishing material with many possible uses. The pad does such diverse jobs as cleaning floors and woodwork, scouring rust from garden tools, light sanding in furniture refinishing, and removing scum from sides and bottoms of boats and pools.

Cleaning baseboards, doors, and aluminum storm windows and doors are other applications. Wrapped around a sponge to provide a reservoir for water and to lessen the cut of the mineral, the pads can be used to wash walls. The pliable pads will also clean stainless-steel sinks and tubs, remove chipped or flaking paint, and restore shine to metal kitchen implements.

Nylon pads will not splinter or shred, and they resist snagging and tearing. They can be used in hot water, with detergents and most solvents, and can be rinsed easily for reuse. They also will not cut or scratch hands and fingernails.

## CLEANING SUPPLIES

Water: Water, especially warm water, is a good cleansing agent. Although it loosens dirt, it should always be used sparingly and wiped off at once. It should never be allowed to stand on floors, walls, furniture, or wood trim, nor soak into seams and cracks. Certain minerals make water "hard" and react with soap, forming a scum or film of insoluble lime. It is very difficult to rinse this scum from fabrics, and hard surfaces need to be rinsed and rubbed to get it off. It is not so necessary, however, to soften water for scrubbing and washing hard surfaces as for cleansing fabrics.

As long as substances remain dissolved in water, they are not likely to interfere with successful laundering. Substances not soluble in water may be deposited on the clothes as unsightly specks and spots. These may come from the sediment stirred up from the bottom of the tub or from the scum formed by the hardness of the water. Filtration and softening are remedies when such conditions exist.

Often objectionable material can be easily filtered out, either with or without previous settling. Allowing the water to stand overnight is especially helpful in case it contains suspended iron compounds, or fastening a salt sack over the spout of the faucet or pump may solve the immediate problem. If the condition is serious, filters of charcoal, sand, and such materials may be worth installing.

**Water Softeners:** Soap will remove calcium and magnesium compounds by forming a scum that can be strained off. However, this is a wasteful and expensive method of softening water, and the scum is difficult to remove effectively.

Trisodium phosphate, borax, and ammonia solution can be used also for softening water. Ammonia is a gas that is bought dissolved in water. So-called household ammonia is often a very weak solution, and a high price is paid for the water and the bottle. It is sometimes more economical to buy concentrated ammonia solution at a druggist and dilute it according to need. This should be done carefully and out of doors, however, as concentrated ammonia solutions are unpleasant to handle.

The great difficulty in using any of these methods is determining the quantity of softening agent required. This cannot be done accurately without knowing the degree of hardness of the water. The addition of too little washing soda or other softening agent for the amount of hardness does not remove it all, whereas the addition of too much renders the water more alkaline than may be advisable. Accurate determinations of hardness are made at all water laboratories, and from their results calculations of the correct amount needed can be made. However, the following method will give a general idea of the condition of the water:

Make a solution of a good neutral soap in denatured or wood alcohol. This should be as strong as it is possible to make it without a jelly forming upon standing. Fill a small glass bottle about half full of water. Fit it with a tight cork or stopper and mark off the level of the surface of the water by scratching the glass lightly with a file or by using a label. Add the soap solution drop by drop (counting the drops) until, when the bottle is shaken violently and placed upon its side, the suds form an unbroken layer over the top of the water and remain that way for 1 minute by the clock. Repeat until the exact number of drops necessary to form the suds has been determined, being careful to use the same quantity of water each time. Compare the quantity of soap needed with that required for producing similar suds in fresh rain water. Vary the quantity of softening agent used each week per tub of water and repeat the above test. When the softened water requires no more soap than the rain water, record the quantity of softening agent placed in each tub of water and thereafter add that same amount.

Soap: Soap emulsifies the oil and grease that make dirt cling to fabrics and finished surfaces, and helps to carry it away. Some soap is the mild, neutral type used for toilet purposes and on fine fabrics. Others contain varying proportions of alkaline salts to produce a better suds in hard water and to aid in the cleansing action. This type is commonly used for laundry and dishwashing.

Most surfaces in the home should be washed only with mild, neutral soap. Soaps containing free alkali or large amounts of alkaline salts may be even more injurious to linoleum, paint, varnish, and lacquer than they are to the skin. Ordinary laundry soap and homemade soaps often contain sufficient free alkali to make their continued use on hard surfaces inadvisable. If more drastic cleaning action is needed than neutral soap and water alone supply, it is safer to add a small quantity of one of the alkaline salts, which also have value as cleansing agents.

Detergents: Some synthetic cleansers are superior to soap for washing, particularly in hard water in which, unlike soap, they can form suds without curd. In hard water localities, it may be advisable to use one of the sulfated fatty alcohols in place of soap, or tetrasodiumpyrophosphate detergent mixture with soap for washing upholstery and rugs.

Detergents are effective whether they create suds or not. Sudless detergents are essential for spinner-type washing machines and save wear and tear on all machines. In addition, they help avoid the back-up of sewerage created when a great deal of suds accumulate in waste systems. Some detergents are available in tablet form, and some with blueing, bleaching, and water softeners added.

**Alkalies:** Many of the alkali cleaning materials are less expensive when bought in bulk. Trisodium phosphate is a moderately strong alkaline salt and one of the most effective. It is seldom sold by its chemical name, so it is well to ask vendors about contents. A half tablespoon to a gallon of water is sufficient to remove any dirt that cannot be loosened with mild soap and water alone. A larger amount will injure surfaces on which it is used. Trisodium phosphate in strong, hot solutions is used as a paint remover.

Washing soda (also called modified soda) is a mildly alkaline salt combining sodium bicarbonate and sodium carbonate. Two tablespoons to a gallon of water are sufficient. Sal soda (sometimes called washing soda or soda crystals) contains about 40 percent of sodium carbonate and about 60 percent of chemically combined water. It will liquefy at high temperatures or humidity, and is expensive.

Borax is a mildly alkaline salt and is not very efficient as a cleansing agent. Use four tablespoons to a gallon of water.

Ammonia may be bought at a drug store in liquid form which is a solution of the gas in water. If water equal to three times the volume of the strong ammonia water is added to it, the same strength will be obtained as household ammonia. Household ammonia is mostly water and the cloudy appearance usually results from the addition of a small amount of soap; it is an expensive way to buy ammonia for cleaning purposes.

Lye, which commonly is caustic soda, is often used to clean drain pipes. However, to prevent the caustic soda from combining with grease and forming hard soap that will clog the pipes, the pipes must be flushed immediately with plenty of hot water. Lye will also damage the glaze on most vitreous china plumbing fixtures and on enameled iron, even that with an acid-resisting finish. Lye is poisonous and injurious to the skin and must be handled with great care.

**Acids:** Bisulfate of soda is used in some preparations for removing the deposits that discolor vitreous china toilet bowls and render them unsanitary. Hydrochloric acid also may be used for this purpose in a 10 to 15 percent solution. These are strong acid compounds and like lye are poisonous, and must be kept out of the reach of children. They will injure enameled iron that is not of the acid-resisting type.

**Abrasives:** Scouring powders and metal polishes owe their effectiveness largely to the action of abrasives. Any abrasive wears down the surface on which it is used, the wear increasing with the amount of pressure applied in rubbing, the type and fineness of the abrasive, and the frequency of application. Consequently, it is well to try first to remove dirt and grease with warm water, soap, trisodium phosphate, or one of the other alkaline salts. Then it is a good rule to start with the finest and mildest abrasives and use a more severe one only when the polishing cannot be accomplished with less drastic action.

The mildness of an abrasive is determined both by the shape and fineness of the particles. Some abrasives, such as diatomaceous earth and feldspar, have particles smooth enough in shape to lessen their abrasive action. Rubbing compound, rottenstone, and pumice are used on furniture, in that order of coarseness. Diatomaceous earth in a fine grade is excellent for polishing a soft metal such as silver; a fine whiting has less abrasive action and takes much longer to do the same polishing job. Such abrasives as volcanic ash, pumicite, and the coarser silicas are much more severe.

Metal polishes on the market combine abrasives with other substances. Thin polishes are wasteful. Silver polishes usually are pastes made with diatomaceous earth, soap, water, and perhaps a little wax, scented oil, and coloring matter. Some metal polishes are made with fine silica, which has sharper particles than diatomaceous earth, combined with such ingredients as water, soap, glycerine, ammonia, oil, or a flammable petroleum product. Sometimes acids are added to loosen the tarnish. These may ruin some metals and will damage most of them unless thoroughly washed off. Since acids cannot be packaged in tin, a polishing compound in a tin container assures freedom from acids.

Some manufacturers claim that their polishes can be used on all metals. If they are adapted to cleaning copper and brass, they are generally too abrasive for silver because it is a softer metal. While a silver polish may be used on other metals, it usually takes longer than a polish adapted to the particular metal. Special polishes are made for silver, copper and brass, and pewter. These are the only metals in the home on which polish needs to be used.

Many recipes are in circulation for home compounding of polishes but they do not always give satisfactory results. When the ingredients are bought in small quantities they are likely to be expensive, and some, such as diatomaceous earth, are known by a variety of names and are difficult to obtain in local stores.

Scouring powders may be of feldspar sold under a brand name, or the commoner volcanic ash or pumicite. Feldspar in a fine grade is less abrasive to the surfaces of plumbing fixtures and metals than the volcanic-ash preparations. Many scouring powders have soap and an alkaline salt added to the abrasives.

Steel wool is another type of abrasive, consisting of fine strands of steel. The finest is No. 00 and is adapted to cleaning some kitchen utensils. It is often sold with a cake of soap, or as steel wool mixed with soap. When straight steel wool is used, the hands may need protection with old gloves to prevent the fine strands from penetrating the skin. Stainless steel wool does not rust but is more expensive. Copper and other metal sponges may be used in place of steel wool.

**Polishes and Waxes:** Waxes protect floor and furniture finishes and keep them looking better than other types of polishes. If the wax on floors is renewed often enough, particularly in the paths of heaviest traffic, the floor can be protected from wear and costly refinishing or replacement.

There are two types of floor waxes: Self-polishing and buffing. The self-polishing waxes are known as water-emulsion waxes and are used primarily on linoleum, cork, vinyl plastic, sealed or varnished wood floors and asphalt, rubber, and mastic tile. These waxes dry to a shine without buffing. Damp mopping with cold water will remove most of the surface dirt. Before re-applying, the floor should be thoroughly cleaned with soap and water.

Buffing-type waxes are paste and liquid cleaning and polishing waxes. They must be buffed when dry to give the surface a bright shine. These waxes are used primarily on wood surfaces but can also be used on linoleum, vinyl plastic, sealed cork, and cement. They should *never* be applied to asphalt or rubber tile as the solvent in these waxes may damage the floor covering. No preparatory cleaning is required when using liquid cleaning and polishing waxes as the solvent in these products dry cleans the surface and removes all dirt as it waxes. These waxes can be removed from floors with commercial wax cleaners, turpentine, or carbon tetrachloride. Wood floors should not be scrubbed with soap and water as the water may penetrate the wood and raise the grain.

Furniture can be maintained with either of the buffing-type waxes, a cream furniture wax or with the newer liquid furniture waxes that do not require rubbing. These polishes will remove the soil and dirt from the surface and impart a hard, dry film of wax. Oil polishes are not desirable for furniture and floors as they leave a smeary film on the surface which collects dust.

Waxed surfaces should never be dusted or mopped with an oil treated rag or mop as the oil tends to soften and streak the wax film.

Dusting and polishing cloths are specially treated to pick up dust, hold, and remove it.


## METHODS OF CLEANING

**Ceilings:** Do ceilings first, beginning in one corner, and work so as not to leave streaks. Use solution of soap and water with ammonia or trisodium phosphate.

**Paint and Varnish:** It is easier to clean and care for painted, varnished, and lacquered surfaces if the types of finishes in use are understood. Each coating applied to wood and plastic is only a few thousandths of an inch thick, and repeated washing soon wears it away.

Wall paints may have a base, or binder, of oil or varnish, emulsified resins, casein or glue. The oil or varnish types have little or no water in them, and they withstand cleaning with soap and water better than the others. The glossier the paint, the more it will withstand cleaning. The emulsified resin type contains water as a thinner, but the dry film does not dissolve in water. Casein and glue (calcimine) bound paints are thinned with water and wash away easily. Caesin paints may be gently washed, but cannot withstand severe scrubbing. Calcimine may be brushed but cannot be washed. Whitewash is a mixture of slaked lime and water, and cannot be washed.

The procedure for washing painted, varnished, or lacquered surfaces is the same whether they are on furniture, wood trim, walls, or floors. Make a light suds with a mild, neutral soap such as that used for fine fabrics. Wash the surface no harder than is necessary to wash off the dirt. Rinse away every trace of soap with clear water, because soapy water leaves a film to catch and hold dirt. Wipe the surface dry with a clean, soft cloth. Use water as sparingly as though it were an expensive cleaning material. Wash only a small area at a time so water will not be left standing on the surface any longer than is absolutely necessary. Floors should never be flooded with water.

When painted walls, wood trim, or wood floors are very dirty, it may be necessary to add a little trisodium phosphate, or other alkaline cleansing agent to the soap and water. These alkaline materials never should be used on furniture or on linoleum or similar floor coverings.

Walls and wood trim should be washed from the bottom up. When water runs down on a soiled surface it leaves streaks that are difficult or impossible to remove. It will not stain a wall that has already been moistened and cleaned. It is easier to wash and rinse these surfaces with soft sponges than with cloths, because good sponges are more absorbent. Two pails should be used, one for suds and one for rinse water. The water should be changed frequently.

After painted walls have been washed, a thin coat of ordinary laundry starch may be applied with a paint brush. The next time the wall needs washing, the job is much easier because the dirt washes off with the starch. Any flat finish will have more gloss after it is washed, for it is impossible not to exert some polishing action.

Floor Maintenance: Wood floors with fine finishes should never be scrubbed with water or unnecessarily brought in contact with water except in connection with refinishing old floors. Sweeping or dry mopping should be all that is necessary for routine cleaning. A soft cotton floor mop kept barely dampened with a mixture of 3 parts of kerosene and 1 part of paraffin oil is excellent for dry mopping. When the mop becomes dirty, it should be washed in hot soap and water, and dried. Exceptional patches of dirt that cannot be removed in this way may be removed by rubbing lightly with fine steel wool moistened with turpentine. Where the finish is a floor seal, badly soiled spots, such as gray spots where water has been allowed to stand on the floor for a time, can be sanded by hand, patched with seal, and buffed with a pad of steel wool. Varnish finish, if kept in good condition, offers better protection against water scars; but if it does become stained it is not so easily repaired.

VARNISHED FLOORS: Brush with soft, long-handled hair brush, and dust with mop.

WAXED FLOORS: Clean with cheesecloth and renew finish with liquid wax. Badly soiled floors may be cleaned by removing old wax with turpentine or carbon tetrachloride on a cloth, and rewaxed.

UNFINISHED WOODEN FLOORS: Remove stains from wood. Scrub with soft brush, sandsoap (or steel wool) following the wood grain pattern. Wipe off cleaners with clear water. Brush if necessary.

Linoleum: Inlaid linoleum should be sealed when first laid to prevent cracking, water seepage, etc. This should be done

### To Prevent Pressure of Furniture Damaging Linoleum

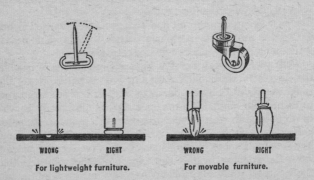

| WRONG      RIGHT | WRONG      RIGHT |
| For lightweight furniture. | For movable furniture. |

professionally. If not sealed, inlaid linoleum should be tacked with moulding at all baseboard edges and tacked with brass seam bindings at other edges. Wax as soon as possible after laying. Wash unwaxed linoleum with solution of mild soap and warm water. Avoid strong soaps that remove essential linoleum oils. Remove spilled water or food from linoleum as soon as possible. Rub waterdrip stains (fresh) with freshly cut lemon. Repair chips with porcelain glaze. To keep linoleum looking well, keep it well waxed, wash it as seldom as possible, wipe up anything spilled immediately. Avoid alkalies and gritty cleaners. Wash with mild suds and lukewarm water. Wait until floor is thoroughly dry before applying wax. To remove marks caused by pressure, rust, etc., apply a jelly of mild soap with fine steel wool, remove and rewax. To remove accumulation of wax on linoleum, allow soapsuds to remain on the floor for 10 minutes. To prevent pressure of chair legs from scarring linoleum, use glass cups or felt pads under furniture legs. To paint linoleum, remove the wax, use ordinary enamel paint. To add lustre, add a half cup of sour milk to the water used in rinsing.

Don't use brushing lacquer, varnish or shellac on resilient floor. Brushing lacquer can be removed from linoleum with ethyl-acetate or lacquer remover, but extreme care must be used because if the remover is not applied correctly, it may ruin the linoleum. Read the directions on the container carefully, and bear in mind the special conditions. Apply the remover to a few square feet of linoleum at a time. Then, when the lacquer has softened, wipe it off with a clean cloth.

**Rubber tile floors:** Wash with clear water and clean mop. Avoid grease which softens rubber.

Don't use an oil mop on floors. It will streak waxed floors. Oil softens rubber tile or asphalt tile floors. If the oil is heavy, it produces a sticky film to which dirt adheres.

**Wallpaper:** Although many wallpapers are sold as washable, the degree of washability varies greatly even on glossy finished paper, and once paper is on the wall, there is no way to distinguish washable from unwashable finishes. It is wise to proceed with caution and to remember that the pigments and other materials applied to wallpaper may be rubbed off. Try suds on a scrap of the paper or in an inconspicuous spot. After determining by test that colors will not run and that the paper is washable, follow the procedure for fabric surfaces. Apply thick suds with a soft sponge to a small space at a time, rubbing as lightly as possible, and rinse with a sponge squeezed out of clear water. Because paper is always absorbent, it is important to use as little water as possible.

Puttylike wallpaper cleaners are safer than soap and water on most finishes. Art gum also may be used. They will remove light soil and sometimes will erase finger marks. Walls need to be brushed before and after their use.

Fresh grease spots may be removed with a clean blotter to which a warm iron is applied; or rub with a cube of laundry starch, then brush off starch; or rub stain with fresh white bread or gum eraser; or a paste solution of magnesium and carbon tetrachloride. The paste should be applied and allowed to remain overnight, then brushed off. Repeat if necessary. Grease spots sometimes may be removed with a paste made of fuller's earth or cornstarch and cleaning fluid applied to the spot, allowed to dry, and then brushed off.

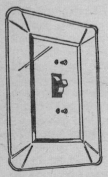

To avoid smudging walls, use plastic switch protectors.

Ink stains or bloodstains may be removed by applying water, rubbing with white magnesia chalk. Allow to dry, then brush off. To remove decals, soak with hot vinegar, or touch them lightly with water and apply a blotter; then treat them with oxalic acid. If the color of the paper is affected, it may be brought back with watercolors or crayons. Or sponge with oxalic acid solution, then apply ammonia.

There are several commercial preparations for surfacing wallpapers to keep them from absorbing dirt and grease easily. Some claim to make wallpaper washable. Lacquer or shellac is recommended by some experts.

To remedy a blemish, paste a patch of the same paper over it, matching the paper carefully.

To remove wallpaper, use a solution of 1 quart of flour paste and 1 pail of hot water, soak thoroughly, scrape, and peel. For quicker treatment, use solution of 4 ounces of pulverized saltpeter to 1 gallon of water.

Furniture: Dust regularly with dry, clean, lintless cloth. (Not oily or damp wax or you remove lustre.) Furniture may be washed with a soft cloth, and a solution of 2 teaspoonfuls of green soap in warm water. Rub with cheesecloth until froth appears, wipe off with tepid water, dry with soft cloth, rub with grain.

Once each week, rub with chamois or flannel cloth, moving with the grain.

Polish or wax once a month. In general, wax is a better protection than polish, is easier to dust. Polish will shine quicker. Remove all wax, with mild soap or lukewarm water or by applying liquid wax and wiping off while still wet. Remove old polish by wiping with cloth dipped in turpentine. Precede waxing or polishing with dusting and rubbing. To apply furniture polish, pour a little onto a slightly dampened clean cheesecloth. Pass lightly over furniture, following grain of wood. Do only a small section at a time on large pieces. Take a clean, dry cloth and polish the surface rapidly, rubbing with the grain. Never allow polish or oil to stand on furniture. Never use harsh cleansing agents (scouring powders, steel wool, lye or household bleach). Avoid solutions containing linseed oil on lacquered surfaces. Carved portions may be cleaned with man's shaving brush or a soft paint brush.

**Scratches:** Light scratches may be removed by removing old oil, applying wax generously in the area, drying, and repolishing the entire surface. If scratches are numerous, remove all wax, sandpaper entire surface lightly with fine paper, moistened with oil, clean with cloth dampened with naphtha, replace finish, allow to dry. For fine furniture call an expert. To remove scratches on light-colored furniture, crumble meat of walnut or pecan (or even better, beeswax) into scratch to fill, then apply wax or polish. A touch-up job can be done by mixing thick oil paints to match color; apply with a match stick. For a deep scratch or any scratch on dark furniture, melt matching sealing wax, smooth and polish. Dents may disappear when treated with hot water applied with moist paper. Hold a hot iron over paper. Small holes may be filled with composition wood and stained to match with a dab of cotton, or sealing wax (available in wide variety of colors). Inlays are best replaced with sealing wax. To remove hot dish marks, apply turpentine, rub with boiled linseed oil, polish. Use clean cloth for each process. (See pages 300, 301.)

### Removing Spots and Stains from Wood

ALCOHOL: If light, rub well; if heavier, rub with rottenstone and liberal amount of lemon oil. Polish with clean cloth and clean oil. Repeat as necessary.

BURNS: If light, rub with felt cloth and furniture polish. If deep, scrape down to lowest mark of the burn and revarnish.

CANDLE WAX: Scrape gently. Remove residue with heated cloth, or apply warm iron over blotting paper. Repeat as necessary. Cleaning fluid on cheesecloth is helpful.

GREASE: Wet with solution of washing soda, allow to stand for 5 minutes, then wash off. This may leave a clean spot which can be removed only by scrubbing or bleaching the entire surface.

INK: Wipe with damp cloth. For old stains, apply oxalic acid solution and ammonia.

LINT: Rub with rottenstone and lemon oil, polish with clean cloth and oil.

MEDICINE: See Alcohol.

MILKY FILM ON VARNISH: (due to absorbed moisture)— Rub with furniture polish and oily cloth or wash with oil and turpentine. If stains persists, wash with solution of a teaspoon of cider vinegar in pint of water, wipe dry, rub and polish. If film still persists, revarnish.

PAINT: Stains may be wiped with cloth dampened with turpentine. Make sure cloth is clean at all times. Old stains may be softened with turpentine or, if necessary, scraped. (This may mar surface.)

PERFUME: See Alcohol.

SHELLAC: Apply alcohol followed quickly by oily cloth.

WATER: (usually a white film)—Rub with 2 drops of alcohol on thumb or solution of ½ teaspoon vinegar in cup of cold water. Or apply blotter and warm iron. (Heat should not be sufficient to damage the varnish.) Alternative—apply cheesecloth dampened with hot water with several drops of ammonia on it, followed immediately by oily cloth and furniture oil.

WATER SPOTS ON FINISHED FLOOR: Rub gently with cloth dampened in alcohol and wipe immediately with oily cloth.

LIGHT STAINS ON VARNISH: Mix light oil and pumice stone to putty consistency, rub briskly with cloth in direction of grain.

Wicker Furniture: Dust with a stiff brush and vacuum occasionally. Water may be applied if the furniture is varnished. Periodic spraying will lessen the chances of wicker furniture drying out and snapping. To darken wicker furniture, apply a thin oil stain. To preserve it, particularly the seats of the chairs, varnish or shellac.

Fabric Surfaces: Upholstery, window shades, and rugs may

all be cleaned at home by a similar method. Remove all the dust possible with a vacuum cleaner, brush, or if necessary, from upholstery and rugs, by beating. Make a thick suds of mild, neutral soap, so thick that the pail seems to be full of suds with almost no water. This will help to keep moisture from soaking through the fabric. For upholstery and window shades, apply the suds to a small area at a time with a sponge or with a piece of turkish toweling or other very absorbent cloth. On window shades, a soft bristle brush may be used instead of a sponge. Remove every trace of soap with a sponge squeezed in clear water and let window shades dry before rolling. (Window shades are most easily cleaned on a large table.) A soft eraser may remove some spots.

If the finish is velvet or other soft finish, apply dry-cleaning fluid on cheesecloth and then stroke with soft brush to replace nap. To remove dust from upholstered section, use vacuum cleaner. If you beat furniture, use a damp cloth over the part so as to absorb the dust. To remove hairs from upholstery or drapery, stroke with damp sandpaper or damp sponge.

Floors: (Non-porous—clay tile, asphalt tile, rubber tile, linoleum, or plastic compositions): Scrub stained surface as soon as possible with soap and water or abrasive cleaner and water. To avoid harming the surface do not scrub linoleum, rubber tile, or the plastics too hard.

(Porous—wood, marble, concrete): Very difficult. Getting removal solution into pores is tough job. So is getting "loosened" stained material out. Waxing will help protect floors by making them nearly non-porous.

Ink on the skin: Don't try to scrub off ink stains. They can be removed without irritating the skin. Following instructions is particularly important in removing ink from children's tender skins.

BALL-POINT INKS: Rub the skin gently with cotton dipped in rubbing alcohol. In addition to removing the stain, the alcohol soothes the skin.

FOUNTAIN-PEN INKS: Wash with soap and water in the usual way. For persistent stains, wash with 5% solution of potassium permanganate and rinse with water. Then apply 5% solution of sodium bisulphite until brown color has disappeared. These materials can be obtained without a prescription at a drugstore.

Don't worry about small ink stains on children's skins. Fountain-pen and ball-point inks won't harm the skin unless poured on in quantity and rubbed in.

**Carpets and Rugs:** Dirt should be removed immediately when it falls. Use carpet sweeper to remove surface dirt daily, vacuum cleaner once a week, thorough "under furniture" cleaning once a month, underside cleaning twice a year, shampooing or drycleaning every year or two. If a vacuum cleaner is not available, sweep once a week. Good rugs, especially hooked rugs, lose their shape if shaken violently. The tacked edges of carpets should be cleaned particularly, as this is a common point of infestation.

For sweeping use a long-handled Tampico fiber brush or sweep with a soft corn broom. Dampen slightly or drop a dustless sweeping material (old, damp tea leaves or moist newspaper strips) before sweeping. Floor underneath matting should not be varnished, as dirt seeps through and tends to spoil the varnish. Matting should be wiped with solution of 1 pail of water to 1 cup of lemon oil, to keep it soft without being greasy. After sweeping, brush gently with the lay of the pile. When vacuuming, work in the direction of the pile. New carpets will give up some excess yarn fibers with vacuuming, but this will not harm the carpet. If tufts work loose, they may be replaced by sewing. If necessary, cut off tufts. Never pull them out. Never shake small rugs by gripping one end and snapping. If dirt causes loss of color, try carbon tetrachloride or other solvent cleaner on small portion. Use as necessary.

Some rugs may be washed—notably string type, sisal, drugget. Wash them in tub, rinse with garden hose, hang to dry. To shampoo a rug, use commercial shampoo or mild soap. Professional handling is recommended. Cloth rugs may be soaked in suds, scrubbed with brush or cloth, then rinsed with a rough cloth dipped in a solution of powdered alum and lukewarm water. To soften a rug, pour solution of sizing in hot water on underside, spread evenly with a broom, allow to dry for 2 days.

Some types of rugs require special treatment. White rugs require special soaps. Frieze or twist rugs should be dry cleaned. Lustre type rugs should be given periodic shampooing in quantities of water in accordance with instructions from manufacturer. If lustre is produced by wax or oils, rug should be re-lustred after a shampoo. Cotton mats may be laundered in warm water with non-alkaline soaps. Rayon rugs should be laundered as directed by the manufacturer.

Professional cleaning at a factory is much more intricate. It involves (1) mechanical beating out of dust; (2) solvent cleaning in large vats and drying; (3) shampooing both sides of the rug, wringing and drying; (4) spot removal. Shampooing can be done on the floor, but this may result in some soap remaining to cause matting and disintegration.

While home cleaning is not recommended as a substitute for a thorough professional job, it will perk up your carpet between cleanings. Three methods of do-it-yourself cleaning are suggested:

## (1) Cleaning with Detergent

This consists of preparing a cleaning solution of two table-spoons of a synthetic detergent (Joy, Glim) or shampoo (Drene, Halo) with a gallon of lukewarm water. Using a sponge, apply the solution sparingly with a gentle wiping motion so as to wet only the face of the carpet. Important: Always work from the outer edges of the stain toward the center.

Help the drying process by opening the windows in warm weather and by keeping the rooms warm in cold weather. (Forced air from fan or vacuum also helps.)

Place squares of cardboard under the legs of furniture to prevent stains. When the carpet is almost dry, brush the pile with quick, easy strokes to restore its lofty appearance. Don't walk on the carpet till it is completely dry.

Home cleaning does not allow adequate rinsing of the carpet, so that cleaning materials accumulate and may cause resoiling to occur more rapidly. For this reason, frequent home cleaning between professional plant cleanings is not recommended.

## (2) Using a Dry-Cleaning Fluid

Apply dry-cleaning fluid sparingly with a gentle wiping motion so that only the top portion of the pile becomes wet. Typical dry-cleaning solvents that are available in most areas are Carbona (carbon tetrachloride), Renuzit, Vythene.

This cleaning method is not recommended for cotton carpets.

In dry-cleaning your carpet, be sure to observe these precautions: (1) read the manufacturer's directions on label; (2) avoid inhaling fumes which are toxic; (3) keep windows open; (4) if cleaner is flammable, avoid having lighted cigarettes or running electrical appliances around during the cleaning operation.

### (3) Using Absorbent Powder Cleaners

A number of absorbent powder cleaners, made especially for cleaning larger areas of carpet, are available. Familiar trade names include Glamorene and Sprinkle Klean. Clear directions for use are given on these packaged cleaners and should be followed carefully.

Carpets properly cleaned and exposed to light should provide no moth problem. However, areas under radiators or heavy furniture, and portions turned under may be attacked by the webbing moth or carpet beetle. Cleaning, shifting furniture, and moth-proofing solutions (as naphthalene or paradichlorobenzene—1 lb. for each 100 sq. ft.) are the best protection. When storing rugs, cleaning and moth-proofing are essential.

Special treatment for rugs are suggested for the following:

To restore pile where furniture has crushed it, apply a hot iron on a damp cloth. Then brush the pile briskly. Repeat as necessary. To flatten curling corners, use the same method on front and back of carpet.

To remove dull spots caused by pressure of furniture, rub French chalk into spots with a small brush, then remove chalk with vacuum cleaner. To prevent such marks, use cups under legs and move furniture from time to time.

Brighten rugs by wiping a cheesecloth dampened with carbon tetrachloride over the rug. When applying, keep windows open to avoid fumes.

Removing Spots from Rugs: Act quickly, before spots set. Blot up liquids with cloth or blotting paper immediately. Scrape off semi-solids with a dull knife. Where the carpet is wet through, lift it to let dry. To hasten drying, insert vacuum cleaner tube under carpet to the spot.

Food stains: Use ordinary washing methods. For radical procedure, add 3 tablespoons ammonia to 2 gallons of suds.

Oil stains: (from fiber rugs), apply cleaning fluid periodically, until stain is removed from rug permanently.

INK STAINS: Flush out stain with water, blot with soft, dry cloth. Or apply fresh milk as quickly after the accident as possible. Cover with cornstarch and remove, then apply solution of milk soap and water. If stain persists, apply paste of milk and cornmeal and allow to remain overnight. If stain still persists, loosen with ink eradicator No. 1 solution, then sponge with oxalic acid, and wash with water to which 3 drops of ammonia have been added, wash with clear water.

PAINT: Apply turpentine, soap and water. If paint has hardened, soften with paint remover, scrape, then apply turpentine. Don't use liquid paint remover if stain is wet.

ARGYROL: Dissolve 2 tablets dichloride of mercury in 1 ounce water. Apply with dropper till stain disappears. Remove solution. Rinse dry.

IODINE: 1 ounce hyposulphite in 3 ounces water. Add ½ ounce ammonia, apply with dropper till stain disappears.

RUST STAINS: Apply a mild solution of oxalic acid and rinse immediately.

SHOE POLISH: Use dry-cleaning fluid, then wash with solution of ammonia, soap and water.

OILY MATERIAL: Butter, grease, oil, hand cream, ball-point pen ink. Remove excess. Sponge with dry-cleaning solution. Allow to dry. Sponge again with dry cleaner, if necessary. Allow to dry. Brush up pile gently.

FOODSTUFFS, ANIMAL MATTER: Coffee, tea, cream, milk, gravy, chocolate, blood, egg, ice cream, sauces, salad dressing, vomit. Remove excess. Sponge with detergent solution. Take up excess solution with clean dry cloth. Dry the carpet. If necessary, apply dry-cleaning fluid to remove remaining spot. Allow to dry. Brush up pile gently.

STARCHES AND SUGARS: Candy, soft drinks, alcoholic beverages. Remove excess. Sponge with detergent solution. Take up excess solution with clean dry cloth. Dry the carpet. If necessary, repeat detergent solution. Dry the carpet again. Brush up pile gently.

FRUIT, WASHABLE INK, URINE, EXCREMENT: Remove excess. Sponge with detergent solution. Take up excess solution with clean dry cloth. Dry the carpet. If necessary, repeat detergent solution. Dry the carpet again. Brush up pile gently.

HEAVY GREASE GUMS: Chewing gum, paint, tar, heavy grease, lipstick, crayon. Remove excess. Sponge with dry-cleaning solution. Follow with detergent solution. Repeat dry-cleaning solution. Dry the carpet. If necessary, repeat entire procedure until all material is removed. When carpet is dry, brush up pile gently.

NAIL POLISH: Remove with ordinary nail polish remover. Caution: Both nail polish and nail polish remover will seriously damage any carpet containing acetate fibers. If yours is an acetate carpet, or contains a percentage of acetate fibers, don't try to remove stain. Call a professional cleaner.

Before attempting to remove stain, test the effect of nail polish remover on some inconspicuous section, or a swatch of the carpet. If you're sure it is safe, proceed as follows:

(1) If polish is still wet, take up excess with clean cloth, being careful not to spread stain.

(2) If dry, apply liquid nail polish remover with eye dropper directly to stain. Allow minute or two to soften. Repeat if necessary.

(3) Apply liquid remover generously to stained area. Sponge up excess. Repeat until stain is entirely removed.

CIGARETTE BURNS: Serious cigarette burns must be rewoven to be completely remedied. However, if surface is merely charred, carefully snip off blackened ends of yarn with small, sharp scissors. Sponge with detergent solution. Dry carpet. Brush up pile gently.

STRONG ACIDS: Strong acids—battery acid, some tile-cleaning compounds, and "laboratory" varieties of acids—require fast action to prevent serious damage. Flush area with plenty of water until acid has been greatly diluted. Sponge up water and apply an alkaline solution of one tablespoon of baking soda to one quart of warm water. Rinse with clear water. Mop up and dry carpet quickly to prevent mildew.

RUST: If stain is fresh, apply detergent solution. Sponge excess. Dry carpet. Repeat. Generally, rust stains are difficult to remove and require the services of a professional cleaner.

For most spots, use warm water and soapless lather detergents. Avoid excessive rubbing. Stains caused by household pets or by spillage of alkaline substances such as soap or cleaning solutions can sometimes be treated successfully with a warm dilute solution of acetic acid or white vinegar. Carpeting in the green, blue and rose taupe shades need particular protection if used where household pets may cause stains, or where other substances may be spilled frequently.

In general, follow instructions for fabrics where applicable. Otherwise, use absorbent powders.

**Leather Surfaces:** Upholstery leather cleaning is similar to that for fabric surfaces. Use thick suds of mild, neutral soap with as little water as possible; wipe off all traces of soap with a damp cloth; then dry and polish the surface with a soft, dry cloth. Never use furniture polish, furniture oils, or varnish on leather. Many of these preparations contain solvents that may soften the finish on upholstery leather and cause it to become sticky. A special commercial leather cleaner and preservative is made of water, wax, and alcohol in a thin solution.

Book bindings may be preserved by working animal or vegetable oils (such as lanolin or castor oil) into them with the hands, especially along the back binding. Mineral oil must never be used on book bindings. A commercial preservative compounded on a formula used in large libraries contains purified lanolin, Japan wax, neat's-foot oil, sodium stearate, and water. It is difficult to obtain the special grades of ingredients necessary for compounding these formulas in the home.

To clean imitation leather or plastic, rub with solution of mild soap and lukewarm water. Apply petroleum jelly to prevent cracking and peeling. To remove burnt spot if only the finish is damaged, rub with pumice and oil (4 or 5 strokes). To cover burnt spot in leather table top, fill hole with matching melted wax, smooth, and allow to harden. To remove white rings, wipe on oil of camphor, rub briskly with dry cloth, polish with wax or polish.

**Wooden Bedsteads:** Old bedsteads which have cracks should be wiped with citronella periodically. Beds which can be taken outside may be doused with gasoline, kerosene, or turpentine. Wait until odor has evaporated before using.

**Enameled Metal Beds:** Wipe with soap and water. Spots may be removed with paste solution of soap, water, and whiting.

**Varnished Beds:** Brush with a mop or rag dampened lightly with lemon oil.

**Brass Beds:** Wipe with a dry cloth, then rub with lemon oil.

**Open Springs:** Use vacuum cleaner, or use a soft, long-handled brush; wipe springs lightly with lemon oil.

**Covered Springs:** Vacuum and give a brushing with a stiff whisk broom.

**Radiators:** Clean with a long-handled stiff brush once a week. Place a damp paper underneath the radiator to collect the dust. Some vacuum cleaners have suitable accessories for this type of cleaning.

**Gilt Frames:** Swab lightly with lintless cloth or soft brush moistened with solution of equal parts of alcohol and ammonia. Apply lemon oil lightly or apply vaseline for 10 minutes, remove with clean cloth.

**Photographs (not colored, not glossy):** Wipe with a damp cloth, allow to dry face down on a smooth dry cloth.

**Oil Paintings:** Rub lightly with petroleum jelly or linseed oil on cheesecloth, or with absorbent cotton dipped in turpentine.

**Artificial Flowers:** Place inside a large paper bag with half a cup of salt; shake well. To clean artificial flowers made of velvet, brush with a shaving brush, rub lightly with fresh rye bread and re-brush. For more radical treatment, steam them over a tea kettle or hot running shower.

**Candles:** Keep in a cool place. Buy non-drip varieties wherever possible. Clean with cloth dampened with alcohol.

**Books:** Keep away from dusty, dry, and hot places, but allow them access to air.

**Pianos:** Have your piano tuned at least three times a year. Do not put the piano near steam pipes, registers, or stoves. Keep in a normal temperature and free from dampness. Close the top of the piano when not in use but expose the keyboard to light—especially if the keys are ivory, which turns yellow if kept continuously from the light.

If the piano is to be left in an unoccupied house for some time, place camphor where it will not touch the metal or wooden parts. Place newspaper in the interior to absorb moisture.

**Piano Keys:** Use denatured alcohol. Or rub with a solution of lemon juice and whiting powder. Avoid getting solution between keys.

**Kerosene Lamps:** Chimneys should be washed daily and char rubbed off the wicks. Glass shades should be dusted daily and washed once a month or oftener. Keep ⅔ full; base may be washed with soap and water. Wicks should be down low and should fit snugly. To insert a new wick, apply a thin layer of candle wax before rolling into the frame. Never cut a wick; pinch off the charred portion. Greasy or dirty wicks may be boiled in soapy water, dried, and re-used. Burners may be cleaned in water and washing soda. Chimneys may be cleaned with a bottle brush and dried with a lintless cloth.

**Lamp Shades:** Where the material is washable and contains no soluble paste, bathe in solution of mild soap and lukewarm water. If shade is pasted or pleated, rub with cheesecloth dipped in dry soapsuds. If material is not washable, rub with cheesecloth dipped in dry-cleaning fluid. To dust a pleated lamp, use a man's shaving brush.

**Lighting Fixtures:** Electric light bulbs and fixtures should be dusted weekly and washed once a month. Cloth or similar types of shades need a regular rubbing off with cleaning fluid. Use cheesecloth dampened in warm water.

**Window Sills:** Brush thoroughly, then wash with hose. Kitchen sills should be washed with soapsuds twice a season and scrubbed. If grease persists, apply dissolved washing soda.

**Fireplace:** Throw salt on fire for a few minutes before cleaning. Use soft brush with hot water and strong soap. For more radical cleaning, apply paste of powdered pumice and ammonia for 2 hours, then scrub with soap and water. To clean tile fireplace, apply salt and rub with raw lemon, then scrub with soap and hot water.

Brick fireplaces are easier to keep clean if front is coated with liquid wax. This gives a slight gloss, a comparatively smooth finish, and fills the porous surface in which dust usually accumulates. Soot and dust can be wiped off more easily.

**Plaster of Paris:** Apply a paste of laundry starch and water. Allow to dry for 1 to 2 hours, then brush off.

**Glass Surfaces:** Windows and mirrors ordinarily can be cleaned with clear warm water, but avoid cleaning mirrors in sunshine. Four tablespoons of dilute ammonia to a gallon of water helps remove oily dirt that accumulates in some localities. Or you may use either a weak alcohol solution or one of the various preparations now on the market for cleaning glass surfaces. These are wiped on with a cloth or sponge or sprayed on with an atomizer. In cold climates, vinegar or ammonia added to the water prevents freezing. In using any fluid containing ammonia or alcohol, care must be taken not to spill the cleaning solution on painted, varnished, or lacquered surfaces.

Chamois may be used for both washing and polishing glass. Dip it in warm water and squeeze it as dry as possible. If the window is very dirty, the chamois may have to be rinsed again before the final polishing. Soft, lintless cloths may be used instead of chamois, but with them it takes more time to dry the glass. Rubber squeegees save time and labor in drying windows and are inexpensive. When windows are only dusty, they may be wiped with soft tissue or newspaper. Sometimes moistened newspaper is used to remove dirt before polishing with chamois or dry cloth or paper.

To pick up broken glass from floor, crumple paper, wet, and allow small pieces to stick. For small areas use absorbent cotton.

To make a special glass polish, dissolve ½ cup of fine soap flakes in one cup of boiling water, stir in one pint of whiting and 1 tablespoon of ammonia solution. Apply with a damp cloth or soft paper, allow to dry, and remove with cloth or soft paper. Rub to polish; avoid allowing water to reach cracks at back of mirror.

To keep mirror from fogging, apply a thin film of soap with moist finger, polish with cloth or tissue. Paint may be removed from window glass with soft cloth dipped in turpentine. If paint is hardened, scrape with razor blade or apply paint remover. To prevent frost from collecting on window, apply alcohol or salt water on exterior. To prevent steam from gathering on windows, apply film of glycerine. To remove adhesive tape or residue, apply cleaning fluid. To replace flaking at back of mirror, cover with tinfoil applied with shellac, glue or dark paint.

**Medicine Chest:** Apply thin coat of nail polish over medicine bottle labels to avoid running of ink when wet. Label poisonous liquids clearly. Put pins in corks to help identification in semi-darkness.

**Venetian Blinds:** Wipe with cloth dipped in sudsy water. Art gum will remove smudges. A pair of sugar tongs set with wool pads enables dusting on both sides at one time.

**Venetian Blind Tapes:** Dust with brush or vacuum cleaner attachment. Scrub with soapy water and brush and rinse. To clean without removing, use white shoe cleaner or cleaning fluid on colored tapes.

**Window Screens:** Apply hose, scrub lightly with brush and soapy water. Preserve with screen paint or clear varnish. To prevent soot from coming through window screen, attach cheesecloth to inner side. To keep metal work shiny, coat with colorless lacquer.

**Shoes:** The electric shoe polisher and buffer is made in various designs and packaged with a choice of brushes and buffers. Some come with long handles to minimize bending.

## WASHING DISHES

Soak in hot, soapy water, for sugary dishes; cold, soapy water for egg, fish and doughs; warm water with soap for greasy dishes, pots and pans. Do not use washing soda on aluminum; it burns it. Change water as it becomes dirty.

Gold-trimmed dishes should never be scraped with metal knife (use rubber scraper or soft paper), and should be washed only in mild soap which contains little alkali. To clean gold borders on plates, scrub with tooth brush dipped in bicarbonate of soda, or in moist alum. If alum is used, allow it to stay on for two hours before washing.

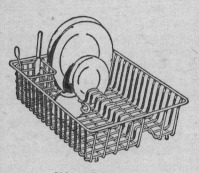

**Dish and silver drainer.**

Glassware should be washed in warm water with a few drops of ammonia added. Do glassware first, and in general, the cleanest dishes first. Wash silverware last; this should be allowed to soak. To add sparkle to glassware, add laundry blueing to water. Rinse with hot water. To remove coffee or tea stains from a cup, wet with vinegar and rub with a damp cloth dipped in salt. Coffee stains respond particularly to baking soda with a spoonful of soap powder added; simmer for 10 minutes. Stack dishes end up (in an ordinary dish drainer if available), to allow maximum air to reach their surface. A spray attached to the hot water faucet may be used to rinse dishes while in a wire drainer. If rinsing water is sufficiently hot, dishes may dry by themselves. However, pots and silver must be wiped.

For bottles, jars, or glassware with a narrow opening, use a long, narrow, flexible bottle brush. If this is not available, insert soft paper inside with a teaspoon, and powder and water. If this method is not practical, fill with cracked egg shells, buckshot, coffee grinds, pebbles, or small hard objects and shake well. To clean the inside of glass drinking straws, use pipe cleaners. To clean the tube of a percolator, add 4 tablespoonfuls of salt to percolating water for 10 minutes; or use a pipe cleaner.

Cut glass should be washed individually in solution of warm water with a few drops of ammonia added. A cloth may be placed at the bottom of the washing pan for protection.

**Baby Bottles:** After each use, rinse and fill with cold water to avoid milk caking on the sides. Rinse nipples and squeeze cold water through holes.

To sterilize, wash with hot water, soap and bottle brush; rinse. (Do same for nipples, nipple covers and bottle caps.) Stack bottles upside down in sterilizer rack. Place nipples, etc. in nipple jar, upside down in proper compartment. Add two inches of hot water. Insert rack. Insert other bottles used for juice and water, funnel, strainer, etc. Place on cover. Boil for 5 minutes. Place ready for making formula.

**Thermos Bottles:** Add a few drops of ammonia to warm water and allow to soak. After being used for milk or cocoa, add baking soda to washing solution. Change the cork frequently. When using, cover the cork with wax paper to prevent absorption, and to allow for easier opening; when not in use, bottle should be uncorked.

**Pots and Pans:** Steel wool is best for scouring. Some substitutes—brown paper crushed into a ball; a sturdy shoe brush with metal bristles clipped way down; coal ashes sifted through a strainer and combined with soap powder and raw potato; a link chain wrapped in a dish towel; crushed egg shells wrapped in cheesecloth.

**Electric Dishwashers:** The most popular electric dishwasher is designed to be attached to home plumbing. Its usefulness depends on its capacity, its number of cycles, its accessories (racks, silverware basket, automatic detergent dispenser). Most modern machines have four cycles: one for small loads, one for pots and pans, one for normal loads, and one for extra health protection needed when someone in the family is ill. Many new models have decorator finishes.

For those who prefer portable, unattached models, rollaway models are made with similar features.

## CLEANING METALS

In general, highly polished metal surfaces require the use of fine abrasives. Less highly burnished surfaces, such as aluminum and iron, may be cleaned with fine steel wool or a feldspar abrasive.

Silver: Requires more care than any other household metal, because sulfur compounds in the air cause it to tarnish. If soap is not rinsed off after washing silver, it tarnishes more quickly. Silver bags and chests sometimes are treated with various salts to retard tarnishing. Air should be kept away from stored silver as much as possible to reduce need for frequent polishing.

The easiest and quickest method for removing tarnish is electrolysis, although this does not produce as bright a lustre as a good silver polish. The tarnish corroding the silver is removed, leaving a dullish, mosslike surface. The "moss" can be reduced by rubbing the silver as it is dried. If this process is used regularly, use a silver polish about every fourth time the silver is cleaned. Electrolysis cannot be used on silver where the dark indented portion is part of the beauty of the design because it removes this oxidation. Where parts are cemented together the hot water may dissolve or loosen the cement.

For cleaning silver by the electrolytic method, fill an aluminum vessel with hot water, or use an enamel pan with a sheet of aluminum or zinc in the bottom. (An aluminum pan will be corroded in the process.) Clean the aluminum by boiling in a weak vinegar solution to keep it bright and active. Add to the hot water in the vessel a teaspoon of salt and a teaspoon of baking soda for each quart of water. Bring the water to a boil and drop in the pieces of silver. If the water is kept boiling, the silver will be brighter. In a few seconds, the time depending on the degree of tarnish, the silver will be bright. It must then be washed in soapy water, rinsed, and polished with a soft, dry cloth.

Silver polishes which act quickly usually are the most abrasive and wear away the silver. It is well to adopt a polish that seems to scratch the least, especially for use on silverplate. Silver pastes should be applied with a soft cloth or brush, thoroughly washed off with soap and water after the tarnish has been removed, and the silver carefully rinsed and dried. (A discarded powder puff is very handy, and more efficient than a cloth for polishing. To polish knives and forks, dip the large end of a cork in polish or powder and rub.

In washing silverware, separate table silver from cutlery to avoid scratching. Soak in soapy warm water but do not allow ivory or bone handles to lie in the water. (They absorb grease and water loosens them.) Rub well and rinse with hot water. Lay silver on clean towel to avoid scratching, then wipe before distributing. To remove egg stains, sprinkle salt on and rub with a wet cloth. If standard polishers are not available soak silver in a solution of rhubarb (a handful to a quart of water), then rinse in hot water and wipe.

Special patented polishing solutions are available. For a homemade cleaning solution, make a jelly solution of 1 cup water, ¼ cup soap flakes, mix with an egg beater until frothy, beat in 2 tablespoons whiting and ½ tablespoon denatured alcohol. Store in tightly covered jar. To obtain a flat polish, without elbow effort, clean silver thoroughly and immerse thoroughly in solution of 1 quart boiling water, 1 tablespoon baking soda, 1 tablespoon cooking salt. Boil for 5 minutes in aluminum kettle. Alkali is a moderately effective silver cleaner.

Long lasting silver polishes and postpolishing sprays eliminate the need to polish for several months.

Ornamental silver should be lacquered to prevent tarnishing. Lacquered silver need only be wiped with a soft cloth.

Oxidized silver should be washed with soap and lukewarm water frequently.

Aluminum: Utensils may be kept clean and stainless with steel wool or feldspar powder. Strong soaps and scouring powders that contain alkaline salts discolor aluminum and should not be used. Discoloration on aluminum may be removed by boiling it in water to which vinegar or cream of tartar has been added.

To wash, soak in solution of water and mild soap. Avoid strong alkalies, washing soda, and potash in washing solutions. If necessary to scrub, use pumice or the finest steel wool. To remove burnt food from an aluminum pot when it does not respond to ordinary scouring, put pot over a low flame without water till food curls up and loosens; or cover scorched portion with vinegar and set the pot in boiling water for 10 minutes before scouring. To remove rust from an aluminum kettle, add 1 tablespoon of sour salt to a pint of water and allow to stand for 10 minutes before rinsing. To remove lime deposits, discolorations, and hard-water scales from aluminum pots, boil vinegar, raw lemon or rhubarb and water for 10 minutes before scouring. Outer surfaces can be treated with fine sandpaper. To prevent scale from forming on the inside of a kettle, keep an oyster shell in the pot until it has accumulated all the scale it can hold. To prevent the bottom from burning, keep two marbles in it at all times. They will rattle when more water is needed.

**Chromium:** Fittings require only frequent wiping with a damp cloth. Use only soap and water. Dry properly to avoid water spots. Avoid polishes or abrasives, as plating is easily rubbed away.

**Copper and Brass:** Clean with a prepared polish. To make a home cleaning preparation, dissolve ½ cup soap flakes in 1 pint of hot water, beat in 3 tablespoons of whiting, and 2 tablespoons of vinegar. Shake before using. Apply with a wad of cotton waste. An emergency cleanser may be made with salt on a piece of lemon. Rinse after cleaning. If copper and brass are not used for foods, they may be lacquered to prevent tarnish. When lacquer begins to peel, it should be removed with denatured alcohol.

**Iron Utensils:** Wash in kitchen soap and hot water. Ammonia may be added. Remove sticky food with soft brush or steel wool. Rinse in hot water, dry thoroughly with cloth. To avoid rust, keep in a warm place or by leaving a film of grease or lard both inside and outside. To remove rust from iron pots, use steel wool with scouring powder or kerosene. Wash thoroughly to remove kerosene odor. Articles which have no contact with food may be rust-proofed by periodic moistening with an oil rag, mineral oil or kerosene, or painted with lead paint. Prevent the grease from going down the drain by placing a paper over the drain before removing contents.

**Monel Metal, Nickel, Nickel-Copper, Stainless Steel:** Wash with warm water, whiting or ammonia solution. Polish with a paste containing similar ingredients. For polishing use feldspar. Avoid abrasive or gritty cleansers. Dry thoroughly.

**Pewter:** Wash in soap and water. Rinse in hot water and wipe thoroughly. Special polishing mixtures should be available. Old pewter, containing a great deal of lead, may be cleaned with a paste solution of whiting and water, rubbed in thoroughly, or with pumice or rottenstone added, or soak in a solution of 1 lump of potash to a quart of water for 24 hours, then rub with olive oil or mineral oil, and dry with a chamois. Avoid strong abrasives as pewter is a soft metal.

**Steel:** Wash in soap and water. Scour with fine sand or fine commercial scouring materials. Use soft wad of paper or large cork instead of dish cloth. Rinse immediately after using for acid foods.

**Tin:** Wash in soapy water and dry thoroughly. To remove burnt food, soak in warm water and allow to stand until food is softened, then scour with feldspar or heat in weak soda solution. Use only fine steel wool for scouring as the tin is usually only a thin coating over an iron base. When it is scratched off, the utensil will rust.

**Zinc:** The coating on galvanized-iron water, scrub, and garbage pails may be cleaned with soap and water and whiting, a volcanic ash or similar abrasive. Feldspar is not quite abrasive enough. Wipe thoroughly to avoid water spots.

**Knife Blades:** Use only for cutting food. Never put into a flame. Avoid having blade rub on metal, as in drawers. (Use a knife rack.) Knives should be kept sharp; best devices are steel sharpening rod or oil-stone sharpener; double-wheel sharpeners may be used on inexpensive cutlery.

**Bread Box:** To remove rust, rub with sandpaper or emery cloth. Apply lard to keep rust-proof.

**Flour Sifter:** Keep in a bag when not in use. To clean it, use a large chicken feather. Avoid washing to avoid flour lumps and rust.

## CLEANING MISCELLANEOUS MATERIALS

**Wooden Utensils:** Do not soak. If shellacked before using, they need only be wiped. To clean natural wood bowls which have no varnish or shellac finish, scrub with dry sand or sandpaper, using circular motion in the direction of the grain, then rinse quickly with cold water and dry.

**Electric Toaster:** Shake gently to remove crumbs; use a chicken feather for brushing.

**Enamel Ware and Agate Ware:** Soap and water are generally satisfactory cleaners. Scour with whiting mixed with soap and water. Use dampened cloth to remove charred or burnt food, soak in washing soda solution. Old fashioned remedy: simmer 3 or 4 potatoes in an inch of water; refill and repeat

3 to 4 times; allow the solution to remain over night; then use scouring powder. If dish is badly chipped, destroy, as these chips are dangerous. To whiten an enamel pot, put 4 tablespoons of bleach in the pot filled with water and allow to stand for a full day. To remove rust stains, rub with a piece of raw lemon, then wash with soap and water. To remove fruit and vegetable stains from a sink, apply a paste solution of bicarbonate of soda and chlorinated lime, and spread on the stains. Allow this to remain for 10 minutes, then wipe off. To remove unidentified stains, fill the sink with a solution of vinegar and laundry bleach, allow to remain over night. To remove stains from enamel faucets, rub with a soft cloth dipped in spirits of ammonia, wash with hot water and soap, and polish with a soft, dry cloth. To remove spots, use full strength ammonia and allow to stand for 30 minutes before washing.

**China and Enamel Surfaces:** Vitreous china and enamel surfaces when new have a smooth, glazed finish. The use of coarse abrasives on them develops tiny scratches that make them harder to keep clean. Soap and water often are sufficient cleansing agents. If an abrasive must be used, select a fine one such as feldspar. Yellow stains on vitreous china plumbing fixtures, caused by iron in the water, may be removed by applying an acid, such as hydrochloric, sparingly on the stain, and rinsing it thoroughly at once. Trisodium phosphate may be used on non-acid resisting enamel.

**Tile Dishes:** Remove soap and allow residue to dry. Scrape out. Wash with cloth soaked in kerosene, allow to dry. Polish with soft cloth.

**Tile, Marble and Granite Surfaces:** Tile, marble and granite surfaces should be cleaned with soap and water and a mild abrasive used only where necessary. Water on tile should be wiped up immediately or it may loosen the tiles.

Powdered marble applied with a brush is used to polish most marble surfaces. For marble statues, scrub with a paste solution of white soap and whiting, wash and dry; or apply solution of sal soda and fuller's earth for 24 hours, then remove.

To remove rust stains on tile, rub with kerosene. If stains are persistent, allow kerosene to soak for 2 hours, then wash with soap and hot water. To brighten, apply laundry starch, allow to dry, and polish with soft cloth. To remove cement or plaster spots, soak with hot water and scrape with razor blade. To remove paint spatters, rub with nail polish remover.

**Outdoor Statuary (granite or concrete):** Scrub with a gritty scouring powder or washing soda, or fine steel wool, and rinse with warm water.

**Toilets:** A disinfectant or hot soapsuds should be used twice a week. Bowl should be cleaned with brush daily, with hot soapsuds dissolved in washing powder. Seats and lids should be wiped with solution of soap or whiting and warm water.

**Plaster:** Sponge with warm water and mild soap powder or flakes. Rinse.

**Cement:** Flush with clear water or scrub with a trisodium phosphate solution after wetting the surface first with clear water. To remove grease, use cleaning fluid. If stain persists, mix cleaning fluid and fuller's earth as a paste; apply, and remove after 1 to 2 hours.

**Ivory:** Rub with denatured alcohol, polish with chamois. To whiten, keep wet with denatured alcohol and allow to dry in sunlight. Alternative: apply salt, rub with lemon. Avoid using water.

**Tortoise Shell:** Apply denatured alcohol, polish with chamois dipped in borax.

**Rubber Articles:** Use mild soap and lukewarm water. Avoid heat, radiators, sunlight, grease or oil. Apply cornstarch or talcum powder after washing. After emptying hot water bottle blow in some air. Repair rips while small. Use adhesive tape for temporary patch, tire patch for permanent repair.

## CARE OF HOUSEHOLD EQUIPMENT

**Stoves:** Stoves should be wiped after each meal. They also need careful cleaning every week, or they become so caked with soot and grease that it is impossible to restore them to their original condition. The porcelain enamel surface that protects the steel beneath is a kind of glass. Though hard, it will break with sudden changes of heat and cold, or hard blows. If the enamel does chip, touch up damaged spots carefully with paint, recommended by your range dealer. It may look patchy but it's better than exposed places that invite rust. Guard against scratches—don't drag pans or anything rough across your enamel range top.

Enamel is easily kept clean with a cloth wrung out of soapy

water. Abrasives roughen the enamel and metal trim, and their use will not be necessary if the stove is wiped after each meal, and if food that boils over is wiped up immediately.

Surface burners need regular, thorough cleaning. Take them out, brush away food or dust particles with a stiff brush. Use a brush also to clean the air shutter. If openings in the burners are clogged, use a fine wire to clean them. Beware of toothpicks; they may break and further clog the burner.

Clean cast-iron burners by boiling them for a short time in a solution of 1 tablespoon of washing soda to 3 quarts of water. Then wash in soap and water. Use a bottle brush to clean the inside of the tube leading to the burner head. Rinse the burners in clear water and wipe dry. Put them upside down in the warm oven for a few minutes to dry thoroughly before replacing.

Burners of materials other than cast iron should not be boiled in soda water. A soap and water bath will usually clean them satisfactorily, with the aid of a scratchless scouring powder and fine steel wool. Clean the pilot light porthole with a fine wire carefully inserted. Clean the top burner pilots with a soft wire brush.

To remove spilled grease from oven, saturate cloths with ammonia solution, place them in oven over night, scrub out spots with soap and water. Repeat if necessary.

To remove fats, heat and pour off while hot. Cool fat may be removed with a rubber scraper, then with paper towel or newspaper.

To remove grease from a single burner, hold it over the flame of another burner. To remove rust from a stove, use fine sandpaper or emery cloth. To blacken or polish a stove, rub with wax paper dipped in stove polish, a few pinches of brown sugar and strong leftover of coffee, and apply the mixture. To prevent rust on a stove, keep the surface covered with mineral oil, kerosene or lard for short periods several times a year. To remove soot from glass door of an oven, wash with baking soda.

Almost all commercial oven cleaners use the power of ammonia plus other chemicals. Some are sprayed, others are rubbed or vaporized to loosen oven dirt. Sprays should be used when the oven is cool.

**Electric Ranges:** The most vital parts of your electric range are the wires that furnish the heat. The wires of open units are easily damaged at any time with sharp objects. Be especially careful not to touch them with any metal object when the current is on. A short circuit—electric shock—blown fuse—burnt-out coil—any or all of these may result. Four things are especially harmful to the wires of an open unit—salt, soda, soap, sugar. Be careful to keep them off the coils; there's danger of burning out the wires.

When food spills over on the surface units, let it char. When the unit is cool, brush off particles with a non-metallic bristle brush. If needed, enclosed units may then be washed off. Keep the pans beneath the surface units clean. Lift them out if they can be removed and wash them like any cooking utensil. If you can't take them out, wipe them with a damp cloth. Keep the drip trays beneath clean—wash them every day if possible. They not only become more difficult to clean if left for a long time, but spilled foods may harm the finish and even cause some drip trays to rust.

New electric ranges are made with push-button controls, automatic heating and timing, self-cleaning ovens, built-in meat thermometers, built-in rotisseries, outlets for other appliances, and integrated hoods.

**Refrigerators:** Refrigerators must be cleaned every week to keep them sweet and sanitary. As soon as anything is spilled in a refrigerator, it should, of course, be wiped up immediately. To prevent rust on refrigerator trays, coat with floor wax.

If the interior is free from spots where food has been spilled, it may be washed with clear warm water in which soda has been dissolved. The use of soda or other equally mild alkali helps to remove odors.

Keep the condenser clean with long-handled brush or vacuum cleaner attachment. Refrigerator should be placed away from heat, with air space at back and top. Some open-type mechanisms require periodic oiling and cleaning. Use a medium heavy oil. A motor should be oiled once in 3 years. If enamel chips or rusts, retouch immediately.

If going away for a short period, turn refrigerator to its warmest setting. If leaving for a long period, remove all food, disconnect, leave door open. When moving, special care must be taken not to jolt or vibrate the mechanisms. In resetting, mechanism should be checked to see that all bolts are fastened.

If refrigerator does not work (1) check that electrical current is coming through; (2) check control switch to make sure it is on; give mechanism a minute to come through; (3) if mechanism runs but does not refrigerate, turn off switch and allow ice to melt, then start mechanism again and check; (4) if mechanism seems to run too much, clean condenser with brush, check to see if too much warm food is being placed in refrigerator or too many ice cubes made, set control for colder temperature.

**Washing Machine:** Tighten and oil. Check occasionally to see that all bolts and screws in the frame are tight. Follow manufacturer's directions for oiling. Some machines are permanently lubricated at the factory. The manufacturer's directions usually tell how much to oil the machine for use once a week. If you wash oftener you may need to oil more often. Too much or the wrong kind of oil is just as harmful as too little oil.

Casters need frequent oiling because they often get wet and the metal parts may rust. Avoil spilling oil on any rubber parts because oil ruins rubber. If washer gets tipped and oil is spilled from around the gears, have a serviceman check the machine and replace spilled oil if needed. Protect machine against bangs, bumps, and jerks that may injure the motor, dent the metal, or chip the finish of the tub.

**Cleaners:** Examine the nozzle and vacuum parts, to tell whether your cleaner cleans by suction alone, or whether it has a sweeping and beating action too. This makes a difference in the way you use and care for the cleaner.

Proper brush length: To test, hold the machine with the nozzle part up. Lay a stiff piece of cardboard across the nozzle. The bristles should come just above the edge of the card—about 1/32 of an inch. To lower the brushes, follow the manufacturer's directions. Usually this is done by adjusting a pin, screw, or lever at each end of the brush roll. Most brushes may be lowered two to five times. As soon as the bristles wear too short after the lowest adjustment, replace the brush or roll.

Store cleaner in a dry place so the metal parts won't rust. This storage place also needs to be cool—away from sun or radiators—for the sake of rubber cord and rubber parts.

**Lawn Mowers:** Wipe blades with oily cloth after each use. Oil bearings and grease wheels once a week. Store in dry place, making certain blades do not touch floor. Never run over walks or stones.

**Garden Hose:** Drain after each use. Store flat in large loose coils, in cool, dry place. If hung, it should be placed over a rounded object. Keep away from oil, heat, and sun. Avoid pinching, bending, running over. Repair leaks with auto tube patch or plastic cement, covered with friction tape. Bad tears may be cut away and hose rejoined with a metal hose mender inserted in each part, and held in place with an outside clamp.

**Clocks, Moving Equipment:** Oil occasionally. Use atomizer, squirt through holes provided.

## PLUMBING CARE

**Drains:** Most drain stoppages could be prevented by the regular use of a good drain pipe solvent, and care in keeping material like grease, lint, hair, coffee grounds, and bits of garbage out of the drain.

**Faucets:** Many leaks are caused by not shutting faucets completely off, or by shutting faucets off too hard. Faucet handles should be turned firmly enough to close the faucet completely yet not hard enough to grind the washer into the seat.

**Fixtures:** Avoid the use of harsh abrasive cleaners for fixtures. Fixtures have a gloss which is virtually glass. Any cleanser which scratches glass will harm the finish of the fixture. Always remove diamond rings when cleaning fixtures. If medicine, acids, or fruit juices are spilled on fixtures, rinse off with water immediately.

**Sinks:** Don't use uncovered sink drainboards as cutting boards. Don't chop ice on sink drainboards. Don't scrape pots or pans across basin or drainboards. Don't let garbage stand in the sink. Don't cut anything on the sink drainboard without protecting the surface. Don't place hot pans in the sink.

**Toilets:** Don't place heavy articles such as jars of cold cream in medicine cabinets over lavatories. Many lavatories have been cracked by jars which slipped out of greasy hands.

**Chromium Platings:** If exposed to salt, salt air, or calcium chloride, chromium plated surfaces should be washed frequently with soap and water. After drying, a protective coating of furniture wax should be applied. Occasional washing with soap and water and drying with soft cloth will ordinarily be sufficient attention.

**Flush Tanks:** Replace worn float valves and old or deformed tank balls. Check flush rim openings for stoppage due to hard water. Keep bowls in sanitary condition by frequent use of cleaner. Avoid cleaning brushes which might mar the finish of the bowl.

**Toilet Seats:** Use soap and water to clean sheet-covered seats and wax or oil to clean painted wooden seats. Polish hinges with metal polish.

**Water Heaters:** Avoid excessive temperatures which hasten corrosion and increase scale deposit from hard water. Have thermostat adjusted to prevent temperatures higher than 140 degrees.

For families of average size (3 to 4 persons), the home water heater should have a storage-rating of from 30 to 50 gallons. Families with four to six members will get best results from a water heater of more than 50 gallons capacity. Three successive loads in automatic clothes washers call for a 50-gallon unit. If there is more than one bathroom, a 50-gallon water heater is essential.

**Hot Water Boiler:** Have soot and fly ash cleaned from exterior flues. Have interior water passageways cleaned with boiler liquids, if required. Have entire hot water heating plant checked in the spring by an experienced heating and piping contractor.

**Oil Burner:** Keep motors and fans clean. Lubricate frequently. Clean burner nozzles and ignition. Clean filters of hot air system once each month with vacuum cleaner. Have heating and piping contractor or oil burner serviceman check controls and air volume.

**Stoker:** Keep motor clean and lubricate frequently. Use care in selection of fuel. Maintain proper firebed depth to protect iron.

**Controls:** Safety controls such as relief valves protect water heaters against damage from explosions. It is important that these valves operate freely. Let water run through them at least twice a year to see that they will act in an emergency.

**Air Valves:** Have air valves on steam heating system checked by heating and piping contractor to be sure they are venting properly. Have defective valves replaced by new multi-venting valves which maintain perfect balance of heat distribution.

**Motors:** Motors on circulators, oil burners, and stokers should be lubricated frequently with grade of oil recommended by manufacturer. Do not oil too freely.

**Indirect Water Heating Coils and Expansion Tank:** Flush sediment from coils at frequent intervals. Have air expelled from expansion tank.

## CARE OF BEDDING

**Mattresses:** Innerspring mattresses should be turned every two weeks—end for end one time and side for side the next. It's advisable to do the same for solid upholstered mattresses every week. To prevent rust marks on mattresses, keep springs well painted.

Opening the windows every morning and throwing back the bed clothes gives the air a chance to penetrate the mattress and keep it fresh. Occasionally, it is a good idea to move the mattress next to the open window and let the sun's rays shine on it. Solar rays keep the upholstery from packing down and act as germ killers. Clean once a month with a vacuum cleaner attachment or a soft brush.

Metal bedsprings can be cleaned with a clean, dry cloth. Some mattress and spring covers can easily be removed for laundering once a month. Innerspring mattresses should never be beaten with a rug beater, and care should be taken never to bend or roll mattresses when moving them.

**Pillows** should be fluffed up every day. When pillow slips are changed, give the air a chance to penetrate the filling before putting on the clean slip. Pillows may be washed but it is usually advisable to have it done by a reliable laundry that has the proper equipment for this service. However, once the feathers have started to deteriorate, even the finest laundering will not put new life into them.

**How to Make a Bed:** (1) Put on a mattress pad. (2) Spread bottom sheet out, with center fold following center of mattress. This leaves equal amounts hanging on both sides. If sheet is too short to allow equal tucking, tuck in more at head than foot. (3) Tuck sheet in top and bottom. Make mitered corners. Start at foot. Grasp sides of sheet about two feet from corner. Lift up straight so as to form triangle and turn back over edge of mattress. Tuck the overhang firmly under mattress with your free hand. Then let the triangle down and tuck under. (4) Miter foot corners of bottom sheet, then pull taut and miter head corners. This smooths and anchors the whole sheet. (5) Spread top sheet so that hem on turn back will be right-side up. Tuck well at foot. If sheet length

How to make a bed.

allows, make a 3" fold all the way across, 8 to 12 inches from the foot of the bed, depending on the sleeper's height. This gives plenty of toe room. Tuck sheet in and miter at foot only. (6) Miter blankets at foot only. If you have a too-short blanket, put it underneath and don't tuck—the well-tucked and mitered top blanket will hold it fast. Keep a spare blanket, folded like an accordion so one pull brings it up, at the foot of the bed. (7) Turn top sheet back over blanket, and tuck sides under. (8) Put on spread, making sure sides are even. Turn back about 10" from top of bed. Fluff up each pillow lightly; hold lengthwise by the corners, and take up slack in one-inch fold. This makes it firmer and neater. Put pillows at head of bed, overlapping the fold of the spread. Pull spread over pillows, easing the crease under them and tucking in at the back.

**Blankets:** Notwithstanding claims of manufacturers, do not machine wash or dry-clean electric blankets. (1) Have your wool and part-wool blankets dry-cleaned if at all possible. This preserves nap and resiliency important to a blanket's insulating power. It also lessens the likelihood of shrinkage. And dry-cleaning costs very little more than having your blanket washed commercially.

(2) If you are washing blankets at home, follow rules exactly. (3) Shake blankets well to remove dust. Wash only one blanket at a time. (4) Use a mild, reliable soap. Have water lukewarm—between 90° and 100°. (5) If you're using

a machine, follow the directions for your particular type of machine exactly. Remove very soiled spots on binding with soft brush. Don't use more soap or detergent than directions call for. Don't overload the machine. (6) If you're washing by hand, put blanket in tub of lukewarm suds. Let stand several minutes, then put through very loose wringer into second tub of suds. Unfold, and let blanket become thoroughly soaked. Return through wringer to first suds, and repeat once or twice. Rinse thoroughly. (7) Never rub a blanket. Never use a washboard. Never twist or wring out by hand. This pounds the wool fibers together, and causes the blanket to "felt-down," become boardy. Always squeeze gently.

(8) Never subject a blanket to temperature shifts. This causes shrinkage. Don't wash blankets in warm room and then hang to dry in very cold air. Wash on warm day if possible. (9) Hang washed blanket over two lines to distribute weight and hasten drying. No clothespins, please. Always hang in shade. (10) Shift blanket often, stretching gently and shaking to fluff up the nap. Now and then squeeze the lower edges where water has collected. (11) When blanket is almost dry, brush lightly to raise the nap. Use a clean whisk broom, or better yet, the sort of wire brush you can buy for this purpose. (12) Press binding with warm iron. Never press blanket itself. (13) Make sure a blanket is just cleansed or washed and thoroughly dry before storing it. Put your favorite moth-preventive in the folds of each blanket. Wrap in heavy paper not more than two blankets to a package, making the package as air-tight as possible. Store in a cool place where the temperature is fairly constant. New blankets should be left in the original package. (14) See that your sheet turns back far enough over blanket to protect it. A 20" turn back is ideal. (15) If you live in a dusty or sooty locality, put blanket covers over blankets at night to avoid soot and dirt that sift in and settle throughout your blankets. (16) To keep outer edges of quilts and comforters clean, sew a washable material along the binding. This can be removed and laundered frequently.

Upholstery Cushions: They keep shape longer if you up-end them every night.

## LAUNDERING

**Soaps:** There are five types of soap used in laundering:

1. Mild white soap contains no alkali, is safe for all fibers.
2. Laundry soap contains a small amount of alkali. It rids clothes of oil, dirt, perspiration and earth. It may be used for all fabrics except wool, rayon, and fine fabrics.
3. Yellow soap is used for clothes which have heavy dirt, oil, grease, etc. It may be used only for white cottons and linens, or those fabrics with fast colors.
4. Bleaching soaps which include bleaching chemicals and other ingredients which overcome the problems of hard water; they should never be used on wool, rayon, silk, or colored fabrics.
5. Detergents or soapless soaps, chemicals which loosen dirt without soap suds. Detergents with high phosphate content were deteriorating the water supply. New low phosphate and no-phosphate biodegradable products are now available.

All types of soaps may come in either cakes, chips, flakes, jellies, or dissolved solutions. In actual practice, it makes little difference which type you use except that some forms save time by dissolving and getting to work more quickly than others. Cake soap lasts twice as long when it is dry as when it is moist. It is bought advantageously in quantity.

To MAKE SOAP: (1) Cover fat with water, cook slowly, and allow to cool. (2) Add two tablespoons powdered borax, 1½ qts. cold water, 1 can of lye to 4 pts. of clean fat. (3) Remove the clean, odorless fat which has risen to the top. (4) If desired, repurify by liquefying and straining through muslin or flannel. (5) While still liquid, pour soap into mold lined with wax paper and allow to harden over night. (6) Cut into bars with fine string.

**Washing Powders:** For value received, washing powders are expensive. They usually contain powdered soap, washing soda, trisodium phosphate, borax, or inert scouring materials alone or in combination. Most washing powders contain too much free alkali and should be used judiciously.

**Detergents:** Some synthetic detergents wash wool faster and cleaner than soap and solve hard-water problems, as no curd is formed and no water softener required. However, even the best of the detergents do not wash cotton as well as soap treated with water softener. Synthetic sponges and sponge cloths make cleaning easier. Some are impregnated with cleaning and polishing compounds.

**Preparing for Laundering:** Tuesday is replacing Monday as a washday. This allows for the extra duties that have accumulated during Sunday, and for preparing the clothes for laundering. Set aside a special day for curtains, blankets, and such pieces requiring particular attention.

Mend all torn places, except the feet of hosiery, and remove stains before washing. Many small tears are made larger, and many otherwise removable stains are set, by laundering. Turn all garments inside out. Place the cotton and linen together and the silk and wool in different piles. Separate the white from the colored in each pile, and also separate the very dirty from the slightly soiled. Notice whether rayon or other synthetic fibers are present in any of the fabrics or trimmings. Rayon is often much weakened by water and must be laundered as a very delicate material. Sort the clothes in a clean place. The practice of throwing soiled clothes on a dirty floor increases the work of laundering. A convenient division of clothes and order of washing is as follows (When the wash is small, some groups are combined.): (1) Cotton and linen: Table linen, doilies, centerpieces. (2) Bed linen, dresser scarfs, towels. (3) Thin white clothing. (4) Heavy white clothing. (5) Handkerchiefs. (6) Slightly soiled, light-colored garments. (7) Slightly soiled dark-colored garments. (8) Very dirty garments. (9) Hosiery. (10) Silks and synthetics.

Some housewives have turned the job over entirely to co-operative or commercial laundries. Many others still do it all at home. In between is a large group that sends out heavy pieces and does the remainder at home.

You can save on laundry by using plastic, paper or fabric place mats, or transparent plastic tablecloths that fit over linens; by using paper tissue for handkerchiefs. Some cities have linen rental services whose charges are as little as normal laundry costs. If your laundry bill is large, investigate putting in your own washing machine or using a laundromat service where the charge is modest.

**Laundry Equipment:** In modern home planning, emphasis is laid on a compact laundry center adapted to the needs of the particular family. Modern equipment and good lighting is important. Doors and windows should be placed to give thorough ventilation, to draw off steam, odors, and heat unavoidable in washing. Walls should be light in color and should be treated so that they are not affected by steam. Several coats of good-quality oil paint give a satisfactory finish. The laundry floor should be of material that wears well, is not too hard for the feet, does not soak up water or get slippery when wet, and is easily cleaned. Of the materials used, wood and concrete are the most common. Concrete is not affected by water, can be fitted with a drain, and is not slippery, but it is more fatiguing to stand on than wood. Rubber mats or low wooden platforms overcome this somewhat.

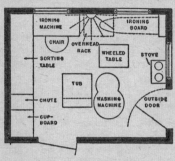

A laundry room (10½ x 8 feet) with modern equipment placed for good routing of the work.

**The Washing Process:** Since white cottons and linens make up the bulk of the family laundry, the general methods of washing and ironing are given for them, and directions for handling colored cottons and linens, woolens, silks, and other materials requiring special care are given separately.

---

### WASHING TEMPERATURES

| | |
|---|---|
| White or colorfast cottons, linens | 140° F. up |
| Non-colorfast fabrics | 110° F. or under |
| Silks | 110° F. or under |
| Wools or Aralac blends | 100° F. or under |
| Rayons (unless labeled for higher temperatures) | 110° F. or under |
| Nylons | 110° F. or under |

---

SOAKING: Soak clothes over night, or even for a shorter time. This loosens dirt, saves time, and lessens wear.

FIRST SUDS: Remove the clothes from the water in which they have been soaked. Wash them either by hand or by machine in plenty of soapsuds as hot as the hand can bear. When the water becomes dirty, drain it off and replace it.

SECOND SUDS: Washing through a second suds is advisable, but not always necessary.

BOILING: Clothes may be boiled if it is desired to disinfect them thoroughly. Under good conditions of washing, rinsing, and drying the boiling may be omitted. If it is done, wring the clothes from the wash water, place in fresh, hot, soapy water, and boil them for 5 to 10 minutes. Longer boiling has a tendency to yellow white fabrics. As the clothes are lifted from the boiler allow them to drain as much as possible.

If the clothes are very dirty or yellowed, kerosene or turpentine may be added in the proportion of 1 to 6 tablespoons for a boilerful of water. The clothes must then be thoroughly rinsed in order to remove the odor.

RINSING: After the clothes have been washed and boiled, rinse them thoroughly in plenty of hot, clear, soft water. Cold water hardens the soap and makes it more difficult to remove. Do not add blueing to this rinse water. It is essential that all soap and washing powders be removed from clothes before they are blued. Thorough rinsing is of great importance. Soap and washing powders weaken and yellow fabrics when allowed to remain on them indefinitely. Wring the clothes from the rinse water as before.

Bleaching: Clothes that are very much discolored from long storage or poor washing may require bleaching. Often merely moistening and spreading them on the grass in the sun is sufficient. If this is not effective, chemicals should be used with proper precautions. In all cases, the bleaching chemicals should be carefully labeled and stored where not accessible to children. The suggestions given below are for white materials only. Avoid using chemical bleaching agents on dyed fabrics. All bleaching agents must be thoroughly rinsed from the fabrics after the desired results are obtained.

JAVELLE WATER is one of the most common bleaches for cotton and linen. It is prepared by dissolving ½ lb. of washing soda to 1 quart of cold water, and adding ¼ lb. of bleaching powder (chloride of lime). An earthenware jar or granite container is best. Allow the mixture to settle, preferably over night, and dip off the top liquid or strain through several thicknesses of cheesecloth so that the solution for bleaching contains no solid particles. Store in tightly closed bottles. When needed, place ½ pint of this mixture in 1 gallon or more of cold or lukewarm water, and immerse the clothes. Allow them to remain until sufficiently bleached (more than ½ hour is likely to be harmful to the fabric). Boiling in Javelle water may also weaken the material. Even the strongest of cotton or linen fabrics can be greatly weakened by a too-concentrated bleaching solution, high temperatures, or long treatment.

Rinse thoroughly in water, and if possible pass into an anti-chlor bath, containing ½ ounce of sodium thiosulphate and ¼ ounce of 36 percent acetic acid per gallon. Sodium thiosulphate (hypo) is used in many homes where amateur photography is being done, or it can be obtained at the drug store.

In using Javelle water, care must be taken with fabrics already weakened, such as curtains. No garment containing silk or wool either as part of the fabric or as stitching or trimming, should be bleached in this way. Silk and wool dissolve in this solution. No fabric containing a colored design should be treated in this way, as many dyes are not fast to chlorine bleaches.

HYDROGEN PEROXIDE is an effective bleach, not harmful to most fabrics. It can be used in various concentrations, depending upon the amount of bleaching required. One pint to a gallon of water is an average quantity. A teaspoon of concentrated ammonia solution or of sodium perborate added to each gallon of the solution makes the action stronger.

OXALIC ACID is a good general bleach, but is used chiefly when ink or rust stains are very widely scattered over the garment. One ounce per gallon of water is a good concentration. Use the solution cold or heated to a temperature that can be comfortably borne by the hand. Place the fabrics in it and leave until bleached. Ten minutes should be sufficient, unless the stains are very persistent. Rinse the fabrics very thoroughly, and, to neutralize any remaining acid, pass them through a bath containing ½ ounce of borax per gallon or through a fairly strong solution of ammonia. Continue the rinsing with clear water until there is no danger of any of the acid being left in the fabric.

## SPECIAL LAUNDERING PROBLEMS

Colored Cottons and Linens: Do not soak unless colors are known to be colorfast. Home color-setting methods are not effective. Handle rapidly.

**Woolens:** Moist wool is sensitive to rubbing and heat. Unless special precautions are taken, it becomes hard and shrunken when laundered and cannot be restored to its original condition. Weak solutions of alkalies increase this tendency, and strong ones tender and often completely dissolve the fabric. Shrinkage is increased by intense heat and also by marked changes in temperature, making it imperative that all water used be lukewarm. Woolens are often washed correctly, but rinsed in cold water, which causes a sudden contraction likely to be permanent. Measure knitted garments and any others likely to shrink, so that they may be stretched later to their original size. If woolens are soaked at all, let it be for only a very short time. Avoid using water that has been softened with large quantities of alkaline compounds. Use only neutral soaps and no strong washing powders. Borax and ammonia solutions are the safest assisting agents. Use soap in the form of a solution or jelly, and do not rub soap directly on the fabric. Have an abundance of lukewarm suds (about 100° F.). Use more water in proportion to bulk for wool than for any other material. Squeeze and work in the suds without rubbing. Press out the excess water and wash in a second suds of the same temperature. Hand washing is less likely than machine washing to shrink woolens and make them lose their softness. If a machine is used, do not crowd the articles and do not agitate them for as long a period as is customary with other materials. Too long and too vigorous agitation is one cause of wool fabrics felting during laundering. Never boil wool materials. Squeeze them from the last suds and rinse free from soap in several changes of lukewarm water as near the temperature of the suds as possible. Wring through a loosely set wringer, being careful not to stretch the fabric.

A dressing is sometimes needed in lightweight wool fabrics and in wool and cotton materials. A dilute glue solution, alone or added to clear boiled starch, may be used. If the fabric is dark, it is better to omit the starch. Have the solution lukewarm, and dry the fabric at a moderate temperature or the glue will show. Dilute solutions of gum arabic and gum tragacanth may also be used.

All wool materials should be dried in a warm place, but not near a fire or in the direct sunlight. Never allow them to freeze. Hang knitted underwear from the shoulders, shaping the garments occasionally and squeezing the water from the bottom. Spread sweaters and similar knitted garments back down with sleeves outstretched on several thicknesses of clean, soft material laid flat. Measure and shape according to the dimensions taken before the garment was wet, and pin in place if necessary. Turn occasionally after it is almost dry. The excess of water may be removed previously by placing it in a sheet suspended in cradle form, but the pad is more satisfactory. Knitted garments may be dried on forms.

Blankets may be placed over a line with a half or fourth on one side. The ends should be squeezed occasionally to remove the excess water. When dry, raise the nap by brushing well with a clean, stiff whisk broom, or with hand cards such as are used for combing wool. The warmth of a blanket depends very largely upon the amount of nap.

Silks: Silks should be washed in the same manner as woolens. Though there is less danger of shrinkage, and they are not so sensitive to alkaline solutions, silks are usually very delicate and must be handled carefully. Hand washing is preferable. If a machine is used, such garments should be placed in net bags and the machine run only a very short time.

For colored silks, the suds should be very heavy and luke-warm or even cooler (about 100° F.). There is less danger of injury to both fabric and color if soap bark is used instead of soap. Do not rub too hard, as the fibers may be broken or the gloss dulled. Careful squeezing or just lifting up and down in the suds is better than rubbing. Avoid strong soap and washing powders and do not twist the fabric to wring out the suds.

Rinse thoroughly in water of the same temperature, and remove the water finally by squeezing and patting between dry towels or heavy cloths. A final rinse in a bath containing a half ounce of 36 percent acetic acid to a gallon of water tends to increase the lustre. Do not wrinkle silks any more than necessary. If an extractor is used, special precautions are needed, as long, hard extraction produces wrinkles very difficult to remove. Gum arabic and gelatin are good stiffening agents for most silks. Dry them as quickly as possible, but never in the sun. Rapid drying before an electric fan prevents watermarks and assists in retaining a good finish.

Synthetics: Before washing, either by hand or by machine, badly soiled areas should be pre-treated to insure best laundering results. For heavily soiled areas, pre-treat by rubbing thoroughly with a heavy-duty liquid detergent or a paste of detergent or soap and water. For spot or stain removal, follow normal procedures for other washable fabrics.

Best results for appearance and ease of care are achieved by washing clothing after each day's wearing. Hand wash if garment has delicate trim or construction.

Remove articles of trim, such as ribbons and bows, which you suspect are probably not washable. This precaution is suggested in order to prevent staining of the fabric by trim which proves to be nonwashable.

If, after washing, touch-up ironing is required, use a steam iron or a dry iron at a rayon or synthetic setting.

HAND WASHING: (1) Wash the garment thoroughly in warm suds (100° F.) of a heavy-duty detergent or soap and a water conditioner such as Calgon, or similar products. Avoid wringing or twisting the garment while washing or rinsing. (2) Give the garment a thorough rinsing in clear warm water. (3) Remove the dripping-wet garment from the rinse water. Place it on a nonstaining hanger and allow it to drip dry. While the garment is still wet, shape the collar, cuffs, and seams with the fingers.

RIBBONS, LACES, AND VEILINGS are restored very nearly to their original finish by dipping in skimmed milk or whey. Be sure the milk-fat has been removed, as it forms grease spots. Stretch over a smooth surface to dry and leave unironed. The odor of milk which is first apparent on the fabric soon disappears.

Some silk prints are not colorfast. A dress of such a fabric should be dried as quickly as possible. Squeeze out the excess water with a turkish towel; then, being careful to keep all folds opened out, hang in the air until just evenly damp. Press on the wrong side. However, do not iron while the hems or any other thick parts are wet. This may make the colors run.

SILK TAFFETAS may often be handled best by lifting them out of the rinse water directly onto a towel to remove most of the water. Squeezing makes lines that are hard to iron out. Iron while fairly wet, since such fabrics tend to dry out before the entire garment can be ironed.

PONGEES are very easily watermarked. Wet spots on the fabric become darker when they are ironed dry. To avoid such difficulties have the dampness very evenly distributed and iron on the wrong side, or iron the dry fabric. Steaming is also effective. Use a double press-cloth and sufficient water to moisten the upper layer. Thus no water reaches the silk, and the steam tends to remove previously formed watermarks. Finally, finish by pressing on the wrong side.

SYNTHETIC FABRICS, such as the rayons, should be laundered with the same care as silks; that is, wash in heavy lukewarm (100° F.) suds of neutral soap. Do not rub. Squeeze and rinse repeatedly until clean. A few types of rayon are weaker when wet and must be handled with particular care. Rinse in water of the same temperature as the suds in order to avoid sharp changes which increase shrinkage. Dry on a clothes hanger or by rolling in a turkish towel. Clothespins tend to tear such materials especially if they are knitted.

Lace Curtains: Measure both dimensions of the curtains before laundering, in order that they may be stretched to the correct size. Handle the curtains carefully in the suds, squeezing and working them rather than rubbing. Many curtains that appear strong have been greatly weakened by sunlight and go to pieces when washed. If a machine is used, enclose the curtains in net or muslin bags.

Rinse and blue white curtains as in washing ordinary fabrics. Cream, ecru, and brown curtains may be retinted. Add a strong solution of tea or coffee, or a combination of the two, slowly to the hot water until the desired tint is produced when tested on a piece of muslin. Brown cotton dyes can be used in very weak solutions, and should be tested on a sample for shade. Remove the curtain as soon as the desired shade is obtained.

Starch the curtains if desired or use gelatin or gum arabic as a stiffener. Dry curtains in stretchers, or spread a sheet on the floor, mark off the size desired, and pin the curtains to it, stretching where necessary. Stretchers that do not form scallops where the pins are inserted are best for straight-edged curtains.

Pillows: Pillows may be washed without removing the feathers. Scrub in a weak washing soda solution, using a good suds. Repeat in a second suds if necessary. Rinse in lukewarm water, changing it two or three times. If an extractor is used, extract, and then dry the pillows on a sheet in a warm place, preferably in the sun. Otherwise, squeeze out as much of the excess water as possible and dry in the same way. Beat the pillows from time to time during drying.

A more satisfactory method is to transfer the feathers to a muslin bag 2 or 3 times the size of the ticking. Sew the edges of the openings of the ticking and the bag together and shake the feathers from one to the other. Wash and dry the bag of feathers in the same way as a whole pillow. After the ticking has been washed separately, apply a very stiff starch mixture to the inside with a sponge to close the pores of the material and prevent the feathers from working through. Refill the ticking in the same way it was emptied.

**Slips:** Use mild soap in lukewarm water. Don't rub. Knit slips should be spread flat, shaped on a towel to dry, and need no ironing. Woven slips should be squeezed (not wrung out), dried away from heat or strong sunlight, ironed with a warm iron on the wrong side, with the weave.

**Bathing Suits:** Rinse in fresh water immediately after each wearing and dry in the shade. They should be washed frequently in a solution of mild soapsuds and lukewarm water. Before packing, make certain the double thicknesses are thoroughly dried. Never pack away wet suits. Never apply hot iron. Avoid sun.

**Foundation Garments:** Follow washing directions on label, if available. Launder frequently, as perspiration deteriorates rubber. Turn garment inside out with all fasteners closed. Immerse in solution of mild soap and lukewarm water. Avoid rubbing, twisting, wringing, too much soaping. To remove spots, use soft brush or turkish towel with soap flakes. Squeeze soapsuds gently through elastic sections, dry with turkish towel inserted between folds and applied on both sides, then roll gently and reshape by stretching as necessary. In hanging on a line, distribute the weight evenly. Bras and lightweight girdles should be smoothed out and hung double over a rod or clothesline. To reshape bra cups, stretch gently along all lines of stitching, such as seams and darts, before hanging and again when nearly dry. Heavier girdles and corsets should be shaped and dried the same way, but their fabric panels can be "touched up" with a warm iron, if desired. Avoid hanging in sunlight or near direct heat. Press, following the line, only fabric sections or lace tops. Do not apply heat to elastic.

**Hosiery:** Prepare suds first, squeeze, don't twist. Remove excess moisture with terry toweling. Shape over sock frames or over a bar away from heat or cold.

**Bathroom Rugs:** Swish in bucket of soapy water, with plumber's plunger.

**Dish Cloths:** To remove coffee and tea stains, keep them in a wide mouth jar half-filled with a laundry bleach solution.

**Crocheted Bed Spreads:** Soak in a mild soap and warm water with occasional swishing. Remove water gently and spread flat to dry. To fasten colors, add acetic acid or a few drops of vinegar to washing water.

**Turkish Towels:** Add a cup of borax to the rinse water, shake well while still wet. Do not iron.

**Fringe:** Shake well while still wet to avoid entanglement.

**Chamois:** Use mild soap and lukewarm water, rinse in soapy water, dry in a towel, rub with fingers before drying is completed to retain softness.

**Infected Clothes:** Clothing and linen used by a person suffering with any contagious disease and handkerchiefs used during a cold, need special treatment and should not be kept or washed with other clothes. Separate bags or other containers that can be sterilized or destroyed. Boiling for 10 minutes is the simplest method of sterilizing but the heat may injure some fibers or set stains and dirt. Clothes may be disinfected before washing by immersion in one of the following solutions for 1 hour:

A 5 percent dilution of the commercial solution of formaldehyde (formalin).

A 1 percent solution of phenol (pure carbolic acid).

A ½ percent solution of liquor cresolis compositus.

Woolen goods may be disinfected by immersing in water 165° F. for 20 minutes. If then carefully washed and dried, no undue shrinkage of the garments should result and most infectious agents will have been destroyed.

The person who handles the infected garments should wear some form of apron to protect the clothing. This apron should be disinfected immediately after the soiled clothes are handled. Hands and forearms should be thoroughly scrubbed with soap, water, and a nail brush for 10 minutes, and thoroughly rinsed in either the phenol solution or the cresolis solution mentioned above, or in a 1 to 1,000 solution of bichloride of mercury.

### BLUEING, STARCHING AND SPECIAL FINISHES

**Blueing:** A fabric that has been properly manufactured and always properly laundered does not need blueing. There are few of these in the average household, but too much rather than too little blueing is usually added. Blueing is used in laundering to cover or neutralize the yellowish tint of white fabrics. It does not remove the cause of the yellow tint, but produces a gray which appears white to the eye. In the case of soluble blues, one of violet cast is required to give the desired effect.

There are two kinds of household blueing available, the soluble and the insoluble. The insoluble is found as balls, cubes, or powders. There are also an enormous number of blue dyes on the market which may be used for blueing. In general, a blueing should give a bright, clear color of a faint violet blue shade, its strength should correspond to its cost, and it should be either soluble in water or composed of such light particles that it will not settle out easily.

**Starches and other finishes:** Starching is an effort to replace the original finish which the textile manufacturer gave to the fabric, and which, in most cases, is removed by laundering. This finish stiffens the fabric, leaves it smooth and pliable, and gives it a certain "feel" which makes it attractive. Starching should, if possible, produce all these results and not just stiffen the garment.

Each kind of starch forms a characteristic paste with boiling water, and even pastes made from the same kind of starch obtained at different times or from several sources may vary. Soft water gives a thicker paste than hard water. The pastes of some starches require longer cooking than others to reach their maximum thickness. The stiffness of the paste, however, is not an indication of the stiffness that a starch will give to a fabric. Natural starches are insoluble in cold water but when mixed with water and heated will dissolve.

The amount of starch needed for garments depends on the kind and construction of fabric, the manner in which they are to be used, the stiffness desired, and whether they are wrung by machine or hand. If put through a wringer after starching, thicker paste is necessary to produce a desired stiffness than if wrung by hand. The wringer removes the excess starch more evenly and leaves the garment drier, but many pieces requiring starch may have trimmings that make it inadvisable to wring them by machine.

The following is a good general starch, and this paste can be thinned with hot water until it gives the stiffness desired for the fabric:

| | |
|---|---|
| 2 to 6 tablespoons corn-<br>starch | ½ teaspoon lard, paraffin,<br>or any white wax |
| ⅓ cup cold water | 1 quart of boiling water. |

Mix the starch and part of the cold water, and stir into the boiling water in a double boiler. Use the remaining water to rinse out the adhering starch. Add the lard or white wax, and cook for 15 to 20 minutes. Strain if lumps have formed.

Starch garments wrong side out, and leave them so until they are sprinkled. For white clothes use the starch as hot as the hands can stand. Hot starch penetrates better and more evenly, and does not leave glazed spots when ironed. Keep the bulk of the starch hot and use only a part of it at a time, replacing it frequently when it becomes cold and thin. More satisfactory results are obtained by having two pans of starch, besides the reserve supply. Dilute one with enough water to make a good paste for the thinner materials, and keep the starch in the other pan sufficiently thick for the heavier materials.

Starch first those garments which are to be stiffest. Garments wrung very dry before starching will be stiffer than wetter ones. Prepared starches are sold for use in cold starching and the directions given on the package should be carefully followed.

### SPECIAL FINISHES FOR DELICATE FABRICS

| Material | Quantity used<br>Ounce | Water<br>Pint | Dilution |
|---|---|---|---|
| Gelatin | 1 | 1 | 1 part solution to 8 to 15 parts hot water |
| Gum arabic | 1 | 1 | 1 part solution to 5 to 10 parts hot water |
| Gum tragacanth | 1/6 | 1 | 1 part solution to 8 to 12 parts hot water |

A little borax added to the solution when first made helps to preserve it. Add the cold water to the gelatin or gum and heat until it has dissolved. Dilute with hot water, the quantity depending on the kind of material and the stiffness desired.

Special finishes are often used on such fabrics as voiles, organdies, batistes, and silks, to restore their crisp new appearance. Dilute solutions of gelatins, gum arabic, and gum tragacanth are all good for this purpose. Avoid using too much of any one of them, or it will give a sticky feel to the fabric.

Hanging and drying: Electrical driers that spin clothes dry are major labor saving devices. Cotton or hemp rope and galvanized or copper wire, either solid or twisted, are used as clotheslines. Boiling a new rope for a few minutes in soapy water softens it and lengthens its life. The wire lines are more permanent, but must be wiped off with a damp cloth before being used and must be free from rust.

Modern home dryers take up to 14-pound wash loads and can be adjusted to the weight of the load, the type of fabric, the room temperature, and the freshening, fluffiness, or dampness desired. A built-in device will report when the load is properly dry. Some models have germicidal lamps. Efficiency depends in large measure on the size of the fan, which may be up to 20 inches.

The clothesline attached by pulleys connecting a distant post with a window ledge or porch makes it possible to hang the clothes without leaving the porch or the house. A revolving outdoor drier with folding arms attached to a post is convenient in drying clothes in a compact space.

There are various kinds and types of devices for winding and storing clothesline, from the small kitchen reel with a ratchet lock to large reels for use in the yard.

If the clothesline has been left out, wipe it carefully with a damp cloth before using. A cloth moistened with kerosene is excellent to remove soot and dirt, but the remaining traces of the oil should be removed with a dry cloth to prevent stains. Clothespins must be perfectly clean.

To avoid a clothesline's getting dirty, remove it when not in use. A clothesline fastened on 2 screw eyes is quickly removed when all the clothes are on, as when a shower comes up. A clothesline fastened to 2 pipes may be made removable by anchoring the pipe in a loose concrete base. To wash a clothesline, coil it around a board, dip in hot soapy water and scrub with a brush. Allow it to dry on the board. If the support for your clothesline tends to slip, place a clothespin on the line on each side of the support.

Hang garments on the straight of the goods and by their

bands where possible. To prevent wet clothes from freezing on the line, add salt to rinse water. To prevent hands from freezing while hanging clothes outdoors, rub in vinegar. Sheets and other large pieces should be placed from a fourth to a half over the line and fastened securely in three or four places. Group similar garments together. Removing the clothes

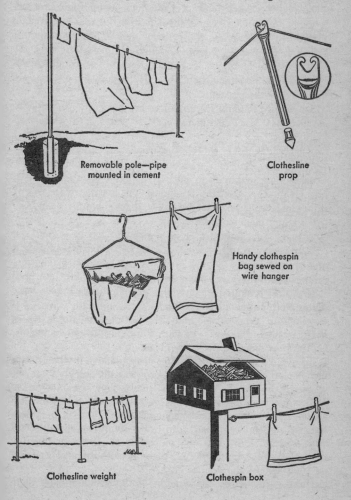

Removable pole—pipe
mounted in cement

Clothesline
prop

Handy clothespin
bag sewed on
wire hanger

Clothesline weight

Clothespin box

from the line in a systematic manner and folding the straight pieces before placing them in the basket will save time later, especially if some are to be put away unironed.

Sunlight is an excellent bleach. To prevent sun from deteriorating curtain fabrics, alternate curtains between sunny and shady spots.

To stretch a newly washed curtain where no curtain stretcher is available, pin large bed sheet to the rug and pin curtain to the bed sheet; allow to dry over night. To hang a quilt to dry, spread over two lines to avoid sliding of innards. To avoid getting slacks out of shape, use metal frames now available. If you must hang them on a line, turn inside out and pin them up by the pockets.

To hang garments where colors are not fast, use separate clothespins. Otherwise stains may be carried to white garments later.

**Sprinkling:** Sprinkle the clothes evenly and thoroughly with warm water. Pull the garments into shape; fold and roll. Cover snugly with a clean cloth and allow to stand for at least half an hour, so that the dampness will become more evenly distributed. Clothes may be allowed to stand over night if there is no danger of mildewing.

A good sprinkling device is a sprinkler top on a bottle, a rubber spray or holes punched in the screwed cap of almost any kind of bottle.

**Ironing machines:** Most household ironing machines are both heated and operated electrically, but there are a few large gas-heated household machines.

Presser type of ironing machine.

There are two types of ironing machines on the market, the presser and the rotary types. With a presser ironer the clothing is arranged on the board, the wrinkles are smoothed out or pleats folded in place, and the shoe then brought down in position to iron them. On the rotary ironer the smoothing is done while the machine is operating.

**Electric hand irons:** The electric hand iron depends for its heat on the presence of a coil of wire which resists the passage of an electric current. In the newer irons, a thermostat is directly connected with the sole plate and a dial and an adjustable switch on the top of the iron. The dial is marked in terms of either temperature or types of fabrics that require different temperatures for ironing, such as rayon, silk, wool, cotton, and linen. The automatic control feature then maintains the heat approximately at the same temperature for hours.

Modern features are permanently connected outlet cords, chromium-plated surfaces, beveled edges with special grooves for ironing under buttons, thumb rests, better shaped large handles, and handles open at one end to facilitate ironing in difficult places like sleeves. The handle should be immovable on its axis for support.

Household irons vary in weight from 4 to 8 lbs., but there is a tendency towards decreasing the weight.

Irons of 800 and 1000-watt rating for faster heating are preferable to those of 600 to 660 watts. The higher wattage provides sufficient heat for maintaining proper temperature.

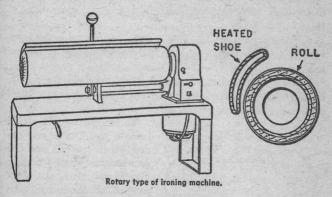

**Rotary type of ironing machine.**

**Ironing:** Use a clean, hot iron as heavy as can be handled comfortably. To keep the iron clean, rub occasionally with wax or paraffin. An iron is hot enough to use when it "spats" when touched with a moistened finger. Too cool an iron may leave a rust stain. With starched clothes, the iron must be hot enough to glaze the starch; otherwise, it will stick and discolor the fabric.

**Steaming:** This is a substitute for pressing fabrics which cannot be ironed. A section of a garment or a seam can be steamed by holding it over an iron covered by a damp cloth.

An entire garment should be hung on a hinge in the bathroom. Let the hot water run for about a half hour to create thick steam. After the room is thoroughly steamed, do not open the door for an hour. Let the garment hang there until thoroughly dry. If you do not have running water hot enough to make steam, you can hang the garment directly over the spout of a boiling teakettle.

**Dry pressing:** This is used to freshen cottons, linens, silks and rayons. Press garment on wrong side without dampening. Be sure iron is not too warm. If not satisfactory, wring water out of a cheesecloth, spread it over the garment and press lightly.

**Damp pressing:** This is used for lightweight fabric. A lightweight cloth is used with a sponge to dampen the fabric slightly. Press on the wrong side. Do not have the cloth too damp or the iron too hot as the fabrics scorch easily through the thin cloth.

**Steam-pressing:** In steam-pressing, you rely on steam rather than pressure to. do the work for you. A wet cloth is placed over the wrong side (except in lined garments). The iron must be kept moving with a rotary motion, never allowed to rest heavily on the fabric. The steam must be allowed to rise. The process is a slow one as the steam must have time to penetrate into the fabric. The wet press-cloth is then replaced by a dry one. Make your iron less hot now but keep it hot enough to create steam in the fabric under the cloth. Watch heat carefully, as scorching goes through the press-cloth very easily. In pressing heavy fabrics, the dry press-cloth should be raised from time to time to allow the steam to escape and to brush the fabric to prevent a flat effect. For worsted fabrics use a stiff brush, for piles a soft brush. Use no brush on rayons. This is continued, section by section, until the fabric is nearly dry. Place the garment on a hanger and allow to dry thoroughly before hanging in closet.

**Iron heat:** Make your iron (1) very hot to create steam for steaming or steam-pressing, or to dry a wet fabric; (2) cotton hot for damp cottons; (3) cotton cool for some rayons, for transparent fabrics; (4) rayon cool for acetate rayons and delicate fabrics; (5) cold for metallic fabrics and similar weaves.

**Preventing clinging in washable garments:** A tendency to cling can be reduced in washable garments of the newer man-made fibers by adding a small amount of a liquid detergent, fabric softener, or special liquid antistatic agent to the final rinse water. Liquid detergents and fabric softeners can be purchased at most food or grocery stores. Liquid antistatic agents can be obtained at notion counters in drug or department stores.

Wash the garments in the usual manner. Then rinse them in a solution of the selected product according to instructions given on the container, or adjust the amount used to suit the needs of the individual.

## SPECIAL TREATMENTS

NYLONS AND SPECIAL FABRICS: Most nylons require no ironing. Squeeze out water gently, hang while wet, and smooth out wrinkles with hands. If you iron, use cool iron (275° F.) on the rayon or nylon setting. Do not allow nylons to lie around wrinkled, especially wet, as this may set the wrinkles. Avoid hanging white nylon in sunlight. Most knitted fabrics can do without ironing. This applies also to seersucker, corduroy, any crinkle crepes.

Dynel (new wool-like fabric) should be ironed at low temperatures. Orlon should be ironed wet at 275° F.

TAFFETA TYPES: Iron while quite wet with rayon-cool iron, on wrong side. Never roll in towel—squeeze or wring—creasing from these will not come out. Iron Celanese taffeta wet for crispness. Have iron almost cold for acetate rayons. For rayon sharkskin, treat like taffeta except roll in towel and place in refrigerator for a while. For wool sharkskin, treat like wool suitings.

WHITE SILK: White silk is easily yellowed by ironing. To prevent this, iron on wrong side with cotton-cool iron and a cheesecloth press-cloth. Use damp cloth, or have cloth dry and silk slightly but evenly damp. A too-hot iron yellows fabric. If fabric is too damp, it irons stiff. If half damp and half dry, it may spot in ironing.

METAL FABRICS: Press when dry with almost cold iron. Protect fabric with tissue paper so iron will not touch it. (Rubber makes metal cloth tarnish.)

Cottons: HEAVY COTTONS: Iron with cotton-hot iron until

thoroughly dry. Dark shades should be ironed on wrong side, to prevent shine.

NAPPED FABRICS: These require no ironing if hung in shade to drip dry and stretched into shape. Never twist or wring, as it mars fabric. If desired, when dry, press lightly on wrong side with cotton-cool iron.

FLANNELS: Require no ironing but, if desired, press when dry with cotton-cool iron.

LIGHTWEIGHT COTTONS: Smooth weave: Iron with cotton-hot iron while slightly damp until dry, on right side for light colors, on wrong side for dark colors. (To finish on right side, protect with tissue paper.) Sateen should be ironed on right side to increase sheen.

NOVELTY WEAVES (brocades): Iron on wrong side when nearly dry with cotton-cool iron over turkish towel padding.

CREPE WEAVES (voile, underwear crepe): Iron with cotton-cool iron when nearly dry—on right side for light colors, on wrong for dark.

CRINKLE CREPE: Iron heat must be less on crinkly material in order not to flatten weave.

SHANTUNG TYPE: Iron on wrong side when very nearly dry (too much dampness stiffens) with cotton-cool iron.

LACES: Heavy lace requires no ironing. Blot excess moisture, stretch into shape on dry towel. Press edges or pull out with fingers. Never hang a lace dress on the line. Before washing, measure and outline on turkish towels laid flat on floor. Medium and fine lace should be ironed with cotton-cool iron on wrong side while slightly damp. Iron over a turkish towel to bring out pattern or weave. Protect from iron with tissue paper.

VEILS: Stiffen by pressing between two sheets of wax paper.

Rayon or Silk: TWILL AND RIBBED WEAVES AND SMOOTH WEAVES: When almost dry, iron with cotton-cool iron on wrong side until thoroughly dry. Rayon fabrics must have careful handling. Never have iron too warm.

NAPPED FABRICS: Rayon corduroy may be ironed on wrong side with rayon-cool iron. Velvet must not be washed or ironed. To freshen, hang to steam.

FLANNELS: Press on wrong side, while slightly damp, with cotton-cool iron.

SMOOTH NAPS: Washable—Roll in turkish towel to blot excess moisture, iron immediately with rayon-cool iron on wrong side (to protect nap finish), stretching slightly in ironing. Fabrics which must be dry cleaned should be pressed with rayon-cool iron on right side to enhance sheen.

NOVELTIES: Shape over turkish towel pad. Iron on wrong side with rayon-cool iron.

CREPE WEAVES: Smooth crepes—Blot out water with turkish towel, stretch to size while damp on straight of grain, then iron on wrong side with rayon-cool iron.

ROUGH CREPES: Wash carefully, as they may draw up. Blot in turkish towel. When almost dry, shape over turkish towel and stretch to measurement when pressing. Always press with grain, on wrong side. Watch texture: if too flat, you are stretching too much; if too crinkly, stretch more.

SHEERS, MARQUISETTE, MOUSSELINE, AND TRANSPARENT CREPES: Blot out excess moisture on turkish towel. Iron with rayon-cool iron on wrong side over turkish towel pad. Don't press too flat.

SEERSUCKER, KNITTED COTTON OR RAYON, OR TERRY CLOTH don't need ironing—save work and cut down on use of electricity.

Woolens: TWILL AND RIBBED WEAVES: Steam press woolens with very hot iron, place on hanger while still damp.

SMOOTH WEAVES: Damp press with cotton-hot iron.

PILE WOOLENS: Hang to steam (as for velvets). Steam press with wet press-cloth and very hot iron. Brush up nap.

FLANNELS: Iron lightweight washable flannels with cotton-cool iron on wrong side while slightly damp, protected with cheesecloth. Suiting flannels are steam pressed with press-cloth.

SMOOTH NAPS: Steam-press with very hot iron. Use wet press-cloth on wrong side except for lined garments. Brush up nap while pressing. Place on hanger still damp. (For very lightweight, damp press.)

NOVELTIES: Press with cheesecloth on wrong side with cool iron.

HEAVY WOOLENS: (1) Make pressing pad of 2 heavy pieces of canvas or denim by removing starch, and making a "pillow case" open at one end. Stuff with old clothes or fabrics. This will hold steam. (2) Lay garment over pad, then cover with damp ticking. (3) Press with hot iron to produce steam. Remove old pleats and set new ones. (4) Hang to dry while still steaming.

Child's Puffed Sleeve

One-Seam Sleeve with Crease

Extended Shoulder Effect

Two-Seam Sleeves

Bias or Uncreased Sleeves

## CHILD'S PUFFED SLEEVE
(1) Iron cuff first.
(2) Fold sleeve back upon itself, matching cuff opening with armhole opening.
(3) Iron sleeve, cuff side first. Work point of iron into fullness at cuff.
(4) Iron shoulder side, working point of iron into fullness at shoulder.

## ONE-SEAM SLEEVE WITH CREASE
(1) Fold sleeve flat with seam on one crease.
(2) Begin at crease, work outward.
(3) Turn and iron on opposite side. Touch up cuff and shoulder.

## FOR EXTENDED SHOULDER EFFECT
(1) Iron sleeve first. Fold top of sleeve at shoulder in crescent shape.
(2) Place hand through neckline and hold body of garment away from crescent area.
(3) Press lightly.

## TWO-SEAM JACKET SLEEVES
(1) Fold sleeve, underarm side up, narrow panel in center. Iron.
(2) Iron outer arm surface up to where underside of sleeve is attached to garment.
(3) Finish top on sleeveboard.

## BIAS OR ANY UNCREASED SLEEVES
(1) Slip sleeve over small end of sleeveboard. Revolve until completely ironed.

## GATHERS AND STRAIGHT GATHERED RUFFLES
(1) Manipulate garment, or iron so that point of iron works into the fullness.
(2) Use in-and-out strokes.
(3) Don't iron over top of gathers.

## BIAS-CUT OR CIRCULAR RUFFLES
(1) Work point of iron from outside edge in toward heading in oblique, crescent curve.
(2) Shift article and repeat until entire ruffle is ironed.

Gathers and Straight Ruffles

Bias or Circular Ruffles

1, 2, 3

Creased Slacks

1-2

3

4

A Man's Shirt

2, 3

4

5

6

7

## CREASED SLACKS AND SHORTS

(1) Lay one leg on board, inner-leg side up, other leg folded back over top.

(2) Fold so creases appear in center front and center back of leg. Iron.

(3) Turn over and iron outer leg up to point where crotch begins.

(4) Repeat with other leg. Finish top over end of board.
Pajamas, etc. may be ironed with legs folded side to side.

## A MAN'S SHIRT

(1) Iron cuffs first; inner surface first, outer surface second.

(2) Iron body of sleeve, cuff opening side first.

(3) Repeat on other sleeve.

(4) Iron yoke. Slip one shoulder over end of board. Iron from center of back to shoulder. Reverse and iron other side of yoke.

(5) Iron body of shirt beginning with one front and continuing to other front (or iron both fronts first if fabric is drying out quickly).

(6) Iron collar, under surface first, upper surface second, working iron inward from edges.

(7) Fold collar down and press over end of board.

Tips for easier ironing: Put together articles that are ironed with a hot iron—those with a somewhat cooler iron.

Heat the iron or ironer hot enough for the fabric before you start ironing—but don't overheat. Iron things that take the least heat first.

Have the ironing board well padded, set at the right height, in a comfortable light; sit to iron, especially with an ironer; have a comfortable chair of right height and shape; have a clothesrack handy for ironed pieces.

Slow, unhurried, well-directed motions give best results with hand ironing. Iron each part thoroughly dry before going on to another. Start with sleeves, collars, ties, and other dangling parts, and iron with the lengthwise thread of the goods whenever possible.

Iron with the thread of the goods and until the garment is dry. Otherwise, it will have a puckered appearance. Iron first those parts of the garment that will hang off the board while the rest is being ironed. For example, when ironing a blouse or a man's shirt, iron the cuffs and sleeves first, then the collar, and then, beginning with one side of the back or the front (depending on where the garment fastens), continue around to the other side. After ironing a garment, look it over carefully and press again where needed. Gloss on hems, tucks, and seams can be removed by sponging lightly with a moist cloth. Scorch is usually removed by moistening the fabric and exposing it to strong sunlight, although bleaches are sometimes necessary.

Iron clothes on the right side, except when it is desired especially to bring out the pattern of the fabric. Embroidery appears best when ironed on the wrong side on a thick, soft pad. Cotton-lace dresses often look best when ironed dry on the wrong side. Flat laces are sewed or pinned in place on a cloth or pad before washing, and do not require ironing.

Remove excess starch by sprinkling salt on newspaper and running iron over it several times. If pressed article is not completely dry, hang over a rack to dry out before storing away.

When pressing nets and flimsy material, never run the iron back and forth, but lift it up after each stroke. Always use a pressing cloth or a double thickness of tissue paper.

To iron straight-edged or long curtains, keep them slightly

damp, pin one end to ironing board, holding the other end tight as you iron.

To iron ribbon, pull it underneath the iron, keeping the iron stationary. An alternative method is to wrap the ribbon around a steam pipe and let it dry.

If your iron sticks, it probably needs waxing or cleaning. To wax an iron, rub with cloth dipped in dry-cleaning fluid while the iron is cold.

**Airing and folding:** All articles should be folded as little as possible, but this depends, of course, upon the space available for storing them. In general, fold pieces lengthwise in the direction of the warp or grain and then very lightly crosswise until a convenient size is reached.

Tablecloths and sheets should be hung on the clothes rack until thoroughly dry before being folded crosswise. Do not iron in the crosswise folds. If arrangements can be made for storage, one lengthwise fold can be made and the tablecloth then rolled

**How to fold a tablecloth and other flat pieces.**

on a short pole or roll of paper. Centerpieces and tray cloths should always be rolled.

Dinner napkins are folded into squares. Two folds each way are customary. These are so arranged that when the napkin is placed on the table at the left of the plate with its edge and selvage parallel to the silver and the table edge, any monogram or embroidered figure is on the outside fold. Luncheon napkins also may be folded square, following the same method, but with only one fold each way. An additional fold making an oblong is sometimes used, the monogram being placed as in the case of the dinner napkin. Luncheon napkins are sometimes folded in triangular and other shapes in order to conserve space on the table or give different effects.

Towels and pillowcases are folded lengthwise into thirds, the center third being left on the outside. The one crosswise fold is not ironed in. Handkerchiefs are often folded into a very small square. A better method is to make one fold each way in a woman's handkerchief and two folds each way in a man's handkerchief. In the woman's one more fold gives an oblong shape that some people prefer. Allow all straight pieces to dry thoroughly before piling them or putting them away.

Garments should be dried well on hangers or the clothes-rack before being folded. Two methods of folding shirts are shown in figures below and can be adapted to most other garments. The first method, however, adapts itself better to shirts and is more commonly used by manufacturers.

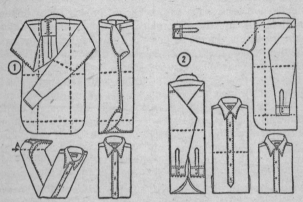

(1) Envelope method of folding a shirt. The part A slips between the upturned cuffs and the shirt.
(2) A simple shirt-folding method that can be applied to many other garments.

## STAIN REMOVAL

**General Rules about Stain Removal:** In removing stains, first determine whether the fabric is washable or not. The process to be used varies radically for each type.

Always try to remove stains while they are fresh. They become increasingly difficult to remove as they grow older. Before you use any chemical on a colored fabric, test to make certain the chemical will not remove the color.

Some chemicals are inflammable, have caused very serious accidents in the past. Many chemicals are poisonous. Label poisonous chemicals plainly. Watch fire hazards. Never smoke while dry cleaning. Highly inflammable chemicals should be used out of doors where possible, or in a room with windows opened and no fire going. Chemicals should be applied sparingly with a light pressure or feathery stroke. Do not rub.

Cloths used should be lint free. In general, use the chemical with the least strength that will do the job. Use the absorbent method on all material too heavy to soak.

**Swabbing Method:** This method is used for applying water, carbon tetrachloride, kerosene, etc. Hold a small piece of fabric, folded sufficiently to absorb all of the chemical used, of the same fabric type as the fabric from which the stain is being removed. Make sure fabric has no lint. Spread garment face down, place absorbent pad or wet blotter underneath the stain. With the swab saturated in cleaning liquid, wipe the stain on the wrong side toward the center with light, quick strokes tapered to prevent a ring. Use as little liquid as practical. Work toward the center of the stain. Change swab as soon as it becomes dirty. Dry the stain by blowing or waving garment.

**Sponging:** This process may be used with water, carbon tetrachloride, or other solvents usually when a cleaning liquid must penetrate the fabric. More of the cleaner is used. Place a pad or blotter under the stain. With a wet pad, saturate the stain with cleaning fluid, soak the fluid into the stain by patting on the wrong side of the fabric. Taper the strokes to avoid a ring. Change the swabs and pad frequently, whenever they appear to be dirty. Remove excess liquid with soft, lintless cloth; then dry by blowing or waving the fabric.

**Floating Method:** When a stain has hardened or resists solvents, a loosener or spot softener like lard or vaseline may be used. With a small piece of cotton wound around a stick, apply the grease or oil floater to be used. After the floater has had a chance to work, use the regular grease-removing method.

**Absorbent Powders—Dry Cleaning:** Make a paste of the absorbent powder to be used. Then work the powder into the stain on the right side of the fabric, rubbing gently with a blunt knife. As soon as the paste discolors, shake it or brush it off and repeat until the stain is removed. Then, remove all trace of powder with a fresh cloth or soft brush.

**Bleaching:** (See page 50.) Bleaches are strong chemicals. They must never be used before testing their effects on the fabric's color. Stretch the stain over a bowl containing lukewarm water and fasten taut with a string or elastic band. Fill one medicine dropper with the acid solution and another medicine dropper with an alkali solution to neutralize it. Apply first one then the other, then apply water (if feasible) or steam from a teakettle. Bleach must be carefully rinsed from the fabric. A glass rod may be used instead of the medicine dropper where smaller quantities and greater care are required.

### Chemicals Helpful In Stain Removal

WATER: The best, most widely used, and usually the most effective stain remover. Before using it on any non-washable fabric, make certain that it will not loosen the color or leave a stain.

CARBON TETRACHLORIDE: An all-purpose cleaning fluid which is useful for removing grease, oil, etc.

DENATURED ALCOHOL (OR ETHER OR CHLOROFORM, OR ACETONE, NAIL POLISH REMOVER): Gum remover which can also be used to remove grease and other stains with the sponging method. Test it on colored fabric before using. All these are inflammable.

VASELINE, TURPENTINE, GASOLINE, KEROSENE, LARD OR BANANA OIL: These are floaters or dirt looseners, useful in softening oil stains and such stains as paint, lipstick, tar. They must be rubbed into the stain and are generally useful only as a first step in stain removal.

ABSORBENTS (CORNSTARCH, FULLER'S EARTH, FRENCH CHALK, CORNMEAL, OR WHITE TALCUM POWDER): These absorb grease, oil, and other stains in a dry-cleaning method, are applied as pastes, allowed to dry, and brushed off.

SALT: This absorbs fresh stains of juice, liquor, etc.

ACETIC ACID, VINEGAR OR AMMONIA (10% AMMONIUM HYDROXIDE): These are color restorers or color fasteners. Test on colored fabrics before using.

BLEACHES: JAVELLE WATER (1 lb. washing soda in 2 qts. cold water. Add ½ lb. chloride of lime. Mix and stir) or HYDROGEN PEROXIDE or SODIUM PERBORATE or OXALIC ACID (teaspoonful oxalic acid crystals to 3 cups of water) or POTASSIUM PERMANGANATE (½ teaspoonful purple crystals to 1 pt. water). These are used to remove persistent stains, must be used with extreme care, and must be tested on colored fabric. They must be removed immediately after using. They are all poisons.

PEPSIN: Used to remove albumen stains. Solution—1 teaspoon to 1 pint lukewarm water.

**Removing stains from non-washable fabrics:** Always test chemicals on fabric before using.

ACIDS: Act quickly. Sponge with mild water. If colored, add drops of ammonia to restore color, or hold over fumes of ammonia. Alternative: sprinkle baking soda on both sides of stain, allow to stand, sponge it off. Before using ammonia, test for color fastness. White vinegar is a good substitute.

ADHESIVE TAPE: Swab or sponge with carbon tetrachloride or benzine.

ALBUMEN: Sponge with cold water.

ALCOHOL: (and alcohol paints): Swab or sponge with denatured alcohol.

ALKALIES: Act quickly. Sponge with lukewarm water, restore color with vinegar.

ASPHALT: See Tar.

BLOOD: Soften with solution of castor oil, sponge with lukewarm water. If persistent, add 3 drops of ammonia to solution. To bleach out, dampen and leave in sun or swab with hydrogen peroxide.

BLUEBERRY: See Fruit. If persistent, use Rust Stain removing process.

BLUEING: See Rust.

BUTTER: See Grease.

CANDLE WAX: Crumble off wax. Place blotter over spot, iron on reverse side. If persistent, swab with carbon tetrachloride.

CHEESE: Swab with cold water.

CHEWING GUM: Swab or sponge with denatured alcohol or carbon tetrachloride.

CHOCOLATE: Sponge with carbon tetrachloride; then with warm water. If stain persists, work pepsin powder into stain, allow it to remain for 30 minutes, then sponge off with water.

COCOA: See Chocolate.

COD LIVER OIL: Swab or sponge with carbon tetrachloride. If persistent, use solution of 2 tablespoons of banana oil in a cup of soap jelly.

COFFEE: Pour boiling water through stain, from reverse side. If persistent, repeat after covering stain with glycerine.

CREAM: See Grease.

CREAM SOUPS: Sponge with warm water. If persistent, swab with carbon tetrachloride or benzine.

DRAWING INK: Swab or sponge with denatured alcohol or carbon tetrachloride.

DYES: Fresh stains may respond to cold water.

EGGS: Use cold water. If persistent, sponge with carbon tetrachloride or other solvent.

FISH: Swab with cold water.

FLOWER STEM: See Vaseline.

FLY PAPER: See Adhesive Tape.

FRUIT (except Peach): Swab with warm water. If persistent, sponge with cold water, rubbing in a few drops of glycerine. Allow to stand for 3 hours, swab with vinegar or oxalic acid, rinse with water.

GLUE: Dampen, then sponge with vinegar or 10 percent acetic acid, then rinse.

GRASS STAIN: Sponge with denatured alcohol or benzine.

GRASSHOPPER: Apply oxalic acid solution; wash immediately.

GRAVY: Swab with carbon tetrachloride. If persistent, apply lukewarm water. Alternative: Use absorbent powder method.

GREASE (food): Spot with carbon tetrachloride, holding gauze under stain to absorb excess of fluid.

GUM: See Chewing Gum.

INDELIBLE PENCIL: See Machine Grease.

INK: First try water. Then try absorbent powder method. If stain persists, apply oxalic acid solution; then apply ammonia to neutralize acid. Repeat if necessary.

IODINE: If still wet, use soap and water; otherwise, use ammonia solution. Alternative: apply dry starch, moistened with cold water.

KEROSENE: Swab with warm water and soap.

LAMPBLACK: See Vaseline.

LEAD PENCIL: Sponge or swab with clear water. If persistent, immerse stain in chloroform or alcohol, brush off with soft cloth.

LIPSTICK: Soften by rubbing in vaseline or lard. Sponge with carbon tetrachloride. If persistent, sponge with denatured alcohol (but not on acetate rayon). Alternative: sponge with mixture of hydrogen peroxide and sodium perborate.

MACHINE GREASE: Rub on a little lard to "float" the stain. Sponge with carbon tetrachloride.

MERCUROCHROME: Sponge with sodium perborate.

MILDEW: If new, wash off, or apply oxalic acid and household bleach.

MILK: See Grease.

MUD: Dry and brush off. If greasy, use grease stain process, then wash or steam garment.

MUSTARD: Apply warm glycerine and sponge with water. If persistent, sponge with diluted denatured alcohol. If stain still persists, use bleaching method.

NAIL POLISH: Apply alcohol or lacquer thinner.

OIL PAINTS: Swab or sponge with carbon tetrachloride, kerosene, turpentine, benzine, or chloroform.

PAINT: Put stain down on pad, apply soft soap jelly on reverse side till color works out. If persistent, apply turpentine.

PEACH: Bleach with oxalic acid and ammonia.

PERSPIRATION: Restore color by holding over open ammonia bottle.

To remove odor, sponge with warm water and ½ teaspoon of vinegar. Then apply pepsin, allow to stand for ½ hour, then brush off.

PITCH: See Chewing Gum.

POLISH (brass or stove): See Machine Grease.

PRINTER'S INK: See Machine Grease.

PROTEINS: See Egg.

RAIN: First rub with rough cloth. Wash, if possible, or steam. Leather coats respond to none of these. On raincoats, apply soap and cold water, with a few drops of ammonia added.

RED INK: Sponge with sodium perborate solution; swab with water immediately to remove chemical.

RINGS RESULTING FROM STAIN REMOVAL: Rub with wet cloth to remove water ring; otherwise, dry clean.

ROUGE: See Lipstick.

RUST: Apply oxalic acid solution, or lemon juice and salt.

SCORCH: Some colored materials which have changed color, may regain their shade when cooled. Woolens and silks may respond to water.

SHELLAC: See Varnish.

SHOE POLISH: Apply carbon tetrachloride or denatured alcohol. If necessary, use lard as a "floater."

SILVER NITRATE: Use ammonia solution.

STARCH: Spot with cold water.

SALAD DRESSING: See Gravy.

SMOKE: See Soot.

SOOT: Sponge with carbon tetrachloride or gasoline, or apply absorbent powders.

SUGAR: See Blood.

TAR: Apply vaseline or lard to soften. Sponge with carbon tetrachloride.

TEA: See Coffee.

TOBACCO: Sponge with cold water, then apply glycerine and lukewarm water. If stain persists, sponge with denatured alcohol.

VARNISH: Apply turpentine or paint remover.

VASELINE: "Float" stain with kerosene, then wash with soap and water.

VERDIGRIS: See Vaseline.

WATERCOLOR PAINTS: Apply turpentine, then swab or sponge with benzol to remove turpentine. Alternative: Sponge with glycerine and lukewarm water.

WAX: Dry and crumble. Iron over blotting paper. Sponge with carbon tetrachloride. If persistent, bleach with Javelle water.

WINE: Apply salt as soon as stain is made; otherwise, bleach with oxaclic acid solution and ammonia. See Fruit.

To Remove Stains from Washable Fabrics: For all stains first try soaking. For persistent stains, use the same process as for removal of stains from non-washable fabrics.

ALCOHOL PAINTS: Soak for 30 minutes in strong ammonia solution, then wash.

ARGYROL: Sponge with warm water, sprinkle powdered pepsin over damp spot and work into cloth. Allow to stand for 30 minutes, then sponge with water.

BLOOD: Soak in cold water till stain lightens; then wash in warm, soapy water.

CHEWING GUM: Hold ice to opposite side till gum freezes, then pick off with fingers. Alternative: soften in carbon tetrachloride or kerosene.

DRAWING INK: Add a few drops of ammonia and plenty of soap suds to washing solution.

DYES: Soak or wash in mild or lukewarm water for 10 or 12 hours; then wash in heavy suds, dry in sun.

EGG: Sponge with cold water. Warm water will set the stain.

GLUE: Soak in warm water.

GRASS: Dip in Javelle water for 1 minute, then rinse.

GREASE: Put soap on stain and soak in cold water.

IODINE: Hold in steam of boiling teakettle.

INK: Rub in glycerine and rinse with cold water; or use absorbent powder.

LEAD PENCIL: First try soft eraser. If persistent, rub soapsuds into stain.

LIPSTICK: Rub in glycerine or vaseline; then wash.

MERCUROCHROME: Sponge with solution of ½ alcohol and ½ water. If persistent, loosen stain with glycerine. Wash in soapsuds and rinse in solution of ammonia and water.

MILDEW: Bleach with Javelle water.

MUSTARD: Rub in glycerine or soap before washing with soap and water.

NAIL POLISH: Sponge with nail-polish remover or peroxide; rinse.

PAINTS: Sponge or immerse in turpentine.

RED INK: Soak for 2 or 3 days in solution of sodium perborate and cold water.

SCORCH: Wash and bleach in sun.

SOOT: Use absorbents, then wash with soap and water.

TOBACCO JUICE: Sponge with cold water, work in glycerine, allow to stand for 30 minutes, then wash with soap and water.

URINE: Soak in warm, soapy water with a few drops of ammonia added. Alternative: Soak in warm water, then hot water, then rinse.

YELLOWING DUE TO AGE: Wash with hot suds, then dry in sun. If persistent, use chlorine bleach according to directions on bottle.


## CARE OF CLOTHING

General rules: Hang garments on suitably shaped hangers immediately after you take them off. Brush dust and lint from the fabric surface frequently, brushing in direction of the nap. Mend small rips and tears before they become larger. Use proper protection against perspiration. Take precaution when you do your nails. (Some nail polishes and removers cause permanent damage to cellulose acetate rayon.) Don't apply perfume or cologne directly to fabric. Keep clothes in cool, dry, airy place. Don't hang in closet while wet. Give entire wardrobe an occasional airing.

Alternating the garments you wear gives the fabric a chance to become free of wrinkles and to return to the shape built into the garment. Remove stains soon after they are made. Have your clothes cleaned frequently. (The longer soil remains in a garment, the more deeply it becomes ground into the fibers and the more vigorous the treatment necessary to remove it.) Never allow a garment to hang uncleaned from one season to the next. (Any stains will become set with age and are difficult, if not impossible, to remove. Soil will also attract moths and insects.)

**Removing garment shine:** Steaming or sponging plus pressing will give temporary remedy. Or, use a pressing cloth dipped in blueing water and wrung out. For more permanent result, sponge with solution half water and half household ammonia. If persistent, rub lightly with suede brush or No. 00 steel wool. To remove shine from blue serge, black silk, crepe, and other materials, apply acetic acid (vinegar will do) with cheesecloth, allow to air to remove odor.

To brighten black rayon, rub spots lightly with mineral oil (or re-dye).

To remove dust from blue serge, use the sticky side of a large piece of adhesive tape.

**Furs:** Furs are apt to show where any article comes in contact with and rubs or cuts the hairs. Heavy jewelry worn where it will rub against the fur may cause friction wear. Wearing the fur high and close around the neck so that movements of the head constantly rub it, and carrying bags or packages under the arms, are likely to wear or cut the fur and cause one section of the garment to wear out prematurely. Friction wear also occurs on the front and bottom edges, at the wrists, and under the sleeves. Riding in an automobile causes friction wear, particularly at the shoulder blades, elbows and lower part of the back of the coat.

Furs deteriorate from heat. Undue or continual exposure to the sun will change the shade of dark furs and cause white fur to turn yellow. Dirt, dust, and grime invite moths which destroy the fur and pelt.

Many furs such as fox, pony, leopard, goat, and kidskin, and furs of similar texture, will shed. Shedding is usually caused by the top hairs breaking off, for which there is no remedy.

Breaks or tears are usually caused by undue strain at the

seam as when the garment is drawn tightly about the body. Motoring, especially driving a car, subjects the coat to much strain. Opening at the seams or tears are no cause for alarm, unless so prevalent as to indicate defective skins. Garments so affected should be reinforced or "re-stayed" at the seams. Loosen up your coat about the body and shoulders when sitting or stooping, in order to avoid undue strain on the leather.

Moisture injures fur unless it is properly cared for. The wet fur should be combed lightly with the flow of the fur and then brushed in same direction. The fur should then be allowed to dry slowly where there is good circulation of cool air, after which it should be beaten lightly and shaken. Proper cleaning and storage increases the life of furs.

Fur garments torn, damaged or noticeably worn should be taken to a reliable firm for repair immediately, so that the repair cost may be minimized and the maximum service obtained from the garment.

Proper shaking is good for fur, but care should be taken not to break the leather or split the seams. Fur coats should be hung on wide end coat hangers, not on a type likely to pierce the skin from the weight of the coat itself.

To freshen fur, rub with cloth dampened in soapy water or rub cornmeal moistened with cleaning fluid into the fur and brush out. To freshen white furs, cornstarch should be rubbed in and shaken out. To bring life to fur, spread out flat and stroke gently with a thin stick.

Hats: Brush periodically with soft bristle brush, preferably after each wearing. Don't hang on rack when wet. Allow sweat band to dry. At season's end, push out crown, turn up the brim, store separately. Remove grease spots from felt and trimming with carbon tetrachloride. Other spots may be removed with carbon tetrachloride or fine manicuring emery cloth. Light-colored hats may be freshened with a dusting of cornmeal or French chalk (see Absorbent Powder Method page 73). In brushing a nap, brush downward counter-clockwise and follow the nap. Avoid artificial heat in drying.

Straw hats exposed to rain should be treated immediately. Push out creases and turn up the brim all around. Turn out the sweat band and allow the hat to dry standing on the sweat band. Avoid artificial heat while drying.

To keep a hat from blowing off, sew comb into rim, teeth down.

**Hosiery:** Hose should not be fastened too tightly, should be rolled on and off the foot, should be washed each night. Dry away from sunlight and artificial heat. Wash silk, nylon, and rayon stockings before the first wearing, and after each wearing, in mild soap flakes and lukewarm water. Allow nylons to dry over night, silk and rayon for 36 hours. Cotton stockings should not be dried in sun or near heat. Woolen stockings should be dried on a drying form.

To prevent undue wear, hose should be of correct size. Keep sheer stockings in a lined box to prevent undue rubbing.

If you tend to wear out stockings at the heel, rub paraffin on the top inside of your shoe. Where hose tends to wear in any one spot, reinforce after first few wearings. Catch runs as soon as possible with transparent run-stopping liquid, dampened soap or collodion; or, in an emergency, use a drop of nail polish (but not on an acetate fabric). Special chemicals (Nylonger) sprayed on hose will increase snag resistance 200 percent. Skilled knitters can repair runs which are not too widespread.

Unmated stockings left over when one of a pair is discarded, if of the same weight and texture, may be dyed a darker shade.

**Footwear:** Polishing preserves shoes. Changing shoes daily prolongs their useful life. Shoes should be kept on trees when not in use. Heels should be replaced when run down to avoid over-wearing the soles. Neolite spots in the heels add durability. Neolite soles are durable but lack flexibility. A pair of good shoes may outlast two pair of cheap ones—and look better.

Shoe trees help keep shoes in their original shape. It is best to have two pairs of shoes for alternate daily wear, thus permitting each pair to dry out between times.

Mud, water, or excessive dryness ruin leather; oil and grease preserve it. The life of boots and shoes may be extended by keeping them clean, pliable, and water-resistant. Those for farm or other heavy outdoor use need greasing. Those for street wear need polishing only, although the soles may be oiled or greased. Frequent polishing, especially with flexible wax polishes, keeps the leather soft and pliable and gives it a finish that helps to turn water and prevent the collection of dust and dirt. A light, even oiling with a little castor oil on a cheesecloth pad once or twice a month helps to keep patent leather uppers from cracking. Neat's-foot oil, tallow, and wool grease are also satisfactory. Shoes thus cared for wear much longer than those that are neglected. Never dry shoes near heat. If dried too fast, leather shrinks, becomes hard, tight, out-of-shape.

## CLEANING LEATHERS

CALF AND COWHIDE: Brush off dry dust and dirt with stiff shoe brush. Wipe on oil-base paste polish in thin, even film using cloth or brush. With soft polishing brush, apply enough force to rub paste into leather, then add a bit more paste and rub to a high polish. Avoid mixing cloths and brushes for different colored polishes. A liquid polish may be applied evenly, then wiped with a flannel when dry, polished with brush and flannel.

SUEDE FINISH, NAPPED FINISH, BUCKSKIN: Brush gently with a stiff brush to remove dust and soil. Brush up the nap gently freeing it of grit. Apply specially prepared liquid dressing for suede or buckskin, following directions on bottle, with a soft, clean cloth or dauber. Wipe off edge of sole with a damp cloth.

PATENT LEATHER: Clean with a mild soap and water. After leather is dry, work in vaseline or cleaning cream to prevent drying or cracking. If high polish is desired, use special patent leather preparation. Apply with soft cloth. Don't allow exposure to heat. Don't apply any preparation containing alkali. Alternative: Apply solution of 2 parts vinegar, 1 part water (or water and petroleum jelly) with soft cloth, polish with dry cloth. To prevent heels from cracking, coat with colorless nail polish.

WHITE SUEDE OR BUCKSKIN: Use specially prepared solutions for these. Follow directions for suede.

LIZARD, SNAKE, ALLIGATOR SKINS: Use only preparations designed for these special types of leather. Apply with soft flannel cloth.

WHITE CANVAS OR LINEN: If muddy, allow to dry. Scrub with soap and water before whitening. Remove spots as for fabric. Apply whitening evenly with stiff brush. Allow to dry. (Preferably stuff with shoe trees or crumpled paper.) Rub with lintless cloth. Do not use polish designed for white leather or suede. Avoid artificial heat.

CREPE, SATIN, GABARDINE: Brush off dirt. Remove spots as for fabric. (See page 72). Avoid using preparations made for leather.

LAMÉ, METAL, GOLD, OR SILVER CLOTH OR EMBROIDERED: Wipe with cloth (not brush). Rub in alum to remove tarnish. Wipe dry. Wrap in black or silver paper when not in use.

WHITE SATIN SHOES: Rub with soft eraser or with soft cloth dipped in vinegar, followed by cloth dipped in cleaning fluid. Alternative method: use solution of alcohol with a few drops of lemon juice.

GALOSHES, RUBBER GALOSHES, OVERSHOES, RUBBER GOODS: Clean with mild soaps and lukewarm water and clean cloth. Apply talcum powder. Wipe and place in ventilated place (away from artificial heat) to dry. Repair rips when small.

## MISCELLANEOUS

To remove squeak from ladies' shoes, rub neat's-foot oil or linseed oil into the sole; or punch 2 or 3 small dents in the sole behind the ball of the shoe with an ice pick.

To keep soles pliable and make them last longer, apply neat's-foot oil or linseed oil to clean soles 2 or 3 times.

To dry water-soaked shoes, stuff them with newspaper, allow them to dry away from any direct source of heat. To restore pliancy, rub with half a raw potato before polishing.

To dye brown shoes black temporarily, polish twice with black polish. To dye white shoes black, apply black enamel paint. Dyes for home use are available. Never dye shoes while on feet. Many preparations contain poisonous nitrobenzene.

Stains on leathers: Butter, lard, vaseline, linseed oil, salad oil, and lubricating oil produce ugly stains on light-colored leather. These spots can often be removed by coating them with a thick solution of rubber in a solvent that evaporates quickly, and then peeling off the rubber coating when it is almost dry, repeating the operation several times if necessary. A solution of finely chopped or shredded unvulcanized rubber (Para or Ceylon) in carbon bisulphide, in the proportion of 1 ounce of rubber to 8 fluid ounces of bisulphide, as well as some of the ready-prepared rubber cements, has been found satisfactory for this purpose.

All oil or grease spots should be removed as quickly as possible, particularly those made by linseed and other paint oils. These oils oxidize as they dry, so that they are soon only slightly soluble in the ordinary liquid solvents.

Milk spots leather and often leaves a white stain—sometimes a brown stain. Soap and water will remove the white stain, but no way of taking out the brown stain is known. The only feasible thing to do is to dye the leather a shade darker than the stain.

Sometimes spots can be removed mechanically by the very delicate manipulation of a sharp edge, such as a safety-razor blade, or with fine emery or crocus cloth. As a rule this produces at least a slightly noticeable blemish. It may not be as unsightly as the stain, however.

Shoe polish sometimes accumulates on uppers. The appearance of such shoes can often be decidedly improved by cleaning with benzene or gasoline and repolishing.

**Waterproofing:** Waterproofed, properly made leather shoes are satisfactory for protecting the feet during rain or snow but do not keep feet perfectly dry. They keep in the perspiration to a large extent, but are better than rubber footwear in this respect. For waterproofing shoes, make solution of 8 oz. natural wool grease, 4 oz. dark petroleum, 4 oz. paraffin wax. Melt ingredients and stir thoroughly. Apply grease while warm, but never hotter than the hand can bear. Let the shoes stand for about 15 minutes in a shallow pan containing enough of the melted waterproofing material to cover entire sole. Rubber heels, however, should not be put in the grease, because grease softens rubber. To waterproof the soles of shoes with rubber heels, use a pie pan to hold the melted grease and set the shoes astraddle the rim of the pan with the heels outside.

**Protection against mildew:** To prevent mildewing, keep shoes in a well-ventilated dry, light place; or apply solution of 1 part copper sulphate in 20 parts water, on cloth, allow to dry, rub on surface. To remove mildew, wash off with soap and warm water, or simply allow leather to dry.

**Protection against alkaline substances:** Lime, Portland cement, lye, and other alkaline substances quickly ruin leather. Shoes will last much longer if kept well greased.

## ACCESSORIES

To wash doeskin, pigskin, capeskin, or other smooth leather

accessories, rinse in a lukewarm solution of water and mild soap, add a spoonful of olive oil to increase softness.

## GLOVE CARE CHART

| How to Wash | How to Dry |
|---|---|
| LEATHER, *in general, and all washables except chamois and doeskin:* Wash on hands in cool suds. Water which is too warm will shrink, change color, harden leather. (Use soft brush for badly soiled spots.) When clean, roll down from wrists without pulling by fingers. Rinse thoroughly in cool water and follow by rinse in light, fresh suds. | Roll in turkish towel from fingertips toward cuff. Knead for few minutes, unroll, and blow into fingers to shape. Hang up to dry. Keep them away from too much heat. Soften leather while still damp by finger-pressing. |
| DOESKIN, CHAMOIS: Follow directions above for washing leather, but wash off the hands. When wet, these are apt to stretch or cut along the stitching. Work the gloves around in the suds, squeezing suds through the leather. Pat out moisture on towel after final rinse in light suds to preserve soft finish. | Follow directions above for leather. Shape and dry on flat surface, or hang on line. Be sure to finger-press while still slightly damp. |
| FABRIC, *ordinary soft glove material, cotton, rayon, silk, etc., woven or knitted:* Wash off the hands in lukewarm water, using mild, gentle action soap to make thick suds. Rinse thoroughly in lukewarm water. If gloves are colored, add vinegar or lemon juice to the rinse water. White gloves with colored trimming must be washed quickly before dye runs. | Pat out moisture in turkish towel without rolling. Ease to shape. Dry slowly indoors, away from sun, heat, wind. With colored stitching or trimming, crumpled tissue paper inside will help prevent streaks. |
| WOOLENS: Draw outline of gloves or mittens on plain paper in pre-washed state. Use lukewarm suds, mild soap. Squeeze suds through fabric without rubbing. Rinse in lukewarm water with clean light suds in last rinse water. Wash quickly to prevent hardening or shrinking. Never soak. Never rub. It | Roll in turkish towel, and knead out moisture. Unroll, and ease into place on pre-washing outline you drew. If necessary, hold in place with rust-proof pins. Dry away from direct heat. If glove |

| How to Wash | How to Dry |
| --- | --- |
| helps mat, felt, and shrink wool. Never use hot water or alkali soap. | tends to shrink, rewet and stretch to size. Never dry over heat or in sunlight. |
| "STRING TYPE," *all types in which shape is easily lost:* Follow directions as above for fabric. Be sure there are no holes before you wash. | Be careful to hang over line evenly—or dry flat on towel. Stretch into shape while drying. |

## HANDBAG AND WALLET CARE CHART

(All handbags should be emptied nightly—inside brushed—contents sorted. When not in use, a little crumpled tissue in handbags prevents flattening.)

| How to Care For | How to Clean |
| --- | --- |
| LEATHER WALLETS, POCKET CASES, HANDBAGS, BRIEFCASES, ETC.: Keep clean. Keep in condition by using special lotion for softening leather, or frequent application of saddle soap at night with polishing in the morning. A special paste wax for bag leather is helpful. Wrap in tissue paper and put in drawer when not in use. Consult section on footwear. Don't keep near heat. | When badly soiled wash with mild soap and water before waxing; or smooth on thick lather of pure white soap, rubbing hard. Let stay a few minutes, then rub off and polish with clean flannel cloth. Dry away from heat. Don't worry if light colors seem to fade a little in washing. They will come back when wax is applied. Constant care will eliminate need for drastic cleaning; don't use drying polish. |
| LEATHER, PATENT LEATHER, BAGS: Keep clean. Wipe off dust frequently. Polish with a soft cloth. A bit of cleansing cream, thoroughly rubbed in, helps soften and polish. (Some people prefer vaseline.) Protect with tissue when putting away. Keep away from heat. Keep away from contact with articles which may scratch. | Wipe with a damp cloth, or wash with lukewarm soapsuds. Frequent polishing with a soft cloth is often all that is necessary. Always wipe thoroughly dry with a soft cloth after using water in cleaning. Proper care prevents drastic cleaning necessity. Keep leather away from heat while drying after cleaning. Don't use too much oil in softening and polishing—it collects dust and dulls. |

| How to Care For | How to Clean |
|---|---|
| LEATHER, SUEDE: See section on footwear. Brush with special sponge to raise nap. Don't store near heat. | When very soiled, use fine emery paper, brushing lightly. For emergency, a manicure emery board will do. Don't use any cleaner or dressing designed for smooth leather. |
| SPECIAL MATERIALS—IMITATION LEATHER, OILCLOTH BAGS, PLASTIC BAGS: Keep clean and dry. Keep away from heat. Put away when not in use in tissue paper. Keep protected from scratching. | Wipe with a damp cloth, or wash with lukewarm soapsuds. Wipe dry and polish with dry cloth. Keep away from heat while drying. Wipe with clean cloth, or use a soft brush. Don't use strong soap for washing. Don't dry near heat. |
| STRAW HANDBAGS, SMALL CASES: Straw is not substantial. Keep clean and handle very carefully. Wrap up when not in use. Colored straw must be kept away from sunlight. Don't allow stains to become set. | Prevention is better than cure. Water should not be used on straw. Don't leave exposed to dust or drying heat or sunlight. Use liquid cleaner, but sparingly. |
| FABRICS—LINEN, CANVAS, GABARDINE, RAYONS, FELT, VELVET, WOOL, ETC.: Brush often, or wipe with soft cloth. Keep clean and free from spots. Wrap in tissue to put away. For wool or felt, see moth protection, page 96. | Use cleaning agents recommended for fabric of which bag is made. For refreshing velvet, see page 64 on steaming. Don't use brush. |
| METAL CLOTH BAGS: Wipe often with soft cloth. Keep wrapped in black paper in box or drawer when not in use. Keep away from dampness whenever possible. | Wipe off with soft cloth. To remove tarnish, rub with powdered (or crumbled) alum. Polishes cannot be used on metal cloth. Don't put away without wiping. |

## HOW TO CLEAN AND CARE FOR JEWELRY

PASTE JEWELRY: Cover with French chalk; rub it in with soft brush and brush out. Polish with chamois. Never wash stones set with paste. Water may soften cement and cause stones to fall out.

RHINESTONES (WITH PASTED-IN STONES), MARCASITE: Scrub with mild soap and water, using soft brush. Dry with soft cloth. Use same method with ammonia, but be sure to rinse thoroughly in clear water. Never leave trace of ammonia, if used in cleaning.

RHINESTONES (HANDSET): Wash with soap and lukewarm water, using soft brush. Rinse and dry with soft cloth. Never use soap and water if stones are set with paste.

CAMEOS: *(Be careful not to drop these. They are breakable.)* Boil cameo in a pan of household ammonia for a few minutes to loosen oily grit and film. Then wash with soap and warm water, rinse and dry. Never try to dig out dirt deposits. Never use a stiff brush.

DIAMONDS, OTHER GEMS: To boiling water in a pan, add a little ammonia. Clean settings and dry thoroughly. Never dig around settings of any stone.

PEARLS: *(Examine string for signs of wear. Restring at least once a year.)* Wash with mild warm soapsuds, using soft brush. Rub them occasionally with a dry soft chamois. Replace flat in case. Never twist pearls while wearing them.

BEADS: To string beads with knots between, lay beads out in graduated sizes, largest beads at the center and the rest graduated. Make a knot at one end of the cord. After each bead, form an ordinary knot, insert a pin while the knot is still loose and draw the pin to the edge of the bead. Withdraw the pin, draw the knot tight, and place the next bead up against it.

SILVER: Use silver polish and a soft clean cloth. Apply polish and let dry. Don't use a coarse abrasive. Use brush for carving and filigree. Remove all powder. Brush powder out after it is dry, or wash in warm soapsuds. Never use too stiff brush. Polish with cloth. (See also page 33.)

GOLD PLATE: Rub often with chamois. If this is not enough try a mild silver polish, and rub very gently in order not to rub through plating. Never expose to salt or perspiration if avoidable. It tarnishes plating. Never leave surface damp.

SIMULATED GOLD: Clean with soap and water. To prevent tarnishing, apply a coat of thin colorless lacquer or nail polish. Never let perfume touch this metal. It destroys the finish.

STEEL BEADS OR BUCKLES: To remove tarnish, use bicarbonate of soda and scrub well.

PEARLS AND AMBER BEADS: Rub with flannel or chamois dipped lightly in olive oil.

RINGS AND SMALL INTRICATE PIECES: Apply soap and water with toothbrush.

PLATINUM: Soak in solution of laundry bleach and water for 30 minutes. To prevent discoloration of costume jewelry or transfer of color to skin, coat the surface with colorless nail polish.

WATCHES: Keep dry. Remove before washing. Wind daily at about the same hour. Do not place near perfume or powder. Use regularly for best time keeping.

Raincoats: Repair holes by patching with special rubber mending tape. Use a patch of the same material where available or auto-top dressing for temporary repair. Rubber tire patches may be applied with rubber cement.

A special kit is necessary for a vulcanized "hot patch." Apply patch to outside, placing special tablet provided, and patch over hole. Clamp together, remove rest of garment as much as possible, light fuse on tablet. Tablet will fuse the materials. Allow to cool and dry.

To apply cold patch, clean with carbon tetrachloride, rinse immediately, roughen edges around hole and around spot, cut patch larger than hole, spread rubber cement on patch and on area surrounding hole, allow to dry slightly, apply second coat, apply patch under pressure.

## MISCELLANEOUS ACCESSORIES

| How to Care For | How to Clean |
|---|---|
| RIBBONS: Keep clean and pressed. Roll on folded paper to put away. Protect from dust in labeled boxes. Don't use hot iron to press. Don't press on right side. Don't fold in creases. | Use 1 tablespoon vinegar in first rinse water in order to set color. Use absorbent method; for both washing and cleaning use methods suited to type of fabric —rayon, velvet, etc. |
| SCARVES: Keep clean and pressed. Fold flat after pressing. | Use absorbent method. Treat according to fabric—rayon, wool, |

| How to Care For | How to Clean |
|---|---|
| Keep protected in covered box. For care and protection of wool scarves, see special directions for washing and packing away of wool fabrics. Don't wear when soiled. Don't put away unpressed. | etc. Don't wash unless sure fabric is washable. |
| TIES: Keep clean and free from spots. Keep wrinkles pressed out. Hang on rack in air to avoid wrinkling. This is especially important for wool ties. Don't keep in drawers. | Don't wash unless fabric is washable. Don't wear when soiled. |
| WHITE TOUCHES: Keep crisp and spotless. Fasten on with buttons or snaps for easy removal. Protect with tissue when freshly laundered and not in use. Don't crowd in drawers. | When washable, use starch for longer wearing freshness. For special stiffening for sheers, see page 60. |
| ARTIFICIAL FLOWERS: Keep clean and fresh. Put away when not in use. Protect from dust and crushing with tissue paper. Keep in special boxes without crowding. Don't put away without protection. | If expensive, send to cleaner. Brush with absorbent powder or dip in cleaning fluid. Dust off frequently with soft brush (shaving brush). Don't use liquid cleaner if flowers are pasted. |
| METAL MESH BAGS, CIGARETTE CASES, COMPACTS, ETC.: Keep clean and untarnished. Protect with chamois bag or black tissue paper when not in use. Put away in special boxes. Don't put away while soiled or tarnished. | Wash frequently with soap and water. Keep special chemically treated cloth for polishing. If badly tarnished, clean with gentle silver polish. |
| PLASTIC ACCESSORIES: Keep clean. Put away in tissue paper when not in use. | Wipe with soft, damp cloth or wash with mild lukewarm soapsuds. Wipe dry with soft cloth. Don't use any cleaner or polish except soap and water. |

## AROMATICS—HOW TO CREATE WELCOME ODORS

For basic freshness: air every room every day, summer and winter. Air blankets, bedclothes, pillows, mattresses. Clean thoroughly, particularly kitchen, bedroom, plumbing, range, oven, refrigerator, garbage can, upholstery, drapes, ash trays, water in flower vase.

Use air deodorizers (Airwick, Tufts). Electric air purifiers add ozone to room air to get rid of odors. Chloride of lime, paradichlorobenzene (moth preventative) and Mil-Du-Rid are good deodorizers for drastic use.

Make a mound of bath salts in a shallow bowl. Place it in a window or place perfume in the water used for humidifying, near or inside the heating unit. Pressurized units that spray are also available.

Remove kerosene odor with vinegar.

ROOMS GENERALLY: Hang perfumed wall brackets or perfumes in hot water pans behind refrigerator. Spray perfume on electric bulbs before lighting.

FURNITURE AND FLOORS: Wipe with cedar oil.

WINDOW SILLS, SHELVES: Paint undersides with scented lacquer.

LINEN CLOSET: Leave scented bath soaps in opened packages.

GIRL'S CLOSET: Hang pomander ball.

BOY'S CLOSET: Hang pine cone painted with pine oil.

GUEST CLOSET: Use cedar lining. Use sachets in coat hanger padding.

BUREAU DRAWERS: Lay scented flannel at bottom. Use lavender bags, sachets, scented lacquers.

BEDS: Insert sachets in pads and mattresses. Use pine pillows.

KITCHEN: Use Airwick, exhaust fan, pine-scented disinfectants. Roast pounded coffee on an iron plate. Burn sugar on hot coals. Boil vinegar with myrrh.

FIRES: Use incense or special fire perfumes. Use aromatic woods—hickory, drift wood, pine cones, cedar chips.

REFRIGERATORS: Keep sauerkraut, fish, ripening cheese, cooked cabbage or broccoli covered. Keep a few drops of oil of wintergreen or piece of charcoal in open box in rear corner.

KNIVES: Remove onion odor by holding over flame for 2 minutes.

Pots: Remove fish odors by sprinkling salt, add hot water, allow to stand for 10 minutes.

Furniture: Scented lacquers on underside.

A potpourri retains aromas. Clip flowers, immediately pull off petals, dry in a ventilated dark place. When petals are dry, pack them in a screw-top glass jar. Store in a dark place. Add a sprinkle of orrisroot between layers. When collection is well filled, brew the mixture of petals. Potpourri may include fragrant flowers, herbs, spices or oils, mixed to desired aroma. Recipes are available.

Pomander balls may be hung in closet or placed between linens. If properly made, they will last several years. Wash an apple or orange carefully. Dry, then wipe with oiled cloth. Cover with rows of cloves. Allow to stand till dried out. Wrap in cellophane and tie with ribbon.

Sachets: Place dried fruit of flowering quince in a gauze bag, or place dried lavender in a cloth bag.

Perfumes: Odor is derived from natural "essential oils," from plants and chemical aromatics. Many have no natural counterparts. Toilet water and Eau de Cologne are diluted perfumes, are less expensive and often more practical to use. Packaging and advertising usually represent a substantial portion of the price.

Odors are floral, woody types, Oriental or French types, or spicy types. Selection is based entirely on personal preferences.

## INSECT PESTS

Repellents: Repellents will minimize your problem. They are effective against some, but not all, pests. Apply on person, clothes, screens, etc. Apply a few drops on palms, smear evenly, then rub on exposed skin to form an oily film. When biting starts again, rub on more. Spraying or daubing clothes will keep mosquitoes from biting through them for several days, water soaking removes effect.

Some repellents irritate the skin. All may cause smarting to mucous membranes, or other tender spots. Repellents will not damage cotton or wool cloth without synthetic fibers, but will dissolve paints, varnishes, synthetic fibers and some plastics.

The great insecticide of the 1950's, DDT, rid most of the world of mosquitoes, flies and other disease-carrying insects but this and carbaryl (Sevin) have special long-range hazards to birds, fish and animal life as well as to human health and the whole world environment. Other formulas like Lindane, DDVP (Vapona) and some containing piperonyl butoxide are also hazardous and should be used with great caution and restraint. Chlordane, which is highly poisonous, is still used in some situations (termite control and occasionally in weed killers) but should be avoided. The less damaging insecticides are: Malathion, dibrom, diazinon and Abate, which are relatively short-lived and low in toxicity. But these are toxic to fish. Rotenone and pyrethrin are natural and relatively low in toxicity to mammals. But pigs are hurt by rotenone. These act and disintegrate quickly. Pyrethrin is often combined with piperonyl butoxide to prolong its life, but the combination is cancer causing to humans.

Methoxychlor is long lasting but living organisms metabolize it and pass it through their digestive chain. It is used to control mosquitoes, flies, and other flying pests.

Carbaryl (Sevin) is teratogenic (monstrosity causing) but is widely used in cities and gardens where some other insecticides are forbidden by law.

Basic formulas for sprays:

**Methoxychlor:** 50% wettable powder—.5% (6 ounces in 5 gallons); 25% emulsifiable concentrate—.5% (1 pint in 5 gallons).

**Malathion:** 25% wettable powder—.5% (12 ounces in 5 gallons); 50% emulsifiable concentrate—.5% (6 ounces in gallons).

**Ronnel:** 24% emulsifiable concentrate 1.0% (1⅔ pints in 5 gallons).

## HOME INSECT CONTROL

Ants: Destroy the colony mound with hot water. Inside old woodwork, use desiccant powder (e.g., Sevin) but avoid contact with skin. Repeat in 2 to 3 weeks. For persistent problem insert 3 teaspoonfuls of carbon disulphide 3 inches into soil, 8 inches apart, around ant hill. Or blow in derris powder containing 5 percent rotenone.

Bedbugs: Nocturnal, they emerge every 3 to 4 days. They live in cracks in furniture, mattresses, bedsteads, and upholstered furniture. A malathion or methoxychlor solution should be sprayed on beds, springs and walls. Repeat after 8 hours.

Centipedes: Practically harmless. Rarely bite man. Normally live in damp outdoors, feed on insects. Eliminate by brushing, cleaning, spraying areas which have contact with ground, with creosote.

CLOTHES MOTHS: Yellowish or buff colored, with a wing spread of ½ inch. 100 to 300 soft white eggs, 1/32 inch long,

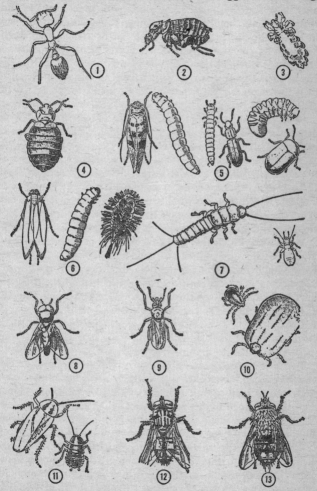

(1) Ant. (2) Flea. (3) Louse. (4) Bedbug. (5) Food pests. (6) Clothes moth. (7) Silver fish. (8) Horse fly. ((9) Sand fly. (10) Tick. (11) Cockroach. (12) Housefly. (13) Wasp.

on the nap of clothing. These hatch in 4 to 8 days in summer, 3 to 4 weeks in cool weather. The hatched worm or larva crawls readily, conceals itself in a silken cocoon, eats wool, lint, hair, fur, casein, feed, meal, dead insects. Remove all clothes and spray walls, door, ceiling with pyrethrin solution, or use Aerosol bombs containing pyrethrum extract. In extreme cases, professionals fumigate with hydrocyanic acid, chloropicrin, or methyl bromide, all of them dangerous to human life. Prevent damage by thorough cleaning and packing in sealed packages containing flake naphthalene or paradichlorobenzene (1 lb. to a trunk) or in cold storage. To mothproof closets, brush clothes thoroughly, seal all openings and cracks, hang, in a muslin bag, 1 lb. of flake naphthalene or paradichlorobenzene to each 100 cubic feet. Cedar-lined chests may be dependable but not cedar-lined closets. Rugs should be kept clean. Upholstery should be brushed frequently.

CLUSTER (HORSE) FLIES: Gather in attics and storerooms. Spray walls, window casings, dark corners with a pyrethrin solution 18 to 36 inches from walls. Have doors and windows closed for 15 minutes following the spraying.

COCKROACHES: Flat bodied, disease carriers. Control with desiccant (drying agent) powder. Spread borax pellets. Spray pyrethrin along baseboards, moldings, crevices, openings around sinks and drains, behind bookcases, around rugs, mattresses, etc. In severe cases use a malathion solution. Remove food and dishes till solution has dried. Effect requires 2 to 7 days. Repeat after 2 weeks if necessary.

CRICKETS: They may eat fabrics, almost anything else. Tend to winter in warm, dark places, will leave in the spring. Dust with pyrethrum or sodium fluoride powder or use Aerosol.

FLEAS: Disease carriers (bubonic plague, typhus), they may be carried by mice, rats, pets. Spray floors on and beneath rugs, and at pets' sleeping places, with malathion (not more than .5%) or methoxychlor (not more than .5%) or rotenone or pyrethrin. To clear an infested house, spray .5% methoxychlor or .2% malathion on floors, baseboards and first 12 inches of wall height. Apply lightly to rugs, upholstery and drapes. A heavy spray will stain. Dust basements, kennels, barns, and other breeding places. Apply a line of dust to dog's back, but do not use on cat except on head. (They lick it off). Ruffle hair with one hand while applying with the other.

FOOD PESTS: (Brown beetles, flour beetles, weevils, bran

bugs, moths): Discard any food badly infested. Don't spray or powder food packets. Valuable food which is only slightly infested may be oven heated to 135° F. for 30 to 60 minutes. After removing food, paint shelves and painted walls with pyrethrin solution.

GNATS (SAND FLIES): Pale yellow, gray or black with spotted wings, small enough to get through screens. Spray both sides of windows and screens, walls, and lighting fixtures with pyrethrin solution or citronella repellent.

HOUSEFLY: Disease bearing. Lays white eggs in manure or garbage. Develop in 10 to 24 hours into white worm-like maggots. These become yellow pupae, then flies which are ready to lay eggs in 2½ to 20 days. Treat with DDT space sprays (½ to 3 percent solutions) or residual sprays on screens, etc. (5 percent solution), or by painting hanging fixtures, beams, doors, windows, etc. with DDT solution. Flypapers, fly poisons, and swatters are also useful. Poison solutions may be made of 3 teaspoons commercial formalin in 1 pint milk or water, with brown sugar added.

LICE (HEAD, BODY, CRAB): Disease carriers (typhus, trench fever). Carried by mice, rats. Dust inner surface of underwear with 10 percent DDT powder, particularly seams and inside of outer clothing. For head or hair lice, rub a teaspoon of powder into hair, repeat after 8 to 10 days.

MOSQUITOES: May transmit diseases (malaria, dengue, yellow fever, filariasis in the tropics, encephalitis in northern U. S.). They are always a pest. Mosquitoes and other flying insects may be repelled by placing 5 drops of spirit of camphor on a lump of sugar. Drain stagnant water areas or spread a light coat of fuel oil over such water in spring breeding system and during summer. Spray with methoxychlor solution. Keep windows closed for 15 minutes following spraying.

PSOCIDS (SILVERFISH, BOOK LICE): Nocturnal, live in damp, dark areas on wallpaper, starchy materials. Common in new "undried" houses. May eat linen, rayon, starched clothing, curtains. Use a water solution where there may be a fire hazard. Alternate insecticides: pyrethrum, sodium fluoride.

SPIDERS: Few bite humans. Only one type is poisonous, the black widow. (These have black shiny, round bodies in two segments, 8 legs, 3 on each side and 2 in front. Males have a yellowish mark on their backs, females one or more red spots on the lower back.) Other spiders are merely a nuisance.

Spray with kerosene, pyrethrum. Sweep off webs. Crush soft white eggs.

TERMITES: These ant-like insects eat wood, can cause a house to collapse. Seldom seen, they live in tunnels eaten through earth or wood, can be detected by the condition of wood or presence of wings. In construction, avoid wood coming within 6 inches of ground. Use wood impregnated with creosote, or sodium arsenate and surround areas of ground contact with these chemicals. In case of infestation, skilled help should be called. Here persistent pesticides are justified. Among the poisons which can be used are chlordane, lindane, and coal-tar creosote.

TICKS: Disease carrier (Rocky Mountain fever). Live in woods and tall grass. Attach to dogs or clothing. Remove (preferably with forceps). Avoid crushing as fluid is dangerous. The brown dog tick is not dangerous but is annoying to dogs. (See Fleas.)

WASPS AND HORNETS: (They live in papery nests, sting). Spray nests, caves, porches, and rafters heavily with DDT solution after dark (when insects are quiet), using caution. Blow dust into nest opening with bellows.

FURNITURE PESTS: Two types of insect infestation are damaging to furniture. One is the dry-wood termite (white ant)

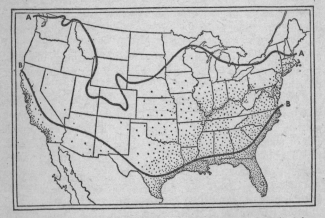

Map showing, by density of stippling, the relative hazard of termite infestations, the northern limit of damage done by subterranean termites in the United States (line A-A), and the northern limit of damage done by dry-wood termites (line B-B).

which thrives in the tropics and extends as far north as Virginia and northern California, and the other, the Lyctus (powder-post beetle). To control the termites, saturate infested furniture with orthodichlorobenzene. If this treatment is not practical, blow dry Paris green into holes bored with an auger, using bellows for blowing.

The powder-post beetle cannot enter wood in which the pores have been sealed, so the best preventive for this type of insect attack is to wax or varnish unfinished portions of the wood or cover with linseed oil. Old furniture may be drenched in kerosene before refinishing. To strengthen a damaged piece of furniture, pour molten paraffin over the wood, wipe off the excess, then refinish.

Upholstered furniture infested with clothes moths, tobacco beetle or book lice should be vacuumed. Bad cases should be sent out for fumigation as sprays do not penetrate sufficiently.

## RODENT PESTS

Rats, mice, ground squirrels, gophers are disease carriers (plague, typhus, food poisoning, infections, jaundice, rat-bite fever, tularemia, Rocky Mountain spotted fever, scrub fever). They also destroy food, clothing, shrubs and trees. They breed at all seasons, 4 to 7 times a year with litters of 6 to 22, reach maturity in 100 to 120 days. One pair of rats in captivity produced 1500 descendants in one year. Nests are found in burrows, buildings, and trees. Control varies with type of animal and location. Most effective are poisoning, trapping, fumigating, eliminating their food supply and shelter, and ratproofing of buildings.

RATS: Avoid open garbage pail. Traps and poisons are usually effective but rats learn to avoid them. Use variety of poisons. One: red squill with water added to paste mixed with fish or chopped meat. Traps may be baited with fresh bread, raw or cooked meat, bacon, fish, melon, apple, carrot, tomato, or nut meats. Fish oil, rancid cheese or rolled oats give added attraction. Rat terriers are effective. Fumigation is most certain method of elimination known.

MICE: The odor of naphthalene flakes repels them. Energetic, well-fed cats are effective eliminators. Mouse seed may be placed under wall boards. Traps should be placed near wall or under table, out of traffic. Bait may be cheese or cereal. Close up entry holes.

SQUIRRELS, CHIPMUNKS: Usually enter houses from tree branches to attic. Metal guards at tree base may prevent this. They dislike odor of moth balls.

BATS: They are harmless, destroy insects, but a nuisance in the attics. Close openings. Leave 2 or 3 openings during the day until the bats have learned to use them, then close several hours after dark when all the bats have left. Bats under floors can be driven out by use of moth flakes. Do not plug openings when bats still remain in the house.

## SPECIAL PROBLEMS

To Make a Fire: (1) Make a bottom layer of crushed paper, dry grass, shavings, etc. (2) Make a second layer of light, dry wood, old boxes, shingles, twigs. (3) When fire is started, add logs or coal. (4) Allow air to get into each level in a steady current. Special chemicals (charcolite) facilitate fast fire-lighting.

COLORED FIRE: For green flames, treat logs with boric acid; for blue flames, with copper sulphate; for red flames with strontium nitrate. Mix 1 lb. of chemical to 1 gallon of water, soak logs for 3 hours, allow to dry.

Check List for Moving Day: (1) Plan moving with company representative. Cost may be based on man hours or weight, plus extras. Arrange for necessary cartons, barrels, old newspapers, cord and other packing materials. Some companies provide portable closets so as to avoid necessity of packing clothing. (2) Check insurance coverage. Some articles, like mirrors, may have to be crated in order to be covered. Most movers take no responsibility unless they pack goods themselves. (3) Check gas, electricity, heat, water, phone, etc., for new home and disconnect old. Arrange for first delivery of food. Inform post office of new address. Also inform magazines to which you subscribe (at least 20 days in advance), charge accounts, motor vehicle bureau, etc. Cancel milk and newspaper deliveries (and arrange for new ones). (4) On moving day, wear old clothes with pockets to hold screw driver, hammer, pliers, thumb tacks, marking crayons, etc. (5) Pack things you will need immediately (toothbrushes, etc.) in a separate package and insert it last in truck. (6) Pack and carry papers and documents personally. (7) Remove and pack separately mirrors, marble tops, casters and loose hardware (properly labeled), breakable articles in drawers. (8) Mirrors and pictures should be packed in papers or sheets. They may be tied to underside of card table after being suitably padded. (9) Fill drawers. Lock, tie or otherwise fasten drawers (as by inserting wad of paper at edges). (10) Pack breakable objects in barrels. (11) Tie books in carriable packages. They need not usually be placed in cartons. Put paper between books to prevent rubbing. Dust before packing. (12) Remove phonograph needle. Tie back movable

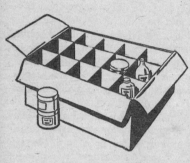

parts. Remove bulbs from lamps. Coil up all wires and extension cords. Pack records and magazines together with records in between pages. (13) Pack bottled inks, preserves, medicines, etc., in partitioned cartons in which bottled goods comes to the grocery store. Secure loose tops with Scotch tape. (14) Disassemble beds. (15)

For moving miscellaneous bottles.

Roll rugs on a pole. (16) Wrap shoes in paper, pack in cartons or laundry bag. (17) Transport portable typewriter as it is. Box or crate a standard typewriter if possible. (18) Roll curtains and drapes on cardboard or wood rollers and pack in boxes. (19) Pack small lamps like dishes. Leave large lamps unpacked. (20) Long-handled brushes, brooms, mops, etc., may be tied into one package. (21) Check to see that all polished surfaces are covered in moving. (22) If cartons are labeled, use a different-colored label for each room. (23) Mark cartons "right side up" where necessary. (24) Number cartons. Make inventory. (25) Have rugs loaded last so they may be relaid first.

**Seasonal Storage:** Draperies should be brushed and aired, and if necessary, cleaned. Wrap in heavy paper or box, provide moth protection where necessary. Upholstered furniture and pillows should be vacuumed or brushed, sunned and aired out of doors, if possible, and mothproofed. Woolens should be brushed and spots removed, cleaned if possible. Pockets and cuffs should be turned out and lint removed. Rugs should be cleaned on both sides and mothproofed, rolled with layers of newspapers; put on paper caps at ends, and cover over all, and tie firmly. Store in dry, clean place. If to be stored on end, roll around a bamboo pole. If proper storage cannot be provided, allow to remain on floor. Furs should be brushed, combed, hung in sunlight, and hung in an airtight bag or tar bag or tar paper, in a cool dry place. Professional storage will provide cleaning and cold storage not available at home. Linens should be cleaned, starch removed, folded lightly to avoid creases (tissue paper between folds helps) and stored in a dry place. Metals should be shined, covered with kerosene or lemon oil (or for such items as irons, paraffin), wrapped in paper for protection against dust and moisture. Lacquered metals need only wrapping. Silver may be placed in specially treated bags or cases.

Closing the House: (1) Clean thoroughly to avoid dust settling, attracting pests. (2) Spray to discourage insects. (3) Spread borax on food shelves. Close up all means of entry, door and window cracks, fireplace, cellar windows. Destroy all unprotected food. Mothproof where necessary. (4) Dispose of perishable foods. (5) Store candlesticks. (6) Remove, clean, and store curtains and draperies. (7) Substitute old window shades for new, to avoid scorch. (8) Close and lock windows with newspaper under sashes. (9) Cover furniture, beds, pillows, bookcases, pictures, statues, and bric-a-brac with dust sheets or newspapers. (10) Take in screens. (11) Remove inflammable liquids—cleaning fluids, varnish, etc., or at least make certain they are safely closed and in a fireproof area; remove oily rags. (12) Store matches in metal containers. (13) Shut off gas, shut off electricity or disconnect lamps and appliances. (14) Clean and protect metals with oil film—grease or vaseline. Clean and dry garbage can. (15) Protect books, etc., against mildew by leaving charcoal to absorb dampness. (16) Shut off water. (17) Lock windows, doors, shutters. Set alarms. (18) Disconnect telephone and arrange for transferring calls. (19) Arrange to leave key with neighbor for emergency use. (20) Check insurance against burglary, fire, etc.

Winter Closing: In addition to above, remove all water from

pipes and traps and shut off intake. Turn faucets to open. Fill traps with crumpled newspaper to avoid sewer gas. Non-alcoholic automobile anti-freeze solutions (1 quart) may be left in pipes. Containers with water should be stored in insulated place or wrapped with newspapers in box or trunk. Flush all toilets, bail and sponge out remaining water. Sponge out bowl traps of toilets and put in 2 quarts of anti-freeze. Disconnect pump and drain. Shut off valve of pressure tank and drain tank.

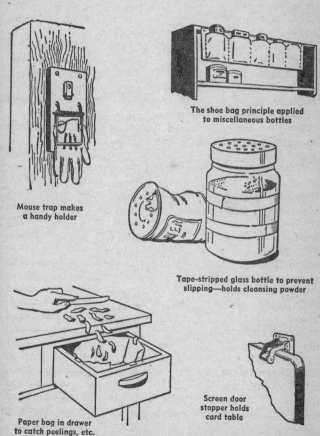

The shoe bag principle applied to miscellaneous bottles

Mouse trap makes a handy holder

Tape-stripped glass bottle to prevent slipping—holds cleansing powder

Paper bag in drawer to catch peelings, etc.

Screen door stopper holds card table

## WRAPPING A PACKAGE

Make certain you've placed the card inside the package.

If a double wrapping is being used (as paper and cellophane) cut and wrap together. Place box on cut sheet, bring paper up, overlapping as near as possible to center of top, and fasten with Scotch tape. If box cannot be turned upside down to wrap, cut paper ½ inch wider and turn the raw edge under. If possible cover the overlap with tying ribbon.

Jars and bottles are best wrapped in tissue paper or cellophane fluff. Cut two squares of sufficient size. Arrange them diagonally under bottle. Bring the paper to the top and arrange in a fluff. Fasten with wire and add ribbons (2).

Fold top ends of paper down and make sharp diagonal pieces on both sides. Fold sides in, then bottom up. Fasten with gummed tape. Repeat at opposite end.

When the box is larger than the paper, cut a second sheet of paper the width of the box and large enough to extend down the sides. Hold in place with gummed tape (3). Then proceed with wrapping of other end to overlap.

*As far as gift wrapping is concerned, it's not a matter of any tricks; it's just practice of a few simple rules.*

Cut the paper to the size needed for package making sure it is wide enough to go around the box and to overlap 1½ inches on top.

Cut off the excess paper, leaving enough at sides to extend over ½ depth of box.

Place the box on the paper face down and bring paper around the box and overlap. To make a clean edge, fold overlapping end in ½ inch.

Fold each side of the ends in neat creases at edges of the box, then fold in flaps at top and bottom of box.

GIFT BOXES: Line gift boxes with tissue paper. Cut paper twice as long as box, pleat it down the center to make it exactly the width of the box. Lay a second sheet across the width and pleat to fit in the same way. Fold long ends over top of gift. Fasten with gum seal or leave loose. For gifts which may be mussed by shifting, crush several sheets of tissue paper loosely, and tuck to hold [Page 104 (3)].

Flat gifts may be wrapped in tissue paper on a slightly larger piece of cardboard. Cardboard may be cut to shape. Wrap, fasten with seals or Scotch tape [Page 104 (4)].

After paper is neatly folded around box it is held in place with matching seals before tying with ribbon.

Plain tying of ribbon on box. After crossing ribbon, bring it around box in opposite direction and tie it with long ends.

It's easy to make a lovely bow. First make a loop between the thumb and first finger, keeping the ribbon flat. A second loop is made by bringing the ribbon from the opposite side. Additional loops can be made same way and tied in middle as shown at right to form multiple bow.

# IDEAS FOR NOVELTY WRAPPINGS

Slogans from
advertisements

Colored picture
cut from magazine

Rickrack Braid
and paste

What a strip of
wallpaper can do

Tied-on toys
or jokes

Pinking shears
will do this

Colored Bias Seam
Tape instead of
ribbon

Tie with yarn

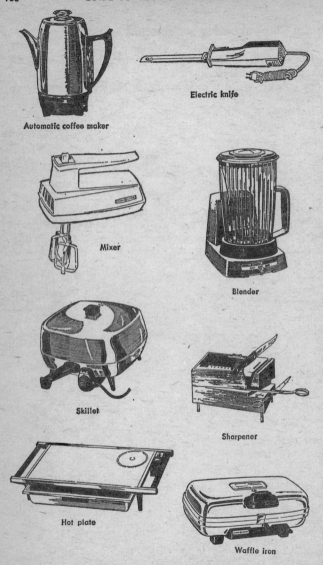

Automatic coffee maker

Electric knife

Mixer

Blender

Skillet

Sharpener

Hot plate

Waffle iron

Electrical Aids for Kitchen Work

## MAKE YOUR OWN KITCHEN GADGETS

**Dish Cloth:** Use mesh sacks from oranges, etc., boiled for 15 minutes in laundry bleach.

**Food Scrapers:** Use cardboard from milk containers, cut to size.

**Overheated Oven:** Insert pans of cold water.

**Pot Covers:** Use a spool or cork, with bolt and washer, to replace loose knobs.

**Pot Holders:** Use old turkish towels.

**Seal Bottles:** When picnicking or traveling, apply nail polish as bottle sealer.

**Shakers:** Use an emptied jar with holes in the cover, adhesive tape around to prevent slipping.

**Sterilizer—Homemade:** Use a can in which meat packers ship livers to your butcher. Boil with soap powder and laundry bleach for 30 minutes. Lace rubber jar covers together to form a shock absorber at bottom.

**Sticky Ice Trays:** Rub in oil or keep wax paper on bottom.

**Uncorking Bottles:** Thump the bottom till the cork comes up enough for a grip. Rubber stoppers may be loosened with a few drops of glycerine allowed to soak in, or wrap hot rag around neck.

# BOOK II

## Home Decorating Guide

**The Spirit of the House:** Good decoration reflects the personality of the people who live in the home. It should, first of all, be distinctive, just as each person is distinctive. A home should have unity not only within each room but throughout the house. Rooms should, to some degree, harmonize with each other. The color and styling of each room, particularly, should fit into the color and styling of the rooms which run out of it.

Attractive home furnishings set the stage for pleasant living. If they are an expression of yourself, you will have a feeling of satisfaction every time you enter your home, and friends will share your enjoyment.

However, furnishings and surroundings expressive of just the right note of restfulness, gay informality, or elegant simplicity are not often assembled by accident. Even enthusiasm alone is not enough. For most home decorators, it takes poring over plans, trying color schemes, finding ingenious ways to make the best of what you have, and shopping around to search out just the right purchases at prices you can afford to pay. But there is keen pleasure in striving for the perfect result, and great satisfaction in achieving it.

The secret is that everything need not be bought at once. Compromise by spending a little money for things intended for temporary use; keeping quality as the first consideration in things you expect to have always.

A successful house and successful rooms will depend upon the proper relationship of each element in it to the others and to the whole. Therefore, in selecting each piece it is well to consider the background, the usage, the draperies, the floor covering, the upholstering materials, the woods, shapes, color scheme, and the "feeling" you prefer for the room.

Work and plan to enjoy your house. Limit the expenditures

of time, effort and money to the extent of your abilities, so that just running the house doesn't dominate your life. Elegance and delicate things may be a drain you can afford only in a limited way. If you can't afford outside help, select a house and furnishings that require less care. Plan your activities so that tumult and upset are limited to a few rooms—an activity room or a bedroom, or a corner of the dining room.

You'll get more pleasure out of a house if you have a hobby connected with it—collecting glass or antiques, gardening or indoor flower growing, ceramics, art, cooking, decorating, flower arrangements, etc. And you'll get more satisfaction and a great deal of help from studying household activities.

## COLOR

**How to Select a Color Scheme:** You can select a pleasing combination of colors from a wallpaper, a fabric, an Oriental rug, a flower or scene, or even a picture in a magazine. If you don't already have the furniture or rugs, it is a good idea to make up a color scheme in this way. Let one color predominate. Limit a color scheme to two or three colors, with white or gray tones. These points will help you: (1) Always choose colors that please you personally—subtle, calm colors if you prefer a restful atmosphere, intense colors if you like liveliness and cheer. (2) Don't be afraid of color. Experimenting on paper will give you confidence. (But remember larger batches of color are more intense.) Try out various color combinations, then "live with them".—look at them frequently before you actually start buying. (3) Colors should harmonize with furniture, draperies, carpets. (4) Colors should be colorful and definite (grass green, lemon yellow, café-au-lait, French gray) not wishy-washy. (5) Generally, darkest colors are lowest in the room. (6) Walls are favored by dark, bright colors, but these should be softened by light colors in furnishings. One, two, or all walls of a room may be papered. Dark walls look richer at night. (7) Ceilings may be white or natural, or they may be tinted with the color of your walls; or they may be wallpapered with the same paper or fabric as the walls; or they may be covered with acoustical board, wall board, or structural glass in the same or lighter color than the walls: or apply decalcomanias or stencil on designs (stars or fairies for a nursery, fish for a bathroom, flowers for bedrooms, medallion for dining room, etc.). If one or two walls are papered, they should be the unbroken walls. The paper should have an important pattern. Painted walls should match the background color. (8) Use the dullest tones for the largest areas (floors, walls, ceilings); next brightest for large pieces of furniture; brightest colors for small accessories.

You can achieve three effects with color. (1) Contrast—different colors used as foils to flatter each other. (2) Blend, in which walls, upholstery and draperies are various tints and shades of the rug color. (3) Accent—gradations of one color, plus one sharp contrasting color for shock value. Contrast may be obtained by using complementary colors; light and dark values; brilliant and/or dull colors; warm and cool colors; pure and grayed-down colors.

Color is made up of: hue or basic color (red, blue, green); value or shade (dark or light blue); and intensity or strength or purity (bright blue, reddish brown).

**The Color Wheel and Color Schemes:** All colors are created out of combinations of three primary colors—red, yellow, and blue —with black or white added. By combining primary colors we get secondary colors, orange, green, and purple. By combinations, in this way, it is possible to make a color wheel of an infinite number of colors.

In making a color scheme, the following combinations may be used effectively:

MONOCHROMATIC: Monochromatic color harmony is the harmony of different tints or shades of one hue. (White added to a color generally produces what is referred to as a tint, and black added to a color produces a shade.) Thus monochromatic harmony is the harmony of different values of the same hue. To produce monochromatic color harmony, white or black is added to a definite hue. This should not be confused with "graying" a color, which changes its strength, but does not result in what is termed a tint or shade. The color scheme is a monotonous, antiseptic combination difficult to use effectively. When used effectively, it can provide a subtle and glamorous background. It is suitable for a very vivid personality. The major color should predominate. Sequence should be gradual. It is usual to add a complementary or contrasting color for accent.

ANALOGOUS: Analogous color harmony is the harmony of colors which are close to one another in the color wheel. Such colors harmonize well if not too widely separated in the spectrum; otherwise they will clash. For instance, blue and purple harmonize since they are close together in the spectrum, while blue and red clash since they are neither close together in the spectrum nor complementary.

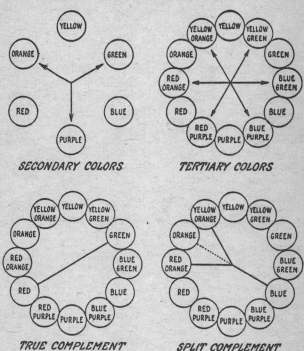

SECONDARY COLORS                    TERTIARY COLORS

TRUE COMPLEMENT                    SPLIT COMPLEMENT

COMPLEMENTARY: Complementary color harmony is the harmony of colors which are directly opposite one another in the color wheel. To achieve complementary harmony, however, judgment must be used as to quantities and position. One color looks best in the presence of a small portion of its complement rather than an equal portion. The best rule to follow is to use the complement of a color sparingly to "set off" the original color.

"SPLIT" COMPLEMENTARY harmony consists of a single hue opposite two nearby hues with the exact complement omitted, for example, blue and red-orange and yellow-orange.

TRIADIC: Triadic color harmony is the harmony of the colors which are at the points of an equilateral triangle superimposed on the color wheel (as green, orange, and purple). By moving the triangle on the wheel, the two triadic harmonizing colors for any hue can be determined. If the triangle is moved so one point is at green-yellow, it is found that orange-red and purple-blue are the colors to combine with green-yellow for triadic harmony.

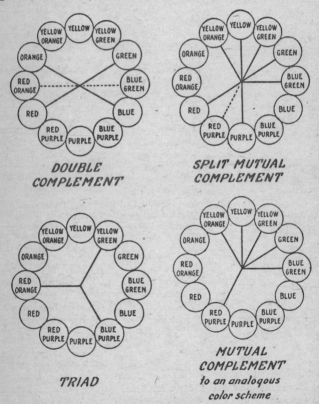

DOUBLE COMPLEMENT

SPLIT MUTUAL COMPLEMENT

TRIAD

MUTUAL COMPLEMENT
to an analogous color scheme

DOUBLE COMPLEMENT: The split complement carried at both ends of the line; e.g. red, orange, green, blue.

MUTUAL COMPLEMENT: A color with a group of colors analogous to its complement.

Split mutual complement: The same principle, with the original color split into its two adjoining colors.

In practice, check off the colors of the rugs, drapes, etc., which you already have. Then choose the scheme which will combine these colors effectively, noting any new colors which may be added to complete the harmonious picture.

One way to select a color scheme you will like is to look through your wardrobe, note the costumes which you like to wear, and use these color schemes as the basis for your room.

## MASTER COLOR CHART

| Color | For Large Areas (Floors, Walls, Large Furniture) Use | For Small Areas (Small Furniture, Accessories) Use |
|---|---|---|
| Black | White, ivory, gray, glass, silver, gold. Pastel colors. | Gold, silver, green, orange, raspberry, peach, yellow. Bright colors. |
| Gray | Light blue, blue, navy, green, purple, lavender, cream, silver. Pastel to dark colors. | Yellow, orange, pink, flame red, maroon. Any bright color, black or white. |
| White | Pastel to dark colors. | Any bright color or black or white. |
| Olive green | Light green, tan, brown, light yellow, copper, white. | Light blue, blue, pink, red, maroon, lavender, cream, rust, copper, yellow, white. |
| Green | Light green, yellow-green, olive, yellow, lavender, gray, tan, copper, white, gold, silver. | Orange, pink, peach, red, maroon, heliotrope, purple, cream, gold, tan, brown, dark brown, white, warm gray. |
| Dark green | White, light yellow, purple, light gray, light green, chartreuse, peach, pink, tan, gold, silver. | Pink, chartreuse, yellow, rust, white. |

| Color | For Large Areas (Floors, Walls, Large Furniture) Use | For Small Areas (Small Furniture, Accessories) Use |
|---|---|---|
| DARK BROWN<br><br>BROWN | Beige, coffee, bisque, olive, yellow, rose, lavender, cream, tan, chartreuse, light gray, light green, light blue, turquoise, silver. Any light color. | Blue, navy, light green, green, white. Any bright color. |
| TAN | Olive, yellow, cream, brown, dark brown, navy, gold, dark green. Any medium or dark color. | Light blue, blue, navy, dark green, light green, maroon, heliotrope, purple, lavender, Any bright color. |
| CREAM | Yellow-orange, pink-gray, tan, brown, dark brown. Any medium to dark color except yellow. | Light blue, blue, navy, dark green, light green, green, olive, red, heliotrope, purple, lavender. Any bright color. |
| GOLDEN YELLOW | Dark purple, dark blue; medium to dark blue-green; medium to dark green; dark yellow-green; tan, brown. | Blue, bright green, turquoise. Bright purples or blues, russet, yellow. |
| YELLOW | Light green, green, olive, orange, cream, tan, brown, dark brown. | Blue, navy, dark green, red, maroon, purple, heliotrope, lavender, gray. |
| ORANGE | Olive, light yellow, red, cream, tan, brown. Purple blue; medium blue-green, gold, silver. | Blue, navy, light green, green, heliotrope, purple, yellow. |
| ROSE | Maroon, heliotrope, purple. | Light blue, light green, green, olive, yellow. Bright blue or bright green. |

| Color | For Large Areas (Floors, Walls, Large Furniture) Use | For Small Areas (Small Furniture, Accessories) Use |
|---|---|---|
| PEACH (YELLOW-RED) | Maroon, heliotrope, brown, dark brown. | Dark violet, pale green, navy, emerald green, light green, green, blue, yellow. Bright blue or bright green. |
| WINE, MAROON | Pink, heliotrope, gray, gold, silver. | Navy, light green, green, olive, butter yellow, gray, white. Bright, light blue, green, yellow or red. |
| RED-PURPLE, (SCARLET) | Turquoise (blue-green), blue-pink, red, maroon, purple, gray, brown, dark brown. | Navy, dark green, light green, green-yellow, orange-cream, tan. |
| BLUE-GREEN (TURQUOISE) | Violet. Blue, navy, myrtle green, light green, green, pink, yellow, heliotrope, lavender, gray, brown, dark brown, chartreuse. Light to medium blue-green. | Scarlet, cherry. Yellow, orange, tan. |
| LAVENDER | Light yellow, blue-violet, light blue, navy, light green, green, pink, purple, gray-brown, dark brown. | Bright turquoise, yellow, purple, purple-red, blue. |
| LIGHT BLUE | Blue, navy, dark green, light green, lavender, gray, beige, yellow, pink, peach, coral, silver, gold. | Red, coral, yellow. |

| Color | For Large Areas (Floors, Walls, Large Furniture) Use | For Small Areas (Small Furniture, Accessories) Use |
|---|---|---|
| BLUE | Light blue, navy, light green, blue-green, green, red-purple, purple, lavender, gray, beige, yellow, pink, peach, coral, silver, gold. | Peach, olive, yellow, orange, cream, tan, brown, dark brown, gray, silver, ivory, cold white. |

## PSYCHOLOGICAL PROPERTIES OF COLOR

In addition to the proper combination of colors, a prime factor in setting the atmosphere of your home will be the psychological properties of the colors you choose. In one sense, selection of colors will reflect your personality as well as your good taste. But in a larger sense, they will create an emotional feeling about your house that will help form the opinion your visitors will have about you and your family.

### Psychological Significance

RED-ORANGE: Heat; stimulation; activity; richness; splendor; dignity.

PINK: Daintiness; gaiety; animation.

YELLOW—YELLOW-GREEN: Dryness; crispness; relaxation; warmth; light; cheer.

GREEN-BLUE: Coldness; spaciousness; passivity; tranquillity.

VIOLET: Coolness; limpness; dullness; daintiness; reservation; femininity.

BROWN: Warmth.

### Decorative Uses and Effects

RED: Stimulating or cheering to the melancholy or lazy; upsetting to the nervous or overactive; attention compelling. (Use in small quantities in dining room, library, kitchen.)

BLUE: Soothing to the nervous; depressing to the morose. Inseparable mentally with illimitability—the cold immensity of space, infinity. It has an intellectual appeal. Symbolically, it is the color of truth, which is the result of calm reflection and never of heated argument.

YELLOW: In certain hues, the sensation of glory, cheerfulness; in other variations, cowardice, cheapness. Connotes splendor, radiance, vividness. It is of great healing value to the brain. (Use in masses or small quantities, where light is poor.)

GREEN: Cooling, not productive of extreme reactions. Symbolic of serenity and rebirth; suggestive of hope.

ORANGE: Associated with life, well-being, energy. (Avoid bright orange in masses.)

BROWN (TAN-GOLDEN BROWN): Depressing if used alone; best combined with orange, yellow, gold. (Use sparingly to avoid drabness, in living room, library.)

PURPLE (PLUM, MAUVE, ORCHID): Associated with heroism, or with passion and mystery, pomp, gorgeousness. It has a soothing influence. (Use sparingly in living room, library.)

LAVENDER, VIOLET: (Lavender may be used in bedrooms.)

PINK: Slightly stimulating. (Use in masses, or in bedroom, or nursery.)

BLACK, WHITE, GRAY: Intensify other colors in room.

**Light Qualities:** Colors may be used to give you more light or more shadow as your decorative scheme and the type of room requires. The amount of light depends on the quantity of light reflected and absorbed. The more light reflected, the greater the visibility, reading and sewing advantages, etc. The following indicates the relative light-conserving powers (reflection) of colors:

| | | | |
|---|---|---|---|
| White reflects | 80% | Peach, Salmon, Light | |
| Ivory (light) | 71% |    pearl-gray | 53% |
| Apricot-Beige | 66% | Pale apple green | 51% |
| Lemon yellow | 65% | Medium gray | 43% |
| Ivory | 59% | Light green, pale blue | 41% |
| Light Buff | 56% | Deep Rose | 12% |
| | Dark Green | 9% | |

**Special Uses of Color:** Grayed or dusty tones sometimes have more character than a color tint. These shades are made by adding the complement of the color to the mixture, and muting the color. They are lovely as background colors, for rugs, for walls, or for covering large pieces of furniture. They are more sophisticated than a true tint.

Strong vivid colors (as vermillion) catch and hold attention. Use them to frame a window, bind the slipcovers, or as trimming contrast: or add a larger accent note in the upholstery of a small chair, or a floor-length cover for a round table.

If you have many windows along one wall, paint the wall to match the background color of the draperies. They blend together and seem to enlarge the room. Just as those colors recede to background softness, so do cool colors, and soft, muted colors.

A bright color (a vermillion, for instance) screams for your attention, but a dull one (a deep tone of red, we'll say) stays quietly in its place. A small area of brilliant color is counterbalanced by a large area of quieter color. The brilliant color has more concentrated attention value. Such positive accents of color are sometimes necessary to give life to an otherwise dull room.

If you want to call attention to your couch and chairs, slipcover them in warm tones. To tie separate parts of the room together, cover a sizable sofa or large chair in the same fabric as the draperies and place it along the opposite wall.

When you plan the color scheme of your rooms, plan one for the winter and another for the summer. The room seems to change completely when you exchange your winter draperies and slipcovers for a sleek summer ensemble. Have warm colors predominate in winter, cool ones in summer. Also notice what different textures do for a room. Dull fabrics look warmer than shiny ones, and sleek surfaces feel cooler to the touch.

For your porch and garden furniture, remember to plan colors very carefully lest you introduce colors that will detract from the exterior appearance of your home rather than enhance its beauty. Take into consideration the color of your roof, the body and trim of your house, as well as the coloring of adjoining houses, if they are close enough to be part of the picture.

## FURNITURE ARRANGEMENT

A great deal of expense can be saved if the rooms are first planned on paper. Draw the room to scale. Make templets of cardboard approximating the shape and size of furniture.

Balance: Furniture and decorations should be arranged in groups for specific purposes—conversation, reading, etc. Groups should be arranged in balance, with several small pieces or bright pieces offsetting larger or heavier-looking

## FUNDAMENTALS OF FURNITURE ARRANGEMENT

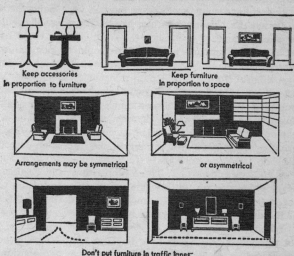

Keep accessories
In proportion to furniture

Keep furniture
In proportion to space

Arrangements may be symmetrical          or asymmetrical

Don't put furniture in traffic lanes

Place large pieces
against the wall

Seating or flat topped pieces may be
placed at right angles or against the wall

Place furniture around a center of interest

pieces. The balance may be formal—that is, symmetrical, or informal, asymmetrical. Formal balance tends to appear stilted, should not be used on more than three groups in a room. Equal balance gives a restful effect to a room, but may become monotonous and dull with too much repetition. Consequently it is good to combine formal and informal balance in the same room.

Line: Lines of furniture and decorations may be straight, curved, parallel, vertical, horizontal or diagonal. They may be delicate or strong, soothing or harsh. Lines should harmonize gracefully. Too many lines, like too many colors, give an air of confusion.

Color: Color schemes for furniture should be planned with consideration of the size, shape, exposure, use, and available furnishings.

Scale and Proportion: Small rooms should have small furniture; large rooms, larger pieces. Small and massive furniture, mixed in one group, tends to clash. Furniture itself and its relation to wall space should be in good proportion. Certain proportions of space are pleasing to the eye, others are displeasing. Good proportions of furniture space to wall space are 2 to 3, 3 to 5, 4 to 7. These proportions may be used in arranging any group, as to height, width or overall mass.

Texture: The roughness or smoothness of materials gives a feeling to a room. Textures may be mingled, should be graduated.

Rhythm: Rhythm is related movement. Architecture has been called "frozen music." In a room, rhythm is a repetition of accent, either by furniture arrangement or by the use of color or design so the eye is carried from one point to another. You may obtain it by a repetition of color, as when the eye is carried from a colorful window drapery to chairs, pictures, and accessories, each repeating in correct proportion the main color scheme of the room.

## SUGGESTIONS FOR VARIOUS ROOMS

The Living Room: There is nothing that makes a room or a single grouping of furniture look more inviting than the appearance that it is used and enjoyed. To achieve this feeling in your home think of the activities that go on in your household and arrange groups or combinations of groups that will take care of all of them. If yours is a house for informal entertaining, arrange conversation groups where two or more can sit cozily, close together. For reading, have enough shelves for books, and a convenient place to keep magazines. Then, a comfortable chair and a reading table with an interesting but effective lamp for good light, create an inviting atmosphere. If your family is musically inclined, you may want one section of the room for the piano with another grouping for the radio-phonograph. Plan storage space for records and sheet music, each convenient to its own unit.

The living room, or drawing room, or sitting room, or parlor, should contain upholstered furniture sufficient to seat all the members of the family plus two or three guests. Each major chair should be within reach of a table containing ash tray, etc., and should be faced so that those entering the room can be seen and welcomed. Tables may also contain lamps, books, and other accessories both for decoration and use. Tables and chairs should harmonize in weight and style. Tall pieces of furniture (breakfronts, secretaries) should be placed against (and parallel with) walls. Seating furniture should be arranged along walls, either parallel or at right angles. Chairs and chaises may also be placed diagonally. Pianos should be placed with straight side parallel to the wall, away from heat, and so as to receive light from the left. (Paper patterns of pianos to lay on the floor for experimental purposes are available from most manufacturers.) Breakfronts may be placed opposite a door of equal height, between two windows, or facing a sofa. This, of course, should be balanced by a large group at the other end of the room. One group is usually centered around a fireplace.

What to do with a corner.

Wherever possible, units should be balanced with pieces of similar or equal design. Pairs of chairs, tables, lamps, etc., help in this. The entire room should be "tied together" with something in common—style of wood, color, period, some design or motif, or just a common feeling.

Lights should be provided for each upholstered chair, and sufficient light for reading in one or two special chairs. Lamps should be at approximately uniform level from the floor—about 50 inches. Lamps may be made from almost any interesting object—vases, statuary, jugs, old kerosene lamps, loving cups, decoys, baby toys. Shades should be simple, translucent, in size and style to harmonize with the base.

Provision for placement of books, souvenirs, collections, magazines, records, writing and sewing materials should be made if they are to be kept in the living room.

One wall of the living room may be set up as an office, with built-in desk (with space for typewriter and fireproof place for valuables). Over the desk a map (or an old-time map), picture, enlarged photograph, or a collection of mementos may be placed. Bookshelves may surround the desk.

The color scheme of the living room should be in quiet shades. Regardless of color, wallpaper should have recessive appearance to accent the furnishings. Two-tone wallpaper makes matching and harmonizing easier. All other designs, imitations of fabrics, bold stripes are all suitable for living room papers.

Accessories are often the most important part in giving personality to the home. Most homes, after years of random accumulations, get cluttered with accessories that add nothing to the decoration. Periodic removal of unnecessary objects is wise. Open shelves with knickknacks, books, hobby items, pictures, lamp bases, ash trays, silver, copper, pewter, chromium, glass, statuary, figurines, pottery, plastics, boxes, and other table decorations may add charm or clutter depending on selection and use. It is usually best to accumulate these as you live in a home.

One decorating trick is to rotate your room's accessories. Guard against monotony by changing living room accessories with the seasons. Use richly colored pottery pieces for fall; warm-colored lamps and handsome oil paintings for winter; gay, fragile vases and a group of vivid water colors for spring; and crystal flower containers, ash trays and lamps for summer.

Avoid antimacassars, runners, table scarves. They are out-of-date, don't protect anything.

To obtain a cool look for summer, minimize accessories. If practical, rugs should be taken up and floors covered with cool, colored linen, glass, rayon, fiber, or cotton summer rugs or left bare. Replace winter draperies with light summer drapes or just white curtains. Slipcovers in cool colors—green, blues, white—should cover upholstered furniture, both as a summer change and as a protection against dust and fading. Furniture should be re-arranged so that chairs catch the breezes. The fireplace may be whitewashed for the summer. (Warm water will remove it in the fall.) Decorative branches may be substituted for logs. Lampshades may be changed. Heavy oil paintings and tapestries may be removed. A sense of bareness is also a sense of coolness.

**The Foyer or Hall:** The entrance hall should be decorated to express warmth, cheer, pleasantness. It should be painted in a warm, cheerful color or papered with big flowery designs and gay checks or bold stripes. However, stripes should be avoided if there is a staircase in the hall. The color scheme should be in harmony with the rooms which run from the hall, with emphasis on the color of the largest room.

The essential quality of the floor is that it should be practical; linoleum, rubber, or washable colored rugs are suitable. However, rugs present a stumble hazard. Furniture may include a table (for packages), a mirror, chair for putting on rubbers, etc., and a chest if the room is large enough. The hall closet is practically essential. Some added suggestions: A tall mirror framed in a wallpaper border will make a hall look lighter and larger; the ceiling and closet may be wallpapered; cut-outs from the wallpaper may be pasted on the chest and shellacked.

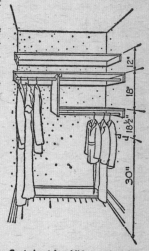

Coat closet for children and adults.

**Dining Area:** Furniture and décor should be adapted to the size, lighting, closeness to the living room, amount and type of entertaining contemplated. Expandable tables are available in drop-leaf, extension console or dining room (leaves are inserted) types. Folding chairs which may be stored eliminate the problem of crowding too many chairs into limited space. Dining chair sets may consist of two upholstered chairs, wing or barrel type, with low arms, and 4 or 6 armless chairs. Color interest may be obtained in chair seats. If the dining area is connected with the living room, the décor (and the rug treatment) should be carried over, or blended.

Dining accessories should not be visible in the living room. The dining room may be separated from the living room by a screen, collapsible walls, wooden curtains, a window shade type of curtain, fiber glass partitions, or sliding doors. If possible only the table should be visible. If the dining-living room are one, the table may be a drop-leaf against the wall. Cupboards should be placed so as not to face important chair groupings. However, a china closet may be made an important decorative piece to display fine bric-a-brac.

What to do with a card table.

A sideboard provides storage space in a dining area. The top may be decorated with candlesticks, flowers, decanters, silver set, etc. Additional storage space may be provided by a corner cupboard. Accessory furniture may include plant stands, small table, tea wagon, etc. The tea wagon is universally applauded as a great serving aid. A folding screen is useful to shut off the view of living room while setting up, or the kitchen while serving. Tables and chairs should be placed in any position in the room so as to interfere least with traffic.

Floor covering should be patterned (to minimize the visibility of spots). Linoleum, rubber tile, braided or hooked rugs, or broadloom are satisfactory.

Wallpaper may be a scenic design, Chinese patterns, small scenes like an English hunting scene or Early American, stripes, fruit or floral design. A chair rail, with solid color paint or paper on the bottom and design on top, is effective.

Windows may be draped, be covered by draw curtains or venetian blinds. (See page 142.)

Many dining rooms today serve several functions. They can still be available for gracious dining and at the same time possess an interesting air of activity and everyday usefulness. Replace the traditional formal background with bright, cheerful and informal colors. Use one corner for dining purposes and turn the rest of the room into groupings to suit the family interests, as of a game or card center, a study corner, a sewing unit, or even a child's playroom if the dining room is located where it gets sunshine. In this case, the lower section of the cupboard can be used as a storage space for toys.

**Bedrooms:** Bedrooms may contain besides bed, dressing table, chest of drawers, chairs, bedside table, chaise longue, bookshelves, writing desk.

The bed may be simply a spring and mattress on four legs; or it may include a frame, headboard, four posts, or even a canopy. Headboards are usually of wood, plain, carved, painted or upholstered; may be purchased separately. Generally the shape, style and upholstery of the headboard sets the style for the room. It may be done in leather, satin, chintz, silk, gingham, or rough fabrics.

Dressing tables may be elaborate or simple unpainted desks suitably covered, with skirts. Mirrors are the most utilitarian part. Three way mirrors are particularly useful in crowded quarters. A full-length mirror on the closet or entrance door is very useful.

Furniture should be arranged so that the bed is easily accessible and not in a draft. Chests should be close to closets. Traffic lanes should be well defined to avoid stumbling in the dark. Fluorescent paint lines or spots are invisible by day but shine at night and are useful if there are occasions for nocturnal emergencies.

Lighting should be provided to suit your habits—reading in bed or on the chaise longue, working at the desk, or making up at the dressing table.

Few bedrooms have enough closets. Accessories help to stretch the space. Decorative touches are added by shelf edging (wood, linoleum or cloth) and hangers.

Wallpaper designs should suggest chintzes or other fabrics. Floral designs are most suitable. Walls may be painted and given a floral wallpaper border. Patterns which can be counted and checks should be avoided as eye straining.

Floors should be covered with rugs. However, bright linoleum with soft scatter rugs or painted floors with hooked rugs are suitable.

Fabric interest may be added in the bedspread and draperies. These should harmonize with the style of the room and the coloring of the furniture. Silks and organdies harmonize with formal furniture, mahogany, etc.; homespuns and rough fabrics with maple, pine, etc. Ready-made spreads are economical, may come with matching draperies. If the spread is not expensive, it may be advisable to buy an extra spread and make draperies from it.

Useful bedroom accessories include radio, ash trays, boxes for jewelry and small accessories, tray and interesting perfume bottles for the dressing table, miniature mirror and drawer combination for a man's dresser, flowers or leaves.

In teen-age room, the bedroomy look may be cleverly concealed to give a sitting room effect. Two couches are placed parallel to one wall and an alcove contrived by building a scalloped valance that extends from wall to wall above the beds. This may serve to hide a track on which draperies could be drawn across the room, concealing beds completely.

Child's Room: Color scheme should be strong and simple. Furniture should be sturdy, accident proof, easily kept clean, and in scale. Ample space for toys and books should be provided.

Walls should be washable paint or paper. Decalcomanias, stencils, cut-outs may be applied. A large bulletin board on which decorative material can be hung, is handy. Pictures should be simple, with a minimum of detail, and colorful.

Pictorial or story maps or pictorial charts are educational decoration. Hang them at eye level. A slate may also be hung.

Linoleum, cork, composition tile, with decorative scatter rugs, are suitable for floor covering.

Furniture should include a junior bed (with removable side rails if necessary) or a full-size bed (a board can be made to fit as a side rail) with a firm mattress; a chip-proof or inexpensive table and one to three chairs; a reading chair and lamp for the older child; adequate shelves and bookcase space; clothes chest and closet; a desk for the school child.

Teen-age room corner.

Good lighting, well planned, is essential. (See page 151.)

Nursery: First needs of the nursery are a crib, with a firm mattress, chifferobe for baby's clothes, and a chest for blankets and linen. The bassinet should be discarded as soon as the baby need no longer be wheeled in it.

A collapsible bathinet of rubber, canvas or aluminum with a top that folds over is important for bathing the baby and dressing him for the first year or so. You will, also, need an extra cabinet in the kitchen for bottles, jars, and baby accessories. A chest, colorful wastebasket, butter tub, or box for baby's toys will be handy after the first six months. A baby chair is necessary at about 4 to 7 months. These now come in table form, 30 inches high, to minimize the danger of a fall. This can later be converted into a play table.

Special colorful window shades, drapes, lamps and accessories are available. Many novelties may be made with wallpaper and decalcomanias on window or lamp shades. Linoleum is the preferred floor covering. Washable cotton or fiber rugs or scatter rugs may be added to give color. Wall coverings, too, should be a washable material—paper, fabric, linoleum or tile.

When baby shares the master bedroom, his area may be

cut off by the arrangement of the furniture, by screens, or even by draw curtains topped by a valance.

Wall plaques for a child's room may be made with an amusing decalcomania. Transfer decalcomania to the glass

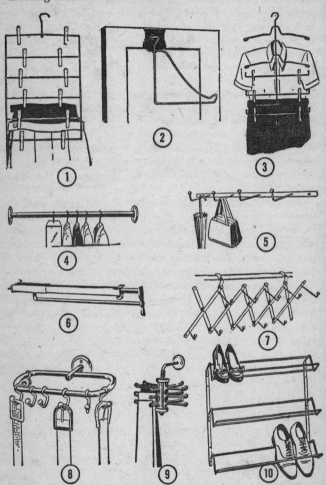

Space saving closet accessories: (1) Shirt hanger. (2) Utility hook. (3) Skirt and blouse hanger. (4) Adjustable clothes pole. (5) Accessory hanger. (6) Sliding clothes rack. (7) Adjustable hat rack. (8) Belt rack. (9) Tie rack. (10) Shoe rack.

and paint the reverse side. Aluminum or bronze paint will reflect the figure as in a mirror. Frame the glass.

**Playrooms:** Attic, basement, guest room or any odd space in a house may be converted into a playroom or hobby room. Unsuitable walls and obstructions may be covered with plywood or wallboard. Pipes or pillars may be painted in bright colors or like barber pole or peppermint stick, and made part of the décor. A theme, based on a hobby or ideal—gun collecting, art, Mexico, the sea, fishing—makes the room interesting. Color scheme may be garish or extreme in any way. Floors may be painted board, linoleum, cork, asphalt tile, or merely filled and sealed. Furniture should be informal in style. Plenty of chairs, game tables, work table, radio, musical instruments, a studio couch, Ping-pong table, folding chairs, ash trays, books, magazines, are suggested. Curtains and drapes may make use of novelty fabrics—monk's cloth, muslins, fishnet, gingham, chintz, etc. Formal accessories should be avoided.

**The Clothes Closets:** To save space, keep closets neat, and protect clothing, use such space-saving devices as garment bags, hat boxes, shoe bags, special hangers, fiberboard drawers, etc. Garment bags or even shelf devices may be sewed onto a wire clothes hanger and hung on a pole. Metal or plastic shoe racks and hat racks may be attached to door. A curtain rod, bent to shape, can be used as a shoe rack.

**Outdoors and Outdoor Rooms:** A terrace or porch may be screened in to provide an added room to the house. An outdoor living room may be delineated by an enclosure of shrubbery, board fence, rustic rail, or a latticed trellis covered with vines, or a row of window boxes. Shade trees, canvas or aluminum awnings, or colorful beach umbrellas may provide overhead protection.

Outdoor furniture may be cast or wrought iron, aluminum, painted steel, wicker, reed, homemade rustic, rattan, redwood or cypress, white pine, or a canvas steamer type. Swings, gliders, chaise longue (they come mounted on wheels) are easily the most used. Seats should be covered with weatherproofed cushions. Hassocks and beach rolls are also handy. Tables in matching materials are available. Iron table furniture comes with glass tops and is useful for formal or informal dining. Unpainted furniture, brightly decorated, will serve in place of any of the more expensive types. An outdoor barbecue makes delicious food and serves as an interesting decoration. It should be placed at some distance from the house. Where outdoor lighting is not available, outdoor lanterns are interesting substitutes.

**Kitchen:** Interesting kitchens may be created around a variety of motifs: Mexican, Early American, ranch type, French Provincial, peasant, Pennsylvania Dutch, etc.

Color should be used on walls to offset the glare of white equipment. Walls may be covered with a washable covering—paper, fabric, plaster, plastic tile, linoleum, or washable wallpaper. Wallpaper should be made washable (page 150), particularly in areas subject to splatter; around sink and stove. Copper, monel metal, stainless steel, Formica type products or glass may be used in these areas. Breakfast nook may harmonize or be papered to contrast in order to create the effect of a separate room.

Inlaid linoleum floors are generally considered best. Other types of linoleum or asphalt tile may also be used. Drapes or curtains should be bright, conceal or reveal according to the worthiness of the view. Curtains or drapes near stove should be non-inflammable.

Modern designers plan kitchen-utility rooms in which there is a kitchen and dining area, also a laundry and heater area which may also include room for a home freezer and even

SEVEN BASIC TYPES OF KITCHENS. Most kitchens lend themselves to one of seven basic arrangements. These may be modified to suit shape and size of room, location of doors, windows and so forth. The "U"-shaped kitchen is the most efficient. The seven basic types of kitchens are:

1. U-Shape  2. Broken U-Shape  3. L-Shape  4. Broken L-Shape  5. Two Wall or Pullman  6. Individual Center  7. One Wall

provide for a sewing machine cabinet. Kitchens do a lot of work in little space. Automatic washers can take care of washing, rinsing and drying clothes in one cabinet, wall ironing boards can fold out of the way when not needed, and cupboards, refrigerators and freezers can take care of all food supplies, sight unseen. Ventilating fans and hoods over stoves do away with the steam and cooking odors. New electrical garbage disposal equipment eliminates food waste down the sink drain.

The basic plan for any convenient kitchen, large or small, simple or with all the latest gadgets, is made up of three main working centers—the sink center, the stove center, and the mixing and food storage center, each conveniently near the other, and, if possible, connected by continuous counters so that the work moves smoothly.

The sink may be double or single. Double sinks cost slightly more but are far more convenient. Six inches is about the right depth for a sink. The only way to be sure of the correct height for your own comfort is to try out sinks at different levels. Ample counters on either side of the sink are important.

Upper cabinets to the left in the direction of the dining room should hold clean dishes, and drawers in cabinets below should hold table silver and clean dish towels. Upper cabinets to the right may hold "kitchen dishes" or food supplies, if the mixing center adjoins the sink center to the right. Under the sink, hidden by ventilated doors, is space for supplies used at the sink, like soap, cleaning powder and dish drainer. The doors may hold racks for wet dish towels or a small covered garbage container with a wall rack attachment. A heat unit under the sink to dry towels is also helpful.

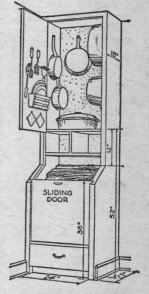

Kitchen utensil closet.

The stove center should be adjacent to the sink center, near the mixing center, and convenient to the dining room or dining area of the kitchen. If possible, there should be counters on either side of the stove finished with heat-proof surfaces for placing hot dishes.

The mixing and storage center is most convenient if located near the outside door. It includes a counter at least 36 inches long, with cabinets above and drawers of various sizes below, and the refrigerator to right or left. The refrigerator door handle should be on the side nearest the counter. (Doors are available with right or left handles.) If you plan to have an electric mixer, be sure to leave a space at least 16 inches between counter and cabinet above. A home freezer can be located in the laundry area of your kitchen-utility room in place of extra shelves or cabinets, or in an open space.

For artificial lighting of the kitchen most designers now recommend fluorescent tubes or filament bulb fixtures, both for general illumination and for direct light on work centers.

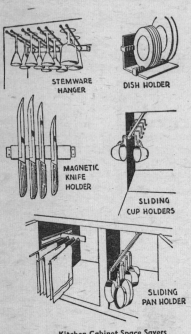

**STEMWARE HANGER**

**DISH HOLDER**

**MAGNETIC KNIFE HOLDER**

**SLIDING CUP HOLDERS**

**SLIDING PAN HOLDER**

Kitchen Cabinet Space Savers

Closet space can hold more if you use some of the commercial or homemade space savers. Cups can be hung from shelf tops by using cup hooks. To make plates stand in back of closet, nail a curtain rod 1 inch from the back of shelf. Shelf coverings and trimmings are available at the dime stores in attractive designs. Discarded window shades make good shelf paper. Glass containers have the advantage of making supplies visible, but they should be kept out of sunlight. Waxed cardboard milk containers, painted or left as they are, are useful for storing breadcrumbs, etc.

**Bathroom:** Bathrooms can be made interesting and colorful, warmer and larger in appearance. Colored tile and fixtures, and decorative materials are available for almost any effect— murals, glass, mirrored, chrome, tile, steel, linoleum, etc. Walls and ceilings may be painted, papered, or covered with a washable material—linoleum, tile or glass. (Wallpaper should not be used in areas subject to constant splash.) Effective wallpapers include large floral designs, undersea flora and fauna, stripes, metallic designs, etc. Window curtains may match shower curtains. Floors usually are tile and walls half tile and half plaster. Linoleum-covered walls and floors are not only attractive but excellent for soundproofing. Some of the new plasticized plywoods developed for torpedo boats and airplanes during the war are providing new finishes for bathrooms.

Other equipment may include besides the medicine chest and hamper, a vanitorium, radio, recessed shelves, or a knick-knack shelf, magazine rack, ash tray, scales, built-in ultra-violet lamps to counteract germs and mold. Electrical appliances near water are dangerous.

The electric toothbrush is a recent addition to the bathroom. Models are made with attached cords and with rechargeable cadmium batteries. Most devices come with four removable brushes, which move in a short up-and-down stroke.

Since plumbing fixtures are immovable, they form the basis of bathroom planning. Points to be considered are the harmony between their color and design and the walls and other parts of the room as a whole. Bathroom fixtures are available in a wide variety of colors, shapes, and designs.

New shower-heads are non-clogging and have adjustments to give different types of showers—from the fine needle spray to the coarse, drenching "overhead bath." Improved mixing valves govern shower temperatures so carefully that the bather cannot be scalded if other faucets in the house are in use at the same time. Pre-fabricated shower cabinets may be installed in a space as small as 32 inches square and 76 inches high.

New tubs are lower, stronger, and safer. Broad, flat rims make it easier to get in and out and are a boon to mothers bathing small children. Square tubs, as small as 42 by 31 inches, are available.

Larger basins are made with counters on either side—like the kitchen counters flanking the sink—to provide for bathing the baby or for a little quick hand laundry. Under the counters, and under the basin, cabinets can be built to provide storage for bathroom supplies—soap, cleaning powder, scrub brushes, rolls of paper. Regular kitchen cabinets may be used for this purpose.

New bathrooms also provide wall cabinets, often full-length cabinets—to hold towels, bath mats and the other supplies that in most homes have to find places outside the room. Washing and dressing center lights should be placed at the side or top of mirrors, to give light on the face rather than on the glass.

A roll-out wooden container may be built to fit under the basin, if a cabinet is not planned there, or a pull-out bin may be part of the full-length cupboard on one wall. A laundry chute is a convenience when the laundry is in the basement. The bathroom is such a convenient place for washing out stockings and lingerie at night that a ceiling rack that folds up or lets down for use will put ceiling space to good use.

## FURNITURE STYLES

**Period styles commonly used today:** There are some 40 eras which have been honored by reproducing the furniture used at those times, but only a dozen have exerted an influence at all profound. Of these five are most common: Gothic, Renaissance, the Baroque, Rococo and the Neoclassic revival which saw a reawakening in classical forms, following the excavation of ancient ruins in Greece and Rome.

Most furniture used today is adapted from the various historic styles. In decorating you may select all or most of the pieces required from the particular style using the same style throughout; or, you may choose individual pieces or groups from a number of styles in which the fundamental relations of colors, woods, proportions, contours, and textures are sufficiently alike to insure harmony.

Furniture should be chosen to suit your tastes and preferences and to match the architectural features of the room in which it is to be used. You might ask yourself some questions: "What do I want this room to be?" "What is the effect I wish to create on my guests, on my family, on myself?" Unsuccessful rooms may be blamed, in general, upon two causes: (1) Too much unification of color, line, and texture resulting in monotony; (2) too much variety, with a hodgepodge of unrelated parts. Since every room is composed of many related parts, it is necessary that there be a certain amount of repetition of the various elements. With a number of easily recognized likenesses, the eye notes the beginnings of harmony. Contrast requires that the grouping be enlivened by the introduction of elements which differ more or less markedly from the prevailing features in color, shape, or tone.

- Woods used together: Blending of woods requires a nice discrimination. The points in which they have similarity are texture, finish, and color. Although it is desirable to have the same or similar woods in most of the furniture for a particular room, it is not always possible.

A brown oak and a brown walnut finished in dark, mellow shades might be very acceptable in adjoining pieces. Likewise a rich red-brown mahogany and a vivid, golden brown figured walnut would have similarity of texture and a pleasant relationship in color. The dark, open-textured oak and the light red, fine-textured mahogany, however, would have little in common. Rosewood and many others listed as rare imported woods are well adapted to use with mahogany or walnut furniture, and may be stained in a tone to match either.

One or two small pieces in red or black lacquer, or in gilt, may add to a room a touch of color which it needs, if most of the furniture is walnut or mahogany. The use of gray-painted furniture, or cream or white enameled pieces in a proper setting, is often very satisfying.

Birch, maple, and cherry are woods which have much in common, and each may be used satisfactorily with walnut. They may be used with the fine or the coarse textured woods if the stain and the lustre provide recognizable likenesses. Care should be taken, however, to avoid that just off-color tone which would be discordant.

Chestnut, as well as walnut, may have enough similarity to oak to be used in conjunction with it, when proper relationships have been established. Wrought iron and brass are likewise suited to use with the heavier woods.

## FURNITURE PERIODS CHART

| Characteristics, Decoration | Decorative Uses |
| --- | --- |
| Louis XIV, *1643-1715 (Baroque)*. *Influenced by Renaissance and Chinese:* Ornate. Straight lines. Massive. Heavy carving. Rectangular forms. Tortoise shell and ebony inlays. Tapestries, velvets. | Very elegant drawing rooms. Occasional pieces. Large homes, hotels. Where dignity is desired. For show. |

| Characteristics, Decoration | Decorative Uses |
|---|---|
| **Louis XV,** *1723-1774 (Rococo). Influenced by Louis XIV, Chinese, Mme. Pompadour, Mme. Du Barry:* Curved lines, shells, female forms, scrolls. Small, graceful. Cabriole legs, inlays. | Feminine rooms. Fastidious elegance. With Oriental rugs. |
| **Louis XVI,** *1774-1793 (Classic). Influenced by Marie Antoinette, Riesener, the English, Italian Renaissance:* Straight, few long curves. Dainty, small, light. Fluted and reed legs. Garlands, urns, wreaths, medallions, cupid's bow, lover's knots. Rectangular and ovals. Delicate damasks, brocades, satins. Cherubs, lovebirds, flowers. | Any room, particularly bedrooms. Feminine rooms. With scenic wallpaper. |
| **French provincial** *1715-1793. Influenced by court styles, climate, cost:* Slender, graceful curves. Ladder back chairs. Center back panel with open work medallion. Cabriole legs, with round and square tapers. Large chests. Walnut, fruit woods; simple styles. | Informal rooms. Bedrooms. With early American and less formal Louis XV. |
| **Directoire** *1795-1799. Influenced by Classic, Louis XIV, Classic Roman, Pompeian, Egyptian:* Broad, straight and curved lines. Lacquer. Lozenges, stars, brass arrows, black and gold and white. Eagles, swags, tassels, cap of Liberty, tri-colored cockade. Square tapering or curved legs without support. | Formal living rooms, dining rooms, bedrooms, library. Simple. Blends with most periods; can be combined with modern. |
| **Empire** *French 1799-1815. Influenced by Napoleon, Roman, Egyptian:* Straight, with ovals. Massive, pompous, heavy. Heavy fabrics, leather. Roman influence. "N" in upholstered wreaths. Military trophies, pineapples, acanthus, eagle, torch, lion's head. | Blends with Phyfe or modern style. Paneling, scenic papers. |
| **Jacobean** *English 1603-1688. Influenced by Elizabethan, French, Spanish, Gothic:* Straight. Sturdy, massive, strong. Geometric patterns, acorns, | Dining rooms, bedrooms. With early American and Queen Anne. Rough textures, plain rough paper. |

| Characteristics, Decoration | Decorative Uses |
|---|---|
| leaves, scrolls. Oak, walnut. Needlepoint, velvet, leather, brocade. Caning. | With paneling, oak trim. |
| WILLIAM AND MARY, QUEEN ANNE *English 1688-1814. Influenced by Dutch, Flemish:* Straight to curved. Lighter. Rectangular, simple. Marquetry. X-stretcher on chairs, tables, chests. Walnut. Needlework, chintz, damask. | Simple, livable rooms. With heavy velvets, tapestry, oak paneling. |
| CHIPPENDALE *English 1710-1779. Influenced by Queen Anne, French Rococo, Chinese, Gothic:* Straight plus flowing curves. Substantial and graceful. Cabriole legs, claw foot, fiddleback. Carved legs, bow shaped ladder backs. Shells, pagodas, foot work, "C" and "S" curves. Mahogany, needlepoint, leather. | Living rooms, dining rooms. With Wilton, American Oriental or plain rugs. Classic and scenic papers. |
| HEPPLEWHITE *English 1765-1795. Influenced by Louis XIV, XV, Classic, Adam brothers:* Curved with straight legs. Delicate, slender, small, sturdy. Straight tapering legs. Honeysuckles, urns, swags, wheatears, lyre. Mahogany, stainwood, rosewood, inlay. Brocades, damasks, haircloth, rush. Shield-backed chairs. | Living room, dining room, bedroom. Widely used. With Wilton, American Oriental, or plain rugs; classic, scenic or satin striped paper; paneling. |
| SHERATON *1751-1806. Influenced by Classic, Directoire:* Straight, few curves. Delicate, slender, narrow, Urns, sunbursts, swags, wheatears, honeysuckles, patera. Stainwood, tulip, inlays, mahogany. Damasks, brocade, haircloth. | Delicate, graceful rooms. With rugs and papers similar to Hepplewhite. |
| ADAM BROS. *English 1760-1792:* Straight, rectangular. Exquisite, graceful. Mahogany, maple, pine. Painted, gilded woods. Brocades, moiré. Oval shield-backed chairs. | F o r m a l backgrounds. With Louis XVI. |
| REGENCY *English 1795-1830. Influenced by Classic, Directoire, Empire:* Straight lines, low curves. Graceful, | Formal living rooms, dining rooms, bedrooms, library. With tiled floors, |

| Characteristics, Decoration | Decorative Uses |
|---|---|
| sturdy. Clear colors, pure forms. Appliquéd metal ornaments, plumes, stars, laurels, Greek key. Black, gold, white. Veneering, inlay. | linoleum, Oriental rugs, plain rugs; Classic, striped wallpapers. Swags. |
| EARLY AMERICAN 1620-1725. *Influenced by Jacobean, Queen Anne, Georgian, limited tools:* Straight. Simple, rough hewn, sturdy, practical. Maple, oak, pine, ash, fruit woods. Little carving. Rush, chintz. | Against rugged backgrounds. With braided rugs, hooked or woven rugs; oak paneling, small figured paper; homespun, printed linen, calico, gingham, chintz, crewel embroidery. |
| COLONIAL *American 1725-1790. Influenced by Queen Anne, Georgian, Federal:* Curved, with straight. Solid, substantial. Mahogany, black walnut. Shell ornaments, winged griffin, laurel, urn, honeysuckle. Chintz, haircloth. | Colonial homes. With Wilton, Oriental rugs; classic or striped wallpaper; paneling. |
| DUNCAN PHYFE *American 1795-1847. Influenced by Sheraton, Directoire, Empire, Greek:* Curved and straight lines. Slender, graceful. Lyre, acanthus, shell, bunches of arrows, lion's head, eagle. Mahogany. Brocade, satin, damask, haircloth, stripes. | Refined background. With Oriental, Wilton or plain rugs. Classic, striped or plain wallpapers. |
| VICTORIAN *English-American 1837-1900. Influenced by Gothic, Napoleon, Louis XV:* Overstuffed, elaborate, homey. Highly patterned and ornamented. Floral motifs, fringe, carving, inlays, gilt, curios. Rosewood, black walnut. Iron furniture. Plush, curves, scrolls, roses, carving. | Playrooms, dens. Occasional pieces. Bleached pieces. As accents in modern rooms or Colonial rooms. Iron furniture for gardens. With figured carpet, floral hooked rugs; small floral wallpapers and cretonnes. |
| MODERN. *Influenced by function, space-saving, skyscrapers, Chinese:* Simple, unadorned lines. Natural and bleached woods, glass. Sectional sofas. Built-in chests. | Formal or informal rooms. With solid-color rugs, tile or linoleum; solid, striped or plaid wallpapers or bold conventionalized designs. |

## DECORATIVE FURNITURE CHART

| Characteristics | Uses |
|---|---|
| LACQUERED: High gloss, smooth finish, beautiful tones. | Modern or Oriental rooms. |
| PAINTED: Usually French or Chinese scenes. | Modern rooms. |
| PEASANT PAINTED: Brightly colored; e.g., Pennsylvania Dutch. | Informal or Early American rooms. |
| CAST IRON: Interesting patterns. Brittle. Must be rustproof painted for outdoor use. May be in any color. White is most popular. | Terraces, gardens, outdoors. Usually in Victorian designs. Formal. |
| WROUGHT IRON: Durable. Must be rustproof finished for outdoor use. Available in any color including Pompeian (antique green) finish. | Terraces, gardens, outdoors. Informal dining, living and bedrooms. |
| CHROME, STEEL, OR COPPER: May be weatherproofed. Tables may have glass tops. Glides, swings, Chinese lounges are common pieces. | Extremely modern rooms, kitchens, porches, playrooms. |
| ALUMINUM: Durable, lightweight, weatherproof if anodized. | Porches, terraces. |
| FORMICA: In wide variety or patterns and colors, including excellent imitations of wood. Heat, stain and acid resistant. | Kitchen and dinette tables, bars. |
| PLYWOOD: Steamed to functional shapes. | Extremely modern rooms. |
| RUSTIC—*Cypress, maple, birch, gum, redwood, pine:* With bark, painted or in natural wood. May be made on wheels for portability. | Lawns, gardens, parks. |
| WICKER, CANE, REED, RATTAN, WILLOW, WOOD SLATS: Lightweight, colorful. Weather resistant if properly treated. May be painted, trimmed with canvas. | Summer rooms, porches, terraces, lawns. May double for playrooms, modern dining rooms in winter. |

| Characteristics | Uses |
| --- | --- |
| DUCK AND CANVAS: Weatherproof. Lightweight. Easily stored. Beach chairs, gliders, hammocks, umbrellas, awnings, are typical. | Lawns, porches, terraces, sundecks. |

## DECORATIVE TREATMENTS

Floors: Floors are usually dark. However, for modern motifs, they may be bleached with ammonia, to a silver-gray color; for gay effects they may be painted in bright colors (possibly with large coin drops or stencil designs). Avoid light, shellacked floors.

Woodwork: If painted white, add a touch of one of the room's colors in the paint; or match woodwork to one color of wallpaper.

Colors should be selected under the conditions of greatest use—under electric light for most rooms. Paint should be viewed when dry, and visualized as somewhat faded, as they will be within a few months.

## WINDOW TREATMENT CHART

| Characteristics | Uses |
| --- | --- |
| ROLLER SHADES—LINEN, CHINTZ, PLASTIC: May be plain, in printed chintz, in solid colors to match or contrast, with designs from draperies or slip-covers pasted on, or with various colored strips pasted on, or with decalcomanias applied. Seasonal designs may be pasted or taped on and later removed. Inexpensive. | For bathrooms, children's rooms, playrooms; with curtains or drapes. |
| VENETIAN BLINDS: Available in aluminum, steel, plastic, and wood in many colors. Tapes may be of matching or contrasting colors. Tend to catch dust. | With draperies or curtains or just a valance. Add width to a room because of horizontal design. |
| SPLIT BAMBOO SHADES: Natural color. May roll up and down or install as vertical traverse curtain. | For informal or Chinese motif. For playrooms, summer rooms. |

| Characteristics | Uses |
|---|---|
| WOVEN WOOD: Available as shades or traverse curtain. Various colors, but usually used in natural tones. | Modern, formal or informal rooms. Playrooms. |
| VERTICAL VENETIAN BLINDS: In fabric, fiber glass or special plastics. Roll up like shades but are generally kept down. Turn 180 degrees to let in light. Translucent. Can be draped. | Very new. Can be used in any type room. |
| NYLON, RAYON OR COTTON CURTAINS—*chiffon, dotted swiss, organdy, embroidered, muslin, voile, dimity:* May be hung in cottage sets (one for each window); full length, ruffled, tied back or tailored to hang straight. Sheer. Admit light. May be too transparent. | With or without shades, blinds, or drapes. For almost any window, particularly in kitchens, dining nooks. |
| GAUZE WITH SATIN STRIPE, NYLON MARQUISETTE | Never hang near a stove or fireplace. |
| PLASTIC FABRIC CURTAINS: Non-inflammable, waterproof, odor proof. | For any window. |
| DUTCH WINDOWS: Wood frames on 4 sides of windows, cut in interesting outline. | Kitchens, playrooms, bedrooms. |
| VALANCES: To hang across one of group of windows. May be stiffened (with buckram or board) or unstiffened; straight, scalloped, ruffled, pleated, swag, cascaded, festooned, etc. Materials may be damask, silk, velvet, brocatelle, chintz, etc., for formal rooms; simple cotton or rayon fabrics for informal rooms. | Formal drapery to floor, over curtains or over curtains and venetian blinds. |
| CORNICES: Wood painted or covered with fabric, shaped or straight at corners. | Formal or informal rooms. |
| DRAPERIES: May be straight, looped back, pinch-pleated at the top, traverse (to close by a pulley and a cord or by | Any room. |

| Characteristics | Uses |
| --- | --- |
| hand drawing). They may be hung from straight or circular rods, from a cornice or a valance. | |
| WINDOW SEATS: Seat cushions may match or tie in with draperies. | For narrow dormers, alcoves, by windows. |
| SHUTTERS: Wood. Seldom used for original purpose of protecting windows from storms. | Color accents on the outside of house. Should be part of background. |
| STORM WINDOWS: Double-hung windows usually have them hung outside. Casement windows may have storm windows inside or outside. In wood or aluminum. Not needed where double-paned windows (Thermopane, Twindows) are used. | Keep cold out in winter, heat out in summer. Reduce condensation. May be combined with screens. Inside storm windows give better insulation, outside windows give better rain protection. |

GROUP OF WINDOWS PLACED TOGETHER: Treat as one. Use pair of curtains for each window, but only one set of draperies for the group with a continuous valance across the top to tie the group together. Draperies should have extra fullness, should look full enough to cover the whole area.

Draperies: Draperies may be the keynote of a room or merely a decorative accessory, depending on other highlights in the room, the view, and your budget. Draperies may be made of almost any fabric. They should be related to the rest of the room in tone, color, and style. The same fabric may be used for slipcovers. Suitable for such purposes are chintz, cretonne, velveteen, sateen, satin, moiré, gingham, corduroy. Draperies should be full. They may be lined with neutral or contrasting materials to make them heavier, look better, hang better. Where draperies must also hold out drafts, flannel interlinings may be used. Ruffles, edgings of tufted cotton balls, fringe, etc., may be used on informal draperies; ruffles or fringe may be used on formal draperies.

Floor covering: For a smooth sweep of color, select a solid color broadloom. Choose twist-weave for texture interest and maximum rug for the dollar. For long, hard, sturdy wear use

Some styles of window draping.

Wilton broadloom. Axminster is easy on the budget; combines good wear with beautiful patterns and colors. For dramatic textured effects, choose sculptured broadlooms. To give your home a feeling of unity, intimacy and greater elegance, run one carpet color through the house. Light-toned, wall-to-wall carpeting makes small rooms look larger. Dark-colored or bold-patterned carpets make large rooms seem smaller.

Printed linoleum is available in three thicknesses, .07", 3/16" and 1/8", in a variety of patterns. Felt base linoleum is lighter and not so durable. Embossed linoleum has a raised pattern. Battleship linoleum is flat looking but inexpensive. Inlaid linoleum is heavy, durable and can be made interesting. Jaspé linoleum has a mottled effect and shows no dirt.

Asphalt tile is resilient, economical, alkali and damp resistant, comes in 6" rolls or tiles. Rubber tile is quieter and has a higher gloss. Vinyl tile is more durable, more easily cleaned and available in dramatic patterns, even with metal inlays. Cork tile is soft and warm in tone and comes in stripes or squares in various thicknesses.

## CARPETING

How will you decide which carpet to buy?

Pile forms the wearing surface of a carpet. It may be loop, cut, or a combination of loop and cut. Variations make possible a wide selection of textured appearances. Natural fibers are not available in continuous-filament yarns. DuPont continuous-filament nylon consists of numerous smooth filaments of continuous length, essentially parallel to one another—running the length of the carpet. This eliminates the short, loose ends (the fuzzy ones) you sometimes see in carpet pile.

Staple yarns are short lengths of fibers spun and twisted to make up carpet yarns. Natural staple fibers are 8″ or less in length; man-made fibers, about 6″ in length. Staple carpet nylon is usually used in cut pile constructions.

Pile density refers to closeness of surface yarns packed together. The denser the pile, the better the wear.

Carpet constructions are usually woven, knitted, or tufted. In woven and knitted carpets, the surface pile and the backing are joined simultaneously. In a tufted construction, the pile yarns are needled into a woven backing.

Broadloom is not a weave. It refers to any seamless carpet made on looms 6 to 18 feet wide.

Backing may be cotton, jute, kraft cord, etc., often coated with latex to secure tufts. Backing holds pile yarns in position. Double backing is required on every tufted carpet.

A room-size rug is a carpet about a foot or more smaller than the dimensions of the room.

You may choose textures ranging from twists to sculptures, from loops to velvets, from tweeds to colorful patterns. Bend a carpet fabric back on itself. If exposed backing shows, the pile may not be dense enough to offer good wear. Pile height is simply a matte of style and personal preference.

Use a rug cushion of wool or rubber to add beauty, comfort, and wear to your floor covering. The cushion is most important on stair treads which take the heaviest blows.

When carpeting steps, lay carpeting with an extra foot of

length folded under against one or two risers at the top of the stairs. Then shift downward an inch or two when the edges start looking worn.

The fiber—wool, cotton or synthetic—is the vital part of a carpet. Combinations of fibers contribute special characteristics.

WOOL: Coarse, wiry, resilient, and long wearing. Blended wools have the right degree of stiffness, resilience and durability. Variety of textures and colors is possible. Colors are muted but lasting.

NYLON: Long wearing, abrasion resistant and resilient, easily cleaned, resists moths and mildew. Colors have a frosty appearance.

CARPET—RAYON: Specially processed to be strong, resilient, and dirt resistant, they may be smooth or crimped. Colors are bright and clear. The closer the tufts, the more resilient the carpet pile.

COTTON: Soft and crushable, giving a shadowed appearance. Dense, firm construction gives the most resilience. Loop pile has great resistance to crushing and is more desirable than cut pile.

ACRILAN: Durable, resistant to moisture, stains, soiling and moths, and easily cleaned. Exceptional resilience and bulkiness.

DYNEL: Long wearing, resilient, and resistant to soiling, moths, and mildew. Most stains are easily removed.

SARAN: Tough, durable, moth resistant, and not affected by soap, water and practically all stains. Permanently crimped fibers give buoyancy and resiliency.

### CARPETING CHART

| Type and Qualities | Uses |
| --- | --- |
| TWIST: Basic weave, no design, wide choice of color. | Any room. |
| AXMINSTER-WILTON VELVET: Thick, closely woven pile, soft to walk on, may have sculptured designs in piling. | Living room, dining room, hall, bedrooms. |

| Type and Qualities | Uses |
|---|---|
| BRUSSELS OR TAPESTRY BROADLOOMS: Hard finish; not receptive to dirt; not so soft to walk on; may have sculptured designs in piling. | Living room, dining room, hall, bedrooms. |
| CHENILLE BROADLOOM: Soft piling, sewn or woven; not durable, expensive. | Living room, dining room. |
| ORIENTAL RUGS, BESSARABIAN RUGS: Fine colors and designs, shiny, expensive, durable. | Living room, dining room, library. |
| FRENCH RUGS (AUBUSSON, SAVONNERIE): Very expensive. | Living room, dining room, library. |
| CHINESE RUGS: Fine colors and designs, shiny, durable, expensive. | Dining room. |
| SHAG RUGS (SHAG, LOOP, WAFFLE WEAVE, NUBBLY, BRAIDED): Heavy pile; difficult to clean; may have two-tone designs. | Bedroom, bathroom, nursery, den, playroom. |
| COTTON AND LINEN RUGS: Inexpensive, washable, variety of styles, colors and weaves. | Bedroom, playroom summer replacement. |
| FIBER RUGS (GRASS, SISAL, COTTON, LINEN OR WOOD PULP): No pile; usually quite colorful, washable. | Playroom, child's room, summer replacement. |
| HOOKED RUGS (RAG, BRAIDED RUGS): Colorful, may be made at home. | Early American or Provincial rooms; good with painted floors. |

## WALL COVERING CHART

| Type and Qualities | Uses |
|---|---|
| PAINT—OIL, CASEIN OR WATER (SEE pp. 261, 262): Choice of colors, inexpensive, may be splatter or novelty painted; or have trim by stencil; or hand-painted design; or decalcomania. | Apartments, particularly where rented for a short period; any room in a home. |
| WALLPAPER—PAPER OR FABRIC EMBOSSED: May be treated to be waterproof, mildew proof, etc.; variety of designs, styles and colors. | Adds tone to any room in the house; may be used on 1, 2, or all walls and ceilings. |

| Type and Qualities | Uses |
|---|---|
| LINOLEUM: Washable, grease resistant, variety of colors and designs. | Kitchen, playroom, bathroom. |
| WOOD PANELING*—KNOTTY PINE, OAK, WALNUT, PECKY CYPRESS, PLYWOOD, STRIATED WOOD: Warmth, quite expensive. | Library, den, living room, dining room, playroom. |
| CORK-SHEETS: Sound and heat insulation. | Playroom, den, bedroom; usually used on the upper ⅔ of a room. |
| TILE—CERAMIC, PORCELAIN COVERED STEEL, PLASTIC: Smooth finish, easy to clean, durable. Resistant to rough treatment. Variety of colors. | Bathrooms, kitchen, showers, bars, utility rooms. |
| PHOTO-MURAL ENLARGED PHOTOGRAPH: Colorful, nostalgic. | Foyer, den, playroom. |
| INSULATED BOARD (PLAIN PATTERNED): Inexpensive, simply nailed to framework, semi-unfinished appearance. | Basement or attic room. |
| FIBER BOARD OR PLASTIC WALL BOARD: High gloss, variety of patterns, imitation tiling. | Over plaster, wood or concrete; in kitchen, bathroom or basement. |
| CEMENT BOARD (ASBESTOS CEMENT): Fireproof, sanitary. | Kitchen, bathroom, playroom. |
| GLASS AND GLASS BRICK: Rich colors, makes room appear larger. | Bathroom, kitchen, enclosed porch. |
| FIBER GLASS: Thin, colorful, variety of designs, plain or corrugated, unbreakable. | Modern rooms, translucent partitions. |
| BRICK: Natural, outdoor appearance. | Fireplace wall, enclosed porch. |

* Similar effect may be obtained by painting wood grains on the wall, using wallpaper, wall linoleum, wall boards with thin veneer of wood, veneers mounted on fabric.

**Pressure-sensitive tapes:** These are made in many colors (including gold, silver, chrome, wood grains, and "invisible") and are available in cloth, plastic, or reflective materials, or in stainless steel. They come in widths for hundreds of special purposes. Their common characteristic is that they don't need wetting to make them stick. Thomas Edison was the inventor of the first of these—the surgical tape. They are now made with one or both sides adhesive, of cellophane, for freezers, electrical insulation, repairing hoses, avoiding a slip in the bath tub, keeping rugs on the floor, hanging weights of as much as three pounds, for mounting wall tile, labeling, weather stripping, decoration, repairs, and scores of other uses. Widths vary from 1/64 inch to 3 inches.

**Wallpaper:** To select a wallpaper to fit your particular decorating scheme, choose a design appropriate to the period of the furniture in your room. Provincial or Early American patterns are small florals or geometric patterns, plaids, and scenic papers; Pennsylvania Dutch colors are blue, yellow or pink with fruit, heart, bird or stencil-type designs; French Provincial incorporates damask papers, floral stripes, floral medallions, *toiles de Jouy;* Eighteenth Century styles—Queen Anne, Chippendale, Hepplewhite, Sheraton and Adam—call for more formal wallpapers; damasks, moiré or brocaded velvet, little chintz patterns, floral garlands in stripe effects. The Empire period in the 19th century used Napoleonic emblems, figures, urns, swags, rosettes, and wreath motifs. Regency was a simpler era of formal stripes and swags. American Federal used wide stripes and panoramic scenes. The Victorians were lavish with oversized florals. Modern décor has adopted stripes, checks, plaids, stylized floral motifs, and textural papers.

Remember that dark shades in a patterned paper shrink a room, light shades enlarge it. Low ceilings seem higher if patterns are vertical on the wall. In a narrow room a scenic wallpaper on one wall gives an illusion of spaciousness.

Vinyl wall coverings are completely washable and stainproof in ordinary use. Vinyls are waterproof and nonpermeable so paste takes longer (some days) to dry. All old wallpaper must usually be completely removed before the new material is hung, but this is not necessary on some vinyls.

Remove all remaining paste by scrubbing with a strong detergent solution. Rough spots should be sanded smooth, and all cracks or holes should be smoothed over with spackling compound or with patching plaster. A glossy enamel should be dulled by sanding or by wiping with a liquid surface preparer. It is important that no air bubbles are left underneath. Butt seams carefully without overlapping because vinyl will not adhere to itself.

## LIGHTING

Lighting should be diffused, not glary. It should be distributed evenly over the room. All bulbs should be covered, if possible. If not covered, frosted or glazed bulbs should be used. Tinted bulbs should be avoided as wasteful.

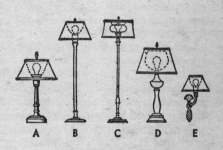

A    B    C    D    E

Large bulbs give more light per watt than smaller ones. Keep bulbs and shades clean.

Special effects can be obtained with cove lighting (built in and concealed), indirect lighting (the light is thrown to the ceiling first), diffused lighting (the light is broken up by globe or shade), fluorescent lighting and spot lighting, high hats (recessed fixtures), and lighting strips which permit spotlightlike fixtures to be focused at will.

Special lamps are available, for reading and for exacting work, which provide high-intensity, concentrated glare-free light with the use of special bulbs and a magnifying glass. Some are portable.

| | Height of Lamp | Shade at Bottom | Bowl | Bulb Size | Placement |
|---|---|---|---|---|---|
| | **LAMPS FOR READING** | | | | |
| A { | 28″ | 18″ | 8″-9″ | 100-150 | Left side of desk or table; table behind sofa end table, bedside. |
| | 24″-27″ | 16″-18″ | 7″-10″ | 50-100-150 | |
| D | 56″-63″ | 16″-20″ | 8″-10″ | 100-300 | Beside and slightly behind armchairs, at piano, centered behind sofa. For low-ceilinged rooms use junior sizes. |
| C | 99″ | 18″ | 9″ | 100-300 | As above. Also, at desk, sewing machine, 12-32 watt close-seeing work areas. |

### FLUORESCENT

| | | | | | |
|---|---|---|---|---|---|
| D | 23" | 16" | 7" | 100 | End tables. (Diffused bulb eliminates glare when viewed from top.) |
| E | 48" at bottom of shade | 12" | 7" | 15-150 | Over beds, chairs, sofa, work table, sewing machines. Especially where floor space is limited. |

### BULBS REQUIRED FOR TYPICAL LIGHTING SITUATIONS

| | | | |
|---|---|---|---|
| 7½ watt | night light | 100-200 | kitchen |
| 3 way | reading light | 75-100 | bath |
| 60-100 | reading | 25-40 | bed head light |
| 100-150 | sewing | 25 | decorative |

Thousands of specially adapted bulbs are made in hundreds of sizes and shapes. Special lamps are made for country homes operated on a battery, for rough service on extension cords and vibrating machines, for high voltage and low voltage, for ovens, refrigerators, automobiles, trains and airplanes, for floodlights, spotlights and electric signs. The following table lists the bulbs used in most households:

### ELECTRIC BULBS AVAILABLE

| Characteristics | Uses |
|---|---|
| A Type: 25, 40, 60, 100 watts. | In clear, frosted, white coated or colors. |
| PS Type: 150, 200, 300, 500 watts. | In clear, frosted, white coated and daylight (blue-green gloss to produce a whiter light). |
| P Type: 15, 25, 40 watts. <br> G Type: 15, 25, 40 watts. | In clear and frosted. <br> Globular. In white, ivory and flame-tint. Ornamental. |
| F Type: 15, 25, 40 watts. | Flame shaped. In clear (for crystal chandeliers), white, ivory and flametint. Ornamental. |
| T Type Tubular: 6 and 10 watts. | Narrow lamps, display cases, ceiling fixtures, lamps with chimneys. Light is reflected upward. |
| Three-light Lamps: 30-70-100, 50-100-150, 100-200-300 watts. | (They have two filaments which light individually or together.) Inside frosted. For floor or table lamps. Use only base down. |

| Characteristics | Uses |
| --- | --- |
| FLUORESCENT BULBS: 2 and 4 watt bulbs in socket. | Screw into an ordinary socket. Night lights, emergencies, industrial. |
| INDIRECT WHITE: 150 watts. | Reflect most light upward. Used in certain fixtures and in lieu of fixtures. |
| S TYPE: 60, 100, 150, 200 watts. | Silvered bowl. The bottom of the bulb has a reflecting surface, gives indirect lighting. |
| LUMILINE: 30, 40, 60 watts. | Long, narrow tubes. In clear, frosted, blue, emerald, orange, pink, straw, white and red. For cool and decorative lighting. |
| FLUORESCENT GENERAL LINE: 6″ to 60″, 4, 6, 8, 13, 14, 15, 20, 30, 40, 85 watts. | In daylight, #4500 white, #3500 white, soft white, pink, blue, green, gold, red. For mirror lights, bathroom, kitchen units, cove lighting, niches. Saves up to ⅓ of electric current. |
| SLIMLINE: 42″, 96″, 16 to 69 watts. | Fluorescent lights with narrower diameters. In white. For concealed lighting. |
| CIRCLINE: 32 watts. | Fluorescent lights in circular form. In #4500 white and blue-white. Portable lamps, kitchens, decorative lighting. |
| SEMI-INDIRECT: 40 watts. | A built-in reflector throws some of the light upward. |
| NEON: ½ to 3 watts. | Withstand vibration and shock. Give off practically no heat. Permanent safety lights, exit lights, switches, pilot lights. Use little current. |
| ULTRAVIOLET SUNLIGHT LAMPS: 100, 275, 400 watts. | A special glass transmits only ultraviolet rays. The 400 watt also gives off infra-red and visible light. For portable sunlamps. |
| FLUORESCENT SUNLAMPS | ($3.50 to $10.00). |

| Characteristics | Uses |
|---|---|
| GERMICIDAL LAMPS: 3, 4, 8, 15, 30, 36 watts. | ($4.75 to $10.00). Require fixtures which protect eyes and skin. To disinfect air in nurseries or sick rooms. |
| LUMINOUS GLASS PANELS | Cold light. Soft, diffused. For clocks. Will be available for walls and ceilings. |

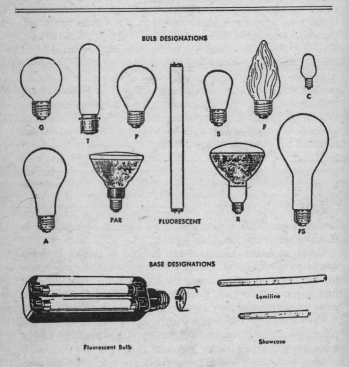

BULB DESIGNATIONS

BASE DESIGNATIONS

Fluorescent Bulb

Lumiline

Showcase

Colored lamps may be outside coated (for indoor use only), inside coated or enameled or natural colored (amber, blue, green, ruby only). Frosting diffuses light. White coated bulbs give better diffusion, but lose 15 percent of the light.

The type of bulb you use will affect the color scheme, inasmuch as colors do not appear the same under artificial light as they do in daylight. Incandescent lights are warm and emphasize the warm colors—reds, yellows, etc. Under incandescent light, blues present special decorating problems. Dark walls look richer under incandescent light.

Fluorescent light tends to intensify the cooler colors—blues, greens, etc. The fluorescent lights are made in various colors to give three variations of this hard white light. A Daylight fluorescent lamp is blue-white, is hard on colors, but gives good illumination to blend with daylight. It is most often recommended for use in kitchens. The "3500 white" is the most efficient in terms of lighting, but gives great emphasis to greens and blues, tends to give skin a greenish look. The Soft White has some red in the light and this should be used when any decorative effect is desired.

Special purpose bulbs and decorative types are made by smaller manufacturers. The Eye Saving Bulb is a blunt modified tubular bulb. Flamescent bulbs have a decorative flame-shaped filament. Some types provide a flickering imitation of gaslight. The Bug-a-Way bulb has a deep yellow finish which is useful for outdoors because yellow light attracts fewer flying insects. The "Odorout" bulb is walnut-sized and designed to provide ultraviolet radiation and thus serve as deodorant. Ultraviolet sterilamp tubes destroy germs in the air. Other bulbs give off infrared heat rays or ultraviolet rays.

**Fireplace:** Most fireplaces are decorative or designed for incidental heating. Heat-circulating devices may be installed so that fire will warm an entire room.

Usual accessory requirements include a screen to keep sparks from spreading, andirons for supporting logs or grate for coal, and fender and tools for handling the fire. Wrought iron requires little care. Brass must be kept polished but is more attractive *and* may be lacquered against tarnish.

**Mantels** may be decorated with a clock, pots of ivy, house plants, matching candlesticks, figurines, large handsome bowls, a tea set, interesting plates, jugs, etc.

**Glass:** It is now made in many forms for use inside and outside the home: glass bricks (room dividers, entrance halls); fiber glass (porch roofs, screens); heat-reflected panels (doors, windows); glare-resistant (pictures, mirrors); one-way mirrors (transparent from one side); fabrics (curtains, drapes); and heat-resistant (cooking utensils).

**Mirrors:** Mirrors may be used effectively in any room. The frame may be in any period style. Mirrors set into a wall are effective in adding light and size to the room. Mirrors should not be hung where the sun shines on them all day. This tends to create a haze in the mirror. An inexpensive way to create a mirrored wall is to mount many small "dime store" mirrors on a board. (Large mirrors cost proportionately more as they must be made of plate glass.)

**Pictures:** A picture is not necessarily good because it is an original or an oil painting. Really good art is available at moderate prices in the form of good reproductions of top quality originals. These reproductions are not "real" in the sense of originality, but they do reproduce the original faithfully. A good reproduction can capture the tangible and intangible qualities of good art.

Original signed etchings and lithographs and good reproductions of contemporary oil and water colors are available at moderate prices from Associated American Artists. Reproductions of masterpieces, including small statuary, are sold by Metropolitan Museum of Art, New York, and the National Gallery of Art, Washington, D. C., for as little as $3.00.

**Picture frames** should be simple so as not to detract from the picture, may be natural wood, tinted, black, or colored to harmonize with the décor. Emphasis may be given to a

small picture by matting. The mat may be white or tinted, 2 inches or more in width all around (slightly more at the bottom). Board, leather, novelty papers, fabrics, etc., may be used. The inside edge of the matting may be colored for additional emphasis. Matting also serves to allow pictures of different sizes to be framed uniformly. The extreme in framing simplicity is a small chrome base or double brace, which holds picture, mat, and glass or plastic cover, with no other frame visible.

A mat adds importance to the picture.

Occasionally the frame itself is to be emphasized. Ornate gold frames, gingerbready frames, painted white or antiqued in a gray and gold pattern, are effective decoration.

If possible, pictures should be hung with no wire or cord showing. Usual height should be eye level. Pictures hung low add height to a room. They should be hung in units of two or three, one over the other, side by side, or in a symmetrical arrangement. Avoid stair-step arrangements except on stair walls. They should, harmonize with furnishings in color and style. An important picture may be the center of attraction in a room. To avoid chipping plaster, apply Scotch tape to wall before driving nail. To make pictures hang straight, attach sandpaper to back.

## SPECIAL ROOM PROBLEMS

**Large rooms:** Use lots of dark colors and bright, contrasting color schemes; large splashy designs in wallpaper and fabrics; large pieces of furniture.

**Small rooms:** Use light shades of cool colors in an analogous or monochromatic color scheme; pale tint on walls, deep tone for the rug, medium value for draperies; small design in wallpaper and fabric. Use small, delicate furniture. Use mirrors lavishly, preferably large and unframed. Assemble group of small mirrors on a wall board or a panel between two windows. Use glass-headed screws. Place these opposite the door, entrance, or on one of the narrow walls. Eliminate unnecessary furniture, pictures. Pictures should have light frame and feeling.

**Narrow rooms:** Decorate the narrow walls in a darker shade. Walls should suggest space with designs of landscape or foliage.

**Long rooms:** Use a definite color tone. Place corner cupboards or bookshelves at end of room. Use bright colors in upholstery and accessories at end of room. Place sofa with end to side wall to make two groupings (perhaps music at one end and library at other).

**Sunny rooms:** Use cool colors (blue, green, gray, white).

**Dark rooms:** Use warm, light colors (reds, yellows, oranges, tans). Refinish one or two pieces of furniture in natural or light colors. Make drapes to begin at edge of window to allow maximum light to enter. Avoid window shades or use light-colored chintz.

**Broken-up rooms:** Use small wallpaper patterns.

**Little furnishing:** Use large wallpaper patterns.

**Large areas:** Use neutral colors (a small piece may be bright red, but not a large wall).

**Cold rooms:** To make room appear warmer, use warm, yellow-tinted colors, heavy textures.

**High ceilings:** Paint or paper the ceiling in a warm or contrasting dark shade and, if necessary, extend the ceiling color to the picture molding. Lower the molding 12 or 18 inches from the ceiling. Run a wallpaper border a few inches below the ceiling. Break up the wall with a chair rail, and decorate the lower portion in a dark shade. Use horizontal effects in wallpaper. Avoid vertical effects on the wall.

**Low ceilings:** Paint or paper ceilings in light shades, contrasted with dark walls. Use vertical effects in wallpaper, either stripes or vertical patterns. Ignore any breaks in the wall, like a picture molding, by painting or papering over it. Hang pictures slightly below eye level. Keep furniture low in scale. Hang curtains high, using cornice at top, extend curtains to floor. Use floor-length curtains tied back ¼ way from top.

Vertical lines add height. Horizontal lines add width.

**Angular attic ceilings:** Paint or paper walls and ceilings in the same color.

**Ceiling beams:** Scrape beams to bare wood and treat decoratively by antiquing, enameling in bright colors, covering with veneer, or painting on a grain. Off-center beams can be matched with a parallel false beam. Or put up a false wallboard ceiling under the beams.

**Wall and ceiling ornaments:** Ornamental plaster on the ceiling harmonizes with early English or Victorian décor. Wall panels look well in a Georgian type home. Otherwise, it is best to remove extra ornamentation.

**Unnecessary windows:** Cover with decorative inside shutters. Cover window with wall board and make bookcase or closet to cover. Place shelves in front of window or create a shadow-box and use as knickknack shelf. Cover with draw curtains in bright colors.

**Large windows:** Cover excess portion with valance and drapes. Shorten the window with a window box.

**Small window:** Hang wide drapes and curtains above and beyond the window margins, and to the floor. Create a border with wallpaper, hanging drapes outside the border.

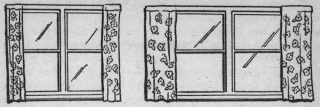

Drapes may make windows wider.

**High narrow windows:** Hang curtains partly outside window frames. Treat group of windows as one with valance or cornice board.

**High windows on the side of the fireplace:** Place or build bookshelves under the windows. Paint them to match the woodwork or walls. Eliminate fussy drapery treatments. Block out windows with shelves or shutter. Make window background for shelves and display colorful glassware. If you don't need the light, the window casing can be used as a frame for a picture backed with plywood.

**Unsightly view:** Screen it with floor-length glass curtains of translucent material, so they let in the light but keep out the view. These curtains may be finished at the bottom with weighted tape so they will stay in place. Or use shelves of glass, holding plants or colored glass vases and bowls. Venetian blinds or bamboo blinds are effective screens.

**Living room to be used as a dining room:** Use different wall treatment at that end. It might be a different color of paint, or a papered wall combined with a painted one. Have the dividing line at a jog in the wall, or at a window or door.

**Side-light where you don't want it:** Have the fixture replaced by a metal plate, and hang a picture or a mirror over the spot.

**Too little wall space for furniture:** An unused door may be locked permanently, and decorated with a textile wall hanging; or a plywood panel can be put over the entire door before papering is done. Groupings of furniture can be brought out into the room. Place desk or table with its end to the wall. Pull the sofa out by the fireplace.

**Too little furniture:** A figured wallpaper will help to furnish a room and draw attention away from the fact that there are too poor or too few pieces of furniture.

**Eyesores:** Pipes, radiators, and irregularities in the wall can be minimized by painting or papering in the wall color. Paint wall a dark color. Use a small, over-all patterned paper for the wall. Try to dramatize the irregularity by tying it into the décor, extending it, paralleling it, or creating a nook out of it.

**Exposed radiators.** Where possible recess or cover with metal or wooden grill, cupboard or bookcases with asbestos sheet protection for the books. Tie in radiator cover with window decoration. Cover with floor-length draperies over a radiator. Use a cornice board extended six to eight inches beyond the side of the window. Draperies will hang free of the radiator and will give a broad look to the window.

## FLOWERS

Fresh flowers or leaves are excellent decorative accessories, need not be expensive. Autumn leaves, pussy willows, cattails (these may be brightly colored) may be kept without water for as much as three months. Huckleberry, laurel, lemon, magnolia, or rhododendron leaves are attractive for 3 to 10 weeks.

**Everlasting:** Colorful, lasting flowers may be used to add to an arrangement, or supplement arrangements, especially for winter decoration. Most are easily grown in the garden.

Ammobium alatum—Winged, white.

Helichrysum bracteatum—Straw flowers, various shades.

Gomphrena globosa—Global, amaranth, purple, white rose.

Helipterum roseum—(Rose Everlasting) pink.

Lunaria annua—(Honesty) seed pods are silky, papery.

Statice latifola—(Sea Lavender) lavender.

Statice sinuata—White or pink.

Physalis Francheti—(Chinese lantern) orange seed pods.

Xeranthemum Annuum—(Immortelle) white, pink, lavender.

**Flower arrangement:** Rule of thumb for height: (a) Tall containers—flowers twice the height of the container: (b) Low containers—add height plus width: (c) Cut stem of choice flower for highest point. For a low design, substitute a line of length for the line of height. Have a design, a pattern. Start with a triangle in three dimensions. Place second flower right and forward; third flower to the left, opposite the second. Add more flowers of different lengths to fill. Let buds and tendrils fall naturally regardless of height or position.

Consider container and flowers as one piece. Work main design lines down to the mouth of the container.

Select a focal point to which the eye should be drawn. Place best blooms at this point. Lines should run toward this point. Focal point should be low in the arrangement. Open roses, gardenias, camellias, make good focal points.

Leave some empty spaces toward edges to avoid confusion in the design.

Basic patterns may evolve around a triangle, a fan effect, column, crescent, oval, circle, S curve, etc. Avoid a square or zigzag line. The design should be similar to or contrasting with the design of the container.

Table centerpieces should be low. Paired arrangements should be made so that, placed together, they would appear as one harmonious display.

The design should be in balance, preferably in an asymmetrical balance. A figure in the container may balance color in a flower, etc. Avoid mathematical precision.

Flowers fall into two groups—round shapes (roses, carnations, tulips, daisies, zinnias, chrysanthemums) and elongated or spear shapes (gladioli, snapdragon, veronica, hollyhocks, delphinium, etc.). A good arrangement combines both. If one shape is not available, leaves or ferns may be of help.

Sort colors first. Colors should be arranged light at the top, dark at the bottom. If you have various shades of one color, graduate them. But if only a few blooms are dark, use them as an accent, at the top or focal point desired. Apply the usual rules of color harmony (See page 111), and color psychology (See page 118).

Flowers should harmonize in texture with each other and with the container and tablecloth; also, if possible, with the furnishings and style of the room itself. Delicate, fine-textured flowers do not mix well with heavy, coarse ones.

Flowers may be held with needle holders, available in various sizes and shapes. A variety of them should be available. Some holders tend to rust. Holders of heavy flowers should be anchored or wired or held together with modeling clay. Green linen thread is useful in tying stems and leaves. Broken stems may be braced with hairpins, wire or tooth picks. Emergency holders may be made of half grapefruit shell, potato, ball of chicken wire, paraffin, etc.

Stones, shells, driftwood, seed pods, gourds, fruit, candles, etc., may add to the display.

Special arrangements may be made with fruit, miniature gardens, gourds, seeds, weeds, etc.

Container may be vase, cup, teapot, mixing bowl, jar, pie plate; pewter, silver or copperware; a soup tureen, a shell, a wooden shoe, old jewel box, wheelbarrow, umbrella stand, etc.

To open a partly open bud, blow vigorously.

**Care of flowers:** All flowers should be arranged so that they fall as nearly as possible in their natural positions. Flowers will never appear cramped in a container if they are allowed to fall carefully in the position they would naturally grow in the garden. If flowers are not to be used as soon as they are received, place them in a bucket of cold water and set them in a cool place for an hour or so. Cut the stem ends as soon as the flowers are received, using a sharp knife, cutting slantwise. Flowers should be cut each day and their ends allowed to heal. When the stems have been cut, place them immediately in a container filled to the brim with fresh and cool water. This is best done in the morning, or at a regular hour each day.

One danger is choking the stems by crowding them into the narrow neck of a container. Remember, flowers must absorb certain elements from the air and through the water. It is much better to distribute the flowers in two containers than crowd them into one where they will wither sooner. Never allow the ends of the stems to touch the bottom of the container. While fresh air is always beneficial to flowers, avoid drafts passing directly over the blossoms. Hot, stuffy rooms are unhealthy for cut flowers. Place cut flowers in a cool shady place, not in direct sunshine. To prolong flower life, keep flowers in a humid room at about 45° F.

If flowers are received by express or other shipment in a seemingly hopeless condition, they can be revived by placing them in a container of water hot enough to steam for a few minutes. Remove them, container and all, to a cool dark place. They should revive in about an hour.

When flowers begin to wilt they can be revived and made to last for days by laying them in a basin or tub so that the water covers the entire stem.

**Preserving cut flowers:** Flowers wilt because they cannot obtain sufficient water through the stems to overcome evaporation through the leaves and flowers. Bacteria multiply in the water, clog and destroy the stem tubes. Charcoal, salt, camphor, Listerine, or ammonia, added to the water in small quantities, slows bacterial growth.

Cut flowers early in the morning or after sundown. Cut stems at an angle to increase water intake. Use a sharp knife in preference to shears. Soak thoroughly before arranging. Cut stems and change water daily. Singe ends by wrapping flowers in bath towel with stems extended. Use Sterno or gas burner.

You can cut a beautiful bloom weeks before a local flower show and preserve the flower perfectly until the show date.

A plastic wrap completely encasing the cut blossom cuts off all air and outside moisture, thus creating a high carbon dioxide concentration inside the "coffin." This action literally keeps the growth and other processes of the cut bloom in suspended animation.

Once the package is opened and certain steps are followed, the growth processes resume, and the cut blossom opens further.

Follow these suggestions:

(1) Blossom must be cut at the stage just prior to the one you desire to display in the show. For example: If show schedule calls for a rose bloom half open, blossom should be cut ¼ open.

(2) Do not place cut bloom in water at any time prior to wrapping.

(3) Prepare cut bloom by washing off foliage with water if necessary. Remove any damaged petal or leaf.

(4) Secure a lightweight cardboard container big enough to encase the entire bloom and stem. Cigarette cartons (minus lid) florists' boxes and other types of boxes should suffice. Inside of container should be clean.

(5) It is best to preserve only one bloom per carton. Be sure to label carton as to variety name and date of cut.

(6) Rose blossoms and other cut flowers which may have thorny stems should be stem wrapped with tissue paper to prevent torn foliage or petals.

(7) Lay cut blossom in container, no part of stem extending beyond container.

(8) Cut a piece of plastic wrap (regular or large size) large enough to encase the filled container completely. Make wrap tight and seal all loose ends.

(9) After a final inspection, place wrapped container flat in your refrigerator at a temperature of 34-36 degrees—not in the freezer section. Wrapped cartons might be placed on top of one another.

(10) Roses should keep well for one or two weeks, other blooms even longer. Try experimenting whenever you can on every type of flower in your garden.

(11) If the flower show—or party—is scheduled for a morning opening, open sealed package the night before; if an afternoon session is scheduled, open package in the morning.

Carefully open plastic wrapping cover and remove cut blossom. Snip off a small section of the cut end of stem and immediately place cut blossom stem in a tall container of warm water (110-120 degrees F). Stem should be immersed up to bloom.

Leave stem in warm water for several hours and then remove and replace in a container filled with cold water and move into a cool location.

Blossom may wilt slightly during any one of these last operations but should regain turgidity and bloom once sufficient water has been taken up into the stem.

Hyacinth, narcissus, etc., should have jelly-like sap squeezed from ends of stems to facilitate their drawing water. Camellias, gardenias, etc., take water only through petals. Wrap these in wet tissue to preserve them and spray while on display. Hydrangeas and other flowers with woody stems should have 2 inches of the bottom of the stem pounded. Ferns may be stored in wet newspapers, in cool, dark place. Water lilies may be forced to remain open by pouring a few drops of warm paraffin in the center, while flower is open.

Cut flowers at proper stage of development. Dahlias when fully open; gladioli when first floret is open; peonies when petals are unfolding; asters when half-open; roses when buds just turn soft.

Scrub containers clean. Keep flowers cool and moist until you are ready to use them. Keep them away from drafts and sunlight. Avoid aluminum containers.

To make the best use of cut flowers—particularly rare ones, you may place the vase before a mirror. This provides double effectiveness. A vase may be set on the floor, so that blooms may be seen from above. Don't crowd flowers in the vase.

Those who make a specialty of preserving cut flowers divide plants into five categories for purposes of handling:

## CONDITIONING SOLUTIONS

### 1. Annuals:

This group includes most of the annual flowering plants—asters, cornflowers, marigolds—and camellias and gardenias.

These hold a great deal of moisture when you cut them and require little water in the vase—not more than three inches. Syringe a small amount of water on the blooms each day.

When these are first cut they should be submerged in water, then "hardened" by being placed in a cool, dark place for several hours or even a day, wrapped in tissue.

### 2. Woody stem plants and shrubs:

These include azaleas, chrysanthemums, hydrangeas, lilacs, apple blossoms, dogwood, etc.

Because wood-stemmed plants have difficulty getting sufficient moisture, it is necessary to smash the ends to expose as much fibrous tissue as possible.

For apple blossoms, a three-minute dip in hydrochloric acid is recommended.

For hydrangeas, place the crushed ends in boiling vinegar for a few minutes, then plunge into cold water. It is wise to cut an additional inch off the stems every three or four days and repeat the preservation process.

Lilacs need leaves surrounding the bloom to conduct moisture.

### 3. Hollow stem plants:

These include dahlias, delphiniums, mignonettes, etc.

Because these plants tend to take up too much moisture, it is necessary to close the tubes slightly and to provide sufficient water.

As soon as the flowers are cut, plunge the stems into boiling water from four to six inches, for about five minutes. Then plunge the stems into cold water. This tends to close the inside of the tubes and restrain moisture absorption.

### 4. Milky sap plants:

This group includes poppies, hollyhocks, heliotropes, hyacinth, wisteria, baby's breath.

Because moisture tends to run out of these plants, the ends must be seared and sealed. First plunge the stems into cold water. Then hold the stems over a flame for half a minute. Replace the stems in cold water. The burn forms a callus which stops the loss of moisture. It is wise to trim the lower leaves, for some of the moisture escapes through these.

### 5. Bulbous flowers:

This group includes tulips, lilies, gladioli, amaryllis, begonias, iris and other flowers that grow from bulbs.

These should be submerged in a deep container immediately after they are cut. Keep the flowers in a cool, dark place for three to eight hours. These require considerable amounts of water in the vase.

Ferns should be kept under water for three to twelve hours before being used.

Autumn leaves require no moisture at all.

Water lilies, lotus and other flowers that close at night may be kept open by dropping a bit of melted parafin into the heart of the flower.

Flowers which absorb a great deal of moisture (chrysanthemums, snapdragons, etc.) should be placed in vases containing at least six inches of water. Roses and carnations require little water. Camellias and carnations need only occasional syringing of the blossoms.

An extensive list of conditioning solutions made from such household items as salt, vinegar, kitchen ammonia, washing soda and alcohol, is described in: *Flower Arranging for the American Home* by Ruth E. Kistner (Macrae Smith Company, Philadelphia).

Bon-sai (potted dwarf tree) is a Japanese system of miniature gardening recently popular in the United States. Growth of plants is controlled by selection, cross fertilization, pruning and training. The appearance of age is fostered by distribution of roots and branches. Trees are planted in pots which restrain their growth, but have holes for drainage.

## HOUSE PLANTS

Keep in mind the conditions under which you expect to grow your plants, and select your varieties accordingly.

**Light:** Light-colored leaves, spindly growth, and few flowers are frequently the result of too little light. There are several species of foliage plants and a few flowering plants that will do well in a north window, or even away from a window if the room is light. In general, east windows that receive full sun until noon are probably best suited for pot plants. South windows get the sun for a longer time than east windows, but often the temperature there is high enough at midday to interfere with plant growth. West windows are seldom so satisfactory as east or south, probably because the temperature fluctuates widely between mid-afternoon and night.

**Temperature:** Most house plants can be grown most successfully when the room temperature is kept below 70° F. during the daytime. There are some exceptions, however. On cold nights move plants away from windows.

**Humidity:** In many houses the relative humidity is too low for the thrifty growth of pot plants. Use room humidifiers to improve growing conditions, or increase the moisture around the plants by placing the pots together on large trays containing wet gravel or sand. Syringing the leaves with water from an atomizer also helps to increase moisture. Do not syringe plants with very hairy or downy foliage.

**Gas:** Manufactured illuminating gas escaping into the air even in small quantities is injurious to most flowering plants. However, this is not true of natural gas which is increasingly used for cooking and heating.

**Containers:** For growing pot plants at home, glazed containers are better than porous clay flower pots as the soil does not dry out so rapidly. In a dry atmosphere, a porous clay pot permits rapid evaporation, whereas the glazed pot does not. Painting the outside of a porous clay pot will give it much the same effect as a glazed pot. Because it is difficult to give plants exactly the right amount of water, it is also advisable to use pots with drainage holes so that the surplus water can drain away.

**Window boxes:** These may be used outside the house for decorative accents, as borders, fences, etc. They may be made of wood, or metal, 8 to 10 inches deep. Hanging baskets may be used as substitutes or in conjunction with boxes. Wicker baskets must be lined with burlap or moss to hold soil and moisture. Plants should be selected on the basis of shade or sun in the location chosen.

**Soils:** Good garden soils when used alone are seldom so satisfactory as a soil mixture for pot plants. The repeated watering and drying cause an ordinary garden soil to become

| Mixture | Loam | Peatmoss, Leafmold or Manure | Sand |
|---|---|---|---|
| No. 1 | 3 parts | 1 | 1 |
| No. 2 | 3 parts | 2 | 1 |
| No. 3 | 1 part | 0 | 1 |

To each mixture add 4 tablespoons bone meal or 20 percent superphosphate per peck.

packed. The addition of humus and sand helps to keep the soil friable. The three following soil mixtures are recommended for potting house plants. Mixture No. 1 is satisfactory for most plants. Mixture No. 2 contains a larger quantity of humus for plants that require a considerable amount of fiber in the soil. Mixture No. 3 is primarily for cacti and some of the succulents that thrive best in a sandy, well-drained soil.

**Potting:** Place a few pebbles or pieces of broken flower pots in the bottom of the pot to improve drainage. Start young plants in small pots and increase the size of the pot gradually as the plant requires it. This avoids excess watering and excessive woody growth. Leave a space between the top of the soil and the top of the pot to make watering easier. In potting or repotting plants, work the soil in thoroughly around the roots so that there will be no large air spaces.

**Fertilizing:** Pot plants that are started in good soil are not likely to need further fertilizing for two or three months. Small fertilizer tablets prepared especially for pot plants are convenient to use. There are also complete commercial fertilizers in bulk form for use on garden and pot plants. Either type should be used in small quantities, and the applications should be made three or four weeks apart. Fresh manure can be soaked in water for several days and the liquid taken off to feed house plants. It should be diluted until it is about the same color as weak tea.

**Watering:** Watering requirements vary with the type of plant, time of year, size of pot, type of soil, and the temperature and humidity. The following points may be helpful:

Lukewarm water should be used instead of cold water.

Newly potted plants do not need watering so often as

Flannel wick waters plants while you're away.

those that have been established for some time. Plants should be watered until the water trickles through the drainage hole at the bottom of the pot. Pots should not be allowed to stand in water in a tray or jardiniere.

A number of house plants go through what is called a rest period, when growth appears to stop and, in some cases, all foliage is dropped. Other plants have no very noticeable rest period. When a plant goes into a normal rest period, waterings should be reduced.

Species vary in their requirements for water. A few thrive in constantly moist soil, and some prefer a very dry soil. The majority do best when the soil is watered thoroughly and then allowed to become reasonably dry, but not baked or crumbly, before the next watering.

One method of judging the moisture of the soil in a pot is to tap the upper rim with a knife handle. If it gives a clear ring, the soil is dry and needs water. When the soil is moist, the sound is dull and heavy.

**To brighten leaves:** Mineral oil rubbed on lightly makes them gleam. Commercial preparations are also available (Ced-O-Flora).

**Pest control:** Much of the trouble with insects on house plants can be prevented by examining each new plant carefully and keeping it under "quarantine" for a few weeks, away from other plants. Following are the most common types of insects that attack house plants:

**Plant lice (aphids):** Small green, brown, or black insects found chiefly in colonies on the underside of the leaves and on terminal growth. They can be controlled by using nicotine sprays: 1 teaspoon nicotine sulphate, 40 percent solution, 1 gallon water, 1 ounce mild soap; dissolve the soap in warm water and add the nicotine.

**Mealybug:** Rounded, soft, fuzzy white insects move about very slowly on their host plants. They are often very serious pests. When plants are completely overrun with mealybugs, it is usually best to discard them. Oil-emulsion sprays and nicotine and soap will help to check this pest, but it is difficult to get rid of them. When infestation is light, dip a pointed camel's-hair brush into alcohol and touch it to the backs of the bugs. Do not let the alcohol touch the plant. If you use an oil emulsion or nicotine and soap spray, take the plants to the basement for spraying, and after an hour thoroughly rinse them with water. Use oil-emulsion sprays according to the manufacturers' recommendations. The nicotine and soap may be mixed as follows: 2½ teaspoons nicotine sulphate, 40 percent solution, 1 gallon water, 1 ounce mild soap. Dissolve the soap in warm water and add the nicotine.

**Scale:** Various brown, rounded, and somewhat flattened

scales adhere closely to the stems and leaves of many plants (usually woody plants). They are difficult to eradicate. Use spray recommended for mealybugs.

Red spider mite: These tiny mites vary in color from red through orange and yellow. Because they are so small, you can usually see the damage they cause before you see the mites themselves. The top of the leaves will be mottled gray and yellow instead of the normal green while the underside will have a crusty, webby appearance. Syringing the foliage, especially the underside, with a forceful stream of water every few days will help to reduce the injury. Insecticides containing from 1 to 1½ percent rotenone will also be effective in controlling red spider on house plants.

## HOUSE PLANTS

| Soil | | Exposure, Comments |
|---|---|---|
| African Violet | 2 | S. or E. Window. Divide and repeat. |
| Amaryllis | 1 | Pot bulbs in fall. |
| Asparagus Ferns | 1 | S. or E. Window. Pinch long shoots to keep bushy. |
| Begonia | 1 | S. or E. Window. |
| Boston Fern | 2 | Needs indirect sunlight. High humidity. |
| Bowstring Hemp | 1 | Withstands adverse conditions. |
| Cactus | 3 | Good drainage essential. |
| Cast Iron Plant | 1 | Withstands heat, dryness, poor light. |
| Coleus | 1 | Needs bright sunlight in winter. |
| Daffodil: (Narcissus) | 1 | These require a cold storage treatment before forcing. As soon as stock is available, plant bulbs in pots in the fall so that the tops are just below the surface of the soil. Good drainage is essential. Place the pots in a cold storage cave or in an outdoor trench. Dig trench 10 to 12 inches deep, and put layer of gravel in bottom for pots to rest on. Then fill in around pots with sand or peat moss and |

| Soil | | Exposure, Comments |
|---|---|---|
| | | cover pots with an inch of same material. A thick layer of straw over all will prevent hard freezing. Keep in storage for 8 to 12 weeks. Then bring indoors and keep in a cool dark room for one or two weeks. Bring into light and continue to keep cool. |
| English Ivy | 1 | N. window or in light away from window. |
| Fuchsia | 1 | Requires a moist atmosphere. |
| Geranium | 1 | Needs full sun for blooming. |
| Gloxinia | 2 | Needs a warm, moist atmosphere during growth and bloom. |
| Grape Ivy | 1 | Full or partial shade. |
| Hydrangea | 2 | Cut back after bloom and grow outdoors in summer. After first frost, place in cellar till Jan., then water and grow in cool room. Fertilize monthly. |
| Impatiens | 1 | Full sun, but in partial shade in summer. |
| Iresine | 1 | Needs bright sunlight in winter. |
| Japanese Rubber Plant | 1 | Can grow in sun or partial shade. Allow soil to dry out well before watering. |
| Oleander | 1 | Rest, then keep fairly dry in cool room during fall and early winter. Rest, water and place in warm room with full sun. |
| Peperomia | 1 | Stands little light and high temperature. |
| Periwinkle | 2 | Withstands high temperature, dry atmosphere. |
| Philodendron | 1 | Withstands high temperatures, without direct sunlight. |
| Poinsettias | 1 | Sensitive to dry atmosphere and temperature changes. |

| Soil | | Exposure, Comments |
|---|---|---|
| Primrose | 2 | Start seed in spring, keep in partial shade indoors in summer. |
| Wandering Jew | | Grows in any soil or water. Needs sunlight in winter. |

# BOOK III

## Lawn and Garden Guide

If you own (or rent) a piece of earth, you will want to grow something on it, either because you want to beautify your home or merely because you like to see things grow.

The ways of nature are quite simple in most things. Growing most plants requires only a few simple conditions, care, patience and adherence to the rules of nature.

### THE SOIL

Basically, there are three types of soil:

SANDY SOIL has less than 20 percent clay or silt. It loses water quickly, absorbs heat, holds excessive air, and draws out fertilizer elements quickly. To cure this condition, add organic matter, or loam, or fertilizer rich in potash, phosphorus, and manure.

CLAY SOIL has very fine particles. It holds too much water, thus remains muddy after a rain. It lacks air. To cure this condition, add sand or fine cinders and organic matter.

LOAM is the type of soil between sand and clay. It is satisfactory for most plantings.

OTHER REQUIREMENTS: Soils also vary in the amount of other chemicals and qualities they have. Certain plants require more of certain chemical components in the soil than others. Some of the other necessary chemicals are lime, nitrogen, phosphorus, potassium, other minerals and water. The other soil and plant requirements include aeration, drainage, shade or sunlight, and suitable temperature.

Soil-test kits, which test for acidity, nitrogen, phosphorus, potash, and other factors, are available for home gardeners. These serve to help in the selection of the proper fertilizer and lime applications.

## SOIL AND PLANT NEEDS

| Need and Explanation | Use or Correction |
|---|---|
| LIME: A necessity for all soils. Lack of it makes a soil acid. Over-supply makes a soil alkali. Most plants require a neutral soil (rated pH 7). | If pH factor (acidity) is low, add lime, usually in the fall. If soil is "sweet," it has too much lime. Apply a mulch or covering of leaves, sawdust, shavings, peat or patented remedies containing sulphur or aluminum sulphate. |
| HUMUS: Result of decomposition of plant or animal residue. Changes structure, texture, water- and air-holding capacity and color of soil. | Add material from compost pile. Spade or plow into soil, preferably in fall. |
| PEAT MOSS: Decomposed vegetable matter. Adds acidity and organic matter, nitrogen; holds moisture. | Apply as mulch in fall, or work into soil in spring. |
| AERATION: Carbon dioxide from decaying bacteria must escape or roots will be injured.<br><br>SOIL CONDITIONER: | Clay soils lack air. Add humus, sand or cinders. Sandy soils contain too much air which tends to dry out plants. Add humus. This clay causes the soil to remain granular and therefore porous. |
| COMMERCIAL FERTILIZERS: Package indicates proportion of nitrogen, phosphorus and potassium (as 5-10-5) in that order. | Various plantings require different proportions so choose accordingly. |
| LIQUID FERTILIZER: Often more effective, speedy in its work, and safer to use than solid fertilizer. | Place fertilizer in a mesh bag and allow it to dissolve in a barrel of water, using one gallon of water for each pound of fertilizer. This may be diluted. |
| COMPOST: A pile of a mixture of straw, leaves, weeds and garden refuse, in 6″ layers, with fertilizer in each layer. After 3 to 4 | Improve it by adding 60 lbs. sulphate of ammonia, 30 lbs. superphosphate, 25 lbs. potassium chloride and 50 lbs. ground |

| Need and Explanation | Use or Correction |
|---|---|
| months of fermentation it is the equivalent of good manure. | limestone to ½ ton of wastes. |
| GREEN MANURE—RYE, ALFALFA, GRASS, COWPEAS, CLOVER, SOY BEANS: Crops grown to be plowed under, to add nitrogen and other plant nutrients to the soil. | Plow in early in fall with fertilizer added. |
| MULCH—PEAT, LEAF MOLD, HUMUS, STRAW, CORN HUSKS, ETC., MANURES, PAPER, COFFEE GROUNDS, SAWDUST: Inert or organic matter used to cover soil, to hold moisture, prevent weed growth, and to keep ground cool. | Cover plants (or grass) with mulch in winter, in dry fall, or late spring. |
| PHOSPHORUS: Many soils lack this essential to plant life. | If lacking, add superphosphate, treble phosphate, or bone meal. |
| POTASSIUM: Necessary for strong stems and roots and general plant health. Usually present where there is plenty of organic matter. | If lacking, add potassium chloride, potassium sulphate, manures, or hardwood ashes. |
| NITROGEN: Normally added to soil from decayed organic matter. | If lacking, add humus or commercial fertilizer—nitrate of soda, sulphate of ammonia, hen or rabbit manure, etc. |
| OTHER MINERALS—CALCIUM, SULPHUR, MAGNESIUM, IRON, SODIUM, MANGANESE, ALUMINUM: Necessary in small amounts. Usually found in sufficient quantity in soils. | If lacking, add commercial fertilizers containing these elements. |
| WATER: Must surround and cling to soil particles to be effective. Clay holds water well; sand has low holding capacity. | Cover sandy soil with organic matter or mulch during dry periods. Plow and spade to soften earth. Keep down weeds which use moisture. |

| Need and Explanation | Use or Correction |
|---|---|
| CULTIVATION: To conserve moisture and incidentally cut down weeds. Moisture is conserved by creating a finely pulverized dust mulch through which water finds difficulty in getting out by capillary action. | Use hand or machine cultivator, preferably after soil has dried following rain. Break up soil into fully pulverized, crumbly dust for 1 to 3 inches depending on type of planting desired. |
| PLOWING: Turning over soil needed for planting, burying vegetation currently growing. | Plow in large gardens (25' x 50' or more) to facilitate planting. Usually done in the fall while ground is not so wet as to make clods, not so dry as to create dust. |

Pruning: Trees and shrubs require pruning to promote vigor, to improve appearance, to remove badly placed branches, to provide sunlight and air circulation, to minimize danger of falling branches, to remove diseased and dead branches, to improve fruit and flowers by giving more nutriment to those remaining, etc. Weak trees and shrubs may sometimes be saved by pruning, inasmuch as this allows the same roots to feed a smaller body. Cut back in season an amount suitable for each plant. Excessive pruning may ruin a plant or hurt flowering. Extensive pruning usually produces larger flowers on longer stems. Pruning should be done annually. Some seasons permit more rapid healing for certain plants.

Generally speaking, prune badly placed branches to increase structural strength, broken, dead or diseased branches (cut back to the nearest healthy crotch), slender shoots growing parallel to trees, branches growing too close to others (especially vertically) to improve form and appearance; to remove excess flower buds (distinguished from leaf buds). Some plants have annual growth removed.

## LANDSCAPING

Trees, shrubs, vines, grasses and flowers should be selected to harmonize with the size of the house, the background, and the functional requirements, as well as the considerations of soil, climate and care required.

Steps in Developing a Landscape Plan for Home Grounds: (1) Prepare a diagram of house, walks and drives, lawns desired, surrounding area, and areas which are to be landscaped. (2) Check general plan with fundamental principles of home landscaping. (3) Provide for adequate drainage.

(4) Indicate location and type of trees, shrubbery, flower beds and flower gardens. As a rule trees are used in the following ways in the home landscape plan: (a) To provide an attractive frame or background for buildings and grounds; (b) To provide shade around buildings and yards; (c) To provide a screen or to soften the outlines of buildings; (d) To provide ornamental effects by shape, foliage, or flowers; (e) To provide protection against wind and snow; (f) To border a long, straight road or driveway.

(5) Indicate arrangement of shrubbery, flower beds and flower gardens. Use shrubs chiefly in: (a) Foundation plantings—low-growing shrubbery massed about the base and corners of buildings—to soften the straight harsh foundation lines; to partially screen foundations; and to "tie" the building to the lawn. Portions of the foundation should be exposed, however, to give an appearance of solidity to the buildings unless pin or open foundations are used; (b) Screen plantings —tall shrubbery—to hide objectionable views, to partially screen fences or buildings, or to give privacy to certain areas; (c) Clumps or groups about the junctions or curves in walks or drives to relieve inartistic lines and to suggest a reason for curves. These should not be so high as to hide traffic at intersections; (d) Groups or masses about the borders and in corners of yards to soften the straight line effect of boundaries; (e) Hedges of various heights to separate property boundaries or different units of a planting design, to form borders in formal gardens, or to seclude one portion of the grounds from another.

(6) Consider the following places for flowers: (a) Small formal flower garden in a more or less secluded portion of the grounds; (b) Informal garden plantings in clumps or in beds of irregular design or arrangement; (c) Border plantings around vegetable garden; (d) Foreground grouping or clumps among the shrubbery plantings; (e) Rock gardens or other special features. Arrange all flower plantings so that they will blend into the general landscape picture, adding touches of color and beauty to the whole design. Avoid isolated or con-

spicuous flower beds that have no relation to other ornamental plantings.

(7) As the plan develops, vines, hedges, ornamental plantings, or special features may be needed. (8) Stake out locations on home grounds. (9) Select suitable plants and seeds from nursery, store, friends. (10) Make planting schedule. Remember planting and frost seasons advance northward approximately 15 miles a day.

## THE LAWN

**Steps in Making and Maintaining a Lawn:** (1) Locate and lay out dimensions of lawn. If one third of a stand of grass is available to start with, it is better to renovate it than to dig it up and start over. Keep the front lawn broad and open in center, framed with trees and shrubs about its borders. Mark off lawn areas with stakes. (2) Grade, level, and provide drainage. Leave natural curves and slopes but grade land sufficiently to get proper drainage away from the buildings and a smooth surface that can be easily mowed. Do not grade land when soil is wet. Round off steep embankments. Keep earth high enough about buildings and walks so that water will drain away from them. Lay tile, if necessary, in tight subsoil, when an outlet is available. (3) Prepare seedbed. Prepare or apply good thick layer of topsoil (4 to 6 inches) free from weeds and high in humus and plant food. Seedbed should be plowed to good depth, well compacted with 1 inch of fine topsoil on top. Plow or spade the ground 4 or 5 inches deep, well in advance of seeding time. Rake or harrow occasionally to destroy weed growth. Pulverize the soil well. Where natural soil is very infertile or sandy or where topsoil has been removed, spread good topsoil, thoroughly disked or properly mixed with the upper soil. For quicker starting apply well-rotted barnyard manure, free from straw, trash and weed seeds. Mix well into soil—about 1 pound per square foot. (4) Secure suitable seed. Purchase the recommended variety or mixture from a reliable source located locally. (5) Sow seed in the morning or evening of a day when there is no wind and just before a rain if possible. Seed in the fall in the northern and eastern states, and in the spring in the southern states. Fall seeding of bluegrass and redtop is generally recommended for all regions. Follow local recommendations for other varieties or mixtures.

Usually quantity of seed required is 1 pound for 400 square feet for re-seeding, 1 pound for 200 square feet for new seeding. Mixtures for most lawns may contain varying quantities of rye grass, fescue, bent, clover, redtop, and Kentucky bluegrass. Fall sowing should be made early enough to allow grass to get a good start before winter. Use plenty of seed. Sow one-half the amount of seed to be used in parallel strips until the entire lawn is covered; sow the remaining one-half of the seed in strips at right angles to the first half sown. After sowing, roll the surface or drag carefully or rake lightly.

(6) Protect and care for new seeding. Prevent slopes from washing. Soak thoroughly if dry weather prevails. Clip the new grass when 3 to 4 inches high. Do not cut too close. (7) Maintain fertility of soil. Apply well-rotted, finely pulverized stable or poultry manure at the rate of 20 to 50 pounds per 1000 square feet, preferably in early fall. Apply, occasionally, top dressings of a compost consisting of about equal parts of manure, sand, and loam which is highly beneficial to lawns. Water the lawn thoroughly after each application of fertilizer. To check the amount of water cast by lawn sprinklers, place three empty coffee cans on the lawn. The depth of the water in the can indicates the equivalent rainfall. (8) Mow the lawn. Cut the grass frequently but not too close. (9) Roll the lawn. One good rolling after the frost is out of the ground is usually sufficient. (10) Water the lawn, soak the lawn thoroughly once a week during dry weather. Evening is the best time to water unless lawns contain bents and fescues which are preferably watered in the early morning.

(11) Control weeds effectively by (a) Securing good drainage; (b) Keeping the lawn well supplied with plant food to insure vigorous growth of grass; (c) Keeping a good thick stand of grass.

To clean up as you mow.

Difficult patches may be layered with sod or prepared seeded sod blankets.

**Lawn care:** Lawns require year round attention. Bare spots should be sowed in February or March, and covered with ¼ inch of sifted soil. In the spring, the lawn should be dressed with compost or other organic fertilizer, moistened and rolled with a 150 to 300 lb. roller. Lawns should be mowed when grass is 2 to 3 inches high.

Weeds: Weeds may be minimized by mulching (p. 176), cultivating and hoeing. They are best killed when just through the ground. Thereafter, they are progressively more difficult to get rid of. During the summer remove weeds and apply chemical weed-killers. In early fall, cut grass close, remove weeds with iron rake, and apply 10 to 25 lbs. of fertilizer per 1000 square feet. Spade up bare spots and make a new seed bed. New seed should be scattered, and covered with sifted top soil. During this season, grass should be cut at 1½ inches, and later at 2 inches, until growth stops. If good sod is available, it may be used to cover small areas.

Broadleaf weeds generally can be controlled by 2,4-D, (sold under many trade names and forms). Follow manufacturer's directions strictly. Sprayers and other containers should be cleaned thoroughly after they have been used to apply 2,4-D. It is wise to have two sets of spraying equipment; one for 2,4-D and one for other purposes. 2,4-D is not harmful to persons or animals. Crabgrass, dandelions, plantain, and chickweed may be partially controlled by hand weeding as the plants appear. Pull or cut dandelions 2 to 3 inches below the surface. Avoid scattering pieces of crabgrass.

Other weed killing chemicals are sodium chlorate, sodium arsenate, iron sulfate oil, and common salt. Weeds are best pulled while young, before roots form thickly or seeds mature. To prevent weeds, have a heavy stand of grass. To fill holes left by pulled weeds, use hormone treated grasses, which germinate faster.

Lead arsenate is poisonous but with care it can be used with relative safety. It is effective against chickweed, Poa annua, and crabgrass in the more acid soils. Apply 20 lbs. per 1000 square feet at any time of year. It is also effective against most insects that live in the soil.

Renovating lawns: Lawns are frequently marred by bare spots, patches in which weeds have taken over, rough places, and areas in which grass has been killed by being covered with an object for a period of time.

These unsightly spots can usually be renovated quite easily and brought to the same rich state as the rest of the turf. These suggestions should be helpful.

# 32 COMMON WEEDS YOU

| | | | |
|---|---|---|---|
| BUCKHORN | BUTTERCUP | CANADA THISTLE | CHICKWEED |
| FLEABANE | GROUND IVY | HEAL-ALL | HORSETAIL |
| MULLEIN | MUSTARD | NUTSEDGE | PENNYWORT |
| RAGWEED | SHEPHERD'S PURSE | SPEEDWELL | SUMAC |

# CAN EASILY CONTROL

| | | | |
|---|---|---|---|
| CINQUEFOIL | CRESS | DANDELION | DOCK |
| JAPANESE HONEYSUCKLE | KNOTWEED | LESPEDEZA | MONEYWORT |
| PEPPERGRASS | PLANTAIN | POISON IVY | POISON OAK |
| VIRGINIA CREEPER | WILD GARLIC | WILD MORNING GLORY | WILD ONION |

**Weed Patches:** Spray the area with weed killer which contains 2,4-D to control the unwanted weeds or spot-treat with weed killer containing 2,4-D and 2,4,5-T. Rake out dead foliage and reseed.

**Bare Spots:** If these spots are due to traffic, divert the traffic or install a walk. If the soil is impacted, hard, dried-out-clay, loosen the soil by turning it over with a tine fork; add peat moss or sand to keep it porous. Level, spread turf food, and reseed the area.

**Killed Spots:** Rake to remove dead vegetation. Feed with turf food, rake surface and reseed with lawn seed.

**Lime:** Grass grows best in neutral or only slightly acid soil in humid areas. Lawn soils are often higher in acid content. This can be decreased by the use of lime, which also adds needed calcium and magnesium.

As lime reacts very slowly in the soil, it is not necessary to apply a large quantity at one time. In rebuilding an old lawn that has been neglected, it is a wise practice to apply 25 to 50 lbs. of agricultural limestone per 1000 square feet every year or every two years in the fall. In building a new lawn, spread 25 to 50 lbs. per 1000 square feet over the surface before harrowing or rototilling or, if new topsoil is used, work this amount of lime into the soil before seeding.

New, specialized soil sterilants control the growth of all kinds of weeds and can kill roots, grasses, or other plants safely and effectively.

**Insects and diseases:** Insects most troublesome in lawns are beetle grubs, army-worms, sod webworms, ants, chinch bugs, and mole crickets. Ticks and chiggers are not harmful to the lawn but they are a nuisance to the lawn owner and his children.

Most insects can be controlled by pyrethrum or rotenone compounds. Ants, mole crickets, and chinch bugs can be checked by the chlordane products.

Most earthworms may be controlled by the use of lead arsenate at the rate of 20 lbs. to 1000 square feet. The growth of algae is a condition caused by standing water on the surface of the soil. Improving the drainage will eliminate this condition. See also p. 242.

Dollarspot, to which bent lawns are susceptible, may be controlled by the use of mercury or cadmium compounds.

**Crabgrass:** This most troublesome of lawn weeds is a coarse annual grass that develops from seed produced in previous summers. Seed germination starts primarily in late spring, but it may occur throughout the summer. The seedlings grow rapidly, and they can destroy desirable grass during summer months if their growth becomes excessively heavy. The mature plants produce large amounts of seed and are killed by frost in the fall; therefore, many bare areas and a new supply of seed result.

Crabgrass

Good management is the first step in crabgrass control. Proper liming, regular fertilizing in September and early spring, and yearly cutting at a height of 1½ inches or higher will produce a turf cover that will usually survive the summer invasion of crabgrass. A dense, high-cut turf is important as crabgrass germinates and grows poorly in the shade. It is very helpful to raise the height of cut to 2½ inches until the crabgrass problem is eliminated.

Watering and fertilizing a crabgrass-infested lawn in summer will encourage an even greater crabgrass problem. Light, frequent watering is particularly bad, as it increases the density and spread of the crabgrass.

Light infestations of crabgrass can be readily controlled by hand-weeding before the plants set seed. Where there are many plants, eradication through the use of selective weed-control chemicals may prove successful. Two methods of chemical control are available. One method involves spreading a chemical on the lawn before the crabgrass begins to grow. The presence of the chemical on the soil surface destroys the crabgrass before or near the time of its germination. This method is known as pre-emergence crabgrass control.

Chemicals that are presently available limit the use of pre-emergence control of crabgrass to certain lawn grasses under specific conditions. You should not consider using this method unless: (1) the lawn is predominantly Kentucky bluegrass or merion Kentucky bluegrass; (2) the lawn is at least one year old; (3) the stand of desirable lawn grasses is satisfactory; (4) the area is sunny; and (5) crabgrass is a definite problem.

Several chemicals are available for pre-emergence crabgrass control. These chemicals vary considerably in their desirability, effectiveness, and safety. Written information on the chemicals and their performance may be obtained from your local Agricultural Experiment Station or from your local county agricultural agent.

The second method of chemical control consists of applying a chemical directly on the crabgrass after it appears in the lawn. Disodium methyl arsonate (and other methyl arsonates), phenyl mercuric acetate . . . and potassium cyanate are among the recommended chemicals that can be employed satisfactorily for this method of crabgrass control. These chemicals are sold under various trade names in varying concentrations at most garden-supply stores.

While the results obtained can be very gratifying, they can be worthless or disastrous for those who do not follow directions. The mercury and the methyl arsonate preparations are the most selective and give best control when used on seedling or small crabgrass plants. Both of these materials can be applied in a liquid or dry form. Three or more applications at seven- to ten-day intervals are usually necessary. As temperature, moisture, and size of crabgrass plants govern the results, it is very important that directions be followed carefully. Do not use phenyl mercury acetate on merion Kentucky bluegrass lawns. The best use of this chemical is for bent grass turf where its fungicidal properties may also give benefit. Potassium cyanate should be restricted to treatment of Kentucky bluegrass-red fescue type lawns in late August and early September. The methyl arsonates can be used at this season also.

Some discoloration usually results from the use of chemicals. This is not always a reason for avoiding chemical treatment, because a lawn with an abundance of crabgrass plants will become brown after the first frost. It is a good practice to test these chemicals on a small section of your lawn until you are familiar with their use and the amount of injury to expect.

Since success in elimination of crabgrass depends on preventing seed production, considerable persistence may be required for several seasons to gain complete control. A few minutes spent removing an occasional plant reduces the chance for a more serious problem next year.

Shaded areas: Densely shaded areas under trees usually present problems. Deep placement of fertilizer around trees and heavy fertilizer applications on the turf may compensate for the scarcity of available plant food. Shade tolerant species (the fescues and trivialis bluegrass in the cool humid regions; and the Zoysia grasses and St. Augustine in the warm humid regions) will overcome the shading effect. Prompt raking or sweeping of fallen leaves prevents any smothering effect which they might have. Grass should be forced into rapid growth during the period when the leaves are off the trees so that strong turf will be established by the time trees begin growth in spring. If, despite good fertilization, grass will not grow in your shaded areas, ground covers like vinca, pachysandra, and thyme are sometimes used.

## FLOWERS

Steps in Growing Flowers About the Home: (1) Mark location and general arrangement of flower plantings. Make your landscape diagram and the actual layout of your home grounds to determine most desirable locations for flower plantings. Work out an arrangement to display all varieties most effectively. If viewed from one side only, the tall plants should be placed in the rear, low plants at the front, with intermediate heights between. If plantings may be viewed from all sides, the tallest plants should be placed in the center, with the lowest around the outer edges.

Your garden can be a continuous riot of color and a constant source of beautiful cut flowers if it is planted with flowering plants whose blooming periods spread over the growing season.

In most areas, continuous bloom requires judicious use of all four varieties of flowering plants:

ANNUALS which grow from seed to flower in a single season. These can be planted from seed, and it is often possible to buy established seedlings from nurserymen.

BIENNIALS whose life-span extends over two years. Usually grown from seed, most biennials do not produce blooms until the second year.

PERENNIALS which live for years, rising each spring, producing blooms, and becoming dormant each fall.

BULBS, also perennial in their life-span, but differing from perennials in the way they grow and multiply. For convenience, flowers grown from corms or tubers are usually classified under bulbs.

(2) Select desirable types and varieties. Make use of all types; annuals, biennials, perennials, bulbs, ferns, mosses, and special grasses. Perennials are the most useful group for ornamentation as they require less work than annuals or biennials and are relatively permanent year after year. But perennials flower only for a few weeks. Annuals require replanting each year but flowers remain all season. Biennials, due to the fact that they produce flowers the second year, are not so generally useful as annuals or perennials. Annuals are the flowers commonly used for color during midsummer; biennials and perennials for spring and fall. Group flowers for mass color effect. Good effects are usually obtained by using the following colors together; scarlet and blue, orange and blue, yellow and purple. Combinations not so pleasing are: orange and purple, bright red and violet, scarlet and pale lavender. White or intermediate colors which blend together are effective in producing a harmonizing color effect. Give consideration to the approximate date of blooming and select varieties that bloom at different dates so as to have a continuous display of flowers somewhere about the grounds or gardens.

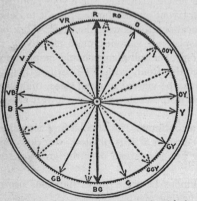

Color wheel: Diagram showing good and bad color combinations. Colors immediately adjacent to one another or opposite one another are appropriate for use together. Those between should be separated by masses of foliage or by white flowers. B=blue, G=green, O=orange, R=red, V=violet, Y=yellow.

(3) Prepare soil—spade to good depth all areas to be planted to flowers. Provide fertile loamy soil high in humus

and well drained. If soil is very poor, excavate the beds to be planted to flowers to a depth of 2 feet and fill with good top soil. The removed soil may be mixed with good soil or well-rotted manure and replaced. If very sandy, mix with clay soils; if very heavy, mix with sand and leafmold or wood ashes. Work into the soil liberal quantities of well-rotted stable manure, hen manure, sheep manure, or cottonseed meal. Small areas which are very poorly drained may be improved by excavating to a depth of 3 feet, placing a thick layer of stones or gravel in the bottom, and replacing the soil above. Work the soil thoroughly to make a fine, closely compacted seed or root bed.

(4) Secure planting material. Provide flower plants for the home garden in the following ways, depending upon the variety and method available: (a) By planting seeds—indoors in boxes and later transplanting in open; or outdoors in late summer in special beds to be replanted later; or outdoors where they are to be grown; (b) By purchase of seedlings ready to transplant; (c) By transplanting whole plants; (d) By transplanting divisions of the crowns of the plant. Each division should have a good portion of root growth; (e) By planting bulbs; (f) By planting stem or leaf cuttings. Most annuals are best started by use of seeds and seedlings. Most perennials are best started by using entire plants or divisions of the roots or bulbs.

(5) Grow seedlings. Study the requirements of the varieties you select. Some plants must be sown where they are to grow since they do not stand being moved. Most plants, however, are improved by transplanting the seedlings. In some cases, the seeds may be sown in beds out of doors; others must be started indoors or in hotbeds for greatest success. For outdoor seeding proceed as follows: (a) Select a favorable location for the seedbed, partially protected from the hot sun and drying winds. (b) Prepare a fine, mellow, well-compacted seedbed that will not become crusty and baked. (c) Sow the seeds in rows 2 to 4 inches apart. Seedlings in rows may be more easily cultivated and weeded. (d) Cover the seeds to proper depth according to size—very lightly or none at all for very small seeds—and compact the soil firmly over them. (e) Sprinkle the surface without washing the soil until thoroughly soaked. (f) Keep crust broken up around seedlings and weeds removed.

FACTS ABOUT ANNUALS

| Popular Name | Botanical Name | Blooming Months | Height | Space Apart | Seeds Germinate (Days) | Colors |
|---|---|---|---|---|---|---|
| African Daisy | Arctotis | 7-10 | 15-24 | 24 | 6 | W, L |
| Alyssum, sweet | Alyssum maritimum | 5- 9 | 8 | 8 | 6 | W |
| Amaranth | Amaranthus | 7- 9 | 18-24 | 18 | 8-12 | C, R, W |
| Amethyst | Browallia | 5-10 | 12-18 | 6-10 | 10 | B, W |
| Annual Mums | Chrysanthemums | 6-10 | 24-36 | 12-19 | 8 | Y, W |
| | | | | | | |
| Baby's Breath | Gypsophila | 7- 9 | 12-24 | 12 | | W |
| Balsam | Imptiens | 7-10 | 12-24 | 8-12 | | P, R, W |
| California Poppy | Eschscholzia | 7- 9 | 12 | 8 | | Y, O, P |
| Calliopsis | Calliopsis | 6-10 | 9-36 | 9-24 | 8 | Y, Br. |
| Candytuft | Iberis | 6-10 | 6-12 | 8 | | C, L, W |
| | | | | | | |
| China Aster | Callistephus | 7-10 | 12-36 | 12-18 | | R, P, W |
| Cockscomb | Celosia | 8-10 | 8-36 | 24 | | C, Y |
| Cornflower | Centaurea | 6- 9 | 18-30 | 10 | | B, R, W |
| Cosmos | Cosmea | 7-10 | 48-72 | 24-40 | 8 | R, P, W |
| Dahlia | Dahlia | 7-10 | 7-60 | 36 | 10-21 | R, W, Y |
| | | | | | | |
| Forget-me-not | Myosotis dissitiflora | 4- 6 | 6-12 | 6 | | B, P, Y |
| Four-o'Clock | Mirabilis jalapa | 7-10 | 24 | 18-24 | 5 | C, Y, W |
| Godetia | Godetia | 6-10 | 12-36 | 24 | | R, P, W |
| Heliotrope | Heliotropium | 7- 9 | 8-12 | 8 | | V, L |
| Holyhock | Althæa rosea | 8-10 | 48-60 | 24 | | W, P, R |
| | | | | | | |
| Larkspur | Delphinium | 7- 8 | 24-28 | 12 | 15 | B, P, W |
| Marigold | Tagetes | 7-10 | 8-36 | 12-24 | 8 | Y, O, Br. |
| Mignonette | Reseda | 7-10 | 6-18 | 12 | | |
| Morning Glory | Ipomoea | 7- 9 | 60 | 12 | | B, R, W |
| Nasturtium, Dwarf | Tropaolum | 6-10 | 8-12 | 10 | | S, O, Y |
| | | | | | | |
| Nemophila | Nemophila | 7-10 | 6-10 | 6-12 | | B & W |
| Painted Tongue | Salphiglosis | 7- 9 | 30 | 12 | 15 | P, C, W |
| Pansy | Viola | 6- 9 | 8 | 8 | 10 | Var. |
| Petunia | Petunia | 6-10 | 6-12 | 12 | 10 | R, P, W |
| Phlox | P. Drummondi | 6- 9 | 15 | 10 | 10 | Var. |
| | | | | | | |
| Pink | Dianthus | 7-10 | 12-18 | 12 | 8 | R, P, W |
| Rose Everlasting | | 1- 8 | 18 | | | P, W |
| Rose Moss | Portulaca | 6-10 | 6 | 8 | 10 | R, W, Y |
| Sage, Scarlet | Salvia | 8-10 | 8-36 | 12-18 | 15 | R |
| Snapdragon | Antirrhinum | 7-10 | 10-36 | 10-16 | 10 | P, Y, M |
| | | | | | | |
| Spiderflower | Cleome Spinosa | 7-10 | 48-60 | | | R, W |
| Strawflower | Helichrysum | 8- 9 | 24-36 | 15-18 | 5 | Y, R, W |
| Sunflower | Helianthus | 6-10 | 36-120 | 36 | | Y, R |
| Sweet Pea | Lathyrus | 6- 9 | 48-82 | 4- 6 | | Var. |
| Vervain | Verbena | 6-10 | 6- 8 | 8-12 | 8 | R, W |
| | | | | | | |
| Zinnia | Zinnia | 6-10 | 6-24 | 12-24 | 5 | R, S, Y |

Colors: B, blue; C, crimson; L, lavender; O, orange; P, pink; R, red; W, white; Y, yellow.
N. No manure, avoid rich soil     E. Everlastings
L. Add lime     M—Moderate

**AND THEIR REQUIREMENTS**

| Used For | | | | Soil | | | | Set | | | | |
|---|---|---|---|---|---|---|---|---|---|---|---|---|
| Border Beds | Rock Garden | Edging | Cut Flowers | Rich Humic | Good Garden | Ordinary | Poor | Sun | Part Shade | Sow by Transplanting | Plant in situ | Hardy |
| X |  | X | X |  | XX |  |  | XX | X |  | X | H |
|  | X |  | E |  |  | XX | XXX | XX |  |  | XX | V, L |
| XX | X |  | X |  | XX |  |  | XX |  | X |  | T |
|  |  |  | X |  |  | XX |  |  |  |  |  | M |
| XX | X |  | X |  |  | XXX | XX | XX | X | X | XX | H |
| XX |  | XX | X |  | XXX | XXX |  | XXX |  |  |  | T |
|  | XX | XX | X |  | XX | XXXX | XX | XXX | X | X | X | V |
| X | XX | X | X |  | X | XX |  | XX | X |  | X | H |
| X | X |  | X | XX | X | XX |  | XXX | X | XX | X | T |
|  |  |  | XXX |  | X | XXX |  | XXX | X | XX |  | T, E |
| XX |  |  | XXX | X | XX |  |  | XXX |  | XX |  | V |
|  |  |  | X |  |  |  |  |  |  |  |  | T |
|  |  |  | X |  | XX | XX |  |  | X | X | X | H |
| XX | XX |  | X |  | XX | XX | X | XX | X | X |  | T |
| XXX |  |  | X | X |  | X |  | X |  |  |  | H |
|  |  | X | X |  |  | X |  | X |  |  |  | M |
| XX |  |  | XX | X | XX | XX |  | XX |  |  | XXXXX | M |
| XXXX |  | XXX | XX | X | XX | X | X | XXXX |  | X | XXXX | V |
|  |  | XXX | XX |  |  |  | X | XXX |  |  | XXXXX | T |
|  |  |  |  |  |  |  |  |  |  |  | X | M |
|  |  |  |  |  |  |  |  |  |  |  | X | H |
| X | X |  |  |  |  | X |  | XX | XX |  |  | H |
|  | XXX | XX | XX | X | XX | XX |  | XXX | XXXX | XX |  | T |
|  | XX | XX | XX | X | XX | XX |  | XXX | XX |  | X | C |
|  |  |  |  |  |  |  |  |  |  |  |  | T |
|  |  |  |  |  |  |  |  |  |  |  |  | T |
|  | X | X | X E | X | X |  |  | XXX |  | X |  | M |
|  | X | X |  | N | XXX |  |  | XXXX |  |  | X | M |
| XX | X | X | X |  | XXX |  |  | XXX | X | XX |  | H |
|  |  |  |  |  |  |  |  |  |  |  |  | T |
|  |  |  |  |  |  |  |  |  |  |  |  | H |
| X | X |  | E |  | X | X |  | XX |  | XXX |  | T |
| X |  |  | X XX | XX |  |  |  | XXX |  | XX | XXX | H |
| XXX |  | XX | XX | N |  | XX | X | XX |  |  | X | H |
|  |  |  |  |  |  |  |  |  |  |  |  | T |
|  |  |  |  |  |  |  |  |  |  |  |  | T |
| X | X | X | X | X |  |  |  | X | X | X | X | H |

---

V—Very
H—Hardy
T—Tender

**C.** Dislikes intense heat. Pansies bloom in spring or fall. Sow spring flowers in August or winter; flowers in June

| Common Name | Genus | Blooming Months | Height (Inches) | Space Apart (Inches) | Seeds Germinate (Days) | Colors |
|---|---|---|---|---|---|---|
| Avens | Geum | 6-9 | 18 | 18 | 10 | R, C |
| Baby's Breath | Gypsophila | 8-9 | 36 | 24 | 10 | W |
| Beard Tongue | Pentstemon | 6-10 | 38 | 10 | 10 | B, S, V, L |
| Bellflower | Campanula | 7-9 | 18 | 18 | 2 | B, P, L, W |
| Blanket Flower | Gaillardia | 6-11 | 30 | 24 | 21 | Y, R, C, P |
| Blue Sage | Salvia | 8-9 | 40 | 10 | 15 | B |
| Bugloss | Anchusa | 6-8 | 48 | 18 | 12 | B |
| Campion | Lychris | 7-9 | 30 | 18 | 10 | B, R |
| Catmint | Nepeta | 5-8 | 12 | 8 | 10 | L |
| Cinbue foil | Potentilla | 6-8 | 18 | 18 | | C, R, O |
| Coatflower | Tunica | 6-9 | 6 | 6 | 5 | L, B |
| Columbine | Aquilegia | 5-7 | 36 | 12 | 30 | Y, W, L, B |
| Coneflower | Rudbeckia | 6-8 | 36 | 15 | 21 | R, W |
| Coralbells | Heuchera | 8-9 | 24 | 8 | 21 | P, W |
| Cornflower | Centaurea | 7-8 | 24 | 10 | 5 | B, R, W, Y |
| Cranesbell | Geranium | 7-8 | 31 | 12 | | C, P |
| Edelweiss | Leontopodium | 6-9 | 4-12 | 6 | | W |
| False Dragon | Physostegia | 7-8 | 36 | 12 | 15 | P, W |
| Feverfew | Matricaria | 7-10 | 15 | 15 | 10 | W |
| Flag | Iris | 5 | 12-48 | 24 | | W, P, L |
| Flax | Linum | 6-7 | 24 | 18 | 10 | B, Y |
| Fleabane | Erigeron | 6-8 | 30 | 12 | 15 | B, P, R, L |
| Foxglove | Digitalis | 6-7 | 36 | 12 | | R, L |
| Gentian | Gentiana | 8-9 | 18 | 18 | | P, B |
| Gay Feather | Liatris | 7-8 | 48 | 12 | 21 | P, W |
| Heliotrope | Valeriana | 6-9 | 21-48 | 12 | 15 | R, W |
| Hollyhock | Althea | 6-8 | 72 | 18 | | P, C, Y, W |
| Larkspur | Delphinium | 5-10 | 70 | 24 | 21 | L, B, P, W |
| Lavender | Lavendula | 7-8 | 18 | 10 | 10 | B |
| Lily of the Valley | Convallaria | 5-6 | 12 | 72 | | W |
| Mallow | Hibiscus | 7-9 | 48 | 36 | | C, W |
| Madwort | Alyssum | 4-5 | 12 | 8 | 7 | Y |
| Michaelmas-daisy | Aster | 6-9 | 12-60 | 12 | | B, V, P |
| Monkshood | Aconitum | 7-10 | 24-84 | 8 | | B, V, L, W |
| Peony | Paenia | 5-6 | 36 | 36 | | C, P, W |
| Pinks | Dianthus | 5-7 | 12 | 8 | 8 | C, W, P, L |
| Phlox | Phlox | 7-8 | 24 | 12 | 10 | P, R, L, O |
| Poppy | Papaver | 6-10 | 12-48 | 48 | 10 | C, W, Y |
| Primrose | Primula | 4-6 | 4-8 | 12 | | W, L, P |
| Sea Lavender | Statice | 6-8 | 8 | 20 | | W, L, P |
| Shasta Daisy | Chrysanthemum | 5-12 | 24 | 12 | 7 | W, Var. |
| Stonecrop | Sedum | 6-8 | 4 | 8 | | Y |
| Sunflower | Helianthus | 8-10 | 48 | 36 | 5 | Y |
| Thrift | Centaurea | 6-8 | 18 | 8 | 10 | Y, B |
| Violet | Viola | 4-10 | 4-8 | 6 | | W, P, Y |
| Verbena | Verbena | 6-10 | 12 | 6 | 10 | R & W |
| Windflower | Anemone | 6-11 | 36 | 18 | D | W, P, R |
| Yarrow | Achillea | 6-8 | 24-38 | 24 | 10 | W, P, O |
| Zinnia | Heliopsis | 7-9 | 40-70 | 12 | 10 | Y, O |

Colors: B, blue; C, crimson; L, lavender; O, orange; P, pink; R, red; W, white; Y, yellow.
All may be set in either spring or fall except Anemone, Lavendula & Pyrethrum.

**NIALS AND THEIR REQUIREMENTS**

| | Used For | | | | Soil | | | | Set | | Propagation | Misc. Notes |
|---|---|---|---|---|---|---|---|---|---|---|---|---|
| Border | Rock | Edging | Cut Flowers | Rich | Good | Ordinary | Light, Sandy Poor | Sun | Part Shade | | |
| X | X | | X X | | X | | | X | | D | b |
| X | X | | X X | | X | X | X | X | | DS | L |
| X | X | X | | | X | X | X | X | | D | |
| X | | | | | X | | | X | | DS | |
| X | | | | | X | X | | | X | CD | 3 |
| X | X | X | | | X | X | | X | | D, S | |
| | X | | | | X | X | | X | | CD | 3 |
| | | | | | X | | | X | | D | |
| | | | | | | | | | | D, S | |
| X | X | X | | X | X | X | | X | X | D | |
| X | X | | X | | X | X | | X | X | DS | |
| X | X | X | | | X | X | | X | X | DS | 3 |
| X | X | | | | X | | | X | | CD | 3 |
| X | X | | | | X | X | | X | | DS | |
| X | X | X | X | | X. | X | | X | X | D | |
| | X | | X | | | X | X | X | X | D, S | L |
| X | X | | | | | X | X | X | | CD | 2 |
| X | X | X | X | | | X | X | X | | D | |
| | | X | X | | | X | | X | X | D, S | |
| X | X | | X | | X | X | | X | X | D | 3 |
| X | | X | X X | X | X | | | | X | S | b |
| | X | | X X | | | | | | X | D | |
| | R | | | | X | X | | X | X | CD | |
| | | X | X | X | X | X | | X | X | S | L |
| X | | | X X | X | | | | X | | DS | |
| X | X | | X X | X | X | X | X | X | | S | |
| | | | X | | X | | | | | CD | |
| | | | | | | | | | | S | |
| X | X | X X | | | X | X | | X | X | S | L |
| X | X | X X | | X | X | | | X | | DS | |
| | | X | | | | | | | X X | S | a |
| X | | X | X | | X | | | X | | S | |
| X | X | X | X | X | X | X | | X | | D | L2 |
| X | X | X | X | | X | X | | X | | DC | |
| X | | X | X | X | X | | | X | | D, S | |
| X | | X | | E | X | | | | X | S | |
| | | | X | X | | | | | X | S, C | |
| X | | X | | | X | X | X | X | | S | 2 |
| X | | | | | X | X | X | X | | CD | |
| X | | | X | | X | X | | X | | D | |
| X | | X | | X | X | | | X | | DS | b |
| X | X | | | | X | X | | X | | S | b |
| N | X | | X X | | X | X | | X | X | D, S | a b |
| X | | | X X | X | X | X | | X | | D | 2 |
| X | | | X X | | X | | | X | | DS | 3 |
| | | X | X | | X | X | | X | | S | a |

C—By cutting   D—By division   S—By seeds
a. Give ample moisture. b. Provide protection after frost. L. Provide ample lime.
2. Dig. divide and replant every 2nd year. 3. Every 3rd year.
E—Everlasting.

A miniature greenhouse may be constructed or purchased for experimentation with seeds and seedlings. These may require only a few square feet of space or as much additional space as the work requires.

For indoor seeding proceed as follows: (a) Provide suitable seeding boxes, or flats, about 3 inches deep. Use hotbed or cold frames if available and if large quantities of plants are to be grown. (b) Fill with fine loamy soil that does not cake readily. Press the soil down firmly and evenly with a small piece of board. When firmed, the surface of the soil should be about ¾ inch below the top of the box. Make shallow narrow trenches about ¼ inch deep crosswise of the box. Scatter seeds in trenches. Cover or sift with fine soil and compact firmly. Depth of covering will vary with size of seeds. Sprinkle carefully to avoid washing, cover box with pane of glass and put where temperature is high enough to start germination. Transplant young seedlings when first true leaves have formed, into other boxes, beds, or pots to give more room for growth and produce better root and top development.

(6) Set out young plants. Since indoor-grown plants should be "hardened" before setting in permanent outdoor locations, expose the plants to outdoor conditions for an hour or two during the warm part of the day. Gradually lengthen this exposure period over several days until they have been exposed the full 24 hours. Set out plants in late afternoon or evening. The best time is following a good rain when the soil is in workable condition. Prepare holes for setting plants to good depth so danger of drying out will be minimized. Remove plants from beds or boxes by cutting around them with a knife, removing a block of soil with the plant roots intact. Place plants in holes and partially cover roots with soil. Press the soil lightly around plants. Pour in a cup of water. When it has soaked away, finish filling up around plant. Space plants with plenty of room for proper development and shape. This usually promotes better flowering and greater ease in cultivating and caring for them.

(7) Set out bulbs and roots: After studying the planting suggestions and seasonal requirements of the plants being considered, set them out in proper season. Methods and time of setting out and handling roots and bulbs vary widely with the different varieties and with the locality.

(8) Cultivate and care for plants: Stir the soil after heavy

**FACTS ABOUT BULBS AND THEIR REQUIREMENTS**

| Flower Name | Botanical Name | Blooming Mos. N. Y. Area | Height | Colors | Planting | | | |
|---|---|---|---|---|---|---|---|---|
| | | | | | Distance Apart | Depth | Planting Months | Sun |
| Anemone | Anemone | 5 | 4 | Var. | 3 | 3 | 9 | L |
| Begonia tuberose | Begonia | 7-9 | 12 | Var. | 8 | 2 | 6 | M |
| Brodiaea | Brodiaea | 3-5 | 8-24 | Var. | 3 | 3 | 9-10 | S |
| Caladium | Caladium | 6-8 | 12 | Var. | 18 | 3 | 5 | S |
| Canna | Canna | 8-10 | 48-60 | W, P, R | 18 | 4 | 4 | S |
| Crocus | Crocus | 4 | 3-4 | P, L, W | 3 | 2 | 9 | L |
| Daffodil | Narcissus | 2-6 | 3-10 | W, Y | 5 | 4 | 9-10 | L |
| Dahlia | Dahlia | 7-11 | 15-60 | Var. | 10 | 5 | 5 | S |
| Dogtooth violet | Erythronium | 4-5 | 8-12 | Var. | 3 | 3 | 4 | Any |
| Fairy lily | Zephranthes | 7-10 | 10-15 | W, Y, R | 3 | 2 | 4 | S |
| Gladioli | Gladioli | 7-9 | 24-48 | Var. | 8 | 3-5 | 3-4 | S |
| Grape hyacinth | Muscari | 3-4 | 7-8 | Y, O, P | 3 | 3 | 9-10 | Any |
| Hyacinth | Hyacinthus | 4-5 | 14-16 | Var. | 6 | 4 | 10 | S |
| Iris | Iris | 3-5 | 6-8 | Var. | 4 | 4 | 7-8 | S |
| Lily | Lilium | 6-9 | 18-60 | W, R, Y, O | 4 | 5 | 3-10 | S |
| Montbretia | Tritonia | 7-9 | 18-36 | Var. | 4 | 3 | 4 | S |
| Oxalis | Oxalis | 7-9 | 6-10 | L, R, S | 3 | 2 | 4 | S |
| Squill | Scilla | 4-8 | 4-16 | Var. | 4 | 3 | 9-10 | M |
| Snowdrop | Galanthus | 1-4 | 4 | W | 2 | 4 | 8 | S |
| Mexican shellflower | Tigridia | 7-9 | 15-24 | W, Y, R | 3 | 3 | 7 | S |
| Tuberose | Polyanthes | 20-36 | 6-8 | W | 10 | pot | 5 | S |
| Tulips | Tulipa | 4 wks | 8-12 | Var. | 6 | 4-6 | 3-10 | L |
| Winter aconite | Eranthis | 1-3 | 4-8 | Y | 6 | 3 | 7-10 | L |
| California quomash | Camassias | 2 wks | 36 | B, W | 8-9 | 4 | 10 | S |
| Zygadenus | Zygadenus | 5 | 18-24 | Y | 6 | 4 | 9-10 | M |

Bulbs prefer well drained, sandy soil, bonemeal fertilizer
S—full sun; L—light; M—moderate; H—heavy.

rains to prevent caking. Do not work soil when too wet. Keep gardens free of weeds. Water thoroughly at frequent intervals during dry weather. A light mulch of leaves or straw will help prevent excessive evaporation and drying of the soil. Follow practices recommended for digging and storing roots and bulbs that must be taken indoors during the winter. A procedure generally recommended is to dig them carefully during dry weather shortly after the first killing frost. Cut off tops, leaving 3 to 4 inches of stem attached to roots or tubers. Leave them on the ground to dry for a few hours. Store in dry, cool place where temperature will not drop below 40°F. during the winter. Burn withered leaves and stems to prevent harboring disease. Protect outdoor flower plants during the winter with a layer of strawy manure, hay, leaves, or coarse ashes after the ground is frozen. (9) Prevent insect and disease damage. (See pages 234–249.)

## SHRUBS, HEDGES AND VINES

**Steps in Selecting, Planting, and Caring for Shrubs:** (1) Mark location and arrangement of shrubbery. Review available literature and plans for ornamental planting. Note how shrubbery can

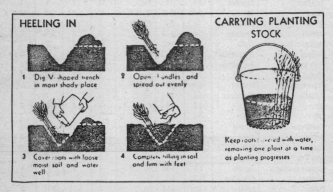

**HEELING IN**

1  Dig V-shaped trench in moist shady place

2  Open bundles and spread out evenly

3  Cover roots with loose moist soil and water well

4  Complete filling in soil and firm with feet

**CARRYING PLANTING STOCK**

Keep roots covered with water, removing one plant at a time as planting progresses

be used most attractively. (2) Select suitable kinds and varieties. Give particular attention to the following factors: (a) Height of growth; (b) Texture of foliage and flowers. (c) Color of leaves, flowers, berries. (d) Winter effect. Use varieties native to your locality as far as possible. Estimate the quantity of each type and variety that you will need. (3) Secure planting stock. Shrubs are generally available from the following sources: (a) Local wild growths in surrounding country. (b) Neighbors who are resetting or thinning out plantings. (c) Nurseries or dealers. Transplant or secure cuttings or seeds of native wild plants. Make special trips about the community, keeping an eye open for suitable materials. Stock should be ordered well in advance of time for setting out. (4) Prepare stock for planting. Cut off smoothly all bruised and broken root ends before planting. Trim out excessive or broken top growth. Keep roots dampened and well covered to prevent drying out while transplanting or while waiting to transplant. If planting is delayed for several

## SHRUBS USED FOR ORNAMENTAL PLANTINGS

[Those marked with asterisk (*) are suitable for hedges]

| Name | Average height in feet | Color of flowers or foliage | Time of blooming or fruiting | Pruning |
|---|---|---|---|---|
| Almond, Flowering (Prunus Communis) | 2-4 | R, W | Early Spring...... | Sparingly after blooming. |
| Althea, Rose of Sharon (Hibiscus Syriacus) | 6-10 | Var. | Midsummer...... | Freely in the spring. |
| Azalea, Flame (Azalea Calendulaces) | 1-5 | Or. | Early Summer.... | Sparingly or none. |
| *Barberry, Japanese (Berberis Thunbergii) | 3-4 | R, b | Late fall and winter | To shape in early spring. |
| Calycanthus (Calycanthus flor dus) | 3-5 | Br. | Early summer..... | None or little. |
| Coral Berry (Symphoricarpos orbiculatur) | 2-4 | R, b | Winter........... | Sparingly in early spring. |
| Cranberry, high bush.......... | 6-8 | R, b | Early winter...... | None or little in spring. |
| *Deutzia (large)............... | 6-8 | W, P | Early spring...... | After blooming for shaping. |
| *Deutzia (dwarf or slender) (Deutzia gracilis) | 2-3 | W | Early spring...... | After blooming for shaping. |
| Dogwood (red) (Cornus florida rubra) | 8-15 | P | Early spring...... | After blooming for shaping. |
| Dogwood (white)............... | 8-15 | W | Early spring...... | After blooming for shaping. |
| Elder, American............... | 8-12 | W | Summer........... | Remove old wood in early spring. |
| Elder, Golden................. | 6-8 | W | Summer........... | Remove old wood in early spring. |
| *Forsythia (Golden Bell)....... | 7-8 | Y | Early spring...... | After blooming, if necessary. |
| Hibiscus. (See Althea.) | | | | |
| Honeysuckle, Fragrant........ | 6-8 | P | Summer........... | Old wood in early spring. |
| Honeysuckle, Tartarian........ | 6-8 | W, P | Early summer..... | Old wood in early spring. |
| Hydrangea.................... | 6-7 | W | Late summer...... | Prune back severely in early spring. |
| *Lilac, common............... | 6-10 | L, W | Early........... | Very little after blooming. Remove wilted flower stems immediately after blooming. |
| Mock Orange................. | 6-8 | W | Spring........... | Sparingly after blooming. |
| *Privet, common............. | 4-15 | W | Summer........... | To shape in early spring. |
| *Privet, Ibota............... | 4-8 | B, f | Late........... | To height in early spring. |
| Quince, Japanese............. | 4-7 | R, P | Early spring...... | Sparingly after blooming. |
| Rhododendron................ | 3-20 | P. W | Early summer..... | Little. |
| Rose, Japanese (Rosa Rugosa) | 4-6 | P, W | Summer........... | Old wood each spring. |
| Rose, Prairie................ | 5-6 | P | Summer........... | Little. |
| Snowball.................... | 6-8 | W | Early........... | Sparingly after blooming. |
| Snowberry................... | 4-5 | W, b | Fall........... | Sparingly in early spring to shape bush. |
| Spirea, Arguta............... | 5-6 | W | Summer........... | Sparingly after blooming. |
| Spirea, Anthony Waterer....... | 2-3 | P | Summer........... | After blooming remove seed heads. |
| Spirea, Bridal Wreath........ | 5-6 | W | Spring........... | After blooming when needed. |
| *Spirea, Van Houttei......... | 5-6 | W | Early........... | Little after flowering. |
| Sumac....................... | 3-6 | W, Y | Early........... | None. |
| Tamarix..................... | 4-7 | P | Spring........... | Cut out old wood. |
| Weigela..................... | 4-7 | W, R | Early summer..... | Very little after flowering. |

Colors: Blue, Brown, Lavender, Orange, Pink, Red, White, Yellow.  b, berries; f, fruit.

days, the plants should be stored in a damp cool place or "heeled in" by burying the roots in a shallow trench and keeping them well moistened. Plants moved in warm or dry weather must be carefully protected against root drying and must be given a more severe top pruning.

(5) Plant shrubs. Avoid planting in heavy soil when too wet. Dig holes sufficiently large to receive all the roots without crowding or bending, and deep enough to allow for filling in with rich top soil under the roots. Place in the hole a layer of rich soil or a small amount of well-rotted manure mixed thoroughly with soil. Place the plant in the hole, making sure that the roots are spread out naturally without bending or breaking. The plant should be set slightly deeper than it stood originally. Work fine topsoil carefully about the roots, packing it down firmly. Make sure that no spaces are left under the roots. Tamp the soil firmly as you fill the hole. Use only topsoil. When hole is about filled, pour a bucket of water slowly around the roots. When it has soaked away, finish filling the hole without additional tamping. (6) Protect new plantings. Water the newly planted shrubs occasionally if the weather is dry. Cultivate around the new plants frequently. Protect with stakes or a wire netting from trampling or other damage.

(7) Prune shrubbery when necessary. The kind and amount of pruning varies with the type of shrub. Shrubs should be kept at their natural height and little top pruning should be done; cut out the dead wood; occasionally remove old branches entirely so that the plant is constantly renewing itself from the bottom. Cut all branches smoothly just above a crotch. The time for pruning depends upon the variety or kind of shrub and the time of blooming. As a general rule, prune any flowering shrub several months before blooming, so that there will be time for new wood to be formed for the following season. Fall-blooming shrubs may be pruned early in the spring. (8) Control pests and disease.

### SHRUBS FOR SPECIAL PURPOSES

FOR HEDGES: Bridal Wreath, Caragana, Cotoneaster, Deutzia, Evergreen, Honeysuckle, Japanese Barberry, Japanese Quince, Privet, Rosa Rugosa.

For border planting:

a. Low Growing: Anthony Waterer Spirea, Coralberry, Japanese Barberry, Slender Deutzia, Snowberry, Thunberg's Spirea.

b. Medium Growing: Bridal Wreath, Deutzia, Rosa Rugosa, Van Houttei Spirea, Yellow Flowering Currant.

c. Tall Growing: Bush Honeysuckle, Caragana, Forsythia, Lilac, Mock Orange or Syringa, Tartarian Honeysuckle, Viburnum, Weigela.

For specimen use: Caragana, Dogwood, Flowering Almond, Japanese Quince, Redbud, Smoketree, Tamarix, White Fringe, Winged Burning Bush.

For shady situations: Azaleas, Calycanthus, Coralberry, Dogwood, Hydrangea, Snowberry, Viburnum.

For steep banks: Coralberry, Drooping Forsythia, Japanese Barberry, Prairie Rose, Regal Privet, Snowberry, Sumac.

**Steps in Selecting and Maintaining a Hedge:** (1) Locate hedge. Hedges may vary in height from a few inches to several feet, depending upon the effect and the purpose for which they are desired. They are commonly used for (a) Boundaries between properties; (b) Boundaries around lawns, gardens, chicken yards, etc.; (c) Ornamental borders along walks in gardens; (d) screening unsightly views, fences, buildings, etc. (2) Select hedge plantings and secure stock. Take into account the following factors in making a choice; (a) Hardiness as to cold, drought, resistance to insects and disease, and the like; (b) Average height of growth for best appearance —plants are usually most effective if maintained at about their natural growth; (c) Flowers or fruits, if any—color, season of appearance; (d) Foliage—color, permanence during growing season; (e) Response to pruning for desired height and shape. (3) Prepare soil. Spade up the soil where the hedge is to be set to a depth of 1 to 18 inches. Apply well-rotted stable manure and mix it thoroughly with the soil to the depth of the spading. Pulverize the soil well to the bottom of the spading and make a compact fine root bed. If soil is very sandy or poor, remove a large portion of it and replace with good topsoil. (4) Set out plants. Dig a trench in the prepared soil deep enough and wide enough to receive the roots without crowding. Keep one side of the trench straight in alignment

and cut squarely. Pile the earth on the opposite side. Place
the plants in a row against the square-cut side of the trench
to make a straight line hedge. Set plants at depth they grew
before or a trifle lower. Privet may be set so the lower branches
of the plant will be covered with earth when the trench is
filled in. Tall-growing kinds are usually planted 3 to 4 feet
apart, medium-growing kinds 2 to 3 feet apart, and low-growing kinds 12 to 18 inches apart. Very low ornamental borders
and privets are usually set closer. Work fine soil in well
around the roots of each plant and tramp firmly. (5) Prune
at planting time according to variety. Privet hedge plants are
usually cut back to about ⅓ of the original height. Barberry
and flowering hedges require little or no pruning at planting
time. Prune very sparingly during the first year. (6) Trim to
desired shape and size when established. Privet hedges may
be pruned as often as desired and in various shapes. Stop
pruning in mid-autumn so that new growth will harden before winter. Always keep the top of the hedge narrower than
the bottom. Flowering hedges should be pruned lightly. (7)
Control insects and disease.

**Steps in Selecting, Planting, and Caring for Vines:** (1) Locate vine
plantings. Vine plants may be (a) woody perennial growers
that do not die down during the winter, such as wisteria,
English ivy, or trumpet vines; or (b) annual growers that
must be seeded annually or which send up new vines each
year, such as morning glories, wild cucumber. Vines are
chiefly useful as: (a) Porch or veranda covers; (b) Climbers
on brick or stone house walls or chimneys; (c) Screens in
places too narrow for shrub plantings; (d) Arbor and pergola
coverings; (e) Coverings for rough banks, rocks, and other
exposed places; (f) Coverings for fences and walls; (g) Coverings for unsightly or distracting features, such as clothesline
posts, light or phone poles, windmill tower, etc. Some vines
climb by twining about a support or trellis and others have
climbing roots for clinging to walls and vertical surfaces;
others have tendrils.

(2) Secure planting stock of kinds and varieties desired.
Careful transplanting of a considerable part of the root with
a portion of the vine attached, but well pruned back, will
ordinarily be successful. (3) Plant vines. Prepare a good
fertile soil. If soil is poor, replace with good loam or mix

properly with well-rotted manure, or leafmold. Do not let manure come in direct contact with roots. Vine seeds require a well-prepared, finely pulverized and well compacted seed-bed. Set plants from 12 to 18 inches from wall in order to obtain better moisture conditions. Set woody vines according to directions for planting shrubs.

(4) Care of vines: Supply plenty of moisture until vines are well established. Occasional heavy soakings with water may be necessary especially if planted under the protection of walls and buildings or in exposed places. Protect young vines from dogs with wire netting or by planting a few barberry bushes around the base. Cultivate the soil occasionally about the vines. They do not thrive in hard, dry soil. Train vines to desired shape and arrangement. Remove dead wood before growth starts in the spring. Provide suitable trellis or support. Do not try to make twining vines climb on stone walls or buildings.

### VINES FOR SPECIAL PURPOSES

FLOWERING VINES: Balloon Vine, Clematis, Purple; Clematis, White; Flame Vine, Honeysuckle, Trumpet Vine, Wisteria, Yellow Jessamine.

VINES FOR COVERING BRICK AND STONE MASONRY: Engleman's Ivy, Boston Ivy, English Ivy, Climbing Euonymus or Trailing Burning Bush.

VINES REQUIRING TRELLIS, FENCE, OR ARBOR SUPPORTS: Ampelopsis, Bittersweet, Clematis, Dutchman's Pipe, Grape, Honeysuckle, Virginia Creeper, Wisteria.

VINES WITH HEAVY FOLIAGE: Bittersweet, Dutchman's Pipe, Honeysuckle, Kudzu, Trumpet Vine, Virginia Creeper, White Clematis, Wild Grape, Wisteria, Chinese; Wisteria, Japanese.

QUICK-GROWING ANNUALS: Gourd, Moon Vine, Morning Glory, Scarlet Runner Bean, Wild Cucumber.

Roses, both hybrids and climbers, also serve the same purposes for which vines are used and should, therefore, be considered where flowering vines are wanted. The Japanese honeysuckle is used commonly on steep slopes.

Steps in Making a Rock Garden: (1) Select the type and location desired. Consider the following: (a) Natural rock outcrops; (b) Steep banks or slopes; (c) Natural mounds or piles of excavated earth; (d) Natural depressions, ravines, or old excavations; (e) Rock piles, old stone walls, etc. appropriately placed; (f) Level ground—depressions can be dug and rocks and soil brought in to make attractive plantings; (g) Keep away from other plantings.

A rock garden should be proportionate in size to the grounds and the other gardens. It should be away from trees where it will get good light and air. Some protection from winter winds is desirable. (2) Prepare the site. The usual purpose is to copy nature by using a natural ledge of porous rock. Make paths between the rocks and make good soil pockets for the plants. Avoid too many small ones. At least ¾ of each rock should be covered. Tilt each stone inward so that the rain and other moisture will soak back into the soil and water the plant roots. Most plants require fertile well-drained soil or leafmold for the soil pockets. Some plants, however, thrive best in sandy or gravelly soils with little organic matter or moisture, but which get plenty of sun. Leave ample soil pockets around the rocks for the plants. Pack well with soil suitable for the plants to be used. Allow the rocks and soil to settle for several days before planting.

(3) Select the plants. Choose low-growing plants for the most part, especially for the foreground and main part of the rockery. Taller plants may be used in the background and for outside borders. Use dwarf varieties of trees. (4) Make the plantings. Follow recommendations for planting flowers, shrubs, and vines. (5) Care for the rock garden: Keep out weeds. Water as needed. Pack new soil around the roots of the plants if necessary after heavy rains. Give some winter protection in cold regions. Control insects and disease.

**Some Widely Used Rockery Plantings:**

ANNUAL FLOWERS: Annual Phlox, Blue Torenia, Cape Marigold, Dwarf Candytuft, Dwarf Nasturtium, Iceplant, Pansy, Portulaca, Alyssum, Twinspur, Verbena.

MEDIUM TO TALL GROWING (for background effect): Bachelor's Button, California Poppy, Cosmos, Larkspur, Petunia, Phlox, Poppy, Salvia, Snapdragon, Zinnia.

PERENNIAL FLOWERS: Low growing—Alyssum, American Pasque Flower, Anemone, Arabis (Rock Cress), Candytuft (Iberis), Caucasian Catnip, Coral Bells, Dwarf Iris, Forget-me-not, Fringed Bleeding Heart, Harebell, Lily-of-the-Valley, Mother of Thyme, Primrose, Rock Aster, Sandwort, Sedum in variety (Stonecrop), Sempervivum in variety (Hen and Chickens), Sweet William, Viola.

MEDIUM TO TALL: Aster, Bleeding Heart, Campanula (Bell-flower), Columbine, Dusty Miller, Ferns, Hardy Phlox, Lupine, Perennial Larkspur, Perennial Poppy, Shasta Daisy, Veronica, Viola, Virginia Bluebells.

VINES: Boston Ivy, Euonymus Radicans, Hall's Japanese Honeysuckle, Trailing Myrtle.

SHRUBS: Anthony Waterer Spirea, Deutzia Gracilis, Spirea Frobelia.

EVERGREENS: Arborvitae (dwarf), Dwarf Japan Yew, Horizontal Juniper, Pfitzer's Juniper.

BULBS: Crocus, Lily, Grape Hyacinth, Narcissus.

Steps in Making a Pool: (1) Excavate: Plan location and shape. (Circular or curving is preferred). Pool should be 18 inches deep. If birds are to use it, area 2 inches deep should be provided. Dig 6 inches deeper and wider than pool is to be made. (2) Provide drainage if pool is to be sizable. Put in hole with tamped gravel or line with chicken wire. (3) Cement with mixture of 1 part cement, 3 parts sand and gravel, for about

## COMMON POOL PLANTS

| Flower | Depth Required | Winter Care |
|---|---|---|
| LOTUS | Plant in large wooden boxes, 12″ deep in warm weather. | Cover roots with heavy covering of leaves, or keep in water 2′ to 3′ deep. |
| WATER HYACINTH | Float in 6″ of water over anchored box containing 6″ of soil. | Bring indoors in container with 3″ to 4″ of soil before frost. Keep at sunny window at 55° to 60°F. |
| WATER LILIES | Plant from end of frost to mid June, 3″ to 6″ water. Heavy rich loam. Cover bottom with soil. Prevent mud by using containers. | Cover pool with boards, then straw or leaves. If water is drained, cover with leaves. Tropical water lilies must be kept in a warm greenhouse. |

SHALLOW WATER PLANTS: Arrowhead, Lizardtail, Papyrus, Pickerel-weed, Water Arum, Water Poppy.

4 inches. Apply finish coat of cement mortar, (1 part cement, 2 parts sand). Allow pool to settle for 2 weeks before putting in fish or plants.

(4) Select and plant background materials: (a) small evergreens, yew, arborvitae, cedar, azalea, cotoneaster, hemlock; (b) flowering shrubs, forsythia, lilac, spirea azalea, rhododendron, laurel; (c) plantings: cardinal flower, Japanese iris, marsh-marigold, rosemallow, astilbe, Siberian iris. (5) Select fish and plants for stocking.

## TREES

Trees fall, generally, into two major classes: deciduous trees which shed their leaves each year; and evergreens which retain their leaves all year round. Trees are useful as windbreaks and screens, for shade, flowers, fruit, bird food, and ornamental specimens.

**Steps in Selecting, Planting, and Caring for Trees:** (1) Mark location and arrangement of tree plantings. Review general principles governing the use of trees for beautifying home grounds. Review available literature, pictures, and diagrams of ornamental planting to see how trees may be used to best advantage. Avoid straight line arrangement except along roads. (2) Select suitable types and varieties of trees. Use, as far as possible, types and varieties that are native to, and representative of your locality which are suitable for your particular situation. Consider: (a) Maximum height and spread when mature. Tall spreading trees are desirable for background or screening effects. (b) Ease of starting. (c) Rapidity of growth. (d) Permanence. (e) Susceptibility to insects or disease. (f) Flower or foliage habits. (g) Amount of shade given. (h) Appearance at various seasons.

(3) Secure planting stock. Select only good, vigorous, healthy specimens with well-shaped top, free from insect or disease damage. Young trees are usually transplanted with greater success than older ones. Plan to transplant native stock selected at the proper season. Order stock from reputable nurseries. Keep roots of planting stock well dampened. Keep stock in a cool damp place or "heel in" if the planting must be delayed for a few days. (4) Prepare holes. Dig holes large enough to receive all the roots when spread in their natural position, without bending or doubling them back, and deep

enough to set the tree at the same depth as before transplanting. Place 3 to 4 inches of rich topsoil, which has been thoroughly pulverized, in the bottom of the hole. (5) Pre-

Average date of the latest killing frost in spring east of the Rocky Mountains.

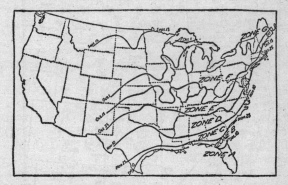

Zone map of the central and eastern part of the United States based on average date of the first killing frost in autumn.

pare the stock for planting. Locally transplanted stock may need some pruning. Remove dead roots. Tops should be pruned back after trees are set.

(6) Plant tree. Set the tree in the hole at about the same depth at which it originally grew, filling under the roots with good soil to bring it to the proper height. Spread the roots as

necessary. Work very fine topsoil well around the roots packing it firmly. Tamp the soil well as you fill the hole. When the hole is about two-thirds full slowly add as much water as will be absorbed readily. Finish filling the hole with topsoil without additional compacting. (7) Protect newly planted trees. Tie young trees securely to a heavy stake or to a framework to prevent loosening by the wind or damage from animals. Large trees should be held firmly in place by guy wires attached to "dead men" on at least three sides. Provide wire screening if there is likelihood of gnawing by rabbits or other pests. Soak the newly planted trees thoroughly at frequent intervals during dry weather. Keep the soil cultivated around the trees and cover with a mulch of manure worked into the surface soil. Feed fertilizer in April and November.

Average date of the last killing frost in spring in the western states.

(8) Control pests and disease. (9) Prune unnecessary or dead branches.

Trees should be selected with the purpose they are to serve in mind, as well as climatic and soil conditions. Chief uses of trees: To serve as a screen (plant closely); to give woodsy privacy (use variety of plantings); to add dignity, balance or background for a house; to provide shade for a specific area; to divert wind or breeze to or away from a specific area; to frame a house or doorway; to accent a lawn or provide a center of attraction in an area; to provide color or flowers; to provide protection for other plantings; to attract birds; to provide fruits or nuts; as street trees, or park or garden trees.

Trees should be visualized as they will grow—as to height,

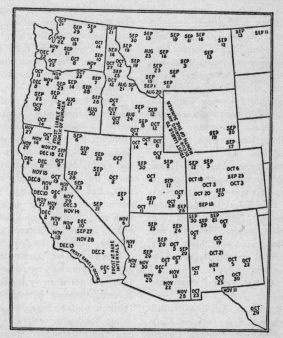

Outline map showing average date of killing frost in the autumn in the western portion of the United States.

silhouette, root development, etc. Some tree roots extend as much as 100 feet and may interfere with water supply or disposal. The danger of falling branches as the tree grows older must also be considered.

## TREES BEST ADAPTED FOR SPECIAL PURPOSES

### Northeastern United States

SHADE TREES FOR SUBURBAN HOMES: EVERGREEN: Canada hemlock, Colorado blue spruce, Eastern white pine, Nikko fir, White fir.

IN NORTHERN PART ONLY: Balsam fir, White spruce.

DECIDUOUS: American hornbeam, American mountain-ash, American yellowwood, European beech, European linden, Littleleaf linden, Norway maple, Panicled goldenrain-tree, Pin oak, Scarlet oak, Schwedler maple, Silver linden, Sugar maple, Sweetgum, Tuliptree, White oak.

ROADSIDE, BOULEVARD, AND AVENUE TREES: EVERGREEN: Canada hemlock, Eastern white pine, Red pine.

DECIDUOUS: American linden, American yellowwood, Black tupelo, Common hackberry, Ginkgo (staminate form), London planetree, Northern red oak, Norway maple, Pin oak, Red maple, Scarlet oak, Silver linden, Schwedler maple, Sugar maple, Sweetgum, Tuliptree.

STREET TREES: EVERGREEN: None.

DECIDUOUS: Ailanthus (pistillate form), Amur corktree, Ginkgo (staminate form), London planetree, Norway maple, Pin

oak, Thornless common honeylocust, Tuliptree.

PARK AND GARDEN TREES (see also SHADE AND ROADSIDE TREES): EVERGREEN: Common Douglas-fir, Oriental spruce, Red pine.

DECIDUOUS: Amur corktree, Bolleana poplar, Common horsechestnut, Cutleaf weeping birch, Eastern black walnut, English elm, Golden weeping willow, Japanese pagodatree, Kentucky coffeetree, Paper birch, Rock elm, Scotch elm, Silverpendent linden, Weeping silverpendent linden, White ash, White oak.

TREES WITH AUTUMN COLOR: American hornbeam (orange, scarlet), American yellowwood (yellow), Black tupelo (scarlet), Ginkgo (yellow), Northern red oak (red), Norway maple (yellow), Pin oak (scarlet, dark red), Red maple (orange, red, scarlet), Scarlet oak (scarlet, dark red), Sugar maple (yellow, orange, scarlet), Sweetgum (red, scarlet), Tuliptree (yellow).

TREES WITH CONSPICUOUS FLOWERS: American mountain-ash (white), American yellowwood (white), Common horsechestnut (pinkish white), Japanese pagodatree (yellowish white), Panicled goldenrain-tree (yellow), Red maple (red), Sugar maple

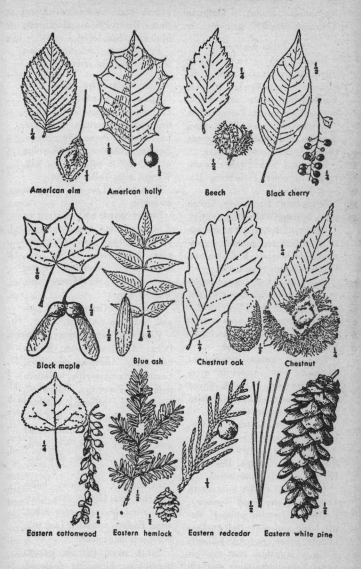

American elm   American holly   Beech   Black cherry

Black maple   Blue ash   Chestnut oak   Chestnut

Eastern cottonwood   Eastern hemlock   Eastern redcedar   Eastern white pine (yellowish green), Tuliptree (greenish yellow).

## Plains Area

SHADE AND PARK TREES: THROUGHOUT PLAINS AREA: DECIDUOUS: American elm, Bur oak, Cottonwood, Green ash, Hackberry, Honeylocust, Russian-olive.

EVERGREEN: Austrian pine, Eastern red cedar, Ponderosa pine, Rocky Mountain cedar.

NEBRASKA NORTHWARD: DECIDUOUS: Boxelder, Hawthorn, Maples, Willows.

EVERGREEN: Douglas-fir, Scotch pine, Spruce, White fir.

NEBRASKA SOUTHWARD: DECIDUOUS: Ailanthus, American sycamore, Black locust, Black walnut, Catalpa, Russian mulberry.

OKLAHOMA AND TEXAS: DECIDUOUS: Chinese elm, Desertwillow, Kentucky coffeetree, Soapberry.

EVERGREEN: Arizona cypress (Texas), Loblolly pine, Shortleaf pine.

STREET TREES: DECIDUOUS: American elm, American sycamore, Boxelder, Bur oak, Green ash, Hackberry, Maples, Russian mulberry, Siberian elm.

EVERGREEN: Austrian pine, Ponderosa pine.

TREES WITH SHOWY FLOWERS: Black locust, Catalpa, Desertwillow, Hawthorn, Honeylocust.

TREES WITH SHOWY FOLIAGE IN AUTUMN: Cottonwood (yellow), Green ash (golden yellow), Maple (gold and red), Oak (yellow to red), Sycamore (clear yellow).

TREES SUITABLE FOR USE ON PHYMATOTRICHUM ROOT ROT INFECTED SOIL: DECIDUOUS: Ailanthus, Desertwillow, Hackberry, Mulberry, Soapberry.

EVERGREENS: Eastern redcedar, Rocky Mountain cedar.

## Southeastern Area

SHADE AND ROADSIDE TREES: DECIDUOUS: American beech, American elm, American sycamore, Laurel oak, Pecan, Sugarberry, Sweetgum, Water oak, Weeping willow, White oak, Willow oak, Winged elm, Yellow-poplar.

EVERGREEN: Live oak, Southern magnolia.

STREET TREES: DECIDUOUS: American elm, American sycamore, Cabbage palmetto, Common crapemyrtle, Laurel oak, Sugarberry, Sweetgum, Water oak, White oak, Willow oak, Winged elm.

EVERGREEN: Camphor-tree, Live oak, Southern magnolia.

PARK AND LAWN TREES: DECIDUOUS: American beech, American elm, American sycamore, Common crapemyrtle, Eastern redbud, Flowering dogwood, Laurel oak, Mimosa, Panicled goldenrain-tree, Pecan, Red maple, Sugarberry, Sweetgum, Water oak, Weeping willow, White oak, Willow oak, Winged elm, Yellow-poplar.

EVERGREEN: American holly, Camphor-tree, Canary date, Carolina laurel-cherry, Eastern arborvitae, Eastern redcedar, Live oak, Southern magnolia.

TREES WITH AUTUMN COLOR: DECIDUOUS: Flowering dogwood,

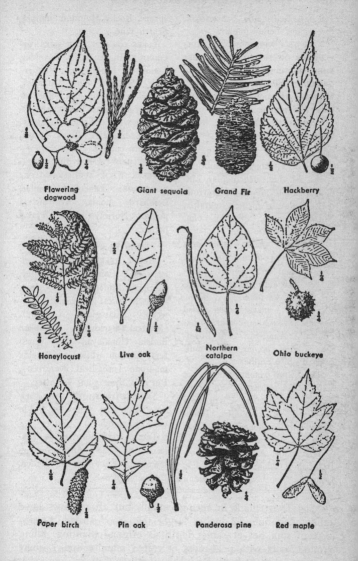

Flowering
dogwood

Giant sequoia

Grand Fir

Hackberry

Honeylocust

Live oak

Northern
catalpa

Ohio buckeye

Paper birch

Pin oak

Ponderosa pine

Red maple

Pin oak, Red maple, Scarlet oak, Sweetgum, Yellow-poplar.

TREES WITH CONSPICUOUS FLOWERS OR FRUITS: DECIDUOUS: Common crapemyrtle, Eastern redbud, Flowering dogwood, Mimosa, Panicled glodenraintree, Red maple.

EVERGREEN: American holly, Southern magnolia.

## Southern Rocky Mountain Region

STREET TREES: DECIDUOUS: Green ash, Lanceleaf poplar, Linden, London planetree, Narrowleaf poplar, Northern catalpa, Norway maple, Siberian elm, Velvet ash, White ash.

ROADSIDE TREES (see also STREET TREES): DECIDUOUS: Black locust, Lombardy poplar. EVERGREEN: Arizona cypress, Eucalyptus, Ponderosa pine.

SHADE TREES (see also STREET AND ROADSIDE TREES): DECIDUOUS: American elm, Boxelder, Plains poplar, Red mulberry, White mulberry.

PARK AND GARDEN TREES (see also STREET, ROADSIDE, AND SHADE TREES): DECIDUOUS: Common hackberry, Russian-olive, Tamarisk, Thornless honeylocust, Tree-of-Heaven ailanthus.

EVERGREEN: Aleppo pine, Austrian pine, Colorado pinyon pine, Colorado spruce, Engelmann spruce, Rocky Mountain juniper, Scotch pine.

TREES FOR DIFFICULT SITES: DECIDUOUS: Black locust, Boxelder, Common hackberry, Russianolive, Siberian elm, Tamarisk, Thornless honeylocust, Tree-of-Heaven ailanthus, Velvet ash.

TREES WITH CONSPICUOUS FLOWERS: DECIDUOUS: Black locust, Northern catalpa.

EVERGREEN: Eucalyptus.

TREES WITH AUTUMN COLOR: DECIDUOUS: Lanceleaf poplar, Lombardy poplar, Narrowleaf poplar, Norway maple, Plains poplar.

## North Pacific Coast Area

STREET TREES: American yellowwood, Common hackberry, European linden, Pin oak.

LAWN TREES: American yellowwood, Atlas-cedar (conifer), Common hackberry, European linden, Himalayan pine (conifer), Oregon white oak, Pacific madrone (broadleaf evergreen), Pin oak, Sweetgum, Tuliptree.

TREES WITH SHOWY FALL FOLIAGE: American yellowwood, Pin oak, Sweetgum.

TREES WITH SHOWY OR FRAGRANT FLOWERS: American yellowwood, European linden, Pacific madrone.

**Planting Trees:** Plant in spring or fall, but after leaves have fallen. Dig hole 12 inches larger than root spread. Loosen bottom soil. Set at same depth as original planting, filling around roots with peat-moss or rotted manure and 1 quart commercial plant food. Soak thoroughly and make depression for holding water. For winter protection, cover ground with

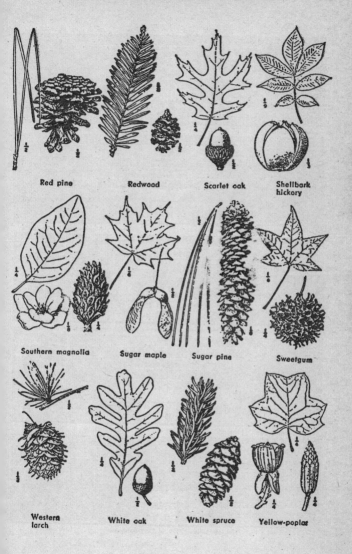

Red pine        Redwood        Scarlet oak      Shellbark
                                                hickory

Southern magnolia    Sugar maple    Sugar pine      Sweetgum

Western        White oak       White spruce     Yellow-poplar
larch

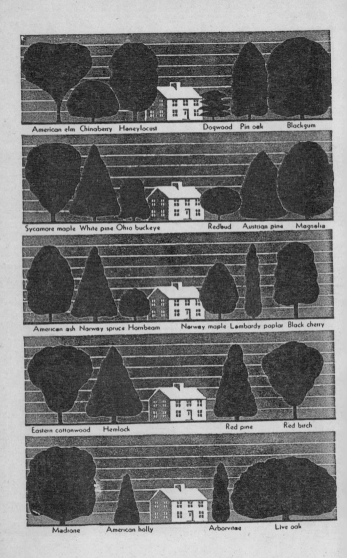

American elm   Chinaberry   Honeylocust      Dogwood   Pin oak      Blackgum

Sycamore maple   White pine   Ohio buckeye      Redbud   Austrian pine    Magnolia

American ash   Norway spruce   Hornbeam     Norway maple   Lombardy poplar   Black cherry

Eastern cottonwood    Hemlock        Red pine       Red birch

Madrone      American holly       Arborvitae     Live oak

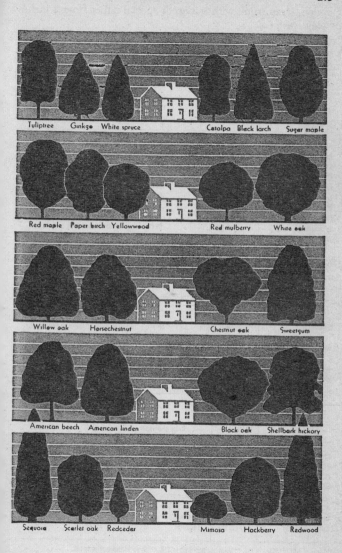

Tuliptree  Ginkgo  White spruce    Catalpa  Black larch  Sugar maple

Red maple  Paper birch  Yellowwood    Red mulberry    White oak

Willow oak    Horsechestnut    Chestnut oak    Sweetgum

American beech  American linden    Black oak    Shellbark hickory

Sequoia    Scarlet oak  Redcedar    Mimosa    Hackberry    Redwood mulch, wrap trunk with burlap or special paper from 2 inches below surface.

SMALL TREES OR LARGE SHRUBS HAVING DISTINCTIVE SHAPE, FOLIAGE, OR FLOWERS USED CHIEFLY FOR ORNAMENTAL PURPOSES:

| Shade Trees | Mature Height | Minimum Planting Distance | Remarks |
|---|---|---|---|
| Ash | 50-75 ft. | 50 ft. | Pink-purple or yellow fall color |
| Ash, Mountain | 20-30 ft. | 30 ft. | Orange-red fruit clusters in fall |
| Chinese Elm | 50-60 ft. | 30 ft. | Resistant to Dutch elm disease |
| Linden | 90-120 ft. | 50 ft. | Difficult to grow grass under |
| Locust, Honey | 60-130 ft. | 50 ft. | Light shade, thorny |
| Locust, Moraine | 80-100 ft. | 50 ft. | Grass thrives under lacy foliage |
| Maple | 90-120 ft. | 50 ft. | Difficult to grow grass under |
| Oak | 80-120 ft. | 50 ft. | Excellent lawn tree |
| Sycamore | 90-125 ft. | 50 ft. | Massive, two-tone bark |
| Walnut | 65-100 ft. | 50 ft. | Roots don't permit growth of nearby plants, other than grass |

| Decorative Trees | Mature Height | Minimum Planting Distance | Remarks |
|---|---|---|---|
| Beech | 90-100 ft. | 50 ft. | Colorful. Impractical to grow any plants under |
| Birch | 60-90 ft. | 10 ft. | Picturesque white trunk, yellow foliage in fall |
| Japanese Maple | 12-25 ft. | 10 ft. | Leaves are green to purple and red |
| Weeping Willow | 40-60 ft. | 30 ft. | Graceful silhouette on large lawn |

| Flowering Trees | Mature Height | Color of Blooms | Blooming Period | Minimum Planting Distance |
|---|---|---|---|---|
| Cherry, Plum* | 8-12 ft. | Pink | Spring | 25 ft. |
| Crabapple** | 8-15 ft. | White, pink | Spring | 25 ft. |
| Dogwood** | 15-20 ft. | White, pink | Spring | 25 ft. |
| Hawthorn** | 15-30 ft. | White, pink | Spring | 25 ft. |
| Horse Chestnut | 30-80 ft. | White, orange, red | Spring | 50 ft. |
| Magnolia — | 25-100 ft. | White, pink | Spring | 50 ft. |
| Oriental Cherry | 18-35 ft. | Pink, white | Spring | 25 ft. |
| Tulip | 40-120 ft. | Yellowish | Spring | 50 tt. |

*Show of purple foliage in fall. **Many produce fruit in fall. ***Show of red berries in fall.

There are numerous varieties of all of the trees listed above, many with widely varying growth habits. Ask the nurseryman for suggestions before planting the trees you buy.

Deciduous: Birch—Cutleaf Weeping, White; Catalpa, Dwarf; Cherry—Black, Choke, Japanese Flowering, Pin; Cockspur Thorn; Crab, Flowering, Bechtel, Double Flowering, Parkman; Crabapple, Wild; Dogwood; Hawthorn; Hoptree, Common; Japanese Lilac; Mock Orange, Sweet; Mountain Ash—American, European, Showy; Nannyberry; Ninebark, Common; Redbud; Russian Olive; Shadblow—Downy, Thicket; Siberian Pea Tree; Sumac—Shining, Shredded, Staghorn; Wahoo; Weeping Willow.

Evergreens: Arborvitae; Holly; Juniper—Chinese, Colorado, Common; Magnolia; Spruce; Yew, Japanese.

**Problems:** Defoliation is usually due to gas poisoning, though it may also be due to temperature change, shock from transplanting, or change from sunlight to darkness. If new shoots remain dwarfed, and branch repeatedly, gas injury is further indicated. Brown leaf tips suggest improper watering. In palm it may be due to root worms or improper food; with ferns, it may be due to insects. Loss of normal color may be due to over-watering, lack of food, or insects. Spotted foliage suggests over-watering or too much sunlight.

**Evergreens:** Evergreens include the narrow-leaved type known as conifers (pine, hemlock, etc.) and the broad-leaved, flowering shrubs (rhododendron, camellia, etc.). Most gardens have some of both types for the year-round green they provide.

NARROW-LEAVED EVERGREENS

Nine types of narrow-leaved evergreens most popular with American gardeners:

|  | Mature Height | Min. Planting Dist. | Average Annual Growth |
|---|---|---|---|
| Arborvitae | 35-60 ft. | 6 ft. | 8-12 in. |
| Cedar, Atlas | 40-75 ft. | 40 ft. | 2-3 ft. |
| Cypress, False | 35-75 ft. | 40 ft. | 24 in. |
| Fir, White | 30-50 ft. | 40 ft. | 2-3 ft. |
| Hemlock, Canada | 30-50 ft. | 40 ft. | 15-24 in. |
| Juniper, Dwarf (many kinds) | 4-5 ft. | 8 ft. | 5 in. |
| Pine (many kinds) | 30-50 ft. | 40 ft. | 15-24 in. |
| Spruce, Norway | 20-40 ft. | 40 ft. | 24 in. |
| Yew (many kinds) | 4-60 ft. | 10 ft. | 5-8 in. |

There are many varieties of each of the above narrow-leaved evergreens, including standard and dwarf, erect and spreading, etc. Consider the purpose for which each is intended, and ask the advice of the nurseryman from whom you buy. The minimum planting distances above are a general indication to prevent overplanting.

BROAD-LEAVED EVERGREENS:

Plants in this family are some of the most stately in the garden world. Rich green the year round, they produce mass color in season in a wide range of hues and shades.

| | Mature Height | Min. Plant Dist. | Color of Blooms | Blooming Period | Aver. Annual Growth |
|---|---|---|---|---|---|
| Andromeda, Japanese | 3-9 ft. | 3 ft. | White | Mid-April | 6 in. |
| Azalea (many kinds) | 6-12 ft. | 3 ft. | White, red, pink, salmon, violet | Spring, early summer | 4 in. |
| Boxwood | 3-20 ft. | 8 in. | insignificant | April-May | 6 in. |
| Camellia (many kinds)* | 6-30 ft. | 3 ft. | White, red, pink | Sept-Apr | 6-8 in. |
| Holly | 8-15 ft. | ** | small white | Red, black yellow berries in Fall | 8 in. |
| Leucothoe | 3-4 ft. | 4 ft. | White | Apr-May | 4-6 in. |
| Mountain Laurel | 6-12 ft. | 3 ft. | White, pink | Late May | 6 in. |
| Ligustrum | 10-15 ft. | ** | White | Late Spring | 8 in. |
| Rhododendron (many kinds) | 6-18 ft. | 5 ft. | Purple, rose, white | Spring to summer | 8 in |
| Skimmia | 1½-4 ft. | 18 in. | White | Apr-May | 4-6 in. |

* Most varieties suitable only to Southern states and Pacific coast.

** According to purpose, individual plants for decoration, plant 3 or more feet apart; for use as hedging, plant 18 inches apart.

There are numerous varieties of each of the broad-leaved evergreens listed above, many with unusual growth characteristics. Ask the nurseryman for suggestions for planting the particular plants you buy.

## FRUITS, NUTS AND BERRIES

Climatic districts: Summer and winter temperatures, rainfall, and prevalence of diseases and insects are all important in determining the fruit and nut varieties that can be grown in the different parts of the country. Varieties of each fruit differ greatly in their adaptation, but some kinds can be grown in almost every home garden.

Home-grown fruits are generally superior to market fruits because they may be grown to maturity. If only a small area is available, small fruits or dwarf trees are usually recommended. Small fruits (strawberries, grapes, currants and gooseberries) are much easier to grow than tree fruits and give the greatest return per square foot of ground. Spring planting is best in severe climates, fall planting in milder climates. Orchards require the same care as vegetable gardens.

**Planting:** Fruit trees should be planted on soil which has been under cultivation. Most suitable soil is of medium texture, to sandy loam, well fertilized. Soil should be cultivated

### COMMON FRUITS, NUTS AND BERRIES

| Type of Plant | Distances Between | | Average Age of Bearing |
|---|---|---|---|
| | Rows (ft) | Plants in Rows (ft) | |
| **FRUIT** | | | |
| Apple | 30-35 | 25-30 | 6-8 |
| Apricot | 20-25 | 10-20 | 3-4 |
| Cherry, Sour | 20-25 | 18-20 | 4 |
| Cherry, Sweet | 20-25 | 18-20 | 6-7 |
| Peach | 20-25 | 18-20 | 3-4 |
| Pear | 20-25 | 18-20 | 4-8 |
| Plum | 18-20 | 16-18 | 4-5 |
| Quince | 8-10 | 8-10 | 5-6 |
| Figs | 16-20 | 15-18 | 2-4 |
| Citrus Fruit | 25-40 | 25-40 | 5-8 |
| Crab Apples | 20-25 | 20-25 | 6-8 |
| **NUTS** | | | |
| Black Walnuts | 30-40 | 25-30 | 8-10 |
| Chinese Chestnuts | 30-40 | 25-30 | 2-6 |
| Filberts (Hazelnuts) | 20-25 | 15-20 | 4-5 |
| Hickory Nuts | 60-75 | 50-60 | 6-8 |
| Pecans | 60-75 | 50-60 | 6-8 |
| Walnuts | 30-40 | 25-30 | 3-6 |
| **SMALL FRUIT** | | | |
| Blackberry | 6-8 | 4-6 | 2-3 |
| Blueberry | 12-15 | 3-4' | 2-4 |
| Currant | 10 | 3-4' | 3-5 |
| Dewberry | 5-8 | 3-4' | 3-5 |
| Gooseberry | 10 | 3-4' | 2-4 |
| Grapes | 15-20 | 8-10' | 3-4 |
| Muscadine Grapes | 15-20 | 8-10' | 3-4 |
| Raspberry | 4-5 | 3-4 | 2-3 |
| Strawberry | 35 | 12-15" | 2-3 |

in the spring through July. A mulch of dust is important to maintain fertility and prevent weed growth. Periodic spraying with lime-sulfur or mineral oil emulsion against diseases and insects is essential in early spring. Arsenate of lead and sulfur dusts may also be used. Pruning is important to thin the fruit and thus produce larger fruit, to maintain ventilation, to remove dead wood, and to shape the tree properly. Branches which are too low should be removed (up to 2 to 3 feet); branches too close to each other should be thinned so that only one remains. Pruning should be done annually in dormant season.

Standard-size fruit trees need plenty of space—figure an area 30 feet square for each tree—in full sunshine all day. Dwarf varieties are practical and require about ⅓ less space.

Cane fruits—blackberries, raspberries, currants, gooseberries, etc.—are best planted in rows 8 feet apart, with 3 feet between plants.

You can harvest a sizable crop of strawberries in a small area, planted in rows 2½ feet apart, with 1 foot between plants.

Planting fruit trees and bushes is done in the same manner as planting trees and shrubs, except that no fertilizer is needed when planting or during the first year. Your trees and bushes will grow with little or no care, but, as the fruits are so attractive to insects and so susceptible to fungus diseases, these blights must be controlled if good, edible fruit is to be harvested. Many of these insects and diseases can be controlled if you spray your fruit trees and bushes regularly and thoroughly.

**Strawberries, Currants, Gooseberries:** Beginning with first leaf growth, spray 10 to 14 days through growing season and after heavy rains. Do not apply within 14 days before picking.

For protection against infestation by scale insects before growth starts and before starting regular spraying schedule, spray fruit trees early.

Mail orders early to a reliable nursery to secure good, true-to-name stock. Be skeptical about catalog descriptions. To facilitate replacements in case of mistakes, keep invoice and leave label on the plant.

## VEGETABLES

**Steps in Setting Up a Vegetable Garden:** (1) Select crops and varieties suitable to the climate and altitude of locality. Consider its convenience for soil preparation and cultivation. (2) Select a suitable garden location near the house to make planting easier. In making plans to plant part of the vegetables with the field crops, remember that certain ones may be attacked by rabbits, ground squirrels, field mice (carrots, cantaloupe, soy beans, parsnips, and salsify), birds (popcorn and sweet corn) or other wildlife. Soil type is less important than convenience in determining location. Most vegetables make satisfactory growth and yield on a wide variety of soil types.

Measure the area that you wish to set aside for vegetables and lay it out on paper. Select the vegetables you wish to plant. Study the chart on the following pages. This will tell you how much space you need for each crop, how long each will require to harvest, how much of each you can expect to harvest, and other crops you can plant when the first harvest is past.

(3) If a majority of the rows are spread 3 feet to 3½ feet apart, a well-kept ¼ to ⅓ acre garden should provide an ample supply of vegetables for the average family (two adults and three children). A dry land garden must be considerably larger than an irrigated one if it is to supply an equal quantity of vegetables. (4) Fertilize with animal manure, if available. Apply before ground is plowed or before the duck-foot cultivator is used. The two most commonly used soil amendments are lime and sulfur. Lime should be used only on acid soils to neutralize organic acids and to improve soil structure by making it less dense or compact.

(5) For tomatoes, peppers, eggplant, cabbage, cauliflower, and other long-season crops to make satisfactory yields, the plants should be started indoors and transplanted to the garden after danger of frost is past. When relatively few plants of each crop are to be grown, as for the home garden, the seed may be sown in shallow boxes, or flats. Any box that is moderately tight and 2 to 3 inches deep is satisfactory. It should be filled within about ½ inch of the top with good garden soil. The soil selected should not contain much manure or other organic matter, because organisms that cause seedling diseases may be present in such materials. A sandy soil or a

FACTS FOR PLANT-

| | Time to Plant (1) | Days to Maturity | Planting Depth | | Distance Apart |
|---|---|---|---|---|---|
| | | | Seeds | Plants | |
| Artichoke (Globe) | Apr | 160 | ½" | 4" | 48" |
| Artichoke (Jerusalem) | Mar | 120 | 3" | | 20" |
| Asparagus | Mar | 3-4 yrs. | 4" | 10" | 16" |
| Snap Beans (pole) | Apr | 70-95 | ½" | | 3" |
| Lima Beans (pole) | Apr-June | 75-90 | 1" | | 8" |
| Snap Beans (bush) | Apr | 55-70 | | | 4" |
| Lima Beans (bush) | Apr | 55-70 | | | 4" |
| Beets | Mar-July | 65-80 | ½" | | 3" |
| Broccoli | Mar-July | 100-120 | ¼" | 4" | 18" |
| Brussels Sprouts | Apr-July | 60-85 | ¼" | 3" | 20" |
| Cabbage | Apr-June | 60-110 | ½" | 3" | 18-24" |
| Chinese Cabbage | Apr-July | 80-90 | ½" | | 16" |
| Carrots | Apr-July | 65-75 | ¼" | | 2" |
| Cauliflower | Apr or June | 55-75 | ¼" | | 20" |
| Celery | Apr or June | 110-130 | 1/16" | | 6" |
| Knob Celery (Celeriac, Root Celery) | July | 60-70 | 1/16" | | 6" |
| Chard | Mar-Apr | 50-65 | | ¾" | 12" |
| Chicory | June | 95 | ¼" | | 3" |
| Chives | Mar-Apr | 60-90 | ¼" | 12" | 2" |
| Collards | Mar or July | 80-100 | ¼" | | 18" |
| Cucumbers | Mar-Apr | 60-80 | ½" | | 36" |
| Dandelion | Mar-Sept | 70 | ¼" | | 8" |
| Eggplant | Mar-Apr | 85-130 | ⅓" | | 48" |
| Endive | Mar or Aug | 75-90 | ⅓" | | 12" |
| Garlic | Mar | 90 | 1-2" | 2" | 4" |
| Horseradish | Mar | 125 | 2" | 4" | 18" |
| Kale | Mar-July | 60-90 | ½" | | 4" |
| Leeks | Mar or Sept | 100 | ⅓" | | 5" |
| Lettuce | Mar or Aug | 40-50 | ¼" | | 15" |
| Muskmelon (Cantaloupe) | After frost | 80-115 | ½" | | 14" |
| Mustard Greens | Mar-July | 40 | ⅓" | | 7" |
| Okra (Gumbo) | Mar | 65-110 | 1" | | 15" |
| Onions | Mar | 55 | ½" | | 2" |
| Parsley | Mar-Apr | 70-75 | ⅓" | | 2" |
| Parsnips | Mar-Apr | 100-140 | ½" | | 3" |
| Peas | Mar | 50-60 | 1" | | 1" |
| Peppers | | 70-115 | ½" | | 20" |
| Popcorn | | 100-120 | | | |
| Potatoes | Mar-Apr | 115 | 4" | | 10" |
| Pumpkins | Mar-July | 65-115 | 1" | | 80" |
| Radishes | Apr-Sept | 25-50 | ½" | | 1" |
| Rhubarb | Mar-Apr | 365-730 | 4" | | 48" |
| Spinach | Mar-Aug | 50-75 | ½" | | 1" |
| Squash (Summer) | Mar | 55-90 | ½" | | 48" |
| Squash (Hubbard) | June | 95-125 | hills | | 84" |
| Sweet Corn | Mar-June | 85 | 1" | | 15" |
| Sweet Potatoes | After frost | 120 | 2-3" | 3" | 16" |
| Tomatoes (not staked) | Mar-Sept | 80-115 | ½" | | 48" |
| Tomatoes (staked) | Mar-Sept | 80-115 | ½" | | 24" |
| Turnips | Mar-Sept | 55-80 | ⅛" | | 2" |
| Watercress | Mar-Apr | | | ¼" | 12" |
| Watermelon | Apr | 90-125 | 1" | | 96" |

1) In Zone N. Subtract 15 days for each 50 miles south.

**ING VEGETABLES**

| Inches Between Rows | Average Yield per 100 ft. Row | Seed per 100 ft. Rows | Growing Conditions Comments |
|---|---|---|---|
| 48 | 250 buds | 25 plants | Grows 3-4 years. Cannot stand cold winters. |
| 36 | 3 bushels | 60 tubers | Best in well-drained rich soil. |
| 30 | 30 lbs. | 75 roots | Plant 1-year old root. Fertile well-drained loam. |
| 30 | 80 quarts | 1/4 lb. | Any soil where nutrients are available. |
| 30 | 80 quarts | 1/4 lb. | Tender. Injured by cold. |
| 28 | 80 quarts | 3/4 lb. | Very tender. |
| 28 | 80 quarts | 3/4 lb. | Tender. |
| 16 | 150 lbs. | 1 oz. | Easy to grow. Will not grow well in acid soil. |
| 30 | 45 heads | 10¢ packet | Same as for cabbage. |
| 30 | 30 quarts | 10¢ packet | Deep cultivation. |
| 30 | 45 heads | 1 oz. | Deep cultivation. Rich well-drained soil. Sow in cold frames or flats for 5-8 weeks. |
| 24 | 100 heads | 1 packet | |
| 15 | 2 bushels | 1/2 oz. | |
| 30 | 60 heads | 70 plants | See cabbage. Cool-weather crop. |
| 28 | 200 stalks | 10¢ packet | Rich. Sweet soil. |
| 28 | 200 roots | 200 plants | Only roots are edible. Rich moist soil. |
| 24 | 50 plants | 10¢ packet | Sow in flats. Well-drained soil. Plant where it is to grow. |
| 24 | 2 1/2 bushels | 1/2 oz. | See carrots. |
| 28 | 80 clumps | 1/2 oz. | Perennial. Replant clumps in Spring. |
| 30 | 4 bushels | 1/4 oz. | See cabbage. |
| 60 | 1 1/2 bushels | 1/2 oz. | Tender. Cannot stand frost. |
| 14 | 2 1/2 bushels | 10¢ packet | Cultivated varieties excel wild. |
| 48 | 125 fruit | 40 plants | Set 6-8 weeks in holes. Rich, moist soil. |
| 20 | 65 plants | 1/4 oz. | Hardy. 3 weeks in seed bed. |
| 24 | 10 lbs. | 1 lb. | Hardy. Plant bulblets. Nitrogen fertilizer. |
| 36 | 30 lbs. | 70 roots | Perennial. Propagate from roots. |
| 20 | 80 quarts | 1 packet | Cannot stand extreme cold. Similar to cabbage. |
| 18 | 200 plants | 1/2 oz. | When plants are 8" tall cut tops and transplant. |
| 16 | 80 heads | 10¢ packet | Sow seeds in flats for 4 weeks, then transplant. Require 58°F., high humidity. |
| 60 | 80 melons | 1/2 oz. | Will not withstand frost. |
| 15 | 4 bushels | 10¢ packet | Best in rich moist soil. |
| 30 | 800 pods | 1/2 oz. | Cannot stand cold. |
| 15 | 1 1/2 bushels | 1/2 oz. | Plant from seeds, sets or young plants. |
| 16 | 90 bunches | 1/4 oz. | Hardy. |
| 18 | 2 bushels | 1/2 oz. | Thin plants to 4 in. apart when young. |
| 18 | 1 bushel | 1 lb. | Light soils or well-drained heavier soils. |
| 36 | 4 bushels | 70 plants | Plant in flats for 5 weeks. |
| 28 | 2-4 bushels | 10¢ packet | Well-drained soil. |
| 30 | 2 1/2 bushels | 1/2 peck | Fertile, well-drained, fairly acid soil. Plant potato pieces with at least one good eye. |
| 60 | 40 heads | 1/2 oz. | Rich, cultivated, well-drained soil. Tender. |
| 12 | 100 bunches | 1/2 oz. | |
| 48 | 200 stems | 25 roots | Perennial. Plant roots. Divide after 5 years. |
| 14 | 3 bushels | 1/2 oz. | Add nitrogen when plants are 1/3 grown. |
| 48 | 400 | 1 oz. | Plant in hills or warm rich well-drained soil. |
| 48 | 100 | 1/2 oz. | |
| 30 | 120 ears | 1/4 lb. | Rich in "milk" state. Tender. |
| 30 | 1 1/2 bushels | 80 plants | Propagate from sprouts. Sandy soil 2-8-10 fertilizer. |
| 48 | 4 bushels | 10¢ packet | Fertile, well-drained soil. Sow in boxes 8 weeks before transplanting. Stakes should be 1 1/2" in diameter, 6" long. |
| 36 | 4 bushels | 51 plants | Tender. |
| 16 | 2 bushels | 1/4 oz. | Hardy—Prefers cold weather. |
| 24 | 100 bunches | 10¢ packet | Requires abundant moisture. Perennial. |
| 96 | 15 melons | 1/2 oz. | Tender, sandy loam soil. |

sandy loam is better than a clay one. After the seed has germinated and the young seedlings are showing their first true leaves, they should be transplanted.

(6) Regardless of how the plants have been started, they should be hardened before they are set in the garden. This is commonly accomplished by withholding water and gradually lowering the temperature until the plants are somewhat checked in growth.

## HERBS COMMONLY USED

| Herbs | Use | Comments |
|---|---|---|
| Anise | flavoring, seasoning | Annuals: at 3″ thin plants to 14″ apart |
| Basil | flavoring vegetable juice, soups, salads | Biennial, produces seeds 2nd year. Grows well in house. |
| Beebalm | scent | Perennial. Hardy. |
| Borage—flowers leaves | garnish, salads, claret cup | Annual, Perennial. |
| Caraway | flavoring | Biennial. |
| Catnip | cooking, cats | Tends to become a weed. |
| Chives | salads, pot cheese | Perennial. Ornamental edging plants |
| Coriander | flavoring bread | Annual. Gather seeds before they scatter. |
| Cress | mustard, salads | Requires running water. |
| Dill | pickling | Annual. Yellow flower. |
| Fennel | garnish, fish sauce | Perennial. |
| Horehound | seasoning, cough remedy | Perennial. Grows in poor soil. |
| Horseradish | fish | Perennial. |
| Lavender | scent, sachets | Propagated by cuttings. Needs mild climate. |

| Herbs | Use | Comments |
|-------|-----|----------|
| Lemon Verbena | scent, tea | Annual. Grows well in house. |
| Mint | tea, sauces, scent | Perennial. It overruns a garden. |
| Mustard | garnish, salads | Annual. Needs rich soil. |
| Parsley | potatoes, chops | Biennial |
| Peppermint | flavoring | Perennial. Grows well in house. |
| Rosemary | meats, chicken | Propagates by cuttings. |
| Rue | bitter, pungent seasoning | Perennial. Tea gives headache relief. |
| Sage | dressing, vegetables, poultry | Perennial. |
| Summer Savory | vegetable seasoning | Annual. Aromatic. |
| Sweet Basil | aromatic seasoning | Annual. Grows from seed. |
| Tarragon | vinegar, salads | Perennial. Grows well in house. |
| Thyme | seasoning sandwiches, salads | Good as an edging plant. |
| Verbena | with mint leaves for tea | Flowers. Start indoors in March. |
| Winter Savory | flavoring | Perennial. |

Mushroom-growing in a basement area at room temperature is a practical operation. Small packaged culture stands are sold so that only water need be added to produce four or five crops.

## HOW TO PROPAGATE PLANTS

**Steps in growing ornamental planting material:** (1) Prepare for production of plant materials. Provide an outdoor space near the house where the soil is fertile, where ample protection can be given, and where there is the least chance for damage to the plants. Set aside an indoor space in the cellar or root house. Make or secure several indoor planting flats, germination boxes, hotbeds, and cold frames. (Cold frames are bottomless boxes with glass tops used to protect plants. A hotbed has a heating device in the box.) Assemble supplies, including sand, leaf mold, fine, fertile topsoil, fertilizers, special tools and other necessary materials. Study the reproductive habits of the plants to be propagated and select the procedure that is recommended by horticultural authorities or that appears to be most likely to be successful.

(2) PROPAGATE BY SEEDS: For plants which can be propagated by seed, collect or obtain fresh-ripened mature seeds. Cut open several seeds to see if kernel is plump and likely to germinate. Seeds in fruits or with pulpy covering are mature when fruit is ripe or well colored. Store seed according to recommendations of authorities for that particular type or variety. Seeds with hard seed coats such as many of the nuts, fruits with hard shelled pits, and many others germinate very slowly and may not come up until the second year without special treatment. One such treatment is called "stratification." Seeds requiring "stratification" are placed in layers in boxes of moist sand as soon as gathered and stored in a damp cool cellar until spring. The sand should be kept damp but not watersoaked. Plant the seed in proper season in flats indoors, in hotbeds, in outdoor beds, or in the places where they are to grow. Where to start the seeds depends upon the type and variety of plant, the climatic conditions of the locality, and the need for quick results. When seedlings are of proper size transplant in outdoor hotbed, cold frame, or in places where they are to continue growth.

If you make a practice of saving flower or vegetable seed from growing season to growing season, place dry, clean seed in plastic-wrap squares of appropriate size. Be sure to seal all edges tightly to exclude air.

Label wrapped seed and place in an envelope to exclude light. The plastic wrap will keep mice from eating stored seed and will, furthermore, increase future germination by maintaining higher humidity inside the wrap.

Chinese Air-Layering: Practically any type of woody shrub, tree or house plant can be propagated by Chinese air-layering.

(1) Use a sharp knife to make a slanting cut (upward) halfway through a healthy stem. Try to cut through a node.

Insert a toothpick or wooden match in the cut to keep it open. Cover cut with a handful of moistened sphagnum moss. Use waxed cord to spiral twist around the moss to hold it in place.

(2) Cover moss with a piece of plastic wrap large enough to extend beyond moss ball. Seal flat edge but twist plastic wrap around stem above and below moss. Seal twisted ends. Continue to water and fertilize plant. Moss should not dry out, but if you do see moss drying, untwist upper end of plastic-wrap cover and add more water to moss.

Once white roots are seen through plastic-wrap cover, the cover may be removed carefully. The rooted cutting can then be cut from parent plant and potted into a soil-filled container—or planted directly into the garden.

It is likely that the parent plant will send out side shoots just below the cut.

(3) PROPAGATE BY CUTTINGS: A cutting is a detached portion of a plant which when inserted in soil or water will send out roots and leaves, thus producing a new plant. Stem cuttings are most commonly used for the majority of plants, although leaf cuttings and root cuttings are most suitable for certain species. Stem cuttings may be: (a) softwood or herbaceous cuttings, made from immature wood or current growth, usually started under glass in summer; (b) hardwood or dormant cuttings, made from previous season's growth during dormant period.

Softwood cuttings: For herbaceous perennials such as geraniums, coleus, etc., take "slips" or portions of branches containing two or more nodes with leaves attached. Remove most of the large leaves. These slips may be taken at any season. Place in water as soon as cut, then transfer promptly to moist sand. For woody plants such as forsythia, crape myrtle, rose, spirea, etc., take cuttings from the new growth that follows the blooming period. Make cuttings 3 to 4 inches long with the lower end cut through a leaf joint. Remove leaves except one or two at top. Place in water as soon as cut, then transfer to moist sand. Plant cuttings upright in wet clean sand, as soon as possible after cutting, in specially prepared boxes indoors, or in greenhouse beds or in hotbeds or cold frames. Pack the sand tightly about the plants. Keep cuttings closely covered with glass and partially shaded to prevent rapid drying and keep sand well moistened. When roots have started, exposure to air may be made gradually to prevent disease developing. Transplant cuttings to larger space when growth is well started. Evergreen cuttings should be made with special care, taking tip branches 3 to 8 inches long. With many plants these shoots should be stripped from their branches so that the base of the cutting includes a "heel" of older wood. Cuttings should be made in the summer when the season's growth is maturing. Evergreens start very slowly, and the cuttings should be well protected during the winter.

(1) HARDWOOD CUTTINGS: Make cuttings during dormant period in early winter, before freezing. Take straight portions of previous season's growth 5 to 8 inches long, including at least two or more buds. Cut the lower end through or just below a bud. Tie cuttings in small bundles for convenience in handling. Pack the bundles in damp moss, sawdust, or sand and store in a cool damp place where they will not freeze during the winter. They may be buried outdoors in a well-drained place if protected from freezing. Keep well dampened but not soaked during winter. Plant the cuttings in the open, early in the spring before growth starts. Prepare fine, well-drained soil. Set cuttings in rows deep enough so that the top bud is at the ground level. Keep well cultivated during the summer. Root and top growth should start and plants should be ready to transplant by the following fall or the next spring.

(2) LEAF CUTTINGS: Some herbaceous plants with thick fleshy leaves, such as begonias, may be started from leaf cuttings. A whole leaf or part of a leaf, which has reached its full development and is in healthy vigorous condition may be used. Insert stem and lower portion in a sand flat, pack sand well, keep well moistened and covered with glass. Some kinds may be pegged flat on the ground.

(3) ROOT CUTTINGS: Root cuttings are usually successful for such plants as apple, cherry, hawthorn, plum, pear, blackberry, some roses, and many other plants which have a tendency to send up suckers readily. Plants from which root cuttings are to be made should be taken up in the fall and stored or heeled-in to keep the roots in good condition. These trees may be reset after the cuttings have been taken. Make cuttings about 3 inches in length from healthy roots from ¼ to ½ inch in diameter. Store in manner similar to hardwood cuttings for few weeks before planting. Set out cuttings in spring in well prepared soil. Leaf buds develop on the end of

the root nearest the parent tree; set out cuttings with this end up.

(4) PROPAGATE BY LAYERING: Layering consists of covering branches or shoots with soil so that they will develop roots while still attached to the parent plant. These newly rooted parts are then severed and treated as new plants. This method is suitable for many types of plants that do not start readily from cuttings, and is simple and easy.

TIP LAYERING: Bend the tip of a branch or cane to the ground. Cover lightly with soil to hold in contact with the damp soil. Roots will develop and a new plant start. The black raspberry is a common example. Sever when well started.

TIP LAYERING

MOUND LAYERING

Examples of tip and mound layering.

VINE LAYERING: Stretch a vine or branch along the ground in the spring before growth starts. Bury it in a shallow trench or cover it well at various points, leaving the rest exposed. Roots will be sent out at these covered points. When well started the vine may be cut apart and each portion handled as a new plant. This is not ordinarily advisable until the following spring.

MOUND OR STOOL LAYERING: This method is suitable for plants that stool freely. Select a healthy vigorous parent plant. Before growth starts in the spring prune it back very severely close to the ground level. When new shoots have started, draw up earth making a mound about the base of the stems. As growth continues, increase the size of the mound. New roots will be formed on these shoots, which can be cut apart and treated as new plants during the fall or following spring.

(5) PROPAGATE BY CROWN OR ROOT DIVISION: This is a

common method of propagating herbaceous perennials and other plants having a tendency to stool and spread. It is similar in effect to mound layering. When plants are dug they may be

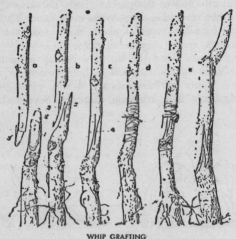

WHIP GRAFTING
The various steps followed in whip grafting.

separated easily into several portions, each having stems or leaves with some roots, which will grow independently if properly planted and cared for.

(6) PROPAGATE BY GRAFTING AND BUDDING: Grafting and budding are methods of propagating many fruit trees and ornamental trees whose seeds do not reproduce true to type or whose cuttings do not root easily, or of establishing plants that are not hardy or adapted to soil and climate. It consists of uniting two parts of different plants of the same or closely related species so that the desired portion, the "scion," develops as the top portion of the plant, while the "stock" or parent plant furnishes the root system. Grafting should be done during the dormant period. Budding is done in the summer after the buds have matured. Many types of grafting and budding are in use. Only the simplest and most common types are considered here.

WHIP OR TONGUE GRAFT: Prepare the scion by selecting smooth straight twigs one season old that have made vigorous growth. Cut in late fall or early winter, 4 to 8 inches long with at least 3 buds. Cut lower and diagonally with single stroke of knife, making a flat surface ¾ to 1¼ inches long. Make a cleft in the cut surface, starting a little back from the tip of the twig and running about half its length to form a thin tongue. Prepare the root stock from roots dug in the fall. Keep stored in moist cool place. Select healthy vigorous roots of approximately the same size as the scion. Cut into 4 to 6 inch lengths. Trim off side roots, leaving stubs. Cut top end of stock in same manner as the scion, including the cleft, so that the two pieces may be fitted together. Unite the scion and stock by pushing the two ends together so that the tongues are interlocked and fit together smoothly. The bark should be in close contact at least on one side. Wrap the joint with raffia or cotton thread which has been dipped in melted wax. Pack the grafts in moist sand or sawdust and store in a damp cool place until spring. Set out grafts in spring in nursery rows and keep cultivated until ready for transplanting.

CLEFT GRAFT: This graft is used for grafting in the open, such as top-working trees, especially when small scions are to be joined to larger branches. Cleft grafting should be done in late winter or early spring while the plants are dormant. Prepare scions from previous season's growth long enough to

### CLEFT GRAFT

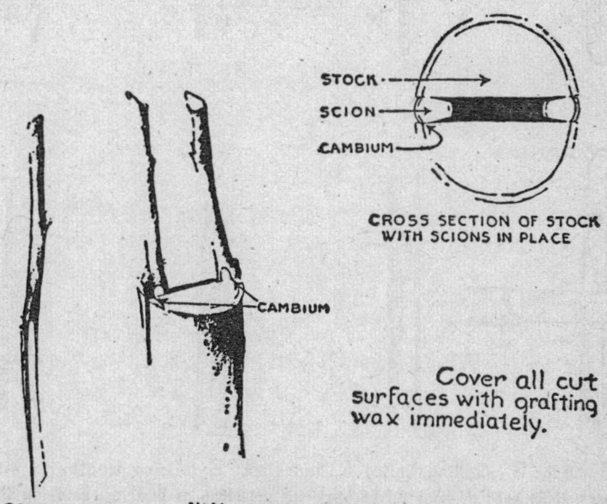

STOCK
SCION
CAMBIUM

CROSS SECTION OF STOCK
WITH SCIONS IN PLACE

CAMBIUM

Cover all cut surfaces with grafting wax immediately.

SCION          Making a cleft graft.

have 2 to 3 good buds. Cut lower end in the shape of a wedge about ¾ to 1¼ inches long, with one edge thicker than the other. Cut so the lowest bud will be just at the top of this wedge. Prepare stock by sawing the branch off squarely without loosening the bark. Split the exposed end with a thin chisel or grafting tool and hold the cleft open while the scions are being inserted. Insert the scion into the cleft of the branch, with the thicker side of the wedge outside so that its bark is held in close contact with the bark of the branch when the cleft closes upon it. If stock is large enough, a scion should be set on each side of the cleft. Both scions should be of the same size so they will both be held in place when the cleft is closed. Cover the end of the branch and all cut surfaces with grafting wax.

BUDDING: Budding consists of using a single bud for a scion.

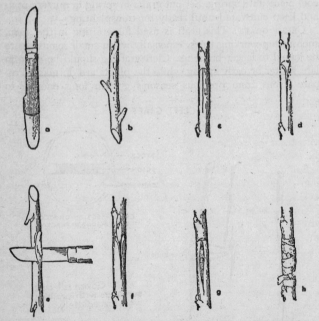

Budding: *a*, budding knife; *b*, bud stick; *c*, incision lengthwise with cross cut at top; *d*, opening of bark for insertion of bud; *e*, removing the bud; *f*, inserting the bud; *g*, bud inserted; *h*, tying in the bud.

It is in common use for a great many fruit and ornamental plants. Budding should be done when the bark slips easily and buds are fully developed. Select buds from wood of the current season's growth. Those near the middle of the twig are best. Buds near the end of the twig are apt to be immature. Slice the bud from the twig so that a shield-shaped portion of the bark with a thin shaving of wood is attached. This is the scion. A portion of the petiole or leaf stem should be left attached to serve as a handle for putting the bud into position. Stock to be budded should be at least as thick as a lead pencil, ordinarily 1 to 2 years old. Make a cut in the bark of the stock near the ground in the shape of a letter T with the top slightly dropped at the ends. The first cut should be made lengthwise of the stem; then with a rolling movement of the knife make the crescent-shaped crosscut. Raise the flaps of bark carefully along the cut edges with the knife. Insert the bud into the crosscut, pushing it down under the bark until it fits smoothly and snugly. Cut off any of the shield which projects above the crosscut. Tie the bud in place by wrapping with raffia, cotton thread, or strips of muslin that have been dipped in melted wax. Remove bandages when tissues have united within a few weeks or at least by the following spring. When growth starts in the spring cut off the stock just above the newly placed bud. Remove all side buds or sprouts which appear below the grafted bud.

CUTTING TENT: A tent of plastic wrap over plant cuttings will speed up rooting processes by retaining moisture inside the enclosure.

Rooting media will not require too frequent watering but, more important, humidity will be kept at a constant high level. This factor will help retain cutting foliage.

To make the tent, bend a wire coat hanger—or any stout wire—into a simple tent framework. Stretch plastic wrap over framework and seal all edges after cuttings have been stuck into the media.

Tent may be periodically loosened to admit air and to remoisten media when necessary.

A PLANT SITTER: Plastic wrap can baby-sit for your house plants while you are on vacation.

To keep pot soil from drying out while you are away, wrap clay pot—or other types of containers—in a large sheet of plastic wrap. Smooth wrap to pot sides, gather up excess wrap at top, and "clinch" loosely around plant base. Do not seal off soil surface completely, as plant roots need some air.

If you water the soil thoroughly before you use the wrap and then place the wrapped pot in a semishaded and cool spot, soil moisture should be optimum for several weeks.

## PEST CONTROL

**Necessity of pest control by the gardener:** The control of the insects and diseases that affect crops is essential to production.

In handling, mixing, and applying poisonous insecticides and fungicides, wear a respirator that protects the entire face. After working with insecticides, wash the hands or any exposed parts of the body thoroughly. Containers in which these materials are kept or stored should be plainly labeled and placed under lock and key.

Unless the poison residues can and will be removed by washing or stripping, do not apply to an edible crop any spray, dust, solution, or bait that contains such materials as paris green, calcium arsenate, cryolite, barium fluosilicate, sodium fluosilicate, sodium fluoride, tartar emetic, corrosive sublimate, calomel, or DDT, when foliage or fruit that is intended to be eaten is on the plants. Apply all chemicals as sparingly as is consistent with effective control. Apply a light, even coating. Some of these (e.g., DDT) should not be used for any purpose.

**General methods of insect control:** Small seedlings may be protected from insects, excepting those living in the soil, by covering the plants with an inverted glass jar or completely covering them with a light paper or muslin hood, about 8 inches in diameter, supported by wire or wooden hoops and sealed to the ground by covering the edge of the hood with soil. Hand-picking of the larger beetles, caterpillars, and plant bugs will often give satisfactory control in a small garden and eliminate the need for applying insecticides. Hand-picking is most effective if begun early enough to catch the first insects attracted to the vegetables.

GOOD GARDEN PRACTICES: The methods of gardening essential to the production of good crops are also an aid in disease control. These practices include (1) the use of fertile, well-drained soils; (2) the proper application of fertilizers of a type suited to the soil and crop; (3) the planting of crops suited to the soil and climate; and (4) clean cultivation.

SANITATION: At the end of the season all diseased crop refuse, including the roots, should be disposed of by burning. Do not compost the remains of diseased plants. Obtain disease-free seed. Where certified seed is available, as with tomatoes and potatoes, endeavor to obtain it. Cabbage, cauliflower, bean, and pea seed grown in the far West is ordinarily free from certain disease-producing organisms. Never save seed from decayed or spotted fruits or from wilted plants. Resistant varieties offer the most effective means of disease control, but such varieties are as yet available in the case of only a few diseases of certain crops. Chemical seed treatment is used for two purposes: (1) protection against decay of seed in the soil and the damping-off of small seedlings, and (2) the disinfection of the seed to kill any parasite fungi or bacteria that may be present on its surface.

DDT is poisonous to higher animals and man and therefore its usage in the garden on leafy vegetables is prohibited. A dust mixture containing nicotine sulphate is effective against the Colorado potato beetle, the potato flea beetle, potato and bean leafhopper, cabbage looper, the imported cabbage worm, the diamondback moth larva, and some species of cutworms which feed on the foliage of cabbage. A higher strength of dust will be needed for the control of aphids on potatoes and thrips on onions.

## GENERAL PLANT PESTS

For fast diagnosis and cure, use this chart:

| Symptom | Trouble | Cure |
|---------|---------|------|
| Curling leaves | Aphids | Nicotine sulphate |
| Yellowing leaves | Aphids or leaf hoppers | Nicotine sulphate |
| Leaves eaten away between veins | Tomato hornworm or blister beetle | Calcium arsenate dust |
| Irregular holes | Cabbage worm Cabbage looper Asiatic beetle or Japanese beetle | Rotenone Pyrethrum Lead arsenate and flour Chlordane |

| Symptom | Trouble | Cure |
|---------|---------|------|
| Holes or small rusty spots | Flea beetle | DDT |
| White fuzzy growth or dark spots | Leaf spot or mildew | Bordeaux |
| Sudden wilting, with holes and "sawdust" | Bores | Inject pyrethrum solution |
| Cut stalks at or below ground | Cutworm | Poison bait |

## INSECT ENEMIES OF VEGETABLES
### DESCRIPTION AND CONTROL SUGGESTIONS

The numeral in parenthesis ( ) indicates approximate enlargement. The bracketed numerals [] indicate the chemical treatment. (See pp. 240.) U indicates application on the under side of leaves. *Avoid poisonous sprays when edible portions have formed.*

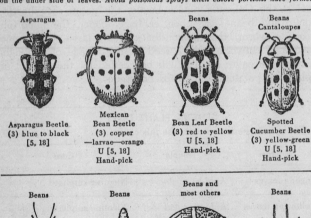

Asparagus

Beans

Beans

Beans
Cantaloupes

Asparagus Beetle
(3) blue to black
[5, 18]

Mexican
Bean Beetle
(3) copper
—larvae—orange
U [5, 18]
Hand-pick

Bean Leaf Beetle
(3) red to yellow
U [5, 18]
Hand-pick

Spotted
Cucumber Beetle
(3) yellow-green
U [5, 18]
Hand-pick

Beans

Beans

Beans and
most others

Beans

Leafhopper
(7) green
U [21]

Seed Corn Maggot
(3) white, legless
Replant

Aphids
(3) small, black
plant lice
[17 or 12]

Red Spiders
(24)
red
sulphur dust

| Beans and many others | Beets | Broccoli, Brussels Sprouts | Cabbage |
|---|---|---|---|
|  |  |  |  |
| Flea Beetles (9) black or striped [18, 5] | Beet Webworm larvae (½) green to brown [19] | Cabbage Caterpillars green before edible parts appear [form 15, 1, or 2 after 18 or 15] | Harlequin Bug (2) red or yellow Hand-pick |

| Cabbage | Cantaloupe and Cucumber | Cantaloupe, Cucumber | Carrots and Parsnips |
|---|---|---|---|
|  |  |  |  |
| Maggots (3) white, legless [13] | Striped Cucumber Beetle (4) yellow and black [15 or 18] | Melon Worm (1) white, green before fruit forms [15 once a week after 18] | Carrot Caterpillar (½) green with black and yellow markings Hand-pick |

| Carrots | Celery | Eggplant | Eggplant |
|---|---|---|---|
|  |  |  |  |
| Carrot Rust (3) Fly Maggot white naphthalene | Celery Leaf Tier (1) green [19, repeat in ½ hour] | Colorado Potato Beetle (2) yellow and black [16, 14, 15, 3, 1] | Hornworm (1/5) green, diagonal lines Hand-pick |

Lettuce

Loopers
(½) green, soft-
bodied
clustered on leaves
[18 or 19]

Onions

Thrips
(15) yellow, small
[4 or 11, 12]

Okra

Corn Earworm
(½) green or
brownish
Hand-pick

Peas, Garden

Weevil
(3) brownish with
white, black or
gray marks
[18]

Peas, Black-eye

Cowpea curculio
(3) black beetle
[2 or 15. Do not
apply within 2
weeks before
picking]

Pepper

Hornworm
(1/5) green with
horn on rear end
Hand-pick

Potato

Colorado
Potato Beetle
(2) yellow and
black striped
[16, 14, 15, 3,
1, 2]

Potato

Blister Beetle
(1) gray or black
[15, 2]

Potato

Potato
Tuber Worm
(2) pinkish-white
cultivation

Rhubarb

Rhubarb curculio
(2) yellow, large
Hand-pick

Squash and
Pumpkin

Squash Bug
(1) brown, flat
backed
Hand-pick, trap

Squash and
Pumpkin

Squash Borer
(1) white
Puncture worms

Strawberry

Strawberry

Strawberry

Strawberry

**Strawberry Weevil**
(8) brown with black spots cryolite and sulphur

**Red Spider**
(24) red sulphur

**Leaf Beetle**
(7) black to red sulphur

**Root Weevil**
(3) brown, black poison bait

Sweet Corn

Sweet Corn

Sweet Potato

Sweet Potato

**Corn Earworm**
(1) green or brown striped mineral oil

**European Corn Borer**
(1) pink and brown
[5, 18]

**Weevil**
(4) antlike beetle
[1 or 14 at 10 day intervals]

**Tortoise Beetles**
(3) yellow
[15]

Tomato

Tomato

Tomato

Turnip

**Tomato Fruitworm**
(½) green or brown striped
[15, 25, at 2 wk. intervals]

**Hornworm**
(1/5) green Hand-pick

**Aphids**
(3) small, green
[17, 4]

**Flea Beetles**
(12) black striped
[18, 5]

GENERAL FEEDERS

Ants
(3) various
special
preparations

Cutworms
(⅔) gray
[24]

Grasshoppers
(⅔) green, brown
[24]

Japanese Beetle
(2) metallic
green
hydrated lime

Millipedes
(⅔) brown, gray
[24, 6]

Mole Crickets
(½) brown
[26]

Slugs and Snails
(½) black, shiny
[8, 24]

Sowbugs
(1) gray
[4, 6]

Vegetable Weevil
(2½) grayish
brown
[28, 1, 2, 15]

White Grubs
(⅔) white,
light yellow
only prevention

Wireworms
(⅔) yellow, white
crude naphthalene

## HOW TO PREPARE INSECTICIDES AND FUNGICIDES FOR
## GARDEN-PEST CONTROL

Insecticides: The following formulas and directions are given
for the preparation of spray and dust mixtures and poisoned
baits needed for the control of the more common insects and
related pests attacking vegetables in farm, suburban, city,

and community gardens. Small measures are given for each of the ingredients in order to guide the gardener in preparing small quantities of the finished insecticide. These are poisons and should be exposed with extreme care to avoid human contact and contact with animal pets.

#### Spray mixture 1: Calcium Arsenate:

Calcium arsenate ............1 ounce (5 level tablespoonfuls)
Hydrated lime ................3 ounces
Water ...............................1 gallon

#### Spray mixture 2: Cryolite:

Cryolite ...........................1 ounce (8 level teaspoonfuls)
Water ...............................1 gallon
Do not use lime or Bordeaux mixture with cryolite.

#### Spray mixture 3: Paris Green:

Paris green .......................2 level teaspoonfuls
Hydrated lime ................3 level tablespoonfuls
Water ...............................1 gallon

#### Spray mixture 4: Nicotine Sulfate:

Nicotine sulfate
   (40 percent) ................1 tablespoonful
Soap (mild laundry
   type) ...........................1 cubic inch cake (or 2 level tablespoonfuls of soap flakes)
Water ...............................1 gallon
Dissolve soap in 1 pint of warm water. Add nicotine sulfate. Stir mixture and add enough water to make 1 gallon.

#### Spray mixture 5: Rotenone:

Derris or cube root
   powder (5 percent
   rotenone content) ......½ ounce (3 level tablespoonfuls)
Water ...............................1 gallon
If the available powder is of lower rotenone content, use proportionately more of it.
Mix the powder first with a small quantity of water, then add it to the rest of the water in the sprayer.

### Spray mixture 6: Pyrethrum:

Use a ready-prepared pyrethrum spray material at the dilution given on the package in which it is sold.

### Spray mixture 7: Nicotine-Pyrethrum:

Add 1 tablespoonful of nicotine sulfate (40 percent) to 1 gallon of water containing spray mixture 6. Mix thoroughly. Stir well all spray mixtures during their preparation, and where a powder and liquid are mixed together, shake the sprayer from time to time during the spraying unless the sprayer is provided with an agitator.

### Spray mixture 8: Bordeaux Mixture:

Bluestone (copper
    sulfate) ........................4 ounces
Hydrated lime ...............4 ounces
Water ..............................3 gallons

Dissolve the bluestone in a wooden, earthenware, or glass vessel (never in metal), using hot water. Dilute with half the total water specified. Make a paste of the lime in a small quantity of water, and add the rest of the water to this. Pour the diluted bluestone and lime solutions together and mix thoroughly. Strain the mixture through a fine cheesecloth directly into the sprayer, and it is ready for use. This mixture should be made fresh each time it is used.

### Spray mixture 9: Bordeaux Mixture-Calcium Arsenate:

Add 3 ounces of calcium arsenate to 3 gallons of Bordeaux mixture, made according to directions just given. Mix thoroughly.

### Spray mixture 11: Tartar Emetic:

Tartar emetic ..................1 ounce (6½ level
                           teaspoonfuls)
Brown sugar ....................2 ounces (6 tablespoonfuls)
Water ..............................3 gallons

Four tablespoonfuls of sirup or molasses may be substituted for the brown sugar.

Dissolve the sugar or sirup in a small quantity of water. Add the tartar emetic slowly while stirring the water. Then dilute with quantity of water required to make 3 gallons. This solution should be made fresh each time it is used.

### Spray mixture 12: Soap:

Soap (mild laundry soap type) ............................2 ounces (4 cubic inch cakes or 8 level tablespoonfuls of soap flakes)

Water ...............................1 gallon

Cut cake soap into very small pieces. Dissolve soap in quart of hot water. Let cool. Add sufficient water to make 1 gallon. Use half strength on very tender plants such as young cabbage, garden peas, and beans.

### Solution 13: Corrosive Sublimate:

Corrosive sublimate (mercuric chloride) ....1/10 ounce (six 7½ grain tablets)

Water ...............................1 gallon

Dissolve the corrosive sublimate in a pint of hot water in a glass or earthenware vessel. Then dilute with quantity of cold water required to make 1 gallon.

Calomel (mercurous chloride) may be substituted for corrosive sublimate at the rate of 1/10 ounce to 1 gallon of water.

### Dust mixture 14: Calcium Arsenate:

Calcium arsenate ............1 pound

Hydrated lime ..................2 to 3 pounds

Place the materials in a tight can or similar container. Add several stones 1 inch in diameter to aid mixing process. Place tightly fitting cover on can. Shake or rotate can for 5 minutes Remove stones by passing mixture through sifter or screen.

### Dust mixture 15: Cryolite:

Cryolite ............................2 pounds

Talc ..................................1 pound

Do not use lime or Bordeaux mixture with cryolite.

### Dust mixture 16: Paris Green:

Paris green ...................... 1 pound

Hydrated lime ................10 pounds

Mix by same method as dust mixture 14.

### Dust mixture 17: Nicotine Sulfate (3 percent):

Nicotine sulfate
(40 percent) ................1 ounce (5 teaspoonfuls)
Hydrated lime ................1 pound

Sift lime to break up lumps. Put sifted lime in tight can. Add several stones 1 inch in diameter to aid mixing process. Pour nicotine sulfate over lime. Place tight-fitting cover on can. Shake or rotate can for 5 minutes. Remove stones by passing mixture through sifter or screen.

### Dust mixture 18: Rotenone:

Use a ready-prepared dust mixture containing at least 0.75 percent of rotenone in the form sold by the dealer.

### Dust mixture 19: Pyrethrum:

Use a ready-prepared pyrethrum dust or dust mixture in the form sold by the dealer. Follow directions given on the package in which it is sold.

To prepare a home-made pyrethrum dust mixture use—
Ground-pyrethrum flow-
ers (1.3 percent total
pyrethrine content) ....1 pound
Talc, pyrophyllite, or to-
bacco dust ...................3 pounds

Mix by same method as dust mixture 14 (above).

### Dust mixture 20: Nicotine-Pyrethrum:

Mix thoroughly equal quantities of dust mixtures 17 and 19.

### Dust mixture 21: Sulfur-Pyrethrum:

Dusting sulfur ..................1½ pounds
Pyrethrum flowers (1.3
percent total pyrethrine
content) ........................1 ounce (5 tablespoonfuls)

Do not use sulfur on squashes, melons, or cucumbers. Mix by same method as dust mixture 14.

### Poisoned bait 24: Cutworm and Slug Bait:

Sodium fluosilicate or
Paris green....................¼ pound
Dry, flaky wheat bran .... 5 pounds (1 peck)
Water to moisten ........... 3 to 4 quarts

Mix thoroughly the poison and the dry bran. Then moisten the mixture with water until each flake of the bran has been wetted. Prepare this bait in the morning and apply it late in the day, so that it will be moist and attractive when the cutworms begin to feed in the evening. Scatter the bait lightly and evenly on the soil surface of the garden or around the bases of plants that have been set out. Repeat application, if necessary.

### Poisoned bait 25: Tomato Fruitworm Bait:

Cryolite ............................ ½ pound
Cornmeal ........................ 5 pounds

Sift cornmeal to break up or remove all lumps. Put one-fourth of cornmeal in bucket or similar container. Add one-fourth of poison to cornmeal. Mix thoroughly. Repeat process until entire quantity is mixed. Scatter the bait lightly and evenly over the leaves of tomato plants, especially the fruit clusters, growing tips, and outer leaves.

### Poisoned bait 26: Mole Cricket Bait:

Sodium fluosilicate .......... ½ pound
Dry wheat bran ............... 5 pounds (1 peck)
Water ........................... 1 to 2 pints

Mix by same general method as poisoned bait 24, but add only sufficient water to the dry bran and poison to cause the bait particles to cling together when squeezed in the hands. Scatter the bait lightly and evenly on the soil surface of infested gardens.

### Poisoned bait 27: Strawberry Root Weevil Bait:

Calcium arsenate ............. ½ pound
Dry wheat bran .............. 5 pounds (1 peck)
Water ............................ 2 quarts

Mix by same method as poisoned bait 24. Scatter bait lightly and evenly around plants as soon as presence of insect is detected.

### Poisoned bait 28: Vegetable Weevil Bait:

Sodium fluoride .............. ½ pound
Fresh, finely chopped carrots or turnips .............. 4 pounds
Dry wheat bran .............. 7 pounds
Water to moisten ........... 3 or 4 quarts

LAWN PESTS AND INSECTICIDES TO USE IN CONTROLLING THEM

| Insecticide and Formulation (See note 1, below) | DOSAGE OF FORMATION PER 1,000 SQUARE FEET (See note 2, below) | | | | | | |
|---|---|---|---|---|---|---|---|
| | Grubs and Ants (See note 3, below) | Sod Web-Worms, Wireworms, Cicada-Killer Wasp, and Wild Bees (See note 4, below) | Chinch Bugs and False Chinch Bugs (See note 5, below) | Armyworms, Cutworms, and Mole Crickets (See note 6, below) | Earwigs, Fiery Skipper and Lucerne Moth (See note 7, below) | Chiggers, Fleas, and Ticks | Leafhoppers, Leaf Bug, and Mites (See note 8, below) |
| **DUSTS** | | | | | | | |
| Aldrin, 2.5 percent | 2¾ pounds | 2¾ pounds | | | | | |
| Chlordane, 5 percent | 5 pounds | 2½ pounds | 5 pounds | 2½ pounds | 2 pounds | 1 pound | 1 pound. |
| Dieldrin, 1.5 percent | 4½ pounds | 4½ pounds | 4½ pounds | 4½ pounds | 4½ pounds | 1⅓ pounds | |
| Heptachlor, 2.5 percent | 2¾ pounds | 2¾ pounds | | 2¾ pounds | | 1 pound | |
| Lindane 1 percent | | | | | | 1 pound | 2 pounds. |
| Malathion, 5 percent | | | | | | 2 pounds | 1 pound. |
| Toxaphene, 10 percent | 5 pounds | | | | | ½ pound | |
| **GRANULES** | | | | | | | |
| Aldrin, 2 percent | 3½ pounds | | | | | | |
| Chlordane, 6 percent | 5 pounds | 2½ pounds | 5 pounds | 2½ pounds | 2 pounds | | |
| Dieldrin, 5 percent | 1⅓ pounds | 1⅓ pounds | 1⅓ pounds | 1⅓ pounds | 1⅓ pounds | | |
| Heptachlor, 2.5 percent | 2¾ pounds | 2¾ pounds | | 2¾ pounds | | | |
| Toxaphene, 10 percent | 5 pounds | | | | | ½ pound | |
| **SPRAYS** Wettable Powders | | | | | | | |
| Aldrin, 25 percent | 4½ ounces | 4½ ounces | | | | | |
| Chlordane, 40 percent | 10 ounces | 5 ounces | 10 ounces | 5 ounces | 4 ounces | 2 ounces | 2 ounces. |
| Diazinon, 50 percent | | | 6 ounces | | | | 1¼ ounces. |
| Dieldrin, 50 percent | 2¼ ounces | 2¼ ounces | 2¼ ounces | 2¼ ounces | 2¼ ounces | ⅔ ounce | |
| Heptachlor, 25 percent | 4½ ounces | 4½ ounces | | 4½ ounces | | 1½ ounces | |

| | | | | | | |
|---|---|---|---|---|---|---|
| Lindane, 25 percent, | 1½ pounds. | | | | ⅓ ounce. | 2 ounces. |
| Malathion, 25 percent, | 5 ounces. | | | | | 5 ounces. |
| Toxaphene, 40 percent, | | | | | 2 ounces. | |
| **Emulsifiable Concentrates** | | | | | | |
| Aldrin, 2 pounds per gallon. | 4½ fluid ounces. | | 2 fluid ounces. | 1½ fluid ounces. | ⅓ fluid ounce. | |
| Chlordane, 75 percent. (8 pounds per gallon). | 4 fluid ounces. | | | | | 1 fluid ounce. |
| Diazinon, 4 pounds per gallon. | 6 fluid ounces. | | 6 fluid ounces. | 1⅓ fluid ounces. | 1¼ fluid ounces. | |
| Dieldrin, 1½ pounds per gallon. | 6 fluid ounces. | | | 1⅔ fluid ounces. | | |
| Heptachlor, 2 pounds per gallon. | 4½ fluid ounces. | | 4½ fluid ounces. | 1½ fluid ounces. | | |
| Lindane, 20 percent, | | | | | ⅓ fluid ounces. | 1½ fluid ounces. |
| Malathion, 5 pounds per gallon. | | | | | 5 fluid ounces. | 1 fluid ounce. |
| Toxaphene, 60 percent (6 pounds per gallon). | 10 fluid ounces. | 12 fluid ounces. | | | 5 fluid ounces. | |
| V—C 13, 75 percent. | 4 fluid ounces. | | | | | |

Note 1.—If you buy a product in which the concentration of insecticide differs from that stated in the table, use proportionately more or less of it. Follow directions on the container label.

Note 2.—To determine the per-acre dosages, multiply the given dosages by 43.

Note 3.—In hot dry areas, lower dosages may be necessary to prevent burning of the grass; consult your State agricultural experiment station. Apply aldrin, dieldrin, or heptachlor to control green June beetle grubs. Use any of the insecticides except DDT to control May beetle grubs and ants. If only a few ant nests are present, treat them individually with an insecticide. Wash the insecticide into the nests or drench the mounds with it. Special treatment is required to control fire and harvester ants; consult your State agricultural experiment station for latest recommendations.

Note 4.—To control sod webworms, apply the insecticide in late afternoon or evening and delay watering until the following morning. To control wireworms, apply chlordane, dieldrin, or heptachlor.

tachlor. To control the cicada-killer wasp and wild bees, apply chlordane. To eliminate a nest of the wasp, pour or spray the insecticide into the nest after dark and seal the entrance with dirt.

Note 5.—To control chinch bugs in the South, use diazinon or V—C 13 in a spray, or consult your county agent or State agricultural experiment station for latest recommendations. A preventive spray program requires treatment about every 6 weeks. In some areas chinch bugs have developed resistance to DDT and possibly to other related insecticides.

Note 6.—To control cutworms, apply the insecticide in late afternoon.

Note 7.—A ready-mixed bait is also effective against earwigs. Follow the directions on the container. Apply the bait in the evening. To control the fiery skipper and lucerne moth, apply chlordane.

Note 8.—To control leafhoppers, apply malathion. To control the leaf bug and mites, apply malathion. To control the eriophyid mite, apply diazinon.

Mix bait by method described for poisoned bait 24. Then mix chopped vegetables with the prepared bait. This bait is more attractive to the weevils if allowed to stand several hours before it is applied. Apply in the late afternoon. The bait is effective only late in the winter and in the spring, since at other times of year the weevils prefer growing crops.

## WEED KILLERS

The best means of controlling weeds in a lawn is the creation of a thick grass base that leaves no sun, bare spots or nourishment for weeds to establish themselves. Pesticides assist in warding off pests; a robust, thick lawn is the best defense against crabgrass and other weeds.

Preliminarily, lawns should be given a pH test by a state agricultural college or county extension agent. Then it should be limed sufficiently to a proper acidity or alkalinity. Your advisor will tell you how much lime to apply. An application of the proper amount of fertilizer—organic or inorganic—repeated in six weeks, and again with organic fertilizer a month afterwards, is essential. The organic fertilizer (urea-formaldehyde or organic sludge) should not be used in summer months to avoid burning the lawn. A fourth application of fertilizer should be made in the fall. Water heavily after each application.

Given a properly maintained lawn, weeds can be controlled with relative ease. Insecticides, fungicides and weed killers may be used even without the old effective DDT preparations which were the mainstay of lawn maintenance in the past.

Weed killers are of two types: pre-emergent controls that prevent germination and hormone type postemergent controls that select weeds and attack them.

Pre-emergent chemicals come in dry form and are often sold in combination with fertilizers and grub-killing insecticides. These save application time. The following are recommended for application in the spring (mid-April in the northeast United States):

D C P A, Trifluralin, Diaphenamid, Amicen, and for large lawns, Siduron.

If weeds emerge, a chemical control may be applied during the summer. Broad-leaved weeds are attacked by 2,4-D. This is often used in combination with 3,4,5-TP (Silvex) and will control not only dandelions (plantain) but also clover and chickweed. In applying, follow package directions carefully. Avoid mowing for several days to allow maximum exposure by the leaves. Be careful to avoid placing the weed killer where wind can carry it to attack other plants.

## FUNGICIDES

Seed decay and damping-off can be controlled by dusting the seed with various chemical compounds, some of which are listed below. *Farmers' Bulletin 1862, Vegetable Seed Treatments,* gives a more complete list of seed treatments and the details of their use with various crops.

## SEED DISINFECTANTS

Various chemicals are used to destroy disease-producing organisms on the seed surface. A complete list is given in *Farmers' Bulletin 1862,* mentioned above.

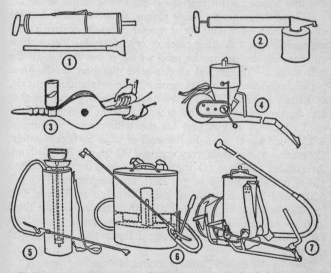

(1) Plunger type of hand duster. (2) Hand atomizer. (3) Simple bellows type of duster. (4) Fan, or blower, duster. (5) Compressed-air sprayer. (6) Knapsack sprayer. (7) Knapsack-bellows duster.

# BOOK IV

## Home Painting Guide

### HOW TO USE PAINT

In general, follow instructions on the can. Work in a well-ventilated, dry, dust-free atmosphere, away from flames. Plan your work, using correct paints, removers, thinners, undercoats, brushes, etc., and color-mixing charts. Cover or mask areas which may be dirtied by paint spots. Allow ample time for drying between coats.

**Preparing the Surface:** Prepare the surface so that it is even, smooth, clean, and dry. Remove hardware where possible. For fine finished work (furniture, etc.) remove old finish.

Sandpaper comes in many shapes, materials, and degrees of coarseness, each best for a special purpose. Square sheets are useful with a sanding block or orbital sander; paper discs and sanding drums may be used with a power drill; belts for belt sanders. The orbital sander gives the best finish. Most popular abrasives are flint, garnet, emery, aluminum oxide, or silicon carbide. The last two are synthetics and tougher and longer-lasting than the others. Aluminum oxide can be used on metal and is best for use with power equipment. Silicon carbide is even harder and is used in floor sanders. Coarseness varies from very coarse (VC or grit 30 of aluminum oxide) to coarse (C or grit 50) for deep cutting, medium (M or grit 80), fine (F or grit 120), and very fine (VF or grit 220) used between coats of paint. Grits go as high as 600 for fine finishing or removing a gloss of fresh varnish. Even finer is rottenstone used with oil. Close-coated papers cut faster and tend to become clogged faster than open-coated papers.

**Removing Old Finish:** Three processes are used.

Scraping-sanding is the most common. If finish is dry and brittle, a sharp scraper may be used on hardwood. Watch out for digs and gouges in surface of softwoods. Grinding off corners of the scraper will help. It may be necessary to sharpen scraper every few minutes while it is in use. Sharpen with burnishing tool and file. An electric scraper is now available that heats and scrapes.

Blowtorch burning is used especially over large areas (floors or sides of buildings). Handle torch carefully to avoid fire. Never use on furniture. Avoid burning paint too deeply and scorching wood. It is best to soften top and then repeat operation until the wood surface appears.

Chemical removers are best for inexperienced workmen. Use of these may raise grain of wood. Sand down when dry. Trisodium phosphate makes a safe remover. Make up a saturated solution in pail of hot water, brush or "mop" onto surface. Or use commercial remover. Neutralize with denatured alcohol. These do not raise grain. Repeat application. Scrub with stiff brush while solvent is at work. Use a scraper after ½ hour. Repeat if necessary. Sand.

To clean surfaces use these.

If old finish is in good condition, has not scaled or cracked, merely apply an undercoat. Sand to a smooth finish and dust. Begin with a coarse abrasive (pumice, rottenstone or sandpaper) if the wood

How to dip a brush.

is rough. Then use finer abrasives for smoothing off and polishing. If sandpaper is used, wrap around a block of wood; if steel wool is used, hold with crushed paper, cloth or rubber gloves.

**Sealing and Filling:** Cover knot holes with shellac. Fill porous wood with wood filler or plastic wood. A paste filler will do for open grain wood, but a liquid filler is necessary for close-grained hardwood. The kind and amount of filler for various types of wood is indicated below:

| Wood | Hardness | Grain | Filler |
| --- | --- | --- | --- |
| Apple | Hard | Close | None |
| Ash | Hard | Close | None |
| Basswood | Soft | Close | Liquid |
| Baywood | Hard | Open | Paste |
| Beech | Hard | Close | Liquid |
| Birch | Hard | Close | Liquid |
| Black Walnut | Hard | Open | Paste |
| Butternut | Hard | Open | Paste |
| Cedar | Soft | Close | Liquid |
| Cherry | Hard | Close | None |
| Cypress | Soft | Close | Liquid |
| Douglas Fir | Soft | Close | Liquid |
| Elm | Hard | Close | None |
| Hemlock | Soft | Close | Liquid |
| Larch | Soft | Close | Liquid |
| Mahogany | Hard | Open | Paste |
| Maple | Hard | Close | None |
| Oak | Hard | Open | Paste |
| Pine (So. Yellow Ga.) | Hard | Close | Liquid |
| Sugar Pine | Soft | Close | Liquid |
| Walnut | Hard | Open | Paste |
| Western Yellow Pine | Soft | Close | Liquid |
| White Fir | Soft | Close | Liquid |
| White Pine | Soft | Close | Liquid |

After a few minutes wipe across grain with rough cloth. Allow to dry for 20 to 30 minutes. Sand lightly.

Wall board may be filled with commercial wall sealer or wall size. Allow to dry. Sand. Floor cracks less than 1/16 inch wide should be filled with wood filler or plastic wood.

(This shrinks as it dries, so repeat if necessary.) Large holes should be filled by shaping matching wood, gluing in, and filling edges with plastic wood or putty. Furniture cracks should be filled with shellac stick or liquid.

**Painting:** Remove loose bristles by ruffling or brushing over palm of hand. Dip the brush 1 to 2 inches into paint but not more than half way. After first dip, wipe paint out of brush against stick laid over paint can to remove other loose bristles. Hold brush handle between thumb and forefinger, as a pencil is held; supporting the wide part of the handle with fingers. For relief, hold the brush as you would a tennis racket. Stroke wood first with the grain, then across grain, and finally with the grain, at a 90° angle.

Paint may be applied over stain if water stain or non-grain raising stain has been used. Otherwise the surface should first be shellacked (1 or 2 coats) or treated with aluminum paint.

SASH TOOL          7/8" OVAL          3" FLAT          4" FLAT
                   PAINT BRUSH       PAINT BRUSH      PAINT BRUSH

1" FLAT
VARNISH BRUSH

1-7/8" OVAL          2-1/2" FLAT          1-1/2" FLAT
VARNISH BRUSH       VARNISH BRUSH        VARNISH BRUSH

Start at the top and work down. Tables and chairs should be turned upside down.

**Paint Brushes:** The best brushes are made of long hog bristles, tough and springy, with center bristles slightly longer, tapering smoothly to a straight, narrow edge. Good brushes are also made of nylon bristles. Cheaper brushes are made of horsehair.

The type of work determines the best brush to be used. Never use a brush used for paint which has been used for varnishing, as it tends to create a cloudy film.

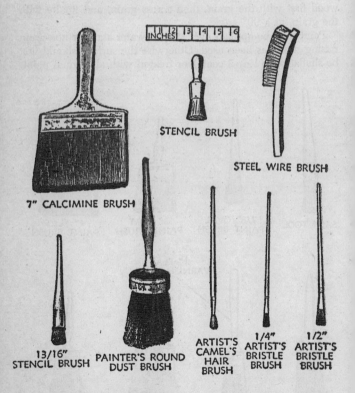

INCHES |1 |2 |3 |4 |5 |6

STENCIL BRUSH

STEEL WIRE BRUSH

7" CALCIMINE BRUSH

13/16" STENCIL BRUSH

PAINTER'S ROUND DUST BRUSH

ARTIST'S CAMEL'S HAIR BRUSH

1/4" ARTIST'S BRISTLE BRUSH

1/2" ARTIST'S BRISTLE BRUSH

### THE PAINTER NEEDS:

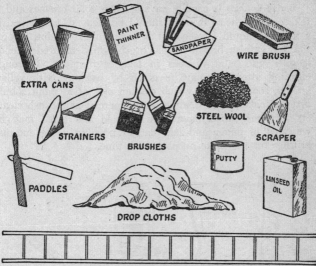

EXTRA CANS — PAINT THINNER — SANDPAPER — WIRE BRUSH — STRAINERS — BRUSHES — STEEL WOOL — SCRAPER — PADDLES — PUTTY — LINSEED OIL — DROP CLOTHS — LADDERS

### WHICH PAINT BRUSH TO USE

| | |
|---|---|
| Ceilings | large flat |
| Floors | large varnish |
| Furniture (Wicker) | 1-2″ flat, spray gun |
| Furniture (Wood) | 1-2″ flat |
| Pipes | oval |
| Radiators | flat |
| Moldings | small varnish, sash tool |
| Trim, narrow edges | varnish, sash tool |
| Walls | 4″, spray gun |
| Windows | small varnish, sash tool |
| Large areas | flat wall brushes 3-5 inches wide or oval brushes |
| Sash work | thin brushes 2-3 inches wide |
| General use | 1½ inches wide |
| Varnish | intermediate with 1-4″ |
| Water Paint | wide brushes with coarse bristles |
| Interior Painting | 6″ or paint rollers (with or without designs) |
| Whitewashing | coarse, vegetable fiber brushes |
| Concrete Paint | coarse, vegetable fiber brushes |

**Storing Brushes:** It usually pays to have good brushes and to take care of them. Brushes should be cleaned, suspended in a thinning liquid (linseed oil or turpentine for paint, turpentine for varnish brush, shellac brushes in denatured alcohol, lacquer gilt paint brushes in lacquer thinner). Thorough cleaning after use may be given by washing with yellow kitchen soap. Brushes which contain old, dried paint should first be soaked in turpentine or commercial paintbrush cleaners. Brushes which have been cleaned and dried may be wrapped in paper and laid flat. If possible, label and use brushes for the same purpose each time.

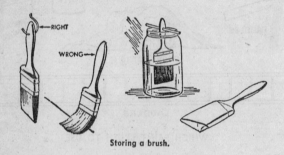

Storing a brush.

Commercial closed containers containing solvents called brush conditioners are available. (Similar containers are easily made.)

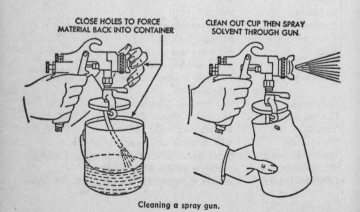

Cleaning a spray gun.

One device available for holding brushes keeps them in a vaporized solvent while in storage, keeping them soft for later use.

**Rollers:** For walls and ceilings, rollers may be substituted for brushes. They are easier for the amateur to handle, take on more paint than a brush, and cover more than twice the area per stroke. They eliminate dripping. A pleasing texture results from this method.

The 7-inch roller is preferred to the 9-inch for extensive work. Narrower rollers are used for trim. Use a ½-inch nap roller for plaster board and other smooth surfaces. Use a ¾-inch nap roller for textured plaster, masonry, stucco, brick, or wire fences. Use a wool or modacrylic fabric for flat paints, a mohair cover for enamels. When you have finished, clean the roller first on old newspapers, then immerse the sleeve in paint thinner.

To use, pour paint in a shallow pan, prop the pan so that

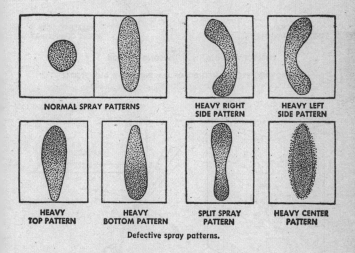

NORMAL SPRAY PATTERNS    HEAVY RIGHT SIDE PATTERN    HEAVY LEFT SIDE PATTERN

HEAVY TOP PATTERN    HEAVY BOTTOM PATTERN    SPLIT SPRAY PATTERN    HEAVY CENTER PATTERN

Defective spray patterns.

paint covers ⅔ of bottom, roll in roller, wipe off excess on the dry ⅓ of the pan. Start 3 feet from the ceiling, work up, then down. Do 3 strips, then apply roller horizontally. Use a small brush to reach corners and edges.

**Spraying:** This saves time, is easy to do, but must be done correctly. Practice before beginning work to get proper distance and technique and to avoid unequal paint distribution. Gun should be held at right angle to surface, 6 to 10 inches away, and moved parallel to the surface. Spraying at an angle or with disproportioned time in one area will give unequal distribution of paint. Regulate thickness of the coat by adjust-

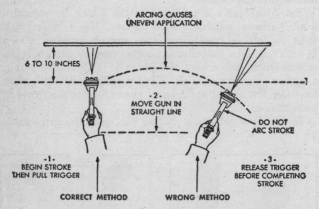

ARCING CAUSES
UNEVEN APPLICATION

6 TO 10 INCHES

· 2 ·
MOVE GUN IN
STRAIGHT LINE

DO NOT
ARC STROKE

· 1 ·
BEGIN STROKE
THEN PULL TRIGGER

· 3 ·
RELEASE TRIGGER
BEFORE COMPLETING
STROKE

CORRECT METHOD          WRONG METHOD

SHOWING PROPER METHOD OF MAKING SPRAY GUN STROKE

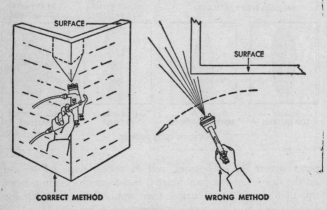

SURFACE

SURFACE

CORRECT METHOD          WRONG METHOD

SPRAY PAINTING CORNERS

Spray gun technique.

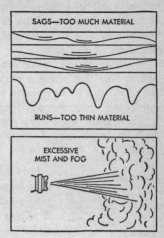

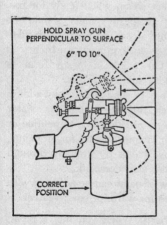

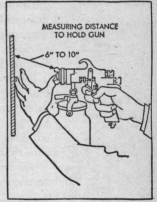

Spray painting faults.

Proper method of making spray gun strokes.

ing the speed of paint flow and trigger action. Keep spray clean.

For small jobs, particularly retouching, a spray can can be used. These are available in white, colors, anti-rust primers, metallics, fluorescent paints which shine in the dark, enamels, and even special finishes.

Painting with a spray can costs considerably more per square foot than using a conventional brush-on paint. However, this is a small price to pay in return for the additional speed and convenience offered on a small job.

These paints have a low pigment ratio in order to come out in a fine even mist. They dry fast; additional coats can be applied in 10 to 20 minutes.

**How to mix thoroughly.**

*Pour off Liquid*

*Stir Remainder Until Smooth*

*Return Liquid Slowly While Stirring Thoroughly*

**Preparing Paint:** Even ready-mixed paints must be well shaken or stirred with a stick before using, as pigments tend to settle. It is best to remove top liquid first and add it back as needed as you mix. Then pour back and forth to insure smooth flow. Paint should have the consistency of heavy sweet cream when ready for use.

Powder or paste paints should be dumped into a can and mixed with lukewarm water until proper consistency is reached. Oil paint in paste form is thinned with mineral spirits.

Paints may be made thinner by adding the proper thinner—water for water paints, casein or calcimine, turpentine or benzine, or lacquer thinner for oil paints, etc. Remove lumps by straining through wire strainer or cheesecloth.

The flow of paint can be adjusted with an additive for warm or cold weather.

**Mixing Paints:** When you mix a paint, make certain to mix enough for the whole job. Check your color when dry under the light in which it will be seen. Keep the color slightly lighter than the effect you want.

Colors come in tubes or small cans. To change the color of a lacquer, a casein or an emulsion paint, combine two or more of the ready-mixed coatings. To mix an oil paint, add a little of the base paint to some of tinting color and mix well. Then add to the large container and mix well. Strain the entire lot through a wire screen or old stocking. Decorators often soften colors by adding the complementary color or a touch of gray to the mixture.

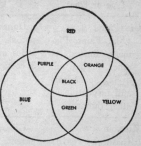

How "pigment" primary colors combine to produce other colors.

## WHERE TO USE EACH TYPE OF PAINT

| Type of Paint | Qualities | Uses |
|---|---|---|
| WHITEWASH (slaked lime, mix with water) | Intensely white, inexpensive. | Plaster, concrete, masonry, stone. |
| CALCIMINE (powdered chalk or whiting, mix with water) | Non-washable, inexpensive, rubs off. Requires undercoat of sizing; 1 coat is sufficient. | Plaster, walls and ceilings. |
| WATER PAINT Resin Emulsion Paints (powdered paints—add to water) | Easy to mix, apply with brush or roller, dries rapidly, leaves no odors. May be washable. Sometimes requires primer. | Summer cottages, cement, concrete, masonry, wood, plaster interiors. |
| CASEIN (pigments mixed with protein binder derived from milk) | Smooth, washable; quick drying. May require undercoat of sizing. 1 coat is sufficient. | Interior plaster walls and ceilings. |

| Type of Paint | Qualities | Uses |
| --- | --- | --- |
| OIL PAINT (Flat Paint. Pigment, linseed or other drying oil, drying chemicals and turpentine or other thinner) | Durable, washable, porous, dull finish. Dries overnight. 1 to 3 coats required. | Inside surfaces—wood, metal, plaster, concrete, masonry or stone. Don't use on floors if grain is to show. |
| VARNISH (natural resins dissolved in drying oils) | Glossy finish; transparent, protective, brings out natural grain and color; special mixtures made for floors and outdoors. | Finishing furniture, floors, woodwork, etc. |
| SHELLAC (resins dissolved in alcohol) | Same as varnish, quick drying. | Finishing furniture and floors. |
| LACQUER | Similar to heavy varnish. Never apply over enamel or paint. | Baseboards, art objects, small furniture pieces, special finishes; undercoating. |
| ENAMEL, GLOSS AND SEMI-GLOSS (pigment added to varnish) | Gives smooth, glossy finish; also available in flat enamels. | Furniture, woodwork; use over 1 to 2 coats of paint or enamel undercoat. |
| PORCH AND DECK ENAMEL | Same as above. | Outdoor floors. |
| PLASTIC FINISHES (available in various types) | May be transparent, resistant to wear, heat, acid, alcohol, etc. May be applied with bombs, sprays. | Furniture, walls, woodwork, etc. |
| ACRYLIC BASE (various types) | Water soluble; dries in 1½ hours; durable; drip proof. | Stucco, concrete, asbestos, masonry, walls, wood. |

| Type of Paint | Qualities | Uses |
|---|---|---|
| STAIN (dyes, pigments mixed with oil, water or alcohol) | Sinks into pores defining grain of soft summer growths and hard winter growths. Provides no protection. | Darkens wood surfaces on furniture, floors, doors, woodwork. |
| ALUMINUM PAINT (microscopic flakes of metal) | Excellent base paint, protective. | On metal, wood, or concrete as base paint or finish; radiators, pipes. |
| CEMENT PAINT (pigment mixed with cement) | Water resistant. | Concrete surfaces, cellar walls. |
| ACRYLIC PAINT (LUCITE) | Extra thick, does not drip, run, splatter. | Irregular walls, walls. |
| RUBBER BASE PAINT | Resistant to wear, moisture, oil. May be applied with roller. | Concrete floors of garages and cellars, asbestos cement siding and shingle. Also interiors. |
| CANVAS PAINT | Requires no undercoat; surface must be clean, dry. | Canvas and duck floors, furniture, awnings, golf bags, etc. |
| CREOSOTE PAINT AND STAINS | Insect resistant. | Roofs, shingles, termite protection. |
| LEAD PAINT | Protects against rust. | Outside iron or woodwork. |
| CHALKING PAINT | Chalk washes away after a year. | Exteriors, clapboard sides, roofs. |
| MILDEW INHIBITORS | Resist mildew. | Damp areas. |
| SUNLIGHT RESISTER | Resists effects of intensive heat. | Certain southern and mountain areas. |

| Type of Paint | Qualities | Uses |
|---|---|---|
| PLASTIC PLASTER (soy bean base) | Heavy, tough, non-porous. Requires no undercoat. Includes finish coat of plaster and paint in one operation. | Over wallpaper, patched walls, plasterboard, concrete, wood, metal. |
| LUMINOUS PAINT | Shines in the dark, in green, yellow, or white. Changes color under light. | Light switches, door posts, furniture edges, flashlight, novelty rooms. |
| SIZING | To seal and form adhesive base for paint. | Must be applied to fresh plaster before painting or papering. |

## HOW TO USE EACH TYPE OF PAINT

**Enamel:** Apply 1 to 2 coats over primer coat. It may be applied over stain, if surface is first shellacked. "Stroke" it on with full brushes in parallel strokes. Working areas should be covered with one brush full, then remove excess. Surface should be smooth with no brush marks. To obtain dull finish, use special enamels or rub with pumice and water or rottenstone and oil. New "liquid sandpaper" may be applied to dull finish.

**Stains:** Stains color wood without concealing the grain. Water stains penetrate deeply, like a dye, may raise the grain and require sanding after drying. Oil stains do not penetrate as deeply. Stains may come mixed with varnish or shellac. To darken a stain, repeat application. To lighten a stain, rub lightly with turpentine, then linseed oil. Allow to dry, then rub with cheesecloth. If ordinary stain was used, add protective coat of varnish or shellac.

**Oil or Water Paints:** Dip brush not more than ½ the length of bristles. Wipe off excess. Divide job into areas of several square feet and stroke brush into center of area. Stroke on thin coats on small areas. Work from the center of an area up and down, first with the grain, then against the grain, finally with the grain. Give a rough coating, then go over the surface laying off any excess paint with a fan stroke. On plaster use a semicircular stroke or a roller.

Work quickly from one area to the next so as not to leave edges. Apply 1 to 2 coats of primer paint for most work. Allow each coat to dry, sand lightly. To obtain a dull finish, rub with powdered pumice and linseed oil or water, using felt pad. To obtain a protective or shiny finish, varnish or use enamel paint.

**How to tint oil base paint.**

*Place small amount of tinting color in mixing cup*

**Calcimine:** Apply as oil paint. Use a special calcimine brush for calcimine.

*Add a little of base paint which has, first, been thoroughly stirred*

**Varnish:** Keep in warm place or it will thicken. Apply with special soft varnish brush (badger or camel hair). "Flow" it on in thin coats. Brush from center of area out, across grain, then with grain, using long, even strokes. Finish with empty brush to remove excess varnish. Allow to dry, and sand lightly. Repeat as desired. To obtain a dull finish, rub with pumice and water or rottenstone and oil. To obtain a more glossy finish, apply solution of 4 parts shellac to 1 part alcohol. Varnish or shellac may be applied over old stain without sanding.

*Combine this mixture carefully*

*Then add gradually to base paint while stirring*

**Shellac:** To obtain a natural finish, use white shellac on light woods, orange shellac on dark woods. Apply 1 to 3 coats. Brush quickly and thinly, in quick long strokes. Allow to dry. Furniture wax or polish may be applied for protection.

**Lacquer:** Undercoat is not usually required. Do not apply over any paint except lacquer. Apply with paintbrush or spray gun, in straight, parallel strokes with the grain. Work rapidly, making sure lacquer runs smoothly. (Otherwise, go over it quickly with thinner.) Allow to dry and sand. Repeat as desired. To obtain a dull finish, rub with powdered pumice and water.

| | Turpentine | Linseed Oil | White Lead | Lead Mixing Oil |
|---|---|---|---|---|
| **MAKE-UP OF PAINT FOR OUTSIDE WORK** | | | | |
| **REPAINT WORK** | | | | |
| Outside Work | | | | |
| 1st coat | 1/4 | 1/4 | 1/2 | |
| Finish coat | | 1/2 | 1/2 | |
| Brick, Stucco, Concrete, Stone | | | | |
| 1st coat | | 5/16 | 3/8 | 5/16 |
| Finish coat | | 1/2 | 1/2 | |
| Woodwork | | | | |
| 1st and Finish coat | | | | |
| (Flat Finish) | | | 1/2 | 1/2 |
| **NEW WORK** | | | | |
| Outside Wood | 2/9 | 4/9 | 3/9 | |
| Interior Wood | 3/8 | 3/8 | 2/8 | |
| Brick | 1/9 | 5/9 | 3/9 | |
| Stucco, Concrete, Stone | | 3/10 | 4/10 | 3/10 |
| Interior Plaster ⎧ | | | 3/7 | 4/7 |
| Wallboard ⎩ | | | | |

Add 1/4 pint drier for each gallon of raw linseed oil used. Boiled oil requires no drier.

## SPECIAL FINISHES

**Wax Finish:** Remove dust. Obtain color desired by bleaching, staining or allowing to remain natural. Apply thin coat with circular motion, wipe off excess with dry cloth. Allow to dry and polish. Rub with steel wool, then chamois. Repeat weekly till wood appears mellow.

**Oil Finish:** Rub in solution of 2 parts linseed oil, 1 part turpentine (they are boiled together, then cooled), with the grain. Allow to dry. Repeat. Then repeat weekly for 3 to 5 weeks.

**Antique Finish:** With paint or floor brush, apply antiquing glaze (amber or raw sienna and lampblack in solution of 3 parts varnish and 1 part turpentine). While still wet, rub with soft cloth, removing glaze in proportion to normal wear—least in the corners, most at the protrusions. Allow to dry. Varnish for protective coat.

Polychroming: This gives a vari-shaded effect in any color. Apply artist's paints thinned with raw linseed oil. Shellac or varnish lightly. Apply thick paste of 1 part rottenstone, 1 part liquid wax, moistened with turpentine (or heavy coat of cream or tan paint). Allow to dry for 10 to 15 minutes, then remove as much paste or paint as desired.

Bleaching: To obtain light-colored (modern) finish, select woods with open grains. Pine comes out a gray; mahogany and cherry, pink. Wipe on bleaching solution (1 lb. oxalic acid crystals plus 1 gal. water for each 10 sq. feet) with old broom. Allow to stand for 15 to 30 minutes. (The longer the lighter.) Mop up with solution of ½ cup ammonia in 1 pail of water, allow to dry. Brush in flat white paint, white lime or white lead, and wipe off immediately with cloth. Apply 1 coat of white shellac and allow to dry. Sand lightly. Apply 3 to 5 coats of liquid wax with soft cloth.

Pickling: Apply flat white or enamel undercoater. Allow to dry for five minutes, then wipe off. Burnt umber for additional color if desired.

Bleaching Old Furniture (Alternative method): Remove all paint. Apply chlorine bleach with cloth or soft brush till correct color is obtained. Apply flat white paint, rub off most of paint immediately. Allow to dry.

Decalcomanias: Buy designs desired. Soak in water or turpentine as directed. Work into position while still wet. Remove base paper. Allow to dry. Similar effect may be obtained by pasting colorful cutouts on the surface.

Freehand Painting: On the outline of the picture to be painted, or a tracing, perforate small holes. Attach original to wall with Scotch tape and rub chalk or powder through holes. Remove drawing and use powder dots as outline. Apply artist's oil paints. After paints have dried, brush off chalk marks. Apply varnish or shellac to protect surface.

Stencil Painting: Buy or cut stencils in design desired. Attach stencil to wall with Scotch tape or heated glue size. With blunt-brush or spray gun, apply special paints. (Tube glazing colors or oil paints thinned with 3 parts turpentine, 1 part linseed oil to a creamy consistency.)

Sand-Float Finish: Apply flat paint. Make a paste of 1 part turpentine, 1 part linseed oil, ½ gallon of flat or exterior paint, 1 quart clear varnish, and strain. Add Torpedo or bank sand and mix into a thick paste. Apply with stiff brush, working

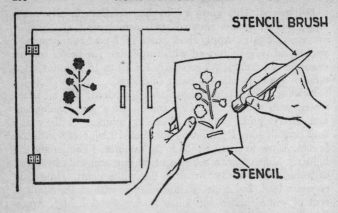

2 to 3 square feet at a time. Stipple in a circular motion, or use trowel or other instrument to create a design.

**Plastic Paint (Alternative):** Plastic paints may be substituted for made paste, using the same technique.

**Highlighting:** Apply bone-white enamel as for ordinary painting. Allow to dry. With a cloth apply a glazing compound mixed with burnt or raw umber oil, color to a rich brown. Remove surplus. Allow to dry.

**Scumbling:** After base paint has dried, apply a second color. Crumple newspaper into a wad, tightly or loosely depending on pattern desired. While second color is still wet, remove some of it by pressing paper into wet paint and removing top color.

Spatterdash.

**Spatterdash:** After protecting surrounding areas, floors, walls, and furniture, divide job into areas. For spatter, prepare regular floor paint which has been thinned only half as much as ordinarily, and pour into saucer. Apply regular base paint, and allow it to half dry to the consistency of glue. Dip stiff brush or broom into spatter paint, taking on moderate amount of paint. Holding spatter brush in left hand, rap it soundly with stick, aiming at center of area to be spattered. Repeat for each area.

**Tiffany Blending:** Prepare 1 to 4 glazing colors in paste form. Apply clear glazing to finished wall. (If wall is hard, add 1 pound of cornstarch per gallon to prevent running.) Apply glazing colors separately with stipple or scumble method.

**Starching:** This is a protective coating used on walls, to reduce gloss. Apply solution of cold water saturated with laundry starch, thinned with cold water to consistency of milk. Apply with flat wall brush.

**Stippling:** This must be done rapidly and is best done with assistance. Place some of final coat paint in saucer in a thick mixture. Apply final coat. While paint is still wet, dip stippling brush deeply into thick paint, and pound wall with brush. Work downward in strips. The same process may be applied in a second color after the base color has dried. Or use dry brush on wet paint, removing excess. Or use stippling roller.

**Sponge Stippling:** A sponge roller may be substituted for the stippling brush. Dip roller into thick paint and roll down the wall.

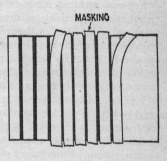

**Stripes:** Mask portions which are not to be painted by attaching strips of board or paper with Scotch tape. Paint or spray as usual. Remove masks. Apply for second color.

**Wheat (Blond) Finish:** Remove other finish. Bleach. Rub with finest sandpaper to a satin smoothness. Dust with cloth dipped in turpentine. Finish with pure white shellac, clear lacquer or a light color.

**Spray cans:** Made to create a great variety of finishes—metallic bronze, copper, silver, gold, aluminum, or a hammer finish, a hard tile finish, a wrinkle finish, an enamel finish, and are used as frosting for glass or to color a green chalk board.

## SPECIAL SURFACE TECHNIQUES

**Walls and Ceilings in General:** Paint applied to new plaster (less than 3 months old) will not last. New plaster tends to develop cracks as it dries and sinks. Temporary coatings may be made with water paint or calcimine (for ceilings) but these are not washable. Best covering is inexpensive wallpaper.

To paint new plaster, seal against moisture with boiled linseed oil thinned with turpentine, then apply paint on oiled surfaces or glue size, either alone or mixed with oil paint.

Surfaces which have been previously painted should be washed with soap and water to remove grease and paint, scraped to remove loose paint, and filled with plaster of Paris to cover cracks or holes. Rough edges should be smoothed with sandpaper. New plaster spots should be allowed to dry and coated with shellac, then apply oil paint in a color desired. For a washable finish, apply a gloss paint.

For new surfaces, apply oil paint in 3 coats: primer sealer tinted with final color; mixture of ½ primer sealer and ½ paint; oil paint in color desired. Some self-priming oil paints are available which require only 1 coat. Wall enamel may be applied in 1 coat for refinishing but requires 3 coats—primer sealer, enamel undercoat tinted with final color, and enamel. Calcimine, water or casein paints are applied in a single coat.

Walls should be painted in yard-wide strips, top to bottom, right to left (if you are righthanded), using a 3½ inch brush for paint and a calcimine brush for calcimine. Work rapidly in horizontal strokes with a semicircular finish. Finish wall in one "sitting." Paint rollers may also be used.

**Ceilings:** Paint these first to avoid spotting finished walls. Ceilings may be painted by placing a plank-scaffold between two ladders. Plank should be placed so head is 6 inches from ceiling. Brush should carry minimum amount of paint at all times to minimize dripping.

**Plaster—Semi-finished:** Apply water paint; or primer-sealer (1 to 2 coats) plus either semi-gloss or high-gloss enamel; or calcimine with sizing added; or primer-sealer, casein, or resin emulsion; or texture (plastic) paints.

**Wall Board (new):** Clean and fill. Cover joints with special tape. Sand lightly. Apply sizing and allow to dry. Sand. Apply prime coat. Apply water paint or oil paint.

**Wall Board (old):** Same as for plaster.

**Wallpapered Walls:** Dust. Apply oil paint.

**Wallpapered Walls (removing paper):** Wet entire paper with warm water to which ½ cup of washing soda to the gallon has been added. Pull paper off in strips, scraping off bits with a putty knife. Rinse wall, allow to dry, sand lightly. Fill holes, sand lightly, apply sizing, allow to dry. Apply oil paint, casein or water paint.

**Hanging vinyl papers:** This requires special care. Walls should be dry and grease-free. Double cutting is the preferred method to follow. Basically this is the procedure:

Hang the first strip of material on the wall without prior trimming. Then paste the adjoining strip and install it so that it overlaps the first by approximately 2 inches. Brush or trowel the strips smooth in the normal manner. Then place a straightedge at the approximate center of the overlapped material. Holding it firmly, use a single-edge razor blade to cut through both layers of vinyl along the line of the intended butting. Hold the blade squarely against the straightedge as nearly perpendicular as possible. Never use a blade with a handle—it can often result in undercutting and an unsightly seam. Do not apply too much pressure to avoid scoring the wall too deeply.

After the cut has been made from the top to the bottom of the strip, gently lift the overlapped cut and remove it. Then use a broadknife to lay the two seams flat. Follow this procedure throughout the room area.

Any adhesive that squeezes out from the seam can be washed away, but avoid excessive use of water. It may dilute the paste. A soft, damp sponge does the job best. Work the seam as cleanly as possible, avoiding paste seepage as much as possible.

**Doors, Window Frames, Trim:** Use enamel which is washable or 3 coats of oil paint—enamel undercoat, undercoat and paint half and half mix, and the finish paint; or apply linseed oil and varnish, shellac, or wax; or linseed oil and thinned semi-gloss paint.

On doors, paint in order—panels, center rail, top and bottom rails, vertical stiles, edges. Sand surface between coats to get a velvet-like finish.

**Furniture:** Remove dirt or scales of previous paint. If paint is glossy, sand lightly to provide rough surface, then dust off. If item is to be stained, or merely varnished or waxed, remove old finish with paint remover, steel wool, wire brush and scraping tool. Fill cracks and nailhead indentations with wood filler. Seal holes with shellac or varnish-type filler. Apply enamel undercoater. Allow to dry, then enamel. Or apply priming paint plus flat paint; or priming plus flat paint plus enamel.

Chairs or small pieces should be first turned upside down, with the top done last.

**Rattan:** Apply spar varnish or exterior enamel.

**Reed, Wicker, Natural Wood Furniture:** Apply oil paint, spar varnish or exterior enamel without too much paint on brush. Keep spaces clear. Apply protective coat of spar varnish. Spraying is easier than brushing on reed and wicker.

**Metal Furniture:** Sand down with wet or dry sandpaper. Remove grease, rust (with turpentine), dirt (with steel wool), scale (with wire brush). Paint entire surface. Apply metal primer. Allow to dry. Rub down with emery cloth. Apply red-lead paint (to prevent rust). Apply oil paint or exterior enamel.

**New Wood Floors:** Surface must be sanded smooth. Apply filler, sealer, and floor wax; or filler, sealer, shellac or varnish; or filler, sealer, and two coats floor enamel.

**Floor Finishing:** Floors may be finished with shellac, sealer or varnish. Shellac is the least desirable of the three, but the most widely used because it dries so rapidly, within 24 hours. The durability of coatings can be improved by waxing. Renew the wax every 4 to 6 months according to the amount of wear on the floor. Wax over a substantial coating of shellac or varnish, however, tends to make a slippery floor unless wax is kept very thin.

The first and most important operation of finishing is scraping or sanding. In sanding, the floor should be gone over several times, first across the grain and then in the direction of the grain. On the first traverse, use No. 2 sandpaper on the machine, graduating down to No. ½, No. 0 and No. 00 on succeeding traverses. On softwood floors, No. ½ sandpaper is often the finest grit practical. After the last sanding, buff with No. 3 steel wool. After the floor has been sanded, sweep it clean and inspect carefully, looking at it across the floor toward the light from a window. Any scratches, undulations, or other blemishes will appear greatly accentuated when the finish is applied.

If the floor is to be stained, this should be done with a penetrating oil stain at this time. Where floor seal is to be used, the stain may be incorporated in the first coat of seal. Floor seals are available in colors or colorless.

Floors of oak or other hardwood with large pores may require filling with paste wood filler before finishing. The filler may be colorless or it may contain pigment. Paste filler is almost always used on oak floors before applying shellac or varnish coatings, but with floor seals the practice varies. When filler is used, care should be taken to see that the excess is wiped off very thoroughly to avoid an uneven, smeared appearance of the final finish. Any imperfections left by poor sanding make it difficult to do a clean job of filling.

**Varnished Floors:** Only floor varnishes should be used for floor finishing. Cleanliness and reasonable control of temperature (70° F. or warmer) and circulation of air are important.

Clean surface, allow to dry, apply spar varnish with a clean flat brush (approximately floor board width). Varnishing should be done in warm, dry weather. First coat should be thinned, following coats may be heavier, but never too heavy to spread. Apply with long, even strokes following the wood grain. Strokes may be made in both directions to spread evenly. Allow to dry and repeat to give 2 to 3 coats.

**Shellacked Floors:** Shellac for floors should be pure and unadulterated, either freshly manufactured or put up in glass containers. The correct thinner is 188-proof No. 1 denatured alcohol. Thin 3 lbs. cut shellac to 3/5 gal. Apply with a wide brush that will cover three boards of strip flooring at one stroke. Put on with long, even strokes, taking care to join the laps smoothly. The first coat requires 15 to 20 minutes to dry, then rub lightly with steel wool or sandpaper and sweep the floor. Apply a second coat, allow 2 to 3 hours to dry, then go over with steel wool or sandpaper, sweep and apply a third coat. The floor should not be put back in service until next morning but may be walked upon in about 3 hours after finishing. If wax is to be used, it should not be applied less than 8 hours after the last coat of shellac and should be a paste wax, not a water-emulsion wax.

**Floor Seals:** Directions for applying floor seals vary widely. In general, floor seals may be brushed on with a wide brush or mopped on with a squeegee or lamb's wool applicator, working first across the grain of the wood and then smoothing out in the direction of the grain. After an interval of about 12 minutes, depending upon the characteristics of the seal, wipe off the excess with clean rags or a rubber squeegee. The floor should then be buffed with No. 2 steel wool by power-driven machine. A second application is generally recommended for new floors or floors that have just been sanded. Sweep clean before making the second application. A correct interval of time between application of the seal and buffing is important. If the manufacturer of the seal does not specify the correct interval determine it by trial on samples of flooring or in some inconspicuous places.

Wax floors with paste floor wax and an electric polishing machine designed for the purpose. Mop paste wax on the floor, allow to stand until the thinner evaporates (15 to 30 minutes), then polish with the machine. The most modern type of floor-waxing machine applies the wax and polishes in the same operation. Water-emulsion floor waxes are merely mopped on the floor and allowed to dry.

Refinishing Old Floors: An old oil finish, embedded in the wood, may cause some difficulties. If a steel-wool buffing machine is available, first try to clean the floor sufficiently by buffing with No. 3 steel wool. If this is not effective, apply an alkali solution of trisodium phosphate, washing soda, or a commercial cleanser solution. If lye is used, care must be taken not to have the solution too strong, because strong alkali swells and softens the wood.

In applying the alkali, flush a small area of the floor at a time and allow to stand for a few minutes, then scrub with a stiff brush or No. 1 steel wool. Next flush with clean water and scrub to remove the soap that has been formed, and finally remove all the water possible by mopping and let the floor dry thoroughly. If the floor turns gray in color as a result of the action of the alkali and water, it may be necessary to bleach it with a saturated solution of oxalic acid in water. Rinse off the oxalic acid thoroughly with clean water, mop, and allow floor to dry completely. Any raised grain or roughening of the surface of the boards that results should be smoothed off with sandpaper or steel wool before new finish is applied.

Floors Originally Finished With Varnish: Old, discolored varnish finish is usually removed most easily by power sanding or it may be removed with liquid varnish remover. Alkaline solutions in water and removers sold in powder form to be dissolved in water should not be used. Follow the directions for using liquid remover carefully. Some old, discolored varnish will remain embedded in the wood, and complete restoration of the natural wood color should not be expected. Traffic channels where the old varnish has long been worn through and dirt ground into the wood should be cleaned by sanding.

**Floors Originally Finished With Shellac:** Old shellac and wax finishes that have merely become soiled by dirt clinging in the coating of wax may be cleaned by going over the floor with steel wool saturated with clean turpentine. White spots in the shellac caused by contact with water may be removed by rubbing lightly with a soft cloth moistened with denatured alcohol, diluted in equal amount of water, but the alcohol must be used with care to avoid cutting the shellac coating. On floors where the dirt is ground into the shellac itself or white spots penetrate all the way through, first, wash the floor with neutral or mildly alkaline soap solution followed by clear water, using as little water as possible in each operation. Scour the floor with No. 3 steel wool and denatured alcohol diluted with equal amount of water. If the floor boards are level and are not warped or cupped, scouring can be done to advantage with a floor-polishing machine fitted with a wire brush to which a pad of the No. 3 steel wool is attached. After the scouring, the floor should be rinsed with a minimum amount of clean water and allowed to dry thoroughly before refinishing with shellac.

**Staining Kitchen Floors:** Otherwise unfinished wood floors may be oil stained after dirt and grease have been removed and floor is dried. Stain should be darker than any spots, but not so dark (mahogany) that it will show footprints.

**Dyeing a Floor Brown:** Apply potassium permanganate dissolved in hot water with a string mop or short-bristle broom. Floor should then be oiled to fill wood. Apply the first coat of varnish thinned with turpentine, brushing lightly following the grain of the wood; repeat. Varnish may be dulled with cloth dampened with denatured alcohol or diluted vinegar.

**Oil Cloth and Linoleum:** Varnish or apply 2 coats floor paint or floor enamel. Special linoleum paints are available.

**To Wax Linoleum:** Apply self-polishing wax to floor. When dry, apply a second coat if additional protection is required.

**Asphalt and Rubber Tile:** Wash with soap and water; wax with nonrubbing wax.

**Fiber Rugs:** Spray occasionally with water to keep from drying out, but do not soak. Treat borders with oil dye, using small brush to apply. Follow with 2 coats of varnish.

**Cement Floors:** Special cement paints are available. Both tile and cement may be waxed, but care should be used in applying wax to cement to avoid danger from slipping.

Commercial hardener or aluminum primer should be applied to tighten up surface. On new floors where lime may be present, applying neutralizing solution of 3 lbs. zinc sulphate in one gallon hot water. Apply rubber base paint. Allow to dry for one week. Apply floor enamel paint, 1 to 2 coats, made for cement or varnish. Allow another week for drying. Dirty floors should first be washed with trisodium phosphate solution, then treated with zinc sulfate solution. Greasy floors should first be cleaned with solution containing lye, alcohol, or gasoline. Cracked floors should be pointed up with fresh cement (1 part cement, 2 parts water).

**Masonry Walls and Ceilings:** Same as plaster; use rubber-base primer.

**Basement Walls:** Apply cement coldwater paint. For fine finish, apply oil paint or concrete finish.

**Pipes, Radiators:** Apply 2 to 3 thin coats of silver, bronze, or gilt paint while radiator is cool, allowing each coat to dry. Last coat may be paint or semi-gloss.

**Enamel Refrigerators, Beds, etc.:** Remove grease, clean surface, and allow to dry. Smooth with steel wool, fill in cracks, and remove loose particles with damp cloth. Allow to dry. Apply 1 to 2 coats of flat paint, then the enamel gloss paint, allowing each coat to dry thoroughly.

**Awnings, Deck Chairs, Lawn Umbrellas:** Apply special awning paint.

**Canvas Furniture and Floor Covering:** Wet canvas. Apply 1 to 3 coats canvas paint in straight, even strokes. Apply special canvas overcoat or allow to stand in sun.

**Outdoor Canvas Floors:** Apply white-lead paste thinned with linseed oil, paste on strip of canvas, press smooth and light. Repeat, strip by strip. Tack edges. Apply 2 to 3 coats varnish or enamel.

**Swimming Pools:** Apply cement water paints, enamel paints with water-resisting varnish or waterproof enamel.

**Toilet Seats:** Remove old finish with paint remover. Sand smooth. Re-coat with quick-drying enamel.

**House Exterior (Wood):** Remove all chalk from previous paint. Shellac or varnish knots. Remove flakes and peels and spot-paint the areas uncovered. Countersink nails and fill holes with putty. Fill cracks and crevices with caulking. Make certain surface is dry. Original painting should be three coats. Single top coats may be given each 3 to 4 years, alternately with 2 coat paintings. Washings and retouchings may be done more frequently. More frequent paintings may not hold if chalking paints have been used unless first brushed down with wire brush. Outdoor work should be done in warm, dry weather, with paint at the same temperature as the atmosphere. Work across, from the top down. Spread paint as thinly as possible. If a color is used, undercoat should contain some pigment; e.g., 1 pint of overcoat to 1 gallon of undercoat. Gray makes a good undercoat covering for all but light colors.

To determine how much paint to use, measure distance around house in linear feet. Multiply by height to eaves. Divide by 600 where surface is in good condition—by 400 if surface is in poor condition. Measure width of gables and multiply by half the height. Add the two figures. This is the number of gallons.

**Shingle Roofs:** Apply stains with a coarse-bristled brush.

**Masonry:** Painting helps in reducing exterior dampness. Do not paint until at least 10 weeks after original construction. If using oil paints, dry walls thoroughly to avoid blisters. (Wait 1 week after rain.) Scrape well with wire-bristle brush. Cement paint may be applied to damp walls. Concrete walls and mortar joints must be moistened before cement paint is applied. Keep cement paint moist for 2 days. Use coarse-fiber brush or spray gun to apply.

**Window Screens:** Black or dark green are the usual colors but white is sometimes used on the interior side to decrease visibility from the outside. Clean thoroughly with soapsuds to remove dirt, washing soda to remove grease, and kerosene to remove dust. Apply special screen paint (or varnish thinned 50 percent with turpentine). Apply evenly on both sides. Frame may be painted with house trim. Rusty spots that show through previously painted metal require a special coating.

(Bar Ox formula 97.) White or light gray screen enamel gives you more privacy. During daylight hours, passersby cannot see clearly a porch that is painted this way. The view for those on the porch, however, is not impeded.

**Exterior Metal (Gutters, railings, trim, etc.):** Clean with paint thinner. Apply a priming coat. Finish with oil paint, enamel or lead paint. Red-lead paint is widely used for priming iron and steel; zinc dust primers are usually used for galvanized iron, copper, bronze; special priming paints are used for aluminum. Apply with brushes. Wire mesh may be painted best with a piece of rug tacked to a wood block. If rust spots show through previous paint, apply special coating. (Bar Ox formula 97.) For dark colors, high gloss, use trim and shutter paint.

**Surfaces Subject to Rot:** Brush or spray liquid wood preservatives—pentachlorophenol, copper naphthenate, zinc naphthenate (available in paint store) in 1 to 2 coats. Wear gloves. Apply second coat before first dries. Apply particularly where wood touches ground, in joints between wood and other materials, before painting or before repainting.

Walls may stain.

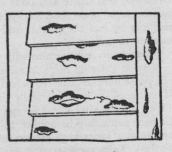

Paint may peel.

## PAINTING MISTAKES AND WHAT TO DO ABOUT THEM

| Defect and Cause | Remedy |
| --- | --- |
| "ALLIGATORING" (INTERLACING CRACKS): Undercoating was soft or not thoroughly dried so outer coat shrinks as it dries. | Allow paint to dry and repaint. |

| Defect and Cause | Remedy |
|---|---|
| BLISTERING: Paint was applied on moist surface.<br><br>or—Hot surface. | Remove cause of dampness. Check ventilation, vapor barrier. Dry. Scrape off blisters. Repaint. Repaint. |
| CHALKING: Normal and desirable for certain paints if not excessive. Paint was applied too thin; heavy rains; frost before paint was dry. | Remove chalk. Repaint. |
| DISCOLORING: Impurities in paints—usually in light colors. | These do not occur in titanium pigment paints. |
| FADING: Some parts of surface are more porous than others.<br>FADING IN RAIN: Pigment was water soluble. | Apply undercoat of special non-penetrating paint. Patch paint spots, discolored areas before repainting. |
| FADING OF COLOR ON PLASTER: Variable porosity of plaster. | Prime before applying more paint. |
| FADING OF COLOR, OUTDOORS: Dirt on surface or in paint. Mildew. Corrosion of copper and bronze screens. | Use mildew resistant paint. Varnish screens before corrosion takes place. |
| GLOSSY SPOTS, THIN SPOTS: Paint or coat was too thin or was applied on too smooth a surface. | Use a tinted undercoat. Patch paint difficult areas. Mix paint more thoroughly to get thicker mixture. Make certain strokes don't overlap. |
| PEELING: Same as blistering; or when surface was too glossy; or when old underpaint was loose. | Roughen surface before repainting or remove old paint. |

**Wallpapers:** Wallpaper is figured in single rolls which contain 37 sq. feet. They may be 18, 22, or 30 inches wide. However, the 18 and 22 inch rolls are actually sold in double rolls and the 30 inch rolls in triple rolls. In calculating paper needs, it is usual to figure 30 square feet of coverage per single roll, and wise to buy an additional roll to provide for waste.

**Wallpapering:** (1) Remove old paper by wetting thoroughly with warm water and scraping from top down. Avoid mess by covering base areas with newspapers or large drop cloths. (2) If wall board is used instead of plaster for the walls, all joints should be covered with a specially gummed tape, covered with glue size and allowed to dry. (3) Line wooden walls with cloth. First, be sure that all boards are nailed tightly with no nails projecting. Greasy surfaces should be scrubbed with a strong soap solution to which a tablespoonful of ammonia has been added. Pitch spots should be scraped or sanded smooth and given a coat of shellac. Over the holes tack a piece of cloth, coated with shellac. (4) Walls originally painted with watercolor or flat paints should be washed off, then given a coat of sizing before being papered. Painted or varnished walls should first be washed with soda, using about a pound of ordinary washing soda to a pail of warm water, then washed with clear warm water to which a small quantity of vinegar has been added to neutralize the free soda which otherwise might remain on the wall and discolor the paper. Fill holes or cracks in plaster. Allow wall to dry. Paper on a dry day. Newly plastered walls, if smooth and dry and unstained, should be sized before they are papered. Check for hot spots (free lime or alkali in the plaster). It is better to cover such spots with a coat of shellac so that your wallpaper will not be stained. The sizing is used to make sure

paper will adhere firmly to the wall. After sizing, wash casings and baseboards to be sure that they are free from the glue sizing. (5) Measure wall and cut strips to size and to match. Match next strip and cut. Most papers have marginal matching marks. (6) Cut off margin first. (7) Apply prepared paste with paste brush, applying evenly over the top strip. Fold back the ends, back to back, for easier handling. (8) Work left to right, with stepladder slightly to right so as not to interfere with hanging.

(9) Mark first straight line in chalk using a chalked plumb line as a guide. Mount first strip straight, with corner touching ceiling and wall. Usual starting point is between two windows so as to have design properly centered. Work from direction of source of light. Brush the paper on with dry brush, a few inches at a time, through the center, then right and left, keeping the rest of the paper away from wall. Do not unfold bottom end until ready to proceed. (10) Paste paper as it goes, allow to dry before trimming on the walls to exact fit. (11) To paper the ceiling, erect a scaffold the width of the room and consisting of two stepladders and a plank. The plank is adjusted so that the hands can comfortably touch the ceiling. The pasted, folded and trimmed paper is carried up to the scaffold over the left arm, but when it is unfolded it is dropped onto the end of the plank farthest away from the point of starting. Drop the short, folded end of paper at the left-hand side of scaffold as you approach it and proceed to unfold the longer fold, allowing the paper to rest on the plank as you walk backward toward the right-hand end of scaffold. When it is unfolded take hold of the end of the paper at right-hand end of scaffold with the left hand and, holding a half roll of paper in the right hand, lift up the loose paper from scaffold, then with the paper resting on the roll in the right hand and left hand supporting top end of paper, lift the paper over the head and place on the ceiling.

Allow an extra inch or two to overlap at the intersection of the ceiling where it joins the wall and secure to the ceiling by pressure of the palm of the right hand, while, at the same time, the left hand (by aid of the roll of paper) is holding up the other portion of paper at arm's length. After you have secured the paper temporarily at the right, brush as in papering wall. After unfolding this, smooth out while you are walking toward the left of scaffold. In hanging ceiling paper, always start on the window side to get maximum light.

Lining papers: Many of the special papers, particularly embossed or pressed papers, require that the walls be covered with a lining paper before applying the special grade of paper. The lining paper is made of special white, porous stock and is hung in the same manner as the ordinary paper.

Borders may be applied over papers, should overlap at least one inch, should be applied last.

Special problems: Sand finish or rough plaster walls require some preparation. Rub the ceiling or wall to remove the cutting edge of the rough plaster and loose sand evenly. Then with a broom, brush the ceiling to be sure that there are no loose particles. The walls are now ready for sizing. For comfort, wear a pair of goggles and tie a handkerchief over your face, and use gloves.

To remove varnished or painted papers, first remove the gloss on varnished or tile papers, painted or oil finished papers, to allow water to soak into the paper. One way is to rub the surface with No. 2 sandpaper. Add a little ammonia or washing soda to the hot water. Guard against defacing woodwork, floors or fixtures with ammonia or soda solutions. Fill up holes and cracks with patching plaster.

To repair wallpaper: Tear matching piece to approximate size of patch, obtaining tapered edges. Cover patch to match with wallpaper. Paste.

To waterproof wallpaper: Apply special preparation or lacquer.

# BOOK V

## Handyman's Home Repair Guide

### TOOLS AND HOW TO USE THEM

**Tool care:** Good tools pay for themselves in lasting longer, working more easily, and doing a better job. Tools must be kept free from rust. Store tools in dry place, handle with dry hands, and wipe with light coat of oil or Vaseline after each use. Keep in box with a piece of charcoal (to absorb moisture). Tools used infrequently should be oiled periodically. Before using, remove oil and accumulated dust with turpentine or kerosene. If sign of rust appears, remove by rubbing with emery cloth. To remove rust, soak in solution of ammonium citrate for two hours, rub with steel wool. Avoid scratching, scraping, bending, excessive friction, or any unnecessary contact with blades. Store planes, chisels or saws with blades free from contact with any hard surface. Use tools for their proper purpose. Prevent warping of handles by wiping or soaking in linseed oil. Sharpen blades when necessary by rubbing diagonally at proper angle on oilstone, then rubbing flat to remove hairline edge, and finishing on a soft leather.

Nails and screws will go in more easily if rubbed with soap.

### TOOLS, THEIR USE AND CARE

AWL: In several varieties. For piercing, to make holes for nails or screws.

BRACE AND BIT: For boring holes. Store bits in case.

AUGER BIT: Used in woodworking. Twist bits to make holes for nails and screws. Sizes for each 32nd of an inch. Foerstner bit is used on thin woods. Sizes for each 1/16th inch.

EXPANDING BIT: Used to cut holes of various sizes. Countersunk bits are used to widen screw holes to sink screws.

CHISELS: Sharp, narrow-bladed knives for carving, notching, leveling, etc. Cold chisels are used for work on stone or metal. They are made from hardened silicon-manganese steel. In ¼ inch sizes, flat or circular. Keep sharp with oil stone. Protect sharpness of blade. A ¼ and ⅞ inch are most used for household work.

CLAMPS: Used to hold two pieces of wood together while glue hardens.

CALIPERS: Used to measure inside or outside of small areas.

COUNTERSINK BIT: Used for enlarging screw holes to allow screws to go below surface.

DRILLS: Operate like an egg beater to make small holes. In 1/64 inch sizes. Some have breast plates so that they may be steadied on the body. Push drills are less expensive, work well for small jobs.

FILES: Available in various sizes, shapes, and coarseness. Most used are flat, half round, round. Clean frequently with wire brush. Remove remaining cuttings with soft metal pin. Used to finish and shape wood and metals.

GOUGES: Chisels with curved blades, used to cut channels in wood.

GIMLETS: Long bits 18 to 24 inches long used to bore holes through thick boards and planks.

GLASS CUTTER: Diamond-chip edged tool for cutting.

GRINDSTONE: Carborundum wheel to sharpen knives, chisels, axes, etc. Handle with care; they break easily. Should be equipped with blotter paper gaskets or safety washer on each side.

HAMMERS: Available in 10, 13, or 16 ounces, etc., and variety of heads. Claws are used to extract nails. Lightweight hammers with magnetized heads are useful for extensive tacking. If handle comes loose, remove it and install larger wedge.

HATCHET: To cut plugs, wedges, kindling wood.

LEVEL: To indicate whether a surface is level.

MALLET (WOOD): Used to hammer on chisels, gouges, etc., where surface might be dented by a hammer.

MARKING GAUGE: To mark straight lines on wood.

MITER BOX: To guide a saw in cutting wood at an angle; it has a swivel arm which can be adjusted from 45° to 90°. Used for making corners of picture frames, cabinets, etc.

NAIL SETS (PUNCHES): Punches to hammer nails below surfaces or push out pins, etc. In ¹⁄₁₆, ⅛, ¼ inch and other sizes. Never use punch with mushroomed head.

OILSTONE, OIL (NEAT'S-FOOT OR MACHINE OIL): Used to sharpen knives, chisels, gouges, plane irons, etc.; rub diagonally on well-oiled stone. Wipe stone clean after each use. When stone becomes glazed, wash with dry-cleaning solvent or ammonia solution.

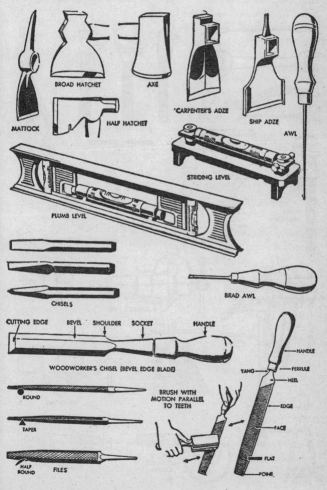

PINCERS: For levering out nails, etc.

PLANES: To smooth or whittle down wood surfaces. Never lay a plane face down. Always plane with grain of wood sloping upward. Hold plane firmly in right hand with left hand on knob.

SMOOTHING PLANE: 8 inches long, work with grain. Used

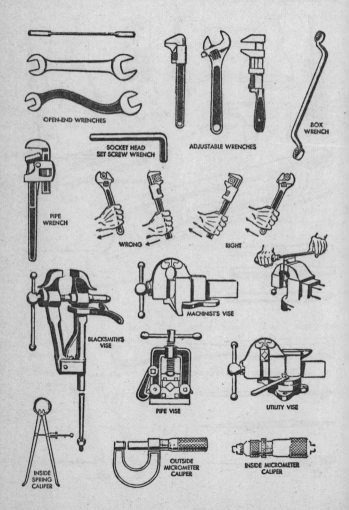

OPEN-END WRENCHES

ADJUSTABLE WRENCHES

BOX WRENCH

SOCKET HEAD SET SCREW WRENCH

PIPE WRENCH

WRONG

RIGHT

BLACKSMITH'S VISE

MACHINIST'S VISE

PIPE VISE

UTILITY VISE

INSIDE SPRING CALIPER

OUTSIDE MICROMETER CALIPER

INSIDE MICROMETER CALIPER

to smooth rough edges where straight edges and sides are not required.

JACK PLANE: 14 inches long. Work with grain. Used to smooth rough edges where straight edges and sides are not required. Not as precise as smooth or fore plane.

FORE PLANE: 18 inches long. Work with grain. Used to make a true edge for accurate work.

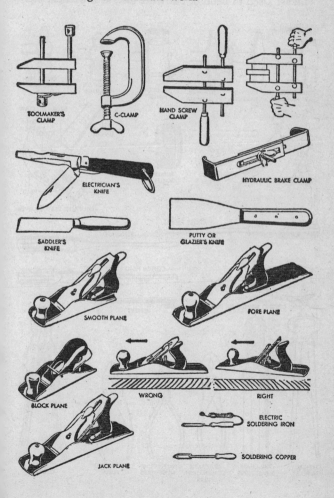

TOOLMAKER'S CLAMP

C-CLAMP

HAND SCREW CLAMP

ELECTRICIAN'S KNIFE

HYDRAULIC BRAKE CLAMP

SADDLER'S KNIFE

PUTTY OR GLAZIER'S KNIFE

SMOOTH PLANE

FORE PLANE

BLOCK PLANE

WRONG

RIGHT

ELECTRIC SOLDERING IRON

SOLDERING COPPER

JACK PLANE

Jointer plane: 22 to 24 inches long. Work with grain.

Block plane: 7 inches long. Work across grain at ends of boards. Use with one hand, making light, short strokes. Do not run over edge of work.

Rabbet plane: Open-sided, to cut grooves or sharp corners.

Combination plane: Irons may be interchanged.

Pliers: Used to bend or cut wire, etc., as a wrench, etc.

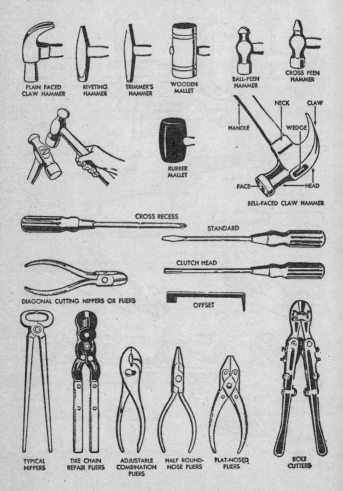

PLAIN FACED CLAW HAMMER — RIVETING HAMMER — TRIMMER'S HAMMER — WOODEN MALLET — BALL-PEEN HAMMER — CROSS PEEN HAMMER

RUBBER MALLET

NECK — CLAW — HANDLE — WEDGE — FACE — HEAD
BELL-FACED CLAW HAMMER

CROSS RECESS — STANDARD

CLUTCH HEAD

DIAGONAL CUTTING NIPPERS OR PLIERS — OFFSET

TYPICAL NIPPERS — TIRE CHAIN REPAIR PLIERS — ADJUSTABLE COMBINATION PLIERS — HALF ROUND-NOSE PLIERS — FLAT-NOSED PLIERS — BOLT CUTTERS

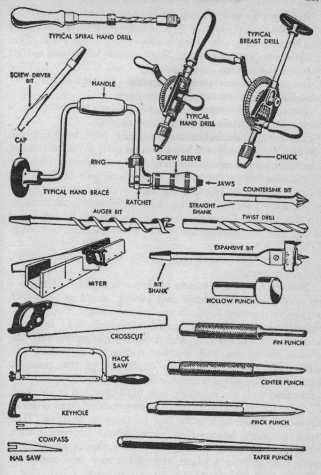

TYPICAL SPIRAL HAND DRILL

SCREW-DRIVER BIT

HANDLE

CAP

RING

TYPICAL HAND BRACE

RATCHET

TYPICAL HAND DRILL

SCREW SLEEVE

JAWS

TYPICAL BREAST DRILL

CHUCK

COUNTERSINK BIT

STRAIGHT SHANK

AUGER BIT

TWIST DRILL

MITER

BIT SHANK

EXPANSIVE BIT

HOLLOW PUNCH

CROSSCUT

PIN PUNCH

HACK SAW

CENTER PUNCH

KEYHOLE

PRICK PUNCH

COMPASS

NAIL SAW

TAPER PUNCH

PUTTY KNIFE: Flexible, dull-bladed knife used to mix and apply putty, plaster, etc.

RULER: Available in folding-wood or self-rewinding flexible tape. Should be marked in $\frac{1}{16}$ inch intervals, to 6 feet.

SAWS:

CROSS-CUT SAW: To saw against grain (7 to 10 teeth to the inch).

RIP SAW: To saw with grain (5½ to 6 teeth to the inch).

COPING SAW: U handle with detachable narrow blades for cutting curves, scrolls, sharp angles.

COMPASS (KEYHOLE) SAW: Short, narrow blade used to start cuts in a flat surface.

BACKSAW (TENON): Small cross cut (14 teeth to the inch) used for cabinet work.

TURNING SAW (WEB): Detachable, narrow blade on a frame, used to make curves close to an edge.

HACKSAW: Detachable, narrow blade used to cut metal. Never saw into nails with wood-cutting saw. Avoid twisting or bending blade. Support waste end till cut through. Use correct blades. In cutting metal, do not use new blade in cut started by another blade. Turn work over and start new cut.

SOLDERING IRON: Irons are heated by acetylene torch or gas stove flame. Copper "irons" are electrically heated. Used to join two metals with lead-tin or silver-tin solders. (See p. 298)

SCRAPER: Wide blade on a handle, used to remove paint, wallpaper, etc.

SCREWS: Come in a variety of shapes and materials adapted for special uses. The heads may be flat, round or oval, with a Phillips recessed head or ornamental design. Copper and brass screws are non-rusting and are widely used for boats and other outdoor work. Nickel plated, chromium and aluminum screws are also weather resistant. Galvanized iron screws will rust, but they are treated to be rust resistant. Iron or steel screws are suitable for most indoor work.

Surform tools are relatively new tools invented in England. They look and act like files, but the cutting edge is much deeper, and so much more can be done in shaping. They come in many forms—files, rasps, planes, curved planes, wheels for the portable drill, etc. Faster than a file or rasp, more flexible than a plane, they fill a new and important place in your tool chest.

SPOKESHAVE: Blade with two handles, for smoothing curved edges.

T-BEVEL: Vertical and adjustable angled edge. Used to mark and test angled edges.

TRY SQUARE: Vertical and horizontal edges used to mark and test right angles. Marked at ⅛ inch intervals.

VISE: Adjustable jaws used to hold or clamp wood.

Wrenches: Monkey Wrench: Adjustable. Used for loosening bolts, faucets, etc. Open-end wrench has fixed openings, usually at each end. Available in sets of 10 or 12 with openings

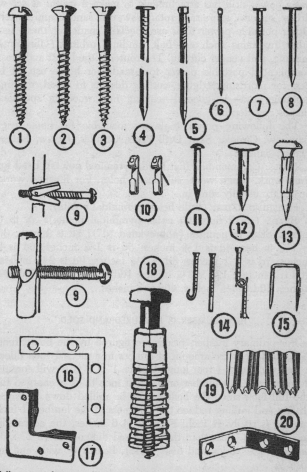

Nails, screws, fasteners: (1) Round head screw. (2) Oval head. (3) Flat head. (4) Common nail. (5) Finishing nail. (6) Wire brad. (7) Plaster board nail. (8) Wire lath nail. (9) Togglebolt. (10) Picture hooks. (11) Brass escutcheon. (12) Roofing nails. (13) Masonry nails. (14) Cobblers clinch nails. (15) Double pointed tacks. (16) Flat corner. (17) Screen brace. (18) Shield. (19) Corrugated fastener. (20) Angle.

from ⅛ to 1 inch. Stillson wrench is adjustable to grip a round pipe.

Portable power tools are made so flexible that most of the tools designed for one use may be adapted for others. The basic power drill has attachments to make it useful as screw driver, surform, sabre saw, rotary saw, disc sander, and router. Other portable power tools are specially made for these and other functions such as—belt sanding, orbital (vibrating) sanding, and veneer cutting. The router is the latest and most complicated portable power tool made for home use. It is best for mortising, edging, cutting designs in wood, making moldings and—in general—cutting into wood in specified shapes and depths.

The following power tools are available for home use: Bandsaw, Circular Saw, Drill Press, Grinder, Jigsaw, Lathe, Planer, Sander.

NAILS: Common nail (flat head, pyramidal points). Used for framework, rough work, sub-floors, holes. For finished work, heads are usually sunk in.

FINISHING NAILS: (little head, pyramidal points).

BRAD: (small finishing nails, pyramidal points): ⅛ to 3 inches. Sizes in pennies (abbreviated "d"): 2d is 1 inch; 3d is 1¼ inches; 4d is 1½ inches; 5d is 1¾ inches; 6d is 2 inches; 7d is 2¼ inches; 8d is 2½ inches; 9d is 2¾ inches; 10d is 3 inches; 12d is 3¼ inches; 16d is 3½ inches; 20d is 4 inches; 30d is 4½ inches; 40d is 5 inches.

## HOW LUMBER IS MEASURED AND SOLD

For ordinary lumber, prices are figured by the board foot. A board foot is the amount of lumber in a piece 1 inch thick, 1 foot wide, and 1 foot long. A piece 1" x 6" x 6' will contain 3 board feet. But lumber only a half inch thick is charged for the full inch since the board must be milled down. Because drying and milling reduce the thickness of the lumber, 1 inch lumber is really ¾ inch. From 2 to 6 inches, the actual dimension is ⅜" less than the expressed dimension; (a 2" x 6" is really 1⅝" thick and 5⅝" wide). Boards 8" wide and up lose ½".

Select close-grained rather than open-grained oak, if you want to do an expert job of finishing. Open-grained woods require a filler.

Some lumber, such as shingles and laths, comes in bunches. Kindling wood is usually sold by the bushel or by the truck-load. Moldings, poles and railings are sold by the running foot. Windows and doors are ready made and are priced according to size and type. Plywood and wall board is sold by square foot or panel.

Wise selection of lumber involves first, singling out the requirements of the job. In general 1 & 2 Clear (also called first and seconds, or B & Better) is highest quality, almost free of blemishes, is used for finest cabinet work. C grade may have pin knots and minor imperfections. Often one side is without blemishes. Grade D is the lowest of the finishing grades. It is a good all-around wood for workshop, for natural-finish shelves or built-in furniture. No. 1 is the first of board grades. It is a good general purpose wood, may have sound, smooth knots up to about 2", but takes paint well. No. 2 is an all-around utility grade. It is used for flooring or knotty paneling, has other blemishes, including larger knots, sometimes loose. No. 3 occasionally has knotholes, a limited amount of pitch and season checking. It is used for rough jobs (shelves for garage or workshop). No. 4 is the lowest board grade you are likely to use. It is used for temporary structures. No. 5 is the poorest quality. It has many imperfections, is used for crating, etc.

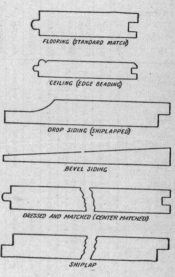

FLOORING (STANDARD MATCH)

CEILING (EDGE BEADING)

DROP SIDING (SHIPLAPPED)

BEVEL SIDING

DRESSED AND MATCHED (CENTER MATCHED)

SHIPLAP

Six typical patterns of lumber.

When ordering three boards 1st quality white oak, 1 inch thick, 6 inches wide, and 12 feet long, smooth on both sides and on both edges, it is written: 3–1x6–12–Fas–Wh. Oak

**BROAD CLASSIFICATION OF WOODS ACCORDING**

A, among the woods relatively high in the particular respect listed;
B, among the woods intermediate in the particular respect listed;

| Kind of wood | Hardness | Weight, dry | Freedom from shrinkage | Freedom from warping | Ease of working | Paint holding | Nail holding | Decay resistance of heartwood | Proportion of heartwood | Amount of figure | Freedom from odor and taste (dry) | Bending strength | Stiffness | Strength as a post | Toughness |
|---|---|---|---|---|---|---|---|---|---|---|---|---|---|---|---|
| Ash: White | A | A | B | B | C | | A | C | C | A | A | A | A | A | A |
| Basswood | C | A | C | C | B | C | A | C | | B | C | A | C | A | A |
| Beech | A | A | C | C | C | | A | A | B | A | A | A | A | A | A |
| Birch, yellow | A | A | C | B | C | | A | A | B | B | B | A | A | B | A |
| Cedar: | | | | | | | | | | | | | | | |
|   Western red | C | C | A | A | A | A | C | A | A | B | C | C | C | B | C |
|   Eastern red | A | A | B | A | A | B | | A | A | B | B | | A | A | B |
| Cherry | A | B | B | A | B | | B | A | B | A | B | B | C | C | B |
| Chestnut | B | B | B | B | B | | A | C | A | C | A | C | C | B | B |
| Cottonwood | C | B | C | C | B | | C | C | B | A | A | B | B | C | B |
| Cypress, southern | B | B | B | C | B | A | C | A | A | A | A | B | A | B | B |
| Douglas fir | B | B | B | B | C | C | B | B | B | A | C | A | A | B | A |
| Elm: Soft | A | A | C | C | C | | B | B | B | A | A | A | A | B | A |
|   Rock | A | C | A | B | B | | B | C | B | B | B | C | B | C | A |
| Fir: Balsam | C | C | C | B | B | B | C | B | C | B | A | B | B | B | C |
|   White | C | C | B | C | B | B | B | C | B | A | B | B | C | B | B |
| Gum, red | B | B | C | B | C | | A | B | C | A | A | B | B | C | A |
| Hackberry | A | A | C | B | C | | A | | B | A | A | | | | |
| Hemlock: | | | | | | | | | | | | | | | |
|   Eastern | B | B | B | B | B | B | B | C | B | B | A | B | B | B | B |
|   Western | B | B | B | B | B | B | B | C | B | B | A | B | B | B | B |
| Hickory: | | | | | | | | | | | | | | | |
|   True | A | A | C | B | C | | A | C | B | B | B | A | A | A | A |
| Pecan | A | A | C | B | C | | A | C | B | A | A | A | A | A | B |
| Larch, western | A | A | B | B | C | C | A | B | A | A | C | A | A | A | A |
| Locust: | | | | | | | | | | | | | | | |
|   Black | A | A | B | B | C | | A | A | A | A | B | A | A | A | A |
|   Honey | A | A | C | B | C | | A | B | B | A | A | A | A | A | A |
| Maple: Hard | A | A | C | B | C | | A | C | B | B | A | A | C | A | A |
|   Soft | A | A | B | B | C | | A | C | C | C | B | A | C | B | A |
| Oak: Red | A | A | C | B | C | | A | C | B | B | A | A | A | B | A |
|   White | A | A | C | B | C | | A | A | B | B | A | A | A | A | A |
| Pine: | | | | | | | | | | | | | | | |
|   Ponderosa | C | B | B | A | B | B | B | (2) | C | C | A | C | A | C | C |
|   Southern yellow | A | A | C | A | A | C | A | B (2) | C | B | A | A | A | A | B |
|   Northern white | C | C | C | A | A | A | A | B (2) | B | C | C | B | C | C | B |
|   Western white | C | C | B | A | A | A | B | B (2) | B | C | C | B | C | C | C |
|   Sugar pine | C | C | B | A | A | A | A | (2) | B | C | C | B | C | C | C |
| Poplar, yellow | C | B | C | A | B | | B | C | A | B | A | B | B | C | B |
| Redwood | B | B | A | A | B | | A | A | A | B | B | B | B | C | B |
| Spruce: | | | | | | | | | | | | | | | |
|   Eastern | C | B | B | A | B | B | B | C | C | B | C | B | B | B | B |
|   Sitka | C | B | B | A | B | B | B | C | C | B | A | B | B | C | B |
|   Engelmann | C | C | A | A | C | | C | C | C | B | B | B | C | B | B |
| Sycamore | A | A | C | C | B | | A | | B | C | B | B | A | B | B |
| Tupelo | A | A | C | B | B | | A | | C | A | | A | A | A | A |
| Walnut | A | A | B | B | C | B | | A | C | B | C | B | A | A | A |

[1] Exclusive of the all-heartwood grades that are available on special order in birch, cedar, cypress, Douglas firred gum, southern yellow pine, redwood, and walnut.

TO CHARACTERISTICS AND PROPERTIES

C, among the woods relatively low in the particular respect listed.

| Surface characteristics of common grades | | | | | | Distinctive uses | |
| --- | --- | --- | --- | --- | --- | --- | --- |
| Number of knots | Size of knots | Number of pitch defects | Size of pitch defects | Number of other defects | Size of other defects | Farm or Home | Commercial |
| C | B | None | ..... | B | B | Handles, Implements............. | Handles vehicles part. |
| C | B | None | ..... | C | B | Woodenware.................... | Fixtures, furniture parts. |
| B | B | None | ..... | A | B | Woodenware, containers, fuel..... | Woodenware, flooring, furniture. |
| C | B | None | ..... | A | B | Millwork, furniture.............. | Millwork, furniture. |
| C | A | None | ..... | C | C | Shingles, siding, posts, and poles.. | Poles, shingles, siding. |
| A | C | None | ..... | C | | Posts......................... | Chests, pencils. |
| C | B | None | ..... | | | Furniture..................... | Electrotype blocks. |
| C | A | None | ..... | A | B | Poles, posts, trim............ | Caskets, poles, core stock. |
| C | B | None | ..... | C | B | Wagon boxes, containers........ | Boxes, cases, and furniture parts. |
| C | B | None | ..... | B | B | Silos, tanks, construction..... | Greenhouses, tanks, construction. |
| B | B | B | B | B | B | Construction.................. | Construction. |
| B | B | None | ..... | B | A | Cheese boxes.................. | Containers. |
| B | C | None | ..... | A | A | Implements.................... | Cooperage. |
| A | C | None | ..... | B | A | Light construction............ | Pulpwood. |
| B | B | None | ..... | B | A | Light construction............ | Light construction, pulpwood. |
| C | B | None | ..... | C | B | Fruit and vegetable boxes...... | Furniture, millwork, containers. |
| C | A | None | ..... | B | B | Furniture..................... | Automobile bodies. |
| B | B | None | ..... | A | A | Construction.................. | Construction. |
| B | B | None | ..... | A | B | Construction.................. | Construction. |
| B | A | None | ..... | B | B | Handles. Implements........... | Implements, handles, sporting goods. |
| C | A | None | ..... | A | A | Wagon and buggy parts......... | Furniture, automobile bodies. |
| A | C | C | C | A | A | Construction.................. | Construction. |
| B | B | None | ..... | B | B | Fence posts................... | Insulator pins. |
| B | B | None | ..... | B | B | | |
| B | B | None | ..... | B | B | Implements, flooring.......... | Flooring, furniture, machine parts. |
| C | B | None | ..... | C | B | Fuel.......................... | Furniture. |
| C | A | None | B | B | B | Implement parts, construction.... | Furniture, flooring. |
| C | A | None | ..... | B | B | Implement parts, posts, construction. | Cooperage, furniture, flooring. |
| B | B | B | B | B | B | Millwork, light construction ...... | Millwork, construction, boxes. |
| C | A | A | A | B | B | Construction.................. | Construction. |
| A | C | A | C | B | B | Millwork, siding.............. | Millwork, containers. |
| A | A | C | C | A | C | Millwork, siding.............. | Millwork, containers. |
| A | C | C | C | B | C | Millwork...................... | Patterns, millwork. |
| C | B | None | ..... | C | B | Millwork...................... | Millwork, furniture. |
| C | A | None | ..... | C | B | Silos, tanks, construction.... | Tanks, construction. |
| A | C | C | C | B | B | Construction.................. | Pulpwood, musical instruments. |
| B | C | C | C | B | B | Ladders, construction......... | Airplanes, construction. |
| A | C | C | C | B | B | Construction.................. | Construction. |
| C | B | None | ..... | B | B | Baskets and boxes............. | Boxes and crates, millwork. |
| C | B | None | ..... | C | C | Fruit and vegetable boxes........ | Factory flooring, boxes and crates. |
| C | B | None | ..... | C | C | Furniture..................... | Furniture, millwork. |

[2] Conflicting opinion and absence of adequate test data preclude a definite rating; the authors recommend against relying on high decay resistance when this wood is used untreated.

S4S. The "Fas" means first and seconds, the top grade in hardwood. The "S4S" means surfaced on all four sides. Lumberyards usually have a power saw that can bevel edges of heavy lumber, rip to specified width when stock sizes won't fit and to exact lengths. Request this if your job calls for a large amount of cutting.

After the requirements have been determined it is relatively easy to check the properties of the different woods to see whether these requirements would be met.

Stockpanels of plywood, masonite, plasterboard, or plastic base are available in a vast variety of finishes. Standard wood patterns are made with veneers or plastic laminations. Some are inlaid, plastic finished, overlaid with a print design or some other texture. Common patterns include shades of walnut, oak, pine, elm, cherry, birch, and mahogany. These are easy to work with, require little upkeep, and make refinishing a room comparatively inexpensive.

## GLUING

To glue wood, remove all old glue with a knife (if there is any danger of removing paint, use alcohol warmed in a deep glass placed in a pan of hot water, not on the stove). Warm new glue in a pan of water and warm wood if possible. Apply glue to both surfaces and allow to dry, binding surfaces together with tape or clamps. (Protect clamp at contact point with a pad of cloth.) Allow to stand till thoroughly dry. Loosen any excess glue with cheesecloth dampened with alcohol.

It is important to know that an adhesive that is good for one job may not be successful on another assignment.

For use with wood, several glues are appropriate. Casein glue needs mixing but is waterproof. Resorcinol glue is waterproof but tricky to mix. Liquid animal glue won't stand much moisture.

For small jobs about the house, such as repairing toys, the house cellulose adhesives are fine. They are generally sold under various brand names as "household cement" and come ready to use in metal fold-up tubes. They are water resistant and flexible.

For heavy jobs, such as fastening fixtures to tile walls, use a rubber-base adhesive. This can be applied directly from a metal tube or by means of a brush or trowel.

The efficiency of glued joints is determined by (1) Kind of wood; (2) Moisture content of wood; (3) Type of joint; (4) Precision with which contact surfaces match; (5) Type of glue and method of preparation, handling, and application; (6) Degree and duration of pressure used in gluing; (7) Method of conditioning glued joints; (8) Service conditions.

The most satisfactory glue for the homecraftsman is the plastic resin type. It comes in powder form to be mixed with water as needed. This glue is waterproof, does not stain and is easily handled. Epoxy glue is made up of a resin base and a hardener.

In general, heavy woods are harder to glue than light woods; hardwoods are harder to glue than softwoods; and heartwoods are harder to glue than sapwoods.

## TYPES OF GLUE JOINTS

SIDE-GRAIN JOINTS: Side-grain surfaces can be glued easily. They are stronger than joints made by gluing surfaces cut at an angle to the grain.

END-BUTT JOINTS: It is almost impossible to make end-butt joints strong enough for ordinary service. With the most careful gluing possible, not more than about 25 percent of the tensile strength of wood parallel to the grain can be obtained.

SCARF JOINTS: Plain scarf joints are recommended when splicing is necessary.

GLUE BLOCKS: Glue blocks increase the strength of joints materially. The standard triangular type is satisfactory for box corners; in frame joints, a splint inserted in a narrow groove in the inside edge of the frame members serves as a block.

DOWEL JOINTS: The insertion of dowels strengthens glued joints appreciably. This is especially true when end-grain pieces are glued to side-grain pieces, and in end-grain butt joints. Dowels also aid in alignment.

(1) Dowels may be any shape. The conventional type is round and is made of birch or maple. A slight rounding of the edge on both ends of a dowel facilitates assembly.

(2) Dowel holes should be laid out carefully to match the companion holes in pieces to be glued. Drill the holes small enough so dowels will not drop out before glue is applied,

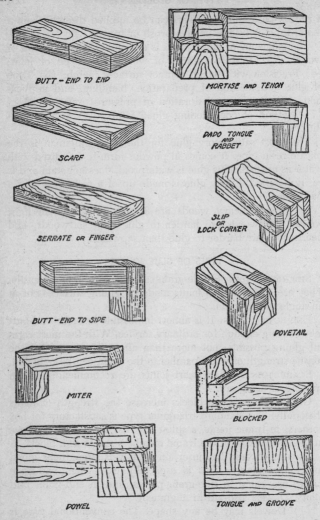

BUTT – END TO END

MORTISE and TENON

SCARF

DADO TONGUE
AND
RABBET

SERRATE or FINGER

SLIP
OR
LOCK CORNER

BUTT – END TO SIDE

DOVETAIL

MITER

BLOCKED

DOWEL

TONGUE AND GROOVE

and slightly deeper than the length of dowel to be inserted. This allows for any surplus of glue. Apply thin film of glue in holes rather than to dowels.

**Soldering:** Two pieces of metal may be joined by a solder of soft metal—usually a lead-tin alloy. The solder must have a lower melting point than the metals to be joined. (1) Remove grease, paint, dirt or corrosion from metals. (2) Apply a flux to surfaces to be joined. This removes oxide coating. Fluxes commonly used are rosin or zinc chloride. (3) File soldering iron clean. Heat soldering iron till it can melt solder. Coat the tip with solder, spread smoothly and evenly. Wipe with a rag to produce even layer of molten solder. (4) Allow solder to flow over edges.

To SOLDER SHEET METAL SEAMS: (5) Bend over edges of each sheet so that edges interlock. (6) Apply flux and solder along seam and allow to melt in.

Or (5a) Apply flux to area to be soldered, masking off the surrounding area with adhesive tape. (6a) Apply beads of solder over the joint and melt. Solder will be contained from spreading by the adhesive tape.

## MISCELLANEOUS HOUSEHOLD REPAIRS

**Cracked Dish:** If not broken, boil in pan of milk for 45 minutes to eliminate crack.

To mend china and glass, dry both edges and apply special cement to both sides, press together firmly, remove excess cement, and bind tightly. Allow to set for 2 to 3 days. Do not soak or heat. If time is available, Ivory White may be used instead of cement on china, but dish must not be used for 12 months. Professional repairers rivet breaks so that they are practically invisible and more permanent than cement.

**Wooden bowls:** Cracks can be filled with shellac. A coat of shellac before using will save time in future cleaning.

**Sharpening scissors:** Cut up a sheet of sandpaper.

**Squeaks:** In apparatus with moving parts—doors, carpet sweepers, etc.—squeaks usually indicate a need for oil at the friction points. Soap, starch, or talcum powder may be used in an emergency. Where equipment comes in contact with food—as an egg beater—use salad oil.

In furniture, squeaks indicate loose parts. Take apart and reglue. (See pages 296, 304.) In floors, squeaks indicate loose boards. (See page 313.)

**Window shades:** If they won't go back, roll up shade and replace. Occasionally spring may require winding at flat end.

**Loose casters:** Remove caster, fill hole with putty, replace caster, scrape off excess putty.

**Mildew:** Molds thrive on heat and damp. If mildew takes hold, remove, scrub surface with solution of ½ oz. bichloride of mercury (at drug stores) or 1 lb. trisodium phosphate or sodium carbonate in 1 gallon of water, rinse, allow to dry, then repaint with mildew retardants added to paint. (See also pages 77, 85 re: stain removal.)

## FURNITURE REPAIR

Major furniture repairs can be largely eliminated by making frequent inspections to detect weak spots, wear, and minor scratches or breaks and repairing them before they become serious.

**Shallow surface defects:** Sand or plane surface to remove shallow defects in solid wood tops. If wood is dented and not chipped, attempt to expand wood with wet pad after removing polish, oil, or wax, so that water may penetrate. Be careful to avoid burning.

To repair a scratch, apply cloth dampened with denatured alcohol if scratch is only shellac deep, or apply furniture polish containing a wood dye, allowing a day to sink in. Rub surface with flannel cloth and furniture polish. If scratch does not respond, remove varnish from the area, rub carefully with fine sandpaper or steel wool, remove the dust, and apply varnish over the surface to be refinished. Build up to the level of the surrounding area. If the new finish leaves a surface shinier than the surrounding area, rub with oil and pumice or fine rottenstone, or with gauze cloth dampened with alcohol.

**Deep defects:** If a defect is too deep to be removed by sanding or planing, repair it with shellac filler of a matching color. Clean out the scratch, removing all loose or crushed wood fiber. Enlarge it if necessary and undercut slightly. Apply stick shellac with a hot knife blade, filling the depression to surface level. Smooth the fill.

**Extensive defects:** If the surface is so damaged that neither of the above procedures is practical, cover the entire surface with plywood or tempered prestwood cemented down with woodworking glue. Remove the finish and sand the old surface until it is smooth and free of irregularities. Cut edges of the covering flush with the old top edge. If the old edge is

marred, use a thin wood banding of the same finish and species as the original surface. Make sure the top edge of the
banding is flush with or very slightly under the surface level

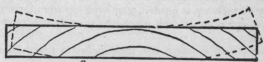

## 1. SOLID BOARD, SHRINKAGE TENDENCY INDICATED BY DOTTED LINES

## 2. GLUED-UP CONSTRUCTION BALANCED STRESSES

To prevent shrinkage shown in (1), rip board into thirds, invert center section, and reglue.

of the new top. Make the banding wide enough to cover both
old edge and surface material. A tempered prestwood surface need not be finished.

A self-adhesive plastic, available in many patterns, may be
used to cover, decorate, and protect any smooth surface; to
waterproof splash areas; to refinish and transform worn surfaces; or in dozens of other ways—from covering a cookbook
in a color to match your kitchen to covering a whole closet in
beautiful pastel. These plastic contact sheets will go on any
clean, dry, smooth surface: wood, plywood, glass, metal, tile,
plastic, most paints, enamel, porcelain. You need no water,
no paste, no tools—just scissors and your imagination. Three
steps are all it takes. (1) Cut to fit. (2) Peel off backing. (3)
Press down and smooth out. The plastic can be lifted and
replaced during application. Some of these plastics come in
long, 36-inch wide rolls.

Some types for use on card tables and desk tops offer a
soft, skidproof surface that's pleasant to the touch. They have
made their appearance on trays, especially those used to carry
drinks—the nylon surface is not only skidproof but waterproof
as well. Contact sheets are useful for picture mats, for panel-

ing cabinet fronts, and for lining all sorts of drawers and boxes that hold silver, jewelry, tools, sewing materials, etc.

**Warped tops:** Replace warped tops. To increase stability, use a glued-up board instead of a solid one. For instance, if an 18 by 36 inch top is needed, glue up a top from three 6 inch pieces, or rip an 18 inch piece into three 6 inch pieces and re-glue.

**Minor defects in veneer:** Use stick shellac to repair minor defects in veneered surfaces.

**Small defective areas in veneer:** If damage is confined to a small area, repair it as follows: (1) Select a patch slightly larger than the damaged section. Apply three or four small spots of glue to the damaged area, press the patch over the glue and allow it to set. (2) With a sharp knife held vertically, cut through both patch and damaged veneer. This cut need not follow a rectangle; it is better to taper it to a point. (3) Detach the patch and clean out the damaged veneer within the cut area. Apply glue, insert patch, and place a weight on it. Remove excess glue from the surface and allow the repair to set.

**Extensive damage in veneer:** If the damaged area is too extensive for repair by these methods, cover the entire surface.

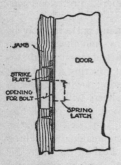

Striking latch bolt.

**Locks and catches:** Minor shrinkage or warpage can make door locks and catches fail to work properly. To correct this condition, shift strike plates or adjust hinge positions.

**Sticking drawers:** Sticking drawers can be freed by sanding or planing sides or bottom. Apply paraffin, soap or powdered soapstone to relieve minor sticking. A slight readjustment of the drawer guides may eliminate a great deal of work on a warped drawer. Unpainted parts may be covered with water paint, shellacked, allowed to dry.

**Loose joints:** If glue joints at corners show signs of loosening, repair them with glue blocks to prevent dovetail corners from breaking. Do not repair loose corners with brads, as this may split the wood.

**Shaky drawers:** Screw metal angle brackets inside drawer, or nail or glue on triangular wood blocks.

**Enlarged screw and nail holes:** Screw or nail holes often become enlarged, with resultant loosening of hinges, strike plates, latches, handles, and similar fittings. Fill such holes with plastic wood or a softwood plug. Replace the fitting and fasten it securely.

**Wear around fittings:** If wood surfaces around a fitting become seriously worn, remove the fitting, inlay a new piece of wood in the worn area, and refasten the fitting. If this is not practicable, relocate fitting. Use the following method to relocate butt hinges for doors or lids:

(1) Mortise door or lid to a depth equal to the double hinge thickness. This eliminates the second mortise and reduces chances of an error in marking or mortising.

(2) Fasten hinges on door or lid. Cut off one screw just long enough to project about $\frac{1}{16}$ inch through the hinge when it is closed and the screw is in place. File a point on this stub and set it in the hinge.

(3) Set door or lid in position and press hinge against frame. Drill screw hole in frame at point marked by stub screw.

(Note. Keep stub-screw marker for future use.)

**Splits or cracks:** Repair lengthwise splits or cracks extending entirely through a piece by forcing glue into crack and then applying pressure to close it. Maintain pressure until glue is dry.

**Broken mortise joints:** To repair broken mortise joints, butt-glue broken ends together. Reinforce joint with a screw or dowel long enough to penetrate at least 1 inch into tenon member. Do not use this method to repair parts under great stress. Replace such parts completely.

**Loose dowels:** Dowels sometimes shrink and become loose at one end, allowing the joint to open. If the dowel cannot be replaced, repair it by one of the following methods:

(1) Make a saw cut lengthwise through shrunken end of dowel. Insert small wedge in cut, with wide end of wedge projecting beyond end of dowel, and force dowel back into joint. This drives wedge deeper into dowel, expanding it and making joint tight.

(2) If wedging is not practicable because the parts cannot

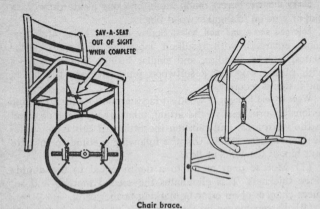

SAV-A-SEAT
OUT OF SIGHT
WHEN COMPLETE

Chair brace.

be disassembled, anchor loose dowel end in the joint with a smaller cross dowel or screw.

**Shaky chairs:** Unsteady chairs are usually caused by loosening of rungs. (1) Remove loose rungs, remove all glue from both rung and hole, apply new glue, bind firmly with cord until glue has set; (2) Metal "rung fasteners" are available to slip over rung which is too narrow; (3) Where several legs are to be repaired, use "chair-bracing sets" to keep legs taut during drying period. When shakiness is caused by loose slat, apply corner splines.

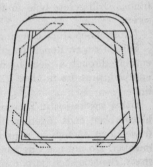

Corner splines.

**Cross-breaks:** Repair cross-breaks by splicing, or replace entire piece. Splicing by scarf joint requires closely fitting contact surfaces. Hand tools can be used with a simple jig, to insure accurate work. Using Jorgensen or C-clamps (page 287), fasten jig, guide, and pieces to be spliced to a work bench, and cut bevel by slicing a hand plane, side down, against edge of the jig base.

**Raising chair:** Glue rubber door stops to legs.

**Sagging chair cane:** To tighten caning, wet cane, allow it to dry, and shrink. Varnish to add life.

## UPHOLSTERED FURNITURE

**Repair problems:** Upholstered furniture consists basically of a frame, strip or cleat webbing, padding, and cover. Some furniture also has spring upholstery. Repairs needed on upholstered furniture generally include recovering, replacement or redistribution of padding, replacement or refastening of webbing, and regluing, reinforcing, or replacing frame parts. With spring construction, replacing, anchoring, and retying springs may also be necessary.

**Recovering:** Replace the entire cover if the covers on seat, back, or arms are torn, soiled, or worn beyond repair. Even with fairly new furniture, it is usually impossible to match new material to worn or faded fabric, so all sections must usually be recovered when one is damaged.

Procedures for recovering upholstered furniture vary with furniture design, but the following general procedure applies to almost all types:

(1) Remove old cover carefully, taking out all tacks.

(2) Using the old cover as a pattern, cut a piece of new material to approximate shape and size.

(3) Smooth out and replace any lumpy or torn padding and lay new cover in place, making certain all four sides have the same amount of surplus material.

(4) Tack center of opposite sides, stretching the material lightly but firmly. Do not drive tacks all the way in. Work from center to edges, stretching material evenly. If wrinkles develop, remove tacks and work the wrinkles out. Note how the older covering was folded and fitted at corners and around legs and arms. If this was satisfactory, fit the new cover the same way. When covering fits smoothly, drive tacks all the way in.

(5) After covering is tacked to the side of the frame, cover tack heads with an edging or gimp. Fasten gimp with large-headed upholstery nails spaced about 2 inches apart. (Note—Whenever covering and padding are removed, overhaul frame, webbing, and springs.)

**Repairing frame:** Tighten loose frame joints with glue blocks, pins and screws, or angle irons. Repair other frame damage using procedures on page 303.

**Repairing Webbing:**
Check strip or cleat webbing for signs of wear or breakage whenever cover is removed. Replace damaged webbing and refasten loose strips. To insure that webbing will hold securely, double it over at the ends to give tacks more gripping power, tighten, and tack so stress is at right angles to tack length. Run webbing in two directions, at right angles to each other.

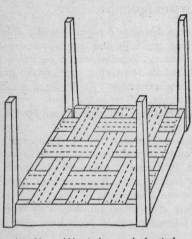

Attaching webbing to framework of a stool.

Closing the entire bottom with webbing is not necessary, but too much webbing is better than to little. If springs are to be anchored to webbing, space the webbing to support spring bases. Similarly, anchor metal strips or wood cleats securely and space them so that springs may be attached.

**Adjusting springs:** Springs may shift, bend, or become damaged otherwise. Re-anchor and retie loose springs; replace those that are damaged.

(a.) Anchoring. Springs are usually attached differently on webbing, on metal strips, or on wood cleats. Fasten spring bases to webbing with heavy flax cord about ⅛ inch in diameter. Anchor springs to metal strips with clamps. If clamps loosen, re-rivet them. Fasten springs to wood cleats with staples or metal straps and nails.

(b.) Retying. After springs are anchored, retie them with heavy flax cord like that used to anchor springs to webbing.

(1) Nail cord to the center of one side of the frame. Pull it over the top of the springs to an opposite anchoring

nail. Allow enough cord to tie two double half-hitches to each spring and cut to this length.

(2) Bring cord up to the top of the first coil spring and tie it with a double half-hitch to the nearest rim of the first spring. Before drawing the knot tight, pull spring down to shape the seat or back. Continue to opposite side of the top on the same spring and tie it.

(3) Continue in like fashion, tying two points on each spring and finally anchoring cord to nail on opposite side of frame. Run cords in both directions (side to side and front to back) at right angles to each other, until all springs are tied in two directions.

(4) Tie springs diagonally in the same manner, beginning at one corner of the frame and anchoring cord on the opposite corner.

(5) Repeat with cord at right angles to the first set of diagonal cords. Tie this cord to spring with two double half-hitches and also tie it

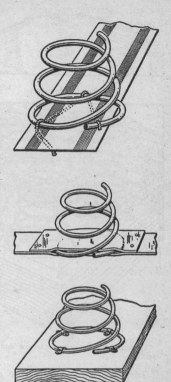

Top: Tying spring to webbing.
Middle: Fastening spring to metal strip.
Bottom: Fastening spring to wood cleat.

to the other three cords at their junction in the center of the coil. Each spring is now tied in eight places and the crossing cords are also tied together. Completely retied springs are shown in illustration.

(6) Replace padding.

**Replacement or redistribution of padding:** Padding of tow, cotton batting, excelsior, or moss is used over the springs in the case of spring construction, or on the webbing in the case of

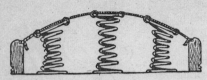

**Springs tied in place.**

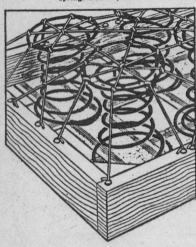

**Springs tied lengthwise, crosswise and diagonally.**

padded construction. When padding shifts or becomes lumpy, remove the cover and redistribute or replace the padding.

To replace padding:

(1) First, remove all old padding and tack a piece of burlap smoothly over the entire surface to be padded.

(2) Spread padding evenly over the burlap, forming a compact cushion about 1½ inches thick.

(3) Cover this with a second piece of burlap or muslin, tacked down securely, and place a 2-inch layer of cotton batting on top. Pull off surplus cotton around the edges; do not cut the cotton since this will make a ridge under the cover.

(4) Tack a cambric cover over the frame bottom to keep padding from working through to springs or webbing and falling out.

(5) Replace cover as described.

### DOORS, WINDOWS AND SCREENS

**Loose doors:** Rattling doors are usually caused by loose "strike plate" of the door lock. Unscrew and remove plate, enlarge the inner edge of the mortised portion, with chisel or knife, and replace closer to the stop. If plate has to be moved any distance, it may be necessary to enlarge hole so that the bolt slats fit. Fill old hole with plastic wood, and sand level when dry.

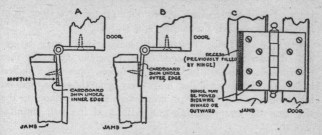

**Hinge readjustments to correct ill fitting doors.**

**Loose hinges:** These may cause a door to sag. To tighten screws, remove screws, fill holes with sticks and plastic wood, allow to dry before replacing. Use longer screws if necessary. If frame is not uniform, insert "shims" of thin wood or cardboard to even out or raise the surface.

**Doors that don't stay closed:** Doors sometimes shrink so they do not reach the frame when closed. Remove lock and add thin strip to the lock-side edge, then replace lock. Simpler alternative: Remove strike plate, add strips of wood or cardboard under plate till it can engage lock.

**Doors that don't close:** Warping and settling may put door or frame out of shape and prevent from closing. (1) Check hinge plates to see if they are fastened firmly. (2) If door is at an angle, remove door (bottom first) and add "shim" of cardboard under one hinge, a thinner strip under the center hinge if there are three hinges, equalize the hinges. (3) If necessary, plane edge which protrudes. Plane as

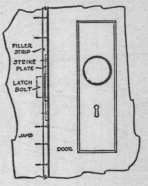

**Door jamb showing filler strips.**

little as possible as a door may shrink as it dries. Top and front edge may be planed without removing door.

**Doors that stick:** To open (1) Check to make certain door is not locked. (2) Pound top, lock edge, and bottom with cloth-covered mallet or hammer (so as not to damage wood); (3) If necessary, remove hinge pins; (4) If door remains jammed, call a carpenter. After opening, remove door from hinges, plane down protruding edges.

**Locked doors:** In an emergency, locked doors may be removed from hinges and eased open. However, this may mar the frame. Almost all locks may be forced open by a skilled locksmith. Spring-cylinder locks may sometimes be opened by forcing a thin piece of metal between the door or the stop and the frame, lifting and pulling at the bolt simultaneously.

**Sprung doors:** If a door has sprung or bent at the hinge edge, add a third hinge to keep door straight. Before removing door from hinges, mark point where hinge is to be attached. If a new hinge is not available, move other hinges closer to point of pressure.

**Broken sash cords:** Sash cords hold up weights which counterbalance the window weight and keep windows from falling

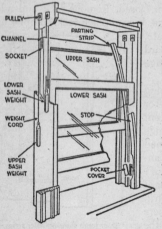

down. They are hidden by a vertical molding, and a metal "pocket cover" which is screwed on. (1) Remove pocket cover, then weight and sash. (2) Replace proper length of sash cord. (3) Attach a weight to the end of the cord and insert over pulley, till it can be reached from pocket. (4) Tie on sash weight. (5) Test to make certain sash weight does not hit bottom or top before window is fully opened or closed. (6) Oil pulleys. (7) Replace cord on other side which is probably equally worn. Chain cords which last a lifetime are available.

**Sticking windows:** Find parts that stick. Dismount window and plane lightly. Chalk or soft pencil edge of window and replace. If binding still occurs, remove and note chalk marks at points of pressure. Sand or plane these points. Repeat as necessary, working gradually. Wait for dry weather. Lubricate with paraffin or graphite solution.

**Sagging screen doors:** Sometimes a few metal corners will do the job. Otherwise, attach a brace to two corners of the door.

**Storing screens:** Number them to save time getting them back in place. (Numbered tacks are available.) Store them carefully, separated, and upright if possible, in a dry, clean place. Wash with a solution of soap, ¼ cup of ammonia, and water

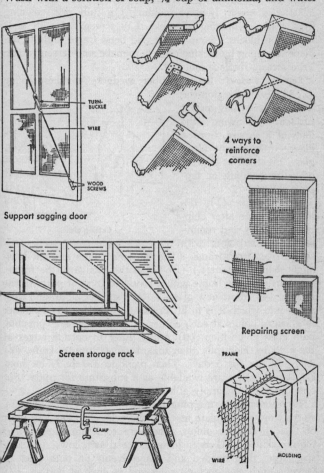

TURN-BUCKLE

WIRE

WOOD SCREWS

Support sagging door

4 ways to reinforce corners

Screen storage rack

Repairing screen

CLAMP

Tacking screen cloth to frame

FRAME

WIRE

MOLDING

Inserting screen

before and after storing. Remove rust with turpentine. Screens may be painted with a special enamel for longer wear, with DDT solution to kill insects, in white enamel on the outside to give maximum privacy.

**Holes in screens:** Make a patch of old screening, leaving free wires all around. Push free wires through holes and fasten.

**Replacing screens:** Remove molding. Carefully pry screening from frame, removing all tacks. Lay screen flat with ends resting on blocks. Clamp center and bend frame slightly. Replace screening by tacking corners to make sure screen is taut. Trim screen. Replace molding.

**Rattling windows:** Insert rubber wedges; weatherproofing (P. 335) will also stop this.

**Cutting glass:** Lay on flat surface. Following the lines of a square, draw a glass cutter firmly along glass. Break off at edge of table by bending or tapping sharply.

Cutting glass.

**Setting glass:** (1) Remove old pane after chipping aff putty and removing glazier's points with screwdriver from frame. (The glazier's points are small triangle-shaped fasteners.) (2) Clean the groove in the frame. (3) Surround the frame with a rope-like layer of putty in the groove. (4) Insert new glass, ⅛ inch smaller all around than space into which it is to fit. Press into position. (5) Hammer in glazier's points at each corner as close to glass as possible, hold glass in position. (6) Apply putty to outside edges of the glass in thick rolls, then smooth off with putty knife. (7) Allow to dry for 5 days. Then paint to match. Note: nonshrinking plastics are available as a substitute for putty. For temporary repair, apply adhesive tape.

**Storm windows·** By trapping air between two panes of glass, storm windows insulate at the point where houses lose most of their heat or coolness. They are sometimes heavy and require skilled workers to hang. Proceed as follows: (1) Buy size larger than needed and plane evenly on both sides to leave ⅟₁₆ inch clearance on sides and ⅜ inch at bottom. (2) Plane gradually to insure that door is perpendicular and that

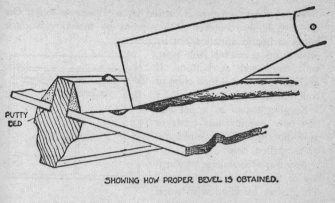

SHOWING HOW PROPER BEVEL IS OBTAINED.

GLAZIERS POINT

ROLL OF PUTTY.

**Glazing.**

both sides are of equal width. (3) Mark out space for gain cut for hinge. Cut gain with sharp knife narrowing from ¼ inch deep to ⅛ inch at jamb. (4) Screw in hinge. Two 3½ inch hinges are usually satisfactory for an ordinary door.

## FLOORS AND STAIRS

**Squeaky floors:** These are due to loose boards, either in the finished floor or in the sub-flooring. Loosening may be due to warping, loose nails.

If the floor is over the basement, and the under side can be seen, it is comparatively easy to locate the trouble between the floor and the beam and to nail the floor board firmly to two or more beams. For the upper floors, it is best to locate the loose beams by sound. (A tap over the beam will not have the hollow ring.) Beams are usually 2 by 8 inches and spaced 16 inches apart.

**Creaky stairs:** Squeaks are caused by space between tread and riser of stair. Screw down tread, after drilling hole large enough to keep head of screw below surface. Drive in screw, and plug hole by gluing in a plug and leveling off with sandpaper. Alternative; nail down tread.

**Sagging floors:** Sagging is caused by weakness in joists. On the first floor, reenforce at key point by inserting wedges between beams and floor, or by setting up a metal jack post, well supported at bottom. If necessary, pour a 6 inch cube of concrete to support jack.

Sagging floors on upper stories may require new joists or new flooring. This would require skilled help.

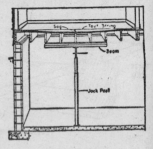

To level sagging floors.

**Floor cracks:** Shrinkage or warping of floors may cause cracks. These may be filled with wood pulp paste which resembles wood when dry. Apply with putty knife, and sand smooth. Cracks more than ¼ inch wide should be first filled with thin sticks, cut to fit, and glued in. Floors in bad repair may be used as a base for new flooring.

**Porch floors:** Because they get more moisture than ordinary floors, porch floors need special treatment. Boards should be painted on both sides and at edges, preferably with aluminum paint. Under side should be ventilated.

**Laying linoleum:** Linoleum is made of ground, colored cork, with a fabric binding. It is available in squares of 6 or 9 inches, or in strips up to 12 feet wide. Enameled linoleum has the design only on the surface. Inlaid linoleum has the design through the entire thickness, thus wears longer and is 2 to 3 times as expensive. In buying linoleum, allow 10 to 20 percent for waste. (1) Sand floor to provide even surface. (Machine can be rented by the day.) If floor is too uneven, lay down a new plywood floor over regular floor. (2) Coat a cord with chalk and lay it along line to make a chalk line guide for first strip. (3) If tiles are to be laid, chalk out each tile. Make necessary provision for pipes, etc., and lay out to insure fit. Cut linoleum to size with linoleum knife. Allow linoleum to lie out for 3 hours to flatten. (4) Coat floor with linoleum cement, using a paste spreader, and press down linoleum. Apply pressure evenly at all points. (Professional workers use a roller which may be rented.)

**Repairing linoleum:** Cut worn spots following pattern line if possible. Insert patch cut to match and cement as a new piece.

Bulges are usually due to poor cementing. Slit in an **X**, fold back, and re-cement. Apply pressure for 6 hours.

To remove persistent stains, sandpaper lightly.

Laying a rug: This is best done by a professional as edges should be bound to prevent raveling. Seams should be flat (to prevent their getting extra wear) and should run in the direction of traffic where possible. Edges may be properly bound and laid without tacks, allowing the rug to be lifted for cleaning. In tackless carpet laying, wall-to-wall or stair carpeting is pulled smooth and taut (without bumpy tacking) by an edging of plywood grippers that work like a curtain stretcher. Many short pins grip carpet flush to walls, hold edges flat and tight. Rug cushions (Ozite) should be laid under rug to add to softness and extend its wear and especially to minimize the effects of uneven floors and marble or cement floors. Rug cushions are best laid with the design down. Sponge rubber underlays are recommended for stairs.

Stair carpeting should be cut a foot longer than necessary with the extra length folded under in one or two risers at the top. The carpet can then be shifted an inch or two downward when it begins to show wear over the nose of the tread. In this way, the carpet can be shifted several times before it will be necessary to replace it. Excess can be folded under at the bottom.

Protect areas of extreme wear by placing scatter rugs over traffic lanes. Or it may be possible to reverse position of rug. To prevent a rug from curling at the edge, sew an L shaped cardboard on the corner.

Floors on which rugs are laid should be even and well padded. Cords under rugs create a ridge which may receive extra wear. Casters and legs of furniture should be placed on pads or coasters.

Carpet fibers require the same humidity as human hair. Excessively dry air is harmful to them. Radiator pans or humidifiers will prolong their life.

Sliding rugs: Liquid brush-on rubber and plastic compounds keep rug from slipping. Some last for life of rug; with others it is necessary to re-treat, periodically.

Scatter-rug-sized sheets of special paper can be placed on floor, trimmed to required dimensions. Treated creped kraft paper grips both surfaces. Two or more side-by-side sheets handle larger rugs. Paper sponges clean.

For emergency treatment, attach jar rubbers on the under side.

If the back needs reglazing to stiffen: (1) Vacuum both sides; (2) Paint wrong side with thin liquid glue, the consistency of maple syrup, using 4-inch paint brush. Avoid penetration or run-off at the edges; (3) Allow to dry thoroughly.

## ELECTRICAL REPAIRS

**Short circuit:** A short circuit is caused when a wire or circuit is overloaded or when two exposed wires touch. Heat is created and the heat melts some part of the circuit. A fuse is placed in the circuit as a safety valve. It contains a soft, easily melted wire which will melt and thus break the circuit, before the heat becomes great enough to melt the copper wire or some valuable part of apparatus, or before the heat causes a fire. A house may have several fuses—one for each circuit, as well as a master fuse for the entire house. These are located in a fuse box. The fuses are designed to carry varying amounts of electricity and are rated in amperes—15 amperes for most new houses, up to 20 amperes where heavy electrical equipment is used. Fuses should be installed which can carry the maximum amperage used on the circuit.

If a short circuit occurs: (1) Find the cause. (2) Disconnect the faulty appliance. (3) Replace the fuse with one of the same rating.

Faulty electrical cords cause most short circuits. They should be handled to avoid rubbing or excessive bending.

### LOAD OF VARIOUS APPLIANCES

| | Watts | | Watts |
|---|---|---|---|
| Incandescent lamps and lamp fixtures | 15-500 | Washing machines | 350 |
| Fluorescent lamps and fixtures | 15-200 | Vacuum cleaners | 400 |
| | | Waffle irons | 650 |
| Fans | 75 | Toasters | 1000 |
| Radios | 100 | Irons | 1000 |
| Television sets | 100 up | Table stoves | 1500 |
| Food mixers | 150 | Hot water heaters | 3000 |
| Refrigerators | 250 | Kitchen ranges | 11500 |

They should be pulled out by the plug, not the wire. They should never be forced or pried out of an outlet with a metal tool. Special cords should be used for heating appliances. Cords or fuses should be designed to carry the load which is demanded of them.

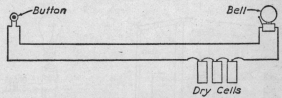

Electric bell system operated by dry cells.

**Doorbells or Chimes:** If your doorbell circuit is run on batteries, probable cause of failure is due to batteries running out. If this is not the cause, tighten connection screws, look for a short circuit. If the bell circuit is connected through a transformer (which steps down voltage from 110 to 6 to 18 volts), test whether transformer is working, check connections. Test bell itself. If not working, it is usually cheaper to replace than to repair.

**Repairing a Cord:** (1) Remove frayed or torn wires. (2) Scrape insulation from each wire for one inch of clean wire. (3) Twist wires of each side to give a firm bundle. (4) Slip both wires through top and tie in a single knot at a point where insulation covers both wires, cover knot with friction tape. (5) Loosen screws at each terminal of plug, removing

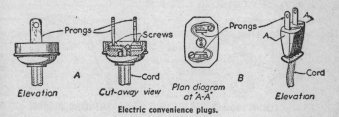

Electric convenience plugs.

old wires. (6) Wind each bundle of wires around one of the terminals, making certain they do not touch each other and that insulation comes up to the terminal posts; cut off loose ends. Tighten screws.

**Switches and Sockets:** Switches and sockets are easily repaired in a manner similar to repair of cords. Make certain main switch is disconnected before work is started. Make certain to replace screws in same place from which they were taken.

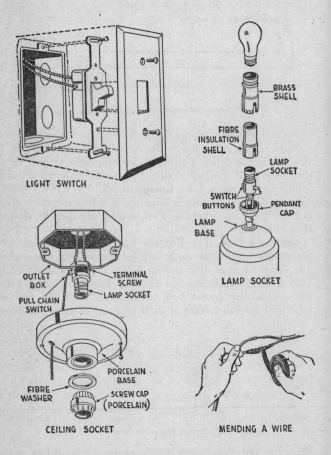

LIGHT SWITCH

BRASS SHELL

FIBRE INSULATION SHELL

LAMP SOCKET

SWITCH BUTTONS

PENDANT CAP

LAMP BASE

LAMP SOCKET

OUTLET BOX

TERMINAL SCREW

LAMP SOCKET

PULL CHAIN SWITCH

PORCELAIN BASE

FIBRE WASHER

SCREW CAP (PORCELAIN)

CEILING SOCKET

MENDING A WIRE

**Three-Way Switches:** Switches are available which allow you to turn lights on or off at either top or bottom of stairs. Installation requires skilled help.

Switches that provide light in varying degrees are available in several forms. The two-way and three-way switches are common in many table lamps. These require special bulbs. Dial-type dimmer switches are made for incandescent or fluorescent lighting, providing all degrees of current from the same bulb, from 10 to 600 watts. Installation is similar to that of ordinary wall switches.

New switches are not only silent, like the mercury switch, but are made to respond to a pressure button and, with a rheostat, to provide current in various degrees, so that lights may be dimmed to the desired brightness.

**Electric Motors:** All appliances with moving parts require periodic oiling. Usually the points to be oiled and the type of oil are specified by the manufacturer. Too much oil may hold dust and hold back the motors. When a motor sparks, it usually means that the carbon "brushes" which carry the current are worn down. They may be replaced by an electrician.

**Rechargeable Equipment:** Electrical equipment which does not require an electrical outlet is now widely made, using rechargeable cadmium batteries. Such equipment is particularly valuable for use around water (avoiding the chance of shock to the user) or outdoors. The electric knife and the electric toothbrush are widely available in battery form. Electric power drills and other tools, hedge cutters, flashlights.

## SIMPLE PLUMBING REPAIRS

Where local or State plumbing regulations are in force, and extensive repairs or alterations are considered, make sure that the work is duly authorized and that it is done by a properly qualified plumber. Afterward, samples of the water should be tested by local or State health authorities.

To tighten an ordinary right-hand screw, nut, or bolt, rotate the tool from left to right, in the same direction that the clock hands move. To unscrew or loosen, rotate the tool counterclockwise. Undue strain should be avoided, as it may result in the part or parts being broken.

**Water Traps:** These are designed to catch dirt to avoid clogging. Modern traps have a screw cap in the lower part of the U. Unscrew and empty into pail, replace tightly. Where there is no screw cap, plumbers may use a force pump.

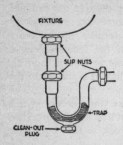

As received from dealers, the nut on the bottom of the plug is generally screwed tight, making it difficult or impossible to turn the handle and plug. Long periods of disuse frequently cause the plug to stick fast in the body. The plug is easily loosened by slightly unscrewing the bottom nut and lightly striking the lower end of the plug a few times with a hammer. Slight leakage caused by wear of the plug or dirt around it may be prevented by cleaning the plug and tightening the bottom nut. A plug badly worn from long or continual use can be reground, but it is usually better and cheaper to get a new plug or a complete new waste cock.

**Leaky or Noisy Faucets:** To repair, replace seat washers. (1) Shut off water at main wheel valve; allow water still remaining in pipes to flow off. (2) Turn faucet screw with monkey

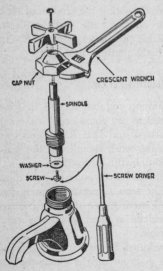

wrench and lift off faucet handle. Place thick cloth in mouth of wrench to avoid marring. (3) Unscrew faucet handle from body of the faucet. Remove washer screw at bottom of stem. If screw is hard to start, apply 2 drops of kerosene or tap lightly. (4) Replace worn washer (usually leather or rubber). (5) Replace faucet and tighten. (6) Test.

If no washer is at hand, a temporary washer may be cut from a piece of leather, rubber, or sheet packing. Leather is preferable on cold-water faucets and rubber on hot-water faucets. A "permanent" brass, bullet-shaped washer is also available.

If the faucet still drips after new washer has been inserted, feel the "seat" behind washer for roughness. Unscrew the stem as above. Ream smooth with a "faucet seat dresser." Screw the adjustable, threaded cone of the tool down into the body of the faucet, thus centering it over the seat. Gently rotate the wheel handle at the top of the tool several times, and the cutter on the bottom of the stem squares the seat. Turn the faucet bottom-side up and shake out the cuttings. If it is not practicable to turn the faucet, the cuttings may be flushed out by turning on the water momentarily. Reassemble and turn on the water to wash out any remaining cuttings.

If leak comes from stem, tighten nut cap. If leak persists, remove nut and replace fibrous packing inside.

A Teflon-coated tape placed around the threads of a faucet will replenish the worn thread, provide permanent lubrication, and stop leaks.

**Thawing Pipes:** The middle of a frozen pipe should never be thawed first, because expansion of the water confined by ice on both sides may burst the pipe. When thawing a water pipe, work from the faucet toward the supply, opening a faucet to show when the flow starts. When thawing a waste or sewer pipe, work upward from the lower end to permit the water to drain away.

It is simple and effective to thaw a frozen pipe with boiling water, hot cloths, hot salt or hot sand or heat from an electric lamp, heater, or special electrical apparatus. Because of the danger of shock, however, electricity should be used only by experienced workers. Where there is no danger of fire a torch or burning newspaper run back and forth along the frozen pipe gives quick results.

Underground or otherwise inaccessible pipes may be thawed as follows: (1) Open the frozen water pipe on the house end. (2) Insert one end of a small pipe or tube. With the aid of a funnel at the other end of the small pipe pour boiling water into it and push it forward as the ice melts. A piece of rubber tubing may be used to connect the funnel to the thaw pipe. Hold the funnel higher than the frozen pipe, so that the hot water has head and forces the cooled water back to the opening, where it may be caught in a pail. (3) The head may be increased and the funnel may be used more conveniently if an elbow and a piece of vertical pipe are added to the outer end of the thaw pipe. Add more thaw pipe at the outer end until a passage is made through the ice. Withdraw the thaw pipe quickly after the flow starts. Do not stop the flow until the thaw pipe is fully removed and the frozen pipe is cleared of ice.

A small force pump is often used instead of a funnel and is much to be preferred for opening a long piece of pipe. If available, a jet of steam may be used instead of hot water; as it is hotter, the thawing is more rapid.

Frozen traps and waste pipes are sometimes thawed by pouring in caustic soda or lye, obtainable at grocery stores. To prevent freezing, the water in the traps of a vacant house should be removed during cold weather, and the traps filled with kerosene, crude glycerine, or a very strong brine made of common salt and water.

**Cleaning Clogged Pipes:** The usual way of clearing ordinary fixture traps is to unscrew the clean-out plug, and wash out the obstructing matter or pull it out with a wire bent to form a hook. Small obstructions are often forced down or drawn up by the use of a simple rubber force cup (the "plumber's friend"). The fixture is partly filled with water and the force cup placed over the fixture outlet. The wood handle of the cup is then worked rapidly down and up, causing alternate expulsion of the water from beneath the cup and suction upward through the waste pipe and trap.

If a trap and the waste pipe from it are clogged with grease, hair, or lint, it is best to open or disconnect the trap and dig out the greasy matter with a stick or a wire.

Rust and dirt in water pipes are more or less successfully removed as follows: (1) Tie a piece of small, stout cord to each end of a 2 inch length of small chain. Each piece of cord should be a little longer than the length of pipe to be cleaned. Attach the free end of one of the cords to a stiff steel wire and push the wire and cord through the pipe. By means of the cords, pull the chain back and forth through the pipe, and then thoroughly flush the pipe with clean water under strong pressure. Long lines may be opened at intervals and cleaned section by section. (2) Or use a swab or wire brush attached to a small steel or brass rod. (3) Or flush with a powerful hand pump. (4) Or fill the pipe with diluted muriatic acid and allow it to stand in the pipe long enough for the acid to act. If the treatment is unsuccessful it should be repeated. A mixture of 1 part of acid and 7 parts of water allowed to stand over night in 1000 feet of badly rusted 1 inch pipe has given good results. After the acid treatment, the pipe should be flushed thoroughly with clean water to remove as fully as possible all dirt, rust, and traces of acid.

When new piping is put in, abrupt turns are sometimes made with T-branches instead of elbows. The unused leg of the branch can be closed with a screw plug, permitting easy access to the interior of the pipe.

CAUTION: When a stop and waste (or valve) on a water service is closed to permit cleaning or repairs, care should be taken to prevent the formation of a vacuum in the high parts of the water piping and the connections to plumbing fixtures; otherwise, siphon action may draw pollution from water closets where the spout (discharge end of the water line) is lower than the fixture rim, or below the fixture overflow.

A variety of inexpensive flexible-coil wire augers and sewer rods are available for removing obstructions—mainly newspapers, rags, toilet articles, grease, garbage, or other solids —from traps, drains, and sewers. The growth of roots in sewers and drains causes much trouble that better workmanship in making the joints would have avoided. Augers and rods come in various sizes and length. Stock lengths for clean-out augers for closet bowls are 3, 6 and 9 feet. Two kinds of flexible augers for general purposes are available. One is 4 feet long and has a small steel cable from the handle to the wire hooks. The hooks can be drawn into the coil, facilitating entry into a trap. Another

Closet auger.

auger is 8 feet long and has the crank handle and corkscrew point generally preferred for closet-bowl work.

Placing a few sheets of toilet paper in the bowl and then flushing usually indicates whether the obstruction has been dislodged.

**Toilet Flush Tanks:** An ordinary compound-lever ball cock. to control the water supply in a flush tank is a simple mecha-

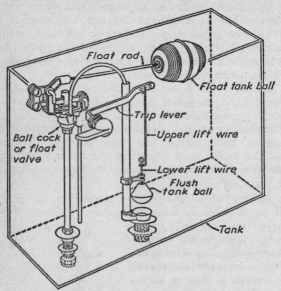

Flush valve mechanism for filling flush tank.

nism. The float ball and the seat washer on the bottom of the plunger are the only parts likely to need repair. The buoyancy of the float is the force that lowers the plunger, shutting off the water as the tank fills. A leaky, water-logged float holds the plunger up, permitting constant flow and waste of water. A small leak in a copper float can be soldered. If in bad condition, the float should be replaced.

The washer should be of soft rubber or leather, because the force that holds it to its seat is not heavy. The cap is thin brass. In replacing the washer, shut off the water and drain the tank. Unscrew the two thumbscrews that pivot the float-rod lever and the plunger lever. Push the two levers to the left, drawing the plunger lever through the head of the plunger. Lift out the plunger, unscrew the cap on the bottom, insert a soft, new washer and reassemble the parts. The cap may be so corroded and weakened that it breaks during removal from the plunger. A new cap is then necessary.

When putting a washer on a ball cock, examine the seat to see that it is free of nicks and grit. The seat may need re-grinding, as explained under compression faucets.

**Adjusting Flush Valves:** Common failings are (a) The hollow rubber ball gets out of shape and fails to drop squarely into the hollowed seat. (b) The handle and lever fail to work smoothly or the lift wires get out of plumb, causing the ball to remain up when it should drop to its seat.

To repair, stop inflow to the tank by holding up the float of the ball cock or supporting it with a stick. Drain the tank by raising the rubber ball. If the ball is worn, is out of shape, or has lost its elasticity, unscrew the lower lift wire from the ball and replace it with a new one. The lift wires should be straight and plumb. The lower lift wire is readily fitted over the center of the valve by means of the adjustable guide holder. By loosening the thumbscrew, the holder is raised, lowered, or rotated about the overflow tube. The horizontal position of the guide is fixed exactly over the center of the valve by loosening the locknut and turning the guide screw. These adjustments are very important. The upper lift wire should loop into the lever armhole nearest to a vertical from the center of the valve. A tank should empty within 10 seconds. Owing to lengthening of the rubber ball and insufficient rise from its seat, the time may be longer than 10 seconds and the flush correspondingly weak. This may be overcome by shortening the loop in the upper lift wire. A drop or two of lubricating oil on the lever mechanism makes it work more smoothly.

**Removing Scale from Water-Backs and Coils:** Hard water causes a limey deposit, or scale, on the inside of water-backs and heating coils, which retards the circulation and heating of the water and may prove dangerous. Continued neglect makes removal increasingly difficult.

The water-back or coil should be removed from the fire-box. At the union or other joints nearest the firebox disconnect all pipes and unscrew them from the coil. If there is a clamp that holds the fire-brick lining against the oven, loosen it and remove side and end linings. Lift out the coil. Soft scale or sludge may be removed by pounding the coil with a mallet or hammer and then flushing with a strong jet of water. A long gouge or chisel is used on surfaces that can be reached. Sometimes the coil is heated in a blacksmith's forge and then pounded, but unless carefully done this treatment may break it.

Waters of varying chemical make-up cause scale differing in composition and hardness. Ordinary limestone (calcium carbonate) scale, if not too thick, may readily be removed with muriatic acid. Gypsum (calcium sulphate) scale is hard and resistant and with other materials in their more compact forms is not affected greatly by muriatic acid. The coil should be laid on the ground or floor and filled with a strong solution of the acid in water. The strength of the solution should vary with the amount of deposit, the ordinary mixture being 1 part of acid and 5 to 7 parts of water. If the deposit is very thick, the acid needs little dilution. Heating the water-back hastens the action of the acid. At the end of an hour or two, or sooner if the deposit is dissolved, pour the solution from the water-back and flush it thoroughly with hot water to clean out the acid. If all the deposit has not been removed, repeat the operation, making sure that the acid is completely washed out before replacing the water-back. It is important to have the water-back level when it is replaced. Use a spirit level for this purpose.

Extreme care should be used in handling acids. Muriatic acid should not be used in water system or waste pipes without professional advice.

Similar methods can be used with copper coils. Place the coil (or heater) on two sticks over a large bowl. With the aid of a lead funnel pour the acid solution through the coil. Dip from the bowl and continue to circulate the solution through the coil until the deposit is dissolved. The coil should then be thoroughly washed out with hot water.

The hot-water flow pipe close to a water-back or coil frequently becomes thickly covered with scale. If the pipe is brass, it may be disconnected and treated with acid and then washed out with hot water. If it is of galvanized iron and in bad condition, it will probably be more satisfactory to replace it.

Pipe Leaks: A small leak in a water pipe can be stopped in an emergency as follows: Place a flat rubber or leather gasket over the leak and hammer a piece of sheet metal to fit over the gasket. Secure both to the pipe with a clamp. A small leak under low pressure is sometimes stopped by shutting off

the water and then embedding the pipe in richly mixed Portland cement mortar or con-
crete. Broken sewer pipe can
be similarly repaired. A wrapping of wire netting embedded in the mortar or concrete
increases its strength. It is
better, however, to re-lay the
sewer and make all joints
watertight and rootproof. A

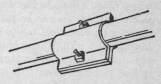

Repairing a pipe leak.

small hole in cast-iron pipe may be tapped for a screw plug.

Where a leaky screw joint cannot be tightened with a pipe
wrench, the leak is sometimes stopped with a blunt chisel
or caulking tool and hammer. Sometimes a crack or hole is
cleaned out and then plugged and caulked with lead or a
commercial iron cement mixed to the consistency of stiff putty.
Sometimes a pipe band, a clamp with two bolts, or a split
sleeve is employed to hold a thin coating of iron cement or
a gasket over a leak. If the leak is at a screw joint, the band
is usually coated inside with one-eighth of an inch of iron
cement and then slipped over the pipe. Keeping the bolt
farthest from the coupling or fitting a little tighter than the
other, tighten both bolts. During the tightening, the band
should be driven with a hammer snugly against the coupling
or fitting.

In addition to these methods and devices, there are several
kinds of good, inexpensive, ready-made pipe and joint repairers available.

**Tank Leaks:** A corroded and leaky spot in a steel tank or
range boiler can be closed with an inexpensive
repair bolt or plug available at dealers. A homemade repairer can be made consisting of a 3/16
by 3 inch toggle bolt and a flat rubber gasket,
brass washer, and nut. The link of the bolt, after
being passed through the hole, takes an upright

position and screwing up the nut forces the gasket tightly
against the outside of the boiler. A small hole must be reamed
or enlarged with a round file to a diameter that will admit the
toggle bolt. The metal beneath the gasket should be firm and
clean. A little candlewick packing may be wrapped around the
bolt to prevent leakage along the bolt. Sometimes a hole is

closed by driving in a tapered steel pin to turn the metal inward, forming a surface that can be tapped for an ordinary screw plug. A hole in the wall of a tank or pipe having considerable thickness can be easily and quickly closed by screwing in a tapered steel tap plug that cuts and threads its way through the wall. These plugs in different sizes are obtainable from dealers, and a monkey wrench is the only tool required to insert them. It is not necessary to shut off or drain the water from the tank or pipe.

A small leak at a seam or rivet can often be closed by merely rubbing a cold chisel along the beveled edge of the joint. Do not attempt to caulk a seam unless the plates have considerable thickness and the rivets are closely spaced and are close to the caulking edge, and then use extreme caution. Run a regular caulking tool or blunt chisel along the beveled edge, tapping the tool very lightly with a light hammer to force edge of upper plate against and into the lower plate.

**Repairing Cracked Laundry Tubs:** Cracks in slate, soapstone, or cement laundry tubs are made watertight with a mixture of litharge and glycerine or a specially prepared commercial cement. The litharge and glycerine are mixed and stirred to form a smooth heavy paste free from lumps. The cracks should be cleaned out to remove all grease and dirt, and the paste should be worked into the crack with a case knife. A paste

SPLIT PIPE COVERING

METAL BAND

Applying split pipe covering around hot-water heating pipes.

of Portland cement and water or of white of egg and fresh lump lime is satisfactory. The crack may also be sealed by packing it with soft cotton cord that has been well covered with white-lead paste.

**Water Pipe Insulation:** Loss of hot water heat (as much as 25 percent) and protection against freezing may be obtained by covering tank and pipes with insulating jackets.

**Sweating Pipes:** This is due to condensation of moisture from warm air on cold pipes. Prevent by winding cork tape spirally around pipes, or coating with cork paint. Shallow metal trays may be placed under toilet tanks where insulation is not practical.

**Knocking Pipes:** This is usually caused by air pockets due to defective valve. Hand-valves in one-pipe system should be either completely open or completely shut.

**Low Water Pressure:** Causes may be small interior pipes, clogging due to rust or scale (particularly in hot water pipes), clogged knuckles. Water softeners, bronze or copper piping, help avoid this. Certain chemicals may help unclog pipes.

**Repairing Garden Hose:** A break in garden hose is quickly repaired or two pieces of hose can be joined with an inexpensive iron or brass hose mender or splicer. Cut off the defective piece of hose, insert the mender in the good ends, and wire or clamp the hose. Menders come to slip inside ½, ¾, or 1 inch hose. The regular brass hose-coupling can also be used for this purpose. Note that most plastic hoses are guaranteed for one year and may be replaceable.

## HEATING SYSTEM CHART

| System and Principal Parts | Common Failings* |
| --- | --- |
| WARM AIR—OIL OR GAS: Firebox or furnace. Metal jacket. Air duct for incoming air. Blowers to force circulation. Ducts to carry warm air to rooms. Ducts for returning air. Dampers for regulating the flow of air into each room. Filters to remove dust from air. Water pan to humidify air. | Joints not airtight. Blower not in adjustment. Noises in blower due to improper insulations. Leaks in furnace. Dust from dirty filters. (Clean filters every month. Replace after one to two years.) |
| STEAM: Firebox. Boiler filled with water (clean annually). Boiler insulation. Steam pipes to conduct steam to radiators where heat is given off and steam condenses. Returning pipes for water. (Water may return via steam pipes.) Air vents to allow air to escape so that steam can replace it. Safety-valve. Boiler flues. (Clean and tighten annually.) | Clogged air vents. (Blow through or wash in washing soda solution.) Broken vents with steam spray or leaks. Hammering in pipes. (This may be due to too small supply line or insufficient pitch. Place blocks under one end.) |

* Where no remedy is suggested, call an expert.

| System and Principal Parts | Common Failings* |
|---|---|
| VAPOR STEAMS: Similar to steam but with vacuum valves to permit air to escape. This holds heat longer. | |
| HOT WATER SYSTEM: Firebox. Jacket containing water. Pipes from jacket to carry warm water. Sometimes pumps to increase circulation of water. Radiator with air vents. Return pipes for cold water. | Insufficient water in system. (Allow to cool before adding water.) Clogged air vents. (Place pan under vent and open to allow air to escape.) Periodic accumulations of muck and scale. |
| SPLIT SYSTEMS: Two systems for various parts of the house, so that one may be shut off. | |
| RADIANT HEATING: Panels of pipes to carry hot water or cold water in summer are laid in floor, wall and ceilings, embedded in concrete or plaster. | Coils not laid level. |
| BASEBOARD HEATING: Hot water system with radiators reduced to a single pipe in the baseboard. | |
| UNIT HEATERS—GAS, COAL, OIL, ELECTRIC, FIREPLACES: Used where central heating is not feasible as where only certain rooms are to be heated. | |
| SOLAR HEAT: Large glass areas of double paned glass which capture winter sun heat. Overhanging eaves which hold out summer sun. | Not sufficient in itself for winter heating. |
| ATTIC LOUVERS AND FANS: Fans draw in air to ventilate attic or air space. This aids in insulation. | For cooling and ventilation. |

* Where no remedy is suggested, call an expert.

Altitude or Pressure Gauge: The dial gauge on a hot-water boiler is to indicate the level of the water in the system. When the tank is first filled, the water level is raised to the proper height in the expansion tank. The red hand on the dial gauge is then set in the same position as the black hand. Thereafter, closeness of the black hand to the red hand will indicate proper filling of the system.

**Boiler-Water Treatment:** Where the water supply is unusually hard, boiler water may require treatment with commercial compounds which are available for this purpose.

Fresh water is frequently treated with lime and soda ash (sodium carbonate) to precipitate scale-forming salts. Commercial water-treating compounds contain proper chemicals.

**Repacking a Leaky Radiator Valve:** Worn or insufficient packing inside the nut or a loose packing nut at the base of the stem may cause a leak. To remedy this, tighten the nuts. If the leak does not stop, it will be necessary to repack the valve.

Many radiator valves are so constructed that the packing nut can be raised without lowering the pressure in the radiator. In a hot-water system where the type of valve used permits water or steam to escape after the valve is closed and the packing nut loosened, the level of the water must be lowered below the height of the valve by opening the drain cock of the system; with a steam system, the pressure should be reduced by allowing the boiler to cool.

Two forms of packing may be used to pack a valve stem, washers of different sizes, or packing cord. If washers are used, remove the valve handle by loosening the screw that holds it. After the handle is removed the packing nut can be withdrawn from the stem. The old packing should be taken out and the new packing washers slipped over the stem. The new washers must be of the right number and size to fill the packing space in the nut. If cord is used, a sufficient amount should be wrapped around the valve stem to fill the packing space in the nut. The nut should be tight enough to prevent water and steam from escaping, but not so tight as to produce excessive friction on the stem when the valve is turned.

For a steam-heating system, let the fire go out, or at least have a low head of steam, before starting work on the valves. Close valve tightly and unscrew the packing nut at the base of the stem, to permit packing the space between the inside of the nut and the stem with metallic packing compound, using a small screwdriver for the purpose. This compound may be purchased in small quantities from a dealer in heating supplies. It may be easier to pack the nut, if it is removed from the stem. To do this, remove the handle and lift the nut from the stem. After the nut has been well packed, screw it down tightly and refill the system.

Cleaning and Repairing Flues: Bricks that fall from the top and lodge at offsets or contracted sections can sometimes be reached and dislodged by a long pole or sections of pipe screwed together. They can be caught on a shingle or piece of sheet metal shoved into a stovepipe hole or removed through a clean-out door. A weighted cement sack filled with straw and attached to the end of a rope may be pulled up and down the flue to remove soot and loose material.

Trouble with creosote and soot is caused by imperfect combustion, usually due to (1) Lack of sufficient air to the fire; (2) Improper mixture of air with furnace gases; (3) Low furnace temperature; (4) Too small combustion space, so that the gases reach the comparatively cool furnace surface before they are completely burned and, as a result, soot or tarry matter condenses and then passes up the chimney in the form of smoke. Soft coal causes more soot trouble than hard coal.

If soot accumulates fast or trouble is experienced with unusual smoke when firing, it is probable that the heating equipment is not being operated properly. Call the manufacturer or installer for proper adjustments.

Soot removers cause soot to burn and are fire hazards. The correct and most thorough method of cleaning a chimney is to do so manually or to employ modern exhaust or vacuum methods used by furnace repairmen. A remover may help to keep the passages of stoves and heaters clear between annual cleanings, if soot accumulates quickly and reduces draft.

Common salt (rock or ice-cream salt) is not the most effective remover, but it is the most widely used because of its cheapness, ease of handling, and general availability. Use two or three teacupfuls per application. Metallic zinc in the form of dust or small granules is often used; however, a mixture of salt and 10 percent zinc dust is more effective than either salt or zinc alone.

Most effective is a mixture of 1 part dry red lead and 5 parts common salt, measured by weight. Shake these together in a can with a tight-fitting lid. As lead is poisonous, wash the hands after using. One or two teacupfuls are used per application.

Old dry-cell batteries contain suitable ingredients and when they are thrown in a hot furnace the soot usually burns. Quicker action can be had if they are chopped up.

Before a remover is used, the fire must be put in good condition with a substantial body of hot fuel on top. Close the ash-pit door and the slots in the firing door and scatter the remover on the hot coals. Close the firing doors and at once reduce the draft by partially closing the pipe dampers. The draft should not be closed so tight as to cause fumes to escape into the cellar. Let the remover "stew" for 10 or 20 minutes or until fumes stop rising from the coals; then make the fire burn fiercely by opening the ash-pit door and the damper. Shaking ashes out will help. The slots in the firing door can be opened or the door itself set ajar. If soot in the furnace will not ignite, throw a little wood or paper on the fire.

Instead of making a special job of cleaning at intervals, one or two cups of salt may be thrown on the fire once a day with the expectation that the furnace will produce a high enough temperature to ignite some of the soot. This is most likely to succeed in cold weather when the furnace temperatures are high.

## INSULATION

Insulation is made in the form of (1) Soft, flexible fibrous materials such as mineral wool and vegetable or animal fiber; (2) Blankets and batts, which are designed to be stretched and tacked between the studs, floor joists, and rafters; (3) Loose or shredded form to be blown or packed into hollow spaces; (4) Stiff board form having some structural strength to be used as sheathing, plaster base, or merely as insulation.

The batt and blanket forms are usually furnished with a vapor-barrier facing made of asphalted paper, and should always be installed with the vapor barrier on the warm side of the insulation. Such reflective metal surfaces as bright aluminum foil (used as a boundary for an air space wider than about one-half inch) are effective as insulation. Only one boundary of the air space need be reflective. It is prefer-able to place reflective surfaces which are also vapor barriers, such as metal foils, on the warm side of the air space.

**Insulating Frame Walls:** For existing frame houses that have not been insulated, loose-fill insulating materials, such as mineral wool or vermiculite, can be poured into the spaces between the studs or joists, where these are accessible. Loose-fill insulating materials can also be blown into place by means of a special blower and air hose designed for the purpose. In such case, it is advisable to have the work done by a reliable firm that has the proper equipment. A guarantee should be required from the installer that no empty pockets exist upon completion of the work. If fire-stopping prevents the space between walls being filled from the attic, openings must be cut in the outside wall covering to admit the hose. After the insulation has been blown into the wall, the holes can be repaired.

**Asbestos-Cement Insulation:** For insulating boilers, valves and joints, where fabricated coverings are not practical, asbestos-cement may be used. (1) Purchase covering material, 1 inch thick, and metal fastenings as needed; also 100 lb. bag of cement for each 20 to 25 sq. feet, 1 inch thick; also, canvas and wire mesh sufficient to cover boiler, and paste for canvas. (2) Mix asbestos-cement with sufficient water to make mixture workable. (3) While pipes or boiler are warm, apply 1 coat of 1 inch of asbestos-cement on boiler, ½ inch on pipes, roughly with plasterer's trowel. After boiler is fairly dry, stretch wire netting over boiler and fasten to first coat. Then apply second coat of asbestos-cement ½ inch thick. Allow to dry. Apply paste and cover with canvas.

**Where and How Much:** 59°F. wall surface temperatures will produce a minimum condition below which discomfort will be experienced.

The major areas of heat loss and heat gain in dwellings are:

|                  | Heat Loss | Heat Gain in Summer |
|------------------|-----------|---------------------|
| Walls            | 33%       | 34%                 |
| Ceiling          | 22%       | 24%                 |
| Floors           | 1%        | 4%                  |
| Glass and doors  | 30%       | 26%                 |
| Infiltration     | 14%       | 12%                 |

**Heat-Saving Suggestions:** Adding ½ inch of insulation is equivalent to 2 feet of stone, may save 20 to 30 percent of your fuel bill. Adding 1 inch of insulation may save 30 to 40 percent. Other fuel savers suggested: (1) Place a ceiling on the cellar; (2) Weatherstrip windows and caulk up cracks; (3) Add storm windows and storm doors; (4) The heater itself should be insulated; (5) Insulate boiler and water storage tank; (6) Weatherstrip bedroom doors; (7) Close the door when you open the window to air a room; (8) Shut off heat in bedrooms at night; (9) Install thermostatic control of temperature; (10) Install proper humidification to give more comfort with less heat; (11) Shut off heat in rooms not used; (12) Replace broken window panes; (13) Use ventilator shields to deflect incoming air, allow better control; (14) Put dampers on the fireplace; (15) Maintain an even temperature; (16) Keep heater, radiators, grills and pipes clean; (17) Place insulating materials (about 3 inches) on the attic floor; (18) Ventilation of the attic will prevent absorption of moisture and promote insulation. This can be accomplished by inserting louvers in the attic wall, available finished at lumber yards. (19) Where homes have no foundation, tack asphalt roofing to outside base, cover with leaves and straw, and anchor with boards weighted with stones; (20) Seal outside cracks created by shrinkage and settling of bricks, with caulking compounds.

Vapor barrier in the attic.

**Weatherstripping:** Seals to prevent drafts and save heat are available in various forms. Felt and metal strips · may be cut to size and tacked or screwed to the frame. Other forms involve interlocking channels which must be installed in grooves, cut into frame of window or door. These require special tools and skilled workmanship.

Doors: Cut 4 pieces. Tack bottom piece to inside face of door with contact edge placed downward and pressed snugly against threshold. Tack side and top pieces to door-stops on the outside with contact edges pressed evenly, but not too tightly against door when closed.

Windows: For upper sash, tack to frame adjoining the sash

on the outside of window. If the flexible type is used, extend the piece around the two sides and top. If rigid type is used, make 3 separate pieces and miter corners to fit. For lower

sash, make 4 pieces. Tack 2 side pieces to face of the top adjoining the sash with contact edge pressed against the face of the sash, extending from the top of the lower sash, so that the contact edge will cover the crack where the upper and lower sash rails meet. It may be necessary to cut piece to provide for window lock. Tack the piece around the bottom to the face of the sash with contact edge placed downward to butt against the top of the stool or inside window sill.

Wood casement windows are weatherstripped as doors.

Cooling rooms: Keep windows closed and shades drawn during the day, open them at night. Upstairs windows should be kept open to allow warm air to escape. Use electric lights at a minimum. (Candles are cooler and pleasanter.) Electric fans are handy for promoting circulation and making you feel cooler. Place a pan of ice cubes in front of a fan for an elementary air conditioner. Scent may be added. The pan may be covered with leaves or flowers for appearance' sake. Good insulation and double-paned windows (Thermopane, Twindows) will keep warmth out in summer as well as keeping it in the house in winter.

Putting the fan to work.

To pull cool night air into a bedroom, place a fan at an open window, at a distance equal to 1½ times the width of the window, facing out. Open other windows. The warm air is thus pushed out.

A fan on the floor of a closet will push stale air out. A fan set at the level of work, but facing away, will cool a work table. Or set a fan at floor level.

Modern fans are available which will turn off—or on—at fixed temperature.

Air-conditioning units for individual rooms or for entire house are available.

## MOISTURE CONTROL

**Moisture Protection:** Uncontrolled moisture is one of the household's worst enemies. It ruins plaster, paint, wood, fabric and most anything around the house. It causes stains, rust, mildew, rot, etc. It may come from the inside, from kitchen or bathroom vapors, or from the condensation of moisture in ordinary warm air as it hits colder objects. Good insulation adds to the problem because it prevents warm moist air from escaping. Best general remedy is good ventilation. Allow air to escape from the window or the door when you take a bath. Have a suction exhaust fan in the kitchen. Keep basement windows open in warm dry weather. Have screened louvers in the attic or attic air space. If you are building anew, prevent exterior moisture from getting into your house by using vapor barriers in the walls.

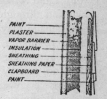

PAINT
PLASTER
VAPOR BARRIER
INSULATION
SHEATHING
SHEATHING PAPER
CLAPBOARD
PAINT

Vapor barrier construction.

Humidity should be kept below 40 percent during winter weather.

Dehumidifiers can remove as much as 14 pints of water in a day. Dehumidifiers keep bedrooms comfortable at night and help maintain furniture at proper humidity.

**Condensation Control:** Moisture contained in warm air will drop out in contact with any cold surface, walls, metals, windows. Dehumidifiers can be made and are available in simple forms such as a container of calcium chloride or other moisture-absorbing chemicals. Other larger commercial units are available. All such units require occasional replacement of chemicals.

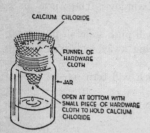

CALCIUM CHLORIDE

FUNNEL OF HARDWARE CLOTH

JAR

OPEN AT BOTTOM WITH SMALL PIECE OF HARDWARE CLOTH TO HOLD CALCIUM CHLORIDE

Condensation of moisture on walls may be prevented by special paints used in priming coats, or by using special building paper as a vapor barrier in wall construction. It is not practical to install such papers in a finished house, but they may be used effectively in an unfinished attic.

**Damp Basements:** Determine basic cause and remedy.

There are many causes of damp or wet cellars. Sometimes the trouble is slight, resulting from an apparent and easily remedied local cause. Sometimes the trouble is serious, resulting from hidden and not easily corrected causes. The cause or causes should always be studied and determined, so that the simplest effective treatment may be employed. The principal causes are as follows:

(1) Land which is flat or slopes toward the cellar wall, down and through which percolates rain and melting snow. The drainage may be over the surface or underground and usually results in damp spots, or standing water at cellar corners and along the junction of floor and walls. The conditions are usually worse in the spring of the year when the ground is very wet; in compact soil having poor natural drainage; on the upper side of sidehill cellars; and in poorly constructed cellars.

(2) Absence of eaves troughs and downspouts, or failure to repair defective ones, frequently resulting in surface depressions, muddy pools, bespattered walls, and water-soaked ground near or against the cellar wall.

(3) Ground water close to the cellar bottom through which water rises by capillarity, producing merely dampness.

(4) Ground water higher than the cellar bottom, causing standing water in the cellar and at times excessive dampness in the rooms above.

(5) Sweating or condensation of atmospheric moisture on walls, floors, and other cold surfaces within the cellar.

(6) Leaky plumbing; drip from ice chests and sill cocks; dense masses of vines, shrubbery, and trees.

These methods of damp-proofing are suggested in increasing order of difficulty:

(1) Where necessary, grade by adding fill against basement wall, grading down to a sharp, smooth slope for 8 to 10 feet from wall. Grow grass, roll firmly and evenly. If grading goes above basement window sill, build a curved or rectangular well of metal, brick, or concrete around window. These may have hinged covers to protect against heavy storm. Where downspouts are not connected to an outlet, place a spatter or good-sized splash block at the outlet to divert water from wall.

(2) For interior waterproofing, cut away 2 to 3 inches at cracks; fill with a stiff putty made of high-early-strength Portland cement, sand and calcium chloride up to 5 percent by weight, mix 1 part cement to 2 to 3 parts sand, then press into opening and hold by a small board.

(3) Bituminous coatings may be applied on the outside of masonry-unit or monolithic walls (not interiors), by either hot or cold methods; or (a) Smooth and dry walls, apply an asphalt primer, with roofer's mop. Mop on 1 to 3 applications of coal-tar pitch, at least ⅛ inch thick; or (b) With trowel apply an asphalt primer with asphalt coatings, and a coal-tar or creosote primer with coal-tar coatings.

(4) Clean and wet walls till saturated, then scrub with a grout coat of Portland cement and water (thick cream consistency). While this is still wet, apply a coating of cement mortar over grout to the outside of masonry-unit walls. Coating consists of 1 or 2 ⅜-inch coats of cement mortar composed of 1 part Portland cement to 2 to 3 parts sand by volume. Roughen first coat with coarse broom before it dries to provide bond for second coat. Keep wall damp for 3 or more days. Apply waterproof coating to outside wall of basement, if possible, otherwise to inside walls.

Specially prepared waterproofing materials are available for this process.

(5) Remove basement floor at junction with wall and place a drain along the inside edge of footing, through or under footing, to an adequate outlet.

(6) In locations where subsoil contains large amount of water, install a drain tile around footings. (a) Dig trench to a

few inches below level of basement floor, but not below the footing level. (b) Lay 4 inch tile pipe with a smooth, steep grade, connected to storm sewer, dry well, open water course, etc. (c) Cover joint cracks with copper screen wire or strips of roofing paper to prevent sediment running into pipe. (d) Surround pipe with gravel, well tamped all around, to prevent settling. Cover with 1 to 2 feet of coarse gravel. Follow with burlap or sod (grass down) before filling with earth.

(7) Lay a concrete gutter 2 to 3 feet wide, 4 inches deep, around house, sloping slightly away from house to some low spot. At point of contact with wall, concrete should be rounded up to meet the face of the wall. Wall should be roughened, cleaned, and moistened to make a good bond.

## ROOFING

**Replacing Wooden Shingles:** (1) Remove defective shingles by cutting nails with a special shingle hook, sliding hook under shingle till it can cut nails. (2) Cut replacement shingle to proper width. They are standard in 16 and 24 inch lengths, but come in random widths. (3) Renail.

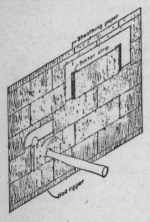

Asbestos-cement shingle siding showing use of nail ripper.

**Replacing Asphalt and Abestos Shingles:** (1) Bend up the layers of shingle above the broken piece and remove nails. Fill nail holes with asphalt cement. (2) Replace and renail with new shingles.

**Replacing Slate Shingles:** (1) Remove broken slate. (2) Drill holes in slate and nail into position. (3) Nail copper strip 1½ inches wide below position of new slate. (4) Insert slate and bend copper cover to hold slate. All slates within 1 foot of the top of the roof should be bedded in flashing cement.

**Flashing Repairs:** All roof joints should be made tight with metal undercoats beneath the shingles because these joints usually receive major weather wear. To locate leaks, look for wet spots on walls or ceiling. In an emergency repair, remove necessary shingles, apply metal patch with mastic cement, replace shingles.

If flashing works loose, cement well before renailing.

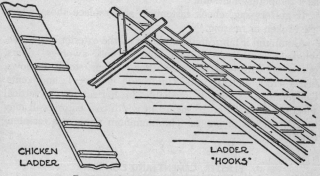

CHICKEN LADDER

LADDER "HOOKS"

Two types of support used in roof repairing.

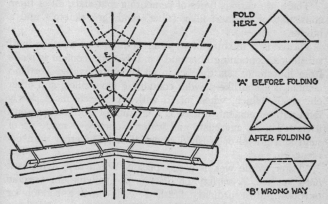

FOLD HERE

"A" BEFORE FOLDING

AFTER FOLDING

"B" WRONG WAY

Method of repairing valley flashing.

To work on a roof, wear sneakers, choose a dry day.

**Gutter Maintenance and Repair:** Keep gutters clean to avoid clogging and consequent overflow which may cause serious damage. Basketlike strainers are available to keep out leaves and debris. Ashes and dirt, if not removed and flushed out, may cause corrosion. Durability may be increased by periodic painting with metal paint.

Buckles or folds may be hammered out with a mallet or padded hammer. Small holes may be repaired with a drop of solder or a patch of matching metal soldered on. Roofing felt or cotton duck may be patched on with flashing cement as a temporary measure.

If gutters sag, check fastenings and replace those which are broken or missing.

Aluminum if fabricated for almost all the exterior of a house, windows, siding, patterned sun screens, awnings, doors, gutters, downspouts, eaves, shutters, screens, storm windows, fascia (roof edges), soffit (underside of eaves), and vents. Conventional siding is available in horizontal or vertical sheets of 5, 8, 12 or 16 inches in width. An entire wall may be constructed of panels. The aluminum minimizes maintenance.

## PLASTER, CEMENT AND CONCRETE

There are various types of cementing materials, all of them consisting of an inert filler (fiber, sand, gravel, etc.) and a binder.

Plaster is a mixture of gypsum or lime and another inert substance, containing fiber and sand. Natural cement is made from limestone, sets quickly in air or under water. Portland cement is a flourlike powder containing lime, silica, and other chemicals, which, when mixed with water, sets more slowly than natural cement. Stucco is a mixture of Portland cement, hydrated lime, aggregate and water. Concrete is made up of sand and gravel or crushed stone, all held together with cement.

Plaster, while wet, is a soft plastic. When dry, it forms a hard surface. A variety of plasters is available for specific purposes. Most ordinary finished walls have a scratch or anchoring coat applied on a wood, fiber, or metal lath; a second brown coat, and a third finishing coat.

Gypsum plaster is most widely used because it hardens quickly. Lime plaster is used for basements and other places where there is much moisture.

Keene's cement—highly moisture-resistant—is used for kitchen and bathrooms.

Applying Plaster: (1) Prepare surface (either a lath or a firm, rough surface; on cracks, or on narrow patches, chisel out an undercut) so that plaster may have a grip. (2) Mix plaster as directed, in small batches in a clean container. (3) Place plaster on a "hawk"—a flat metal plate with a handle—and apply with steel trowel. (4) Apply scratch coat over entire area, allow to dry slightly, then scratch surface with wooden comb. (5) When scratch coat is thoroughly dried, apply ¼ inch of brown plaster to approximate final surface. Allow to dry. (6) Apply final coat of white or colored plaster about 1/16 inch thick, and smooth with a trowel. (7) A special "rough" finish may be given by sweeping the surface with a "float" trowel covered with carpeting or sponge rubber.

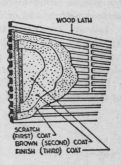

Three coats of plaster.

Small patches may be made more simply by using "patching plaster," available in mixes ready for water. Very thin cracks may be filled with a creamy mixture of white lead and turpentine, applied with a cloth and sanded smooth. If plaster is drying too quickly a few drops of vinegar will slow the hardening.

Wall tiles are usually set in a mortar of 1 part Portland cement, 2 parts sand, and water. Floor tiles are set in a similar mixture with 15 percent hydrated lime added.

**Replastering a Wall or Ceiling:** (1) Cover joists with furring strips for lath. Nail strips over old surface in line with joists. (2) Nail plasterboard to strips to form smooth surface. Place sheets so that joists are staggered. (3) Attach strips of metal lath over joists. (4) Apply first coat of plaster about ¼ inch thick and while still soft, roughen with a whiskbroom to provide a hold for second coat. (5) Apply second coat, ¼ inch thick after first coat is dry. Press to adhere to the rough surface of first coat. (6) On a three-coat job, roughen second coat. (7) Apply a "setting" coat, about ⅛ inch thick, when second coat is nearly dry. Trowel to a hard finish or "sand-float" with a wooden trowel in a circular motion.

**Basement Ceilings:** Ceilings add fire resistance, cleanliness and appearance to basements. (1) Close all openings to upper floors—around pipes, studs, registers, etc. (2) Nail up gypsum or asbestos board, or metal lath for plastering. Finish by plastering, painting as desired. (3) Material within 2 feet of boiler or furnace or 1 foot of smoke pipe should be protected by a loose-fitting metal shield, set 1 to 2 inches from wall surface with blocks of non-combustible materials.

**Basement Partitions:** (1) Construct a framework of 2" x 4" lumber, placing studs 16 or 24 inches apart. (2) Attach wall board or tongued and grooved ¾ inch boards; (3) Or construct wall of brick, concrete blocks or hollow tile.

**Closing Joint Cracks:** To close up joints between corner walls or wall and window, a plastic material is used. The process is

known as caulking. Caulking materials are usually available in clay-like ropes. Apply at window or door cracks, with putty knife. Other forms are applied with pump guns in the same way that grease is inserted into cups. Caulking materials may be used to fill cracks in walls, roofs, etc., in wood, masonry or metal surfaces.

Caulking gun.

New silicone rubber adhesive caulks are useful for sealing around casement windows, faucets, shower stalls, bathtubs, air-conditioning and exhaust-fan casings, auto windows; for adhering and sealing gutters and downspouts, ceramic and plastic tile, tears in tents, awnings, and tarpaulins.

**Wall Board:** Prepared wall boards in a variety of finishes may be substituted for plastering. These may be tacked to studs with broad-headed nails, meeting halfway at the stud. Fill joints and cracks. Space nails 4" apart at edges, 6" apart in center. Nails should be depressed slightly below the surface and holes filled. An allowance of ⅛" may be made for expansion between sheets. Metal strips are available for joints. Smooth, sandpaper, size, then paper or paint. If board is finished, a molding may be placed over joints. If wall board gets wet and bulges, replace.

## WALLS AND WALL BOARD

GYPSUM: Plaster covered with tough paper, fire resistant.

PLYWOOD: Laminated wood veneers laid with grains at right angle. For finished or semi-finished rooms.

FIBERBOARD: Hardboard or insulating board.

ASBESTOS CEMENT BOARD: Portland cement and asbestos fiber. Non-combustible. Water-resistant, smooth, hard surface; plain or colored, or with fabric finish. For finished walls or ceilings or unfinished rooms.

WOOD PANELING: In almost any wood, natural, pickled, stained or varnished. For finished or informal rooms.

WALL TILE: Waterproof, looks like tile. For bathrooms, kitchens.

FORMICA and similar laminated products: Laminated papers treated with resins, under extreme heat and pressure. Scratch, water, alcohol, acid, insect, etc., resistant. For kitchen, counters, splash boards, bathrooms, table tops.

Stucco Cracks: (1) Chip away and clean damaged parts with a cold chisel, to form groove wider on inside than outside. (2) Try to use same brand and the same mix of cement as was originally used. Mix patching cement of 3 parts sand, 1 part ordinary cement, 1/10 part hydrated lime by volume. Mix dry till uniform in color, then add water to a putty consistency. (3) Ram and tamp into crack with putty knife or trowel. Keep surface damp for 3 days to allow cement to set.

If stucco bulges or cracks in large areas, remove affected portion and re-stucco in 3 coats.

Refinishing Stucco: Wash old surface with clear water and then with a solution of 1 part muriatic acid and 6 parts water. Apply with stiff bristle brush. Rinse and allow to dry. Moisten and apply new coat in color or texture desired.

Crumbling Mortar: Replace mortar, a process known as pointing. Mix 3 parts sand, 1 part ordinary cement, 1/10 part hydrated lime, by volume. Apply with a pointed trowel, tamping into joint. Scrape off excess. Keep damp for 3 days.

Concrete Work: Concrete is a mix of various sizes of gravel or stone and sand (aggregate) and Portland cement. Materials should be clean and uniform. Mix with water in a wooden trough or on watertight platform. Small batches may be mixed in a wheelbarrow. Machine mixers are available at moderate cost or they may be rented. However, this work can be done by hand. For ordinary use a 1:2:3 solution by volume of cement, sand and gravel with 6 gallons of water per sack of cement is satisfactory. Proportion of water depends on the condition and quality of sand.

On a platform, spread sand evenly, add and mix cement, till uniform. Add and mix in gravel. Add water gradually into a depression in the pile of dry mix. (Not more than 6 gallons per sack of cement.) Mix to a paste consistency with the

**SAND**
fine aggregate

**GRAVEL
OR CRUSHED STONE**
coarse aggregate

**PORTLAND CEMENT**

**SHOVEL**

**MEASURING PAIL**

**WOOD FLOAT**

**MEASURING BOX**

Materials needed
for concrete work.

gravel worked well into the mixture. Pour into previously prepared wood framework, or apply with trowel within 30 minutes after it is mixed. Work one section at a time. As soon as top moisture begins to disappear, level off with smooth board. For any large, flat area, make one side slightly higher than the other to provide drainage. This is done by making one side of forms higher. For smoother surface, tamp with a float, a flat board to which a handle has been attached. Keep damp for 5 days.

Concrete walks are first laid out in 3 or 4 foot sections, with taut parallel strings, spaced to allow for setting form boards. Excavate 6 inches and set form boards into place. 2" x 4" boards braced by stakes are usually used. Divider boards are placed between sections and moved as work progresses. The surface should be 1 inch above grade and pitched ¼ inch for drainage. Insert tar paper or felt ½ to ¾ inch thick in section joints to absorb expansion of concrete on hot days. Finish grooves with a trowel. The same principles apply to floors, terraces, curbs, pools, etc.

When repairing concrete or adding to a portion already finished, a bonding agent should be brushed, rolled, or sprayed on the surface before the repair concrete is laid.

**Stepping Stones:** Forms for steps should be made of 2 inch lumber braced by 2" x 2" cleats. Use concrete which is not too wet. Fill the first step and make it compact, then follow with each other step in turn. Allow to settle for ½ to ¾ hour. Level and finish with wood float. Round tread with trowel.

**Flagstone Walks:** To construct a flagstone type or a stepping-stone type of walk, make simple forms for flagstones of concrete. The various sizes of stone may be placed in any one

### CONCRETE MIXES

| Purpose | Sacks of Cement | Cu. Ft. Sand | Cu. Ft. Gravel | Gal. Water |
|---|---|---|---|---|
| General use, pavements | 1 | 2¼ | 3 | 5 |
| Foundations, thick sections | 1 | 2¾ | 4 | 5½ |
| 2″ to 4″ reinforced concrete | 1 | 2¼ | 2½ | 6 |
| Thin concrete such as finish coat on 2-layer pavements | 1 | 1¾ | 2¼ | 4 |

### HOW TO ESTIMATE MATERIALS REQUIRED FOR 100 SQ. FT. OF CONCRETE OF VARIOUS THICKNESSES

| Thickness of concrete, in. | Amount of concrete, cu. yd. | 1:1¾:2 mix | | | 1:2¼:3 mix | | | 1:2¾:4 mix | | |
|---|---|---|---|---|---|---|---|---|---|---|
| | | Cement, sacks | Fine, cu. ft. | Coarse, cu. ft. | Cement, sacks | Fine, cu. ft. | Coarse, cu. ft. | Cement, sacks | Fine, cu. ft. | Coarse, cu. ft. |
| 3 | 0.92 | 7.5 | 12.9 | 14.7 | 5.8 | 12.9 | 17.5 | 4.6 | 12.9 | 18.4 |
| 4 | 1.24 | 10.0 | 17.3 | 19.9 | 7.8 | 17.3 | 23.6 | 6.2 | 17.3 | 24.8 |
| 5 | 1.56 | 12.5 | 21.9 | 25.0 | 9.8 | 21.7 | 29.6 | 7.8 | 21.8 | 31.2 |
| 6 | 1.85 | 15.0 | 25.8 | 29.4 | 11.5 | 26.0 | 35.2 | 9.3 | 26.0 | 37.0 |
| 8 | 2.46 | 20.0 | 34.6 | 39.8 | 15.4 | 34.4 | 46.8 | 12.3 | 34.4 | 49.3 |
| 10 | 3.08 | 25.0 | 43.8 | 50.0 | 19.3 | 43.2 | 58.5 | 15.4 | 43.2 | 61.6 |
| 12 | 3.70 | 30.0 | 51.6 | 58.8 | 23.1 | 51.8 | 70.4 | 18.5 | 51.8 | 74.0 |

Quantities may vary 10 percent either way, depending upon character of aggregate used. No allowance made in table for waste.

of a number of designs, in rectangular or broken effect. Since the forms will be used several times, they should be assembled so that they may be taken apart easily. Oil them well before concreting.

In making stepping stones irregular holes may be dug in the ground in position. The concrete is then poured into these forms, smoothed off and allowed to cure.

Mixing concrete

Pouring concrete

Making flagstones

Making steps

Making a curb

Patching

Making a walk

Making a garden pool

**Patching:** Cracks or areas to be patched should be cleaned and roughened with a chisel. Undercut lightly (in an inverted V). Remove dust. Dampen. Mix a thick creamy mixture of Portland cement, sand, and water and brush onto surface. Then apply patch while it is still wet. Patch is made by mixing a mortar of 1 part cement, 3 parts sand. Allow this mixture to stand for 30 minutes with occasional mixing. Tamp firmly into crack. Smooth off lightly with a wood float. When concrete begins to stiffen, finish with trowel or wood float. Keep patch damp for 5 days.

**Attaching Fixtures** to plaster, cement, stucco, brick, stone, marble, concrete, glass or plastic requires a screw anchor. The usual procedure is to drill a hole in the base material, insert an expanding anchor or shield into the hole, expand the anchor to make it hold tight, and screw into the anchor. The anchor may be metal with suitable grooves to catch the screw, or a woody material. Rawl plugs are made of lead cases surrounded by a cork-like substance. They expand as the screw is inserted and hold tight. Other anchors are made of tapering soft metal which expands as the screw is inserted. The screw anchor and tampin contains a lead shell which expands under hammering, and holds in a grooved center.

## ESSENTIAL PARTS OF A HOUSE

(1) Gable end.
(2) Louver.
(3) Interior trim.
(4) Shingles.
(5) Chimney cap.
(6) Flue linings.
(7) Flashing.
(8) Roofing felt.

(9) Roof sheathing.
(10) Ridge board.
(11) Rafters.
(12) Roof valley.
(13) Dormer window.
(14) Interior wall finish.
(15) Studs.

(16) Insulation.
(17) Diagonal sheathing.
(18) Sheathing paper.
(19) Window frame and sash.
(20) Corner board.
(21) Siding.

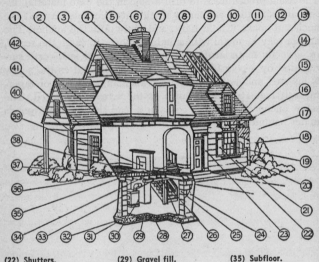

(22) Shutters.
(23) Exterior trim.
(24) Waterproofing.
(25) Foundation wall.
(26) Column.
(27) Joists.
(28) Basement floor.

(29) Gravel fill.
(30) Heating plant.
(31) Footing.
(32) Drain tile.
(33) Girder.
(34) Stairway.
(36) Hearth.

(35) Subfloor.
(37) Building paper.
(38) Finish floor.
(39) Fireplace.
(40) Downspout.
(41) Gutter.
(42) Bridging.

# BOOK VI

## Every Woman's Mending Guide

Sewing can be an exciting hobby as well as a means of having handsomer clothes and a more beautiful home. Moreover, sewing at home can be a real money-saver for you. The average hour in labor that goes into a store dress is reflected in the price not only for the amount paid to the worker, but also for manufacturer's selling cost, overhead, taxes and profit, a retailer's selling cost, overhead and profit plus your own shopping time and your own income taxes. Thus, the $2 an hour which the stitcher gets may mean $8 at the retail counter and $10 when you have to earn the money yourself. At the very least every woman should know the basic mending techniques to make what she has go farther, look better, and last longer.

Sewing, like most home tasks has been made easier with the years. New attachments to the sewing machine, new electric machines, new threads and patterns have all helped to make sewing easier, more pleasant and more interesting.

### SEWING TOOLS

First step is to set up your sewing kit. You will need:

SHEARS: The longer the blade, the longer and better your strokes; 9 inch is good, 4 inch will do. Old shears should be cleaned, sharpened and tightened.

NEEDLES: Have several sizes for hand and machine. Needles should suit the weight of the material. Size 10 is best for most dresses, for small stitches. Sizes 7 and 8 are best for basting, for heavy materials. 10 is finest, 7 and 8 medium, 4 and 5 coarse.

PINS: Use size 5 with sharp points. Get a pincushion or clear box with a lid. If the pincushion is filled with wax paper, you'll help avoid rusting. A magnet will help you collect stray pins.

THREAD: Use mercerized cotton thread on wash fabrics and on all dull-surfaced materials. Keep a variety of colors on hand for mending—black, brown, white, to match hose and other clothes, etc. Buy threads in a shade darker than your material as it usually works in lighter when it's stitched.

### NEEDLE AND THREAD GUIDE

| Types of Fabrics | Thread | Hand Needles | Machine Needles | Number of Machine Stitches Per Inch | |
| --- | --- | --- | --- | --- | --- |
| | | | | Seam | Outside |
| Canvas, duck, upholstery fabrics | 8, 10, 12 Black and White, Heavy Duty Mercerized | 3 | Coarsest | 6 | 9 |
| Gabardine, rep, corduroy velveteen, wool fleece, twill, linen crash; sewing on buttons | 30, 36, 40, 50 Black and White. Heavy Duty Mercerized | 6 | Medium Coarse | 10 | 12 |
| Gingham, chambray, sheer wool, crepe, taffeta | 60, 70, 80 Black and White. Mercerized. Nylon thread | 8 | Fine | 12 | 18 |
| Lawn, dimity, voile, batiste, chiffon, rayon crepe, rayon sheer | 80 to 100 Black and White. Mercerized | 9 | Fine | 16 | 20 |
| Net, ninon, batiste, organdy, marquisette, fine lace | 100 Black and White. Mercerized | 10 | Finest | 16 | 20 |
| Poplin, bengaline, faille, wool, flannel, wool jersey, rayon jersey, pique, moire, wool crepe, percale, chintz | 50, 60, 70 Black and White, Mercerized. Nylon thread | 7 or 8 | Medium | 12 | 18 |
| Sailcloth, denim, ticking, drapery fabrics | 16, 20, 24 Black and White. Heavy Duty Mercerized | 4 or 5 | Coarse | 8 | 10 |

For worked buttonholes on tailored wool garments use buttonhole twist. For silks, rayon or wool, silk or mercerized cotton is recommended.

For embroidery, use cotton. For decorative stitching use cotton on the bobbin and stitch wrong side up.

THIMBLE: It should fit your middle finger. Be sure there are no rough edges that might snag materials.

60-INCH TAPE MEASURE, 36-INCH YARDSTICK, AND 6-INCH RULER: Use the yardstick on the table and for measuring

## BASIC MENDING STITCHES

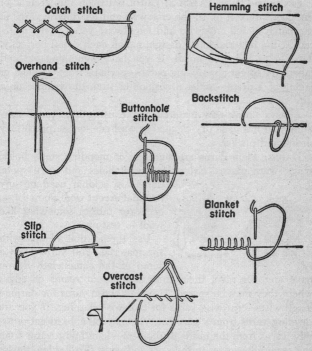

distances to the floor, the ruler for measuring hems, buttonholes, and other short distances.

TAILOR'S CHALK: Get white and colored chalk. Don't use wax pencils which may leave a stain.

IRON, IRONING BOARD, PRESSCLOTHS: Boards should be sturdy, well padded. Heavy and lightweight muslin cloths should be handy. Special boards, like a sleeve board, will be helpful.

SEWING MACHINE: If you have a choice get a modern electric machine with as many attachments as you can use.

If you have trouble threading a needle, hold a piece of white paper behind the eye. Or get one of the automatic threading gadgets.

## MENDING

**Patches and Darns.** PATCHES: Cut a patch on the straight of the goods. Sew it on so the crosswise and lengthwise yarns in the patch match crosswise and lengthwise yarns in the material. If the material has a design, match each detail perfectly. That helps hide the mend. If you have something old and faded, try to get a matching patch—perhaps from the hem or facing of a dress—under a cushion or from the valance on a slip cover.

Always shrink new material before using it to patch anything that has been dry-cleaned or washed—or the patch may shrink and pucker.

DARNS: Plain darns are suitable for mending small holes, snags, worn places. Except for small holes and worn spots,

  darns are seldom used on any material except wool, some laces, or heavy fabrics somewhat like wool in texture.

Plain darn      Pattern darn

Use thread that blends with the material. Pull yarns from a scrap of the same cloth if you

have any. Or ravel them from straight-cut seams or edges where they may be spared. Use lengthwise yarns for darning lengthwise—crosswise yarns for crosswise darning. If you are raveling yarns from a garment, you may be able to get crosswise yarns from the inside of the hem—lengthwise yarns from the seam allowances in the skirt and waist. To get lengthwise yarns for darning a drapery or bedspread, trim off a selvage or rip a side hem, ravel off a few yarns, trim, and refinish the edge. Take the crosswise yarns from one end.

If you can't get self yarn, use dull sewing thread that blends with the material. Thread usually works up lighter than it appears on the spool, so it is better to buy slightly darker thread.

Study the weave of the fabric. Repeat it as closely as you can. Work under a strong light.

Use a fine needle and short thread. Long thread pulled back and forth across a tear or hole tends to pull and stretch a darn out of shape.

Work for flatness. If the yarns are pulled up tight, the finished darn puckers and looks drawn. Too loose stitching, on the other hand, makes the darn look "puffy."

Draw the mending yarn through the yarns in the cloth itself when you can. Take tiny stitches and be especially careful not to pull them too taut when you make a turn. Run the stitches unevenly into the cloth around the edge of the darn —so there is no definite line where the darn starts.

Pull ends of darning yarns to the inside of the garment and cut them off—but not too closely. Be sure that all raw edges of the hole or tear are on the under side of the darn.

Usually it's better to darn on the right side of the material, so you can see how well you are blending the darn into the fabric.

Press the finished darn. Steam-press on the wrong side. Brush darns on wool on the right side to lift the nap.

STRAIGHT TEARS—DIAGONAL CUTS: When a fabric tears, it always breaks straight along crosswise or lengthwise yarns. The simplest tear is the straight tear in one direction.

Unlike a tear, a cut seldom breaks the material straight along crosswise or lengthwise yarns. More often it breaks the material diagonally—cutting yarns in both directions with one slit. Such a cut stretches and loses shape if not mended right away.

Washable Materials: Materials that fray in dry cleaning: Clothes and household articles that must go through many tubbings and those which fray easily need sturdy mends. Most suitable repairs, unless the hole is very small, are the hemmed patch, lapped patch, and pressed-on or thermoplastic patch.

HEMMED PATCH: This is a sturdy mend done by hand. Cut the smallest possible square or rectangle that will remove the snag, hole, cut or tear. Cut along crosswise and lengthwise yarns. Then clip this hole diagonally at each corner— about ¼ inch. Turn under slightly beyond the ends of these clips. Crease sharply or press but be very careful not to stretch the material.

Slide a piece of matching material under the hole until the

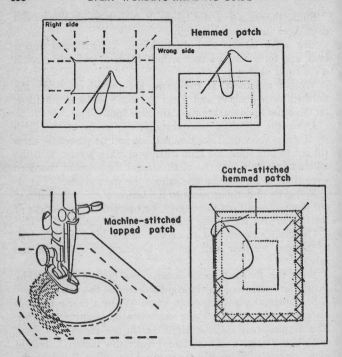

design matches exactly. Cut a patch about 1 inch larger all around than the hole. Baste the patch in place—then from the right side hem with very fine stitches, especially at the corners. Let these stitches catch in the very edge of the crease.

Now turn to the wrong side. If the material is a lightweight washable, turn the patch piece under about ¼ inch. Snip off the corners to avoid thick lumps. Baste and hem with stitches so tiny they will not be noticeable on the right side. This patch is good for tubbables, such as house dresses, play and work clothes.

For heavy, less firmly woven materials, such as some drapery and slipcover fabrics, damasklike bedspreads, and thin blankets, the catch-stitched hemmed patch is less bulky. Cut the patch as described above. Machine stitch twice around the outside of the patch—once close to the edge, again a little further in. Then baste the patch in place. Hem on the right side, turn to the under side and catch-stitch the raw edge of the patch to the article being repaired.

LAPPED PATCH: This is used when sturdiness is more important than appearance. Cut away ragged edges and make a round hole. Lay a matched piece of cloth underneath and baste it in place. Then on the right side, stitch back and forth over the cut edge until it is firm and secure with no rough ends. Cut away extra material on the under side not caught in the stitching. Or if the fabric around the hole is weak, leave on this extra goods and fasten it with tailor's tacks. They hold the material flat and do not show on the right side.

Stitch a lapped patch by machine if you are mending shirts, children's play clothes, overalls, sheets, or dish towels, by hand, on thick materials, as blankets or bath towels, where there is less strain. Hand darning makes the mend less stiff.

When patching heavily napped blankets—cotton or wool— shear some of the fuzz from both the under side of the blanket and the top of the patch where the two overlap.

PATCHES TO PRESS ON: These are made of various types of materials, treated on one side so that they may be pressed on to the material. They are best suited to men's shirts, women's uniforms, and woven cotton underwear. If you cut out your own patches from treated material, make corners rounded rather than sharp. They stick better and more smoothly. These patches may be bought at many notion counters.

DRY-CLEANABLE SILKS AND RAYONS: An inset patch is a good mend for most silks and rayons that will be dry-cleaned instead of washed. Hemmed or lapped patches may also be used but they show more on silks and rayons than the inset patch.

INSET PATCH: Cut around the damaged place with the grain of the goods so that it forms a square or rectangle. Clip the corners as for a hemmed patch—turn the edges under evenly and exactly with the grain of the goods all around. Press, do not crease with your fingernail, because that stretches soft materials.

If the fabric is printed, shift the patch piece around under the hole until you find the exact spot that matches. Then pin it in place so you can mark the exact size of the inset. From this point, there are two ways to go ahead with the patch.

First way to finish is to check the exact size patch that fits the hole. Do this by pushing in a pin through the patch at

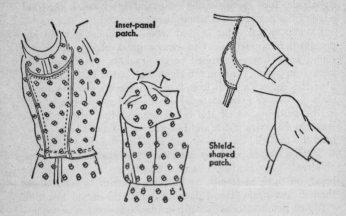

Inset-panel patch.

Shield-shaped patch.

each corner, then turn under between pins, press, and trim off the extra material, leaving only a small seam allowance. The amount you leave depends on the material—more seam allowance is necessary for materials that fray. Check again to make sure that patch fits the hole exactly. From the wrong side, overhand the patch into the hole with tiny stitches caught through the two folded edges. When the patch is done, press it flat with the seams open. Overcast the raw edges so they won't fray in cleaning.

Another way to finish the inset patch after matching the patch to the hole is as follows: Use long hemming stitches and contrasting thread to baste the patch in place. Let these stitches catch only in the edge of the fold. They serve as a guide for the inside stitching and will be pulled out later. Now turn to the wrong side and stitch by machine exactly on this line of hand stitching. Trim off extra material—clip off thick corners. Steam-press with the seams open.

**Wool:** A plain weave hand darn is the best way to mend most small tears or cuts in wool material. For a larger hole, use a darned-in patch or an inset patch. The inset patch is better for thinner wools—the darned-in patch for thick ones. A lapped patch is more suitable for thick reversible wools such as blankets.

STRAIGHT-TEAR HAND DARN: To darn a straight tear in wools, start and finish about one-quarter inch beyond the tear. With matching thread and a fine needle, stitch back and forth across the tear on the right side with tiny stitches. Keep the stitches exactly in line with the yarns in the cloth. The darn will show less if you extend the rows of stitching unevenly into the fabric. As you turn to stitch in the opposite direction, let the thread go in easily—do not pull it tight. To make the mend stronger darn over a piece of the same cloth or any thin material basted to the under side. If the tear is frayed, weave over and under the loose yarns. Let the ends of broken yarns go to the under side.

To darn a tear in heavy reversible materials, such as blankets, snip off short ravelings, draw torn edges together, matching the design if there is one, and pin to a piece of tough paper. Catch the two edges with a needle and matching sewing thread. Darn across the slit, following lengthwise and crosswise yarns in the material or the pattern in the weave— whichever shows the least.

DIAGONAL HAND-DARN: To darn a diagonal cut, first baste a piece of the same material or net on the under side to keep the cut from stretching. Then with fine needle and matching thread or yarns, work from the right side and weave back and forth across the cut, following the yarns in the cloth as for a straight tear. In some twilled materials the darn shows

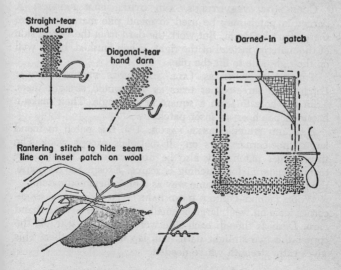

Straight-tear hand darn

Diagonal-tear hand darn

Darned-in patch

Rantering stitch to hide seam line on inset patch on wool

less if stitches follow the diagonal pattern in the weave rather than yarns of the cloth.

On heavy, reversible materials such as blankets, pin a piece of tough paper to the under side to hold a diagonal cut in shape while you darn.

DARNED-IN PATCH: If the cloth does not fray, use a darned-in patch where a plain darn or patch might not look right. It is a fairly sturdy mend—not so bulky and easily noticed on thick wool as a hemmed patch. Trim the hole so it is either square or rectangular. Cut the patch to fit the hole exactly, also to match the pattern and grain of the cloth. Baste the patch to net, fit the hole down over the patch, then baste to hold all together while you work. Use dull matching thread, and darn each of the four sides of the patch as you would straight tears. Overlap the darns at the corners to strengthen them.

INSET PATCH: To make this mend on lightweight wools, follow directions for the machine-seamed inset patch. You can hide the seam line with a rantering stitch. Pinch the seam line on the right side between thumb and forefinger. Stitch back and forth over the seam, being careful to catch only one yarn on each side of the seam. Pull the thread up close. When steam-pressed, this patch is hardly noticeable.

CORDUROYS, VELVETEENS, AND OTHER PILE FABRICS: A darned-in patch may be used to mend pile materials where there won't be strain. But work the darn from the wrong side of the material instead of the right. When finished, brush well on the right side to lift the pile.

THREE-CORNER TEARS (ALL MATERIALS EXCEPT WOOL): Patch small three-corner tears as you would straight tears. Trim the hole to form a square or rectangle. Then make a hemmed patch or an inset patch.

HEMMED THREE-CORNER PATCH: Use this patch to mend large three-corner tears on all materials except wool. The three-corner patch may also be used on small three-corner tears if material for patching is scarce. Except for its shape, the patch is made the same way as a plain hemmed patch.

WOOL (THREE-CORNER HAND DARN): To mend most three-corner tears on wool, large or small, use the three-corner hand darn. Darn as though each side were a straight tear. At the corner the two straight darns will lap over each other. This gives extra strength where needed.

**Hemmed three-corner patch**

Like a straight darn, this one may be worked over net or a piece of cloth laid on the under side for strength. Work with special care where the darns lap at the corner or your mend may be bulky and show.

**Three-corner hand darn**

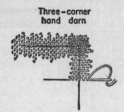
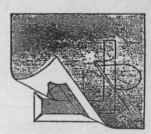

## SNAGS AND SMALL HOLES

WOVEN MATERIALS: These materials may be mended with a plain hand darn or by reweaving. Reweaving is nothing more than a darn done carefully with matched yarn, so that it reproduces the original almost exactly.

PLAIN DARN: To darn small holes, first get matching thread. If you ravel yarn from a piece of self material, use crosswise yarns for crosswise darning, lengthwise yarns for lengthwise stitches.

Leave the hole in its original shape, which usually is round. Trim off the ragged edges. Fill in new lengthwise yarns. Then, keeping the darn flat, work with small stitches back and forth across the hole—and far enough into the fabric to strengthen the thin area around the hole.

PATTERN DARN: For materials with a distinct weave, a pattern darn which repeats the weave of the cloth shows less than a plain darn. The simplest pattern darn shows how the darning produces the diagonal in a twill. To make other pattern darns, first study the weave in the cloth to see how the lengthwise and crosswise yarns are interwoven—then reproduce it as nearly as possible. The pattern darn is suitable for blankets, loosely woven suitings, and damask tablecloths.

KNITS: In knit material, snags or breaks stretch to form holes. Mend these while they are still small. The following mends will take care of most knit repair. For any of these mends you'll need matching yarn. Ravel out a pocket or some

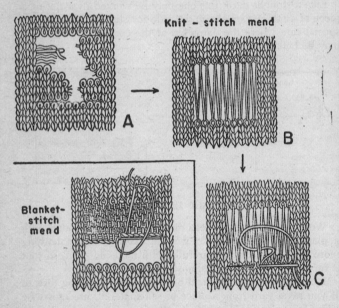

**Knit - stitch mend**

A

B

**Blanket-stitch mend**

C

other part of the garment you can do without—or you may be able to buy a matching skein.

To keep a simple break in the knitting from growing, catch the end of each loop with a needle and matching thread. Tie off securely on the wrong side.

KNIT-STITCH MEND: If the knit is plain, you can copy the stitch with a knit stitch. This mend hardly shows, and it will "give" as much as the rest of the garment.

First make two horizontal cuts—one above the hole, one

below it. Ravel the knit to the ends of the cuts. A thread may be run through the loops at the top and bottom of the hole to be sure they won't ravel. Thread each loose end and run it back through the fabric on the under side.

Then with matching yarn zigzag across the hole lengthwise. Work the knit stitch as shown on page 362.

BLANKET-STITCH MEND: This is easier to do than the knit stitch, but it shows more and has no "give." Use this stitch only where the garment will not be stretched in use.

Ravel out a square hole as illustrated for the knit-stitch mend (A). Thread each loose end and run it back through the fabric on the under side. Then pull in a crosswise yarn and work back over it with loose blanket stitches—one for each knitting stitch. Pull another yarn crosswise. Work back over it with blanket stitches and continue until the hole is filled.

## SPECIAL MENDS

WORN SPOTS: As soon as you see worn spots on the elbows of a garment or in other places that get wear, do some preventive darning to make the garment wear longer and save yourself more difficult mending later on. Use matching thread —weave it in and out to look as much like the material as possible.

Reinforce the under side of the thin spot with a piece of matching or similar material. Sometimes you can cut a piece from the hem if no scraps are available. Darn back and forth, through, and slightly beyond the thin spot, with tiny stitches on the right side. Keep the rows of stitching parallel to the lengthwise and crosswise yarns of the fabric. Sometimes it is enough to stitch back and forth with matching yarn raveled from the seams or a scrap of material. On knits, reinforce thin places by darning on the inside of the garment.

If elbows of sweaters and knit dresses wear through, cut off the sleeves above the elbow and move the wristlets up to finish off the short sleeves. Stretch the cut edges as you sew on a wristlet, so the stitching won't break when worn. Seam and finish so the knit stitches can't ravel.

If elbows on children's, men's, and boys' sweaters wear through, sew oval patches of felt or leather-like materials on the outside. Old gloves, old handbags, felt hats, or ready-made patches sold at novelty counters can be used.

LINGERIE: Lingerie, net or lace will wear a little longer if you machine stitch back and forth over small breaks or worn places. If broken places are large, baste to a piece of net footing, then stitch by machine. Mend broken edges of lace with a short blanket stitch. Use thread of matching weight.

Mend small holes in lace girdles with loose darns of matching thread.

Pulled-out shoulder straps on slips and brassieres often take pieces of the garment with them. Mend these by setting in

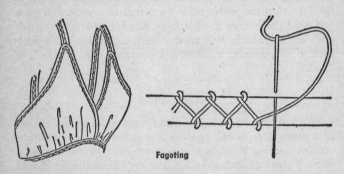

Fagoting

little patches. Try to make them an attractive part of the garment. Put them on in diamond or triangular pieces. Finish with Bermuda fagoting (hemstitching without pulled threads).

Fagoting on slips and gowns often breaks long before the garment wears out. When these breaks start, you can refagot them easily as shown. Baste the two edges to be reworked to a piece of strong paper—leaving space for fagoting. Cut and pick out the old fagoting—then restitch to make it look as much like the original as possible. Another way to mend broken fagoting is to rip out about an inch of fagoting at a time—then follow with new stitches. Buttonhole twist matches best the thread used in lingerie fagoting.

PULLED-OUT SEAMS: When a seam pulls out, the garment usually is already too close-fitting to allow for deeper seams. On a tailored dress with outside stitching you can mend pulled-out seams with an outside-stitch seam. First, re-seam the garment even though there is scarcely any seam. Then, on the under side of the seam, lay a piece of narrow matching tape. Stitch on the outside along both sides of the seam line, so the finished effect looks right with the rest of the dress.

If you have extra scraps of material, you sometimes can mend broken seams with small insets. Put the insets in to look as though they were part of the original dress design. Thus you can enlarge the garment at the same time you mend the seams.

HOSIERY: To darn a hole in a stocking foot, leave the hole in the round shape it took as it developed. Snip away ragged edges. Then, with a darner or your hand in the stocking, work with small stitches back and forth across the hole and far enough into the fabric around the hole to strengthen the thin, weak spot there. Darn in one direction, then the other, weaving in and out to make a plain weave.

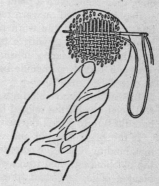

Darning hose.

Use only as many strands of the darning yarn as you need to match the weight of the stocking. The darn will look better and wear longer if you use yarn of the correct weight.

Patches that press on may also be used—these are most suitable for holes or weak spots in stocking feet where they will not show.

When new hose run, they may be mended to look like new at shops that specialize in this work. If you mend your own, take a fine needle and fine matching thread. First catch the stitch that is making the run. Then, using the overhand stitch and working from the wrong side, mend the stocking a little beyond the ends of the run. Tie your mending thread securely when you finish. A special hook is available for re-knitting runs, but it requires time and much patience to develop skill in using it.

SHIRT COLLARS: Rip off the collar; turn and resew it; for white shirts, it is easier and usually more practical to buy new collars at the notion counters. Try to match the quality of shirt broadcloth in the new collar. You won't be able to buy matching collars for colored shirts.

Towels and mats: When the selvage first begins to fray, stitch it to a narrow tape—or if the selvage is wide enough, turn it down once and stitch two or three times on the machine.

Darn small holes in the body of a terry towel with darning cotton. Clip off the loose loop yarns even with the edge of the hole, then mend with a plain darn.

Repair damaged or worn terry bath mats the same as bath towels. Or cut off the worn part, if it is near the edge, and bind the new edge with a twilled tape, carpet binding, or straight piece of heavy muslin.

Repair tufted or chenille bath mats and curtains the same as tufted bedspreads.

Blankets: When bindings wear out on blankets that are still good, rip off the ragged binding, and replace with a new one. Be sure to shrink the new binding before you use it.

If the blanket is old and worn and not worth putting on new binding, finish the edge with a blanket stitch. First rip off the old binding, then trim away any ravelings, straighten the blanket edge, and steam-press. On a thick blanket, stitch a couple of times on the machine—once close to the edge, again about ¼-inch farther in. On lightweight blankets, first baste in a narrow hem, then sew with the blanket stitching.

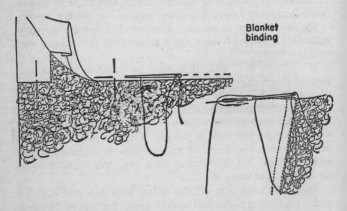

Blanket binding

Bedspreads: When you need patching material take it from the corners at the foot or from one end of an extra long spread. Face or hem raw edges where you cut out the pieces.

To mend chenille and tufted bedspreads, set in a piece cut from the corner, if the design is the same—or patch with muslin similar in weight to the foundation fabric. Sometimes on straight tears the edges can just be overhanded together. Then put in new tufts and the mend will scarcely show. If you can't get tufting yarn to match, six-strand embroidery floss will do. Double it enough times to make tufts the same size as those in the rest of the spread.

Darn lace bedspreads as you would a lace curtain. If badly torn, set in a piece of net as nearly like that in the spread as you can find.

SHEETS AND PILLOWCASES: When hems split along the fold, trim off the frayed edges, turn them in and overhand the two together. Or if there is extra length, rip out the old hem, cut off along the old fold, and turn a new hem.

For triangular rips, baste or pin paper under rips; have edges meet but not overlap. Use thread approximately same size as threads woven in sheet. If you mend by hand, use a running stitch back and forth across rip. You can do this by machine, too. Continue sewing ¼-inch beyond rip in each direction. Tear out paper. Patch a worn-thin spot before the threads break. Cut out a circular section of the worn part; make four slits at equal distances. Turn edges under so hole appears square; back with square patch of similar material (the side portions of old sheets are good). Make sure lengthwise and crosswise threads go in the same direction as those of the sheet. Make double row of stitching around patch for

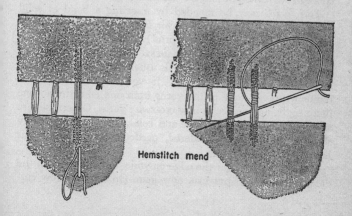

Hemstitch mend

strength. This is the system for cigarette burns, too. When sheets begin to wear along the center (you can tell by holding them against the light) tear them in half lengthwise and sew the selvages, or outer sides, together. Join with a flat seam. Hem outside edge. When sheets finally give out beyond repair, cut them up for bassinet sheets, pillowcases, sheet-covers for the linen closet, bandages, aprons, kitchen curtains, dust or cleaning cloths. Tear (don't cut) to the size desired, so fabric will keep its shape through launderings.

When pillowcases are worn along the side folds, rip out the end hem where it crosses the folds, take a seam deep enough to catch the line of wear, then restitch the hem.

If hemstitching breaks in a place or two before the pillowcase or sheet wears out, fill in the "spokes" with a needle and thread.

When hemstitching breaks in several places, trim the "points" close to the fabric, turn down a narrow edge, and fagot the old hem back on. Or insert rickrack braid, white or colored, to join the hem and sheet or pillowcase.

TABLECLOTHS: Mend small holes in good linen tablecloths or napkins with yarns from the linen even if you have to sacrifice a napkin to get them.

For larger holes, take patching material from an old tablecloth similar in pattern and weight, or from a matching napkin. If the patch comes in a suitable place, work a monogram over it. Choose one large enough to extend beyond the edge of the patch and the repair will be almost entirely concealed—it then becomes a decoration instead of a blemish.

Torn hems may be mended by inserting a band of solid color percale or a gay print. Cover small holes with appliqués (stars, flowers, figures from a print).

CURTAINS AND WINDOW SHADES: Curtains of lace, net, marquisette, and similar materials usually split lengthwise before they wear out crosswise. If you have any left-over remnants, ravel some of the yarns from one end, thread one in a needle, and weave in new crosswise yarns. Otherwise, use sewing thread of similar size and color. These repairs rarely show after they are laundered, particularly if the curtains hang full at the window.

If the holes are near the edge on wide curtains, trim off the damaged part and put in a new hem. On some narrow curtains, a ruffle of net, a contrasting applied hem or facing, is suitable. Sometimes narrow strips from two or three curtains can be tinted different harmonizing colors and sewed together.

Mend tears or splits in window shades with transparent adhesive tape or by pasting a strip of matching cloth or paper to the under side. Lay the shade on any flat surface, wrong side up. Draw the torn edges together, then apply the patch. Cut off torn hems and rehem the end. If the shade pulls off the roller, take out the tacks, cut off the ragged edge, and retack in place.

SHOWER CURTAINS: Use adhesive tape to mend oiled silk and plastic shower curtains. To repair a split or a three-corner tear, lay the shower curtain on a flat surface, draw the torn edges together, and apply the tape—transparent for thin or colored curtains, regular adhesive for the heavier white opaque ones.

Also use the tape to set in patches in shower curtains of this type. Cut a patch the same size as the hole from a corner of the curtain, the lower edge if the curtain is plenty long, or perhaps from a matching window drapery. Lay the curtain wrong side up on a table, fit the patch in place, then put a strip of adhesive over the raw edges just as though it were a tear. Repeat on all sides.

Patch canvas or duck curtains with an inset patch, a machine-stitched lapped patch, or one of the new patches that can be pressed on. Use an inset patch to mend a rayon curtain.

In patching rubberized items, sew a patch of similar fabric over a tear or a hole on the outside of the item, using two rows of stitches, one row at the edge of the tear or hole and one row on the edge of the patch. Then clean and rough up the patched area on the inside of the garment. Using a good grade of rubber cement, coat a second patch or strapping (previously cleaned and roughened) and also coat the patched area on the inside of the item. When the cemented surface is tacky, roll or press this patch firmly in place. Do not place strain on the patch for at least 24 hours. The outer patch gives strength; the inner patch imparts waterproofing qualities.

In patching synthetic resin-coated garments, use the same method as that used for patching the rubberized items except for the cement; use a hycar-neoprene base cement.

SLIP COVERS AND UPHOLSTERY: Replace worn cording in slip covers or take the cording out and stitch a plain seam.

If you have no left-over pieces, or the material has faded, use the valance or take patching material from a place where the fabric you substitute won't show, such as the under side of the cushion or the outside back.

To repair cuts and tears in upholstery where it gets little strain, use a patch that can be pressed on, or a piece of adhesive carpet binding. Cut the patch about an inch longer and wider than the hole—slip it under the hole, sticky side up —draw the upholstery together—cover with a cloth and press with a warm iron.

On the seat or back where there will be considerable strain, a sewed-on patch wears better. Choose the kind of patch best suited to the fabric, then loosen the upholstery, patch the hole, and retack the material to the furniture frame. For a large hole or a thin area, cut the patch large enough to extend well beyond the worn place, turn edges under on all sides, match the pattern, and slip stitch the patch to the upholstery on the right side.

Mend pile upholstery fabrics the same as other pile materials.

Re-cover worn chair arms. Get material for this, as well as for patching, from the outside back or from the under side of a cushion. You can replace the upholstery removed for repair with a material or a remnant of upholstery fabric that harmonizes even though it doesn't match exactly.

## HOW TO KNIT

A ball of yarn and two needles are the only equipment necessary for the basic knitting stitches; the knit stitch and the purl stitch.

(1) Casting on or putting the first line of stitches on the needle: Make a slip loop—approximately 16 inches from the end of the yarn for 20 stitches (Fig. 1)—place the loop on the needle (Fig. 2) and holding the needle in the right hand gently pull the ends of the yarn (Fig. 3). Keep the loop near the pointed end of the needle and with the point of the needle draw in the yarn (Fig. 4) which has been made into a loop around the left thumb (Fig. 5), through the under side

of the loop (Fig. 6) and then through the loop on the needle (Fig. 7). It is this loop which becomes the stitch. Repeat until you have the required number of stitches.

(2) Knit or garter stitch: Hold the needle with the cast on stitches in the left hand—holding the first stitch lightly with the index finger. The other needle is held like a pencil in the right hand (Fig. 8). Insert the point of the right hand needle through the first loop from left to right (Fig. 9). Put the yarn under and around the point of the right hand needle and draw the loop thus made through the loop on the left needle forming a new loop on the right needle (Fig. 10, 11 and 12). This is the first stitch. Repeat until all the loops on the left needle have been used. This is the first row and should contain the same number of stitches that were cast on. Change needles into opposite hands and start the next row. Keep pushing your work so that the stitch you are working on is near the tip of the needle.

(3) Purl stitch: Hold the needles exactly as for knitting but insert the needle from—*right to left*. Always keep your yarn in front of your needle. That is the essential

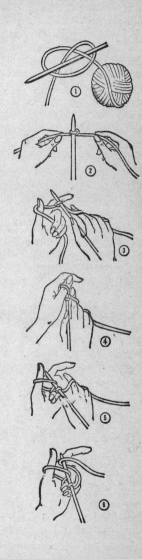

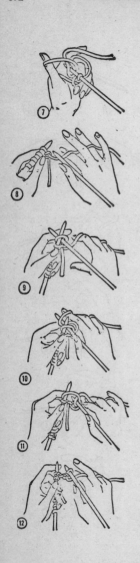

difference between knitting and purling.

(4) Increasing and decreasing: The simplest way to increase is to knit into the front of a stitch to make one stitch and then knit into the back of the same stitch thus making two stitches to transfer to the right needle. To decrease, merely knit two stitches together.

(5) Stockinette stitch is made by knitting one row and purling the next. Garter stitch is made by knitting every row.

(6) Binding off: When the desired number of rows have been worked you end by slipping the first stitch off the left needle onto the right needle. Knit the second stitch very loosely thus leaving two stitches on the right needle. Insert the left needle through the left side of the first stitch bringing the first stitch forward over the second stitch and over the tip of the needle so that you have one stitch instead of two. Knit the next stitch loosely and keep repeating. At the last stitch cut the yarn and pull the loose end through the last stitch very tightly. The important thing to remember is to bind off loosely.

# BOOK VII

## Value Guide for Good Shopping

### HOW TO BUY MORE FOR YOUR MONEY

Your dollar will buy more if you know how to shop, when to shop, and something about the quality of the things you buy. If you are on a budget, you'll find these simple hints helpful in making your dollar do more for you. (1) Compare values. Similar merchandise is priced differently at various stores. (2) Buy according to your own needs. Learn what will fill your needs most effectively. Don't buy what you don't need—oversize equipment because it has been reduced, silk where cotton will do as well, rayon where nylon will last longer. (3) Buy staples that can serve more than one purpose and more than one season. Avoid fads and extreme styles in clothes, decoration, etc. Consider upkeep needed, washability, etc. (4) Avoid low-end and luxury lines. The low-end goods don't generally wear, the luxury lines are generally over-priced and you don't get the advantages of mass production. (5) Buy staples in large quantities to take advantage of lower unit costs. The 70c tube of toothpaste contains 10 times as much as the 15c tube. (6) Where you can, pool your buying with friends and neighbors to take advantage of bulk buying. (7) Avoid instalment buying. It limits your ability to choose the best value and generally costs more. (8) Watch for better values in private brands. They often represent the same merchandise offered by a nationally advertised brand, without the cost of advertising added. (9) Wait for out of season merchandise, for post-holiday clearances, for sales generally, for "special buys," for price wars, etc.

## MONTHS WHEN SALES USUALLY OCCUR

APPLIANCES: Feb.

APRONS: Apr., May, June, July, Oct., Nov.

ARMCHAIRS: Feb., Aug.

ART SUPPLIES: Jan., Feb.

BABY CLOTHES: Jan., Mar., July.

BANDAGES: Jan., Feb., July, Dec.

BEDS: Feb., Aug.

BEDDING: Jan., May.

BEDSPREADS: Jan., May.

BIBLES: Feb.

BICYCLES: Jan., Feb., Sept., Oct., Nov.

BINDERS, LOOSELEAF: Feb.

BLANKETS: Jan., May, Nov., Dec.

BLOUSES, BOYS': Jan., Mar., Apr., Dec.

  GIRLS': Aug., Dec.

  WOMEN'S: Jan., Feb., Apr., May, June, July, Nov.

BOOKS: Feb.

BOWLS, GLASS: Jan., Feb., Sept.

BRASSIERES: Apr., May, June, July, Oct., Nov.

BRIEFCASES: Feb.

CABINETS, KITCHEN: Jan., Feb., Sept.

CARRIAGES, BABY: Feb., Aug.

CARRIAGE BLANKETS: Jan., May.

CHILDREN'S WEAR: July, Dec.

CHINA: Jan., Feb., Sept.

CLOTHS, DISH AND TABLE: Jan., May.

CLOTHING, BOYS': Jan., Mar., Apr., June, Dec.

  MEN'S: Jan., Mar., Apr., Aug., Dec.

COATS, INFANTS': Jan., Apr.

BOYS': Jan., Mar., Apr., June, Dec.

  GIRLS': Jan., May, Aug.

  MEN'S: Jan., Mar., Apr., June, Dec.

  WOMEN'S CLOTH: Jan., Feb., Apr., May, Aug.

  WOMEN'S FUR: Jan., Feb., Apr., May, Aug.

COFFEE MAKERS: Jan., Feb., Sept.

COFFEE MAKERS, ELEC.: Feb.

COMPACTS: Jan., Feb.

COOKING UTENSILS: Jan., Feb., Sept.

CORSETS: Feb., Aug.

COSMETICS: Jan., Feb., July.

COSTUME JEWELRY: Jan.

COTTON BLANKETS: Jan., Nov., Dec.

CURTAINS, DRAPES: Jan., Feb., May, July, Aug., Nov.

CUTLERY: Jan., Feb., Sept.

DISHES: Jan., Feb., Sept.

DRAPERIES: Jan., Feb., May, July, Aug., Nov.

DRESSES, INFANTS': Jan., Mar.

  GIRLS': July, Dec.

  WOMEN'S: Jan., Feb., Apr., May, June, July.

DRUG SUNDRIES: Jan., Feb., July, Dec.

ENAMELWARE: Jan., Feb., Sept.

FLOOR COVERING: Jan., Feb., July, Aug.

FURNITURE: Feb., Aug.

FURNITURE, SUMMER: Jan., July.

GAMES: Jan., Feb., July.

GIRDLES: Feb., Aug.

GLASSWARE: Jan., Feb., Sept.

HANDBAGS: Jan., May, July.

HATS, CHILDREN'S: July, Dec.
  MEN'S: Jan., July.
  WOMEN'S: Feb., May, July.
HOSIERY: Mar., Oct.
HOUSECOATS: Apr., May, June, July, Oct., Nov.
HOUSEWARES: Jan., Feb., Sept.
IRONS, ELECTRIC: Feb.
JEWELRY: Jan.
KNIVES: Jan., Feb., Sept.
LAMPS: Feb., Aug.
LINENS: Jan., May.
LINGERIE: Apr., May, June, July, Oct., Nov.
LINOLEUM: Jan., Feb., July, Aug.
MILLINERY: Feb., after Easter, July.
NOTIONS: Feb.
NURSERY FURNITURE: Jan., July, Dec.
PANTIES, INFANTS': Jan., Apr.
  WOMEN'S: Apr., May, June, July, Nov., Dec.
PANTS, BOYS': Jan., Mar., Apr., June.
  MEN'S: Jan., Mar., Apr., Aug.
PILLOWS AND CASES: Jan., May.
PLAY CLOTHES, CHILDREN'S: Aug., Dec.
  WOMEN'S: Feb., July.
QUILTS: Jan., Nov., Dec.
RACKETS, TENNIS: July, Aug.
RADIOS: Jan., Feb., July.
RANGES, REFRIGERATORS, ELEC.: Feb.
RUGS: Jan., Feb., July, Aug.

SHIRTS, INFANTS': Jan., Apr.
  BOYS': Jan., Mar., Apr., June, Dec.
  MEN'S: Jan., July.
SHOES, INFANTS': Jan., Apr.
  BOYS': Jan., Mar., July.
  GIRLS': Jan., Mar., July.
  MEN'S: Jan., July, Nov., Dec.
  WOMEN'S: Jan., July, Nov., Dec.
SILVERWARE: Feb.
SLACK SUITS, MEN'S: Jan., July.
  WOMEN'S: Feb., July.
SPORTSWEAR: Feb., July.
STATIONERY: Feb.
SUITS, BOYS': Jan., Mar., Apr., June, Dec.
  GIRLS': Jan., Feb., Apr., May, Aug.
  MEN'S: Jan., Mar., Apr., July, Dec.
  WOMEN'S: Jan., Feb., Apr., May, Aug.
TABLES: Feb., Aug.
TOASTERS, ELECTRIC: Feb.
TOILETRIES: Jan., Feb., July.
TOYS: Jan., Feb.
UNDERWEAR, BOYS': Jan., Mar., Apr., June, Dec.
  MEN'S: Jan., June.
  GIRLS': Apr., May, June, July, Oct., Nov.
  WOMEN'S: Apr., May, June, July, Oct., Nov.
WASHING MACHINES, ELEC.: Feb.

(10) Shop in reputable stores which make a point of cutting price—some department stores, specialty chain stores for shoes, clothes, auto supplies, food chains like A & P and Safeway Stores, variety chains like the dime store. Mail-order catalogues are a handy means of shopping. In most large cities, there are discount houses which sell nationally adver-

tised products at a discount. Some such houses carry only sample stocks. They are usually located in out-of-the-way places, poorly advertised. Avoid so-called wholesalers, manufacturers, sample houses or outlet houses who sell at retail, etc., unless you can compare prices. (11) Avoid paying for extra services you don't use. Some stores specialize in delivery, credit accounts and other services at no extra charge. The charge for these services is in the price. (12) Read the labels. Most merchandise must be labeled to indicate what is in it. The quantity of wool in a garment, hair in a mattress, or the U. S. Standard of quality of a food product is plainly marked. (13) Know your merchandise. You can compare values better if you know what makes quality. (14) In general: Choose reputable dealers. Even the best quality merchandise may have hidden defects. Check government inspection labels wherever they are available.

## JUDGING FABRIC QUALITY

Satisfactory quality as well as attractive appearance is important in the selection of textiles you buy in clothing and household items. Stores offer a wide variety of fabrics in myriad hues, textures, designs, and weaves. The person who buys a fabric wants to know what it is made of, what service it can reasonably be expected to give, whether it will hold its color, whether it can be laundered or dry-cleaned, whether it is warm or cool as compared with others of its kind, whether it will shrink or stretch and, if so, how much.

The characteristics of a fabric depend on the fiber content, how it is spun into a yarn, how it is woven or knit, and how it is finished. The more common practice is to combine two, three, or even more fibers into a yarn. This makes fiber identification difficult.

### Animal Fibers:

ALPACA: A fine, glossy, thick, long filling used for men's office jackets and for filling.

CAMEL HAIR: A soft, lustrous fiber used for coats, jackets and sportswear.

CASHMERE, VICUNA: An extremely soft, fine fiber used for overcoats, suits, shawls, etc.

MOHAIR: Short, coarse, soft, durable goat's wool used for upholstery.

SILK: Fine, long, strong strands of 800 to 1200 yards from the cocoon of the silk worm.

SPUN SILK: Short ends of silk spun to make a soft yarn.

## Vegetable Fibers:

COTTON: Absorbent, heat resistant, versatile, inexpensive fiber from cotton pods.

LINEN: Strong, inelastic, hard, smooth, absorbent, washable, mothproof, quick drying.

HEMP: Long, strong, pliable fiber used for fabrics and coarse ropes.

JUTE: Woody, brittle. Used for horse blankets, or mixed with wool.

RAMIE: Lustrous, inelastic fiber similar to linen.

## Synthetic Fibers:

VISCOSE and CUPRAMMONIUM RAYON: Both are made of cellulose. Similar to cotton, but weaker when wet.

ACETATE RAYON: Burns readily; puckers and melts under heat. Dissolves in acetone (nail polish) and chloroform (in spot removers).

NYLON: Strong, durable, shrink resistant, synthetic made from coal air, and water.

ORLON: Lustrous, fast drying, inelastic, wrinkle resistant, acid resistant synthetic made from natural gas.

DACRON: Wool-like, wrinkle and crease resistant, resilient, shrinkproof, quick drying synthetic made from coal tar.

DYNEL: Soft, wool-like shrinkproof, synthetic made from natural gas and acetylene.

SARAN: Acid and chemical resistant, durable synthetic made from petroleum and brine.

TERGAL: Used for curtains.

ULTRASUEDE: Looks like suede but is washable.

GLASS FIBRES: Thin, smooth, lustrous, fireproof, moisture and decay proof fiber made of glass.

## New Fabrics for Traveling:

SYNTHETIC FABRICS are nonabsorbent and should be laundered frequently. For best cleaning choose the higher wash water temperatures. Less wrinkling will result with the use of lower temperature. Good "wash-and-wear" synthetic fabric garments must have a high percentage of synthetic fibers. The following minimum percentages are necessary:

| | |
|---|---|
| 65% or more Dacron with cotton | 80% or more Acrilan with cotton |
| 55% or more Dacron with rayon | 70% or more Acrilan with rayon |
| 50% or more Dacron with Orlon | 70% or more Acrilan with wool |
| 75% or more Orlon with rayon | 50% or more Kodel with rayon |
| 70% or more Orlon with wool | 50% or more Kodel with cotton |
| 80% or more Orlon with cotton | 50% or more Kodel with wool |

Garments made of 100% Dacron, Orlon, Acrilan and nylon, as well as 100% cotton, if properly resin treated, will also give good wash-and-wear performance.

| | WATER TEMPERATURE | |
|---|---|---|
| FABRICS | WASH | RINSE |
| Acetate | Warm or Cold | Cold |
| Acrilan | Warm or Cold | Cold |
| Arnel | Hot, Warm, or Cold | Cold |
| Blends* | According to minor fiber | Cold |
| Dacron | Hot, Warm, or Cold | Cold |
| Dynel | Hot, Warm, or Cold | Cold |
| Fortisan | Do not wash in machine | |
| Nylon | Hot, Warm, or Cold | Cold |
| Orlon | Hot, Warm, or Cold | Cold |
| Rayon | Hot, Warm, or Cold | Cold |
| Vicara | Warm or Cold | Cold |
| Spandex | Warm | Cold |

*Note: If blend contains wool, use a warm wash and a cold rinse, unless manufacturer specifies otherwise.

Fabrics are treated with water resistant polyurethene for light, waterproof wearability.

Yarns: Knowing what fiber is used does not solve all problems of textile selection. The quality of the fibers, the way they are spun, the amount of twist, and the ply of the yarn all have a great deal to do with the wearing quality of the cloth. The manner in which the yarns are interlaced to produce the material is largely responsible for its firmness and its resistance to snagging, fraying, and stretching. Good fibers and good yarns generally make good serviceable fabrics, provided the weave is suitable. Sometimes, however, poor fibers and poor yarns, if carefully spun and woven, will produce a material that will wear reasonably well for certain purposes and, if the price is in relation to the service that can be obtained from it, may prove to be a satisfactory purchase.

In being made into a yarn, fibers are carded (foreign matter is removed by combing), combed (very short fibers are removed by further combing) and spun (twisted into firm, hard threads). Long fibers—like the man-made fibers—may be woven or knit as filaments, without further spinning. In general, combed, hard-twisted yarns are thinner, stronger, and more durable than loose yarns.

Fibers are spun into many types of yarns—some simple, others more complex. Single yarns are made by spinning many fibers together into one continuous length. Sometimes two or more single yarns are twisted together to form a ply yarn. Thus a yarn made by twisting two single yarns together is a two-ply yarn; one made by combining three single yarns is a three-ply and so on. These multi-ply yarns must not be confused with multi-filament. A multi-filament yarn is a single rayon yarn composed of many continuous strands which are held together with very little twist.

Core yarns, a type of complex yarn, consists of loose fibers wrapped around a tightly twisted central core. The core gives strength and lessens expense. It is generally of cotton. The so-called metallic yarns used in metal cloth and the filling yarn in some cotton and wool blankets are familiar examples.

Bouclé and ratiné yarns are also of the complex type. They are made by twisting single and plied yarns together under different tensions so that little kinks or bumps occur along the surface. Both the color and the fiber are often varied to produce novel and beautiful effects.

The amount of twist put into a yarn governs its size as well as its strength. As a rule, tightly twisted yarns wear better than those that are soft and loosely twisted.

A special mercerized finish may be given to cotton to add strength, luster, a soft feel, and better dyeing qualities.

**Making the Fabric:** In weaving, the threads that run lengthwise are described as the warp, the threads that run crosswise are called the weft or the fill. The number of crossings is the pick. The count of a cloth is given as 70x60, or 70 warp threads and 60 fill threads. The pick is the product of these two numbers—4200. The higher the count of a fabric, the stronger and more durable it will be.

Fibers may be made directly into fabric by felting. Fibers are pressed under steam so that they interlock to make felt.

After a yarn is made, it may be made into a fabric in a variety of ways:

TWISTING: Yarns are twisted in a pattern to make lace.

KNOTTING: Yarns are knotted by machine to make nets.

BRAIDING: Flat or tubular fabrics are sometimes braided.

KNITTING: Yarns are looped together to make elastic knit fabric.

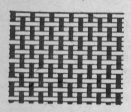

Plain Weave

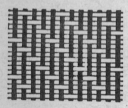

Twill Weave

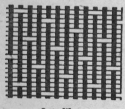

Satin Weave

WEAVING: Fabrics are woven to make most fabrics. The weaving may be in one of many types. The plain, or over-and-under weave, is the simplest and perhaps the most durable type of construction. It is used in fabrics designed for hard wear. Muslin, gingham, percale, voile, and taffeta are examples of fabrics with a plain weave. The twill weave, identified by diagonal ridges, wears well and resists tearing, but it tends to stretch more than a plain weave because the yarns are not held so securely in place. Denim and serge are examples of the twill weave. Changing the direction of the ridges, as in a herringbone design, or varying their width, results in interesting patterns. The satin weave produces a smooth, lustrous fabric that drapes well. Since a warp yarn is crossed by only every fifth to eighth filling the warp seems to float on the surface of the cloth. When the floats are made by the filling yarns, the weave is called a sateen weave. In either satin or sateen, the loose floating yarns get more wear, and the surface is apt to roughen or to catch and snag easily. Also, where there are too few yarns in either direction, there is danger of shifting.

These four fundamental weaves have many variations which make almost countless fancy designs and textures.

Jacquard looms weave elaborate and intricate designs on the loom under the regulation of a board punched with holes. The board regulates rods and cords which raise and lower the loom so that the fill may skip some threads in the warp, thus creating the design.

From the basic weaves, various developments have been made to produce pile fabrics, swivel and lappet effects which give the appearance of embroidery, multiple layer cloth, corded weaves, and leno weaves (strong and open as in mesh fabrics).

Look for firm weaves when long service is desired. Ordinarily, a closely woven fabric keeps its shape better, shrinks less, pulls less at the seams, and wears longer than a loosely woven cloth of similar texture and weight. To judge the firmness of a cloth, first hold it up to a strong light. Notice whether the yarns, both warp and filling, are uniformly spun, practically the same size, and evenly spaced. Then try to shift the yarns. Grasp the cloth with thumb and first finger of each hand and pull gently. Try this in both the lengthwise and crosswise direction. If the yarns shift easily or if the fabric becomes puffy in places, it will pull along the stitching lines. Look also at the cut edge of yard goods and at the seams of ready-made articles. The amount of frayage is often an indication of the looseness of the weave. Fraying may also be due to the fiber from which the fabric is made. Some types of rayon fray more than other fibers woven in a similar construction. Sometimes, however, excessive frayage does not show up until after the fabric is washed because sizing materials hold the yarns in place while the cloth is new.

Good balance in a fabric (approximately the same number and size of warp and filling yarns in an inch of cloth) makes a good wearing cloth. However, in some cases, the very nature of the fabric makes an equally balanced construction impossible. For example, a true broadcloth always has from one and a half to two times as many warp yarns as filling yarns.

**Woven-in Designs:** Designs and patterns may be produced by the weave or by contrasting yarns. These usually last as long as the material holds together. Weave alone, not color, produces some patterns. These are sometimes called textural designs: corded and ribbed effects in dimity, poplin, and broadcloth.

A true crepe is another example of a woven-in textural design. The crepe effect comes from a difference in the tension on groups of warp yarns during weaving, as in seersucker, or from a difference in the direction the yarns are twisted. Such crepes are permanent and remain as long as the fabric lasts. Imitation crepes are made by embossing or by printing cloth with an alkali which causes shrinking wherever it touches the fabric. These crepes are not permanent. To determine whether or not a crepe is permanent, stretch the fabric between the hands. If it stretches out smooth, the crepe will disappear with wear or washing.

Sometimes the woven-in crepe is exaggerated by various finishing methods. Such heavily creped fabrics, stretched and dried under tensions during finishing, are likely to shrink greatly in washing or dry cleaning.

Surface designs such as printed patterns, paste dots, moiré, and some embroidered dots and figures are applied after the cloth is woven. Some designs applied in this way last as long as the fabric holds together; others are not permanent. White dots or small designs on a dark background are often made by printing on the dyed cloth a chemical that removes the color.

Warp-knitted Fabrics: There are several types of warp-knitting machines: Tricot, Milanese, Raschel, Kayloon, Simplex, and variations of these. It is the tricot machine, however, that accounts for the major share of warp-knit fabric production. There are two main types of tricot jersey, one-bar and two-bar. In one-bar tricot, one thread is fed to the fabric from the warp beam or spool for each row of loops. The fabric created is run-resistant. In two-bar tricot, two separate warp threads are fed to the fabric from the warp beams for each row of loops. Every loop of the material is interlocked by this intricate process, making the fabric run-proof. This also produces a richer texture, gives a greater range of stability, which means that the draping qualities and resistance to shrinking and stretching can be predetermined and built into a two-bar tricot fabric.

Knit fabrics have several advantages: Elasticity enables

knit fabrics to conform to body contours without tight tailoring. Porosity permits a circulation of air next the skin—keeping you comfortable, summer and winter. Suppleness of knit fabrics make them highly drapeable, exceptionally wrinkle-resistant. Bulk without weight is characteristic of knit fabrics, which means they may have good "body" without feeling heavy. Softness is inherent in knit fabrics, making them particularly good for intimate apparel. Ease of laundry is possible because the flexibility of the construction permits the dirt to be loosened and flushed away with a minimum of effort.

**Colorfastness:** The fastness of dyes depends upon the type of dye-stuff and the method used in dyeing. Once a fabric is dyed, little can be done to set the color. The common household practice of soaking in a solution of salt, vinegar, or sugar of lead is usually almost useless.

Vat dyes are most satisfactory for cotton. Such dyes are developed right on the fiber and become a part of it. They are fast to washing, light, acids, alkalies, and in some cases to bleaching agents. Whether the dye is applied to fiber, yarn, or a piece of woven cloth determines to some extent the colorfastness of a fabric. As a rule, in-the-fiber dyeing gives better penetration than does either yarn or piece dyeing.

Sometimes the method of dyeing can be determined from the finished cloth. Ravel a yarn from the material and look at it closely. If white or light spots occur at regular intervals, the fabric was piece-dyed, and only the surface of the yarns took the dye. If the fabric shows no evidence of piece-dyeing, untwist the yarn. If the center is white or lighter than the surface, the dye was probably applied to the yarn.

Dyes should be fast to the conditions under which the fabric will be used. These may include one or more of the following: light, washing, perspiration, bleaching, ironing, steaming, or dry cleaning.

**Shrinkage Control:** Even though a woven cotton fabric is labeled "fully shrunk," "shrinkproof," etc. it can under certain treatments practically always be made to shrink further. To be of real help, the label should give the upper limit for the amount of shrinkage remaining after it is washed a specified way.

Pre-shrinking is generally considered to apply only to cotton, but some methods that produce shrink-resisting wool fabrics are now in use. One method of steaming and pressing is used principally on women's coat, suit, and dress materials. Another method, known as the chlorination process, removes some of the fiber scales.

**Special Finishes:** Before a fabric is ready for the retail market, it goes through many finishing processes to enhance its appearance and to make it more useful. After they are woven, fabrics are finished. This processing may include: giving a moiré effect, shrinking, glazing, weighting, starching, mercerizing, making the fabric water repellent, waterproof, spot and stain resistant, absorbent, crisp, fire resistant, non-inflammable, resistant to perspiration or mildew or germs or rot or wind, crease and wrinkle resistant. Some other fabric finishes:

BLEACHING: Used on cotton and linen to whiten it. It weakens the cloth.

SELVAGE: This places a binding on the fabric, prevents raveling.

WEIGHTING: Powdered metals are added to give weight, body and feel to a fabric. This slowly washes out.

SIZING: Starch is added to give weight and luster. This comes out after a few washings.

NAPPING: This raises the fibers on one or both sides to give softness, as in blankets.

CALENDERING: The fabric is run under pressure between two rollers to give it a hard, lustrous finish.

DYEING: This gives fabrics color. It may be done in the yarn or in the fabric.

PRINTING: This may add either color or a design.

EMBOSSING: The fabric is run under pressure between two rollers with designs in them. The result is a raised design in the fabric.

## SYNTHETIC MATERIALS

New materials have become the chief ingredients in many home products. Some of them are best known by their trade names, others by their generic names.

NYLON, originally a DuPont development, is now widely made (from carbon, hydrogen, nitrogen, and oxygen). It is a polyamide fiber, noted for strength and long wear. It is used for stockings, carpets, clothing, rugs, brushes, and many industrial products.

DACRON, a DuPont synthetic polyester fiber (from coal, air,

and petroleum), is noted for resistance to wrinkling, ruggedness, and washability. It is used for men's wear, fire hoses, sewing thread, filtering fabrics, and fill for pillows.

ORLON, is a DuPont acrylic- or vinyl-type fiber used for knit goods and in blends with wool, rayon, and cotton. It may appear with a deep pile, as in blankets, or with soft feet as in sweaters. It is noted for its resistance to chemicals and its strength, but it is not as strong as nylon. It is washable and requires a minimum of ironing.

ACRILAN is the trade name of an acrylonitrile, bulky, mothproof, usually crimped, quick-drying fiber which resists moths, mildew, fungi, wrinkling, and spotting; is light, resilient, and warm (used in blankets and rugs). It is often blended with wool, cotton, nylon, or Orlon.

VECTRA is a fiber made of polypropylene, used for snag-resistant stockings.

SPANDEX (trade names are Lycra, Spandelle, Vyrene, Neuma, Blue Sea, etc.) is a synthetic, elastic fiber that stretches and snaps back. It is used for women's undergarments, bathing suits, ski pants, etc.

LASTEX, the trademark of a yarn combined with rubber, is used for bathing suits, foundation garments, and support hose.

FIBERGLAS, the trademark for a fiber made of molten-glass filaments, is used for draperies, curtains, panels, and translucent roofing.

VINYL is a synthetic product of ethylene, used in making fibers, wall and floor covering, phonograph records, interlinings, leather substitutes, etc. Vinyl fabrics are made in all thicknesses, from thin coatings to sheets for wall covering and heavy imitation leathers for luggage and upholstery. Finishes imitate rugs, marble, wood, brick, stone, terrazzo, and scores of special designs. The material is elastic, washable, durable, and scuff resistant. Nonwoven vinyls, include Velon, Naugahyde and Koroseal. Sheet vinyl products may be laminated to a fabric backing, printed, or embossed.

FABRICORD, the trademark for pyroxylin, is a coated fabric used for belts, bookbinding, footwear, and luggage.

FUR FABRICS are made in imitation astrakhan, beaver, Persian lamb, leopard, etc., with a pile weave of mohair, nylon, rayon, Dynel, Orlon, or spun silk. These are used for coats, linings, trimmings, and toys.

ARNEL, a synthetic, warm, bulky fiber with the feel of wool, highly resistant to moths, carpet beetles, mildew, and abrasion, is used for knit outerwear and drip-dry clothes.

SARAN is a generic term for a transparent plastic used for textiles, wrapping, pipe, film packaging, and interliners.

MYLAR is the trademark of a synthetic film, sometimes transparent, used for electrical insulation, repairs, storm windows, and packaging.

SANFORIZED is a trademark applied to fabric processed to eliminate shrinkage.

METALLIC YARNS (Mylar, Lurex) are laminations of clear-plastic film and aluminum foil or metalized film. They are washable, may be dry-cleaned, and do not tarnish. Other metallic fabrics used for clothing are lamé, Metlon, Raymet. These fabrics are used for draperies and women's clothing. Other fabrics may be printed with lacquer and coated with pulverized gold, silver, or copper.

MILIUM, the trademark of a heat-insulating lining fabric based on aluminum flakes which reflect body heat, is used as a lining for clothing.

FLAMEPROOFED FABRICS chemically treated not to burst into flame, are available in widths up to 108 inches, in muslins and other materials, for decorative uses in public places.

CRUSH-RESISTANT FABRICS are pile-treated and used in women's coats.

DRIP-DRY FABRICS (Arnel, cotton-Dacron mixtures, etc.) require no ironing, regain their shape in hanging. They should not be tumbled.

Crease and wrinkle resistance is the built-in ability of a fabric to spring back from a crease or a fold. Synthetic fabrics are made crease resistant by treatment with synthetic resins or by "curing" or steaming in pleats after the garment is finished. Before dry-cleaning, such garments must be properly rinsed or they will lose their quality. Wool, silk, and polyester fabrics are naturally resistant to wrinkling.

Stain- and spot-resistant finishes (including water-repellent finishes) do not allow waterborne stains—and to some extent oil-borne stains—to penetrate the fabric. This is accomplished by treatment with resins which closes the pores of the fabric. However, when stains do penetrate, they are dislodged only with great difficulty.

Water-repellent and waterproof finishes may have any of a variety of resin, silicone, or plastic finishes or coatings. Continuous exposure to water will eliminate resistance to it, so cleaning must be done with special care.

Moth-resistant finishes make wool and other animal fibers unfit for larvae, but soiled garments are always vulnerable. Most finishes will survive washing and dry-cleaning.

Mildew-resistant finishes are chemicals applied to cotton, wool, linen, silk, leather, and paper. Ordinarily synthetic fibers, while clean, are naturally resistant to mildew.

Antibacterial finishes (Cyana Guard, Sanitize, Eversan) are applied especially to resist bacteria and fungi.

Antistatic finishes are applied especially to acetates, acrylics, modacrylics, nylons, polyesters, and sometimes to wool through a thermosetting resin which absorbs or contains moisture. Moisture helps dissipate an electrical charge. Fabric softeners in rinse water are effective antistatic agents. Dry-cleaning may invalidate these finishes.

## GUIDES IN BUYING CLOTHING

**Clothing in General:** To save money on clothes, plan your wardrobe. Select clothes which go together and can be interchanged. Stick to a few conservative colors and classic styles. Avoid fashion fads. Budget your clothing so that you don't get overstocked on accessories and can't afford the basics. Buy out-of-season, at the end of the season, and at sales. Go to sales on the first day to get the best selection. Avoid "phony" sales by merchants perpetually going out of business.

**Women's Dresses:** Select styles in simple, classic, functional lines, styles which are inexpensive to keep up, to clean, etc. Pleating, shirring, tucking, embroidery, add to upkeep costs. Extreme style fads date a dress, may make it obsolete in a year. Select a style easy to get into and out of. Select the fabric best suited to the use you plan for the dress, considering particularly durability and washability. Check the size by fitting. (Sizes vary among manufacturers.) Allow for shrinkage. Seams are a good gauge of workmanship. They should be at least ⅜ inches, finished to avoid unraveling. The number of stitches to the inch varies from 7 in cheap dresses to 15 in expensive dresses. Stitching should look the same on both sides. Hems should be wide to provide for adjustments (2 inches is good). Dresses to be dry-cleaned should have binding at the edges; wash dresses should be stitched and hemstitched. Plackets should be 10 inches or more in length, inconspicuous, and well secured (zippers or metal fasteners). Buttons, buttonholes, and shoulder pads are indications of a manufacturer's care. Reinforcements and tape should be placed at the pockets and under the buttons. Material should be cut so that patterns match and flow symmetrically from the seams. The way the grain of the material runs is important. Sleeves should run with the length of the fabric. Trimmings are not usually important, as they may be changed, but the additional cost should be considered. Collars and cuffs should be well finished. Trimmings of contrasting color should be detachable for cleaning.

Fabric should be of close and even weave. Label should indicate cleaning, washing, and ironing procedure. Stitching should be firm and even, similar on right and wrong sides.

Select sizes to fit without alteration if possible. For short or medium figure with small frame and short waist, junior sizes, 7 or 9 to 15 is the range.

For the 5 feet 5 inches or under, with small frame, *petite* sizes are proportioned to fit.

For the "average" height figure, small to medium frame and long waist, misses sizes range from 10 to 20.

For short, fuller proportioned women with short waist-lines, half sizes, 12½ to 22½ is the range. These come in both youthful and mature styles.

For medium to tall women, with medium to large frame and long waist, women's sizes, 28 to 52 will be right.

No one can afford to buy clothes which will not be a joy to wear. Nothing can take the place of "trying on." Walk around, stretch, reach and sit down. Check with the mirror from all angles. If you are doubtful, don't take anyone's word for it except a fitter's. Even though you plan to alter it yourself, in many stores a fitter will pin-fit a dress for you and tell you how to sew it without charge. When you try it on, use this Check List for fit:

Shoulder line and armholes are major lines, and must fit. Is there space to move without straining the seams? Raise your arms and swing them forward to check.

Notice if shoulder pads are the right size and shape.

Shoulders are too wide if the armhole rides down on the arm unless so styled.

Shoulders are too narrow if the seam is in from the shoulder edge. It will feel uncomfortably snug and make the shoulder appear too narrow. Don't buy this.

Think a long time before having alterations made in shoulder line. This type of alteration is expensive, may be disappointing.

Sleeves should be sewed in the armhole so crosswise threads of the fabric in upper sleeve run parallel with the floor.

Fullness at the top of the armhole should be evenly distributed.

To check length, bend your arm, fist closed and palm side toward your chest. The sleeve should be even with the knob of your wrist. Remember that sleeves become shorter with wear. Length is not hard to alter unless sleeve has elbow fullness and is too short or too long from shoulder to elbow.

Waistline of a one-piece dress should come to your normal waistline. If it is too short or too long waisted try a different size range.

Too loose at the waist? Requires a simple alteration. If belt is set in, it may be tedious but not risky.

Waistband will wrinkle less and be more comfortable if an easy fit. A waistband liner will keep blouse tucked in.

Skirt length should depend on your most becoming length. Modify style trend to your height and the shape of your legs.

**House Dresses:** Fabric should be a firm cotton with a hard (dirt resisting) finish (percale, chambray, glazed chintz). Pattern should not show spots (small figures on a dark background, etc.). Style should be simple, with minimum of trim to avoid catching, washing problems, etc. They should be easy to get into and out of (wrap around, button front, ample neckline), ample in size to avoid binding, washable, with good, firmly sewed pockets at the right level.

**Cloth Coats:** Warmth, comfort, service, and pleasing appearance are what a woman looks for when she selects a cloth coat. Materials, designs, and workmanship affect these qualities. To be sure of satisfaction, read informative labels and check such points as the following:

An outer cloth of good quality fibers and well-constructed yarns.

Firm, close weave that will not stretch out of shape or snag.

Lining of firm construction, without excessive weighting.

Lightweight interlining proportionate in warmth to the type of coat.

All materials thoroughly shrunk.

Colors fast to sun, rain, cleaning, and perspiration.

All parts cut accurately with the grain of the goods.

Precise workmanship, short stitches, and strong thread.

Thorough pressing done as the coat was put together.

Tape and fabric stays at all points likely to stretch.

Trim and fastenings equal to coat in wearing qualities and colorfastness.

A becoming design that keeps out cold, and allows ample freedom of activity.

**Underwear:** Underwear should be washable, pre-shrunk, of firmly woven strong fabric with reinforced seams, of correct size. Knitted garments absorb perspiration, give both greater warmth and coolness. Fabrics in order of durability are nylon, wool-cotton mixtures, cotton, rayon. Tricot knits do not run, are easy to wash, require no ironing.

**Slips:** Nylons are far and away the most durable, outlast several knit rayons. Tricot knit nylons need only a rinsing, no ironing. Satins of the same quality are usually stronger than crepes. Bias-cut slips are best for slim figures as they are more elastic and hug the form better (but size should be ample); straight-cut slips are recommended for larger figures. These have less tendency to ride up or slip. Slips with front and back panels cut on the bias have the advantages of both types. Seams and straps should be securely stitched. The finish at the top and hem are good indications of workmanship. Knit rayons seldom run, or do not run in more than one direction. It is wise to fit slips, as the sizes vary widely in proportions. Inset midriff gives sleeker fit. Select proper length, suitable top (brassiere top, strapless or bodice top).

**Women's Hosiery:** Get stockings of correct size, proportions, length and sheerness, in neutral shades. Buy two or more pair of the same shade and sheerness so that you can substitute if one of a pair runs. Notice ample width, reinforcements at heel and toe, fineness of seam, stretch of hems. Full fashioned hose has best proportions, looks best. Seamless hose will eliminate danger of crooked seam. No-run hose give good wear even if sheer. Lace or net stockings are distinctive.

Denier refers to the thickness of the yarn. Gauge refers to the number of yarns to the 1½ inch space. Sheerness is due to denier. Higher gauged stockings fit better, look better and wear better. Recommended weights: for evening or dressy wear 15-20 denier; for daytime wear 30-40 denier; for heavy duty 60-70 denier. Seamless hose give a barelegged effect. In this type of hose, needle count has the same meaning as gauge, varies from 300 (in 40 denier) to 400 (in 15 denier).

Buying several pairs in the same shade avoids being left with too many "odd" stockings.

**Men's Suits and Overcoats:** Value depends on fabric, style, and workmanship. Workmanship may be gauged by the amount of hand stitching at key points, where collar joins the lapel, at buttonholes, sleeve linings, trouser linings, inside the lapel (the lapel should be springy). Lapels should be pliable and drape well. Sleeves should be full from shoulder to elbow. Half-lined coats should have a double lining across the shoulder. Alterations should be made from a larger size to a smaller. If major alterations are necessary, a made-to-order suit may offer better value. Fabric wears best if it is hand finished, tightly woven, and resilient (worsted cheviots, gabardines, twills, sharkskins). Highly resilient fabrics spring back quickly when crushed. Other details to look for: quality of linings (rayon twill is good), fabric and stitching of pockets, ample seams in trousers to allow for letting out. Fabric has warmth if it has a high nap (cashmere, velour, montagnac, Polo cloth) but this wears quickly. Harder overcoat cloths are heavier for the same warmth (melton, mackinaw, homespun). Worsteds with a soft nap attempt to combine warmth with wear.

Avoid poor qualities of woolens: They may be made of fibers reworked to such an extent that they are uneven, harsh, and stubby, with most of the natural qualities of wool destroyed. These fabrics feel heavy and boardy, and have little or no resiliency. They also look dull and matted. Such fabrics soon become baggy, the finish wears away, and breaks may come at the elbows, across the hips, and other places where there is strain and rubbing. However, there are both good and poor qualities in reworked wool. If wool left-overs from the garment cutters are of high-grade virgin wool, they might, when reclaimed, make better cloth than would inferior qualities of new or virgin fibers.

High-grade suits are full cut, with no piecings or defective cloth. This means higher production costs, as more cloth is required for each suit. In low-grade suits, materials are not inspected. Small flaws are ignored, others mended or made to fall in seams. Sizes are skimped and piecings used, most often in the crotch, to make the goods go as far as possible. In the best suits, stripes and plaids are cut so that the pattern matches precisely. In low-grade suits patterns are matched in only one direction, and not always with exactness. Precise pattern matching adds nothing to the wear life of a suit, but is important to its appearance.

The term "hand tailored" applied to a suit doesn't mean that every stitch is hand sewed. For practical reasons all seams are machine stitched. To carry a "hand tailored" label, a coat must be made with at least 21 specified hand operations. In many very fine suits, hand operations number more than 21, and many suits with fewer than 21 are serviceable and good buys. In fact, some hand work is not as long wearing as machine sewing, and unless done by an expert, may not look as well. Hand operations skillfully done add to appearance and to the softness that makes a comfortable suit. The silk thread used in high-grade suits also adds to softness because of its elasticity.

After every important sewing operation in a factory that makes high-grade clothes, experts skillfully shrink and shape the coat with hand steam irons. In this way shaping can't come out—it is sewed in by operations that follow and it is there for the life of the suit. By the time such a suit is finished it seems to need little additional pressing, but even so it receives a very careful inspection and a final press.

In best quality suits, the lining is smoothly fitted and finely stitched by hand with matching silk thread. The lower edge of the coat is bound—"piped," the trade calls it—and fastened over the lining. A small pleat for "give" is left along the lower edge of the lining.

Look for neat, strong buttonholes. Best in appearance and most flexible are those hand-worked with silk twist, but high-grade machine buttonholing is better than poor hand work. Examine both sides of buttonholes. In high-grade suits they are worked with close, even stitches, with a strong bar opposite the eyelet end. Without the bar, buttonholes tear with use.

Best buttons, and the standard for judging all others, are tip horn. You can tell them by their transparency, dark veining, and natural soft polish. They are expensive, so ivory buttons are more commonly used. These wear and look very well. Least expensive are synthetics.

**Men's Shirts and Pajamas:** Value depends on fabric, washability, workmanship and cut. They should be guaranteed pre-shrunk and color-fast. High thread-count in fabric determines durability. Workmanship and cut can be gauged at the collar and cuffs (flat, evenly cut, matched in pattern and stitched), front panel (2 rows of stitching, interlining of same material), fullness of the body and tail, tucks at the

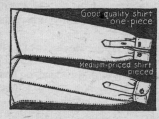

Shirt backs rounded high at the center and having evenly distributed gathers or pleats fit better over the shoulders.

shoulder blade, sleeve fullness, seams, buttons (smooth, even, firmly sewn pearl with 4 holes), collar stitching (18 to 20 to the inch).

Broadcloth is the most common fabric, and is graded by the single or double-ply yarns used, 1 x 1, 2 x 1, 2 x 2, etc. The 2 x 2 ply gives a smooth, silky finish. Pajama fabrics are gauged by thread to the square inch. (80x60 count is good). Trimmings on pajamas are a major factor in bringing up costs. Fabric should be closely woven. Sizing may be added to give the fabric body, but this washes out.

Shirt fabrics popularly used are: nylon, silk, rayon, percale, madras, poplin, chambray, oxford cloth, broadcloth.

**Men's Underwear:** Ribbed or knit types are resilient, absorbent, more comfortable. Woven types are less expensive, more durable, especially if cut on the bias. Winter underwear should be a combination of wool and cotton. Underwear should be washable, pre-shrunk, of firmly woven strong fibers, of correct size, with reinforced and ample seams. Crotch and waist should be reinforced.

**Men's Hats:** Quality depends on the amount of long-haired fur in the felt. A good hat body is smooth, flexible, elastic, supple, shows good workmanship (e.g., stiff cloth or oil silk between sweatband and felt), is not spongy, stiff or grainy, is even in color. No dye powder should show when you flick the hat.

**Men's Hosiery:** Quality depends on fabric, closeness of knit, elasticity. Ribbed tops hold their shape best. Size should be ½ inch longer than foot. Hose should be full-fashioned. Toes and heels should be reinforced or double woven. Instep should be able to stretch to 7 inches. Seams should be well trimmed. Top should be elastic. Dyes should be fast. Fabric should be pre-shrunk. Buy several pairs of the same color to avoid having odd socks when one of a pair wears out. Mend at first sign of wear. Wash socks daily for best care.

Most popular hosiery fabrics are: nylon (longest wearing, most expensive); wool (they should be shrink-resistant); lisle (long-staple cotton twisted hard); mercerized cotton (cotton made shiny and stronger by caustic soda treatment); rayon (some cotton will give it added strength).

**Men's Ties:** Quality depends on fabric, lining, sewing, and exclusiveness of design. Knit ties, silk, wool and cotton shed wrinkles in the order named. Even inexpensive ties can be of good construction; the reason one tie costs a dollar and another $7.50 is due largely to the exclusiveness of the pattern and the superior quality of the fabric.

Hold the tie away from the body by the narrow end. It should hang with perfect balance, in a straight even line. Stitching should be neat with no threads hanging. The back seam should be sewn in a straight line. At the point where the folds meet, the tie should be bar tacked for greater strength. Careful pressing at the factory gently folds the fabric, does not mar it at the edges with a permanent line. Good ties have wool lining which helps keep shape.

Grasp the tie in the middle between both hands. Tug gently. A good tie is cut on the bias and will pull evenly without puckering. There should be some give—but it should not be excessive. Fine ties are often "tipped" with silk. Windsor knot ties should be at least 50 inches long.

**Work Clothes:** Value depends on weight of cloth and workmanship. A good normal weight is 2.20 yards of 28 inch cloth to the pound. All material should be pre-shrunk.

**Boys' Suits:** Buying a suit for a boy is different from buying a suit for a man. A boy is more active and growing, so two seasons' wear—sometimes only one—is about all that can be expected. Best suits for boys are, as a rule, comparable with medium quality suits for men.

Materials should be sturdy. Outer cloth should have weaves that are firm, strong, and not likely to snag, with texture that is soft and comfortable, takes a good press, does not wrinkle readily, and is of a color that does not show spots quickly, and should be thoroughly shrunk. Color permanence is essential.

Fabrics of wool, cotton, and of mixed fibers are the three main types of suitings used for boys' garments.

Knit clothing for men and women is non-crushable and often completely washable.

THINGS TO NOTE IN THE JACKET: Fabric pattern matched; cut accurately with grain; fine, close stitching; collar smoothly shaped to fit neck; front softly rolled; flexible; armholes smoothly pressed; buttonholes firmly worked; buttons handsewed; pockets precisely tailored and reinforced; pressed thoroughly; lining only in coat fronts; exposed seams bound; hand-felled at armholes, neck and shoulders; taping at armholes and along front and lower edges and roll or revers; fabric stays at pocket mouths; seams at least three-eighths inch wide; outlets in body and hems of sleeves and coat; front stayed with shape-retaining interlining; padding of flexible material, secure, not excessive.

THINGS TO NOTE IN THE TROUSERS: Cut full and straight; pockets bar-tacked; fly neat and flat; belt loops evenly placed; waistband fastened with two buttons; buttons of lasting quality; cut with no piecings; waist, bias-faced; pockets of twill cotton, twice-stitched seams; stayed openings, clean finish; seams, serged; outlets, at back rise and cuffs; fly facing extended to crotch; linings, smoothly fitted.

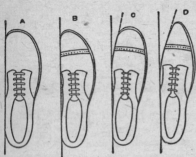

**Shoes:** Fit and durability and appearance should be considered. Leather should be pliant, soft, close fibered and firm. Toes should be roomy, heel snug, instep comfortable.

Construction should be all-leather, except lining and inside toe reinforcement. Good shoes have lining of kid or finer portions of cowhide. Lining should be neat and smooth fit. Best for patent leathers are enameled colt or

Shoes made on proper and improper lines:
A, B: Satisfactory. Note the straight inner line and rounded toe characteristic of the normal foot.
C, D: Objectionable. Note the curve outward from the naturally straight inner line of the foot; also the too pointed toe. D.

horsehide. Insoles should be made of lightweight, even-grained leather. Stitches should be small and even, properly caught in the leather. In good shoes, there should be 2 to 3 rows of stitching.

Leather should be pliant and show no signs of cracking when bent, but not elastic or loose fibered. Watch out for sheepskin which is soft but wears poorly.

Outsole, finish at the edge should be firm, smooth and neat. There should be no space between sole and seat of the heel.

In welt construction, sole and upper are joined by being mutually stitched to a leather strip or welt. This type wears best, repairs most easily.

In women's shoes, heels should taper, are best for health at minimum heights. (Army nurses' heels are 1⅛ inches high.)

The size of a shoe is its length for a standard width. The width is expressed in letters and the length in numbers. Stock widths range from triple A, the narrowest, to triple E, the widest. Whole sizes increase in length by one-third of an inch. The American size-system runs from 0 to 13½ in the first series and continues from 1 on in the second series. In the first series, size 0 is 4 inches long and size 13½ is 8½ inches long. The second series, size 1 is 8 2/3 inches long and size 12 is 12 1/3 inches long.

Shoes of correct shape are broad and round at the toe and straight along the inner edge. A pair of normal feet placed together touch at the heels and also from just in back of the big joints of the big toes up to the ends of these toes. The inner edges of the soles of a pair of properly made shoes do likewise. The more these edges diverge or curve toward the outside of the shoe, the more unnatural the shoe's shape and the greater the wearer's discomfort.

Shoes should always be fitted with the entire weight of the body on the feet, as the feet are then at their largest. New shoes, if a correct fit, are comfortable from the start. They do not need "breaking in."

The "swing" or general direction, of the shoe should be the same as that of the foot; it should not tend to twist the foot out of its normal position. If the "swing" is not right, the shoe can not fit correctly. It will be too loose in one place and too tight in another. The one-sided appearance of a worn shoe is usually due to an incorrect "swing," which has caused the ball of the foot to rest at one side of the shoe, rather than straight in the middle.

There should be a good half-inch of empty space beyond the toes in a broad or well-rounded shoe. In more pointed shoes there should be more space. The broadest part should be at the end of the little toe. It is essential that the big joint of the big toe should come just at the rounding-in of the sole on the inside edge near the instep. The vamp seam should not press upon the top of the foot back of the toes. Here there should always be a little, although not much, free space. The counter, which holds the back part of the shoe upper in

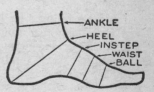

Where to measure the foot.

shape, should center the heel of the foot in the heel seat of the shoe. It should fit the foot snugly and yet be wide enough to be comfortable when the whole weight of the body is borne by the feet for some time.

Corfam poromeric material is DuPont's man-made breathable shoe upper, available in high-fashion women's footwear and some men's shoes. Corfam can be wiped or washed to remove normal soil. Even in its softly napped version, Corfam cleans well with soap and water. Smooth and grained types require only occasional polishing with conventional colored wax or cream polishes to heighten the shine and mask any heavy surface mars.

Neither a plastic nor a coated fabric, Corfam is a complex chemical structure that breathes freely and wears well, flexing easily with each step. It is resistant to scuff and abrasion, indifferent to weather, color fast, light, and it retains shape.

It is available in three distinct surface textures—a smooth, glowing surface; a series of several rich grains; and a napped surface, unique to Corfam, which is soft to the touch.

A Teflon-coated sole is available for bowling shoes and other shoes which require a sliding surface.

## COMMON SHOE LEATHERS

ALLIGATOR: Scales can almost be lifted.

CALFSKIN: Sturdiest, most waterproof. Should be close-grained.

KID AND GOAT: Soft and pliable.

REPTILE: Durable. Requires little care.

SHEEPSKIN: Suitable only for lining.

SNAKESKIN, LIZARD SKIN: Vary widely in design and coloring.

SUEDE (CALF WITH NAP): The flesh side of calf is buffed to provide a nap.

Leather substitutes for footwear now provide better wear and adaptability than natural products. Corfam (DuPont) is a high-fashion, durable product for shoe tops on both men's and women's shoes. Turlite, Permagrain, and Neolite (Goodyear) are sole materials, with great durability and variations.

Gloves: Best leather is kidskin. Calfskin (capeskin), pigskin and ostrich are also widely used and good wearing. Goatskin and sheepskin are also used. Table-cut gloves carry the mark of the National Association of Leather Glove Manufacturers subject to specifications. Such gloves have grain running with the fingers, are usually brush-dyed on one side only. Block-cut gloves are cut regardless of grain, are usually vat-dyed both inside and out. Stitches should be small and even. The type of seaming and the gusset are no hallmarks of quality.

**Children's Clothes:** Economy can be obtained by avoiding ruffles, embroideries, pleats, and stressing durable fabric, construction and good design. Simple clothes, button-down-the-front, also aid in teaching children to dress themselves. Sizes should be checked, may vary among manufacturers. Ample room should be allowed. Material for letting out at hems, seams, and cuffs should be available. Good fabrics: corduroy, chambray, cotton covert, denim, gabardine, jean cloth, moleskin, poplin; for summer, seersucker, covert, khaki, corduroy; for underwear, combed yarns; for outer clothing, water repellent Byrd cloth, poplin, melton or mackinaw cloths.

Cotton should have a close weave; knitted goods should be elastic; all should be color fast and pre-shrunk. Construction should be noted particularly at seams (close stitching, sufficient overlap); reinforcements (bar-tacking at ends of seams, pockets, etc.); linings (sturdy material); buttons and buttonholes; cuffs (elastic).

Consider a child's activities, his measurements and proportions and the changes growth will soon make. Look for clothes built for comfort and for tubbings.

Collarless indoor winter clothes won't catch in snow suits.

Seats with extra length allow spread for stooping.

Trouser legs should be snug enough to appear neat, never bind.

Shoulder support is best. Bib-tops and shaped straps stay in place.

Dresses well above the knees won't be stepped on.

Elasticized waists, tucks, gathers, circular cuts provide ease through body and shoulders.

Raglan sleeves, roomy armholes, short sleeves loose at cuff or long sleeves bloused with knit cuff permit reaching.

Pockets are needed for hanky and treasures. Patch type with slanting top is durable and handy to use.

**Children's Shoes:** Value depends on fit (very important), style, workmanship and materials. Fit should be made with full weight on both feet, with both shoes laced. The large toe should be ½ to ¾ inch from the tip. Shoes should not gap, should be wide over the toes and at the heel, should be loose at the vamp. Shoes should not be passed from one child to another.

**Infants' Shoes:** Durability is not important for the first year, but size and workmanship are important. When purchased, shoes should be ½ inch longer and ¼ inch wider than the foot. Leather should be flexible, light. Heels should be snug.

The first walking shoes should have flexible but firm soles, unpolished, preferably slightly buffed, and broad enough to be a steady platform under each foot. The toes of the uppers should be full or puffy and not so flat that the leather pulls straight back from the end of the sole and cramps the baby's toes.

**Diapers:** It is generally wise to select the items you need. Diapers may be flannel (softest), birdseye (not so absorbent, fast drying), gauze (least absorbent, easy to wash). About 36 is the minimum required. Diaper service, which supplies and cleans, is available in most cities. Disposable diapers and diaper pads are about equally expensive and less comfortable than cloth. Soiled diapers should be flushed in the toilet and kept in a closed, interlined can.

**Furs:** The selection of fur trim or a fur coat should consider durability, warmth, use (casual, formal or trim), and price. Fur prices vary widely—as much as 50 percent—according to variations in demand and style.

There is often a difference in the serviceability of furs of the same species. For example, many species of skins are graded 1, 2, 3, and 4 and the quality is indicated by the fullness and texture of hair as compared with peltries of the same kind. The prime skins (No. 1) are soft, heavily furred, because taken in the season when the fur is naturally at its best.

Minks, sables, raccoon, etc., may be top blended to improve the color. Examine the fur carefully through the underfur to detect top blending. Top spotted furs, as in imitation of leopard or leopard cat, may be detected by brushing the fur against the grain to tell whether the spots are on top or run through the pelt. Some cheap furs, as in cheap raccoons, may be heavily dyed or painted to give stripes or pattern. To detect such, rub your hand over the fur. Heavily top painted fur may feel sticky rather than smooth and clean or may even be apparent to the eye.

Edges subject to hard friction wear, such as front edges, cuffs, sleeves, pockets, back of neck, bottom edges should

## FURS COMMONLY USED FOR CLOTHING
(L, low; M, moderate; H, high)

| FURS | Service-ability | Price Range | Remarks |
|------|-----------------|-------------|---------|
| ALASKA SEAL | M-H | M-H | Beautiful fur suitable for most purposes. Very warm. Dyed in logwood brown, "Safari" brown, Matara brown, or black. Finer skins are unscarred, close-furred, and even of pile with supple leather. |
| BROADTAIL LAMB | L | H | Light or dress wear. New-born or very young lambs of Persian or Karakul type; flat haired, light weight, thin leather. Best type has beautiful moire markings throughout; often dyed. |
| AMERICAN BROADTAIL PROCESSED LAMB | L | L-M | Light or dress wear. Young South American Lamb sheared to reveal natural flat moire pattern resembling Broadtail Lamb, and dyed. |
| BEAVER | M | M-H | Sports and dress wear. Very warm. Inclined to mat when repeatedly exposed to dampness but easily corrected. Medium weight with medium length, medium brown silky hair or dyed. Sheared beaver makes a coat that is less bulky and less inclined to mat. |
| CALF | L-M | L | Sports or dress wear. Often used as a substitute for pony, dyed, or stenciled to imitate leopard, ocelot, etc., but has brittle hair. |
| CARACUL-DYED LAMB | L-M | L-H | Mostly for dress wear. Short to long hairs of various textures. Skins graded according to curl and lustre, the flattest moire skins with the highest lustre and silkiest texture being the best but generally poorest in serviceability<br>CARACUL PAWS—Made of paws and leg pieces—are not serviceable. |
| CARACUL-DYED KID | L | L-M | Dress wear. Type of dyed Kidskins having loose curls and resembling caracul; sometimes has moire markings. |
| CHINA MINK CHINESE MINK | M | M-H | Everyday or dress wear. Coarse haired, yellowish peltry but commonly dyed. Incorrectly called "Chinese Weasel." Heaviest qualities known as Kolinsky. |
| CHINCHILLA | L | H | Dress wear. Beautiful but delicate. Pelts are very light and thin, very silky, soft beautiful gray, short to medium length fur. |
| CONEY (See Rabbit) | | | |
| ERMINE | M | H | Dress wear. Species of weasel from Canada and Russia, the latter being denser furred and more expensive. Dainty, delicate light fur. Natural Winter color is white but certain types turn naturally grayish. "Summer Ermine" is not ermine, but brown weasel. White ermine sometimes dyed shades of brown. |

## FURS COMMONLY USED FOR CLOTHING

| FUR | Service-ability | Price Range | Remarks |
|---|---|---|---|
| FISHERS | M-H | H | Large species of marten. Makes beautiful scarfs. Rich dark brown, long black over-hairs, or dyed. Coarse-haired types give better service. |
| FOX | L-M | L-H | Dress wear. Soft, full-furred, silky in better grades, to coarse hair for low grade. Readily dyed to harmonize all colors or used naturally. Tendency to shed.<br>BLUE FOX—Combination of dark gray, brown and misty blue color; some have heavy elusive purple tinge and others are brown with gray underfur, the most expensive skins having the most bluish tinge.<br>CROSS FOX—A black type of the red fox and of reddish tinge, having a distinct black cross at neck and across shoulders and down the back of skin.<br>RED FOX—Darker shades in natural state wear better. Commonly dyed in other colors.<br>SILVER FOX—Blue-black with silvery hairs. The lower part of each silvery hair is black, the next part white and the tip black. (In pointed fox the inserted hairs are generally all white.) Best grade is lustrous blue-black with bright silver hairs covering from half to almost full length of skin. |
| JAP MINK | L-M | M-H | Every day or dress wear. Soft, silky, short-haired fur, dyed in rich shades of brown. Coats commonly made by "resetting" or "let-out" process, working skins in diagonal or vertical effects. Inferior grades are coarse and have fewer guard hairs. |
| KID | L | L-M | Sports or dress wear. Natural color or dyed. Glossy, flat-haired; some resembling caracul, called "caracul-dyed kid." Character, color, varies. Thin leather apt to tear easily. |
| KOLINSKY | M | M | Everyday or dress wear. Heaviest grades of long-haired, silky Chinese or China mink. Generally dyed in brown tones. |
| LAMB | L-M | L-H | There are many varieties or species of lamb peltries used for fur, ranging from the common variety to Persian Lamb, ranging correspondingly in price. Serviceability ranges from low to good depending on the type of lamb, the numerous varieties and grades in each type, method of processing, manufacture, etc. "Mouton" is a trade name for "Mouton-dyed Lamb," an inexpensive fur. |
| KRIMMER | M | M | Dress wear. Cross-bred species of Persian lamb type. Gray and black color, showing much variation in the character of the curl. Tendency to peel when leather becomes dry. Commonly dyed |
| LAPIN (See Rabbit) | L-M | | "Lapin-processed Rabbit";—closely sheared and dyed. |

## FURS COMMONLY USED FOR CLOTHING

| FURS | Service-ability | Price Range | Remarks |
|---|---|---|---|
| LEOPARD | L-M | M-H | Sports or dress wear. Sheds. Mostly pale fawn or reddish, brownish red buff, spotted over with dark brown or black rosettes or broken rings. Better quality has flat, silky hair and more contrast between spots and body color. Long coarse hair less desirable. |
| MARMOT | L-M | L | Light or dress wear. Often dyed or top blended to resemble mink. Best grades have long fine, silky fur. |
| MARTEN | | | Light or dress wear. Sometimes incorrectly called "Hudson Bay Sable." |
| | M | M | BAUM MARTEN—Generally for scarfs and trimmings; yellowish brown naturally, but usually blended in deep brown tones. Somewhat coarser and less lustrous than sable. |
| | L-M | L | JAP MARTEN—Tends to yellow color naturally, thin, short-haired, to heavy. Generally dyed sable color. Generally less expensive than baum or stone marten. |
| | M | L-M | STONE MARTEN—Slightly coarser than Baum Marten but handsome with conspicuous whitish underfur and ashy-gray or brown guard hairs. Usually used natural. |
| MINK | M-H | H | Suitable for most purposes. Serviceability good except for very cheap, lowest grades. Fairly light weight with short, fine, brown hair. Used natural color, dyed or blended. Silkier, fuller-furred and softer fur pelts the best. Coats generally made by "resetting," "let-out" or "dropping" process. |
| MOLE | L | L-M | Dress wear. Grace and beauty. Fairly light weight with fine dark hair, or dyed. Light, supple, velvety, lustrous. |
| MOUTON-DYED LAMB | M | L-M | "MOUTON" is a trade name for "Mouton-dyed Lamb." The pelts are sheared, processed, and dyed to produce a soft, flexible, close-haired fur. The leather is strong. Commonly dyed dark brown, but various brown tones and lighter colors available. Better "Moutons" are of lighter weight and supple; and distinguished by smooth even texture or shearing, free from "wavy" or shaggy surface appearance, and free from conspicuous "breaks" in the smooth surface. |
| MUSKRAT | M-H | L-M | Sports or dress wear. Medium weight with chestnut or medium brown hair, or dyed. Long top hairs with heavy underfur. |
| MUSKRAT (Silver) | L | L-M | Sports or dress wear. Usually made of bellies; shorter haired, lighter in color and apt to be more tender than Muskrat. |

## FURS COMMONLY USED FOR CLOTHING

| FURS | Service-ability | Price Range | Remarks |
|---|---|---|---|
| MUSKRAT (Hudson Seal-dyed Muskrat) | M-H | M | Sports or dress wear. Fairly light weight with short line, black-dyed fur. Sheared and dyed to resemble Alaska Seal. Best coats judged by uniformly thick fur, brilliant lustre, less noticeable joining of pelts. |
| NUTRIA | M | M | Sports or casual wear. Water rodent. Resembles beaver, but has weaker leather and shorter fur. Long hairs plucked; dense underfur inclined to mat, but easily corrected. Commonly dyed. |
| OCELOT | M | M | Sports wear. Spotted cat. Elongated spots or blotches of black and brown. Pale peltries more desirable. |
| OPOSSUM | M | L-M | Sports wear. Inclined to mat. Medium weight with medium length yellowish brown or gray colored hairs. Pliable skins if properly dressed. Quality of skin and fur may vary in single pelt. AMERICAN OPOSSUM—Underfur coarse, fuzzy, and almost white mixed with long bluish gray and sometimes with silvery or dark guard hairs. Used in natural colors or dyed. Inexpensive. Inclined to shed. AUSTRALIAN OPOSSUM—Close, even, soft fur. From most desirable full-furred natural clear blue-gray to less desirable thin-furred natural yellowish muddy gray. Used more extensively than American Opossum. |
| OTTER | M | M-H | General use. Medium weight with medium length gray, brown or dark brown hair with stiff silver or shiny guard hairs which are often plucked leaving short, dense underfur, or dyed. |
| PERSIAN LAMB | L-H | M-H | Every day and dress wear. Young lamb of the Karakul breed, a fat-tailed sheep with hair in regular curls lying close to the pelt; but not including Krimmer, or other cross breeds of Karakul, or cross breeds of Bessarabia, Shiraz, and Krimmer, or other types such as caracul. Natural gray color is sometimes undyed, but otherwise the peltry is commonly dyed a lustrous black. Leather should be soft, light weight and pliable, but the pelt may crack or peel. Finest type has silky, complete curls of firm bodied, lustrous character, varying in size from small to fairly large. Cross breeds of Karakul must not be designated as "Persian Lamb," but as "Cross Persian Lamb." The latter may be woolly, loosely curled and less lustrous than Persian Lamb. |
| PONY | L-M | L | Sports wear. Coarse haired pony wears "fair," but flat, or moire type not as durable. Used in natural color or dyed. |

## FURS COMMONLY USED FOR CLOTHING

| FURS* | Service-ability | Price Range | Remarks |
|---|---|---|---|
| RABBIT | L-M | L | Light dress or sports wear. Treated to resemble many other furs. Dyed various colors. Certain type, light weight and tender; other skins are thicker, furred, heavier and stronger in leather. "Coney" and "Lapin" are trade names for rabbit. |
| RACCOON | M | L-M | Sports wear. Heavy weight with long, silvery, black-tipped top hairs, dense, woolly underfur. Used in natural color or commonly blended to darken the stripes. More expensive grades have definite silvery cast throughout rather than brownish or reddish cast. Skins should be well matched according to color and depth of hair. Good grades have heavy underfur and plenty of guard hairs. Bellies and sides are lighter in color naturally and will not wear as well. |
| RUSSIAN SABLE | M | H | Dress wear. Marten family. Medium weight, medium length, medium brown hair. Best grades have very deep soft pile in lustrous blue cast brown color; silky guard hairs which in many cases have white tips naturally. Often blended a darker shade if the natural color is light. |
| SKUNK | M | M | General use. Heavy with long, coarse black hair and white stripes. Sometimes dyed, or white stripes usually cut out and pelts sewn together. |
| SPOTTED SKUNK | M | L-M | Sports wear. Short, thick, dark underfur with top hair silky, tender leather and black with white stripes or patches. Erroneously called "Civet cat," Civet or "Civet skunk." Commonly dyed. |
| SQUIRREL | L-M | M | Dress wear. Fairly light weight with short, fine, light to dark color hair. Not suited to hard usage. Finest squirrel has clear, blue-gray cast and dense fur. Less expensive has flatter gray fur with brownish streaks. Matching of pelts for color and density of fur an indication of value. Low grades dyed brown and gray. Squirrel belly plates not serviceable and used mostly for trimmings. |
| WOLF | M | M | Used for trimmings and scarfs. Sheds. Heavy with long, coarse hair but wide variety in species and texture. Used in natural color or dyed. |
| WOLVERINE | M | M | Large species of weasel. Durable long hair, thick, deep, woolly underfur with heavy coat of long, coarse top hair varying from deep coffee to blackish brown. Dark skins most valuable. Very light colors are usually dyed. |

* Fabrics which imitate most furs are available in various weights.

be adequately protected by full, thick hair, and in long-haired furs by plenty of guard hairs.

The better qualities in most furs are bright and lustrous.

Linings should be good, strong, and serviceable; should resist friction wear, particularly under the arms and at bottom edges.

Furs and fur pieces vary in price according to the way they have been dressed, treated, and styled. All furs are dressed—prepared from the original animal skins by tanning and other treatments. Some are sheared—the hair is cut down to give a better texture. Let-out furs are cut into narrow strips to take maximum advantage of natural beauty of the fur, and to give the effect of stripes. This involves extensive labor and increases the cost of the coat.

Generally, furs should be well matched, lustrous, uniform in texture, not matted or scarred, with joinings scarcely noticeable, and leather firm and pliable. Fit should be ample.

**Luggage, Leather Goods:** The best wearing leathers for luggage are: cowhide, calf, seal, pig, goat, and reptiles. "Leathers" labeled alligator finish, etc., usually indicate cheaper leather suitably finished. Top grain is the outer side of the hide which contains the grain. A split is one of the inner layers after the top has been removed. Deep buff is the top layer after top grain. A split has no natural grain, a coarse fiber, and is substantially less durable than top grain leather. Pyroxylin, a water repellent coated fabric, is usually superior to all but top grained leathers. Value in leather goods depends on the leather, blemishes, stitching, lining, hardware, color fastness, lack of elasticity, pliability. Good top grain leather can be doubled over with the grain, without cracking.

Best frames are made of 3-ply (or 5-ply) basswood or 3-ply (or 5-ply) plywood, or aluminum. Molded plastic and fiberboard are also used. Wood base throughout is better construction than covered frames.

## JEWELRY

Jewelry depends, for value, on the stone, the setting, and the design. Most costume jewelry contains imitation or simulated stones made of colored glass. Better grades of jewelry contain synthetic stones made from the same chemical elements as natural stones. Genuine or real stones are natural.

Emeralds, rubies, diamonds, sapphires, and genuine pearls are precious stones or gems; others are semi-precious stones. Gems are weighed in karats; 100 points equal 1 karat, about 4 grains troy weight. All stones may be cut in various ways to bring out their best features. Quality of genuine pearls depends on luster, color, shape, flawlessness and size. The quality of simulated pearls depends on the thickness of the coating and the amount of hand polishing given. Quality of cultivated pearls depends on thickness of pearl around bead, shape, luster, flawlessness. The facets of a stone are the flat, polished surfaces. The more facets cut into the stone, the more brilliant it appears.

Cameos are carved figures raised above the surface of the stone. Quartz and onyx are cut in this way. Intaglios are

Brilliant cut    Emerald cut    Baguette    Marquise    Cabochon cut    Pear shape

carved figures indented into the stone, the opposite of cameos. Cloisonné is an enamel type of decoration in which designs are stamped into metal, and the indentations filled with various colored enamels. Filigree work is lacelike work in metal.

Precious metals are gold, platinum and silver. Equally expensive, and sometimes used, is palladium. These precious metals may be mixed with or laid over a base metal, usually copper, zinc, tin, antimony, nickel, aluminum, lead, chromium, rhodium or iron. A mixture of metals is an alloy. The alloy may be used to attain greater durability, hardness, tarnish-resistance, or some special effect. Or it may be used to decrease cost.

Solid (24-karat) gold contains no copper to each 24 parts of gold. This is too soft for most jewelry purposes. 14-karat gold contains 14 parts gold and 10 parts copper, 10-karat gold contains 10 parts gold, 14 parts copper, etc. Gold-filled metal contains a thin sheet or covering of 12-karat gold, usually (soldered, welded, or brazed on) 1/10th to 1/20th the thickness of the metal. Rolled gold may have a coating of 1/30th to 1/40th the thickness of the metal. Gold-flashed or gold-washed metals may have a gold thickness of 1/100,000th of an inch. Gold-plated metals have a thin layer of gold coated by an electroplating process. White gold, red gold, and green gold are made by adding other metals in the plating process. They may be of solid gold, plated, etc.

Sterling silver is 92½ percent silver, 7½ percent copper. Pure silver is too soft for ordinary use. Silverplate has a coating of silver over a base metal. Antiqued silver has been oxidized (tarnished) to add to the design.

## JEWELRY STONES

| Name (and "Popular Names") and Hardness Number* | Usual Colors | Comment |
| --- | --- | --- |
| AGATE (7) | green; also red, yellow and brown | May have white or gray bands; moss agate has dark markings. |
| ALEXANDRITE (7) | greenish | Appears reddish under artificial light. |
| AMBER (2.5) | yellow | Translucent, warm to the touch; imitated in plastics. |
| AMETHYST (7) | violet | Transparent; rich purple is most valuable. |
| AQUAMARINE (7.5) | bluish-green | Transparent; deeper colors most valuable. |
| BLOODSTONE (7) | dark green with red spots | Opaque; usually cut flat. Often engraved. |
| CARNELIAN (7) | orange-red | Translucent; color can be changed by heating. |
| CHALCEDONY (7) (Blue or Green Onyx) | gray-blue | Translucent. |
| CHRYSOPRASE (7) | apple green, pale yellow | Color fades in light and heat. |

*Hardness number indicates relative hardness based on an arbitrary scale in which a diamond is 10, talc is one. The harder the stone, the better is the polish possible.

| Name (and "Popular Names") and Hardness Number | Usual Colors | Comment |
| --- | --- | --- |
| CINNABAR | red | Opaque; inexpensive, usually elaborately carved by Chinese craftsmen and used in brooches, etc. |
| CORAL (4) | pinkish-red, white, pink, red | Opaque; from microscopic sea life; often carved; ox blood color is the most valuable. |
| DIAMOND (10) | colorless, also yellow, pink, green, blue, black | Transparent; hardest and most brilliant of all stones; clear colorless blue-white is the most valuable color; is considered flawless or perfect if there are no flaws in it when seen under 10-power magnification. |
| EMERALD (8) | green | Transparent; good quality more expensive than a diamond; the deeper the color the more valuable. |
| GARNET (7.5) | red; also translucent and opaque green, blue, red, rose, brown and black | Transparent; "Carbuncle" was a garnet cut in rounded form. |
| JADE (7) | green; also pink, violet, pale blue, etc. | Translucent green is the most valuable. |
| JET (4) | black | Opaque; takes a high polish. |
| LAPIS LAZULI | blue | Opaque; rich royal blue coloring is the most valuable. |

| Name (and "Popular Names") and Hardness Number* | Usual Colors | Comment |
|---|---|---|
| Moonstone (6) | colorless | Translucent, poor luster; normally cut cabochon; the bluer the stone the more valuable; imitated in plastics. |
| Onyx (7) | black; also brown or red, green, white | Opaque. |
| Opal (6) | white | Translucent; iridescent, cut cabochon for best play of colors. |
| Oriental cats-eye (8.5) | yellow-brown, gray, green | Looks like blinking eye when cut cabochon. |
| Peridot (7) | olive-green | Transparent. |
| Precious topaz (8) | yellow-brown; also colorless, pale blue, green, pink and red | Transparent, rare. |
| Rhinestone (7) | colorless | Made from crystal glass; identifiable by gold or silver coated mirrored base, cut and polished to give diamond-like brilliance. |
| Rose quartz (7) | rose | Opaque. |
| Rock crystal (7) | colorless | Transparent. |
| Ruby (9) | red | Transparent; deep (pigeon blood) red is most valuable; "Star Ruby" reflects six-rayed star. |

*Hardness number indicates relative hardness based on an arbitrary scale in which a diamond is 10, talc is one. The harder the stone, the better is the polish possible.

| Name (and "Popular Names") and Hardness Number | Usual Colors | Comment |
|---|---|---|
| SAPPHIRE (9) | blue; also colorless, yellow, green, purple, pink | Transparent; Kashmir (rich blue) is most valuable. "Star Sapphire" reflects six-rayed star. Synthetically made from titanium rutile. |
| SARDONYX (7) | brown | Opaque form of agate. |
| SPINEL (8) "Balas Ruby" | rose-red; also purple, blue, orange | Transparent. |
| TOPAZ (7) Quartz Topaz Citrine | yellow-brown | Transparent. |
| TOURMALINE (7.5) | various | Greens and pinks are most common. |
| TURQUOISE (6) | blue; also gray, green | Opaque; sky blue is the most valuable color. |
| ZIRCON (7.5) | colorless, blue, also golden brown, red, reddish-brown and pale yellow | Colorless stones cut and polished to look like diamond. |

## PEARLS

| | | |
|---|---|---|
| GENUINE PEARLS OR ORIENTAL PEARLS | creamy white; also, pink, blue, gray or black | Grows within oyster as protection against irritating foreign body. |
| CULTURED PEARLS | six main colors, of which the rarest is a pink-white called rainbow. Other recognized colors are white, cream, pink, green, gold, and black | Made by inserting mother of pearl bead in oysters, in controlled beds. Pearls take 3 to 7 years to develop. |

## MISCELLANEOUS MATERIALS

| Name | Usual Colors | Comment |
| --- | --- | --- |
| Ivory | white | From animal tusks. |
| Marcasites | gray | Iron pyrites cut to reflect light, like diamonds. |
| Mother of pearl | iridescent | From shell of pearl oyster. |
| Tortoise shell | mottled brown | From shell of tortoise. |

## GUIDES IN BUYING HOUSEHOLD ITEMS

**Pots and Pans:** A good minimum selection will serve well, keep your kitchen uncluttered. A good selection might include: saucepans—1 qt., 2 qt., 3 qt.; coffee-maker—6 cup, 2 cup; tea kettle, 1½ qt. double boiler; frying pan—6"; baking pan—15"; roasting pan—18"; pudding pan—1 qt.; pie plate—10"; cast-iron skillet—10"; mixing bowl—3 piece set; colander; waterless cooker or pressure cooker.

Durability, cleanability, heating efficiency, ability to withstand chipping and breaking, and ultimate appearance should be considered. Bottom should be wide and flat; sides straight. Double boilers and pots that fit into each other for cooking or storing have special advantages.

**Non-stick cookware:** A permanent solid lubricant, Teflon, prevents food from sticking to cooking utensils (metal and glass) without the use of fats or oil and is particularly useful for grease-free diets.

Nonstick cookware is made possible by a permanent, greaseless, lubricant coating, Teflon. Fry pans, skillets, sauce pans, ovens, spatulas, cake and pie pans, casserole dishes, dutch ovens, waffle irons, griddles, even rolling pins are available with this coating from many manufacturers. Cooking processes with this equipment are identical to ordinary processes, but with a few exceptions food does not stick to the utensil.

**Knives:** Best blades are hollow-ground (giving a concave surface behind the cutting edge), of highly tempered carbon vanadium-steel alloys. Flat-ground knives are satisfactory for most purposes. Handles should be securely fastened. Tangs which project into the handle are best.

Judge a knife as a tool. Pick it up. See how it fits in your hand. The handles should be solidly riveted with either two or three rivets. Handles made of Pakka-wood (densified wood and plastic produced under 600 tons of pressure) or hard rubber are sturdy.

Silver: Hollow-ware pieces useful in serving include: chop plate, vegetable dish, gravy boats, well and tree platter, sauce boats, water pitcher, bread tray, bread and butter plates, tea

## KITCHEN UTENSIL MATERIALS
(L, low; M, moderate; H, high.)

| Material | Comments | Cost | Durability | Cleanability | Cooking Efficiency | Use |
|---|---|---|---|---|---|---|
| **ALUMINUM** | | | | | | |
| Cast | Alloy is used. Heavy | M | H | L | H | Heavy frying pans. |
| Chromium Plated | Fine, shiny appearance | H | H | H | H | Frying pans, pots. |
| Stamped | Light | L-M | H | H | H | Frying pans, pots. |
| **CERAMICS** | May use for serving "in casserole" | L-M | M | M | M-H | Baking dishes, mixing bowls. |
| **COPPER** | Avoid using for salty or acid foods. Usually has inset of another metal | H | H | L | M-H | Frying, cooking, baking, decoration. |
| **ENAMELWARE** 1 to 3 coats porcelain | Chips easily, especially if overheated | L-M | L | M-H | M-H | General, but not for waterless cookery. |
| **GLASS** (Pyrex) | Breakable. Requires time to cool | L-M | M | H | H | Coffee making, baking, mixing. |
| **IRON** | | | | | | |
| Cast | May be lacquered to improve cleanability. Heavy | L | H | L | H | Kettles, frying pans. |
| Sheet | May be chrome plated | L | M | L | H | Frying pans. |
| Oxide Coated | Avoid scratching off coating | L-M | M | L | M | Oven pans. |
| Galvanized | Not for cooking | L-M | M | M | | Pails. |
| **STAINLESS STEEL** | Use low flame, under 350° F. | M-H | M | H | M | Frying pans, pots, knives. |
| Copper Inset | | H | H | H | H | Pots, frying pans. |
| **TIN** | Really tin over steel. Avoid scratching off tin | L | M | M | M | Baking pans. |

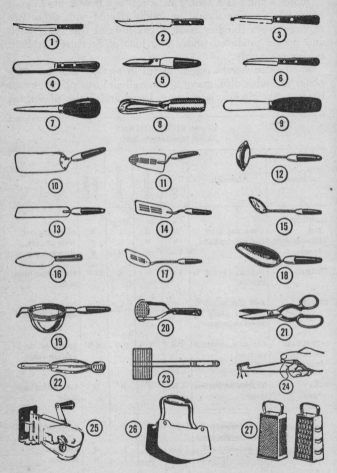

**USEFUL KITCHEN AIDS:** (1) Roast slicer. (2) Bread knife. (3) Paring knife. (4) Spreader. (5) Apple corer. (6) Grapefruit knife. (7) Oyster knife. (8) Fish scaler. (9) Clam knife. (10) Flexible spatula. (11) Pie server. (12) Oval ladle. (13) Narrow spatula. (14) Wide spatula. (15) Mixing spoon. (16) Pastry server. (17) Cake turner. (18) Sugar scoop. (19) Bowl strainer. (20) Masher. (21) Kitchen shears. (22) Vegetable peeler. (23) Bar-B-Q broiler. (24) Gas lighter. (25) Can opener. (26) Mincing knife. (27) Grater.

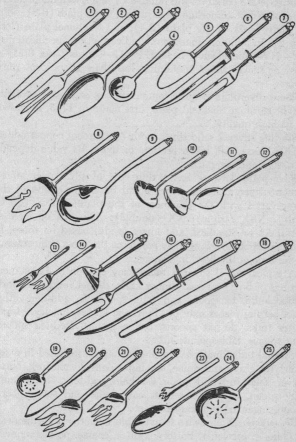

**SILVER FLATWARE AVAILABLE:** (1) Letter opener. (2 and 3) Salad set. (4) Sugar spoon. (5) Cheese server. (6 and 7) Steak set. (8) Salad or serving fork. (9) Berry or serving spoon. (10) Cream or sauce ladle. (11) Gravy ladle. (12) Jelly server. (13) Lemon fork. (14) Olive-pickle fork. (15) Pastry server. (16, 17 and 18) Roast set. (19) Nut or bon-bon spoon. (20) Butter knife. (21) Large cold-meat fork. (22) Cold-meat fork. (23) Sugar tongs. (24) Table serving spoon. (25) Round server.

and coffee service, serving trays, candlesticks. The grades of silverplate are based on the number of pennyweights of silver per square foot. Superfine (8 or more), triple plate (6-8), double plate (4-6), single plate (2-4), and fractional plate (less than 2). In addition, marks may indicate other specifications: E P—N S—nickel-silver base; E P—C—copper base; Brass—brass or nickel silver containing less than 10 percent pure silver.

Some silverplate is quite famous and as expensive as lightweight sterling; Sheffield plate, first made in 1743, is known for its high quality.

Sterling silver is solid silver (with 7½ percent copper added for hardness), will last a lifetime or more. Its value depends on design and weight.

Silverplate flatware has a thin coat of silver over an 18 percent silver nickel or other metal base. The grade of the silver varies with the thickness of the plate; XXXX (quadruple); XXX (triple); XX (double); AA; A1x or A1X or Extra; A1 or Standard, and lower grades based on these. In addition, spot "overlays" may reenforce the spots of most wear, as the base of the bowl in a spoon.

A typical set of silver flatware may contain 8, 12 or more settings of 5 or 6 pieces: dinner knife, dinner fork, salad fork, butter knife, teaspoon, and soup spoon. In addition, other place-setting pieces may be: luncheon knives, luncheon forks, oyster forks, dessert spoons, coffee spoons, iced-tea spoons, fruit spoons, tablespoons, etc.

Special individual serving pieces may be included in a set: ladles for gravy and sauce, serving spoons, lemon fork, butter server, salad fork and spoon, fish knife and fork, cheese knife, jelly spoon, asparagus server, cake knife and server, berry spoon, sugar tongs, carving set, etc.

Dinnerware: Dinnerware is available in pottery, earthenware or china (porcelain). Pottery is thick, coarse, porous, uneven, opaque, soft and brittle. It is suitable for inexpensive decorative pieces that got little handling. Earthenware may be coarse or semi-hardened (semi-vitreous). It is quite porous; may look very much like china.

China or porcelain is translucent, smooth, hard, and has a distinctive ring when struck on the edge. Porcelains vary with the type of materials used and the firing process. Three chief types are hard-paste porcelain, bone porcelain, and

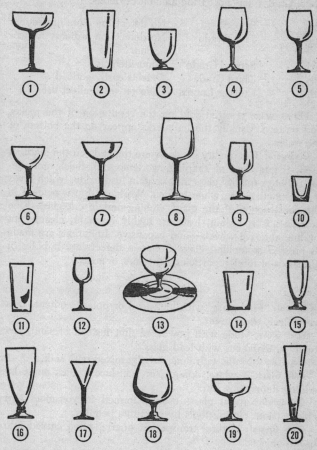

GLASSWARE: (1) Hollow-stem champagne. (2) 10-12-14 oz. highball. (3) Oyster cocktail (fruit cocktail). (4) Low goblet. (5) Claret. (6) Cocktail. (7) High sherbet (saucer champagne). (8) Tall goblet. (9) Wine glass. (10) Whisky. (11) Seltzer or whisky sour. (12) Cordial or liqueur. (13) Plate. 14) Old fashioned. (15) Footed juice glass. (16) Footed iced tea. (17) Sherry. (18) Brandy inhaler. (19) Low sherbet. (20) Pilsner.

soft-paste porcelain. Practically all dinnerware has some defects. Grades depend on the amount of defect.

| | | |
|---|---|---|
| 1st | Selects | No defects on close inspection. |
| 2nd | First Grade | No defects on ordinary inspection. |
| 3rd | Second Grade | Minor defects. |
| 4th | Third Grade | Defects easily noticed. |
| 5th | Culls or Lumps | Defects which affect use. |

Dinnerware is often sold on the reputation of the maker and pattern. Usually the hallmarks appear on the bottom of the wares.

**Glassware:** The quality of glassware depends on the material used, the method of shaping, workmanship, finish, and defects. Better quality glass may contain lead oxide, which gives it a distinctive ring when tapped. Workmanship is evident in the construction of the glass, etching and in cut glass. Fine cut glass is sparkling, lustrous, highly resonant, cleanly cut by fine abrasive wheels—and expensive. Imitations are made in pressed or molded glass. Common defects are bubbles of air, seeds of foreign particles, off colors, or scars.

### GLASS DICTIONARY

**Crystal:** "Fine glass" with high lead or potash content. It is very clear, transparent.

**Flint Glass:** Made with powdered flint instead of sand, virtually synonymous with lead glass.

**Lime Glass:** Made with lime, usually mixed with soda.

**Milk Glass:** A white, opaque, or translucent glass made by adding fluorspar or tin.

**Obsidian:** Natural glass, usually formed in volcanoes and chipped into cutting tools by primitive peoples.

**Rock Crystal:** Natural transparent quartz, often carved into useful objects.

**Soda Glass:** Lime glass, has heavy soda content, used mainly for chemical apparatuses, etc.

*How It's Made and Decorated:*

The three methods of forming glass are blowing, drawing, and pressing. Some other glass-making terms:

**Air-Twist:** Spiral hollows in a stem, produced by piercing the heated stem with rods, then twisting.

**Annealing:** Reheating and cooling of glass to remove stresses built up during the first fast cooling.

**Blow-and-Blow:** Both the preliminary and the final shaping are formed by air pressure.

**Cameo Glass:** White glass blown layer-on-layer onto dark glass, then cut away in cameo style.

**Cased Glass** (or overlay glass): A layer of colored glass is placed over a layer of clear glass. Sometimes part of the colored layer is cut away to produce a two-color effect called case-cut.

**Cut Glass:** Patterns cut by hand or abrasive wheels, then polished. Unpolished patterns are called gray cuttings.

**Enameled Glass:** Decorated with an opaque vitreous ceramic.

**Engraving:** Delicate designs are cut in glass with fine abrasive tools.

**Etching:** A satinlike finish on part of a glass is put on by attacking it with acid.

**Fluting:** Upright lines are impressed on blown glass by a mold. When the raised part is thinner than the trough, it is fluted; when it is wider, it is ribbed.

**Iridescent Glass:** Glass with a distinctive colorful radiance, produced by adding certain chemicals and heating in a carbonaceous flame.

**Millefiore Glass:** Objects made from bundles of varicolored rods fused together; when viewed on end, the rods resemble clusters of flowers.

**Mold-Blown:** Glass blown into, and shaped in, a mold.

**Press-and-Blow:** Shaping in which the preliminary form is both pressed and blown and the final form is pressed.

**Prunt:** Blobs of glass applied to the surface, in which monograms or other designs may be impressed.

**Sandblasting:** A method of rough-texturing glass by blowing fine sand across it.

**Threaded Glass:** Glass decorated with fine applied threads not impressed into the surface.

*Names in Glassware History:*

**John F. Amelung:** A German immigrant who produced a well-known cut glass line in this country in the Bohemian and Swiss style (1784-1894).

**Murano:** Island near Venice, where the industry has flourished since 1292.

**George Ravenscroft:** English chemist who produced the first practical lead glass (1676).

**Sandwich Glass Co.:** Produced glass of many types. Famous for pressed glass (1825-1886).

**Henry W. Steigel:** German immigrant who produced fine blown and enameled glass, in Pennsylvania, in the 18th century.

**Waterford:** Irish glass, originally produced 1729-1851, has characteristic cuttings and clarity.

**Mattresses:** There are two types of mattresses—the innerspring and the solid upholstered. The way in which the coils are held together divides all innerspring mattresses into two groups. In one, the coils are individually encased in cloth pockets which are sewed together. In the other, the coils are fastened to one another by small helical springs or metal ties. The coils in the metal-tied units are usually larger and made of heavier wire than those in pocketed types. In innerspring mattresses, filling material consists of felted cotton layers, curled hair, or a combination of both. Various types of insulation, including sisal, quilted or stitched pads and other special patented devices are used between the coil unit and the padding to keep it from working down into the coils and to keep the coil from the sleeper.

Rubber mattresses made from the milk of rubber trees and synthetic combinations into a foam-like substance are of good quality and durability.

High quality curled hair makes a good mattress for anyone who prefers a very firm sleep foundation. Horse tail and cattle tail hair are best, with horse mane second. Hog hair is rather stiff and less resilient.

Kapok, which comes from the pod of a tropical tree, makes a soft, light, easy to handle mattress. However, kapok fiber is extremely perishable and there is little demand for kapok mattresses today.

Quality mattresses have strong reenforced borders to keep their edges erect and neat, ventilators for free passage of air, and firmly attached handles for easy turning.

Crib mattresses are available with the same filling materials as adult-size mattresses, but the construction is firmer, in accordance with doctors' recommendations.

In all mattresses, ticking should be strong enough so that

it will not stretch with use. In tickings, closeness of weave and smoothness of finish are important.

Bedsprings: There are three classifications of bedsprings—box springs, coil springs and flat springs. In box springs, the coils are mounted on a wood base, top upholstered with felt and covered with ticking to match the mattress. The coils of box springs are tied to each other, to the base and to the border with a special twine, metal ties or small helical springs. The twine-tied box springs employ larger-gauge coils, while the metal-tied have more coils of finer gauge.

Because an innerspring mattress is designed to provide two-thirds of the total resilience, it should be combined with a box spring, a coil spring equipped with a platform top, or one built with convolute coils. These are all firmer than open coil springs, but they can be used with solid upholstered mattresses if an especially firm foundation is preferred.

The platform top bedspring has metal bands running lengthwise and/or crosswise on the top of the spring frame at frequent intervals. Convolute coils are those with several extra turns of wire at the top so that when depressed, they furnish a closed surface.

The open top coil spring provides more resiliency and is generally preferred for use with a solid upholstered mattress.

Pillows: There are four types of fillings used in good quality pillows: All-down, a combination of down and waterfowl feathers, all-waterfowl feathers, and foam rubber. An all-down pillow is the most expensive, but is really too soft for comfort as it lacks the buoyancy supplied by waterfowl feathers. The mixture of down and waterfowl feathers is an ideal combination, and the least expensive of the three—all-waterfowl feathers—is also very satisfactory.

Crushed, chopped or artificially curved waterfowl feathers are generally less desirable because these processes destroy the natural resiliency of the feathers. Goose and duck feathers are springy and resilient. They are full and fluffy, and their shafts are naturally curved and buoyant. Although goose feathers are considered better, because they are stronger and fluffier, a good quality duck feather is often better than a low grade goose feather.

Chicken and turkey feathers have straight shafts which must be artificially curled to give them resilience. After a few years, the curl is lost, and the feathers become dead and lifeless.

Foam rubber pillows are preferred by many, particularly those affected by allergies. They are highly resilient, resistant to insects, mildew, germs, and deterioration, and are washable.

Pillows should have closely woven ticking to keep the feathers from working through. However, extremely soft pillows such as those filled entirely with down should be covered with a lightweight, finely woven cotton ticking which has a linen finish.

Sleeping comfort is enhanced by special face pillows for people who sleep on their stomach.

**Sheets:** Durability and appearance of sheets are determined by thread count, tensile strength, adequate size, hemstitching, weight (after removal of sizing), shrinkage.

Grade labeling is compulsory. Grades are in 4 types, according to thread count before bleaching. After bleaching, the count is somewhat higher.

Government purchasing agents require bleached cotton sheets to have a minimum breaking strength of 70 lbs. in both warp and filling. The highest counts give a fine smooth finish.

---

### SHEET QUALITY GUIDE

| Grade | Weave or Thread Count | Points to Consider in Buying | Price |
|-------|----------------------|------------------------------|-------|
| BACK FILLED MUSLIN | Less than 112 threads to each square inch. | Loosely woven; excess starch washes out, leaves sheets sleazy. | Lowest |
| LIGHT-WEIGHT MUSLIN | Not less than 112 threads to each square inch. | Wears well considering low price. For limited household service. | Low |
| MEDIUM WEIGHT MUSLIN | Not less than 128 threads to each square inch. | Strong; gives satisfactory wear. Widely used for everyday service. | Medium |

| Grade | Weave or Thread Count | Points to Consider in Buying | Price |
|-------|----------------------|----------------------------|-------|
| HEAVY WEIGHT MUSLIN | Not less than 140 threads to each square inch. | Sturdy; longest wearing muslin. Used where durability is prime consideration, as in hospitals, many hotels, etc. Makes a neat bed. | Highest Price Muslin |
| PERCALE (CARDED) | *Carded* yarns not less than 180 threads to each square inch. | Lightweight; durable. Smooth, pleasant to sleep on. Easy and economical to launder. | Medium |
| PERCALE (COMBED) | *All combed* yarns. Not less than 180 threads to each square inch. | Lightweight, extremely strong and durable. Soft and unusually smooth. Easy and economical to launder. | Medium |
| FINEST QUALITY PERCALE | Not less than 200 threads to each square inch. | The finest, most luxurious sheets available. Light, fine, soft texture, beautiful appearance. Made of finest all combed yarns. | Highest Price Percale |

(Dacron polyester sheets equal to percale require no ironing.)

Seconds must be so labeled. Any sheet under 112 count is substandard. Inspection should also reveal uniformity of fiber thickness, thin spots, knots, excess sizing (this adds weight, covers faults, but washes out).

TESTS FOR DETERMINING SHEET QUALITY:

(1) Stretch sheet tightly between your hands, and hold it to the light. The fabric should be closely woven, tight and even. Beware of sheet threads which show knots, unevenness or puckers, or missing warp threads.

(2) Hold sheet flat on a level with your eye. Look for smooth, flat finish—with very little fuzz.

(3) Look for small stitches along the hem (12 to 14 to the inch) caught securely at both ends of the hem. Look at the tailoring detail. Hems should be smooth, flat, neat, never puckered, should average 2 inches in width.

(4) Rub parts of the sheet together. Sizing should not come off on your hands. More than 6 percent sizing is not desirable.

(5) Examine the selvage. It should be finely woven—with tape-like sturdiness.

(6) Sheets should be torn in the proper sizes. Sheets that are cut won't keep their shape as well after laundering.

(7) Sheet widths should be 63 inches for single beds, 72 inches for ¾ beds and 81 to 90 inches for double beds. Satisfactory lengths are 99 to 108 inches. Measurements should be printed on the sheet. Sheets tend to shrink in the direction in which they are ironed.

Colored sheets add a charming modern touch to any room. They are available in peach, aqua, rose, maize, blue, spring green and pink.

Towels: Look for a firm, close underweave for strength and maximum durability; for close, thick loops for absorbency and quick drying. Select towels of soft, medium-soft, or rough texture, as preferred. Select sizes suitable to the size of the user, suitable for the purpose. Select sizes and weights easy for home washing, economical at laundry pound rates. Consider bathroom decoration and color harmony.

Bath towels should have thick, long loops which provide absorbency; firm, close weaving of the base cloth provides sturdiness. Selvage should be firm, visible on both sides. Government purchasing standards require 82 warp threads and 42 filling threads to the inch. A 22 x 44 inch towel should weigh 7 oz. Standard sizes are 16x30, 18x36, 20x40, 22x44, 24x46, 24x48.

Face towels may be huck (most widely used), crash (for guest towels), waffle weave (good), damask (mostly for show), or cambric.

Best dish towels are linen (strong and lint free). Cotton or cotton-linen combinations are less expensive. Knitted towels are highly absorbent. Gauze towels are absorbent, lint free but not durable. Rayon towels are not usually satisfactory.

Table Linen: Government specifications for linen cloths require a minimum of 84 threads each in the warp and in the filling.

**Blankets:** Quality is visible in a close and even weave, even distribution and firmness of the nap; securely fastened binding. There should be no color streaks. A guarantee as to washability and maximum shrinkage (10 percent is fair) is important. The blanket should feel springy and firm, should snap back when squeezed. When pulled taut, there should be little slipping of the weave. Weight should be 11 to 12 ounces to the square yard. Strength of weave may be tested by lifting the blanket by the nap. It should support its own weight. Sizes recommended: for single beds, 60 inches wide, 80, 84 or 90 inches long; for ¾ beds, 66x80, 70x80, or 72x84, 72x90; for double beds, 72x84, 72x90, 80x90.

**Electric Blankets:** These are lighter in weight than the several blankets which may be required in cold temperatures, may be automatically self-adjusting to room temperatures. There are washable models made so that each section may be set at a different temperature. For freezing temperatures, additional blanket may be required. There is little shock or fire hazard. Electricity cost is approximately 3¢ a night.

**Electric Heating Pads:** They have been for many years a standard replacement for the hot-water bottle. New models are now inflatable to varying degrees of firmness and are equipped with 3-heat push-button controls, waterproof covers, and decorator-designed fabrics.

Electric mattress pads, electric foot warmers, electric sheets, and electric blanket covers are also made—each with variables for double-bed sleeping.

## FURNITURE AND APPLIANCES

**Furniture:** Government grades are: standard, medium, and low. The two top grades are satisfactory for home use.

Wood furniture should be examined with regard to style, wood and finish, and structure. Simple lines, good classic designs, size in proportion to the living area, and style to harmonize are prime factors in getting good value. Cheap lines (boral furniture), large sets, and highly ornamented pieces, should generally be avoided. A so-called bargain piece that does not fit in is no bargain. The type of wood will tell you a great deal about the value, durability and workmanship of your piece. The finish, or the surface you see, will indicate how much work has gone into preparing the wood. This is principally handwork and is expensive.

Most furniture surfaces are covered with a paper-thin cut of finely grained wood or veneer, over a strong, less expensive base wood. Veneers reduce the cost of a fine-surfaced piece of furniture, are satisfactory if the veneer has been applied properly. However, sometimes inferior wood may be hidden underneath. If the veneer chips, a different type of wood with a poor finish shows through. If veneers are selected, they should be well-matched, in grain and color, well glued on in a smooth finish.

Furniture should show no warping, bulging, or cracking in the veneers. Where possible (chairs, beds, etc.) furniture should be tried by sitting or lying on it. Ornamental features tend to raise furniture costs considerably. Unpainted and knock-down furniture offer opportunities for substantial savings. Auctions sometimes offer such opportunities, but furniture offered at auctions should be examined closely before the sale. Old furniture may often be altered, refinished, recovered, or redecorated to bring it up-to-date in style, finish and function. Various books are available on this subject.

Inlay is a design in the surface of wood formed by inserting woods, ivory, or other materials of contrasting color. Marquetry is a name given to an entire surface of inlaid work when colored pieces of wood, ivory, shells, etc., of several colors are fitted into surfaces forming an artistic design. Carved portions glued or otherwise affixed to furniture rather than carved from it, are often seen. There is obviously a considerable difference in the cost and value of solid carving and glued-on carving.

Joinery: Best constructed pieces are held together with mortise and tenon joints. In this type of joint a wooden tongue fits tightly into a slot. Dowel joints may also be used in the framework joinery and frames of upholstered pieces. Round wooden pins, sometimes with spiral grooves, fit into matching sockets and are glued into place for extra strength. Spiral grooving helps to hold the glue. In fine-quality pieces, double dowels are sometimes used at points of great strain.

Fitting and grooving of wood panels contributes to strength of the frame. The side panel should fit snugly into a grooved corner post. In the best drawer construction, bottoms are similarly fitted into matching grooves on the four sides of the drawer.

Dovetailed corner joints are indications of sturdy construction and made by interlocking and gluing wedge-shaped tenons.

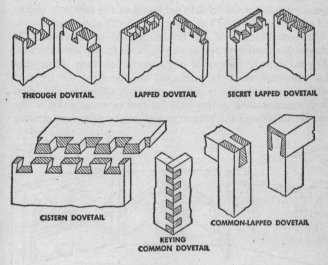

THROUGH DOVETAIL     LAPPED DOVETAIL     SECRET LAPPED DOVETAIL

CISTERN DOVETAIL          KEYING COMMON DOVETAIL          COMMON-LAPPED DOVETAIL

Dovetail joints.

**Chairs:** Most of the structural details of a piece of furniture are hidden. The "upside down" test should give some general indications about the entire piece. If the bottom of the piece is sanded and shows no splinters, and if it is given a coat of finish to prevent atmospheric and insect invasion, it is probably good. Back posts of chairs and the legs of beds, tables, and cabinets show workmanship. Shake the pieces to see if they stand squarely upon the floor. In order to be strong and durable, furniture should be securely framed and braced throughout, and mortised and tenoned or doweled.

Chair legs should have corner blocks (triangular reinforcements) fastened with counter-blocked screws. Legs should be braced with cross pieces, should run with the grain. Nails used anywhere are an indication of skimping. Additional rigidity and less squeaks may be obtained by stay braces in the hidden parts under chairs and beds. These may be tightened by turnbuckle at will. In the best furniture the stretchers should be carefully centered in the posts or legs.

**Tables:** Table legs should be constructed similar to chair legs. Tops usually have the edges bound with an edging strip of solid wood or veneers. Specification for Army officers' quarters calls for a solid strip not less than 1½ inches in width. The edges of the solid top should be smooth and even.

**Drawers:** Bottoms of the drawer should be substantial. It should be possible to rest one's weight on the inverted drawer. A good drawer bottom is a quarter of an inch thick, may be composed of 3-ply laminated construction, the exposed surface made of good quality face veneer, although solid wood is sometimes used. A tiny block or two of wood glued to the sides will prevent the bottom as well as the sides from getting

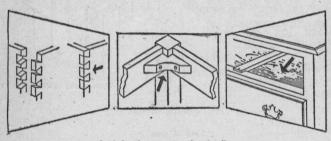

Look for these construction details.

Buttoning.    Slot screwing.    Dovetail keying.

out of position. Center or side drawer slides on the under side should be fastened to front and back cross rails and glued to the bottom of the drawer. Groove rails upon which the drawer glides should be fastened to both the front and the back of the drawer. Between drawers there should be a "dust" panel at least 3/16 inch thick.

**Antiques:** Antiques are desirable because of fine workmanship and style or sentiment, as collectors' items, and conversation pieces. They may be used to advantage in home decoration, but their cost is usually much higher than that of comparable reproductions or modern furniture.

Prices of antiques vary with fads which affect demand, inasmuch as supply is limited. "Officially," by customs-law definition, an antique was manufactured prior to 1830. However, anything "old" and of interest may be accepted as an "antique."

There are so many clever imitations of antiques that it is difficult to tell the spurious from the genuine. Much of the so-called early American furniture of New England and of southern colonial styles on the market today unquestionably consists wholly or in part of reproductions. The fact that a piece of furniture may be a hundred or more years old is no guarantee that it will beautify the home. Much ugly furniture was produced in the early days, and unless an antique has historic interest or artistic value it will detract from, rather than add to, the beauty of a home.

Mirrors: The commercial standard grades of mirrors are designated in a descending quality scale, as follows: "AA," "A," No. 1, No. 2 and No. 3, which may be accompanied with labels in the following respective colors: white, red, blue, green, and yellow.

The "AA" mirrors are entirely free from major defects and as nearly perfect as it is possible to manufacture them. "A" mirrors have no major defects in their central area, but may contain a few well-scattered bubbles and other very minor defects. No. 1 mirrors contain limited numbers of defects which are inherent in practically all plate glass. This quality of mirror will adequately suit the needs of most homes. No. 2 quality contains more frequent defects and those more readily seen, as occasional coarse seed, light wavy lines, known as strings, and a wavy defect known as "bull's-eye." This type of mirror is serviceable and is found in much of the popular-priced furniture. No. 3 quality mirrors may contain all of the defects which are naturally found in plate glass and must be bought only after careful examination.

The silvering of all commercial standard quality mirrors is usually guaranteed for one year from the date of manufacture unless exposed to unusual conditions, such as open weather, moist walls, steamy rooms, and direct sunlight.

Upholstered Furniture: Spending emphasis should go on quality of key living-room pieces—the sofa and upholstered chairs. These will probably be re-covered and last for your lifetime. Hardwood frames (mahogany, ash, birch, hard maple) are best; gum is softer, cheaper. Soft or white elm, pecan, hick-

## COMMON FURNITURE WOODS

| Wood | Color of Heartwood | Color of Sapwood | Pattern Figure | Warpage | Strength | Uses |
|---|---|---|---|---|---|---|
| Alder, red (Alnus rubra) | Light pinkish brown to white | Same | Obscure | M | M | Panel cores, table tops, sides, drawer fronts, exposed parts of kitchen furniture. Stains readily in imitation of mahogany or walnut. |
| Ash, green, black, white (Fraxinus) | Light grayish brown | White | Pronounced | M | H | Solid tables, dressers, wardrobes; wooden refrigerators. |
| Beech (Fagus grandifolia) | White to slightly reddish | Same | Obscure | H | H | Chairs and exterior parts of painted furniture. Bends easily and is well adapted for curved parts such as chair backs. Also used for sides, guides, and backs of drawers, and for other substantial interior parts. |
| Birch, yellow and black (Betula) | Light to dark reddish brown | White | Varying from a stripe to curly | M | H | Solid and veneered furniture. Same uses as hard maple. |
| Cherry, black (Prunus serotina) | Light to dark reddish brown | White | Obscure | M | M | Solid furniture. Relative scarcity causes it to be quite expensive |
| Chestnut (Castanea dentata) | Grayish brown | White | Conspicuous | M | M | Cores of tables and dresser tops, drawer fronts, and other veneered panels. Used with oak in solid furniture. |
| Elm, American and rock (Ulmus) | Light grayish brown often tinted with red | White | Conspicuous | H | H | Used for exposed parts of highgrade upholstered furniture. Easily bent to curved shapes such as chair backs. |
| Gum, red (Liquidambar styraciflua) | Reddish brown | Pinkish white | Obscure to figured | M | M | Gum furniture may be stained to resemble walnut or mahogany. Also used in combination with these woods. |

H, high; M, moderate; L, Low

## COMMON FURNITURE WOODS

| Wood | Color of Heartwood | Color of Sapwood | Pattern Figure | Warpage | Strength | Uses |
|---|---|---|---|---|---|---|
| Gum, tupelo (Nyssa aquatica) | Pale brownish gray | White | Obscure to striped | H | M | Cores of veneered panels, interior parts, framework of upholstered articles. |
| Mahogany (Swietema, Khaya) | Pale to deep reddish brown | White to light brown | Ribbon or stripe | L | M | All solid and veneered high-grade furniture, boat construction, and cabinet work. |
| Maple, hard (Acer saccharum) | Light reddish brown | White | Obscure to figured | L | M | Bedroom, kitchen, dining and living room solid furniture. Some veneer (highly figured) is used. Most furniture is given a natural finish. |
| Oak, red and white (Quercus) | Grayish brown | White | Conspicuous | M | H | Solid and veneered furniture of all types. Quartered-oak furniture compares favorably with walnut and mahogany pieces. |
| Pine, ponderosa (Pinus ponderosa) | Light reddish | White | Obscure | L | M | Painted kitchen furniture. |
| Poplar, yellow (Liriodendron tulipifera) | Light yellow to dark olive | White | Obscure | L | M | Cross banding of veneers, inexpensive painted furniture, interior portions of more expensive furniture, frames of upholstered articles. |
| Rosewood (Dalbergia nigra) | Dark reddish brown with black streaks | White | Obscure streaked | L | H | Piano cases, musical instruments, handles, and so on. |
| Sycamore (Platanus occidentalis) | Reddish brown | Pale reddish brown | Obscure flake | H | H | Drawer sides, interior parts, frame work of upholstered articles. |
| Tanquile (Shorea) | Pale to dark reddish brown | Pale grayish to reddish brown | Ribbon or stripe | L | M | Similar to true mahogany. |
| Walnut, black (Juglans nigra) | Light to dark chocolate brown | Pale brown | Varying from a stripe to a wave | M | H | All types of solid and veneered furniture. |

H, High; M. Moderate; L, Low

ory, pine and yellow poplar are sometimes used. Frames should be well glued, doweled, tenoned, and corner-blocked, not nailed together.

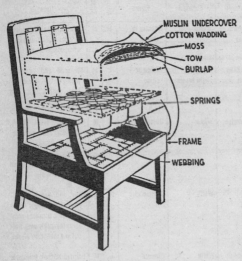

MUSLIN UNDERCOVER
COTTON WADDING
MOSS
TOW
BURLAP
SPRINGS
FRAME
WEBBING

Three different types of materials may be used as the base for springs: textile webbing; tempered-steel webbing, and foundation of wooden slats. The webbing has a certain amount of resiliency. If the webbing sags when springs are depressed, it will permit the use of a deep spring, upon which depends a great deal of the resiliency. Tempered-steel webbing provides a base which has resiliency and does not stretch; it may be compared to the common type of bedspring. Cone-shaped coil springs are usually used in connection with the steel or wire base.

High-tempered steel wire, enameled to prevent corrosion, should be used for the coiled springs, which vary in size according to their use; deep springs in the seat, shallow ones at the edges of the seat, tiny springs are used in the arms; medium-sized ones in the back. These springs may be tied in two, four or eight positions, the more the better.

Stuffing is set over the fabric-topped springs. The following materials are, in order of quality, used as stuffing: foam rubber; long curled hair (horsehair is preferred to pig hair); short hair, or hair and moss; down; kapok; African palm fiber; Spanish moss; tow; cotton, and excelsior. New stuffing should be used.

TEXTILE COVERINGS: The coverings used for upholstered furniture are mainly concerned with color and patterns but, to the purchaser, texture and fabric construction are equally important. Utility, durability, materials and weave are the most important considerations. Commonly used are: mohair, horsehair, cretonnes, chintzes, damasks, matelassé, brocades, brocatelles, armures, reps, tapestries, velvets, velours, plushes, friezes, satins and sateens, embroideries, needlepoint and leather.

Slip-Covers: Fabrics should be close-woven, pre-shrunk, washable. Fabrics suggested: chintz, crash, cretonne, homespun, twill, whipcord, denim and sailcloth. Special finishes that make fabrics crush- and moisture-proof are especially desirable. Remnants may be used. Slip-covers may be purchased ready-made or custom made or they may be made at home.

## FLOOR COVERINGS

Rugs: Wool makes the best rugs. Rugs of nylon, rayon, cotton, and combinations of these fibers are also made. Hemp, cotton, jute, cotton or paper yarns may be used for backing. Jute and paper yarns tend to deteriorate when wet.

Wear in a rug depends generally on three things—the compactness of the weave, the thickness and density of the pile, and the materials used by the manufacturer. Wool is the best-wearing fabric. In general, the best buy in rugs is a simple twist weave. Special weaves and sculptured carpets tend to become specialties less subject to competitive pricing. Places which receive heavy traffic should get good quality rugs or overlays of carpeting. The compactness, thickness and density are affected by the number of tufts per square inch. Fine Oriental rugs may have 500, good Wilton rugs 120, good Axminster and Velvets 80, medium-grade rugs may have 25 percent less. Poor rugs may have as little as 25. Combed yarns wear better than uncombed yarns. Twisted yarns of two or more piles wear better than untwisted. Better grades of cheap rugs are better values than poor grades of good types. Broadloom is a term for any rug woven 54 inches or wider, is suitable for wall-to-wall carpeting.

Rug padding of sponge rubber, jute, or coarse hair on a latex base (or ozite) gives better wear and softer tread to rugs.

## CHIEF TYPES OF RUGS

| Type and Construction | Appearance, etc. |
| --- | --- |
| AXMINSTER: Tufts are attached by heavy threads. Pile from ⅛ to ⅜ inch. 28 to 77 tufts to the square inch. | Many colors; usually figured. May be rolled only lengthwise. In broadloom. |
| VELVET: Cut pile weave. 42 to 80 tufts to the square inch. Design may be printed on or dyed in yarn. | Simple weave. Textured effects, are called frieze velvets. In broadloom. |
| WILTON: Cut pile weave. Close, compact, durable. ⅛ to 1¼ inch pile. Imbedded in backing. 50 to 130 tufts to the square inch. | Up to 6 colors. Thick, luxurious. Small, conservative patterns. In broadloom. |
| BRUSSELS: Looped pile. | Not widely used. |
| TAPESTRY: Short, uncut pile. 48 to 63 tufts to the square inch. | Not widely used. |
| CHENILLE: Densely woven. 60 to 150 tufts to the square inch. Tufts sewed in rows, then sewed together. | Lustrous, shaggy, luxurious, usually not durable. In broadloom. |
| AMERICAN ORIENTAL: Usually densely woven and of good quality. | Lustrous. Imitation of Orientals. |
| REVERSIBLE: ORIENTAL, CHINESE, AUBUSSON, SAVONNERIE: Pile on both sides. Handwoven. Tufts individually knotted. Designs vary with locality and tradition. Many colors. 100 to 400 tufts per square inch. | May be turned. Lustrous, long wearing. Imperfections due to hand work. |
| RAG: Cotton or silk rags, sewed. | Inexpensive. |
| FELT: Matted jute, wool, hair, etc., with rubber or plastic backing. | Inexpensive. |
| COTTON: May be shaggy, waffleweave, braided, nubby, tufted, tweedy. Washable, not usually durable. | Informal. |

| Type and Construction | Appearance, etc. |
|---|---|
| HOOKED: In all sizes, machine made. May be homemade by pulling narrow strips of wool or cotton through a coarse burlap or linen, with a hook. | Colorful, in variety of designs and shapes. For scatter rugs. Homey. |
| OZITE (also used as rug underlay): Weather resistant. | Comes in many colors. Used for putting greens, screened porches, summer houses. |

## APPLIANCES

**Gas Ranges:** Look for the seal of the American Gas Association, a blue star in a circle for minimum standards, a C.P. (for certified performance) for better grades. Factors to evaluate: insulation (rock wool, fiber glass, thick oven walls); burners (ribbon flame is least wasteful); trays easy to pull out and clean; space between burners; oven thermostat; oven space; barbecuer and broiler attachments; griddle; work space; clock and timing devices; electrical attachments.

**Electric Ranges:** CONSTRUCTION: Outside body should be of reenforced sheet steel, porcelain enameled. Oven should also be porcelain enameled. Rounded corners make cleaning easier.

SURFACE UNITS: Check number of different heats available. Five heats are best for greatest flexibility and economy. Check ease of complete cleaning. Some tops are under glass. Microwave ovens cut cooking time by 90 percent.

INSULATION: Must be moisture-proof, resistant to settling. Oven door must be well insulated and fit tightly.

SPECIAL FEATURES: Choose a range with automatic timing devices and signal lights for oven and surface units. Select a deep well cooker which will best suit your needs.

GUARANTEE: Read and save guarantee.

**The Blender** and **Osterizer** have opened new methods of preparing foods by breaking down ingredients and homogenizing them. Models come with speed and time controls, in various sizes.

**Electric Fans:** Electric fans have the single purpose of moving air. Effect depends on speed of motion and size. Generally 10-inch size is more satisfactory than 8-inch size. Oscillating fans cool a wider area and avoid creating a continuous draft.

Look for a rigid wire guard, safety factor in stopping oscillation, number of speeds, noise, location of switch.

**Refrigerators:** Ample space is important. Standard equipment comes in 4 cu. feet to 18.5 cu. feet. Recent improvements include: automatic defroster (it may be attached to older models); this works so quickly, food has no chance to thaw; high humidity with minimum of air circulation from the evaporator into the lower chamber; self-filling ice trays; doors which have shelf space; built-in freezers; multiple ice cube makers; nonbreakable drip trays; handles which may be opened while hands are full; high humidity; crispers for vegetables; variety of temperatures—as special place for butter; magnetic, self-closing doors; variety of colors; accessible temperature control; easily removable freezing compartments and trays. Various models have some disadvantages: some require periodic oiling; some make noise in operation; some refrigerants are toxic or inflammable; some are difficult to service. Two manufacturers make refrigerators which operate on gas.

All electrical appliances and appliance cords should have the label of approval from the Underwriters Laboratories or the name of a reputable manufacturer.

**Washing machines:** An automatic machine saves time and labor. You set the controls, add soap, the machine fills itself with water at the right temperature, washes the clothes, rinses them, spins them damp-dry. The tub is cleaned and drained during the drying process; only the trap needs to be cleaned of lint. Successful results depend on a plentiful supply of running hot and cold water, reasonably soft, with sufficient water pressure.

The performance of a washing machine is judged by how much washing it can do at one time and how well it does the job. The capacity of a machine is measured in terms of the pounds of clothes the machine will wash effectively in one load. A moderate-sized machine holds between 5 and 8 pounds of dry clothes. The larger machines built for household use hold from 9 to 16 pounds. Small machines for lighter work, such as baby clothing or fine lingerie, have a capacity of only 2 pounds.

Automatic washing devices are chiefly of three types:

AGITATOR: The most commonly used washing device is the agitator. It consists of fins or blades on a central post. Fitted over a shaft in the tub, the agitator turns back and forth,

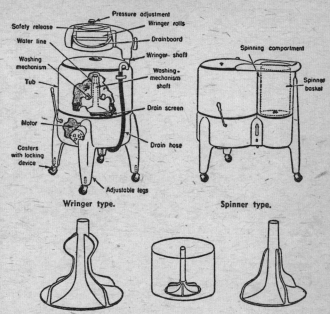

Wringer type.  Spinner type.

Various forms of blades or vanes in the agitator type washer.

swishing clothes through the water. Agitators differ in size, shape, number, arrangement of blades, and are called by various names.

CYLINDER: This mechanism is a cylinder with holes; it fits into the tub and holds the clothes. The cylinder revolves— usually reversing its direction at intervals—and the water is forced in and out through the holes. Projections or "baffles" inside the cylinder carry the clothes along. Cylinders, like agitators, vary in design.

VACUUM CUP: The vacuum-cup device works like the plunger or "funnel-on-a-stick" sometimes used as an aid when washing by hand. Bell-shaped cups, usually three or four in number, are fastened to arms on a center shaft. They move up and down, and may have a circular motion also. The cups pull the clothes up through the water, then drop them back.

A well-built washer, whatever the type, is made from sturdy materials, well-braced and welded. It is free from sharp edges and rough screw and rivet heads that might tear

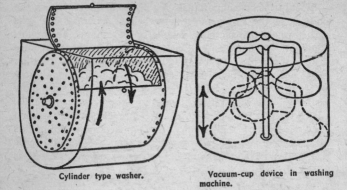

Cylinder type washer.          Vacuum-cup device in washing
                               machine.

clothes. Parts that come in contact with clothes are rustproof.
Gears are enclosed so that nothing can get caught in them.
Tub and motor are mounted on rubber or hung on springs
to lessen vibration and noise. Tubs are sometimes made of
aluminum or nickeled copper, both long-wearing materials.
Nickeled copper is easy to keep bright and shiny. The finish
most used on washing machine framework and cabinets is
synthetic enamel. This is easy to care for and wears well. If
scratched or nicked it can be touched up.

Many washers have motors with sealed-in lubricant and
need no re-oiling. A desirable feature on the motor is a protective device that cuts off the electric current if the machine
is overloaded.

Non-automatic or "standard" type washers may be a
wringer or a spinner type. There are many wringer models, a
few machines with spinners. A spinner takes care of a whole
tubful of clothes at once; with a wringer the clothes are fed
in piece by piece. The spinner, a metal basket, forces water
from the clothes as it whirls at high speed. In most models
the spinner has its own tub, separate from the washer tub.
When using this type you lift the clothes by hand from one
tub to the other. The machine is designed so you can use
both washer and spinner at once and so save time—one load
of clothes can be damp-dried while another is being washed.
In the spinner there's no danger of tearing off buttons or
damaging buckles, hooks, and zippers. The spinner leaves the
clothes less wrinkled than does a wringer.

Safety is of first importance in a power wringer. Check the position of the emergency release which separates the rolls and stops them if clothing, fingers or hair should be caught. Some wringers have an automatic control that keeps pressure the same whether the article going through is thick or thin. On a wringer without this feature, you'll find a handscrew to regulate pressure. Sometimes there's a scale to show how far to turn the screw for light, medium, and heavy materials. Check the balance of the empty machine with wringer in each position. Be sure the machine won't upset when wringer is swung away from it. Present-day wringers have drainboards that adjust automatically when the direction of the rolls is reversed.

FOR HOMES WITHOUT ELECTRICITY, there are washers operated by gasoline engines. Otherwise, they are like the electric machines.

Some manufacturers make twin-tub wringer machines that give double capacity and speed up the washday job. For small washings there are portable machines that hold 2 to 3 lbs. of clothes.

Modern washing machines have from 2- to 14-pound capacity devices to filter dirt; varied lengths of soak, wash, spin, rinse and damp-dry cycles; temperature controls; and detergent, bleach, and softener dispensers.

**Electric irons:** Weight may be 3 to 6 lbs., but 4 lbs. is most popular. Wattage may be 660 to 1000 watts. The top figure is best.

Good modern irons have adjustable heat controls for various fabrics, even heating all over the bottom plate, large ironing plate surface, good balance, heat-resistant handles, narrow points, good back rest solidly attached to the iron. The cord may be covered with rubber, cotton, or rayon, in declining desirability. A gold label from the Underwriters Laboratories (U.L.) indicates the cord can stand 3 times as much flexing as the red label (satisfactory). Also, look for thumb rests on the handles, cooler plastic rather than wooden handles; chrome-plated steel alloy (most durable) or hard aluminum alloy (lighter and quicker heating).

**Travel irons:** Compact, portable, lightweight irons are available for travel. They should be usable on A.C. or D.C. For foreign travel, get irons adapted to voltage used in other countries.

**Steam irons:** These are useful for steaming woolens, as a sewing aid. They may be self-contained or be attachments to a dry iron. The water may drip out drop by drop (gravity feed type) or come out as in a teakettle (pressure type). Thermostats regulate heat and steam pressure.

**Garbage disposer:** This device placed under the sink shreds all kinds of food waste into a fine pulp and flushes it quickly down the drain. Check local laws before installing.

**Vacuum Cleaners:** Uprights usually have more power than tank types. Tank types, with attachments, are easier to use. Combinations of both are available.

In selecting, note: cleaning power; weight and ease of handling; how easily is dust bag removed; is cord long enough; what attachments that you need are available and how easy are they to insert; on an upright, can adjustment be made for different pile heights in rug.

**Electric Heaters:** Although these are not a substitute for home heating, they serve to remove a chill, for drying, and for emergency and supplementary service. Best types have a blower to circulate hot air. Next best are steam electric radiators, which create steam. (These require 10 to 20 minutes to work up.) Radiation heaters, though not efficient for room heating, are satisfactory for the immediate area. Convection types heat only area above them.

**Radios:** Quality depends on fidelity (ability to reproduce fine changes, particularly in bass); sensitivity (ability to receive weak stations); selectivity (ability to tune out nearby wave lengths). Other factors to evaluate: maximum volume, tuning range, tone control, automatic volume control, tendency to drift from a station (especially on FM), alignment of dial with actual station frequencies. Best fidelity is obtained from large speakers, many tubes.

FM (frequency modulation) stations broadcast on different wave lengths. Reception from FM stations is comparatively static free. Some sets can tune-in foreign wave lengths.

**Home Entertainment Devices:** Music, readings, drama, poetry, and educational courses can now come into your home in great variety, through color and black-and-white television, radio, tape, and phonograph recordings. High-fidelity and stereophonic recordings are reproduced with great detail on modern equipment.

In essence, the four elements of sound reproduction are:

THE TUNER, which takes sound from the air. Multiple tuners which can make fine wave-length distinctions are included in better sets.

THE AMPLIFIER, which converts the electrical energy into sound waves. The recommended minimum-power set should be at least 25 watts (50 watts on stereo). Newest types are transistorized.

THE SPEAKERS, which reproduce the sound waves. Multiple speakers provide specialized reproduction of treble (tweeter) and bass (woofer). Stereophonic speakers separate sounds to provide three-dimensional reproduction. Some sets are equipped with as many as 12 speakers.

Record players are available to play up to ten records, and some models make it possible to play both sides without manual help. Records made in recent years are usually long-playing discs, turning 45 or 33⅓ rotations per minute.

Needles on record players should be changed twice each year if the machine has average use. Blunted needles wear out and destroy the fidelity of records. Diamond needles are best because they may have a finer point; sapphire needles are only a little less efficient and are usable for long playing periods.

Record players are enhanced with the addition of a tuner, which brings in radio broadcasts and reproduces them in full stereo. More expensive tuners allow for the reception of stereo broadcasts, which are being programmed with increasing frequency.

A tape recorder allows you to capture great radio performances of speeches, plays, concerts, operas, etc. and add them to your own private and unique recording library.

Tape recorders can be used as message centers, to record living history, to provide continuous music for a party, for teaching, for narration of home movies, and for a tie-in with telephone, radio, or television (use a clock switch).

Home communications centers may be installed to provide intercom service to various rooms and radio tuning to a limited number of stations.

Plastics: The term plastics is applied to a large number of synthetic products with widely different characteristics.

## TYPES OF PLASTICS

| Type | Characteristics | Uses |
|---|---|---|
| ACRYLICS | Transparent, difficult to break, sparkling appearance, weighs half as much as glass. May scratch. | Salad bowls, hairbrushes, combs, handbags, control panels, trays, skylights. |
| CASEIN | Noninflammable, can be dry-cleaned but not washed. Based on milk. | Belt buckles, knitting needles, costume jewelry. |
| CELLULOSICS | Five different types. Variety of colors. | Lawn-mower handles, lamp-shades. |
| MELAMINE AND UREA | Colorfast, break-resistant, heat resistant, rigid. | Tableware, counter tops, appliance parts. |
| NYLON | Withstands washing with hot water and dry cleaning. But stains should be wiped off immediately. | Slide fasteners, tumblers, hosiery, bristles, dishes, gears, combs. |
| PHENOLICS | Very heat resistant, lustrous. Do not transmit electricity. | Light-switch plates, radio cabinets. |
| POLYETHYLENE | Odorless, tasteless, flexible, milky white, translucent. | Flexible kitchen mixing bowls, squeeze bottles, "rubber" backing, toys. |
| POLYSTYRENE | Tasteless and odorless, brittle. | Refrigerator boxes, toys. |
| VINYLS | Tough. Resist stains. Easily wiped off with warm water and soap, have a slight odor. Avoid contact with moth repellents, flame or heat. | Raincoats, phonograph records, upholstery fabrics. |
| VINYLIDENE CHLORIDE | Transparent or colored. | Packaging films, outdoor furniture, pipes, parts. |
| POLYTETRAFLUORO-ETHYLENE (Teflon) | Solid, flexible, slippery. | Coating for greaseless cooking ware, permanent lubricants. |
| POLYURETHANE | Resilient, moisture resistant. | Rug underlays, cushioning, mattresses. |
| REINFORCED POLYESTERS | Water, sun and scratch resistant. | Luggage, awnings, roofing, shower doors, lamp shades. |
| SILICONES | Rubbery, liquid or film; wet resistant. | Water proofing, laminations. |
| CELLULOSE ACETATE | Transparent or colored. | Safety goggles, spools, instrument panels and parts. |
| CELLULOSE ACETATE BUTYRATE (Tenite) | Strong, transparent or colored. | Tool handles, rods, electrical parts. |
| ETHYL CELLULOSE | Lightweight, transparent or translucent. Keep from heat, alcohol. | Flashlights, radio cabinets, boxes, eyeglass frames. |
| CELLOSE NITRATE | Film. | Photo and X-ray films, tool handles, fountain pens, transparent sheets. |

# BOOK VIII

## Food Selection and Buying Guide

### GOOD EATING FOR LESS MONEY

It has been estimated that, knowing all factors, it is possible to save 25 percent on a food budget. Some general rules to help cut your food costs: (1) Balance your food spending, 25 percent for fruit and vegetables; 25 percent for milk and cheese; 20 percent for grain products; 15 percent for meat, fish and eggs; 15 percent for coffee, soda, sugar, condiments, etc. (2) Buy in bulk rather than in packages. (3) Buy fresh foods in season rather than canned foods. (4) Buy all foods considering their seasonal price changes. (5) Serve more of fewer courses. (6) Buy the grade and type of food for the particular dish you plan to make; e.g., cheaper grades of meat may make an equally delicious stew. (7) Prepare as close to serving time as possible to avoid nutriment losses. (8) Investigate the fun and saving of home baking.

Food is generally classified into three groups: fats, carbohydrates and proteins. In addition, food provides vitamins, minerals and enzymes to promote body functions.

### FOOD FUNCTIONS

FATS: Provide energy (9 calories per gram). Found in butter, cream, bacon.

CARBOHYDRATES (STARCHES): Provide energy (4 calories per gram). Found in bread, potatoes, cereal.

PROTEINS: Provide energy (4 calories per gram), repair and build tissue. Found in milk, lean meat, fish, eggs, cheese, beans, dried peas.

## VITAMIN NEEDS CHART

| Benefits Derived | Important Sources |
| --- | --- |
| VITAMIN A: Helps body build resistance to infection. Keeps certain eye tissues and mucous surfaces healthy. Prevents night blindness. Promotes growth. Keeps skin healthy. | In green leafy* and yellow vegetables, dairy products, fish liver oils, eggs, liver, kidney, dried prunes, apricots. |
| VITAMIN B₁ (THIAMIN): Promotes growth, stimulates appetite, and good digestion. Keeps nerves healthy. | In green leafy* and yellow vegetables, yeast, whole-grain cereals and breads, nuts, beans, peas, peanut butter, lean pork, egg yolks, oysters, liver, kidney, fruits (especially oranges and bananas), oatmeal, "enriched breads." An alkaline substance destroys Vitamin B. Never add soda to green vegetables to preserve their color. |
| NICOTINIC ACID (VITAMIN B COMPLEX): Lack causes pellagra. | Liver, yeast, meats. |
| PANTOTHENIC ACID: Lack has caused hair to turn gray in experiments on animals. | Yeast, liver, egg yolk, rice polishings. |
| VITAMIN C (ASCORBIC ACID): Builds bone and tooth structure and healthy gums. Strengthens walls of blood vessels. Lack retards growth. | In citrus fruits (oranges, lemons, grapefruit, etc.), tomatoes, green peppers; most fruits (bananas, strawberries, etc.); *green vegetables if eaten fresh, quickly cooked or commercially canned. |
| VITAMIN D: Builds and preserves bones and teeth. Normalizes blood. Insufficient amount in diet of children results in rickets. | In sunlight; cod and halibut liver oils, egg yolk, salmon, sardines, mackerel, tuna, herring, oysters; beef, lamb or pork liver, butter, cream; irradiated (Vitamin D fortified) milk and butter. |

* Swiss chard, broccoli, salad greens, pepper.

| Benefits Derived | Important Sources |
| --- | --- |
| VITAMIN G (RIBOFLAVIN): Necessary for growth, health and for the process of cell breathing. Helps prevent loss of weight. Essential for healthy eyes and skin, for proper co-ordination of muscles. Helps increase life span. | In green leafy vegetables,* peas, beans, soy beans, beet tops, yeast, eggs, milk, lean meats, liver and kidneys, most fruits, oysters. |
| VITAMIN K: Helps prevent hemorrhages. Important in the building of prothrombin, a substance essential for normal blood clotting. | In green leafy vegetables, particularly cabbage, kale, spinach. |

## MINERAL NEEDS CHART

| Mineral and Benefits | Important Sources |
| --- | --- |
| CALCIUM: Builds bones and teeth. Necessary for growth, normal muscle and nerve response, blood clotting. | Milk, cheese, skimmed milk, green leafy vegetables, grapes. |
| PHOSPHORUS: Essential for cell life. Necessary for bones, teeth, normal growth. | Milk, cheese, oatmeal, beans, cereals, eggs, meat, fish, green leafy vegetables. |
| IRON: Essential for cell life. Necessary for formation of hemoglobin (red cells which carry oxygen). Helps prevent anemia. | Oatmeal, molasses, egg yolk, beef, liver, oysters, dried fruits, beans, green leafy vegetables. |
| COPPER: Necessary for iron to work properly in blood. | Same as for iron. |
| IODINE: Necessary for thyroid gland. Lack will cause goiter. | Saltwater fish, seafood. Vegetables grown where soil contains iodine. |
| SALT: Controls flow of water in and out of tissues. | Most foods. Table salt. |

* Swiss chard, broccoli, salad greens, pepper.

NUTRIENT VALUES
Amount of various necessary food ele-

| | UNIT | Food Energy (Calories) | Protein (Grams) | Fat (Grams) | Total Carbohydrates (Grams) |
|---|---|---|---|---|---|
| **DAIRY PRODUCTS** | | | | | |
| Milk, fresh, whole | 1 cup | 166 | 8.5 | 9.5 | 12.0 |
| Cream—light | 1 tablespoon | 30 | .4 | 3.0 | .6 |
| Ice Cream | 1 slice | 167 | 3.2 | 10.1 | 16.7 |
| Butter | 1 pat | 50 | .0 | 5.7 | .0 |
| Cheddar Cheese | 1 oz. | 113 | 7.1 | 9.1 | .6 |
| Cottage Cheese | 1 oz. | 27 | 5.5 | .1 | .6 |
| Eggs—fresh | 1 medium | 77 | 6.1 | 5.5 | .3 |
| **MEATS** | | | | | |
| Beef—roasting | 3 oz. | 266 | 20 | 20 | 0 |
| chopped | 3 oz. | 316 | 19 | 26 | 0 |
| steak—Porterhouse | 3 oz. | 293 | 20 | 23 | 0 |
| Lamb—leg, roast | 3 oz. | 230 | 20 | 16 | 0 |
| Pork chops | 3 oz. | 284 | 20 | 22 | 0 |
| Ham—fresh | 3 oz. | 338 | 20 | 28 | 0 |
| Bacon | 2 slices | 97 | 4 | 8.8 | .2 |
| Veal—roast | 3 oz. | 193 | 24 | 19 | 0 |
| Bologna | 1 inch piece | 467 | 31.2 | 33.5 | 7.6 |
| Frankfurters | 1 | 124 | 7 | 10 | 1 |
| Tongue—beef | 4 oz. | 235 | 18.6 | 17 | .5 |
| Chicken—roast | 4 oz. | 227 | 22.9 | 14.3 | 0 |
| Turkey | 4 oz. | 304 | 22.8 | 22.9 | 0 |
| **FISH** | | | | | |
| Mackerel | 3 oz. | 155 | 16.4 | 9.4 | 0 |
| Salmon | 1 steak | 204 | 33.6 | 8.7 | .2 |
| **VEGETABLES—FRESH, COOKED** | | | | | |
| Asparagus | 1 cup | 36 | 4.2 | .4 | 6.3 |
| Beans—lima | 1 cup | 152 | 8.0 | .6 | 29.3 |
| green | 1 cup | 27 | 1.8 | .2 | 5.9 |
| Beets | 1 cup | 68 | 1.6 | .2 | 16.2 |
| Brussels Sprouts | 1 cup | 60 | 5.7 | .6 | 11.6 |
| Cabbage | 1 cup | 40 | 2.4 | .3 | 9.0 |
| Carrots | 1 cup | 44 | .9 | .7 | 9.3 |
| Cauliflower | 1 cup | 30 | 2.9 | .2 | 5.9 |
| Celery | 1 large stalk | 7 | .5 | .1 | 1.5 |
| Corn—sweet | 1 ear | 84 | 2.7 | .7 | 20 |
| Cucumber | large | 25 | 1.4 | .2 | 5.5 |
| Kale | 1 cup | 45 | 4.3 | .7 | 7.9 |
| Lettuce | 4 sm. leaves | 7 | .6 | .1 | 1.4 |
| Mushrooms | 1 cup | 28 | 3.4 | .5 | 9.0 |
| Onions | 1 cup | 79 | 2.1 | .4 | 18.3 |
| Peas | 1 cup | 111 | 7.8 | .6 | 19.4 |
| Peppers—green | 1 medium | 16 | .8 | .1 | 3.6 |
| Potatoes—baked | 1 medium | 97 | 2.4 | .1 | 22.3 |
| Spinach | 1 cup | 46 | 5.6 | 1.1 | 6.5 |
| Tomatoes | 1 medium | 30 | 1.5 | .4 | 6.0 |
| Turnips | 1 cup | 42 | 1.2 | .3 | 9.3 |

**OF TYPICAL FOODS**
ments contained in common portions of

| Calcium (Mg.) | Phosphorus (Mg.) | Iron (Mg.) | Vitamin A Value I. U. | Thiamine (Vitamin $B_1$) (Mg.) | Riboflavin (Vitamin $B_2$ or G) (Mg.) | Niacin (Mg.) | Ascorbic Acid (Vitamin C) (Mg.) |
|---|---|---|---|---|---|---|---|
| 288 | 227 | .2 | 390 | .09 | .42 | .3 | 3 |
| 15 | 12 | .0 | 120 | Trace | .02 | Trace | Trace |
| 100 | 80 | .1 | 420 | .03 | .15 | .1 | 1 |
| 1 | 1 | .0 | 230 | Trace | Trace | Trace | 0 |
| 206 | 140 | .3 | 400 | .01 | .12 | Trace | 0 |
| 27 | 54 | .1 | 10 | .01 | .09 | Trace | 0 |
| 26 | 101 | 1.3 | 550 | .05 | .14 | Trace | 0 |
| 9 | 157 | 2.6 | 0 | .05 | .15 | 3.6 | 0 |
| 8 | 134 | 2.4 | 0 | .07 | .16 | 4.1 | 0 |
| 9 | 145 | 2.6 | 0 | .05 | .15 | 4.0 | 0 |
| 9 | 219 | 2.6 | 0 | .12 | .21 | 4.4 | 0 |
| 9 | 200 | 2.6 | 0 | .71 | .20 | 4.3 | 0 |
| 9 | 202 | 2.8 | 0 | .45 | .20 | 4.0 | 0 |
| 4 | 41 | .5 | 0 | .08 | .05 | .8 | 0 |
| 10 | 219 | 3.1 | 0 | .11 | .27 | 6.7 | 0 |
| 19 | 236 | 4.6 | 0 | .37 | .40 | 5.7 | 0 |
| 3 | 25 | .6 | 0 | .08 | .09 | 1.3 | 0 |
| 10 | 212 | 3.2 | 0 | .14 | .33 | 5.7 | 0 |
| 16 | 227 | 1.7 | 0 | .09 | .18 | 9.1 | 0 |
| 26 | 363 | 4.3 | Trace | .10 | .16 | 9.1 | 0 |
| 157 | 233 | 1.8 | 370 | .05 | .18 | 4.9 | — |
| — | 500 | 1.4 | — | .12 | .33 | 9.8 | — |
| 33 | 93 | 1.8 | 1820 | .23 | .30 | 2.1 | 40 |
| 46 | 123 | 2.7 | 460 | .22 | .14 | 1.8 | 24 |
| 45 | 29 | .9 | 830 | .09 | .12 | .6 | 18 |
| 35 | 51 | 1.2 | 30 | .03 | .07 | .5 | 11 |
| 44 | 101 | 1.7 | 520 | .05 | .16 | .6 | 61 |
| 78 | 53 | .8 | 150 | .08 | .08 | .5 | 53 |
| 38 | 38 | .9 | 18130 | .07 | .07 | .7 | 6 |
| 26 | 86 | 1.3 | 108 | .07 | .10 | .6 | 34 |
| 20 | 16 | .2 | 0 | .02 | .02 | .2 | 3 |
| 5 | 51 | .6 | 390 | .11 | .10 | 1.4 | 8 |
| 20 | 43 | .6 | 0 | .07 | .09 | .4 | 17 |
| 248 | 68 | 2.4 | 9220 | .08 | .25 | 1.9 | 56 |
| 11 | 12 | .2 | 270 | .02 | .04 | .1 | 4 |
| 17 | 220 | 2.0 | 0 | .04 | .60 | 4.8 | — |
| 67 | 92 | 1.0 | 110 | .04 | .06 | .4 | 13 |
| 35 | 195 | 3.0 | 1150 | .40 | .22 | 3.7 | 24 |
| 7 | 16 | .3 | 400 | .02 | .04 | .2 | 77 |
| 13 | 65 | .8 | 20 | .11 | .05 | 1.4 | 17 |
| 223 | 59 | 3.6 | 21200 | .14 | .36 | 1.1 | 54 |
| 16 | 40 | .9 | 1640 | .08 | .06 | .8 | 35 |
| 62 | 53 | .8 | Trace | .06 | .09 | .6 | 28 |

**NUTRIENT VALUES**
Amount of various necessary food ele-

| | UNIT | Food Energy (Calories) | Protein (Grams) | Fat (Grams) | Total Carbohydrates (Grams) |
|---|---|---|---|---|---|
| **VEGETABLES—CANNED** | | | | | |
| Asparagus | 1 cup | 42 | 4.5 | .7 | 6.9 |
| Beans—snap | 1 cup | 43 | 2.4 | .2 | 10.0 |
| Peas | 1 cup | 145 | 7.2 | 1.0 | 27.5 |
| | | | | | |
| **FRUITS—FRESH** | | | | | |
| Apples | medium | 76 | .4 | .5 | 19.7 |
| Bananas | medium | 88 | 1.2 | .2 | 23 |
| Cranberry sauce | 1 cup | 549 | 0.3 | 0.8 | 142.4 |
| Grapefruit | ½ medium | 75 | .9 | .4 | 19.0 |
| Lemons | medium | 20 | .6 | .4 | 5.4 |
| | | | | | |
| Muskmelons | ½ melon | 37 | 1.1 | .4 | 8.3 |
| Oranges | medium | 70 | 1.4 | .3 | 17.4 |
| Peaches | medium | 46 | .5 | .1 | 12.0 |
| Pears | medium | 95 | 1.1 | .6 | 23.9 |
| Pineapples | 1 slice | 44 | .3 | .2 | 11.5 |
| | | | | | |
| Plums | medium | 29 | .4 | .1 | 7.4 |
| Raspberries—red | 1 cup | 70 | 1.5 | .5 | 17.0 |
| Rhubarb—cooked | 1 cup | 383 | 1.1 | .3 | 97.9 |
| Strawberries | 1 cup | 54 | 1.2 | .7 | 12.4 |
| Watermelons | 1/16 melon | 120 | 2.1 | .9 | 29.4 |
| | | | | | |
| **FRUIT—CANNED (in syrup)** | | | | | |
| Peaches | 2 halves | 79 | .5 | .1 | 21.3 |
| Pears | 2 halves | 79 | .2 | .1 | 21.5 |
| Pineapples | 1 lg. slice | 95 | .5 | .1 | 25.7 |
| Plums | 3 plums | 92 | .5 | .1 | 24.9 |
| | | | | | |
| **GRAIN PRODUCTS** | | | | | |
| Bread—white | 1 slice | 64 | 1.9 | .8 | 12.0 |
| Rolls | 1 roll | 118 | 3.4 | 2.1 | 20.9 |
| Bran—cereal | 1 cup | 145 | 7.2 | 2.0 | 44.5 |
| Macaroni—cooked | 1 cup | 209 | 7.1 | .8 | 42.3 |
| Farina | 1 cup | 104 | 3.1 | .2 | 21.7 |
| | | | | | |
| Rice—white | 1 cup | 201 | 4.2 | .2 | 44.0 |
| Crackers—plain soda | 2 crackers | 47 | 1.1 | 1.1 | 8.0 |
| | | | | | |
| **MISCELLANEOUS** | | | | | |
| Beer | 1 cup | 48 | 1.4 | .0 | 10.6 |
| Cake, plain and cup cakes | 1 cup cake | 131 | 2.6 | 3.3 | 22.8 |
| Milk Chocolate | 1 oz. | 143 | 2 | 9.5 | 15.8 |
| Gelatin | 1 cup | 155 | 3.8 | .0 | 36.3 |
| Peanuts | 1 cup | 805 | 38.7 | 63.6 | 34.0 |
| | | | | | |
| Soups—Bouillon | 1 cup | 9 | 2 | — | 0 |
| Chicken | 1 cup | 75 | 3.5 | 2.5 | 9.5 |
| Vegetable | 1 cup | 82 | 4.2 | 1.8 | 14.5 |
| Sugar | 1 teaspoon | 16 | 0 | 0 | 4.2 |
| Yeast | 1 oz. | 24 | 3 | .1 | 3.7 |

**OF TYPICAL FOODS**
ments contained in common portions of

| Calcium (Mg.) | Phosphorous (Mg.) | Iron (Mg.) | Vitamin A Value I.U. | Thiamine (Mg.) | Riboflavin (Vitamin $B_1$) (Mg.) | Niacin (Vitamin $B_2$ or G) (Mg.) | Ascorbic Acid (Vitamin C) (Mg.) |
|---|---|---|---|---|---|---|---|
| 43 | 103 | 4.1 | 1450 | .16 | .23 | 2.1 | 35 |
| 65 | 45 | 3.3 | 990 | .08 | .10 | .7 | 9 |
| 51 | 123 | 3.4 | 1070 | .19 | .10 | 1.6 | 15 |
| 8 | 13 | .4 | 120 | .05 | .04 | .2 | 6 |
| 8 | 28 | .6 | 430 | .04 | .05 | .7 | 10 |
| 22 | 19 | .8 | 80 | .06 | .06 | .3 | 5 |
| 41 | 34 | .4 | 20 | .07 | .04 | .4 | 76 |
| 25 | 14 | .4 | 0 | .03 | Trace | .1 | 31 |
| 31 | 29 | .7 | 6190 | .09 | .07 | .9 | 59 |
| 51 | 36 | .6 | 290 | .12 | .04 | .4 | 77 |
| 8 | 22 | .6 | 880 | .02 | .05 | .9 | 8 |
| 20 | 24 | .5 | 30 | .03 | .06 | .2 | 6 |
| 13 | 9 | .3 | 110 | .07 | .02 | .2 | 20 |
| 10 | 11 | .3 | 200 | .04 | .02 | .3 | 3 |
| 49 | 46 | 1.1 | 160 | .03 | .08 | .4 | 29 |
| 112 | 54 | 1.1 | 70 | .02 | — | .2 | 17 |
| 42 | 40 | 1.2 | 90 | .04 | .10 | .4 | 89 |
| 30 | 51 | .9 | 2530 | .20 | .22 | .7 | 26 |
| 6 | 16 | .5 | 530 | .01 | .02 | .8 | 5 |
| 9 | 12 | .2 | Trace | .01 | .02 | .2 | 2 |
| 35 | 9 | .7 | 100 | .09 | .02 | .2 | 11 |
| 10 | 15 | 1.3 | 280 | .03 | .03 | .5 | 1 |
| 15 | 19 | .1 | 0 | .06 | .04 | .5 | 0 |
| 21 | 36 | .7 | 0 | .09 | .06 | .8 | 0 |
| 56 | 787 | 6.2 | 0 | .22 | .23 | 11.5 | 0 |
| 13 | 91 | .8 | 0 | .03 | .02 | .7 | 0 |
| 7 | 31 | .2 | 0 | .01 | .02 | .2 | 0 |
| 13 | 76 | .5 | 0 | .02 | .01 | .7 | 0 |
| 2 | 11 | .1 | 0 | .01 | .01 | .1 | 0 |
| 10 | 62 | .0 | 0 | Trace | .06 | .4 | 0 |
| 62 | 55 | .2 | 50 | .01 | .03 | .1 | 0 |
| 61 | 80 | .6 | 40 | .03 | .11 | .2 | 0 |
| 0 | 0 | 0 | 0 | 0 | 0 | 0 | 0 |
| 107 | 566 | 2.7 | 0 | .42 | .19 | 23.3 | 0 |
| 2 | 24 | .1 | 0 | 0 | .05 | .6 | 0 |
| 20 | 20 | .5 | — | .02 | .12 | 1.5 | — |
| 32 | 50 | 1.4 | — | .05 | .08 | 1.0 | 8 |
| 7 | 172 | 1.4 | 0 | .13 | .59 | 8.0 | 0 |

### DAILY ENERGY NEEDS

| Age (Years) | Calories Per Day | | Type of Work | Calories Per Day | |
|---|---|---|---|---|---|
| | Boys | Girls | | Men | Women |
| 1- 3 | 1200 | 1200 | Sedentary | 2100-2500 | 1800-2100 |
| 4- 6 | 1600 | 1600 | Light | 2500-2800 | 2100-2400 |
| 7- 9 | 2000 | 2000 | Moderate | 2800-3100 | 2400-2700 |
| 10-12 | 2500 | 2500 | Active | 3100-3500 | 2700-3000 |
| 13-15 | 3200 | 2800 | Muscular | 3500-4500 | |
| | | | Extreme | | |
| 16-20 | 3800 | 2400 | Muscular | 4500-6000 | |

The amounts of protein recommended are as follows:

For children under 1 year of age, 3 to 4 grams per kilogram of body weight per day; 1 to 3 years, 40 grams protein a day; 4 to 6 years, 50 grams; 7 to 9 years, 60 grams; 10 to 12 years, 70 grams; boys 13 to 15, 85 grams; boys 16 to 20, 100 grams; men regardless of the degree of activity, 70 grams; girls 13 to 15, 80 grams; girls 16 to 20, 75 grams; women, regardless of muscular or mental activity, 60 grams, rising to 85 grams in pregnancy, and to 100 grams in lactation.

### DAILY MINERAL NEEDS (in Grams)

| | Calcium | Phosphorus | Iron | Copper | Iodine | Salt* |
|---|---|---|---|---|---|---|
| Adults.............................. | .8 | 1.32 | .012 | .002 | .00014 | 15 |
| Children to 12 yrs.................... | 1.0 | 1.0 | .006-.012 | .002 | .00014 plus | 8 |
| Children over 12 yrs................. | 1 to 1.4 | 1.0 | .015 | .002 | .00014 plus | 10 |
| Pregnant women..................... | 1.5 | 1.65 | .015 | .002 | .00014 plus | 15 |
| Nursing women...................... | 2.0 | 1.65 | .015 | .002 | .00014 | 15 |

Potassium, sulphur, magnesium, manganese, cobalt, and zinc are also necessary in small amounts at all ages. Aluminum and silicon may be necessary for healthy tooth enamel.

*Increased amounts needed during periods of excessive perspiration.

Cholesterol is an alcoholic fat which is present in many foods, particularly butter, milk, meat and eggs. It is required by the body for the synthesis of Vitamin D. Most doctors agree that cholesterol forms an irreversible coating on the arteries and veins, thickening them and making them less flexible. This is a major factor in causing arteriosclerosis and hastening heart disease and senility. Certain polyunsaturated oils (principally fish oils) help reduce the amount of cholesterol in the blood stream and thus lessen the deposits of the coating.

## SEASONS FOR PERISHABLE FOODS

X, in season; L, lowest price season

| | Jan. | Feb. | Mar. | Apr. | May | June | July | Aug. | Sept. | Oct. | Nov. | Dec. |
|---|---|---|---|---|---|---|---|---|---|---|---|---|
| **FRUITS** | | | | | | | | | | | | |
| Apples | X | X | X | | | | | | X | L | X | X |
| Apricots | | | | | | X | X | X | | | | |
| Avocados | X | X | | | | | | | | X | X | X |
| Bananas | | | | | | L | | | | | | |
| Berries | | | | X | X | X | X | X | X | | | |
| Cherries | | | | | X | L | X | X | | | | |
| Cranberries | | | | | | | | | | X | L | X |
| Gooseberries | | | | | | L | X | | | | | |
| Grapefruit | X | X | L | X | X | | | | | | | |
| Grapes | | | | | | | | | X | L | X | |
| Lemons | X | X | X | X | X | L | X | X | X | X | X | X |
| Limes | | | | | | L | | | | | | |
| Oranges | | | | | | | | | | | | |
| Florida | L | L | X | X | X | | | | | X | X | X |
| California | L | L | X | X | X | | | | | | X | X |
| Melons | | | | | | X | L | X | X | | | |
| Casabas | | | | | | | | | | X | | |
| Peaches | | | | | | X | X | L | X | | | |
| Pears | | | | | | | | L | X | X | | |
| Pineapple | | | L | | | | | | | | | |
| Plums | | | | | | X | X | X | X | X | | |
| Raspberries | | | | | | L | X | | | | | |
| Rhubarb | | | X | L | X | | | | | | | |
| Tangerines | X | | | | | | | | | | | L |
| **VEGETABLES** | | | | | | | | | | | | |
| Artichoke | | | | X | | | | | | | | |
| Beans, Lima | | | | | | | X | X | X | | | |
| Beets | | | | | | X | X | X | X | | | |
| Brussels Sprouts | X | X | X | X | | | | | | | X | X |
| Broccoli | X | X | X | X | | | | | | | | |
| Celery | | | | | | | | | X | X | X | X |
| Corn | | | | | | X | X | X | X | | | |
| Cucumbers | | | | | X | X | X | | | | | |
| Eggplant | | | X | X | X | X | X | X | X | X | | |
| Kale | X | X | X | | | | | | | | X | X |
| Kohlrabi | | | | | | X | X | X | X | | | |
| Leeks | | | | X | X | X | | | | | | |
| Mushrooms | | | | | | | | | | X | X | X |
| Onions | | | X | X | X | X | | | | | | |
| Okra | | | | | | X | X | X | X | | | |

These lists do not include perishable foods such as carrots, potatoes, etc., which are available all year round at more or less stable prices.

## SEASONS FOR PERISHABLE FOODS

X, in season; L, lowest price season

| | Jan. | Feb. | Mar. | Apr. | May | June | July | Aug. | Sept. | Oct. | Nov. | Dec. |
|---|---|---|---|---|---|---|---|---|---|---|---|---|
| Peas | | | X | X | X | X | X | | | | | |
| Pumpkin | | | | | | | | | X | X | X | X |
| Rhubarb | | X | L | X | | | | | | | | |
| Scallions | | | | X | X | X | | | | | | |
| Spinach | X | X | X | X | X | | | | | | | |
| **Squash** | | | | | | | | | | | | |
| Acorn | X | | | | | | | X | X | X | X | X |
| Hubbard | X | X | | | | | | X | X | X | X | X |
| Summer | | | | | X | X | X | | | | | |
| Swiss Chard | | | | | X | X | X | X | | | | |
| Tomatoes | | | | | X | X | X | X | X | | | |
| **Turnips** | | | | | | | | | | | | |
| White | | | | X | X | X | X | X | X | | | |
| Yellow | | | | | | | | | | X | X | |
| **MEATS** | | | | | | | | | | | | |
| Beef | X | L | X | | | | | | | | | X |
| Lamb | | | | | X | X | X | | | | | |
| Pork | | | | | | | | | X | L | X | X |
| Veal | | | | | X | L | X | | | | | |
| **POULTRY** | | | | | | | | | | | | |
| Capons | X | X | | | | | | | | | | X |
| Ducks | | | | | X | X | X | X | X | X | X | X |
| Fowl | X | | | | | | | | | X | X | X |
| Fryers | | | | | X | X | X | X | | | | |
| Geese | X | | | | | | | | | | X | X |
| Roasters | X | | | | | | | | X | X | X | X |
| Squabs | | | | | X | X | X | X | | | | |
| Turkeys | X | | | | | | | | | X | X | X |
| Guineas | | | | | | | | X | X | X | | |
| **FISH** | | | | | | | | | | | | |
| Alewives | X | X | X | X | X | X | | | | | | |
| Barracuda | | X | X | X | X | X | | | | | | |
| Bluefish | X | X | X | X | X | X | X | X | X | X | X | X |
| Blue pike (Jack salmon) | | | X | X | X | X | X | X | X | X | X | X |
| Blue runner | X | X | X | X | | | | | | | X | X |
| Buffalo fish | X | X | X | X | X | | | | X | X | X | X |
| Butterfish | X | X | X | X | X | X | X | X | X | X | X | X |
| Carp | X | X | X | | | | | | X | X | X | X |
| Catfish | X | X | X | X | X | X | X | X | X | X | X | X |
| Chubs | X | X | X | X | X | X | X | X | X | X | X | X |
| Cisco (lake herring) | | X | X | X | X | X | X | X | X | X | X | X |

These lists do not include perishable foods such as carrots, potatoes, etc., which are available all year round at more or less stable prices.

## SEASONS FOR PERISHABLE FOODS

X, in season; L, lowest price season

| | Jan. | Feb. | Mar. | Apr. | May | June | July | Aug. | Sept. | Oct. | Nov. | Dec. |
|---|---|---|---|---|---|---|---|---|---|---|---|---|
| Cod | X | X | X | X | X | X | X | X | X | X | X | X |
| Crappie | X | X | X | X | X | X | X | X | X | X | X | X |
| Croaker | X | X | X | X | X | X | X | X | X | X | X | X |
| Cusk | X | X | X | X | X | X | X | X | X | X | X | X |
| Drum, red (redfish, channel bass) | X | X | X | X | X | | | | | | X | X |
| Eels | X | X | X | X | X | X | X | X | X | X | X | X |
| Flounder | X | X | X | X | X | X | X | X | X | X | X | X |
| Grouper | X | X | X | X | X | | | | | | X | X |
| Haddock | X | X | X | X | X | X | X | X | X | X | X | X |
| Hake | X | X | X | X | X | X | X | X | X | X | X | X |
| Halibut | X | X | X | X | X | X | X | X | X | X | X | X |
| Herring, lake | X | X | X | X | X | X | X | X | X | X | X | X |
| Herring, sea | X | X | X | X | X | X | X | X | X | X | X | X |
| Kingfish | X | X | X | X | X | X | | | | | | |
| King whiting | X | X | X | X | X | X | X | X | X | | X | X |
| Lake trout | X | X | X | X | X | X | X | X | X | X | X | X |
| Lingcod | X | X | X | X | X | X | X | X | X | X | X | X |
| Mackerel, Boston | | | | | X | X | X | X | X | | | |
| Florida | X | X | X | X | X | | | | | | X | X |
| Cal. | X | X | X | X | X | X | X | X | X | X | X | X |
| Mullet (popeye) | X | X | X | X | X | X | X | | | | X | X |
| Pilchard (sardine) | X | X | X | | | | | X | X | X | X | X |
| Pike | X | X | X | X | X | X | X | X | X | X | X | X |
| Pollock | X | X | X | X | X | X | X | X | X | X | X | X |
| Pompano | X | X | X | X | X | X | X | X | X | X | X | X |
| Porgie | X | X | X | X | X | X | X | X | X | X | X | X |
| Red Snapper | X | X | X | X | X | X | X | X | X | X | X | X |
| Sablefish | X | X | X | X | X | X | X | X | X | X | X | X |
| Salmon | X | X | X | X | X | X | X | X | X | X | X | X |
| Scup | X | X | X | X | X | X | X | X | X | X | | |
| Sea bass (blackfish) | X | X | X | X | X | X | X | X | X | X | X | X |
| Shad | X | X | X | X | X | X | X | | | | | X |
| Sheepshead (river drum, gaspergou) | X | X | X | X | X | X | X | X | X | X | X | X |
| Smelt | X | X | X | X | X | | | | X | X | X | X |
| Sole | X | X | X | X | X | X | X | X | X | X | X | X |
| Spot (Cape May goodie) | | | | | | X | X | X | X | X | | |
| Spotted trout | X | X | | | | X | X | X | | X | X | X |
| Striped bass (rock) | X | X | X | X | X | X | X | X | X | X | X | X |
| Sturgeon | X | | X | X | X | X | X | X | X | X | X | X |

These lists do not include perishable foods such as carrots, potatoes, etc., which are available all year round at more or less stable prices.

## SEASONS FOR PERISHABLE FOODS

X, in season; L, lowest price season

| | Jan. | Feb. | Mar. | Apr. | May | June | July | Aug. | Sept. | Oct. | Nov. | Dec. |
|---|---|---|---|---|---|---|---|---|---|---|---|---|
| Sucker | X | X | X | X | X | X | | | | | | X |
| Sunfish | | | | X | X | X | X | X | X | X | | |
| Swordfish | | | | | | X | X | X | X | X | | |
| Tuna | X | X | X | X | X | X | X | X | X | X | X | X |
| Weakfish (gray trout, sea trout) | | | | X | X | X | X | X | X | X | | |
| White Bass | X | X | X | X | X | X | X | X | X | X | X | X |
| Whitefish | X | X | X | X | X | X | X | X | X | X | X | X |
| Whiting (silver hake) | | | | | X | X | X | X | X | X | X | X |
| Wolf fish (ocean catfish) | X | X | X | X | X | | | | | X | X | X |
| Yellow perch | X | X | X | X | X | X | X | X | X | X | X | X |
| Yellow pike | X | X | X | X | X | X | X | X | X | X | X | X |
| Yellowtail | X | X | X | X | X | X | X | X | X | X | X | X |
| **SHELLFISH** | | | | | | | | | | | | |
| Clams | X | X | X | X | X | X | X | X | X | X | X | X |
| Crabs | | | | | | | | | | | | |
|   Hard-shelled | X | X | X | X | X | X | X | X | X | X | X | X |
|   Soft-shelled | | | | X | X | X | X | X | | | | |
| Lobsters | | | X | X | X | X | X | X | X | X | | |
| Oysters | X | X | X | X | | | | | X | X | X | X |
| Scallops | X | X | | | | | | | X | X | X | X |
| Shrimps | X | X | X | X | X | X | X | X | X | X | X | X |

These lists do not include perishable foods such as carrots, potatoes, etc., which are available all year round at more or less stable prices.

## AVERAGE DAILY VITAMIN NEEDS

| | A Intl. Units | Thiamin (B₁) Mg. | C Mg. | D I. U. | Riboflavin G or K₃ Mg. |
|---|---|---|---|---|---|
| Men | 5000 | 1.2 to 2.0 | 75 | Unknown | 1.6 to 2.6 |
| Women | 5000 | 1.1 to 1.5 | 70 | Unknown | 1.5 to 2.0 |
| Pregnant Women | 6000 | 1.8 | 100 | 800 | 2.6 |
| Women in Lactation | 8000 | 2.0 | 150 | 800 | 3.0 |
| Children under 1 | 1500 | .4 | 30 | 400 | .8 |
| Children 1 to 3 | 2000 | .6 | 35 | 400 | .9 |
| Children 4 to 6 | 2500 | .8 | 50 | 400 | 1.2 |
| Children 7 to 9 | 3500 | 1.0 | 60 | 400 | 1.5 |
| Children 10 to 12 | 4500 | 1.2 | 75 | 400 | 1.8 |
| Girls 13 to 18 | 5000 | 1.3 | 80 | 400 | 2.0 |
| Girls 16 to 20 | 5000 | 1.2 | 80 | 400 | 1.8 |
| Boys 13 to 15 | 5000 | 1.5 | 90 | 400 | 2.0 |
| Boys 16 to 20 | 6000 | 1.8 | 100 | 400 | 2.5 |

## FAMILY FOOD PLAN AT MODERATE COST

Weekly Quantities of Food for Each Member of Family

| Family Members | Milk | Potatoes, sweet potatoes | Dry beans and peas, nuts | Citrus fruit, tomatoes | Green, yellow vegetables | Other vegetables and fruit | Eggs | Meat, poultry, fish | Flour, cereals | Fats and oils | Sugar, sirups, preserves |
|---|---|---|---|---|---|---|---|---|---|---|---|
| | qt. | lb. oz. | lb. oz. | lb. oz. | lb. oz. | lb. oz. | no. | lb. oz. | lb. oz. | lb. oz. | lb. oz. |
| CHILDREN 9-12 months..... | 7 | 0-8 | ...... | 2-0 | 1-8 | 0-8 | 5 | 0-2 | 0-8 | 0-1 | 9-1 |
| 1-3 years................. | 5½ | 0-8 | 0-1 | 2-0 | 2-0 | 2-0 | 6 | 0-8 | 1-4 | 0-4 | 0-2 |
| 4-6 years................. | 5½ | 1-4 | 0-1 | 2-0 | 2-0 | 2-0 | 6 | 1-0 | 1-12 | 0-6 | 0-8 |
| 7-9 years................. | 5 | 2-0 | 0-1 | 2-0 | 2-0 | 3-0 | 6 | 1-8 | 2-4 | 0-10 | 0-10 |
| 10-12 years............... | 6 | 2-8 | 0-2 | 2-4 | 2-0 | 3-0 | 6 | 2-4 | 3-0 | 0-12 | 0-12 |
| GIRLS 13-15 years.......... | 7 | 2-8 | 0-4 | 2-4 | 2-0 | 4-0 | 6 | 2-8 | 3-0 | 0-12 | 0-14 |
| 16-20 years............... | 5 | 3-0 | 0-4 | 2-4 | 2-0 | 4-0 | 6 | 2-8 | 3-0 | 0-12 | 0-14 |
| BOYS 13-15 years.......... | 7 | 3-8 | 0-4 | 2-8 | 3-0 | 4-0 | 6 | 2-12 | 4-0 | 1-0 | 1-0 |
| 16-20 years............... | 6 | 4-8 | 0-8 | 2-8 | 3-0 | 5-0 | 6 | 3-0 | 5-8 | 1-6 | 1-0 |
| WOMEN Moderately active... | 4½ | 2-8 | 0-4 | 2-8 | 3-8 | 4-0 | 6 | 3-0 | 2-8 | 0-14 | 1-0 |
| Very active.............. | 4½ | 3-0 | 0-6 | 2-8 | 3-8 | 4-0 | 6 | 3-0 | 3-12 | 1-2 | 1-0 |
| Sedentary................ | 4½ | 2-0 | 0-2 | 2-8 | 3-8 | 4-0 | 6 | 2-8 | 2-0 | 0-10 | 0-14 |
| Pregnant................. | 8 | 2-0 | 0-2 | 3-0 | 4-0 | 4-0 | 6 | 3-0 | 2-8 | 0-12 | 0-12 |
| Nursing.................. | 10½ | 3-0 | 0-4 | 3-0 | 4-0 | 4-8 | 6 | 3-0 | 2-8 | 0-12 | 0-12 |
| MEN Moderately active..... | 4½ | 3-0 | 0-6 | 2-8 | 3-8 | 4-0 | 6 | 3-0 | 3-12 | 1-2 | 1-0 |
| Very active.............. | 5½ | 4-8 | 0-8 | 2-8 | 3-8 | 5-0 | 6 | 3-8 | 7-4 | 1-14 | 1-0 |
| Sedentary................ | 4½ | 2-8 | 0-4 | 2-8 | 3-8 | 4-0 | 6 | 3-0 | 2-8 | 0-14 | 1-0 |

## GUIDES TO MEAT BUYING

Three guides to be considered in buying meat are: (1) The inspection stamp, which certifies that the meat has been inspected and is free from disease, (2) the grade stamp, and (3) the appearance of the meat itself.

Meat grade and brand stamps: The grade and brand stamps which are affixed to meat and meat products are of two types: (1) The grade or brand names of the individual packers, and (2) the grade names of the United States Department of Agriculture. Meat products which pass federal inspection standards are marked, or stamped, in abbreviated form, "U. S. Inspected and Passed." This stamp also bears the official number of the establishment. The marking fluid used for this stamp is a vegetable coloring and is harmless. It need not be trimmed from the meat.

The United States official grades, in their respective order for the different kinds of meat, are: 1st grade, U.S. Prime; 2nd grade, U.S. Choice; 3rd grade, U.S. Good; 4th grade, U.S. Standard; 5th grade, U.S. Commercial; 6th grade, U.S. Utility.

The grades known as cutter, canner, and cull are not sold at retail. There is little or no difference in the food value of various grades and cuts of meat, and inexpensive meat may be prepared tastily.

The grades of beef, veal, pork, lamb, and mutton are determined by the (1) conformation, (2) finish, and (3) quality of the individual carcasses or wholesale cuts.

Following is a brief description of each of the seven grades of beef. With two exceptions these descriptions also apply quite closely to veal, pork, lamb, and mutton. The exceptions

This stamp shows that the meat was federally graded.

The round purple stamp used for marking meat to show that it has passed federal inspection. The number of the establishment appears in the space occupied by three ciphers.

Look for the labels that help you buy wisely.

are: (1) Veal does not have the firmness of flesh or as much fat, either as an outside covering or deposited in the lean, as the comparable grades of beef. (2) The figures concerning the comparative amounts of fat in the various grades are not necessarily the same for the other kinds of meat.

PRIME is the highest grade of beef obtainable. The meat is firm and the cut surface shows a pronounced marbling of or intermingling of fat with the lean. A smooth, heavy outside covering of fat and liberal deposits of fat in the lean are the outstanding characteristics of prime beef. The very limited quantity of this grade (probably less than 1 percent of the total beef supply) is used largely in exclusive restaurants, hotels and clubs.

CHOICE is the highest grade of beef widely available throughout the year. It has a smooth, moderately thick fat covering and there is an extensive marbling of fat with the lean. Fifteen percent, or less, of the total supply of beef comes within this grade.

GOOD is the most popular grade of beef. It normally represents from 25 to 35 percent of the total beef supply, or more than twice the total tonnage of the prime and choice grades combined. The fat covering is usually slightly thinner and the marbling less extensive than in the next higher grade.

COMMERCIAL ranks fourth in the grading scale, second in the total tonnage of beef sold at retail. This grade is popular with those who want leaner and lower-priced meat. The fat covering is usually thin and the cut surface may show practically no marbling. The cuts from the rib and loin may be roasted and broiled. The other cuts should be cooked by moist heat.

Appearance of meat: The more important characteristics of meat are conformation, finish, and quality. Conformation refers to the general build, form, shape, contour, or outline of the carcass, side or cut. Good conformation implies short necks and shanks, deep plump rounds, thick backs with full loins, and well-fleshed ribs and shoulders.

The term "finish" refers specifically to the quality, amount, color, and distribution of fat. The best finish implies abundant marbling (intermingling of fat with lean) and a smooth even covering of firm fat over the exterior surface of the carcass, side or cut. The fat of meat is very important because palata-

---

## SELECTION OF BEEF CUTS

---

| CHARACTERISTICS | COOKING METHODS |
|---|---|
| **ROUND**—Round Steak (full cut): Round or oval shape with small round bone. One large muscle, three smaller ones. | B |
| Top Round Steak: Most tender portion of round. Is one large muscle. | Br; Pb; Pf; B |
| Bottom Round Steak: Not so tender as top round. Distinguished from top round by having two muscles. | B |
| Tip Roast or Steak: Triangular cut; roast may contain kneecap. Steaks are boneless. | R; Br; Pb; Pf; B |
| Standing Rump: Triangular in shape; contains portions of aitch (rump) bone and tailbone. Knuckle end of leg (round) bone usually removed. | B, R |
| Rolled Rump: Boneless roll. | B, R |
| Heel of Round: Boneless wedge-shaped cut from lower part of round. Weighs 4 to 6 lbs. Has very little fat and is least tender cut of round. | B, C |
| Hind Shank: Bony, considerable connective tissue, rich in extractives. | B; C |
| **SIRLOIN**—Sirloin Steak: Contains portions of back bone and hip bone. Wide variation in bone and muscle structure of the various steaks. | Br; Pb; Pf |
| Pin bone Sirloin Steak: Lies next to the porterhouse. Contains pin bone which is the forward end of hip bone. | Br; Pb; Pf |
| Boneless Sirloin Steak: Any boneless steak from the sirloin. | Br; Pb; Pf |
| **SHORT LOIN**—Porterhouse Steak: Largest muscle above T-bone. Tenderloin muscle is largest in this steak. Deposit of fat between flank (tail) and tenderloin. Cut across the grain | Br; Pb; Pf |
| T-Bone Steak: Somewhat smaller in area than porterhouse. Tenderloin muscle gradually growing smaller. | Br; Pb; Pf |
| Club Steak: Triangular shaped, smallest steak in short loin. Tenderloin has practically disappeared. | Br; Pb; Pf |
| **TENDERLOIN**—Tenderloin Roast or Steak: Tender; boneless. | R; Br; Pb; Pf |
| **FLANK**—Flank Steak: Oval shaped boneless steak weighing ¾ to 1½ pounds. Muscles run lengthwise; usually scored to shorten fibers. Less tender cut. | B |
| Flank Meat: Boneless, coarse fibers. | B; C |
| **RIB**—Standing Rib (10" ribs): Contains usually two or more ribs. The rib eye is largest in the 12th rib numbering from the neck back. | R |
| Standing Rib (7" ribs): Referred to as a short cut rib roast because the ribs are cut 7 inches long instead of 10 inches. | R |
| Rolled Rib: Bones are removed and the thin portion rolled around the rib eye and tied securely. | R |
| Rib Steak: Contains rib eye and may contain rib bone. | Br; Pb; Pf |
| Short Ribs: Cut from ends of ribs; layers of lean and fat. | B; C |
| **SHORT PLATE**—Plate Beef: Cut across plate parallel with ribs. | B; C |
| Boneless Plate: When rolled, the absence of the rib eye distinguishes this cut from the rolled rib. | B; C |
| Short Ribs: Cut from ends of ribs; layers of lean and fat. | B; C |
| **REGULAR CHUCK**—Arm Pot-roast or Steak: Has a round bone and cross sections of 3 to 5 ribs. A small round muscle near the round bone is surrounded by connective tissue | B |
| Blade Pot-roast or Steak: Pot-roast contains portions of rib and blade bones. Steaks cut between ribs will not contain rib bone. | B |
| Boneless Chuck: Any part of the regular chuck (except the neck) from which the bones have been removed. | B |
| Boneless Neck: Any part of the neck without the neck bone. | B; C |
| English (Boston) Cut: A rectangular piece cut across 2 or 3 chuck ribs. | B |
| **BRISKET**—Brisket: Layers of lean and fat. Presence of breast bone sure indication that cut is from the brisket. | B; C |
| Boneless Brisket: Same as above with ribs and breast bone removed. | B; C |
| **FORE SHANK**—Shank Knuckle: Knuckle or upper end of fore shank. | B; C |
| Shank Cross-Cuts: Small pieces cut across shank bone. | B; C |
| **GROUND BEEF**—Loaf and Patties: Usually made from flank, shanks, plate and chuck. | R; Br; Pb; Pf |

B, Braise; Br, Broil; C, Cook in liquid; Pb, Panbroil; Pf, Panfry; R, Roast

# Meat Cuts and How to Cook Them
## BEEF CHART

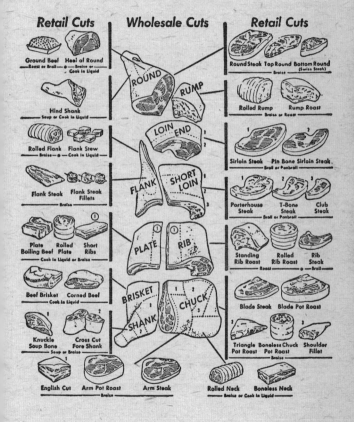

### Retail Cuts

Ground Beef — Heel of Round
Roast or Broil — Braise or Cook in Liquid

Hind Shank
Soup or Cook in Liquid

Rolled Flank — Flank Stew
Braise — Cook in Liquid

Flank Steak — Flank Steak Fillets
Braise

Plate Boiling Beef — Rolled Plate — Short Ribs
Cook in Liquid or Braise

Beef Brisket — Corned Beef
Cook in Liquid

Knuckle Soup Bone — Cross Cut Fore Shank
Soup or Braise

English Cut — Arm Pot Roast — Arm Steak
Braise

### Wholesale Cuts

ROUND
RUMP
LOIN END
FLANK — SHORT LOIN
PLATE — RIB
BRISKET — CHUCK
SHANK

### Retail Cuts

Round Steak — Top Round — Bottom Round (Swiss Steak)
Braise

Rolled Rump — Rump Roast
Braise or Roast

Sirloin Steak — Pin Bone Sirloin Steak
Broil or Panbroil

Porterhouse Steak — T-Bone Steak — Club Steak
Broil or Panbroil

Standing Rib Roast — Rolled Rib Roast — Rib Steak
Roast — Broil

Blade Steak — Blade Pot Roast

Triangle Pot Roast — Boneless Chuck Pot Roast — Shoulder Fillet
Braise

Rolled Neck — Boneless Neck
Braise or Cook in Liquid

## SELECTION OF VEAL CUTS

| CHARACTERISTICS | COOKING METHODS |
|---|---|
| **LEG**—Leg: May be cut long or short. Long cut leg includes the sirloin, while the short cut leg corresponds to beef round. | R; B |
| Leg, Rump Off: Includes the shank and center sections of either the long cut or short cut leg. | R; B |
| Shank Half of Leg: Lower half of leg. | R; B |
| Rump Half of Leg: Upper half of leg. | R; B |
| Center Cut of Leg (Round): Leg with rump and shank off. | R; B |
| Round Steaks (Cutlets): Same muscle and bone structure as beef round steaks. | B; Pf |
| Sirloin Roast: Corresponds to sirloin of beef. Contains hip and back bones. | R; B |
| Sirloin Steaks: Same as above except cut into steaks. | B; Pf |
| Sirloin-Rump Roast: Includes the sirloin and rump sections of the long cut leg. Contains pelvic (hip and aitch) bone, tail bone and part of back bone. | R; B |
| Standing Rump: Contains aitch or rump bone, tail bone, and usually a part of leg bone | R; B |
| Boneless Rump: Boneless roll. | R; B |
| Heel of Round: Wedge-shaped boneless piece—same as in beef. | R; B; C |
| Hind Shank: Considerable bone and connective tissue. | C |
| **LOIN**—Loin Roast: Corresponds to beef short loin. Contains back bone and three separate muscles—loin eye, tenderloin and flank. | R; B |
| Loin Chops: Same as above except cut into chops. Corresponds to porterhouse, T-bone and club beef steaks. | B; Pf |
| Kidney Chops: Cut to contain cross section of kidney. Made from rib end of loin. | B; Pf |
| Flank: Comparable to beef flank. | B; C |
| **FORESADDLE**—Standing Rib Roast: Similar to standing beef rib roast. | R; B |
| Rib Chops: Same as above except cut into chops. Contains rib bone and rib eye, except chops cut between ribs have no rib bone. | B; Pf |
| Blade Roast: Includes that section of the shoulder which contains the blade bone. | R; B |
| Blade Steaks (Chops): Contain blade bone and rib bone except chops cut between ribs have no rib bone. | B; Pf |
| Arm Roast: Includes arm section of shoulder. Contains arm bone and cross sections of 4 or 5 ribs. | R; B |
| Arm Steaks (Chops): Same as above except cut into slices. | B; Pf |
| Square Cut Shoulder: Thickest part of forequarter. Shoulder with standing rib, breast, and fore shank removed. Neck may be removed. | R; B |
| Rolled Shoulder: Boneless roll. | R; B |
| Breast: Corresponds to short plate and brisket of beef. Thin, flat cut containing rib ends and breast bone. | B; C |
| Breast with pocket: Same as above with pocket cut between ribs and lean. | R; B |
| Riblets: Breast bone is removed (usually). Breast is separated into riblets by cutting between ribs. | B; C |
| Fore Shank: Contains considerable bone and connective tissue. Varying amounts of lean. Rich in gelatin-forming substance. | B; C |
| City Chicken: Boneless cubes of veal fastened together on a wooden or metal skewer | B |
| **GROUND VEAL**—Loaf and Patties: Usually made from flank, breast, shank and neck. | R; B; Pf |
| Mock Chicken Legs: Ground veal molded into shape of chicken legs with wooden skewer to represent leg bone. | B; Pf |

B, Braise; Br, Broil; C, Cook in liquid; Pb, Panbroil; Pf, Panfry; R, Roast.

# Meat Cuts and How to Cook Them

# VEAL CHART

**Retail Cuts**

Veal Rump Roast — Rolled Veal Rump Roast
— Roast or Braise —

Loin Veal Chop — Sirloin Veal Steak — Kidney Veal Chop
— Braise —

Veal Crown Roast — Veal Rib Chop (Frenched) — Veal Rib Roast
— Roast — — Braise — — Roast —

Blade Veal Roast — Arm Veal Roast
— Roast or Braise —

Blade Veal Steak — Arm Veal Steak
— Braise —

Rolled Veal Shoulder Roast — City Chicken
— Braise or Roast — — Braise —

**Wholesale Cuts**

ROUND
LOIN
RIB
BREAST
SHOULDER
SHANK

**Retail Cuts**

Heel of Veal Round — Veal Hind Shank
— Braise or Cook in Liquid —

Veal Round Steak (Cutlet) — Veal Round Roast
— Braise — — Braise or Roast —

Veal Scallops — Veal Rosettes
— Braise —

Veal Breast
— Braise or Cook in Liquid —

Mock Chicken Legs — Veal Loaf
— Braise — — Roast —

Veal Riblets — Veal Stew
— Braise or Cook in Liquid — — Cook in Liquid —

Veal Fore Shank — Veal Patties
— Cook in Liquid — — Braise —

## SELECTION OF LAMB CUTS

| CHARACTERISTICS | COOKING METHODS |
|---|---|
| **LEG**—Long Cut Leg: Corresponds to the round and sirloin of beef................... | R |
| Short Cut Leg: Same as above except with sirloin section removed.................. | R |
| Shank Half of Leg: Lower half of leg............................................... | R |
| Sirloin Half of Leg: Upper half of leg; usually includes sirloin section............ | R |
| Leg Chops (Steaks): Round cut with small round bone. Comparable to beef round steaks | Br; Pb; Pf |
| Sirloin Chops: Correspond to beef sirloin steaks. Pinbone chops have considerable bone | Br; Pb; Pf |
| Boneless Sirloin Roast: Two unsplit sirloins with bones removed and meat sewed or tied into shape. | R |
| **LOIN**—Loin Roast: Corresponds to beef short loin. It can be the unsplit loin but is usually one side of the split loin. | R |
| Loin Chops: Contain T-shaped bones; correspond to porterhouse, T-bone, and club beef steaks. | Br; Pb; Pf |
| English Chops: Cut across the unsplit loin. Back bone removed and boneless chop skewered into shape. | Br; Pb; Pf |
| Flank: Corresponds to beef flank.................................................. | C |
| **RACK**—Rib Roast: Contains rib bones and rib eye muscle.......................... | R |
| Crown Roast: Ribs are "frenched" that is, meat is removed from rib ends, then two or more rib sections are shaped and tied into a "crown" | R |
| Rib Chops: Contain rib bone and rib eye muscle.................................. | Br; Pb; Pf |
| Frenched Chops: Same as rib chops except meat is removed from ends of ribs........ | Br; Pb; Pf |
| **YOKE (Triangle)**—Triangle: Forequarter with rack (rib) removed. Includes shoulder, neck, breast, and fore shank. | R; B |
| Rolled Triangle: Same as above except with bones removed and meat tied into a boneless roll. | R; B |
| Cross Cut Shoulder: Forward section of forequarter including shoulder, neck, fore shank, and tip of breast. Contains 3 to 5 ribs. | R; B |
| Mock Duck: Outer portion of shoulder with blade and arm bones removed but shank bone left in. Shaped like a duck. | R |
| **BREAST AND SHANK**—Breast: Corresponds to short plate and brisket of beef. Narrow strip of meat containing breast bone and ends of 12 ribs. | R; B; C |
| Breast with Pocket: Same as above but with pocket between ribs and lean.......... | R; B |
| Rolled Breast: Small boneless roll. Alternating layers of lean and fat............ | R; B |
| Riblets: Breast bone removed and breast cut between ribs. Each small piece contains part of a rib bone. | B; C |
| Fore Shank: Contains shank and elbow bones...................................... | B; C |
| **4-RIB SHOULDER**—Square Cut Shoulder: Thickest part of forequarter, with shank, breast rib (rack), and neck removed. | R |
| Rolled Shoulder: Boneless roll made from square cut shoulder.................... | R |
| Cushion Shoulder: Boned and left flat. Sewed on two sides. One side may be left open or stuffing, then skewered and sewed. | R |
| Arm Chops: Contain small round bone and usually the cross section of 4 or 5 rib bones | Br; Pb; Pf; B |
| Blade Chops: Contain portions of rib, back and blade bones...................... | Br; Ph; Pf; B |
| Neck Slices: Round slice with neck vertebrae in center......................... | B; C |
| **GROUND LAMB**—Loaf and Patties: Usually made from flank, breast, shank, and neck.. | R; Br; Pb; Pf |

B, Braise; Br, Broil; C, Cook in liquid; Pb, Panbroil; Pf, Panfry; R, Roast.

# Meat Cuts and How to Cook Them

## LAMB CHART

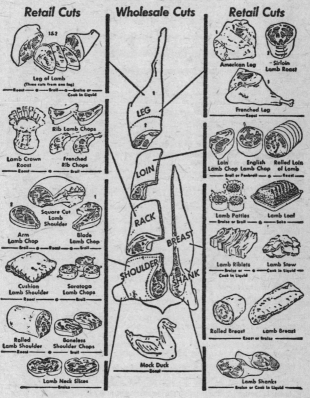

**Retail Cuts**  **Wholesale Cuts**  **Retail Cuts**

1&2

Leg of Lamb
(These cuts from one leg)
— Roast — ● — Broil — ● — Braise or —
Cook in Liquid

Rib Lamb Chops

Lamb Crown Roast
— Roast —

Frenched Rib Chops
— Broil —

Square Cut Lamb Shoulder

Arm Lamb Chop
— Broil — ● — Roast —

Blade Lamb Chop
— Broil —

Cushion Lamb Shoulder
— Roast —

Saratoga Lamb Chops
— Broil —

Rolled Lamb Shoulder
— Roast —

Boneless Shoulder Chops
— Broil —

Lamb Neck Slices
— Braise —

LEG

LOIN

RACK

BREAST

SHOULDER

SHANK

Mock Duck
— Roast —

American Leg

Sirloin Lamb Roast

Frenched Leg
— Roast —

Loin Lamb Chop

English Lamb Chop
— Broil or Panbroil —

Rolled Loin of Lamb
— Roast —

Lamb Patties
— Braise or Broil —

Lamb Loaf
— Bake —

Lamb Riblets
— Braise or Cook in Liquid —

Lamb Stew
— Cook in Liquid —

Rolled Breast
— Roast or Braise —

Lamb Breast

Lamb Shanks
— Braise or Cook in Liquid —

## SELECTION OF PORK CUTS

| CHARACTERISTICS | COOKING METHODS |
|---|---|
| **HAM (Leg)—Ham (smoked):** Corresponds to beef round with tail bone and portion of back bone removed. Heavier outer covering of fat than other meats. Outer skin or rind is left on regular ham and is removed from skinned ham... | R (bake); C |
| Ham or Leg (fresh): Same as above except not cured and smoked.................. | R |
| Rolled Fresh Ham (Leg) Roast: Boneless roll................................... | R |
| Half Ham (Leg), shank end (smoked or fresh): Shank, or lower half of smoked ham or fresh leg of pork | |
| Ham Shank or Hock (smoked or fresh): Wedge-shaped piece. Contains shank bones | R (bake); C |
| | C |
| Center Cut Ham (Leg) Roast or Steaks (smoked or fresh): Oval shape with small bone. | Smoked: R; Br; Pb; Fresh: R; B; Pf |
| Half Ham (Leg), Butt end (smoked or fresh): Adjacent to loin. Contains aitch bone and part of leg bone................................................ | R (bake); C |
| Ham (Leg) Butt (smoked or fresh): Same as above except this cut contains practically none of the center cut section of the ham or leg.................................. | R (bake); C |
| Ham (Leg) Butt Slices (Steaks) (smoked or fresh): Slices from the cut above. More bone than center slice................................................ | Smoked: Br; P Pf Fresh: B; Pf |
| **LOIN—Loin:** Corresponds to the rib, short loin, and sirloin of beef. Extends from shoulder to fresh ham or leg. Contains the tenderloin and the boneless back strip (eye or back muscle). | R |
| Tenderloin (whole or frenched): Long, tapering round muscle. Weighs about ½ to ¾ lb. | Whole—R Frenched—B; Pf |
| Boneless Loin Roast: Consists of the back strip or eye of the loin. Two strips are often tied together to form a roll from which various size roasts may be cut.................. | R |
| Canadian Style Bacon: Boneless back strip or eye of loin, cured and smoked........ | R; Br; Pb; Pf |
| Butterfly Pork Chops: Double chops cut from the boneless back strip............. | B; Pf |
| Half Loin (ham end): Corresponds to the trimmed full loin of beef—that is, the short loin and sirloin................................................ | R |
| Sirloin Roast or Chops: Ham end of the loin containing the hip bone............... | R; B; Pf |
| Half Loin (shoulder end): Corresponds to shortcut beef rib roast, contains more ribs... | R |
| Blade Loin Roast or Chops: Shoulder end of the loin containing the blade bone....... | R; B; Pf |
| Center Cut Loin Roast: Section of loin between hip bone and blade bone........... | R; B; Pf |
| Loin Chops: Loin chops may be cut from any section of the loin but the true loin chops are those corresponding to porterhouse, T-bone and club beef steaks.................. | B; Pf |
| Rib Chops: Contain the eye muscle or back strip. When cut thick each chop will have a rib bone; cut thin, every other chop will have a rib bone.......................... | B; Pf |
| Crown Roast: Made from two or more rib sections. Corresponds to the crown lamb roast | R |
| **SHOULDER—Shoulder Roast:** Whole shoulder includes both the picnic shoulder and the Boston Butt................................................ | R |
| Shoulder, hock off: Includes the Boston butt and the picnic shoulder, without the hock. Contains arm and blade bones................................ | R |
| **PICNIC SHOULDER—Picnic Shoulder (smoked or fresh):** Lower half of the shoulder. Contains arm and fore shank (hock) bones.................................. | R; C |
| Cushion Picnic Shoulder: Arm section of picnic shoulder. Does not include hock. Arm bone removed and opening left to insert stuffing.............................. | R |
| Rolled Picnic Shoulder: Boneless roll. May include meat from hock (shank)........ | R |
| Arm Steaks (Chops): Oval at one end and squared off at other. Small round bone..... | B; Pf |
| Shoulder Hock (smoked or fresh): Wedge-shaped. Contains fore shank (hock) bones | B; Pf |
| **BOSTON BUTT—Boston Butt Roast:** Upper half of shoulder. Contains blade bone...... | R |
| Rolled Boston Butt: Made by boning and rolling Boston butt........................ | R |
| Blade Steaks (Chops): Made from Boston butt. Most steaks contain section of blade bone | B; Pf |
| Smoked Shoulder Butt: Eye of Boston butt. Boneless roll weighing 3 to 5 pounds...... | Whole—R (bake); C Sliced—Br; P Pf |
| **SIDE (Belly)—Bacon (sliced or in the piece):** Corresponds to the flank, short plate and brisket of beef. Spareribs are removed leaving boneless piece, the bacon strip, which is cured and smoked................................................ | Br; Pb; Pf; C |
| Side Pork (fresh or salt): Same as above except fresh, or cured in salt, but not smoked | Fresh—B; Pf Salt—C; Pf |
| **SPARERIBS—Spareribs:** Ribs and breast bone which have been removed from bacon strip | R; B; C |

# Meat Cuts and How to Cook Them

## PORK CHART

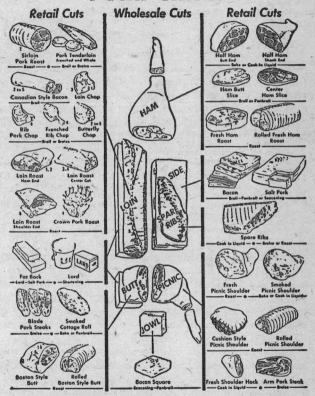

**Retail Cuts** — **Wholesale Cuts** — **Retail Cuts**

Sirloin Pork Roast — Roast

Pork Tenderloin Frenched and Whole — Broil or Braise

Canadian Style Bacon — Broil

Loin Chop

Rib Pork Chop

Frenched Rib Chop

Butterfly Chop — Broil or Braise

Loin Roast Ham End

Loin Roast Center Cut

Loin Roast Shoulder End

Crown Pork Roast — Roast

Fat Back — Lard · Salt Pork

Lard — Shortening

Blade Pork Steaks — Braise

Smoked Cottage Roll — Bake or Panbroil

Boston Style Butt

Rolled Boston Style Butt — Roast

HAM

LOIN

SIDE

SPARE RIBS

BUTT

PICNIC

JOWL

Bacon Square — Seasoning · Panbroil

Half Ham Butt End

Half Ham Shank End — Bake or Cook in Liquid

Ham Butt Slice

Center Ham Slice — Broil or Panbroil

Fresh Ham Roast

Rolled Fresh Ham Roast — Roast

Bacon — Broil · Panbroil or Seasoning

Salt Pork

Spare Ribs — Cook in Liquid · Braise or Roast

Fresh Picnic Shoulder — Roast

Smoked Picnic Shoulder — Bake or Cook in Liquid

Cushion Style Picnic Shoulder

Rolled Picnic Shoulder — Roast

Fresh Shoulder Hock — Cook in Liquid

Arm Pork Steak — Braise

---

JOWL—Jowl Bacon Square: Made from the trimmed jowl, cured and smoked.......... C; Br; Pb; Pf
FEET—Pig's Feet: Either fresh, or pickled and ready to eat............................. Fresh—C; B

B, Braise; Br, Broil; C, Cook in liquid; Pb, Panbroil; Pf, Panfry; R, Roast.

bility, which includes juiciness, depends upon a certain proportion of fat being present.

The term quality has to do with the factors which affect the palatability of the cooked meat. Quality refers to certain characteristics of the lean and fat. It is related primarily to the firmness and strength of the muscle fibers and connective tissue, since these affect the tenderness of the meat. It also involves the amount, consistency, and character of the juices and extractives. Although cooked meat should yield a high proportion of juice, the uncooked meat should be of such a consistency that the flesh when chilled remains firm and resilient. Best quality implies a well-marbled lean, fine-grained meat, with color typical of the meat being judged.

The factors of conformation, finish, and quality are the measuring sticks used in judging beef, veal, pork, lamb, and mutton, but they will differ to some extent with each of the five meats. For example, veal shows practically no marbling of fat with the lean; consequently the flesh is less firm than is found in comparable grades of beef. Veal also has a moderately thin outside covering of fat as compared with beef. The firmness and color of the fat varies with the five meats and from grade to grade for each kind of meat. Generally speaking, the fat of each kind of meat is progressively firmer as the meat increases in grade. Lamb and mutton produce the hardest fat with the highest melting point, while pork fat is the softest with the lowest melting point.

Pork is merchandised somewhat differently than the other meats since it is almost completely processed into relatively small cuts, lard, and sausage products before leaving the packing plant. This meat does not come under the official grading service, but is graded by the packer on a quality and weight basis. Many of the cuts, especially those which have been cured and smoked, carry identifiable packer brands.

Pork should be firm and marbled, greyish pink in color. Hams should be short and plump with smooth, thin skins free from hair. Pork should always be cooked thoroughly, until it is white clear through. This kills trichinae which frequently infest pork. Trichinae are also killed by refrigeration (5° F. for 20 days).

Aging of meat: Meat is sometimes aged to develop palatability, tenderness and flavor. The meats most frequently aged are high quality beef and mutton. Lamb of high quality is sometimes aged, but aging does not improve veal and pork. To be suitable for aging the meat must have a fairly thick covering of fat to prevent discoloration of the lean and to keep evaporation at a minimum. Only the higher grades of beef, mutton and lamb have a sufficiently thick fat covering to stand aging for the necessary period (3 to 6 weeks at temperatures of from 34° F. to 38° F.).

## MEAT, POULTRY AND FISH LOSS CHART

The real cost of meat and fish is not in the price per pound at the butcher shop. Meats lose poundage in fats, bones, and waste products as well as in cooking. The following table indicates percentage of average food waste between counter and table. Amount of bone and fat trimmed off will, of course, affect each purchase differently.

### PERCENT OF WASTE AND LOSS

**Meat**

Beef
- Rib roast, medium ........57
- Plate pot roast ............53
- Porterhouse steak .........40
- Bottom round, stew ........38

Lamb
- Leg, roast .................58
- Loin chops ................56
- Breast, stew ..............51

Veal
- Cutlet ....................51
- Breast, stew ..............60

**Fish**

- Halibut steak, baked ........29
- Flounder, pan fried .........49
- Mackerel, baked. ............40
- Cod steaks, steamed .........39
- Salmon steak, baked ........48

**Fowl**

- Hens (Fowl) ................36
- Roaster ....................37
- Broiler ....................39
- Turkey ....................32

### HOW MUCH TO BUY PER PORTION

**Meat**

Large amount of bone
   and gristle ........½- 1 lb.

Moderate amount of
   bone and gristle ...⅓-½ lb.

Little bone and
   gristle ............¼-⅓ lb.

Chopped meat .......¼-⅓ lb.

**Fish**

Whole or round fish .. 1 lb.
Large fish, dressed
   (head off, cleaned) .½ lb.
Steaks or fillets .......⅓ lb.

**Poultry**

For broiling .......¼-½ bird
For frying .........¾- 1 lb.
For stewing .......⅓-¾ lb.

Number of persons served with two pounds of meat: Boneless meats (flank steaks, hamburgers, rolled roasts, tenderloin, liver, kidneys, sausages, brains, sweetbreads, most canned meats), serve 8.

Meats with little bone (leg of lamb, round rib, breast of veal or lamb, pot roast, ham), serve 6.

Meats with substantial bone (shoulder cuts, spare ribs, short ribs, chops, breast, brisket, plate, most steaks), serve 4.

## POULTRY CHART

| | Age in Weeks | Weight In Lbs. | Quantity to buy per person | How to Prepare | | | | |
|---|---|---|---|---|---|---|---|---|
| | | | | Broil | Fry | Roast | Stew | Braise |
| **CHICKEN** | | | | | | | | |
| Broilers (1) | 6-14 | 1-2½ | ¼ to ½ bird | X | X | X | | |
| Fryers (2) | 14-20 | 2½-3½ | ¾-1 lb. | | X | X | | |
| Roasters (3) | 21-39 | 3½ plus | ½-¾ lb. | | X | X | | |
| Capons (4) | 17-44 | 6 plus | ½-¾ lb. | | | X | | |
| Pullets (5) | 17-39 | 2½-5½ | ½-¾ lb. | | X | X | | |
| Fowls (Hens) (6) | 52 plus | 3-8 | ¼-¾ lb. | | | | X | X |
| Roosters | 104-156 | 4-10 | ½-1 lb. | | | | X | X |
| **TURKEYS** | | | | | | | | |
| Young Toms | 26-52 | 12-21 | ¾-1 lb. | | | X | | |
| Young Hens | 26-52 | 6-16 | ¾-1 lb. | | | X | | |
| Old Toms | 52 plus | 16-30 | ¾-1 lb. | | | X | | |
| Old Hens | 52 plus | 10-18 | ¾-1 lb. | | | X | | |
| Ducks | 6-12 | 3½-6 | 1 lb. | | | X | | X |
| Geese | 14-52 | 10-12 | 1¼-1½ lb. | | | X | | X |
| Guineas | 6-12 | 2-3½ | 1 bird | X | | X | | |
| Squabs | 14 | ¾-1¼ | 1 bird | X | | X | | |

CHARACTERISTICS:

(1) Smooth, thin skin; tender muscles; very thin connective tissue; little fat under skin, over the back; flexible tipped breastbone.

(2) Same as above except size and age, enough meat to be disjointed and cut into serving pieces. Noticeable layering of fat beneath skin.

(3) Tender, soft-meated muscles. Smooth skin. Large enough and meaty enough to be roasted whole. Excellent layering of fat beneath skin. Flexible tipped breastbone. Connective tissue thin but slightly more developed than in fryer.

(4) Excellent in finish, flavor and tenderness brought about by caponizing. Full-breasted with high proportion of white meat.

(5) Similar to roaster except body is shorter and plumper. Flexible tipped breastbone; smaller weights often marketed as fryers.

(6) Less Tender Meat: Thick, coarse skin. Muscles well-developed with thick connective tissue. High proportion of fat beneath skin. Breastbone not flexible.

## HOW TO BUY POULTRY

Correct selection is the first step to delicious chicken. The use to which it is put and the style of service determine the kind of bird to be purchased.

In selecting poultry look for pliable cartilage at the bottom of the breastbone, yellow fat under the skin, firm meat, ample flesh and fat on breast and legs. Birds properly dressed have clean skins, feet, crop, and no pinfeathers, bruises, or discoloration of the wings. Body should be plump and full-breasted, with firm tender skin, white or yellow in color. In young birds, breastbone should be soft and flexible, leg scabs should be soft, smooth and yellow, claws should be sharp and long. Large birds have more meat in relation to bone and are usually better buys. Deterioration begins under the wings and can usually be detected by odor or stickiness. Government grades are Grade AA, U. S. Prime (Grade A), U. S. Choice (Grade B), and U. S. Commercial (Grade C).

Chicken styles available: READY-TO-COOK CHICKEN (EVISCERATED): This style is drawn and cleaned ready for cooking. It may be fresh or frozen fresh and is usually government inspected and individually packaged. It may be whole, disjointed, halved, or quartered. Ready-to-cook chickens are also sold by-the-piece either fresh or frozen fresh. This style allows the purchase of any part of the chicken in any amount.

DRESSED (FORMERLY NEW YORK DRESSED): This style has head and feet on, the feathers are removed but bird is not drawn. The retailer will usually draw and cut the chicken.

## HOW TO BUY FISH

How to select fish: Insist upon freshness. A fresh fish may be recognized by the following: firm and elastic flesh, scales that cling to the skin in most species, reddish gills free from disagreeable odor, eyes bright and full, not sunken. In selecting shellfish like clams and oysters, be sure that the shells are tightly shut, indicating that the animals are alive, unless you prefer to buy the meat separately as shucked shellfish. Crabs and lobsters should be bought alive or as cooked meat. However, uncooked shrimp may be bought in the shell provided it feels firm to the touch. Cooked shrimp is sold either with or without the shell, with the heads already removed.

## FRESH WATER FISH

| Name | Sold | Weight in lbs. | Fat or lean | Broil | Bake | Fry | Panfry | Steam |
|------|------|----------------|-------------|-------|------|-----|--------|-------|
| Buffalo Fish | R, D, Dr, S | 5-15 | F | | X | X | | X |
| Carp | R, F | 2-8 | F | | X | X | | X |
| Catfish | R, Dr | 1-10 | F | | X | X | X | |
| Lake Herring | R, D, F | ⅓-1 | L | X | X | | | |
| Lake Trout | D, Dr, F | 1½-10 | F | X | X | X | X | |
| Smelts | R | 1/12-⅛ | F | X | X | X | | |
| Whitefish | R, D, Dr, F | 2-6 | F | X | X | | | |
| Yellow Perch | R, F | ½-1 | L | X | X | | X | |
| Yellow Pike | R, Dr, F | 1½-10 | L | | X | | | X |

## SALT WATER FISH

| Name | Sold | Weight in lbs. | Fat or lean | Broil | Bake | Fry | Panfry | Steam |
|------|------|----------------|-------------|-------|------|-----|--------|-------|
| Bluefish | R, D | 1-7 | L | X | X | X | X | |
| Butterfish | R, P | ¼-1¼ | F | X | X | X | | |
| Cod | D, Dr, S, F | 3-20 | L | X | X | | X | X |
| Flounder | R, Dr, P, S, F | ¾-6 | L | X | X | | X | X |
| Haddock | R, D, F, S | 1½-7 | L | X | X | | X | X |
| Hake | Dr, S, F | 2-5 | L | X | X | | X | |
| Halibut | S | 8-75 | L | X | | | | |
| Mackerel | R, Dr, F | ¾-3 | F | X | X | | X | X |
| Mullet | R | ½-5 | L | X | X | | X | X |
| Pollack | D, Dr, S, F | 3-14 | L | X | X | X | | X |
| Pompano | R, P | ½-3 | F | X | X | | | X |
| Porgie | R, Dr, F | ½-2 | F | X | X | | | |
| Red Snapper | D, S | 2-15 | L | X | X | X | | |
| Rosefish | F | ½-1¼ | | X | X | | | |
| Salmon | D, Dr, S, F | 5-30 | F | X | X | | | X |
| Sea Bass | R, P, F | ¼-4 | L | X | X | X | X | X |
| Sea Trout | R, D, F | 1-6 | F | X | X | | | |
| Shad | R, D, Dr, F | 1-6 | F | X | X | | | |
| Smelt | R | 1/12-⅛ | F | X | X | X | X | |
| Striped Bass | R, F | 2-15 | F | X | X | X | X | |
| Swordfish | Dr, S, P | 60-700 | L | X | X | X | X | |
| Tuna | S | 10-700 | F | X | X | | | X |
| Weakfish | R, F | 2-12 | L | X | X | X | X | X |
| Whiting | D, Dr, F | ½-1½ | L | X | X | | X | |

R, round; D, drawn; P, pan dressed; S, steaks; F, fillets. Dr, dressed

**When to buy:** In general, the fish of any species are of highest food quality when most abundant, for at these periods fishermen are making their catches in the shortest time and shipping them promptly. Usually, but not always, fish are cheapest when most abundant.

**Common market forms:** FRESH (refrigerated) fish and completely frozen fish should be equally good if the freezing is done by the modern methods. Both are marketed in a variety of convenient forms, as follows:

WHOLE OR ROUND FISH are those marketed in the form in which they come from the water, and are of three kinds: fish that keep as well or better without dressing, e.g., small fishes, or the small sizes of larger species. Before cooking, whole or round fish are eviscerated, and in all but the very small sizes, the heads, scales and sometimes the fins are removed.

DRAWN FISH are those marketed with only the entrails removed. To prepare these fish for cooking, the heads, scales, and (if desired) the fins are removed, and the fish may be split or cut into serving portions if too large to be cooked whole.

FILLETS are meaty slices cut lengthwise from the sides of the fish. Fillets contain no bones or other waste. Their weight varies with the size of the fish from which they are cut.

STOCKS are crosswise or lengthwise cuts of fillets.

CANNED FISH: Besides the familiar canned salmon, tuna, and sardines, many kinds of fish are canned for use in main dishes and appetizers.

SALT OR SMOKED FISH: Variations in the menu are provided by salt or smoked fish. Salt fish ordinarily requires one-half to several hours' soaking before further preparation. Smoked fish usually is ready to eat as it is, or may be heated.

**Fat content of fish:** For best results in preparing a fresh fish, it is always desirable to know whether it is fat or lean. Fat fish are especially suitable for baking, and may also be broiled, while lean fish are best adapted to steaming, boiling, and frying. Medium fat fish are prepared like the lean, or may be dressed with strips of salt pork or bacon and baked.

## COMMENTS ON CANNED FISH

CLAMS: Should have a bright color when opened. Dark color indicates staleness, bad flavor.

CRABS: Colors rapidly when canned. Shredded. Good flavor.

JAPANESE CRABMEAT: Solid pieces. Good flavor.

CODFISH: Many varieties of fish are canned under this label.

LOBSTER: Discoloration is common. Flavor is not generally good.

OYSTERS: Flavor is good. Watch out for unfilled cans.

SALMON:

    CHINOOK: Pink to red. Oil content 20 percent. Large flakes. Best flavor. For salads.

    RED: High oil content. Good flavor. For salads.

    COHO: Orange. For salads or cooking.

    PINK: Pink. Little oil. For salads, sandwiches, cooking. Good flavor.

    CHUM: White to pink. Oil content 4 percent. For cooking, catfood.

TUNA: Available as fancy, standard, flakes, pieces, shredded and grated. There are four official grades.

SHRIMP: Not as tasty as fresh shrimp, but satisfactory.

SARDINES: Most sardines are domestic. Others are imported from France, Spain, Portugal and Scandinavia. These may be pilchards, sprats, bristlings, or young herring. They may be boneless and skinless, in olive oil, or with spices.

## HOW TO BUY EGGS

The quality of eggs depends on freshness (or freshness at the time they were cold storaged). There is no difference in quality between white and brown eggs—merely local prejudice. Yolk colors may also vary without regard to quality. Commercial eggs are graded U. S. Special (nearly fresh), which are seldom available; U. S. Extra (Grade A); U. S. Standard (Grade B); U. S. Trade, which are useful where flavor is not important. Grading is done in a dark room by holding the egg up to the light, a process known as candling. This shows the size of the air-cell and the condition of the yolk, white

An electric light and a tin can with removable top make a cheap and easily constructed egg candle.

and germ. Top grade eggs have large, dark, highly curved yolks, well centered in a thick white, little air space in the egg, slightly better flavors.

Grade B eggs are suitable for eating, are equal to Grade A for frying, cooking, or baking. Biological abnormalities sometimes appear in eggs as blood spots—bright or dark specks. They occur very infrequently. They may be lifted out of the egg before cooking. They do not alter the nutritive value or the cooking performance.

Large, medium or small eggs vary widely in price according to quantities which come on the market.

| Jumbo | 30 oz. per dozen |
|---|---|
| Extra Large | 27 oz. per dozen |
| Large (Standard) | 24 oz. per dozen |
| Medium | 21 oz. per dozen |
| Small | 18 oz. per dozen |

Small eggs are usually more plentiful in the late summer and fall months. The size does not affect the quality but does affect price. The various qualities of eggs may be found in all sizes. Weight for weight, the nutritive value and the cooking performance of small eggs are equal to those of large eggs of the same quality. Comparative dollar values are shown below:

| When large eggs are | Buy medium eggs at | Buy small eggs at |
|---|---|---|
| 50c | 43c | 37c |
| 60c | 52c | 45c |
| 70c | 61c | 52c |
| 80c | 70c | 59c |
| 90c | 78c | 66c |
| $1.00 | 86c | 74c |

Eggs should not be washed until they are to be used; the porous shell absorbs water which may spoil the egg.

## DAIRY PRODUCTS

**Milk:** The quality of milk is determined by the bacterial count, amount of milk solids (must be more than 8 percent), and amount of butterfat (must be more than 3¼ percent).

| Kind | Origin | Hardness | | | Color | |
|------|--------|------|-----------|------|---------|--------|
| | | Hard | Semi-hard | Soft | Outside | Inside |
| American Cheddar.... | England............ | ...... | X | ...... | Yellow Brown | White to Yellow |
| Bel Paese............. | Italy............... | ...... | ...... | X | Slate Gray | Light Yellow |
| Blue................. | France............. | ...... | X | ...... | | Green Mold |
| Brick................ | U. S. A............ | ...... | X | ...... | Yellowish Brown | Creamy Yellow |
| Brie................. | France............. | ...... | ...... | X | Russet Brown | Creamy Yellow |
| Cacciacavallo......... | Italy............... | X | ...... | ...... | Clay | Light |
| Camembert........... | France............. | ...... | ...... | X | Gray White | Creamy |
| Cottage.............. | Unknown.......... | ...... | ...... | X | White | White |
| Cream............... | U. S. A........... | ...... | ...... | X | White to Cream | White to Cream |
| Edam................ | Holland............ | ...... | ...... | X | Red Coated | Creamy |
| Gjetost.............. | Norway............ | ...... | X | ...... | Light Brown | Light Brown |
| Gorgonzola........... | Italy............... | ...... | X | ...... | Clay | Yellow with green mold |
| Gouda............... | Holland............ | ...... | X | ...... | Red Coated | Creamy |
| Gruyère.............. | France............. | ...... | X | ...... | Light Yellow | Light Yellow |
| Monterey Jack........ | California.......... | ...... | ...... | X | Grayish White | White |
| Liederkranz.......... | U. S. A............ | ...... | ...... | X | Russet | Creamy |
| Limburger............ | Belgian............ | ...... | X | ...... | Grayish Brown | Creamy |
| Muenster............ | Germany........... | ...... | X | ...... | Yellow Tan | Creamy |
| Mysost (Primost)...... | Scandinavia........ | ...... | X | ...... | Light Brown | Light Brown |
| Neufchatel........... | France............. | ...... | ...... | X | White | White |
| Oka (Port du Salut).... | Canada............ | ...... | X | ...... | Russet | Creamy |
| Parmesan (Parmigiano). | Italy............... | X | ...... | ...... | Dark Green | Yellowish White |
| Pineapple............ | U. S. A............ | X | ...... | ...... | Waxed Orange | Deep Yellow |
| Romano.............. | Italy............... | X | ...... | ...... | Greenish Black | Yellowish White |
| Provolone............ | Italy............... | X | ...... | ...... | Light Brown | Light Yellow |
| Roquefort............ | France............. | ...... | X | ...... | | Green Mold |
| Sapsago.............. | Swiss.............. | X | ...... | ...... | Green | |
| Sbrinz............... | Argentine.......... | X | ...... | ...... | Grayish Green | White |
| Stilton............... | England............ | ...... | X | ...... | Creamy | Green Mold |
| Swiss................ | Switzerland........ | ...... | X | ...... | Grayish Brown | Light Yellow |

OF CHEESE

| Weight in lbs. | Shape | Use | Usual Ripening Period |
|---|---|---|---|
| 10-70 lbs. | Circular | General, Table, Processing | 1 mo. to 2 years |
| 1 lb. | Circular—2 inches high | Table—Dessert | 3 months |
| 5 lbs. | Cylindrical—6 inches diameter—4½ inches high | Canapes—Table Dessert | 2 to 9 months |
| 5 lbs. | Rectangular | Table—Sandwich— Processing | 2 to 9 months |
| 2 and 4 lbs. | Circular—2 to 3 inches | Table—Dessert | 4 weeks |
| 3-5 lbs. | Like a beet or ten pin | Table—Grating | Eaten fresh or cured several months |
| 1½ oz. portion | Circular | Trays—Table | 4 weeks |
| 3 oz. cake | | Dessert | |
| bulk and ind. pkg. | | Salads—Table | None |
| 3-6 oz. pkg. | Varies | Salads—Sandwiches | None |
| 2-3 lb. loaf | | Table | |
| 5-6 lbs. | Loaf or Cannon ball | Trays—Table | 1 to 2 months |
| 8 oz. | Cubical | Table | 4 to 8 months |
| 1 lb. | Rectangular | Dessert | |
| 16-19 lbs. | Cylindrical | Table—Dessert | 3 months to 1 year |
| 12-16 oz. | Ball shaped—flat top and bottom | Cheese Trays | 6 to 8 months |
| 2-5 lbs. | | Table | |
| 8 oz. | Circular in triangular portions | Table—Dessert | None |
| 6-7 lbs. | Circular | Table—Dessert | 3 to 4 weeks |
| 4 oz. | Rectangular | Cheese Trays—Dessert | 4 weeks |
| 8 oz.-1 lb. | Cubical, Rectangular in jars | Table | 1 to 2 months |
| 6-16 oz. jars | | | |
| 5-6 lbs. | Circular and block | Sandwiches—Table | None |
| 8 oz. | Cubical | Table | 6 to 8 months |
| 1 lb. | Cylindrical | | |
| 2 to 3 lbs. | Loaf | Salads—Sandwiches | None |
| 1 to 5 lbs. | Circular | Canapes—Table Table—Dessert | 5 to 6 weeks |
| 50 to 60 lbs. | Cylindrical | Grating | Several years |
| 10 oz. to 5 lbs. | Pineapple with shiny, corrugated surface | Table | 6 to 8 months |
| 12 to 15 lbs. | Circular | Table—Grating | 8 to 12 months |
| 2 to 3 lbs. | Like Sausage link | Table | 2 to 3 months |
| 4½ to 6 lbs. | Cylindrical | Canapes—Table Dessert | 3 to 9 months |
| 4 oz. | Conical | Table—Grating | 6 months to 2 years |
| 12 lbs. | Circular | Grating | 6 months to 2 years |
| 12 to 15 lbs. | Circular | Table | 6 months to 2 years |
| 175 to 225 lbs. | Circular Block | Sandwich—Table— Processing | 3 to 9 months |

The maximum bacterial count for pasteurized Grade A milk is 30,000 per cubic centimeter, for Grade B, 50,000, and for Grade C, 1,000,000.

Homogenized milk has had the fat broken down and thoroughly mixed. It has no nutritional advantage but tastes richer. Vitamin D milk has been treated by irradiation (sunlamps) or by special feeding of the cow. Cream contains not less than 18 percent milk fat. Whipping cream should contain 30 percent fat.

Skimmed milk has had some of its butterfat removed. Buttermilk has had the fat entirely removed in the process of churning and contains not less than 8 percent milk solids. Cultured buttermilk is made by souring a lactic-acid culture of milk. Most buttermilk sold in cities is not cultured.

Milk can be obtained most economically as dried milk (which can be mixed to taste exactly like milk). Non-fat dry milk solids (which, when mixed with water makes skim milk) is even more inexpensive, lacks only fat and Vitamin A. Evaporated milk is also somewhat less expensive than whole milk. Sweet condensed milk is more highly concentrated than evaporated milk and contains more sugar. It is useful for recipes where sweetening is desirable.

Where pasteurized milk is not available, certified milk or Grade A raw milk may be used. It may be pasteurized by heating to 155° F., stirring constantly, and cooling suddenly by placing the pot in cold water and stirring until the milk is cool.

Butter: Best butter is made of fresh, sweet, pasteurized cream. The score of butter is rated on flavor (45 percent), body (25 percent), color (15 percent), salt (10 percent) and package (5 percent). Butter must score 92 or more to be certified. If it scores 75 or less, it is classified as grease butter, and unfit for food. Butter must contain 80 percent fat to be considered unadulterated. Color is no indication of quality, but the color should be uniform throughout. Cold storage butter, if it has been properly handled, is equal to fresh butter. Tub butter is lower in price than print butter, but scores are not as readily ascertainable. Three grades are generally sold: 93-score, 92-score (suitable for table), and 91-score (suitable for cooking).

Cheese: The official grades of American Cheese are U. S. Extra Fancy, U. S. Fancy, U. S. No. 1, U. S. No. 2, U. S.

No. 3, and culls. The top two grades are not widely available. The grades are based on flavor (30 percent), body and texture (40 percent), finish and appearance (20 percent), and color (10 percent). Cheese should have a desirable flavor, be reasonably free of gas holes, have a smooth and waxy texture, have no mold or cracks in the rind.

The best Swiss cheese has eyes ½ inch in diameter, with a shiny surface. It should have no pinholes or cracks.

Processed cheese is made of different lots of cheese melted together with emulsifiers and flavoring, and pasteurized. It does not have as much food value as natural cheeses.

Hard cheese keeps better than soft cheese, has higher values in calcium, phosphorus and protein.

Yogurt is a cultured milk product which can be purchased or made at home.

## GUIDE TO BUYING VEGETABLES

**Artichokes:** Name is applied to two vegetables, French (Globe) allied to the thistle; and Jerusalem, a potato-like plant related to the sunflower, not widely used. French artichokes should be compact, heavy, plump, globular, with large tightly clinging, fleshy leaf scales, of good green color. Avoid brownish color, which indicates age or injury; spreading leaves (which indicate over-maturity), fuzzy or dark pink center, hard tips; vegetables with even small worm injuries. The size does not affect quality or flavor.

**Asparagus:** Available in two varieties, blanched (white), and green. The white part is grown under the ground, the green above ground. The underground portion begins to toughen as soon as green part begins to grow, so green spears should have little white part. Best when purchased fresh, tender, firm, with close compact tips. Avoid angular stalks, wilted or spreading tips. Usually sold in a bunch, but also by weight.

**Beans (lima, faba):** Available in two types—large "potato" type and "butter bean" type. They deteriorate rapidly after shelling. Pods should be well filled, clean, bright, fresh, dark green in color. The bean should be plump, with tender green or greenish-white color. Avoid dried, shriveled, spotted, yellowed, or flabby pods. Irregular sunken areas, which may contain mold, indicate decay. Hard, tough skins indicate immaturity.

**Beans (snap):** Available in many varieties, of both green and wax or yellow pod. Beans should be firm, crisp, tender, and should snap readily when broken. Pods in which seeds are immature are best. Length is not important. Large seeds or pods tend to be tough and stringy. Avoid stringy, dull or wilted beans. A moldy or soft watery condition indicates decay.

**Beets:** Sold in bunches, 3 to 5 in a bunch, with tops attached or cut to 4 inches. Fresh tops make excellent greens after discolored or ragged leaves have been removed. Avoid slimy tops. Late crops are marketed with tops removed, unwashed and suitable for storage. Medium sized beets are best. Beets should be smooth, free from blemish, may have some soil on them. Avoid rough beets with growth cracks, soft, flabby or shriveled beets. Bunched beets that have become tough because of lying too long in the field have a short neck covered with deep scars or several circles of leaf scars around the top. A soft form of rot indicates decay. Condition of leaves is no indication of condition of the beet.

**Broccoli** (Italian sprouting): Should be fresh, clean, not over-mature, with firm and tender stalks. Buds in the heads should be compact and green. Avoid yellowed or damaged leaves, wilted or flabby broccoli. Bud clusters which show yellow or purple blossoms indicate over-maturity and toughness.

**Brussels sprouts:** These are really miniature cabbages. They should be firm, compact, fresh, bright and of good green color. Puffy sprouts are of poor quality. Avoid wilted or yellow leaves, riddled leaves (which indicate worm injury), smudgy, dirty appearance (which indicates plant lice).

**Cabbage:** Varieties include the pointed (new cabbage), Danish (hard, tight leaved, used for winter storage), domestic (round or flat heads), savory (crumpled leaves), and red.

Prime heads should be solid, hard and heavy for their size. Stems should be trimmed close to the head, and all except 3 to 4 outer leaves should be removed. Early cabbage is not so firm as later varieties, but freshness is more important for this variety. Soft heads are of poorer quality. Avoid heads which are badly affected by worm injury, decay, yellow leaves or burst heads.

**Carrots:** Early or new carrots are sold in bunches of 5 to 8 with tops attached or clipped. Late crop is sold with tops removed. Early carrots should be smaller, brighter in color, milder in flavor. Late varieties may be woody at the heart.

Carrots should be firm, clean, fresh in appearance, smooth, well-shaped, and of good color. Poor color sometimes means poor quality. Avoid carrots that are wilted, flabby, soft or shriveled, as they lack flavor. Forked or rough carrots are wasteful. Carrots with thick masses of leaf stems at the neck usually have undesirably large cores. Soft or watersoaked areas indicate decay.

Cauliflower: Quality is indicated by white, clean, heavy, firm, compact curd, with outer leaves fresh, turgid and green. Avoid plants where the flower clusters have developed enough to cause a separation of the clusters. Yellowing leaves may indicate age. Avoid spotted, speckled, or bruised curd as wasteful. Smudgy or spotted appearance indicates plant lice. Leaves which have grown through curd do not detract from quality.

Celery: Available in two types, Golden type (white), and Pascal type (green with thick midriffs). Sold trimmed, or with hearts removed for soup greens, or hearts alone. Best quality is medium length, with thickness and solidity, and brittle stalks. Avoid stringy or pithy celery. Black-rot disease or insects can be detected in the heart by separating the branches.

Chard (Swiss chard): This is a form of beet grown for the tops only. Leaves should be crisp, tender, fresh, free from insect injury. Stalks should be fleshy and crisp. Yellow or wilted stalks are tough and stringy. Coarse stalks are pithy.

Chicory, Endive, Escarole: Endive has a narrow, finely divided leaf, grows flat; escarole a broad leaf, grows flat; chicory has a broad leaf, grows upright. Blanched chicory is sold as Witloof chicory and as French or Belgian endive. Good quality is indicated by crispness, freshness, and tenderness. Wilted plants may be freshened by being placed in water. Avoid tough, coarse plants. Browning of leaves or slimy rot may indicate decay.

Collards: This form of cabbage has large leaves, slightly curled at the edges, but does not form a head. Sold by weight. Should be fresh, crisp, clean, and free from insect injury. Avoid wilted or yellow leaves (indicating age) or perforated leaves (indicating worm injury).

Corn: Grown in two varieties: Field corn, or roasting ears, which matures early, is not notably sweet. Sweet corn, which is smaller, with darker green husk, has ribbon-like tassels.

Both varieties may be white or yellow. Slender ears may have as many kernels as large, coarse ears. Cobs should be filled with bright, plump, milky kernels, rather firm. Husk should be fresh and green. Dry, yellowed, or straw-colored husks indicate age or heat damage and dry kernels. Small kernels indicate immaturity, lack flavor. Corn loses flavor rapidly after being picked. Worm injury may be removed if at the tips.

**Cucumbers:** Should be firm, fresh, bright, well-shaped, of good color. Avoid withered or shriveled cucumbers which are tough, rubbery, and bitter. Puffiness and dull color indicates over-maturity and toughness. These, however, are suitable for pickling. Irregular dark, sunken areas indicate decay.

**Dandelions:** Best quality is large, tender-leaved, and fresh. Wilted, flabby, yellow, or tough leaves indicate age of damage and are wasteful.

**Eggplants:** Best qualities are heavy, firm, free from blemish, and of uniform dark color. Wilted, shriveled, soft or flabby condition indicates age, poor handling, or staleness, and consequently poor flavor or bitterness. Worm injury is self-evident, can usually be cut away. Dark-brown spots on the surface indicate decay.

**Garlic:** The bulb has a number of cloves, each in its own skin, and all enclosed in an outer skin. If the outer skin is split, the bulbs are called "splits" or doubles. There is no difference in quality. Garlic is usually sold in strings of 50 or 100, in red or white varieties. They should be dry, clean, not soft, with outer skin intact. Decay may appear in the form of mold or rot. Dryrot causes shrinking and shriveling and works downward.

**Greens:** Beet tops, broccoli, chard, chicory, collards, cress, dandelions, endive, escarole, kale, mustard, sorrel, spinach and turnip tops are available on most markets. They should be clean, fresh, young, green and tender. Flabby or wilted plants indicate age or damage. They may sometimes be restored by trimming and placing them in water. Seed stems indicate age and toughness.

**Kale:** Color is usually dark or bluish green, clean and fresh. Brownish appearance may indicate growth in cold weather, but does not affect quality. Avoid plants with yellow or wilted leaves as wasteful.

**Lettuce:** Four varieties are marketed—crisp head (Iceberg), butter head (Big Boston), romaine, and leaf lettuce. Crisp heads are firmer, larger, and crisper than butter heads. Romaine is elongated, has a coarser leaf and a stronger flavor. Leaf lettuce does not head, has a curled or smooth leaf and a crisp texture. Head lettuce should be fresh, crisp, tender, and firm to hand, with only a few wrapper leaves, and free from decay. Lettuce with well-developed seed stems at the knob of the head usually has a bitter flavor and is wasteful. Dead or discolored areas on the outer leaves may indicate decay. Sometimes a soft rot penetrates to the interior of the head. Broken, ragged, bruised, or wilted leaves usually do not affect quality. Even decay, if not deep, may be removed by trimming.

Mustard: Greens should be fresh, tender, crisp, and of good green color. Wilted, dirty, discolored, or spotted leaves indicate poor quality, are usually wasteful. Seed stems indicate age and toughness.

Okra (gumbo): Pods should be young, tender, fresh, clean, and of small-to-medium size. They should snap easily when broken, be punctured easily. Pods past their prime are dull, dry, hard, woody, fibrous, and the seeds are hard. Those that have been held too long are likely to be shriveled and discolored.

Onions: Two general classes are sold: Bermuda and Spanish (Valencia) types; and domestic American type.

THE BERMUDA is a flat type, in white, yellow, and red varieties. Popular sizes are 2½ to 2¾ inches in diameter.

THE SPANISH type is large, sweet, and either white or yellowish brown. It is usually globular but may be oval in shape.

DOMESTIC onions are globular, may be yellow, red, white or brown. They keep well and are available year round. White varieties are mildest.

"BOILER" is a small-sized onion, 1 to 2 inches in diameter, either domestic or Bermuda. Those under 1 inch, particularly white ones, are used for pickling.

All onions should be bright, clean, hard, well-shaped, with dry skins. Where seed stems have developed (accompanied by thick, woody stem) they are undesirable. Rot may attack either the outer scales or the center scales. Moisture at the neck is an indication of decay. Misshapen onions (usually splits) tend to be wasteful.

Leeks, green onions, shallots: These are blanched leaf bases or incompletely developed bulbs, with green portion of leaves. Leek is a plant similar to onion, with broad, dark green leaves, and a thick, white neck about 1 inch in diameter. It is used cooked or raw, usually for flavoring.

The shallot is related to the onion. It grows in oblong clusters, is pulled before maturity.

All should have green fresh tops, medium sized necks which are well blanched for 2 to 3 inches from the root, which should be crisp and tender. Bruised, yellow, wilted, or otherwise damaged tops may indicate poor quality, age, or tough fibrous necks. This condition may be ascertained by puncturing with thumbnail and twisting. Bruised tops are unimportant, as they may be trimmed.

**Parsley:** Available in three types—plain or flat leaf, curled leaf, and Hamburg (turnip-rooted). Hamburg roots are valuable for flavoring. These should all be of good appearance, bright, green, fresh, and free from dirt or yellowed leaves. Slightly wilted stock may be revived by placing in water, but badly wilted stock is practically worthless.

**Parsnips:** These develop flavor only at near-freezing temperature, are sold in winter and spring. They should be smooth, firm, well-shaped, of small to medium size. Large, coarse roots tend to be woody. Soft, flabby, or shriveled roots are usually pithy or fibrous. Decay may be indicated by softness, gray mold or watery soft rot. Misshapen roots may be wasteful.

**Peas:** Peas lose sweetness and flavor as they mature. Best quality are young, fresh, tender, sweet, of good color and bright green pods, velvety to the touch. Some varieties of pods are naturally puffed out, and appear unfilled although well developed. Immature peas are flat, dark green, and wilted. Over-mature pods are swollen, of poor color, and appear wilted or flecked with gray specks. Yellowness indicates age or damage, poor flavor, and toughness. Avoid water-soaked pods or those with evidence of mildew.

**Peppers:** These are available in sweet or in hot varieties. Sweet peppers, bell or bullnose in shape, are shipped green but turn red as they mature. Hot or pungent varieties may be either green or red. They may be small (chili) to large. Chili, cayenne, and other varieties may be dried and strung before being sold. Peppers should be mature, firm, well-shaped, thick-fleshed, of good color and not shriveled, limp or pliable. Seeds should be developed and hard. Bad shapes may be wasteful, but are otherwise not objectionable. Avoid peppers with surface blemishes; bleached, discolored or blistered surfaces may be wasteful.

**Potatoes:** New potatoes are dug before maturity, will not stand rough handling, may be discolored or feathery. Late potatoes are more mature, are usually stored for winter or spring sale.

Potatoes should be sound, smooth, shallow-eyed, and reasonably clean. Dirt does not injure eating quality. Varieties vary in shape, size, color, and cooking qualities. Medium sized potatoes are usually most desirable, but this may depend on anticipated use. Uniformity in size and variety is desirable. Wilted, leathery, discolored potatoes should be avoided. Sunburned potatoes show a green color on the surface and are usually bitter and inedible. Some potatoes may have a "hollow heart," which may not be wasteful, or black heart which is wasteful, and particularly objectionable in potatoes used for baking. Wet and leaky potatoes have been frozen. These usually have a black ring or black flesh when cooked. They lack flavor. Wet rot, dryrot or other decay may be cut away, but is wasteful. Small perforations indicate wire worms which are extremely wasteful. In late spring or early summer, old potatoes may be shriveled, soft or spongy, or may have sprouted. These are wasteful and may not cook satisfactorily.

**Radishes:** These vary in color, shape, and size. A good radish is well formed, smooth, firm, tender, crisp, and mild. Leaves give little indication of quality. Old radishes may be coarse, dry, or yellow, are usually strong in flavor, and may be woody. Avoid radishes which are pithy or spongy.

Common Varieties:

SPRING: bunches of small red, long white "icicles."

SUMMER: round, pungent, white, up to 4 inches in diameter; long types, 3 to 10 inches long.

WINTER: largest, strongest, long-root types.

**Rhubarb:** Local, fieldgrown rhubarb is usually rich dark red, with deep green foliage. Forced rhubarb is light pink with yellowish foliage. Leaves are not edible and may be harmful. Rhubarb should be fresh, firm, crisp, and tender, with thick stalks of good color. Stale rhubarb is wilted and flabby, may be stringy and of poor flavor. Old rhubarb is pithy, tough, and stringy, is usually wasteful.

Salsify (oyster plant): These are similar to parsnips. They should be smooth, firm, well-shaped, and of medium size. Avoid soft, flabby or shriveled roots, which are usually fibrous. Softness may indicate decay, which may be a gray mold or soft watery rot. Large, coarse roots may have woody cores.

Spinach: Should be fresh, crisp, crinkly, clean, of good green color, and free from sand. Small, straggly, or overgrown stalks are often tough. Bruised or crushed leaves may be wasteful. Plants with yellow leaves, seed stems, or very coarse leaf stems may be tough and yellow. Decay, in the form of soft, slimy rot, may be indicated by wilting or yellowing.

Squash: White varieties are usually disk-shaped and known as cymblings or patty pans. Yellow varieties are usually long, with straight or crooked necks, with rough rinds. Winter varieties have dark green or orange colored rind, rather coarse.

Summer squash should be fresh, heavy for its size, free from blemish, with a rind tender enough to be punctured easily. Winter squash should be heavy for its size, free from blemish, with a hard rind. Hard-rind summer squash has hard seeds, stringy flesh. Soft-rind winter squash is usually immature, thin-fleshed, watery, and lacking in flavor. Bruised or injured squash may be decayed. Watery areas, black or brown mold-like growths, may often be cut away without undue waste.

Sweet potatoes: These are two varieties, one with mealy flesh when cooked, yellowish skin and yellow or orange flesh; the other, with a moist flesh (incorrectly called yams), have reddish flesh with green, yellow, or orange tint. Sweet potatoes should be smooth, well-shaped, firm, and bright. Watch for decay, misshape, growth cracks and wire-worm injury. Decay spreads quickly and gives a disagreeable flavor, may appear as soft wet rot, or dry, shriveled, discolored, sunken area. Dampness may indicate bad handling or freezing. Clay-colored spots affect the skin only.

Tomatoes: Should be firm, not overripe, well-formed, plump, smooth, of good color and free from blemish. Many defects are not serious but may be wasteful—as catfaces or scars around the blossom. Avoid tomatoes which have been attacked by worms. Those with growth cracks are suitable only if to be consumed immediately. Watery fruit is wasteful.

**Turnips:** Early turnips are small. Late crops are stored and sold in winter. Rutabagas are a large, elongated variety with yellow flesh. Turnips should be smooth, firm, with few leaf scars around the crown, and few fibrous roots. Fresh, green, young, turgid condition of tops is an indication of quality. Yellow or wilted tops indicate staleness or damage. Large, coarse turnips, especially those light for their size, may be tough, woody, pithy, hollow, or strong in flavor.

**Turnip tops** (for greens or salad) are sold separately. A form of turnip top is sold as broccoli greens. This consists of leaves and seed stems of a variety grown only for the greens. Greens should be fresh, clean, crisp, and tender. Watch for aphids or plant lice and for decay.

## GUIDE TO BUYING FRUITS

**Apples:** Should be firm, of good color, and desirable flavor. Watch for "scald," a brown tinting of the skin caused by gases given off by the apples themselves. This seriously affects the quality of the fruit. Internal breakdown may cause the apples to be mealy or brown, particularly winter varieties. Avoid soft, mealy, overripe, tough-skinned apples, or those with bruised or brown surfaces. Best buys are those of medium size.

**Apricots:** Best flavors are in those which have ripened on the tree, but these are available only close to growing areas. Should be plump, fairly firm, and uniformly golden yellowish, with a juicy flesh. Extremely perishable. Avoid bruised, shrunken, shriveled, or injured fruit.

**Avocados:** Vary widely in shape, size, color, in appearance, from 3 to 5 per pound. Ripen in warm, humid place for 2 to 3 days. Should be bright, fresh looking, just beginning to soften. Flesh should be soft, buttery, or marrow-like. If not soft, they may be held for ripening. Avoid bruised fruit. Light-brown "scab" does not affect the quality, but dark, sunken spots indicate decay.

**Bananas:** Should be plump and yellow or red, depending on the variety; avoid badly discolored skin and soft or mushy texture. Blackened bananas may still be good eating. Avoid bruised fruit with mold on a darkened skin.

**Blackberries, dewberries, loganberries, raspberries:** Quality is indicated by bright, clean, fresh appearance; solid, full color;

plumpness. Berries should be free from dirt. Avoid overripe, decayed, or bruised berries which are soft and leaky. Berries with caps attached are usually immature.

**Blueberries and huckleberries:** Should be plump, fresh, clean, dry, free from leaves and trash, and fairly uniform in size; of deep, full color. May be blue, black, or purplish. Avoid berries which show heavy moisture, signs of mold or mechanical injury.

**Cherries:** Varieties include light-fleshed (Napoleon, Royal Ann) and dark fleshed (Black tartarian, Bing, Republican, Lambert, Windsor and Schmidt) type; sour varieties (Montmorency, English Morello or Early Richmond). Cherries should be bright, fresh, plump, and of good color; fairly firm, juicy, with a well-developed flavor. Avoid injured, hard, poor-color fruit and soft, dull, shriveled, or leaky fruit. Examine for worm injury and for circular spots which indicate decay. Damp, stained, and leaky boxes also indicate decay. Break open a few, for worminess generally runs through a lot.

**Cranberries:** Usual varieties are large, bright red, and small darker kinds. Look for fresh, plump appearance, high luster and firmness. Avoid shriveled, dull, sticky, tough or soft fruit, or fruit with discolored flecks. Dampness does not indicate poor quality unless caused by injury, indicated by sticky fluid.

**Figs:** Look for ripe, soft fruit. Colors depend on variety. Extremely perishable. Avoid bruised fruit.

**Grapefruit:** Should be firm, springy to the touch, well shaped, heavy; not soft, wilted or flabby. Heavier fruit contains more juice. Avoid fruit with watersoaked area, discoloration on the peel, soft spots; russeting, scaly scars, scratches, and ordinary discoloration do not affect the quality of the fruit.

**Grapes:** The American types are grown in the East (Concord, Catawba), the European types in the West (Tokay, Flame, Malaga, Thompson, Seedless, Emperor). Eastern types are used for jelly, etc. Concord is used for juice purposes. Western types are best for eating. Grapes should be fresh, mature, plump, firmly attached to the stems, of good color. Amber indicates sweetness, although some varieties remain green when ripe. Avoid grapes with dull appearance, substantial shriveling or milky opaque pulp. Leaky berries indicate decay. A few wrinkled, raisined, or unripened grapes do not affect the quality of the bunch.

**Lemons, Limes:** Should have a fine-textured skin, be heavy for their size. Deep yellow lemons are more mature and not so acidy. Generally thinner-skinned varieties have more juice. Avoid shriveled or hard skin, or soft fruit. Decay is indicated by discolored soft area at the stem. Spots from purple to brown are caused by "scald" and do not affect the quality of the fruit.

**Melons:** (Casaba, cantaloupe, Christmas, cranshaw, honeydew, honeyball, Persian, watermelon). For melons other than watermelons, full color and distinctive, characteristic odor indicate ripeness. In ripe melons, the blossom end smells sweet and is soft when pressed gently.

The netting on the rind of a good cantaloupe is coarse, and stands out. Melons with thin netting are not sweet. A sunken and callused scar on the stem end shows that the melon was picked when ripe rather than ripened in storage, indicating superior quality. Large watermelons are usually better than small ones, and have a much higher proportion of flesh to rind. A ripe watermelon is rich green, with yellow under side.

**Oranges:** Most desirable sizes range from 126 to 216 per box, with 176 to 200 preferred. Tangerine types are popular, from 144 to 196 to the box. Fruit should be firm, heavy, with thin-textured skin. Avoid puffy oranges. Decay is indicated by soft areas that appear to be watersoaked. Avoid wilted, shriveled, or flabby fruit.

Varieties vary in season. Some California varieties (Washington Navels and Thompson Navels) are seedless. Florida varieties (Parson-Burn, Valencia) are usually good for juice. Heavy fruit tends to have more juice. Satsumas, King and Mandarin types are flattened at the ends and have thick skins which are easily removed, tend to feel puffy.

**Peaches:** White flesh and yellow flesh. Both have clingstones and freestones. Fruit should be firm, free from blemishes, with a fresh appearance, with flesh fairly firm to firm. Avoid soft, overripe, bruised, or wormy fruit. Brown, circular spots usually indicate decay.

**Pears:** Storage-ripened pears usually have a fine texture, while tree-ripened fruit may be fine, coarse, or gritty. Fruit should be fairly firm to firm, but not hard; free from blemish, clean, not misshapen, wilted or shriveled. Avoid wilted, shriveled, watersoaked, mushy fruit. Scald may make the fruit unattractive and sometimes affects the flesh. Popular varieties in-

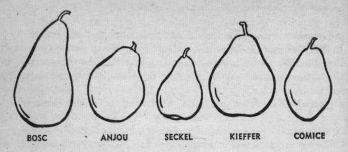

BOSC    ANJOU    SECKEL    KIEFFER    COMICE

clude Bartlett, Clapp, Bosc, Comice, Seckel, Anjou, Winter Nelis, Kieffer, Garber, and Leconte.

**Pineapples:** Should be of good color and odor, fresh and clean, with distinctive dark orange color. Eyes should be flat and almost hollow. Heavy fruit is best. Avoid bruised fruit or fruit with discolored or soft, watery areas. Sometimes blackened color indicates decay, particularly around the eyes on the side of the fruit. Sometimes a sour odor is noticeable. Sunburn may affect one side of the fruit, causing flesh to be hard, pithy, and dry.

**Plums and prunes:** The prune is a variety of the plum suited for drying. Fruit should be plump, clean, fresh looking, full-colored, and soft enough to yield to slight pressure. Avoid shriveled, soft, bruised, or leaky fruit. Evidence of moisture indicates injury to the fruit or some form of decay. Brownish or reddish color indicates sunburn and poor quality. Growth cracks may indicate decay.

**Quinces:** Fruit may have heavy, fuzzy skin which may be wiped off. Should be firm to hard, free from blemish, greenish-yellow or golden yellow in color. Avoid hard, green, or shriveled bruised fruit, worm-injured fruit, and fruit with black skin. Circular spots are extremely wasteful.

**Strawberries:** Should be of good appearance, fresh, clean, bright; solid red in color, free from moisture, dirt; with cap attached. Large berries are preferred. Small, misshapen berries are usually of poor quality. Avoid overripe or underripe, shrunken, wet, or leaky berries. Presence of mold or decay is self-evident. Strawberries without caps are probably overripe.

## EDIBLE WEEDS

Dandelion for salads. Milkweed shoots (picked before June), cook like asparagus, for salads. Shepherd's purse, cook like spinach. Marshmallow leaves (young) cook like spinach. Cowslip, for salads. Wild chicory, for salads. Carroway, for salads; roots are edible. Brake ferns (early sprouts), cook like asparagus. Watercress, salads.

## PROCESSED FOODS

You can buy many types of processed foods, created by new technologies, often at less cost than home-prepared foods of the same quality. Prepared foods, some by famous chefs who have included a great variety of ingredients, are offered in special packaged form. Most popular are:

FROZEN: vegetables in sauces, frozen in bags which are dropped into boiling water; dried turkey or beef in gravy, frozen in bags; seasoned vegetables in interesting combinations; raw, peeled potatoes; mushrooms, chopped onions, and green peppers (use just the amount needed, and keep the rest frozen). Wide variety of TV dinners.

FREEZE-DRIED: shrimp, mushrooms, green beans, bananas, some meats.

DEHYDRATED: soups, seasonings, sauces, milk, cream, potatoes.

CRYSTALIZED: crystals of citrus juices and other drinks—add water to reconstitute.

Other food processes include:

LOW-CALORIE AND DIETETIC FOODS.

LOW-CALORIE SODAS.

FROZEN DOUGH, CAKES, BREAD, BISCUITS.

REFRIGERATOR DOUGH—PUFF PASTES THAT WOULD OTHERWISE TAKE HOURS TO MAKE.

QUALITY PREPARED FOODS—PIES, CAKES.

Wrap frozen products in moisture-proof paper to seal in moisture and prevent burning.

Fruits and vegetables which have been preserved by canning, drying, dehydrating, and freezing and other food-processing methods, are usually graded by the United States Department of Agriculture.

Grade A, or United States Fancy, processed fruits and vegetables are high quality foods. They are very carefully selected as to size, color, and maturity.

Grade B, or U. S. Extra Standard, vegetables are usually more mature than those in Grade A. Fruits in this grade are not so uniform in color, size, or maturity as those in Grade A. This grade is very satisfactory for general household and institutional purposes.

Grade C, or U. S. Standard, fruits and vegetables are good, wholesome products. The products used in this grade may not be so carefully selected as to size, color and maturity as in the higher grades but in many instances are just as nutritious and should sell at lower prices.

Some canned fruits and vegetables that fail to meet the requirements of Grade C in certain respects may be wholesome, nutritious, and acceptable in flavor, and if properly labeled may be sold on the retail market.

Swelled or bulged cans contain spoiled food. Dented cans are all right.

**Peas:** Two types are canned, early varieties which are starchy, round and smooth; and late varieties which are wrinkled, oval, tougher, and sweet. Cloudy liquid indicates a tougher pea. The liquid is valuable for soups or sauces.

**Peaches:** Yellow clingstone are even and of good color and texture. Freestone peaches taste better.

**Frozen vegetables:** These cost less than out-of-season fresh vegetables, but more than canned vegetables. Quality varies widely, but is generally good. Keep frozen, never re-freeze.

**Dried fruit:** Apricots, apples, peaches, and prunes are dried without substantial loss of food value. Dried fruits and vegetables should be soaked overnight to lessen cooking time (and fuel costs).

## CEREALS—WHAT THEY ARE, HOW THEY'RE MADE

BRAN FLAKES: Winter wheat rolled into flat pieces and bran added; flavored, cooked under steam pressure, dried, rolled into flakes, and toasted.

CORN FLAKES: Inner part of the kernel, called hominy grits, of corn, flavored, cooked under steam pressure, dried, then flaked and toasted until brown.

CORN SOYA SHREDS: Blend of hominy grits from corn and soybean flakes, flavored, cooked under steam pressure, dried,

## STANDARD CAN SIZES—VEGETABLE AND FRUIT SERVINGS

### STANDARD CANS FRUITS AND VEGETABLES

| Size of Can | Average Weight | Number of Cups |
|---|---|---|
| 8 oz. Tall Can | ½ | 1 |
| No. 1 Tall | 1 lb. | 2 |
| No. 303 | 1 lb. | 2 |
| No. 2 | 1 lb. 4 oz. | 2½ |
| No. 2½ | 1 lb. 12 oz. | 3½ |
| No. 10 | 6 lbs. 14 oz. | 13½ |

### JUICES

| | | |
|---|---|---|
| No. 2 | 1 pt. 2 fl. oz. | 2½ |
| No. 303 Cylinder | 1 pt. 4 fl. oz. | 2¾ |
| No. 2 Cylinder | 1 pt. 8 fl. oz. | 3 |
| No. 3 Cylinder | 1 qt. 14 fl. oz. | 5¾ |
| No. 10 | 3 qt. 7 fl. oz. | 13½ |

### VEGETABLE AND FRUIT SERVINGS

| Vegetable | Size of Serving | Servings (2) per pound |
|---|---|---|
| Asparagus: | | |
| Cut | ½ cup | 4 |
| Spears | 4-5 stalks | 4 |
| Beans, lima | ½ cup | (3) 2 |
| Beans, snap | ½ cup | 6 |
| Beets, diced | ½ cup | 4 |
| Broccoli | 2 stalks | 3-4 |
| Brussels sprouts | ½ cup | 5-8 |
| Cabbage: | | |
| Raw, shredded | ½ cup | 7-8 |
| Cooked | ½ cup | 4-5 |
| Carrots: | | |
| Raw, shredded | ½ cup | 8 |
| Cooked | ½ cup | 5 |
| Cauliflower | ½ cup | 3 |
| Celery, cooked | ½ cup | 3-4 |
| Collards | ½ cup | 2 |
| Corn, cut | ½ cup | (4) 2 |
| Eggplant | ½ cup | 4 |

| Vegetable | Size of Serving | Servings per pound(2) |
|---|---|---|
| Onions, cooked | ½ cup | 4 |
| Parsnips | ½ cup | 4 |
| Peas | ½ cup | (3) 2 |
| Potatoes | ½ cup | 4-5 |
| Spinach | ½ cup | 3-4 |
| Squash | ½ cup | 2-3 |
| Sweet potatoes | ½ cup | 3-4 |
| Turnips | ½ cup | 4 |

| Fruit | Size of Serving | Servings per pound(2) |
|---|---|---|
| Apricots | 2 medium | 5-6 |
| Berries, raw | ½ cup | 4-5 |
| Cherries, pitted cooked | ½ cup | 2 |
| Plums | 2 large | 4 |
| Rhubarb, cooked | ½ cup | 4 |

For apples, bananas, oranges and pears, count on about 3 to a pound; peaches 4 to a pound.

**Dried**

| | | |
|---|---|---|
| Dry beans | ¾ cup | 9 |
| Dry peas, lentils | ¾ cup | 7 |

| Canned | | Servings Per Can |
|---|---|---|
| 8 oz. can | ½ cup | 2 |
| No. 2 can | ½ cup | 4-5 |
| No. 2½ can | ½ cup | 6-7 |
| No. 3 Cylinder (46 oz.) | ½ cup | 11-12 |

| Frozen | | Servings Per package |
|---|---|---|
| Family-size packages | ½ cup | 3-4 |
| Juices, concentrated 6 fluid oz. | ½ cup | 6 |

(2) As purchased  (3) In pod  (4) In husk

ground, and run through grooved rolls to form shreds, then toasted.

CRISP CORN CEREAL: Corn meal, with sugar, salt, and vegetable oil added, mixed into a dough, cooked, formed into pellets, dried, then expanded by sudden application of heat.

CRISP OAT CEREAL: Oat flour with sugar, salt, and flavoring added, mixed into a dough, cooked, formed into pellets, dried, then expanded by sudden application of heat.

OVEN-POPPED RICE CEREAL: White rice, cleaned, mixed with flavoring, and steam cooked, then dried and allowed to "cure" until the moisture is evenly distributed; lightly rolled into thick flakes, then dried and allowed to "cure" again; toasted to emerge popped to several times their normal size.

PUFFED RICE: White rice, cooked and steamed in a closed vessel called a "gun." During this period of heating the moisture in the grain turns to steam. When the pressure is suddenly released the starch granules explode and puff the grains.

FARINA: Substantially pure wheat endosperm of hard wheat. The bran, outer coating, and germ of the wheat kernel are removed.

GRANULAR WHEAT CEREAL, BROWN: Kernel of whole wheat, with or without added flavoring, ground.

ROLLED OATS: Oats cleaned and hulled, leaving the whole oat kernel, steamed and then passed through heavy steel rolls. The cooked product is oatmeal.

ROLLED WHEAT: Whole wheat kernels, steamed and rolled into flat flakes.

WHEAT AND OAT CEREAL: Whole wheat blended with oat kernels, steamed and rolled into thin flakes. Quick-cooking. Wheat germ is available concentrated.

PUFFED WHEAT: Wheat prepared as is puffed rice.

RAISIN BRAN FLAKES: Bran flakes to which are added specially processed raisins.

RICE FLAKES: White rice processed as is oven-popped rice except kernels are rolled into thin flakes, then toasted.

SHREDDED WHEAT: Winter wheat washed, cooked with or without flavoring, then partially dried and shredded by passing between groover rolls. Shreds are molded and cut into oblong, round or bite-size biscuits, oven-baked and toasted.

WHEAT AND BARLEY KERNELS: Flours, principally wheat with added melted barley, mixed into a stiff dough with yeast, salt, and water. The dough is baked, cooled, then broken into small pieces, rebaked, ground to size.

WHEAT FLAKES: Winter wheat cleaned, mixed with flavoring, cooked under steam pressure. Flakes are formed by rolling between heavy rollers. The flakes are then toasted.

WHEAT SHREDS: Soft winter wheat, cleaned, rolled, mixed with malt flavoring, sugar, and salt; cooked, ground, and passed between grooved rolls to form ribbon-like shreds which are then dried and toasted.

WHOLE BRAN: Bran from soft winter wheat, cleaned, cooked with flavorings, dried, finely shredded, and toasted.

### CEREALS AND CEREAL PRODUCTS—SERVINGS

| | Size of Serving | Servings per pound | | Size of Serving | Servings per pound |
|---|---|---|---|---|---|
| Flaked corn cereals | 1 cup | 18-24 | Oatmeal | ¾ cup | 13 |
| Other flaked cereals | ¾ cup | 21 | Hominy grits | ½ cup | 20 |
| Puffed cereals | 1 cup | 32-38 | Macaroni and | | |
| Cornmeal | ¾ cup | 16 | noodles | ¾ cup | 12 |
| Wheat cereals: | | | Rice | ½ cup | 18 |
| Coarse | ¾ cup | 12 | Spaghetti | ¾ cup | 13 |
| Fine | ¾ cup | 16-22 | | | |

Breads: The following types of bread are widely available: Apricot, Boston Brown, Cheese, Cracked Wheat, French Loaf, Gluten, Italian Loaf, Milk, Nut, Orange, Potato, Prune, Pullman Loaf (for sandwiches), Raisin, Raisin Nut, Raisin Nut Date, Salt Free, Sour Rye, Sweet Rye, Swedish, Vienna, White, Whole Wheat.

Rolls: The following types of rolls are widely available: Bread Sticks, Butterfly, Clover Leaf, Dinner, Finger, Frankfurter, Parker House, Poppy Seed, Twist.

Crackers: The following types of crackers are widely available: Animal, Arrowroot, Butter, Cheese, Filled, Graham, Oyster, Pilot, Pretzels, Rusk, Rye Wafers, Saltines, Soda, Soya, Triscuits, Water Biscuits, Whole Wheat Wafers.

Cookies: The following types of cookies are widely available at bakeries: Butter, Butterscotch Drops, Chocolate Chip, Fudge Bars, Gingerbread, Hermits, Macaroons, Molasses, Oatmeal, Petit Fours, Refrigerator Type.

The following types are available packaged: Chocolate

Chip, Chocolate Wafers, Fig Bars, Gingersnaps, Lemon, Marzipan, Macaroons, Rum, Shortbread, Sugar Wafers, Vanilla Drops.

## MISCELLANEOUS FOODS

Oils, shortening: Vegetable oils which may be used as shortening are olive oil, peanut oil, mixture of 4 parts peanut oil to 1 part olive oil, cottonseed oil, corn oil (this has a strong odor), soybean oil (this sometimes gets a fishy taste).

Fats used in cooking vary in the jobs they do most effectively. Proper choice may mean economy as well as a better cooking job.

### SHORTENING AND OILS

| Product | Characteristics of Best Quality | Uses |
|---|---|---|
| LARD | Mild color and taste. Firm when cool. | B, S, D, F |
| HYDROGENATED LARD | Odorless, tasteless, creamy. | B, D |
| HYDROGENATED VEGETABLE FATS | Solid, odorless, plastic. | B, S, D, F |
| POULTRY FAT | Yellow, flavorful. | B, S, W |
| BEEF SUET | White, flavorful. | (1) |
| CORN OIL | Yellow, odorless, flavorless. | C, T |
| COTTONSEED OIL | Yellow, tasteless. | W |
| OLIVE OIL | Straw yellow, flavorful, aromatic. | C, T |
| PEANUT OIL | Inexpensive. | C, T |
| SOYBEAN OIL | Strong odor and flavor. | Commercial |
| MARGARINE | Colorless unless color is added to make it resemble butter. Inexpensive. May be vitamin enriched. | C, T |

| | | |
|---|---|---|
| B—Baking | C—Cooking | D—Deep frying |
| F—Frying | S—Sautéing | T—Table use |
| W—Bread spreads | (1)—For larding meats; steam puddings | |

Most shortenings are mixtures of blended animal and vegetable fats and hydrogenated vegetable oils. They are used for baking or frying.

## SWEETENERS

| Type | Characteristics | Uses |
| --- | --- | --- |
| BROWN SUGAR (DARK) | Has distinct flavor. | Cakes, cookies. |
| BROWN SUGAR (LIGHT) | Milder color, flavor. | Cakes, cookies. |
| COARSE SUGAR | Large crystals, may be colored. | Decoration on cookies, garnish. |
| CONFECTIONERS' SUGAR | Fine, sometimes mixed with cornstarch, velvety. | Frosting, icing, dusting. |
| CORN SUGAR | Crystalized corn syrup, yellow, in lumps or granulated. | Substitute for sugar. |
| LUMP SUGAR | Cubes. | Teas, formal meals. |
| MAPLE SUGAR | Maple flavor, expensive. | Candy, special cooking. |
| POWDERED SUGAR | Fine, granulated sugar. | Iced drinks, fruits, berries, special cooking. |
| MAPLE SYRUP | Maple flavor, 65 percent sugar. Four grades: Fancy, No. 1, No. 2, and No. 3. Lightest colors with delicate flavor are best. | Pancakes, cooking. |
| CANE SYRUP | Sap of sugar, thin. | Pancakes, cooking. |
| CORN SYRUP | Glucose, colorless or brown. | Cooking, table use. |

| Type | Characteristics | Uses |
|---|---|---|
| MOLASSES | From sugar cane. Lighter colors, delicate flavors, are best. | Table, cooking. |
| PANCAKE SYRUP | Mixture of corn, maple and molasses syrup. Less expensive. | Pancakes. |
| SORGHUM CANE SYRUP | Stronger flavor than corn syrup. | Pancakes, cooking. |
| HONEY | From bees. Lighter colors have milder flavors. | Pancakes, table, cooking. |
| JELLIES | Clear, transparent. From fruits or berries. | Table, bread spreads. |
| JAMS | Small fruits or berries preserved. | Table, bread spreads. |
| PRESERVES | Whole fruits preserved. | Desserts, bread spreads. |
| MARMALADES | Thin slices of citrus fruit preserved. | Desserts, bread spreads. |
| APPLE BUTTER, APPLE CIDER BUTTER | Thin, spiced. | Bread spreads. |

## NUTS

| Type | Characteristics | Uses |
|---|---|---|
| ALMONDS | Hard or soft shell, flattened ovals. | Table, cooking, baking. |
| BRAZIL NUTS | Hard shell, white meat, triangular shape. | Table, cooking, baking. |
| CASHEW | Crescent shaped, inexpensive. | Table. |

| Type | Characteristics | Uses |
|------|-----------------|------|
| CHESTNUTS | Round, flattened. | Roasted, preserved, dried, canned, stuffing. |
| COCONUTS | Large, white meat. | Cooking, dessert. garnish. |
| HAZELNUTS (FILBERTS) | Small, round. | Cooking. |
| HICKORY NUTS | Round, smaller than walnuts. | Cooking. |
| LITCHI | Round, sweet, white meat. | Dessert. |
| MACADAMIA | Golden brown; rare; similar to almond in flavor. | Table. |
| MIXED | Usually walnuts, almonds, pecans, filberts, cashews, peanuts. | Table, cooking. |
| PEANUTS | Inexpensive, long. | Confections, cooking. |
| PECANS | Thin shelled, oval. | Confections, cooking. |
| PINE NUTS | Small, delicate flavor. | Table. |
| PISTACHIO | Green, almond-shaped, small. | Confections, cooking. |
| WALNUTS | Round, sweet, thin-shelled. | Table, cooking |

**Tea:** Black teas, most commonly used, have been crushed, fermented and dried. Green teas, popular in England and China, have been steamed, rolled and dried. Their aroma is heavier, their flavor tangier. Oolong tea is partially fermented before drying. Quality of tea depends on the climate and soil where it is grown, and processing. Tea bags, though more convenient, are 2 to 3 times as expensive as bulk tea efficiently used.

Quality of tea depends on the conditions of growth of the various types used in the blend. The sizes of the leaf are sometimes used as designations, though they do not refer to quality. From smallest leaf up they are flowery, orange pekoe, pekoe, souchong. The pieces which break off in preparation are called fannings, and are used in tea bags.

Powdered tea which may be added to tap water to make iced tea, or to hot water to make hot tea, is also available.

**Coffee** is best when freshly roasted and ground. Most coffees are a blend of the following types:

SANTOS (Brazil)—Heavy body. Medium, mild flavor.

RIOS (Brazil)—Heavy body. Strong flavor.

JAVA (East Indies)—Expensive.

MOCHA (Arabia—Fragrant. Rich flavor.

BOGOTÁ (Colombia)—Expensive.

MARACAIBO (Venezuela)—Expensive.

Chicory may be added in the blending. Roasting may be light, medium, or dark. Dark roasts are best for demitasse. French coffee is made best from overroasted beans.

Coffee is also available in powdered, liquid, or frozen forms to which hot water is added; in decaffeinated forms similar to ordinary coffee, or in powder form. Parched grains with roasted flavor (Postum) are offered as substitutes.

## HOW TO STORE AND PRESERVE FOOD

BLACK WALNUTS, (FRESHLY PICKED): Keep in sun for several days.

CANNED GOODS (OPENED): May be stored in the same can as well as in another container, if can is covered. However, acid foods may get a tinny taste.

CANDY: In an airtight jar.

CHICKEN (COOKED): Serve chicken promptly after cooking. Refrigerate leftover chicken and gravy, well-covered, as soon as possible after the meal. Remove any stuffing from stuffed birds and refrigerate it separately, well-covered.

CHICKEN (UNCOOKED): Keep frozen till ready for use. Wrap fresh-drawn chicken loosely in wax paper.

CITRON: In an airtight jar.

EGGS: Eggs may be stored in waterglass. Mix 1 part of mixture with 9 parts of water which has been boiled and cooled. Put eggs in a covered stone crock and add mixture to 2 inches above. Store in a cool place. This will keep for several months. A 5-gallon crock will hold 15 dozen eggs.

EGGS, RAW YOLKS: Cover with water, shortening, or melted butter. In refrigerator.

FRUIT CAKE: Cover with damp or wine-soaked towel.

ICE: The more there is, the longer it lasts per pound.

NUTS: In airtight jars.

STEWED FRUIT: Covered, in refrigerator. If souring, add a pinch of baking soda and reboil for 5 minutes.

SWEET POTATOES (PEELED): Cover with ice-cold water.

TOMATOES: Do not chill for lunch or picnic box. Will shrivel soon after being removed from refrigerator.

WATERCRESS: Damp in closed glass container, in refrigerator. Remove discolored leaves daily.

## HOW LONG FROZEN FOOD MAY BE KEPT

| | | | |
|---|---|---|---|
| Fresh beef | 6 to 9 mos. | Poultry | 6 to 9 mos. |
| Fresh pork | 3 to 6 mos. | Steaks, chops, roasts | 6 to 9 mos. |
| Fresh veal | 6 to 9 mos. | Fish | 3 to 6 mos. |
| Fresh lamb | 6 to 9 mos. | Eggs | 6 to 9 mos. |
| Cooked hams | 3 to 4 mos. | Bread and cakes | 2 to 8 mos. |
| Ground fresh meats | 1 to 3 mos. | Fruits and vegetables | 1 season |

## WHERE TO PUT IT IN YOUR REFRIGERATOR:

(1) Milk, cream, table fats: Cover tightly. Remove only amount to be used at one time. Keep away from foods with strong odors and flavors. Wash milk bottles before storing. Do not leave bottles standing on the doorstep, as vitamins are lost.

(2) Raw meat: Remove store wrapping and cover lightly with waxed paper.

(3) Ground raw meat: Wrap tightly in waxed paper and freeze or use within twenty-four to forty-eight hours.

(4) Opened packages of ready-mixes which contain fat (muffin mix, cake mix, biscuit mix).

(5) Cut lemons, grapefruit: Will keep moist for awhile if placed cut side down on a saucer.

(6) Salad dressings, vegetable oils (except olive oil), peanut butter, opened jars of relishes, coffee, opened cans of milk.

(7) Opened cans of fruit and vegetables: Leave in original containers; cover.

(8) Eggs: Retain quality longest in hydrator or covered container. Never wash except just before using. Remove only number to be used.

(9) Bacon: Wrap in waxed paper. Remove only amount to be used at one time.

(10) Fresh greens and vegetables without natural protective covering: Store in hydrator or vegetable bag. Wash and trim before storage.

(11) Frozen foods: Keep in freezing compartment. Follow package directions for defrosting.

(12) Cantaloupe: Wrap tightly, store on top shelf.

(13) Fish: Wrap tightly or leave in store wrapping. Cook at once if possible, or keep frozen or very cold.

(14) Liver and organ meat: Use on day of purchase.

(15) Poultry: Wrap drawn or cut-up poultry in waxed paper and store same as raw meat.

(16) Nuts: Store covered in refrigerator.

(17) Cooked meat, leftovers, used fat: Cool rapidly; cover and refrigerate immediately. Do not cut or slice meat until ready to use, then use quickly.

(18) Cheese: Wrap tightly in waxed paper. Use soft cheese quickly.

(19) Berries and cherries: Spread on shallow plate, do not hull or wash until ready to serve.

(20) Bread: Wrap well and refrigerate in warm weather to delay mold formation.

(21) Dishes made with milk or cream: Cool quickly, refrigerate immediately and use within eighteen to twenty-four hours.

(22) Other fruits: Finish ripening at room temperature, then refrigerate. Do not cut until used.

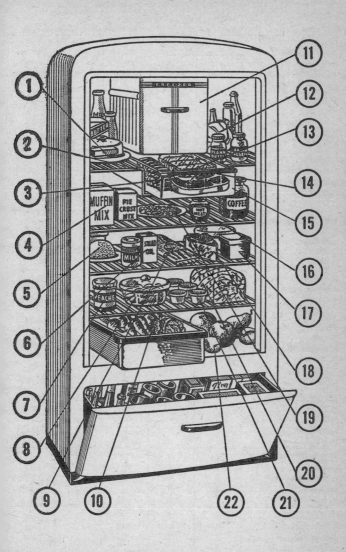

### HOW TO KEEP FOOD PROPERLY

| Foods<br><br>(Numbers indicate footnotes, p. 501) | Humidity | | Temperature Fahrenheit | Away from Sun | Maximum Period (months) |
|---|---|---|---|---|---|
| | Covered | Percent | | | |
| Apples (1, 2) | | 85 | 30-38 | X | 2 to 8 |
| Apricots | X | 80 | 32 | X | ½ |
| Artichokes (4, 7, 9) | | 90 | 32 | X | 2 to 5 |
| Asparagus (3) | X | 85 | 32 | X | 1 |
| Avocados (8) | | | 85 | X | 1 to 1½ |
| Baking Powder | | | Room | | |
| Bananas (5, 8) | | 90 | 56 | X | ⅓ |
| Beans (Dried) | X | 65 | 32 | | 12 |
| Beans (Green) | X | 85 | 32 | | 1 |
| Beans (Lima) (2) | X | 85 | 32 | X | 1 |
| Beans (Soy) (2) | X | X | Cool | X | |
| Beer | | | 40 | X | 3 to 5 |
| Beets | X | 85 | 32 | X | ¼ to 3 |
| Berries | | 80 | 32 | X | ⅕ to ⅓ |
| Bread | X | | Cool | X | |
| Broccoli | X | 85 | 32 | X | ⅓ to ½ |
| Brussels Sprouts | X | 85 | 32 | X | ⅓ to ½ |
| Butter (1) | X | 80 | 0 | X | 8 to 12 |
| Buttermilk (1) | X | | Cold | X | |
| Cabbage (9) | | 90 | 32 | X | 3 to 5 |
| Candy | | 60 | 32 | | 2 to 5 |
| Canned Foods | | | | | |
| (7) in Jars | | | | | |
| (8) open cans | | | Cool | X | |
| Cantaloupes (5) | | 80 | 32 | X | ⅕ to ⅓ |
| Carbonated Beverages | X | | 0 | X | 3 to 5 |
| Carrots (topped) (9) | | 90 | 32 | X | 4 to 6 |
| Catsup | X | | Cool | X | |
| Cauliflower | | 85 | 32 | X | ½ to ⅔ |
| Celeriac (7) | | | 32 | X | |
| Celery (6) | X | 90 | 32 | X | 3 to 4 |
| Cereals | X | 75 | 32 | X | 2 to 5 |
| Cheese—American (4) | X | 85 | 32 | X | 2 to 20 |
| Cherries | X | 80 | 32 | X | ⅓ to ⅔ |
| Chili Sauce | X | | Cool | X | |
| Chocolate | X | 50 | 50 | X | 3 to 5 |
| Cider | X | 80 | 32 | X | 6 to 8 |
| Citron Peel | X | 80 | 32 | X | 2 to 4 |
| Cocoa | X | | | X | |
| Coffee (1) | X | 85 | 40 | | 2 to 4 |

## HOW TO KEEP FOOD PROPERLY

| Foods (Numbers indicate footnotes, p. 501) | Humidity | | Temperature Fahrenheit | Away from Sun | Maximum Period (months) |
|---|---|---|---|---|---|
| | Covered | Percent | | | |
| Corn (2) | X | 85 | 32 | X | ¼ to ½ |
| Cornmeal | X | 80 | 32 | X | 2 to 5 |
| Cornstarch | X | | | X | |
| Cottage Cheese (4) | X | — | 0 | X | 2 to 6 |
| Crackers (4) | X | | | X | |
| Cranberries | | 85 | 32 | X | 1 to 4 |
| Cream | X | 85 | 32 | X | 10 days |
| Cream Cheese (4) | X | 85 | 32 | X | 12 to 20 |
| Cucumbers (2) | | 80 | 38 | X | ⅓ |
| Dates | | 70 | 32 | | 10 to 12 |
| Dates (Dried) (8) | X | | Warm | X | |
| Dried Fruits (1) | X | 65 | 32 | X | 12 |
| Eggplant | X | 85 | 38 | | ⅛ to ⅓ |
| Eggs (1) | X | 85 | 29 | X | 8 to 10 |
| Figs | | 85 | 28 | X | ½ to 1½ |
| Fish—Frozen | X | 75 | 0 | X | 12 |
| Flour | X | 75 | 32 | X | 2 to 5 |
| Frozen Foods (4) | X | | 5 | X | 6 to 12 |
| Garlic | X | 70 | 30 | X | 6 to 8 |
| Ginger Ale | | — | 40 | X | 3 to 5 |
| Grapefruit | | 85 | 32 | X | 1½ to 2 |
| Grapes | X | 85 | 32 | X | 1 |
| Grated Cheese | | 80 | 32 | X | 8 to 12 |
| Honey | | 85 | 40 | X | 3 |
| Ice Cream | | 60 | 0 | | 2 to 4 |
| Jams | X | | 32 | X | |
| Lard | X | 80 | 32 | X | 6 to 8 |
| Leeks | X | 85 | 32 | | 1 to 3 |
| Lemons | | 85 | 55 | X | 3 to 5 |
| Lettuce (6) | | 90 | 32 | X | 1 |
| Limes | | 85 | 50 | | 1½ to 2 |
| Mayonnaise | X | | | X | |
| Meats (4) | X | | 0 | X | 6 to 8 |
| Melons (4, 5) | | 75 | 35 | X | ½ |
| Milk | X | | 32 | X | |
| Mushrooms (7) | X | Dry | 32 | | 3 days |
| Nectarines | | 85 | 32 | | 1 to 2 |
| Oatmeal | X | 75 | 32 | X | 6 to 12 |
| Okra | X | 85 | 32 | X | ½ to 1 |
| Oleomargarine | X | 80 | 35 | X | 1 to 1½ |

## HOW TO KEEP FOOD PROPERLY

| Foods | Humidity | | Temperature Fahrenheit | Away from Sun | Maximum Period (months) |
| | Covered | Percent | | | |
|---|---|---|---|---|---|
| Olive Oil (8) | X | 85 | 40 | X | 3 to 5 |
| Onions (1) | | 75 | 32 | X | 5 to 8 |
| Oranges | | 85 | 32 | X | 2 to 3 |
| Parsnips (7) | | 85 | 32 | X | 2 to 4 |
| Peaches (5) | X | 85 | 32 | X | 1 |
| Peanut Butter | X | 82 | 34 | X | 3 to 5 |
| Pears (5, 7) | | 85 | 32 | X | 2 to 7 |
| Peas (2) | | 85 | 32 | X | 1 |
| Pineapple (5) | | 85 | 40 | X | 1 |
| Plums (10) | | 85 | 32 | X | ½ to 1 |
| Potatoes (7, 9) | | 85 | 40 | X | 6 to 8 |
| Poultry | | — | 0 | | 12 |
| Pumpkins (7) | | 75 | 50 | | ½ to 2 |
| Quinces (7) | | 80 | 32 | | 3 to 4 |
| Radishes (2) | | 90 | 32 | X | 2 to 4 |
| Raisins | X | 70 | 28 | | 12 |
| Rhubarb (6) | | 85 | 32 | X | 1 |
| Rice | X | 75 | 32 | X | 4 to 8 |
| Rutabaga (7) | | 90 | 32 | | 2 to 4 |
| Smoked Meats (4a) | X | 75 | 32 | X | 2 to 4 |
| Squash (7) | | 70 | 50 | X | 2 to 6 |
| Strawberries (3) | | 80 | 32 | X | ⅛ to ⅓ |
| Sugar | X | 80 | 40 | | 1 to 5 |
| Sweet Potatoes (8) | | 80 | 50 | X | 4 to 6 |
| Sirups | X | 75 | 40 | X | 3 to 5 |
| Tangerines (7) | | 80 | 32 | X | 1 to 3 |
| Tea (1) | X | | | | |
| Tomatoes (5) | | 85 | 50 | | 1 to 3 |
| Turnip, winter (7) | | 90 | 32 | | 2 to 4 |
| Vinegar (8) | X | | | X | |
| Watercress | | 85 | 40 | X | |
| Watermelon (4) | | 80 | 40 | X | ½ to 1 |
| Wines | | 75 | 45 | | 3 to 5 |
| Yeast (4) | | 85 | 32 | X | ⅓ to ½ |

Notes: (1) Keep away from foods with strong odors. (2) Do not cut or shell till ready to serve. (3) Do not wet till ready to prepare for serving. (4) Cover exposed flesh with wax paper. (5) Ripen at room temperature. (6) Revive by placing in cold water. (7) Keep in dark place. (8) Avoid extreme cold. (9) Keep in ventilated spot. (10) Avoid drafts. (11) Keep in hydrator or moisture proof bag.

# BOOK IX

## Guide to Entertainment and
## Good Social Usage

Social life is important not only for the personal satisfactions it brings and the business relationships it fosters, but also because it establishes and maintains your reputation for culture, intelligence and hospitality. It keeps you from being "left out of things," fosters your personal friendships, and gives you an opportunity to be gracious to your acquaintances.

Good social usage is merely the simplest and best method of acting toward others in a pleasant way, and so as to avoid causing offense or embarrassment.

### HOW TO MAKE FRIENDS

Making and keeping friendships is an art which comes naturally to some, and with difficulty to others. Dale Carnegie won national fame with his best seller, *How to Win Friends and Influence People*. Some of his suggestions:

1. Become genuinely interested in other people.
2. Smile.
3. Remember that a man's name is, to him, the most important sound in the English language.
4. Be a good listener. Encourage others to talk about themselves.
5. Talk in terms of the other man's interests.
6. Make the other person feel important—and do it sincerely.
7. Show respect for another man's opinions. Never tell a man he is wrong.

**Introductions:** Always introduce

    a man to a woman (except high dignitaries or the very old)

    a woman to an older woman

    girls to married women.

The most common ways: May I introduce Mr. Friend? Or: I want you to meet Mrs. Friend.

Visiting: Among close friends, visits are not counted or returned as a matter of "turn." Some visits should be made as a matter of formality:

1. Return of first visit made, after an invitation.

2. A visit of condolence upon a death. But a lady sends a note of sympathy to a man.

3. A visit to a convalescent friend. (Bring a gift.)

4. A lady's visit to the fiancee of a close male relative.

5. A visit of congratulations to a new mother. (Bring a gift.)

6. A visit to a neighbor recently moved in.

## POINTERS FOR GIVING A PARTY

Select guests who will mix well. Try to add one person to a party for your guests to meet.

Tell your guests what the party will be about, who will be there, how formal it will be (so they don't dress out of place).

Plan your menu with something interesting but don't experiment on your guests. Select dishes that go together in balanced diet, formality, etc.

Try to remember the diet likes and needs of your guests, particularly as to sweets, drinks, calories, etc. Provide for food for children—for meals and between meals.

Plan your menu so that serving will be easy. If you have no help, a casserole meal may be simplest.

Plan details in advance—center piece, leaves and flowers, place cards, napkins, toothpicks, silver, crystal, ash trays, candles, matches, cigarettes, liquor, ice, soft drinks, candy, the fire in the fireplace, housecleaning, your own clothes, help, seating, provision for coats, what to do with the children, bathroom accessories, etc. Do as much of the preparation in advance as possible, so as to avoid last-minute rush, and get a chance for a nap before guests arrive. Little things to remember: filling sugar bowls, salt shakers; slicing lemons for tea.

In your invitation, give explicit instructions on how to get to your house. (Some families have a map printed on their letterheads!) Give a phone number so that guests may call in an emergency. If there will be a parking problem, explain where and how it can be met. Give an indication of what time guests are expected to arrive.

Greet each guest personally if you can. Make as many introductions as time will allow or arrange for someone else to introduce new friends.

**Conversation:** For general conversation, a party should be limited to 8. It is wise to select guests with something in common, but include someone who is new to the group. Avoid inviting guests who dominate the conversation (unless they are funny or otherwise worth listening to), who chatter endlessly, or who sit moodily. Steer conversation away from extremely controversial subjects or subjects which might embarrass some guest. Break up a "lecture" when it begins to bore. Keep the topics of conversation shifting. When conversation lags, bring up a subject of general interest. Avoid discussions of your personal ills, the exploits of your children, your new car, home, etc. Break up twosomes or cliques. A safe subject is always what is happening to the other person.

**The Kind of Party:** Parties suitable for celebrating any of the early wedding anniversaries are a housewarming, calico fancy-dress party, barn dance, surprise party, treasure hunt, stork shower, or any imaginative informal party. The later years suggest more formal gatherings. These are more fittingly celebrated by a big dinner or entertainment—as a musicale or a garden party. The golden wedding anniversary (50 years), is most usually celebrated by a formal family dinner with friends and neighbors visiting to offer congratulations. Guests should not be made to feel that a present is obligatory, especially when the anniversary year is one which suggests an item of value. Intimate friends, however, usually bring or send something if possible. Flowers are of course always appropriate.

**Suggestions for Special Parties:** New Year's, Christmas, Halloween, Thanksgiving, Lincoln's Birthday, Washington's Birthday, Valentine's Day, July 4th, Easter, St. Patrick's Day.

Come as What You'd Like to Be; Circus Party; Hay Ride; Sleigh Ride; Housewarming; Anniversaries; Showers (for engaged girls, expectant mothers, on opening of a home, etc.).

**Suggested Ways of Entertaining:** BREAKFAST PARTIES: Sunday noon or 1 P.M. Informal. Not more than 8.

LUNCHEON: Light, simple food. Usually for ladies only. May precede cards or games.

TEA PARTIES: Simple and intimate. Light, simple food. May be small or large.

AT HOME: Tea at home at the same time each day or week.

COCKTAIL PARTIES: An easy, comparatively inexpensive method of entertaining large groups but may be used for small groups. Usually 5 to 7 P.M. May precede a larger, more formal gathering.

DINNER PARTIES: Elaborate. Inexpensive menu may be selected but quality and preparation should be good. For general conversation, party should be limited to 8.

BUFFET SUPPERS: Requires minimum service for large group and generally less expensive than dinners. Menu may include choice of two main dishes. Provide as many small tables as may be needed (nests, card tables, etc.) at which guests may be seated.

PARTIES IN THE EVENING: For entertaining large groups, almost anything goes as to food: sandwiches, tea and cake, cocktails. Arrange for games.

THE BOYS FOR AN EVENING: Provide ample food, drinks, smokes, ash trays, card tables, etc. The hostess should be inconspicuous.

OUTDOOR PARTIES: If you have the space, you can entertain large groups in this way in season. Party may be centered around an outdoor fireplace.

## HINTS ON GIVING A CHILDREN'S PARTY

At Age 5: Wait till 3 days before to invite guests to make certain there is no illness at home. Limit party to 8 guests. Guests should be between 4 and 6. Best party time is 4 to 6 o'clock. The shorter the party, the better. Let the child help with the plans. Menu should give choice of two things—e.g. creamed chicken or jelly sandwiches. Food should be cut, lettuce shredded. Provide extra milk, simple cake, extra sandwiches, etc., for mothers, ice cream for nurses. Children's portions should be small. Ice cream should be neither too soft nor too hard. (Bricks are best.)

Souvenirs should be provided for each guest. Each place should have small baskets of assorted candy, streamers, balloons, paper hat. Games may include pin the donkey's tail (or put the carrot in the rabbit's mouth); peanut hunt; fishing for presents over a screen (but make sure each child get the right present). Entertainment may include home movies. Provide paper bags so that the party miscellany may be taken home in comfort. For a birthday party, instruct your child on not saying: "I got one already," etc.

**At Age 8:** Guests should be of one sex. Party should be held on Friday or Saturday afternoon. Menu should be simple to prepare and eat, but with some novelty. (Croutons with chicken soup; ice cream cones for dessert.) Games may include lollypop hunt, treasure hunt, quizzes, charades, going to Jerusalem. Never ask: "Shall we play ——?" A single negative will sour the suggestion. Don't announce that there will be a booby prize. Souvenirs should be original, preferably not from local dime store. (Riddle books, magic or joke material, miniatures in glass or china, puzzles.)

**For Adolescents:** Parents should be present but inconspicuous. Provide phonograph with plenty of records.

## PARTY GAMES FOR ADULTS

**Charades:** The group is divided into teams of 4 or 5. All but one member of the team leave the room while the group selects a word, a name, or a place, a nursery rhyme or a proverb, or the title for a song. The member of the team who remains with the group then attempts to act out the selected word (as Ten-I-See) while his teammates guess at it. Three to five minutes may be allowed.

**Introduction:** This is very good to familiarize everyone with the names of others. The guests are all seated. The one chosen to be leader rises and says, "It's a pleasure to meet you all. My name is Jones." The next person stands and says, "How do you do, Mr. Jones. My name is Miss So and So." The next stands and says "How do you do, Mr. Jones and Miss So and So. My name is," etc. Each person must repeat in turn all the names which have been mentioned.

## PARTY GAMES FOR TEENAGERS

**Adverbs:** One player chooses an adverb and proceeds to act in the manner that the adverb implies. The other members of the group can ask him to do various things in the manner of the adverb until the word is guessed. The one who guesses the word is the next actor. Example—timidly: One member can ask him to shake hands in the manner of the adverb. He would then proceed to shake hands in a shy manner.

**Teakettle:** One person is chosen to leave the room. The remaining players choose any words which are pronounced alike such as: neigh and nay—beat and beet, and to, two, too. The person who is out is then called in and is greeted with a sentence in which teakettle is substituted for the words which were chosen.

> *Example:* I can go teakettle the movies.
> Phil and I can go teakettle the movies teakettle.
> I can go teakettle the movies teakettle times a week.

**Coffeepot:** One player leaves the room. The remaining players choose a verb. The one who left returns and ask questions substituting the word coffeepot to represent the activity. Example: Where do you coffeepot? How often do you coffeepot? The players must answer truthfully. The questioning continues until the word is guessed or until he gives up. The person who made the last remark leaves the room next.

**Catch the Balloon:** The players are seated on the floor. Have them number off and the highest number is put in the center to act as "it." "It" holds a balloon. He suddenly drops the balloon and instantaneously calls a number. The holder of that number tries to catch the balloon before it touches the floor. If he succeeds, "it" calls another number until the one who loses takes his place. If the one who catches the balloon breaks it, he loses.

## PARTY GAMES FOR INTERMEDIATES

**Shadows:** Hang a sheet by two corners, the lower side touching the floor with a bright light several feet behind it. Divide the players into two groups. One watches while the others go behind the sheet. Let each player pass slowly between the sheet and the light. He may disguise himself by making faces, stooping, etc. The watchers try to identify the shadows. Each group takes a turn. The group identifying the most shadows wins.

**Animal Blindman's Bluff:** One player is blindfolded and given a cane. The others walk in a circle around him. When the blind man taps his cane twice the players stand still. The blind man then points his cane at one of the players who grasps it; the blind man commands him to make a noise like some animal. The player imitates the call of the animal named. If the blind man can identify the name of the player, they change places; if not, he remains blind man until he guesses a player.

**Sniff Sniff:** Select a judge. The players leave the room while the judge collects a number of articles that have a distinctive odor—soap, powder, flowers, fruit, coffee, chocolate, tobacco, etc. When all is ready, the judge calls one player in at a time, blindfolding him before he enters. The judge then lets him smell each item and he must identify it by its odor. The player with the highest score wins.

**The Handkerchief:** Divide the players into two teams. A handkerchief is given to each team. The teams face each other. At the signal, the first player of each team ties the handkerchief to the arm of the one next to him, who must untie it and tie it onto the arm of the next player and so on to the end; then the last player must tie it back onto the arm of the first player. The team that finishes first, wins.

## PARTY GAMES FOR YOUNG CHILDREN

**Blind Man's Bluff:** One child is blindfolded. He imitates the sound of an animal, at the same time touching one of the children in the circle. That child repeats the sound and the blind man must guess who the child is. If he guesses correctly, that child becomes the blind man.

**Fruit Basket:** The children are seated in a circle. The children are given the names of fruits—a few children have the same name. One child stands in the center and calls the name of a fruit. The children having the same name change seats and as they do so the one in the center tries to get a seat. If he succeeds, the one left out stands in the center. If he calls Fruit Basket, everyone changes seats. There should always be one seat less than the number playing.

**Guess the Animal:** Fill a basket with a variety of small animals, cookies or plastic ones wrapped in paper. One child takes a package and leaves the room to see what animal he has chosen. He returns and acts in the way he thinks the animal would. The children try to guess and the one who guesses correctly is the next one to act.

**March on the Newspapers:** Place newspapers about 3 feet apart on the floor from room to room. The children march to music along the line of these newspapers. When the music suddenly stops any children whose feet are on the newspapers drops out of the game. The game ends when only one child is left.

**Hide the Thimble:** One child leaves the room. When he leaves, the others hide a thimble. The child is then called back and tries to find the thimble. The others clap their hands softly if he is far away from where the thimble is and louder as he gets near it. (Music may be used instead of clapping.)

**I Went to the City:** Choose a leader. The players gather around him in a circle. The leader says to the first player, "I went to the city." The first player replies, "What did you buy?" The leader says, "I bought a pair of shoes," and wiggles his feet. The movement is repeated by everyone and must be continued throughout the game. Each time it is the leader's turn, he mentions a new article and adds a new movement. The game ends when all but one player has been dropped for errors.

## TOYS CHILDREN LIKE

**1-YEAR-OLD:** Toys painted in bright colors in vegetable paints, rattles, teething rings, dolls, stuffed animals, bath toys. Nothing small enough to swallow.

**2-YEAR-OLD:** Toys painted in bright colors in vegetable paints, dolls, washable stuffed animals, blocks, pull toys, simple put-one-into-another toys, brightly colored small balls, doll carriages, rockers.

**3-TO-4-YEAR OLD:** Simple put-it-together sets. Wagons, tricycle, wheelbarrows, doll carriages, blocks, miniatures of anything used around the house, simple jigsaw puzzles, picture books, table and chair, paint sets, cutouts, beads, tracing sets, coloring books, balls, doll house.

**5-TO-6-YEAR OLD:** Bicycle (with stabilizers), sled, tinker toys, big blocks, paint and tool sets, weaving and sewing sets, miniature household appliances, doll houses, child's phonograph and records, roller skates, electric trains, books.

**6-TO-8-YEAR OLD:** Construction sets, tools, electric trains, miniature household appliances, games, books, records.

OVER 8: Hobby material—collections, model making, tools, sporting equipment, painting equipment, chemistry set, games, puzzles, books, records, bicycle.

## CHECK LISTS FOR IMPORTANT OCCASIONS

**Check List for the Bride and Her Family:** Write to close relations to let them know of engagement before it is publicly announced.

Announce engagement by telephoning society editors of local papers. If bride would like to have her picture published, she should have one ready. (8 x 10 inches, glossy, preferred.) A party may be given. Guests are told as they arrive, by the girl or her mother. At the party, the host may propose a toast which is also an announcement.

Invite the groom's family to lunch, tea or dinner.

Return visits of groom's relatives.

The engagement ring is usually first worn in public on the day of the public announcement of the engagement.

Friends may give bride a shower.

Plan the wedding—type, time, number of guests, maid of honor, attendants, etc.

Select and arrange for invitations to the wedding.

Bride's mother consults with groom or his mother regarding wedding list for (1) those who are to be asked to the house; (2) those who are to be asked to church only; (3) those who should receive announcements. Invitations may be sent even to those too far away to come.

ARRANGE FOR: Church, *music at church, *decorative flowers at church, clergyman, *clothes for bride, *bridesmaids, flower girls, pages; *flowers for the bridesmaids, *clothes for bridesmaids (paid for by the wearer), decorative flowers for home, *music at home, *seating, wedding cake, food, *menu cards, liquors or punch, trousseau; gifts for bridesmaids (usually given the day before the wedding); wedding rehearsal (but the bride does not take part); *gift for the groom, gifts for attendants, last minute hairdressing.

Presents may be shown at the wedding reception.

Record the gifts.

Send acknowledgments and thanks, personally written.

---

\* Almost all items are optional. Those indicated are often eliminated.

**Check List for the Groom and His Family:**

Propose and be accepted.

Inform bride's father and obtain consent.

Arrange with jeweler to show engagement rings in price range you can afford; bring bride to make selection. (It need not be a diamond. It may be postponed.)

Write to close relatives to let them know of engagement before it is publicly announced.

Have parents (and close relatives) call on bride and her family or write.

If your family is in the habit of entertaining, invite fiancee to lunch or dinner.

Consult with bride's mother regarding invitations.

Arrange for: license, clergyman's fee to be given to best man, wedding ring or double rings; gift for the bride, best man, ushers, and their instructions; liquor, clothes for the wedding, pictures of the wedding, gifts for the best man and ushers, honeymoon, own clothes for the honeymoon, wedding ties and boutonnieres and gloves for best man and ushers, boutonniere for self, bouquet for the bride or "wear away" corsage, *flowers for the bride's mother and his own, *bachelor dinner.

**Check List for the Best Man:**

Arrange for clothing for the wedding similar to groom's.

At the ceremony: See that everything is ready for departing on the honeymoon.

a. "Wear away" clothing at bride's house or local hotel.

b. Transportation and delivery of luggage to the local hotel if this is first stop, or to railroad station.

c. Luggage packed and loaded for both bride and groom if they are leaving by car.

d. Register at local hotel.

e. Obtain wedding ring and clergyman's fee and pay the clergyman after the wedding.

**Things to Do in Case of Death:**

Notify members of the immediate family and 1 or 2 intimate friends who will be of help.

Place notice of death in the newspapers, including state-

---

* Almost all items are optional. Those indicated are often eliminated.

ment of the time of funeral. Type of notice can be selected from those which appear daily.

If only intimate friends are to attend, the notice should say "private funeral" and notification of time and place should be sent to intimate friends.

The person who is to take charge of arrangements should make such arrangements with a funeral director. Obtain from the funeral director an itemized list of the costs; e.g., (1) casket, (2) vehicles.

Select a plot.

Select a clergyman from the church of which the family is a member.

If desired, select 6 or 8 close friends as pallbearers.

The funeral director may hang streamers or make some other indication of a death.

A friend or member of the family should be appointed to be in charge of the arrangements and to answer questions.

Have friend of the family examine wardrobe to see what is necessary if mourning is to be worn.

Arrange for the collection of cards and notices which accompany flowers. Write on each card a description of the flowers sent.

Arrange for someone to go to church to arrange flowers if this is to be done.

If desired, a memorial service may be held instead of a funeral.

Acknowledge messages of sympathy.

## SPECIAL HINTS ABOUT LETTERS

Long letters to friends may be typewritten and all business letters should be typewritten, but never typewrite an invitation, acceptance, regret, or formal social note.

Avoid underscoring and postscripts, unmatched paper and envelopes, writing with a pencil, or sending a letter with a blot on it.

Avoid excessive use of French, Italian, or any other foreign words, in a letter written in English.

## SUGGESTED TELEGRAMS FROM THE WESTERN UNION COLLECTION

BIRTHS:

Congratulations to both of you and happiness and health to the new arrival.

Best wishes to the new arrival and its proud parents.

Happy to hear the good news. Good health and good fortune for the new member of your family.

We are happy in your happiness. Love and best wishes to mother and the baby.

Wanted you to be among the first to know. Just arrived —— pounds ——ounces boy (girl). Mother and daughter (son) doing fine.

Thrilled and happy to hear the good news. Here's just a small token of welcome for the new arrival.

### BIRTHDAYS:

The best of everything to you, today and always.

Wishing you health and happiness on your birthday and for many years to come.

Love and greetings to the best mother (dad) in the world on her (his) birthday.

Hope this gift will add in some small measure to all the joy and happiness I wish you on your birthday.

### WEDDINGS:

Congratulations and best wishes for a long life, prosperity, health and happiness.

Congratulations and best wishes. A long life and a happy one to you both.

Heartiest congratulations. May all your days be as happy as this one.

### ANNIVERSARIES:

Best wishes and love to you on your anniversary.

Congratulations on your wedding anniversary. May many years to come be as happy as those that have passed.

Our heartiest congratulations on your wedding anniversary.

Love and congratulations on your wedding anniversary.

Sorry we can't be with you to help celebrate. Heartiest congratulations. Please accept this little token of friendship and affection.

### ENGAGEMENTS:

Delighted to hear the good news and wish you great happiness.

Congratulations on your engagement. Please accept our best wishes for your every happiness.

Very happy to hear of your engagement. Congratulations and much happiness to you both.

### COMMENCEMENT:

Congratulations and best wishes. May the years ahead of you bring the fulfillment of your fondest hopes.

May your graduation day be the commencement of a continued series of upward steps to success.

We are sorry we cannot be there to applaud you when you take your diploma, but our glad hearts are with you.

Best wishes and congratulations on your graduation. May the road ahead be one of health, happiness and great accomplishment.

### BON VOYAGE:

Bon Voyage and the happiest journey to you.

Bon Voyage. Here's hoping that happiness and good health will accompany you.

Goodbye, good luck, good riddance to all cares and a good warm welcome when you come home again.

### CONVALESCENCE:

Was sorry to hear of your illness but glad to know you are improving. Hope you continue to make rapid progress.

Sorry to hear of your illness. Best wishes for a speedy recovery.

Don't take too long to get well. We are anxious to see you around again soon.

### THANK YOU:

Thanks for a lovely evening. We had a grand time.

Thank you for your lovely gift. It was a delightful surprise.

Thank you for the pleasure of a wonderful visit. I enjoyed every minute of your warm hospitality.

No one could ask for more—you're the world's best party thrower. Many thanks for a grand time.

### CONFIRMATION:

May the blessings of this Holy Confirmation day be multiplied throughout the years.

Our thoughts and prayers are with you on this your Confirmation day.

CONDOLENCES:

My (our) heartfelt sympathy in your great sorrow. ———— joins me in the expression of our deepest sympathy.

Our hearts are with you in love and sympathy. May your happy memories of the past bring you a measure of comfort and peace. Lovingly.

We are grieved beyond expression to learn of your loss. God bless you and comfort you.

My (our) deepest sympathy in your great loss. If there is anything I (we) can do, do not hesitate to let me (us) know.

## ON THE CARD

When you send flowers to a funeral: on your card "with sympathy" or "with deepest sympathy."

When you visit the house of a sick friend who could not see you: on your card "to inquire."

When you visit a friend not at home: on your card "sorry not to see you" or "sorry I missed you."

## MISCELLANEOUS NOTES

CONGRATULATIONS:

*Dear Mrs. Friend:*

*We were both delighted to hear the good news of Sid's success. It was a great accomplishment and we are proud of him and happy for you.*

*Please give him our love and congratulations.*

*Affectionately,*

CONDOLENCES:

*My dear Mrs. Friend:*

*John and I were shocked to hear of the sorrow that has come to you.*

*If there is anything either of us can do, I earnestly hope that you will send us a message.*

*With deepest sympathy,*

Acknowledgment of a note of condolence or flowers:
*Thank you for the beautiful flowers and your sweet letter of sympathy.*

For a Prominent Person:
> *The Commissioner and Mrs. Sound wish gratefully to acknowledge your kind expression of sympathy.*

Recommendation of employees:

*..................................................................has been in my employ*
*..........................................years as...........................................*
*I have found her..............................................................She is leaving because.....................................................................*
*Special Remarks:*

> *..............................................*
> *(Mrs. ...........................)*

## TABLE SEATING AND SETTING

**Seating:** The host sits at the head of the table, and the hostess sits at the other end of the table. The guest of honor sits at the right of the host and is always served first at every course.

**The Setting:** Cloths and mats should be immaculate.

Candles may be used at dinner, but not at lunch. Use at least two candelabra or four candles.

Settings should be geometric, with centerpiece in exact center, candlesticks and settings balanced, parallel, and at equal distance from the edge. Plates, glasses, silver, and individual pieces should be in identical relationship for each setting.

Place silver 2 inches from edge of table in parallel lines. Plate should have designs straight for the person in front of it.

Forks (except small cocktail fork) are placed left of the plate. Knives, spoons, cocktail fork, etc., go to the right of the plate, in reverse order of use. Those to be used first are placed farthest from the plate.

Water glass is placed at the tip of the dinner knife. Bread-and-butter plate is placed to the upper left of the plate, with butter knife either horizontally or vertically across it.

Napkins are usually placed to the left of the fork. For formal or semiformal settings, napkin is placed on a place plate.

**Suggestions for Serving:** All food should be passed, placed, and removed from the left. All beverages are placed, poured, and removed at the right.

Dishes containing food should be held low enough to make it easy for the person to whom it is being passed to help himself. Serving fork and spoon should have handles toward the guest, with fork to the left of the spoon. A waitress should hold serving dish on a folded napkin in her left hand, never at edge of dish or with two hands.

Dinner plate should be removed with the right hand and the bread-and-butter plate or salad plate with the left hand.

Fill water glasses without removing them from the table. Hold a napkin in the left hand slightly under the mouth of the pitcher.

Serve guest of honor or hostess first. Continue around table to right of the first person served. The guest of honor is at the right of the host.

Use left hand in serving from the left, right hand in serving from the right.

Pass dishes in order: main dish, vegetables, sauces, bread, relishes, and salad if part of main course.

Remove dishes from main course in following order: roast, accompanying dishes, dinner, bread-and-butter plates or salad plates together, relishes, and salts and peppers. Use small tray or a folded napkin in removing salts and peppers. Never stack one on another. Remove crumbs from table after main course. Crumb the table with a folded napkin and plate, if necessary, after the main or salad course.

Use a napkin, folded in a square, in placing and removing dishes.

Where help is limited to one maid, six persons is maximum service. Courses should be limited to three or four. The first course may be at the setting before the meal. For informal service, the main course may be carved in the kitchen and served with vegetables in one serving plate. If vegetables are served separately, a double serving dish will save a trip to the kitchen.

AFTER THE FIRST COURSE: If the main course is to be carved at the table, remove all plates after first course. If the main course is carved in the kitchen, and the dinner plate is already on the table, remove sherbet glass and soup bowls only. If a place plate has been used, remove the place plate and substitute dinner plate.

If host carves, waitress places hot dinner plates in front of him, and meat platter just beyond dinner plates. When he has

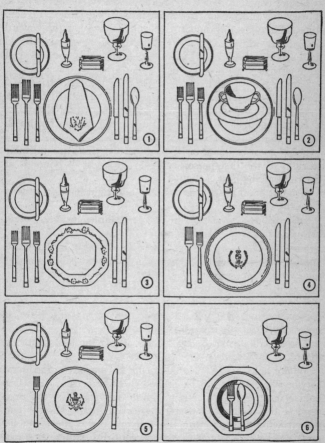

**CORRECT SETTING FOR EACH LUNCH COURSE:** (1) Bread and butter plate is in place as luncheon is served. (2) The bouillon cup replaces the service plate. (3) The plate for the entree follows on the rare occasions when two courses come before the meat. (4) For the meat course. (5) Then the salad plate. (6) Only the glasses remain when dessert is served.

served the dinner plate, he passes it first to the right, then around the table. Vegetables are served by the waitress in the same order. If carving is done in the kitchen, the main course may be served from one platter, or the meat first and the vegetables following.

DESSERT: The dessert is best served whole at the table with

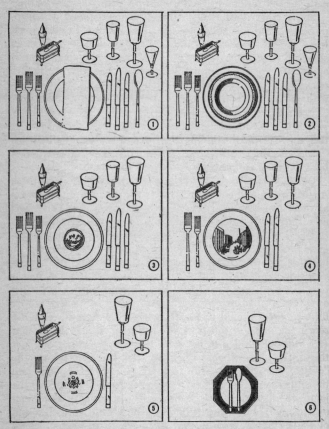

CORRECT SETTING FOR EACH COURSE OF A FORMAL DINNER: (1) There is no bread and butter plate at a formal dinner. (2) The soup plate has a rim, is of the same color, but of different design. (3) The fish plate replaces soup and service plates. Sherry glass is removed. (4) The meat plate follows. (5) A salad knife is provided with the salad plate. (6) Only the glasses remain when dessert is served.

serving fork and spoon, so that each person may help himself. The portions may be cut in advance, retaining the whole form. Place individual dessert plates, dessert fork, and spoon at each place, then bring in the dessert. The hostess may serve the dessert. Place a pile of dessert plates in front of hostess. The hostess fills each plate and waitress serves it. In such case, dessert fork and spoon should be in the original setting.

SERVING WITHOUT HELP: A meal can be planned which requires no outside assistance, and where the hostess must leave the table on a minimum number of occasions. Courses should be limited to two or three. All silver should be placed at the setting before the meal. Bread-and-butter trays are placed on the table in advance. Main course should be planned to be served from one platter.

Used plates may be removed by passing from person to person to the hostess, and placed by her on a tea cart, or they may be removed by the hostess and placed on a tea cart.

The hostess serves the dessert on plates piled in front of her, and they are passed from person to person.

**Carving Roast Chicken:** The standard carving set may be used. A steak set is particularly good for carving small birds. Above all, a sharp knife is necessary to good carving. (1) Place bird according to the side that carver chooses to carve—legs to the right if the side away from the carver is being carved, or to the left if the near side is being carved. Remove leg by holding drumstick with left hand. Cut through skin around thigh drawing knife from left to right down to the socket near the backbone. With the flat side of the knife, press leg away from chicken. When roaster is cooked to the proper turn, the joint should break. Sever leg by cutting through the remaining skin on the back. Remove leg to service platter. (2) Still holding leg in left hand, disjoint the drumstick and thigh. This makes two servings of dark meat. (3) Ease the "oyster" out with the point of a knife or with a spoon from the spoon-shaped bone near the backbone and just above the joint where the leg was removed. There is one oyster, an oval-shaped, tender muscle of choice dark meat, on either side of the backbone. (4) If the wings are to be served, carve them with a fairly good piece of breast meat attached. Insert fork firmly into the wing section that joins the body. Place knife blade lengthwise the length of the bird and at a point on the breast about 1½ inches from the wing. Strike the wing joint by cutting down and through breast at a 45° angle. (5) To remove wishbone piece, straddle keel bone firmly with fork. Insert knife crosswise of the chicken and just beyond the end of the keel bone. Cut straight downward to the bone. Then turn blade at an angle cutting down and toward the wing joint. With the flat side of the blade, press wishbone piece away from the body, at the same time snapping the joints to free the wishbone. Removing the wishbone piece may be omitted. (6) Breast meat may be sliced in two ways: (a) Insert fork to straddle the keel bone, or into rib section in the side opposite to the side being carved. Start the first slice just above the point where the wing was removed. Continue slicing diagonally toward the back, holding the knife blade flat and using a sawing motion. From 6 to 10 slices may be cut from one side depending upon size of the bird. (b) Or, run point of knife around the breast from left to right along the side of the keel bone, completely circling the breast. Slip flat of blade along keel bone to loosen the breast meat so it can be removed in one piece. Cut crosswise slices of meat. (7) Reverse platter to carve the second side. (8) Remove dressing from body cavity, enlarging the opening if necessary. For each serving, serve dressing, dark and white meat, unless preference is indicated. For a left-handed person reverse these positions.

To carve whole stewed chicken, proceed as described above. A sharp knife is necessary to do a good job since the meat, when properly done, tends to flake or shred.

### TABLE SETTING PLAN FOR BUFFET SUPPER

**Buffet Party:** Buffet parties are simplest to give without help. The table is set with as much color and taste as possible. Coffee, water, or dessert may be placed at a separate table.

Food should be prepared to require no cutting. Breads should be buttered in the kitchen. Avoid stemware or delicate glasses. Provide as many individual tables as possible. (Nests of tables are particularly handy. Bridge tables can seat four.) These should be removed after the meal.

### SERVING WINE

The host may pour, or pass bottle around table. Guests should have opportunity of seeing label. The host pours a lit-

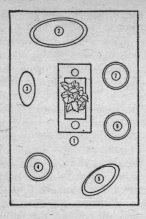

| 1 Center piece | 9 Water Glasses |
| 2 Meat Platter | (on tray) |
| 3 Hot Buttered | 10 Napkins |
| Rolls | 11 Plates |
| 4 Hors D'oeuvres | 12 Lemon & Sugar |
| 5 Macaroni or Rice | 13 Iced-Tea Spoons |
| 6 Salad | 14 Forks |
| 7 Vegetable | 15 Butter Spreaders |
| 8 Iced-Tea Glasses | |
| (on tray) | |

tle wine into his own glass to remove any sediment. He then fills each glass ¾ full. To catch any drops from the bottle, he holds a folded napkin under the bottle mouth. The bottle is then placed on the buffet or serving table, wrapped in a napkin or cradled in a wicker basket.

Serve appetizer or dessert wines in a cocktail glass, white wines in a medium-sized glass, red wines in a goblet. Sparkling wines should be served in a medium-sized or large stemmed glass.

Toasting glasses should be as thin as possible and also large. Never fill them more than partially, in order to let the bouquet escape freely.

If it is an old wine it is better to decant it beforehand to separate the deposit which results from age and to allow the aromas to develop freely.

Aperitifs (Vermouth, Dubonnet, Sherry) or cocktails (Martini, Manhattan) may be served before the meal. White wines (Sauterne, Rhine) are served with fish or shellfish or poultry.

Meat, paté de foie gras, cheese and nuts bring out the qualities of a red wine. Avoid salads dressed with vinegar, sweet vegetables, and any other sweet dishes.

Sweet wines (Port, Madeira) or cordials are served with desserts, or after the meal.

If several wines are to be served, begin with the "younger" or newer vintages, leading up to the old and noble bottles.

Serve dry wines before sweet wines; white wines before red ones; light wines before heavier ones.

**How to Serve Wines and Liquors:**

Serve cold (42°-45°): White wines, sparkling wines, pink wines, beers, cocktails, most mixed drinks, spirits used as aperitifs, very dry Sherry or Madeira.

Serve at room temperature (70°-75°): All red wines, medium and rich Sherry, Madeira, Port, Marsala, spirits taken neat, gin, rum, whisky, brandy, liqueurs.

These are merely common preferences. Exceptions may be made on hot days, or to comply with personal tastes.

**How to Open a Bottle of Wine: 1.** Cut and remove capsule below bulge. Wipe off mold or dirt. 2. Drive corkscrew as far as possible into center of cork, lever out with even motion. Avoid jerking. 3. With T corkscrew, hold between knees, with shoulder of bottle in palm of left hand, pull slowly and evenly with right hand, turning slightly to the right. 4. Wipe bottle mouth, inside and out.

# BOOK X

## Home Medical Guide

### HOW TO KEEP HEALTHY

People who live in it are the most important part of a household. To keep them healthy, to repair their minor ills, and to protect them from major dangers are all parts of good household management.

**Preventive Medicine:**

These rules of preventive medicine will help you keep your family well.

1. AVOID FATIGUE: At first signs of physical or nervous fatigue get more rest.

2. EAT SENSIBLY: Eat the foods which meet your nutritional needs. Eat regular meals at regular times. Don't overeat. When you are overly tired or emotionally upset, rest before eating.

3. DRESS SENSIBLY: Your clothes should protect you against extremes of weather.

4. CHOOSE SHELTER WISELY: The cleanliness, warmth, comfort and the airiness of your living quarters are important.

5. PREVENT ACCIDENTS: Be conscious of accident hazards and provide safety measures in your home.

6. LEARN WHAT TO DO: Courses are available in first aid, home nursing, nutrition, water safety, accident prevention. These will teach you how to take care of yourself and your family more skillfully. Be prepared for emergencies with a well-stocked medicine chest.

7. HELP YOUR DOCTOR HELP YOU: Take periodic medical examinations, particularly at middle age and later, even though you feel well. Have your eyes examined often enough to be sure your glasses are right for you. Visit your dentist twice a year and have your teeth cleaned professionally.

8. LEARN WHAT IMMUNIZATION YOUR CHILDREN NEED and when they need it. Immunization protects against certain infectious diseases such as smallpox, diphtheria, whooping cough, scarlet fever and others.

9. AT FIRST SIGNS OF A COLD keep warm, rest, and drink generous amounts of citrus fruit juices and other liquids. If you have chills or a fever call your doctor.

10. CONSULT YOUR PHYSICIAN at first signs of any abnormal conditions.

When an illness is serious enough to require more than temporary relief or simple home remedies, it needs expert diagnosis. No single symptom indicates one disease and only one, and a given disease may appear in any one of several forms. If you rely on your own diagnosis and treatment, you may postpone proper treatment until a serious condition develops.


## MENTAL HEALTH

A large proportion of illnesses have been found to be caused by emotional disturbances which seem to have absolutely no relation to the disease itself. Some of us are fortunate enough to be able to control our emotions, others, on the contrary, allow them to run rampant or suppress them unduly.

Here are some hints that may prove helpful in maintaining good mental health.

### Some Rules for Mental Health:

1. Try not to worry. Time minimizes all troubles. Postpone until tomorrow what you are worrying about today.

2. Don't brood over the past. Think about the rosy future.

3. Make the best of each situation. Nothing is really as bad as it appears at first.

4. Envy is a natural feeling. Try, nevertheless, to limit your desires to things which are reasonably obtainable.

5. Cultivate a tolerance for the opinions and emotions of others. Remember that other people have emotions very similar to yours.

6. Cultivate a sense of humor.

7. Find an interesting hobby. Above all, keep busy, and you will find you have no time for emotional upsets.

8. If you have something bothering you, let it out. Keeping it to yourself makes it grow.

9. If something's gone wrong, don't look for a scapegoat to let it out on. Take a walk till you're relaxed.

10. Remember everybody needs love and appreciation. A few kind extra words or a surprise gift will do wonders.

11. If you have something unpleasant to do, do it immediately and get it over with. Worrying about it will probably bother you more than doing it.

12. Families are important, but remember, every member of the family has a life of his own to lead.

## SAVING YOUR ENERGY

Some hints on doing housework with a minimum of waste of effort:

1. Plan your work to do as much of it in a sitting position as possible. Plan your kitchen to do as little walking as possible.

2. Stand straight with weight borne by bony framework. This puts minimum strain on muscles and ligaments. Sit straight from hips to neck.

3. Bend at knees or hips; save the back.

4. Use leg and shoulder muscles, not back muscles.

5. Use whole body at center of any weight to be moved.

6. Take ten-minute rest period after every hour's work.

7. Have tables and working surface at right height.

8. Keep things within easy reach.

9. When carrying packages, keep the body in balance.

10. Use the best tools for the job. Use labor-saving devices when you can.

## THE MEDICINE CHEST

A well-stocked medicine chest should contain the following:
ANTISEPTICS
    Iodine (not more than 3 months old)
    Boric Acid (mix 1 teaspoonful to 1 pint water)
    Tincture of Green Soap (for cleansing wounds)
    Tincture of Benzoin Compound
FOR BURNS, ETC.

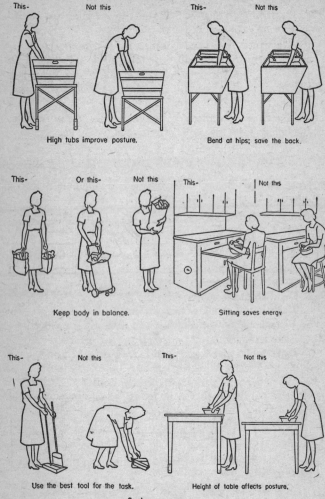

This-    Not this      This-    Not this

High tubs improve posture.     Bend at hips; save the back.

This-    Or this-    Not this    This-    Not this

Keep body in balance.     Sitting saves energy

This-    Not this      This-    Not this

Use the best tool for the task.     Height of table affects posture.

**Saving your energy.**

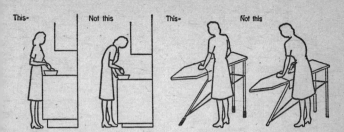

This-     Not this     This-     Not this

Height of working surface affects posture.     Correct height makes ironing easier.

This-     Not this     This-     Not this

Substitute leg muscles for back muscles.     Use whole body at center of weight to be moved.

This-     Not this     This-

Not this

Back bending is back breaking.     Use of labor—saving equipment improves posture.

Saving your energy.

Picric Acid—3 percent aqueous solution
Sodium Bicarbonate (solution)
Gauze (unopened packages, ⅔, 1, and 2 inches)
Adhesive tape

INHALANTS
Tincture of Benzoin Compound (Loses strength after 3 months)

MOUTHWASHES
Dobell's Solution
Sodium Perborate

CATHARTICS
Cascara Sagrada (liquid or tablet form)—Probably most efficient of all.
Castor Oil
Epsom Salts—Should not be taken habitually without medical supervision.

LIGHT CATHARTICS
Calcium Carbonate
Rhubarb and Soda
Milk of Magnesia (Caking indicates deterioration.)

COLDS
Acetylsalicylic acid (aspirin)
Vinegar (Odor indicates deterioration.)

COUGH MIXTURES
Stokes' Expectorant and Brown Mixture—Usually combined half and half.
Wine of Ipecac (for children)—Especially useful in sudden attacks of croup. Dose, one teaspoonful.
Evaporation, color or odor change indicates deterioration.

SALVES
Lanolin (base of cold cream)
Zinc oxide
Castor Oil (good for the skin if you can stand the odor.) (Heat causes discoloration or separation showing deterioration.)
Petrolatum (vaseline)
Calamine Lotion

THERMOMETER

"PATENT MEDICINES" are formulas of secret composition and should be avoided unless prescribed by physicians.

"PROPRIETARY MEDICINES" are recognized formulas listed in the official United States Pharmacopoeia (published every 10 years) or the New and Non-Official Remedies, published by the American Medical Association, but the "proprietor" has given it a trade name and advertised it.

Most proprietary medicines may be purchased at lower cost by their true names than by their trade-marked names.

DENTIFRICES: Most brands of baking soda and bicarbonate of soda are inexpensive and effective dentifrices. These serve three purposes: polishing, making teeth brushing more agreeable, and some we now know, medicinal. They usually contain abrasive to rub, detergent to loosen, and flavoring.

TOOTHBRUSHES: Most effective brushes are small and narrow, with level head. Stiffness of bristles varies with taste.

TO BRUSH TEETH: Use a downward motion on upper teeth, an upward motion on lower teeth. Brush inside, chewing, and outside surfaces. Never brush across. Rinse mouth thoroughly after brushing, with warm water.

---

### WHAT TO DO IN CASE OF ACCIDENT OR ILLNESS

*The First Things to Do in Case of Accident:*

Keep cool. Send for a doctor at once.

Stop bleeding. Cover wounds.

In case of fractures, apply a splint.

Move the patient to a quiet, airy place.

Keep bystanders at a distance.

Place him in a comfortable position. Handle gently and quietly.

Unless the head is injured, place it on the same level as the body.

Loosen the collar, waist-band or belt.

In case of vomiting, turn patient on one side with the head low.

---

### SIGNS OF DANGER

*If you see these symptoms, call a doctor at once. They mean that something may be seriously wrong.*

FEVERS: A fever of 101° can often indicate far more serious disease than one of 105°. The danger signs associated with any fever are—pallor, listlessness, somnolence, excessive dryness of the skin, convulsions (muscular twitchings associated with unconsciousness).

PAIN: Severe chest pain in any man over 30 years of age if persistent for more than an hour. Abdominal pain of steady rather than cramplike nature, especially if accompanied by tenderness (pain can be elicited by pressing one's hand against the abdomen). Pain in extremities or back following a fall or accident (most fractures cannot be diagnosed simply by examination of the injured limb, but require X-ray studies) Seemingly trivial sprains or falls, especially suspicions of fracture if there is considerable swelling, blueness, pain, or disability of the limb.

HEADACHE: if associated with fever or mental changes.

SEVERE CRAMPS that persist all day, especially if a hernia is known to exist or if the abdomen becomes distended.

VOMITING if persistent for several hours or if associated with dry skin, high fever, bright flush, abdominal pain or tenderness, abdomen held rigid.

DIARRHEA (watery stools, not simply frequent formed movements) when persistent for 48 hours or if associated with severe cramps, boardlike rigidity of abdomen or cold sweat. In adults, frequently recurring bouts of mild diarrhea should be investigated. In infants, notify doctor if diarrhea lasts even for several hours, especially if skin becomes dry and crinkly.

COUGH: if associated with fever, even if only a daily rise to 100° over a period of days. Croup (crowing or gasping respirations) in babies or children.

RAPID PULSE—over 110 in adults when checked over a full minute while at rest.

BLOODY OR COFFEE COLORED URINE or markedly diminished urine output, especially if swelling of ankles or eyes develop

UNCONSCIOUSNESS—of any sort. Don't administer anything by mouth. Usually best to slope body slightly toward head.

BLEEDING—if more than a pint (2 glassfuls) from whatever cause, or if pulsating in character and incapable of being stopped by steady pressure over bleeding point for 10-1 minutes. Or if pallor, cold sweat, rapid pulse or breathing, and listlessness develop.

## HOME REMEDIES FOR MINOR AILMENTS

| Ailment—*Causes* Symptoms | Treatment |
| --- | --- |
| ABRASIONS (skin rubbings) tiny pin-point bleeding spots, fluid | Disinfect and treat as wound. |
| ACNE *caused by inflammation of skin glands.* Papules — usually around nose, chin, and forehead. | Prevent by washing with soap and water, using soft nail brush several times daily. Dry with rough towel, rub to promote circulation. In acute cases, call a doctor. Empty papules by squeezing. Change clothing frequently to avoid re-infection. Minimize carbohydrate and greasy foods and oils in diet. Exercise. (*But,* perspiration is bad for acne.) Bathe frequently. |
| AIR OR MOUNTAIN SICKNESS *unaccustomed low air-pressure.* Rapid heartbeat, paleness, weakness. | Prevent by taking dramamine tablets. Keep patient lying down and warm. |
| ALCOHOLISM *alcohol poisoning.* Respiration is deep, slightly snoring, muscles twitch, patient can be aroused. | Give emetic (soapy water, salt water, mustard in water). Give hot coffee, solution of 2 tablespoonfuls of Epsom salts in glass of water. But give nothing by mouth if patient cannot be roused. |
| DELIRIUM TREMENS | Avoid physical restraint. If necessary, place in "strong" emptied room. Large doses of sedatives may be given. Give diet high in calories and vitamins as soon as practical. CURE: Antabuse, a new drug, produces a hangover effect if a small amount of alcohol is taken. It tends to wean away from alcohol. |

| Ailment—Causes Symptoms | Treatment |
|---|---|
| HANGOVER | Give Epsom salts or 1 tablespoonful of bicarbonate of soda in glass of water; liquid diet; sedative; strong black coffee; cold shower. |
| ALLERGIES, HAY FEVER *sensitivity (allergy) to some particular pollen, dust, or other substance.* Tickling, stuffiness, and a watery discharge in the nose, sneezing, and redness and itching of the eyes and face. | Injections will often reduce the sensitivity and prevent further attacks for some time. The injections must be given each year, a few days apart, during the months before the season when symptoms appear. Antihistamines are available in tablet or liquid form for temporary relief of symptoms. See your doctor. Removal of pollens from the air, particularly in sleeping room, may help. Use an air filter, an air-conditioning unit, an electric pollen remover, a filter mask, or small filter worn in the nose. |
| APOPLEXY *unconsciousness,* snoring, dilated pupils, sometimes bluish face, partial paralysis. | Call a doctor. Remove clothing from neck and chest. Do not give stimulants. Apply cold cloth or ice pack to head and back of neck. Remove false teeth. Avoid movement. |
| ATHLETE'S FOOT RINGWORM *fungus which attacks hair, skin and nails.* Burning, itching, cracking of skin usually around toes. | To prevent, avoid walking barefoot around showers, swimming pools, etc. Don't wear other person's socks or shoes. Soak feet for 10 minutes, morning and night, in solution of 2 tablespoons of sodium hyposulphite in 1 quart of water. Allow to dry on feet. Dust with powder made of 1 part sodium hyposulphite mixed with 4 parts powdered boric acid before putting on socks. Keep infected toes separated with absorbent cotton. (Burn cotton after using.) |
| AUTOMOBILE SICKNESS | To prevent, take one or two dramamine tablets. |

| Ailment—Causes Symptoms | Treatment |
| --- | --- |
| TES—*Animal* dogs, cats, rats, any warm-blooded animal | Call a doctor for antitetanus injection. If tetanus develops, it is usually fatal. Drench wound with boiled water and treat as any other wound. Animal should be observed for hydrophobia if possible. |
| *Ant* | Apply theophrin ointment (5 percent). |
| *Bees, wasps, hornets, yellow jackets* | Not dangerous unless around mouth or throat and thus interfere with breathing. Remove stingers. Apply 2 drops of solution of bicarbonate of soda or dilute ammonia water. Apply ice or cold cloth wrung with boric acid solution to relieve swelling or pain. Avoid fingering, squeezing, etc. |
| *Black Widow, Spiders* local pain spreads rapidly. Fever, perspiration | Call a doctor. Keep patient warm. Treat as snake bite if possible. |
| *Chiggers* | Apply drop of kerosene or tincture of iodine; or paint with ethyl aminobenzoate, 30 grains, with flexible collodion, ½ oz. |

**Chigger attached to skin at hair follicle.**

| | |
| --- | --- |
| *Flea* | Apply alcohol, camphor water, or calamine lotion. |
| *Human* | These may cause infection. Scrub wound copiously with soap and water. Apply antiseptic and wet salt solution. |
| *Low forms of marine life* | Clean. Wash with solution of 1 part ammonia, 1 part water. Apply paste of bicarbonate of soda in cold cream. |
| *Mosquito* | Prevent by anointing with pyrethrum in oil (33 percent pyrethrum extract, 52 per- |

| Ailment—*Causes* Symptoms | Treatment |
|---|---|
| | cent mineral or castor oil, 15 percent oil pennyroyal). Treat with theophorin ointment 5 percent. |
| *Sandflies* | Remove eggs with sterilized needle. Apply antiseptic. |
| *Scorpion* | Treat as for bee bite. If swelling appears apply a tourniquet above wound (see 542), suck out as in snake bite. Wash wound with potassium permanganate solution (2½ grains in 1 quart of cool water. Apply paste of baking soda and water. Apply hot or cold compresses to reduce swelling. |
| *Snake* pain, swelling, discoloration. L a t e r, nausea, v o m i t i n g, rapid heartbeat, convulsions, paralysis | To prevent: Snakes rarely attack unless molested. Watch where you walk or climb. In the U. S. the four poisonous snakes are cottonmouth moccasin, copperhead moccasin, rattlesnake and coral snake. Large blackfanged snakes are dangerous. They are most active at night, spend most of days lying in the shade of a rock or ditch or buried in sand. |
| | Treat for shock: Keep patient quiet and warm. Call a doctor. Apply bandage above wound (toward heart) tight enough to make veins swell. Sterilize knife and cross cut in form of an X above fang marks to cause free bleeding, but do not sever artery. Suck wound (with suction cup or mouth) and spit out fluid. Repeat for ½ hour. If swelling continues, make additional cross-cuts in semicircle above fang marks and apply suction for 15 minutes at each point. When swelling ceases, apply strong solution of potassium permanganate or other available antiseptic on wound. Give coffee or aromatic spirits of ammonia for nausea or faintness. |

| Ailment—Causes Symptoms | Treatment |
|---|---|
| *Tarantula* | Call a doctor. Wash and treat as snake bite. |
| *Woodtick* | Apply cold compress and cloth wrung in lead water and alcohol. |
| BLEEDING | See CUTS. |
| BLISTERS *caused by rubbing* | To prevent, wear gloves while working in job that may cause blisters. Apply tincture of benzoin on areas which may be affected. Do not use adhesive plaster. <br><br> Wipe blister with alcohol and antiseptic. Open with sterile needle (sterilize in flame or alcohol), at the edge rather than the top, with a minimum break. Apply antiseptic and sterile gauze. |
| BOILS | Apply mild antiseptic in a moist blotter-like poultice. Or paint edges with 2 percent tincture of iodine, followed by a moist pack of 1 part glycerol and 1 part alcohol. Hot, moist antiseptic dressings will hasten bringing it to a head. Do not open within the nose. This may end fatally. Incisions may be made by a doctor after pus has formed. |
| BRUISES *blow or fall* black and blue marks "black eye" | Apply cold compresses several times a day to reduce swelling. Then apply hot cloths or heating pad to promote healing. In case of major bleeding or multiple bruises, call a doctor to determine if there is internal injury. <br><br> A bump near eye will usually be followed by swelling or discoloration unless treated. Only time will cure a black eye. |
| BUNIONS *pressure of ill-fitted shoe causes enlargement at a joint* | Get special shoes with metatarsal bar. Foot exercises will help. |

| Ailment—*Causes* Symptoms | Treatment |
| --- | --- |
| BURNS<br>  scalds, sunburn,<br>  1st degree—redness,<br>  2nd degree—blisters,<br>  3rd degree—deep tissue destruction | If burn covers large area, call a docto as this may cause shock. Cover burnt are (nerve endings) with thick paste of bakin soda and water. For first aid, use ointmen or jellies containing tannic acid on 1 degree burns; use only jellies on 2nd d gree burns. Never use tannic acid ne eyes. Call a doctor. Remove clothing, whe it does not stick to skin. Do not use oils ointments. Cover burned area with moi gauze until the doctor comes. In seve cases, place patient in bath of salt solutio at 95 to 100° F., even with clothing. Ad tional dangers are shock or poisoning. |
| ACID BURNS<br>*nitric, sulphuric, carbolic* | Remove acid quickly by drenching wi water, then apply solution of 2 teaspoo bicarbonate of soda in full glass of wat (or dilute ammonia water). Treat as bu |
| ALKALI BURNS<br>*caustic soda, lye, ammonia, cleaning powders* | Remove alkali quickly by drenching wi water, then apply diluted vinegar or lem juice. Treat as burn. |
| CALLUS | Soak feet in solution of ½ cup of soda in gallon of water, morning and nig remove by scraping with sterilized kni Apply antiseptic dressing. |
| CHARLEYHORSE<br>  sore muscles | Rest, apply heat, liniments. After so recovery, exercise actively. |
| CHILBLAIN<br>*too rapid warming of frozen parts*<br>inflammation, itching, burning, swelling, sores | Call a doctor. Rub affected area w alcohol. Massage. |
| CHILLS | Put patient to bed with heating pad feet. Give hot drinks. If accompanied fever, call a doctor. |

| Ailment—Causes Symptoms | Treatment |
|---|---|
| **COLDS** | Put patient to bed. Give hot baths, warm drinks, light diet, laxative, aspirin. If colds recur, take vaccine injections. Antihistamines may be helpful in early stages but should not be used habitually without doctor's instructions. |
| **COLD SORE** at lips, usually in fevers | Apply camphor ice. |
| **COMA** *(loss of consciousness) alcohol, epilepsy, head injuries, brain diseases, meningitis, encephalitis, tumors, narcotics, chronic kidney disease, diabetes* severe fever, hemorrhage, heat, hysteria | Call a doctor. Keep patient horizontal or slope body slightly toward head. Do not give anything by mouth. Give complete rest in darkened, well-ventilated room. |
| **CONVULSIONS** *internal poisoning during pregnancy, tetanus, meningitis, epilepsy (5 to 30 minutes daily to infrequently, may be accompanied by loss of consciousness)* twitching or spasm of muscles in arms, legs, or other parts of body. | Call a doctor. Put patient to bed in quiet, darkened room. Place small piece of wood (clothespin) between patient's teeth to avoid biting lips. Raise head on pillow. Loosen clothing. Do not leave patient alone. |
| **IN CHILDREN**—*tetanus, Vitamin D deficiency or beginning of infection* | Insert cloth roll between teeth. Place in tub of lukewarm water for 5 to 10 minutes. Apply cold cloth to head. Dry. Put to bed in quiet, darkened room with hot water bag at feet. |

| Ailment—Causes Symptoms | Treatment |
|---|---|
| CORN | Surgical removal is considered wisest. |
| CONSTIPATION | Laxatives should not be taken regularly without consulting a doctor. Most widely accepted are cascara sagrada (liquid or tablets), castor oil, Epsom salts. |
| COUGHS | If coughs persist, see a doctor. For emergency remedy, use solution 1 part Stokes' Expectorant, 1 part Brown Mixture. For children, 1 teaspoonful wine of ipecac. |

## MAKING A TOURNIQUET

1. Make a loop around the limb.

2. Pass a stick under the loop.

3. Tighten tourniquet just enough to stop bleeding.

4. Bind free end to limb to keep tourniquet from unwinding.

| Ailment—*Causes* Symptoms | Treatment |
|---|---|
| **CUTS** open wounds | If a nerve is cut (accompanied by loss of motion or sensation) or cut is jagged or deep (with tetanus danger), call a doctor. Wash away dirt outside wound with alcohol but do not try to wash out dirt in wound.<br><br>Apply antiseptic (2 percent solution of iodine, mercurochrome, tincture of metaphen). Apply iodine in one stroke, allow to dry before bandaging. Then apply sterile gauze and affix with tape to press cut edges together. Never apply iodine near eyes or body cavities. Never apply adhesive tape directly over iodine.<br><br>If deep wound is bleeding freely, apply pressure at wound with gauze. (Scalp and face wounds usually do.) If blood spurts from a wound, a severed artery is indicated. Close by applying pressure at pressure points near wound. If this does not succeed, make a tourniquet, but this must not be left on for more than 15 minutes. At the end of the 15 minutes, loosen for 1 minute or 2, or until it is necessary to re-tighten. If vein is cut (blood is dark red), apply pressure at point away from heart. A tourniquet may be applied, but is seldom necessary.<br><br>If tourniquet is not effective in stopping bleeding, call a doctor to apply a hemostat. |

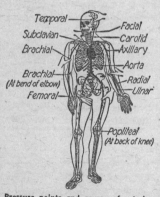

Temporal
Subclavian
Brachial
Brachial (At bend of elbow)
Femoral
Facial
Carotid
Axillary
Aorta
Radial
Ulnar
Popliteal (At back of knee)

**Pressure points and course of arteries.**

| | |
|---|---|
| **DIARRHEA** (many liquid bowel movements) *unwise eating, excitement* | Cathartics. No food for 24 hours. Then, boiled milk in diet. If persistent, call a doctor. |

| Ailment—*Causes* Symptoms | Treatment |
|---|---|
| accompanied by pain, loss of weight, or other symptoms | Appendicitis: Give no food. After acute symptoms pass, give weak tea every 3 to 4 hours for 12 hours. Then give only soft foods—cereals, toast, eggs, custard. |
| DISLOCATIONS<br>t o r n  l i g a m e n t s (shoulder, hip, jaw, fingers); this causes pain, stiffness and swelling, followed by discoloration | Call a doctor to replace bones. Apply cold compresses. The doctor may bandage or apply a plaster of Paris cast. |
| DROWNING | Give artificial respiration. (See p. 558.) |
| EARACHE<br>*infection of middle ear. May follow cold, influenza, measles, diphtheria, etc.* | Call a doctor, especially if in a child suffering from a disease. Report temperature and pulse. Keep head raised. If difficulty persists, call a doctor. Put nothing in ear until examined by doctor. |
| *boil in external ear foreign body wax in ear* | Have a doctor flush out with a syringe. Do not pick it out with fingers or sharp instrument. |
| ECZEMA<br>*external irritations or faulty metabolism* | See a doctor. Bathe in borax solution and dry by blotting. (Do not rub skin.) Take light diet. Rest. Clean scales by dabbing on olive oil. |
| ELECTRIC SHOCK<br>*lightning, touching live wires* | Remove live wire (or patient from live wire) with dry stick, rubber gloves, dry cloth or newspaper as insulation. Give artificial respiration if necessary. When conscious, give solution of 1 teaspoonful of aromatic spirits of ammonia in glass of water. Keep patient quiet. Provide ample ventilation. Place pillow at neck so head falls backward. Loosen clothing. Rub arms and legs vigorously. Call a doctor. |

| Ailment—Causes Symptoms | Treatment |
|---|---|
| EYE—FOREIGN BODY IN THE EYE *cinder, dirt, steel* | Remove as quickly as possible to avoid abrasion, scars, etc. Do not rub eye. Winking or pulling lid down may loosen material or drift it to edge of eye, where it may be removed with clean cotton. |

To remove object, place matchstick over lid with one hand, lift lid with thumb and forefinger of other hand and pull gently over matchstick. Locate dirt and remove with sterile cotton at edge of toothpick. A few drops of castor oil or medicinal paraffin may be applied to cotton to help pick up dirt, or apply boric acid solution with medicine dropper, allowing solution to run from nose outward. If material is imbedded or cannot be located, call a doctor. Cover both eyes with gauze soaked in cold water. Doctor may anesthetize the eyeball to work more effectively.

1. Inspect eyeball and lower lid; gently remove object with a moist clean corner of handkerchief.

2. If object is not in lower lid, inspect upper lid; grasp eyelashes with thumb and index finger; place matchstick or small twig over lid.

3. Pull lid up over stick; examine inside of lid while person looks down; gently remove particle with a clean corner of handkerchief.

| | |
|---|---|
| STY — Inflammation of eyelid membrane. *searing, pus, irritation, itching* | Wash with solution of boric acid to keep eye free of secretions. Penicillin ointment applied on the inner eyelid usually clears condition in a few days. |
| FAINTING *vomiting, weakness, fatigue, fright, excessive joy* | If patient is sitting, place head between knees; lying down, keep head or shoulders below body. Allow ample ventilation. Loosen clothes. Hold smelling salts or am- |

| Ailment—*Causes* *Symptoms* | Treatment |
|---|---|
| (cold, clammy skin, weak, rapid pulse, shallow breathing) | monia to nostrils, but not too close. Dash cold water in patient's face. When patient recovers consciousness, give him water or ¼ glass of water with 1½ teaspoons of aromatic spirits of ammonia. Patient should be kept lying till fully recovered. |
| FEVER 98.6° F. is normal; 101° to 103° moderate; 104° to 105°, call the doctor immediately | Sponge bath. Prevent chilling by covering patient with sheet or light blanket. Sponge and dry small areas at a time (chest, abdomen, legs) keeping rest of body covered. Take 5 to 10 minutes. Alcohol rub may improve comfort. Ask doctor's permission. Apply wet packs: Place patient on large bath towel covered with sheet previously soaked in lukewarm water. Wrap patient for 10 minutes, covered with light blanket. Remove sheet and dry. Cover patient. Drugs: Aspirin for relief, but not for cure. |

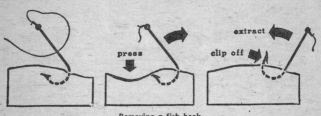

Removing a fish hook.

| | |
|---|---|
| FISHHOOK WOUNDS | If possible, avoid pulling out. Push hook out at another point and cut off the barb. Apply tincture of iodine and sterile gauze. If hook is dirty or deeply imbedded, call a doctor to avoid tetanus. |
| FRACTURES (crack or break in bone) compound | Don't move patient except when necessary. Call a doctor to X-ray and set bone, and apply a splint. For first aid, a board, |

| Ailment—*Causes*<br>Symptoms | Treatment |
|---|---|
| fracture: when skin is broken by bone. Always accompanied by pain, especially when injured part is moved, usually by swelling and discoloration | newspaper, pillow or blanket may be made into a splint and bandages tied to it, except at the point of break. If spine is injured, particularly avoid movement or changing position. If neck is broken, transport lying on back. If back is broken, transport lying on stomach. In placing on stretcher, move body as a unit, applying tension to head. If elbow is broken, do not change position. Wounds should be treated as such, first. |
| FREEZING<br>(frostbite) ears, nose, fingers, toes, etc., numbness | Keep in cool or cold place until affected parts have thawed to a red or normal color. Wrap in cotton or treat as first-degree burn. If skin blisters, call a doctor. |
| GAS POISONING<br>*inhalation of carbon monoxide from illuminating gas, sewer gas, motorcar exhaust, etc.*<br>headache, dizziness, drowsiness, rapid heartbeat, nausea, vomiting, sometimes unconsciousness | To avoid, use a safety lamp which will go out in poor oxygen. Place patient outdoors or in best-ventilated position available. Keep warm with blankets and heating pads. Loosen clothing. In severe cases, call a doctor. Place rolled blanket or pillow under neck so that head falls back. Rub arms and legs vigorously. If breathing is weak, apply artificial respiration. (See p. 558.) Caution: Carbon monoxide is odorless. Rescuer should use precaution so as not to be affected. |
| HALITOSIS<br>(unpleasant breath) *recent eating, excessive fat in diet, menstrual period, excessive smoking, digestive disturbances* | If due to recent food eaten, use a mouth wash. Remedy the basic causing condition. |
| HANGNAIL<br>split outer skin at side of nail | Flatten filament with flexible collodion. With sterile blade, notch skin in wedge-shape near hangnail, removing flap of tissue. Treat as cut. |

| Ailment—*Causes* Symptoms | Treatment |
|---|---|
| **HEADACHES** *various* Usually a symptom, not a disease. | If fever is present, call a doctor. |
| **MIGRAINE:** usually on one side of head, accompanied by nausea and vomiting | Give aspirin. Doctor may prescribe morphine. Keep bowels open. Keep patient quiet in darkened room. |
| **HEAD INJURY** (unconsciousness) *skull fracture, blow at jaw, blow at lower spine* slow heartbeat and breathing; sometimes bleeding from nose or ears | Call a doctor. Place patient on a flat surface, head elevated. Apply ice packs to head. Treat wound. (But never use iodine on a skull injury.) Do not attempt to stop ear or nose bleeding. If nose fluid is clear or bloodstained, and patient is not in shock or unconscious, sit him up. If ear bleeds, place that ear downward. Keep patient quiet. If patient must be moved, transport lying. Avoid stimulants. |
| **HEAT EXHAUSTION** *(usually due to loss of salts and fluids)* *tiredness, profuse sweating* faintness, cramps, diarrhea, rapid but weak heartbeat, subnormal temperature | To prevent, take salt tablets, drink water. Call a doctor. Place patient on back near open window, head level or low. Loosen clothing. Rub arms and legs vigorously. Give salt tablets or teaspoonful of table salt with pint of water or in orange juice. In severe cases, give ½ teaspoonful of aromatic spirits of ammonia in ¼ glass of water, or tea or coffee. Place heating pad at feet. Keep patient quiet. Diet should be easily digestible. |
| **HIVES** *allergic reaction, usually to foods* tingling or itching reddish elevations on the skin | Take cathartic. Apply carbolized calamine lotion or solution of bicarbonate of soda to relieve itching. |

| Ailment—*Causes* *Symptoms* | Treatment |
| --- | --- |
| HYSTERIA | Do not act solicitous. Be firm. A strong command may serve to stop it. Hold strong ammonia inhalant close to nose. Consult a doctor for underlying cause. |
| INDIGESTION | Distinguish from heart attack. Apply heating pad to upper abdomen. Give bicarbonate of soda in water, then peppermint water. Give enema. |
| INFECTIONS | Call a doctor. Apply hot compresses made of 6 tablespoons of salt to 1 quart boiling water. If possible, soak infected area in the solution. Keep compresses hot. |
| INSOMNIA | Stop worrying by getting your mind on pleasant things. Spend the half hour before going to bed in mild recreation. Take a tepid bath. Open windows on the dark side of the house. (Cool air tends to deepen sleep.) Avoid light hitting your face. Minimize noise. Wear loose night clothes. Use sheets and blankets of sufficient length. Use a comfortable mattress, a buoyant pillow. |
| NASAL DISCHARGE *Cold, sinus infection* | Doctor may prescribe ephedrin in water. Do not use oil solutions in drops or sprays. Apply cloth soaked in hot water. |
| ALLERGIC RHINITIS (hay fever) | See Allergies. |
| NAUSEA *In Pregnancy* (2nd or 3rd months) *whooping cough, nervous disorder* | Try breakfast or crackers in bed. Place cracked ice in mouth. Give solution of 1 teaspoonful of sodium bicarbonate in $\frac{1}{4}$ glass of water. |

| Ailment—Causes Symptoms | Treatment |
|---|---|
| **NOSE, FOREIGN BODIES IN THE** | Do not blow out. Irrigate with solution of ½ teaspoonful of salt in warm water. If object would absorb water, try a few drops of olive oil or mineral oil. If persistent, call a doctor. |
| **NOSEBLEED** *blows, crying, tumors, menstruation, kidney disease, high blood pressure, skull fracture, etc.* | Press nostrils together for 5 minutes. Seat patient and apply cold cloths. Keep head elevated and back. Raise arms over head. (Patient may clasp them.) Patient should breathe through mouth and expectorate blood. Apply cloth wrung in cold water, or press nostrils gently with fingers. If bleeding persists, insert cotton plugs, call a doctor. |
| **POISON IVY** *plant poisoning, poison oak, poison sumac.* *red rash, itching, burning* | To prevent, scrub with strong soap and warm water as soon after suspected contact as possible. Dry and apply solution of 2 teaspoonfuls of baking soda in pint of water or solution of Epsom salts, or apply solution of 1 tablespoonful Burow's solution in 2 glasses of water. Some persons have limited immunity. Mild cases usually subside in a few days. Treat with 10 percent |

Poison Oak: Is common on the Pacific Coast. It grows as a vine or bush, has leaves divided into three leaflets.

Poison Ivy: Common east of the Rockies. It grows as a vine or a shrub, is divided into three leaflets, has grayish berries in season.

Poison Sumac: Grows in boglands as a low tree. It has 7 to 13 pairs of leaflets; pale, waxy berries in season.

| Ailment—*Causes* *Symptoms* | Treatment |
|---|---|
| | solution of tannic acid in alcohol. Rub tops of blisters. Open large blisters with sterile needle. Repeat 3 to 4 times at 6-hour intervals. Or apply calamine lotion with 2 percent phenol added. Inflamed areas should be exposed to air but avoid contact with others. *See also* following section, SPECIAL TREATMENTS, for antidotes for common poisons. |
| POISON *swallowed* | Call a doctor. (1) Dilute the poison by making patient drink liquids. (2) Cause vomiting till stomach liquids are clear in color. This can be done by putting fingers down throat or giving an emetic. (Teaspoon of dry, ground mustard in pint of warm water; half strength for children. Soap suds from soap, not flakes; salt or baking soda in water.) Repeat as necessary. (3) Give an antidote after stomach has been washed out. In cases where ammonia, monkshood (aconite, friar's cowl, wolfsbane), strychnine are swallowed, avoid emetics. |
| SKIN ERUPTIONS *sensitivity to chemicals, poison ivy, oak poisoning* | Calamine solution to relieve itching. |
| ALLERGIES *hives, eczema* | See page 536. |
| INFECTIONS | Call a doctor. Apply hot salt solution compresses made with 4 tablespoons of salt in quart of boiling water. Change compresses to keep hot. |

| Ailment—*Causes* Symptoms | Treatment |
| --- | --- |
| PARASITES scales, ringworm | Apply iodine or ammoniated mercury. If in difficult area, see a doctor. |
| SHINGLES blisters along the course of a nerve | See a doctor. |
| SPLINTERS imbedded foreign bodies | Wash area with soap and water and alcohol or antiseptic. Sterilize needle over flame or in alcohol. Remove splinter by pricking skin over it or pull with sterilized tweezers. Apply antiseptic. If splinter is deeply imbedded see a doctor. |
| SPRAINS (tear or stretch of ligaments) | X-ray to determine absence of fracture. Elevate injured joint and keep immobile. Apply cold compresses to reduce swelling, then apply heat to promote healing. If able, apply a snug bandage after swelling has subsided. |
| STIFF NECK | Apply hot compresses or pad and massage gently with liniment two or three times a day. Take two or three aspirins. If other symptoms occur, see a doctor. |
| STAINS ON SKIN | To prevent fingernails getting dirty in gardening, etc., fill with soap before starting. Remove iodine with lemon juice or slice of potato; adhesive tape with cleaning fluid or nail-polish remover. |
| STOMACH PAIN *eating spoiled food, particularly in summer* Often with nausea, diarrhea, no fever | Rest. Do not apply hot or cold compresses. Do not give food. Do not take laxative. (This may lead to ruptured appendix.) If persistent, call a doctor. |

| Ailment—*Causes* Symptoms | Treatment |
| --- | --- |
| *Appendicitis* Severe and persistent pain (usually with fever, nausea, vomiting). Rapid pulse. After some hours, pain tends to localize in right lower abdomen. Stomach muscles contract, become rigid and tender | Call a doctor. Rest. Avoid food or drink. Avoid laxative or enema. |
| *Ulcers* usually act up 1 to 3 hours after meals | Relieved by taking food or some alkali (bicarbonate of soda). Call a doctor. |
| *Gall Bladder* in upper abdomen, just beneath ribs; usually with vomiting and nausea | Call a doctor. |
| *Kidney Disease* in lower abdomen. Sharp or persistent attacks, also pain in back below ribs | Give sitz bath and sedative. Rest. After pain passes massage abdomen and return to full diet. |
| CRAMPLIKE PAINS *disturbances of ovaries and tubes* If accompanied by fever | Rest in bed with knees bent and hot water bags over lower abdomen and under back. Sit in hot bath. Hot drinks. Call doctor immediately. |
| STRAINS *injuries to muscles, ligaments, tendons.* | Rub gently, to stimulate circulation. Rub toward heart. |
| SUNSTROKE flushed face, enlarged | Place patient in cool place with head elevated. Call a doctor. Remove clothing. |

| Ailment—Causes Symptoms | Treatment |
|---|---|
| pupils, dry skin, headache or dizziness, nausea, vomiting, unconsciousness. Fever 102° to 110°F. | Sponge body with cool water. When conscious, give patient cold water to drink. Avoid stimulants. Apply cold compresses or cracked ice at head. In severe cases, immerse patient in cold bath or wrap in cold, wet sheets and fan him. Continue ice bags. |
| SWALLOWING FOREIGN OBJECT | Call doctor and X-ray to determine location and danger. Most objects will pass through bowels. Take soft foods (potatoes, bread, cereals) to cover object. |
| THROAT—FOREIGN BODY IN THROAT in air passages, gasping for breath, bulging eyes. In larynx or windpipe, choking, coughing, difficulty in breathing. In food passages, choking, coughing. | Place patient with shoulders hanging down over couch. Slap vigorously between shoulders to dislodge object. If it can be seen, grasp with fingers. Produce vomiting to expel it. (A child may be held upside down, following same procedure.) Call a doctor, even if symptoms have disappeared, to ascertain that object has not slipped into windpipe or lung. |
| TOOTHACHE | Consult a dentist. To relieve pain, clean cavity with sterile cotton, soak cotton with oil of cloves and apply to cavity. Apply heating pad or, in some cases, cold compress. Give aspirin or pyramidon. |
| VOMITING | Find the cause. Rest stomach for a few hours. Give cereal decoctions (sweetened barley water, etc.). Discontinue giving milk. If persistent, call a doctor. Vomiting may be a symptom of a serious disorder, particularly if catapulted out. |

## RESCUE BREATHING

Rescue breathing is the use of one person's breath to revive another who is unable to breathe for himself. It is the oldest and most effective method of resuscitation.

Absence of breathing movements or blue color of lips, tongue, and fingernails are danger signs indicating a lack of oxygen in the blood and the need for help with breathing. When in doubt, begin rescue breathing. No harm can come from its use, but grave consequences follow if it is not used promptly.

Whether or not the unconscious person is trying to breathe, chances are that his breathing is fully or partially blocked by his tongue. Tilting the head backward or displacing the jaw forward moves the tongue out of the throat and allows air to reach the lungs.

The air you breathe is not "spent." It contains enough oxygen to save a person's life. If you breathe twice as deeply as usual, your exhaled breath contains more than enough oxygen for any adult victim. When each inflation expands the victim's chest, you can be sure rescue breathing is working. Inflate the adult's chest at least 10 times each minute. Infants require smaller and more frequent inflations, at least 20 times per minute.

*Don't waste time.* Only a short time without oxygen can cause serious damage to the brain.

If practical, place the victim on his back or halfway on his side. If not, leave him as he is and start breathing for him. Rescue breathing can be accomplished with the victim sitting in an automobile, pinned under debris, suspended on a safety belt on an electric power line, or floating face-up in the water, as long as you have access to his nose or mouth.

If the first inflation effort fails, make sure the tongue or some foreign object is not blocking air flow to the lungs. Sweep your fingers through his throat to clear any obstructions.

If aspiration of a foreign body is suspected in an adult after failure to move air into the lungs by mouth-to-mouth ventilation, place the victim on his side and give a sharp blow between the shoulders. The rescuer's fingers should sweep through the victim's mouth to remove any such material. An asphyxiated small child should be suspended momentarily by the ankles, or over an arm, and given three sharp pats between the shoulder blades to dislodge obstructing material.

You can prevent tongue obstruction by holding the victim's

head and neck in any position which lifts the jaw and tongue forward.

The head tilt involves holding the victim's head tilted as far back as you can—until the skin over the throat is stretched tight. Use one hand to hold the crown of his head firmly and push backward. Pull his chin upward with the other hand. Close his mouth during inflation through his nose and open it slightly for mouth-to-mouth rescue breathing.

Two other ways to prevent tongue obstruction are: Lift chin up by grasping lower teeth; and lift jaw upward from both corners of jawbone near the earlobe.

Whenever possible, put an infant on his back. Lift the neck gently and tilt the head back until the skin over the throat is stretched. This opens the mouth. With the other hand, pull the chin, keeping the lips slightly open with your thumb. Open your mouth wide. Seal your lips around the infant's mouth and nose. Blow air gently until you are sure the chest expands. It takes only a little air. Stop blowing as soon as the chest starts to rise.

Then remove your mouth and let him breathe out by himself while you breathe in fresh air. It's time for the next breath as soon as you hear him breathe out.

Continue inflations at least 20 times a minute. Take an occasional deep breath if you feel the need for more air.

Rescue breathing for an older child uses either the nose or mouth when you cannot cover both with your mouth.

Excess air may be blown into the stomach. Some victims will burp by themselves. In others, the excess air is noted by an increasing bulge of the stomach between the ribs and navel. To remove air, press the victim's stomach gently. Check the throat for stomach contents before the next inflation. Prevent accumulation of excess air by keeping one hand on the stomach. Keep the head lower than the chest to prevent fluids from entering the lungs.

Lift the neck and tilt the head back. Hold the head tilted so that the skin over the throat is stretched tight. One hand pushes the crown of the head, the other pulls the chin. This prevents obstruction.

Take a deep breath. Open your mouth wide.

MOUTH-TO-NOSE BREATHING: Seal your lips widely on the victim's cheeks around his nose. Be sure your lips don't clos his nostrils. Close his mouth with your thumb on his lower lip.

If his head is not tilted enough, the soft palate allows inflation through the mouth. If this happens, tilt more, or part his lips with your thumb, after each inflation.

Mouth-to-mouth breathing: Seal your lips widely around the victim's mouth. Fold his lower lip down to keep his mouth open during inflation and exhalation. To prevent leakage, press your cheek against his nostrils during inflation.

Blow air into the victim until you see the chest rise. Then remove your mouth to let him breathe out. Take your next breath as you listen to the sound of his breath escaping. Reinflate his lungs again as soon as he has exhaled. Continue inflations at least 10 times a minute.

Gurgling or noisy breathing indicates the need to repeat the steps for clearing the throat and improving the head-tilt position. The choice between mouth-to-nose and mouth-to-mouth usually is not important. However, in some instances only one of these methods will work. Use mouth-to-nose breathing if the victim is convulsing, if his mouth is difficult to open, or if his stomach gets inflated too much during mouth-to-mouth breathing. Use mouth-to-mouth breathing if the nasal air passage is blocked, or if you have to use one hand to control the victim's body (as in the water).

Rescue breathing can be started in the water—as soon as you can reach the victim's mouth with your mouth and you are able to stand with your head out of the water. Some experts can rescue breathe while treading in deep water. Grasp the crown of his head with one hand and tilt his head back until his mouth opens. To keep the air passage open with one hand, you must keep the head tilted far back. Inflate his lungs using the mouth-to-mouth method, sealing his nostrils with your cheek. Your other hand or arm should be locked in his armpit to keep control of his body.

The first 10 breaths should be given as quickly as possible. Don't be concerned if the first few breaths cause water to spurt from his nose and mouth. As you carry him ashore, breathe for him at least once every 10 seconds. If he does not recover breathing by the time you reach shore, don't struggle to get him out of the water into the hot sun. Leave him in shallow water as you continue to breathe for him. The cool water reduces his need for oxygen. Also, in shallow water,

*Essentials of*

# RESCUE BREATHING

**1** *Prevent Obstruction*

Tilt head...

or Lift Chin

or Lift Jaw

**2** *Inflate Lungs*

Thru Nose...

or Mouth...

or Both

Begin rescue breathing as soon as possible.

Even while victim is still in water.

# relaxed tongue obstructs breathing

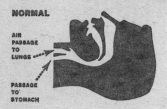

**NORMAL**

AIR
PASSAGE
TO
LUNGS

PASSAGE
TO
STOMACH

**UNCONSCIOUS**

TONGUE
AGAINST
THROAT

## CLEARING VICTIM'S THROAT

To loosen an object stuck in an infant's throat, hold him by his ankles, open his mouth and let any fluid or solids fall out. Suspend the child head down over one arm. Apply several sharp pats between the shoulder blades. Then clear his throat with your fingers and resume rescue breathing.

he'll be easier to pick up by stretcher or by hand when help arrives. You can kneel in the water and rest his head on your knee. Now you can use both hands to hold his head tilted back fully and his chin pulled upward. Also, in this position, you can switch from mouth-to-mouth to mouth-to-nose breathing if too much air is being blown into his stomach.

When he begins to recover, get him ashore so you can take better care of him if there are complications. He may vomit food or sea water. If so, drain his throat each time to make sure the material does not enter his lungs. If possible, keep his head lower than his chest so any liquid will run out of his mouth. To aid this drainage, pull his shoulder up over your knee to raise his chest. You may clean his throat of mucus, vomit, or water with a cloth around your fingers.

During recovery he may have a convulsive seizure. If this happens, give him mouth-to-nose rescue breathing—enough to keep him pink. Watch his breathing carefully. If he lapses back to shallow breathing or turns blue, rescue breathe in rhythm with him. Rescue breathing may be needed in the ambulance. Continue to breathe for him until medical help takes over.

Don't worry about getting him into the boat or getting ashore until he has had five minutes of rescue breathing.

## CARE OF THE SICK

**Emetic:** Used to cause vomiting. In emergency, put fingers down throat. Or give solution of soapy water, salt water, or mustard in water. Or 1 teaspoonful ipecac powder in glass of water or as a syrup; or 2 grams zinc sulphate in glass of water.

**Enema:** In case of abdominal pains, this should be done only on the advice of a physician. For infant or small child, use a rubber air syringe with a soft rubber tip. Regular enema bag with rubber tube and hard tip may be used for older children. Bulb should be completely filled so that no air remains in it. Cover tip with vaseline or cold cream. Insert 1 to 2 inches. Allow water to flow slowly. Hold bag 1 to 2 feet above level of buttocks. Stop flow occasionally to permit person to rest. Patient should hold solution 5 to 10 minutes if possible. A high enema is given by inserting the lubricated tip 4 to 5 inches; low enema 1 to 2 inches. Usually an enema solution contains 1 to 2 quarts soapy water. A cleansing enema may contain ordinary tap water or salt solution (1 teaspoon-ful to 1 pint distilled water). Use 2 to 3 pints for a child, 3 to 4 pints for an adult, at 100 to 105°F. A soapsuds enema should contain 3 pints at 105°F. castile or other mild soap-suds.

**Ice Pack:** Used to check inflammation, reduce swelling, re-lieve pain, or to check bleeding. Fill rubber bag with ice cubes (after removing sharp edges under warm water). Ex-pel excess air. Screw on cover. Dry and apply.

**Poultice:** A poultice is used to draw substance from the skin. Starch poultice may be used for removing scabs; linseed poultice to relieve pain as a counter irritant (with mustard added), or to relieve congestion of an internal organ.

To make a starch poultice, mix starch paste with water, boil for 2 minutes while stirring. Pour into gauze and fold into cloth. Apply when cool. To make a linseed poultice, crush 3 cupfuls on wooden board. Pour into boiling water while stir-ring. Spread this paste on flannel ½-inch thick and fold in. Apply hot, covered with wool and bandages.

**Tourniquet:** (See page 542.)

**Pulse:** Hold inner surface of wrist, 1 inch above joint or any other point where artery is close to skin and passes over a bone (as at temple or front of ear). Press tips of index, 2nd and 3rd finger (not the thumb) at one of these points, with slight pressure. Count number of beats of the pulse in 60 seconds. Normal rates are: men, 60 to 70; women, 70 to 80; babies under 1 year, 115 to 130; 1 to 5 years old, 100 to 115; children 7 to 14, 80 to 90.

**Temperature** (how to take temperature): Temperature may be taken in the rectum (normal 99.4), mouth (98.4), armpit (97.2) or fold of the groin. Temperature is usually one degree lower in the morning than later in the day. It should not be taken directly after a bath, a cold drink, or exertion. Usually registering time is ½ to 2 minutes.

Rectal thermometer should be inserted with the patient lying down, preferably on his side. The thermometer should be clean, lubricated with vaseline and shaken down to be-low 96°. Insert in rectum about 1½ inches. An oral (mouth) thermometer should be inserted sidewise under the tongue after being shaken down. Never wash in hot water. Either thermometer can be used under the armpit.

The reading of a thermometer is indicated at the point

where the mercury (silver) shows on the scale. Usually only the even degrees, 94, 96, 98, etc., are numbered, because of lack of space. "Normal" is usually marked with a red mark. No person's temperature is absolutely steady, and a variation of 1 to 2 degrees should not cause concern.

**Persons Caring for the Sick:** Persons caring for the sick should maintain a cheerful and sympathetic attitude at all times. Only clothing that can be laundered and kept scrupulously clean should be worn. The hands should be washed with soap and running water immediately after each handling of the patient. When running water is not available, an assistant may pour water over the hands of the attendant.

Under no circumstances should an attempt be made to diagnose or to treat the patient. The attendant should obtain orders from the physician regarding the care of the patient. Any suggestions offered by "well-meaning" visitors should be ignored.

It is a good practice to write down the physician's orders so that details will not be forgotten.

**· Observations Helpful to the Physician:** When there is illness in the home, the physician may appreciate a written record of observations made during his absence. These observations may include:

1. Temperature—morning, afternoon, and evening.
2. Quality and duration of sleep.
3. Number and kind of bowel movements.
4. Amount of urine passed in 24 hours.
5. Items and amount of food eaten.
6. Amount of liquids taken (including water, fruit juices, tea, milk, etc.).
7. Attitude of patient (irritable, fearful, cheerful, contented, etc.).
8. Any complaints the patient may have (headache, abdominal pain, etc.).

**Changing Sheet Under Patient:**

1. Gently roll patient over to one side of bed.
2. Fold soiled sheet close up against the body.
3. Fold the clean sheet in narrow pleats and adjust to the mattress as close to the patient as possible, and tuck well at the side, the head and the foot of the bed.
4. Gently roll patient to the side of the bed covered by the clean sheet.

5. Withdraw soiled sheet, and pull the clean sheet in place.

6. Smooth sheet of wrinkles and tuck tightly on that side and at the head and foot of the bed.

7. All of these changes can be accomplished without uncovering the patient.

**Preparation of Patient for the Day:** The face and hands should be washed, the teeth brushed and the hair combed soon after the patient has fully awakened. A daily sponge bath is both refreshing and stimulating. Upon completion of the toilet, the patient should be rubbed with alcohol, especially those places on which the weight falls—the back, shoulders, heels, and elbows. This will help maintain good circulation of blood and may prevent the development at these pressure spots of "bedsores," which are very painful and heal slowly.

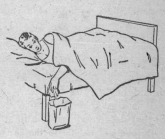

Paper bag for used tissues.

**Communicable Diseases:** Most communicable diseases are more "catching" during the first days of illness, and frequently before the diagnosis has been established. Consider every illness communicable until the physician has decided otherwise.

Wash all eating and drinking utensils with soap and water, scald with boiling water after each use by the patient and keep them separate from utensils used by other members of the family unless they are boiled for five minutes after each use.

**Contagion Protection and Fumigation:** Contact with patients should, if possible, be limited to doctor and one other person. An overdress, smock or coverall apron should be worn on going into sickroom and removed when leaving, hung on entrance door. Sprinkle with antiseptic. Entrance way should be covered with sheet, wet with antiseptic solution. Remove metal particles and jewelry after giving them an antiseptic bath.

Fumigation should follow illness. Burn ½ lb. sulphur candle in sealed room, making certain cracks are sealed with cloth or paper. Candle should be set on fireproof support (a can in a basin containing water at candle level), lighted, and all living things removed. Some odor will seep through, otherwise check if burning. Allow 3 hours; then, with mouth and nose covered, open windows and re-close door. Allow 3 hours for fumes to dissipate, several days for odor to leave. Removable fabrics may be deodorized in the sun.

In extremely contagious diseases (scarlet fever, smallpox, etc.) linen, mattress, and clothing should be burned.

## SPECIAL FOOD NEEDS

FLUID OR LIQUID DIET: Fruit and vegetable juices, milk and milk drinks, cereal gruels, soups, coffee, tea or cocoa, raw eggs.

SOFT, BLAND OR SMOOTH DIET: Any above, plus pureed vegetables, toast, cereals, custard, eggs, ice cream, gelatin desserts.

LIGHT DIET: Any above, plus baked or stewed fruits, baked potato, green vegetables, chopped veal, chicken, lamb chop, simple desserts.

DIABETIC DIET: Minimum sugar and calories, limited proteins.

CARDIAC DIET: Minimum salt.

ANTI-CONSTIPATION DIET: Bulky foods, whole cereals, fruits, vegetables; maximum fluids.

HIGH CALORIC DIET: Foods that help create appetite. Large portions of starches and fats.

LOW CALORIC DIET: Minimum fats, starches, sugar. Leafy green vegetables. Substitute saccharine for sugar.

## CHOOSING THE DOCTOR

The doctor you will usually call on is your family doctor, a general practitioner who has completed at least a four-year course in medicine, a year or two as an interne at a hospital, and has had the experience of hundreds of cases.

Most doctors are M.D.'s. Some doctors may, however, be Osteopathic Doctors who belong to a school of medicine which emphasizes normal body mechanics. Their degree is called D.O. instead of M.D.

If your illness is a serious or complicated one, your doctor may call on a specialist.

Twenty-six specialties are listed in the Directory of the American Medical Association:

ALLERGY: Conditions caused by sensitiveness to foods, pollens, etc.; hay fever, hives, asthma.

ANAESTHESIOLOGY: Administering anesthetics by inhalation or injection.

BACTERIOLOGY: Diagnosis of infectious agents in blood and excretions, preparing vaccines, etc.

CARDIOVASCULAR DISEASE: Diseases of heart and blood vessels.

CLINICAL PATHOLOGY: Examination of blood, excretions, and secretions, in the laboratory.

DERMATOLOGY: Skin diseases, syphilis.

GASTROENTEROLOGY: Diseases of stomach and intestines.

GYNECOLOGY: Diseases of the female generative organs; usually combined with obstetrics.

INDUSTRIAL MEDICINE: Prevention of industrial diseases.

INTERNAL MEDICINE: Diagnosis and treatment of disease by other than surgical means.

NEUROLOGY: Diseases of brain, nerves, or spinal cord; may be combined with psychiatry.

NEURO-SURGERY: Surgery of brain, nerves or spinal cord.

OBSTETRICS: Assisting at births.

OPHTHALMOLOGY: Diseases of the eye.

ORTHOPEDIC SURGERY: Surgery of bones, joints, deformities.

OTOLOGY, LARYNGOLOGY, RHINOLOGY: Diseases of ear, throat and nose.

PATHOLOGY: Study of the changes in tissues caused by disease.

PEDIATRICS: Diseases of infants and children.

PLASTIC SURGERY: Corrective and cosmetic surgery.

PSYCHIATRY: Mental and emotional disturbances.

PROCTOLOGY: Diseases of the rectum.

PUBLIC HEALTH: Sanitation, prevention, and control of communicable diseases.

RADIOLOGY, ROENTGENOLOGY: X-ray diagnosis and treatment.

SURGERY: Major operations of the abdomen, chest, thyroid, etc.; treatment of wounds and fractures.

TUBERCULOSIS: Treatment of tuberculosis.

Urology: Deals with diseases of the genital and urinary organs.

Your Eyes: The oculist or eye physician is known technically as an ophthalmologist or as an ophthalmic physician. He is a licensed physician who has specialized in diagnosis and treatment of the eye. He diagnoses optical defects and any primary cause of defective vision brought about by one's physical condition, fits or prescribes lenses, or administers or prescribes any other form of treatment for the eyes, including drugs or surgery when necessary.

An optometrist is a person who has specialized in diagnosis and non-medical treatment of the visual system. Before an optometrist is permitted to practice, all states require that he shall have been graduated from an accepted school of optometry, and pass an examination covering the anatomy, pathology, function, and abnormalities of the eye.

The optician does not examine eyes or prescribe for eyeglasses. He is one who manufactures and deals in lenses, or optical instruments, fills prescriptions for eyeglasses written by oculists and optometrists.

Dentists usually receive two to four years of specialized training and must pass strict examinations before they are permitted to practice. Most dentists are general practitioners and will take care of any mouth problem. However, the American Dental Association recognizes the following types of dental specialists:

| Specialty | Dealing with |
|---|---|
| Exodontia | extractions |
| Oral surgery | cysts, tumors, fractured jaw, mouth surgery |
| Peridontia | soft tissues, pyorrhea |
| Orthodontia | position of teeth |
| Prosthodontia | replacements, bridges, crowns, dentures |
| Pedontia | children's problems |
| Radiodontia | X-rays, diagnosis (usually practiced by oral surgeons) |

Dental hygienists are specially-trained assistants to dentists, may clean and polish teeth, help give anesthetics, and act as a nurse does for a doctor.

## OTHER MEDICAL PRACTITIONERS

A chiropractor uses a system of mechanical therapeutics to relieve pressure on the nerves and thus relieve certain ills. They should not be confused with medical and osteopathic doctors.

A chiropodist is a foot physician and surgeon, specializing in the diagnosis and treatment of medical, physical, and surgical conditions involving the foot and its surrounding structures.

A physiotherapist uses various types of apparatus to help cure ills. This treatment may consist of massage, medicated baths, colonic irrigation, exercises, heat or electric treatments.

Clinics: In some communities, and for some cases, clinic care may cost less than private care. There are three types of clinics for medical care:

PRIVATE CLINICS: Sometimes groups of physicians pool their equipment and resources to establish private clinics. Such groups often include specialists and offer fairly complete services. Usually the patient is assigned to one physician. Other specialists are called in when consultation is necessary. Often the fee is set according to the patient's ability to pay.

MEDICAL SCHOOL CLINICS: Privately-endowed medical school clinics generally charge for services according to what the patient can afford.

HOSPITAL AND INSTITUTIONAL CLINICS: Hospitals and other institutions maintain clinics and wards. Patients who cannot pay may have the best medical supervision available, especially when the clinic or ward is in an institution used for medical training.

## PERSONAL HEALTH CHECK-UP

Ask yourself these questions, mark the answers, then examine the "No" column for clues to bettering your health.

|  | Yes | No |
|---|---|---|
| 1. Do you feel well? | ☐ | ☐ |
| 2. Do you look well? | ☐ | ☐ |
| 3. Is your weight right for your age, height and build? | ☐ | ☐ |
| 4. Are you full of pep? | ☐ | ☐ |

|  | Yes | No |
|---|---|---|
| 5. Do you have some energy after a day's work is done? | ☐ | ☐ |
| 6. Do you feel rested when you wake in the morning? | ☐ | ☐ |
| 7. Do you get some exercise daily? | ☐ | ☐ |
| 8. Is your elimination regular without aid? | ☐ | ☐ |
| 9. Are you free from infections, aches or defects? | ☐ | ☐ |
| 10. Do you avoid catching colds? | ☐ | ☐ |
| 11. Do you breathe deeply? | ☐ | ☐ |
| 12. Do you breathe with mouth closed? | ☐ | ☐ |

EYES:

| | | |
|---|---|---|
| 13. Can you read this page from a distance of 15 inches? | ☐ | ☐ |
| 14. Do you avoid headaches, dizziness or blurred vision from eye strain? | ☐ | ☐ |
| 15. Do you get proper lighting when you use your eyes? | ☐ | ☐ |
| 16. Do you rest your eyes periodically while doing close work? | ☐ | ☐ |
| 17. Do you avoid reading constantly in bus or train? | ☐ | ☐ |

EARS:

| | | |
|---|---|---|
| 18. Can you hear an ordinary conversation at 15 feet? | ☐ | ☐ |
| 19. Are your ears free from aches, unusual noises, or discharges? | ☐ | ☐ |

TEETH:

| | | |
|---|---|---|
| 20. Do you brush your teeth twice daily? | ☐ | ☐ |
| 21. Have you seen a dentist in the last six months? | ☐ | ☐ |
| 22. Is your mouth free from bad odors? | ☐ | ☐ |
| 23. Are your teeth free from cavities or breaks? | ☐ | ☐ |
| 24. Do your gums bleed when you brush your teeth? | ☐ | ☐ |

HANDS:

| | | |
|---|---|---|
| 25. Do you wash your hands before handling food, dishes, dish towels, the baby, etc.? | ☐ | ☐ |
| 26. Do you wash your hands after going to the toilet, changing the baby, combing your hair, brushing teeth, handling soiled handkerchiefs or linens, or handling animals? | ☐ | ☐ |
| 27. Are your nails trimmed and clean? | ☐ | ☐ |

SKIN:

| | | |
|---|---|---|
| 28. Is your skin clear, soft and smooth? | ☐ | ☐ |
| 29. Is your flesh firm and not flabby? | ☐ | ☐ |

|  | Yes | No |
|---|---|---|

POSTURE:

30. Are your shoulders even in height? ☐ ☐
31. Abdomen flat? ☐ ☐
32. Stance erect? Shoulders up? Body symmetrical? ☐ ☐
33. Do you stand with feet evenly placed on the floor with toes pointed out? ☐ ☐
34. Are your shoes of proper size, shape and style for your feet? ☐ ☐

YOUR BODY:

35. Is your body clean and free from odors? ☐ ☐

MENTAL HEALTH:

36. Are you cheerful and free from worry? ☐ ☐
37. Do you have confidence in yourself? ☐ ☐
38. Do you have a sense of humor? ☐ ☐
39. Do you lose courage when faced with difficulties? ☐ ☐
40. Do you control your temper? ☐ ☐
41. Do you rely on accomplishments rather than dreams for your satisfaction? ☐ ☐
42. Do you get along well with your family? ☐ ☐
43. Do you get along well with others? ☐ ☐
44. Do you make friends easily? ☐ ☐
45. Do you respect the opinions and attitudes of others? ☐ ☐

## NORMAL HEALTH

| WEIGHT FOR HEIGHT AT THE AGE OF 30 YEARS | | | | | |
|---|---|---|---|---|---|
| Height | Women lbs. | Men lbs. | Height | Women lbs. | Men lbs. |
| 4 feet 10 inches | 116 |  | 5 feet 8 inches | 146 | 152 |
| 4 feet 11 inches | 118 |  | 5 feet 9 inches | 150 | 156 |
| 5 feet | 120 | 126 | 5 feet 10 inches | 154 | 161 |
| 5 feet 1 inch | 122 | 128 | 5 feet 11 inches | 157 | 166 |
| 5 feet 2 inches | 124 | 130 | 6 feet | 161 | 172 |
| 5 feet 3 inches | 127 | 133 | 6 feet 1 inch |  | 178 |
| 5 feet 4 inches | 131 | 137 | 6 feet 2 inches |  | 184 |
| 5 feet 5 inches | 134 | 140 | 6 feet 3 inches |  | 190 |
| 5 feet 6 inches | 138 | 144 | 6 feet 4 inches |  | 196 |
| 5 feet 7 inches | 142 | 148 |  |  |  |

In this table, the height includes ordinary shoe heels and the weight includes indoor clothing.

Below the age of 30 a majority of people tend to be underweight and would do well to build themselves up to the weight-for-height shown in this table. On the other hand, as they enter middle age most people should be on guard that they do not let their body weight run too much above the standard for their height.

Normal rate of respiration is 16 to 20 per minute for adults, 20 to 25 for children, 30 to 35 for infants. Normal blood pressure (systolic) varies with age and activity, roughly calculated as 100 plus the age of a person. The normal diastolic pressure is more constant, roughly equal to 70 to 80 mm. of mercury. Normal blood count is 5000 to 8000.

| NORMAL SLEEP REQUIREMENTS | | | |
|---|---|---|---|
| Age | Hours | Age | Hours |
| 1st month | 22 | 4 to 5 years | 12½ to 11 |
| 1 to 3 months | 20 | 5 to 6 years | 12 to 10¾ |
| 3 to 6 months | 18 to 16 | 6 to 10 years | 11½ to 10½ |
| 6 to 12 months | 16 to 14 | 10 to 15 years | 10½ to 10 |
| 1 to 3 years | 14 to 12½ | Adults | 8 to 7 |
| 3 to 4 years | 13 to 11½ | | |

# BOOK XI

## Family Business and Legal Guide

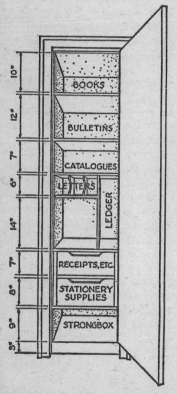

**Closet for business materials.**

**The Family Office:** Every home needs an office. It may have a reference file including phone numbers, addresses of vendors and repair men, receipted bills, canceled checks, clippings on home problems and affairs, reference books, accounts, etc. The telephone, typewriter, budget books, date books, etc., may also be in this section. A bulletin board or slate for shopping lists and reminders may be hung on one wall. Readily available should be emergency phone numbers, where everyone in the family may be reached (especially husband and mother), the doctor's office and home, fire, police, gas, electric and furnace repairs, plumber, etc.

## POINTERS FOR THE "FAMILY BUSINESS" OFFICE

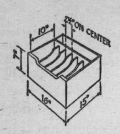

Detail of drawer for receipts.

Keep accounts—so that you will know where the money went, so that you can plan to use it better. Appoint one member of the family for the job.

Keep receipted bills on all major purchases and all canceled checks for seven years.

Take a household inventory, room by room, periodically. It is necessary for collecting on burglary or fire insurance. Booklets for inventory taking are available from fire insurance companies.

Keep a reference file of instruction booklets on your appliances, catalogues, addresses, books on home problems.

Keep insured and keep an inventory of your insurance. (See p. 578.)

Make a will—for both husband and wife.

Guiding Family Spending: As a first step in drawing up a spending plan, a family needs to get a sense of its goals, then to decide how the money likely to be available should be divided. Some people like to write down their goals. Others find it enough to mull them over, and to discuss them informally at mealtime or around the fireplace. A spending plan is off to a good start when family members agree that a plan is needed. Planning is a process of matching means and ends. In making a plan for next year's spending, last year's purchases provide a good starting point, even if spending habits have not been entirely satisfactory. In estimating next year's expenditures, it may be important first of all to consider whether prices are likely to be higher or lower than those paid during the past year. Knowing what other families do may give a family some help in spending, even though needs and preferences vary so widely that good spending for one family may be very poor spending for another.

## TYPICAL FAMILY BUDGET

| Percent of Income | | Percent of Income | |
|---|---|---|---|
| Shelter | 20-25 | Home operation | 10-15 |
| Food | 33 | Savings | 12½ |
| Clothing | 10-15 | Amusement | 10 |

## SOME GENERAL HINTS ON AVOIDING UNNECESSARY SPENDING

Care for your appliances, equipment and furnishings properly. Follow manufacturers' directions on the use. Re-read directions from time to time. Save original directions and guarantees. (See Book 1.)

Buy wisely, carefully, and with a plan. Before you buy, study the product, the substitutes, the advantages of each type, the places where it can be bought to best advantage. Avoid buying a more expensive quality than you need, or a quality that will not stand up for the job to be done or the length of time it will be needed. (See Book 7.)

Learn how to make your own repairs. With skilled labor so expensive (doubly so if a contractor has to pay for office, billing, supervision, etc.), with a good portion of your earned dollar going for taxes, it may pay to do it yourself. (See Books IV, V and VI.)

Learn how to salvage from what you have. Some people furnish a home from a junk yard and it *doesn't* look it. Old furniture remade, old clothes transformed, old toys renovated, may mean substantial saving.

Buy things which are easy and economical to keep up. A compact home, brick or low-scaled exterior, moderate grounds, a smaller car, etc., will be easier on the budget.

Get the most out of your community activities and facilities —for entertainment, relaxation, education, better health, social activities.

Choose a low-tax community to live in. Often the taxes in neighboring areas vary as much as $100 a year, with the better-run town giving more service for less taxes.

Avoid a neighborhood where you can't keep up with the neighbors. As much as you think you won't, the things your neighbors have exert a pressure on your budget.

Don't be immodest. Many professionals fix their charges on what you lead them to think you can afford.

Seek advice. The storekeeper, your more experienced neighbors, the carpenter, plumber, garage or service man know more about many things than you do. Experts on insurance and income taxes may save, rather than cost, you money.

Buy and use facilities that will save you money: a refrigerator with a freezer that will allow you to store more food longer and thus buy more economically; storm windows and insulation that will save on heating; a better furnace that will save on heating by the use of less fuel, and which won't have to be forced; equipment for washing, storing, hanging, and caring for clothes and equipment.

Plan your wardrobe with staples and separates, to allow changes, special clothes for hard work, etc. (See Book VII.)

Substitute imagination for lavishness in your entertaining. (See Book IX.)

Plan your vacation in off seasons, at out-of-the-way places, where fun may be substituted for fashionableness.

## HOW TO PAY BILLS

| How It Works | Advantages |
| --- | --- |
| CHECK: An order to the bank to pay out money from your checking account. Regular checking accounts require a minimum balance of $300, $500, or $1000, depending on the rules of the bank. Special checking accounts are available under which no minimum balance is necessary. Charges for such accounts are usually made for each check. | If you pay bills by check, you can send payment through the mails without risk of loss. Checks give you a good record of what you spend, help you plan and keep your budget. A returned check is evidence of payment equivalent to a receipt. You may stop payment on a check even after you have given it, but you should have a good reason. |
| CERTIFIED CHECK: A bank will certify your check upon request. The bank then sets aside the money from your account for payment and guarantees payment. | In transactions where cash is necessary, a certified check may usually be used as a substitute. |

| How It Works | Advantages |
|---|---|
| CASHIER'S CHECK: If you do not have a checking account, the bank may issue its own check for you for a small fee. Such checks may be made out to you, to another bank, or to any person specified. | If you withdraw large sums from a savings account, and wish to avoid carrying cash, this is a good way of doing so. |
| TRAVELERS' CHECK: This is a check guaranteed by a well-known bank or company which has your signature on it for identification. When you sign a second time, you make the check transferable. | Because these checks require a second signature, they are valueless if stolen or lost. These are safer to carry than cash. |
| MONEY ORDERS: The United States Post Office issues these "checks" for a fee. They are the equivalent of checks from the United States Government. | If you have no checking account, these are useful in sending payments through the mails. |

## SOME BANKING SERVICES

SAFE DEPOSIT BOXES: The safe deposit department of a bank offers facilities for the safekeeping and protection of valuables and personal possessions. Each box has its own door and key. Locks are changed every time there is a new renter. The renter of the box is the only one who has a key to it, and without the key the box cannot be unlocked. The customer can remove his box to a private room for examination at any time he wishes to do so. Only the renter has the authority to state who is to have access to the box and it is under his absolute control at all times.

Papers you should keep: PERMANENTLY: Birth certificates, marriage records, Social Security cards, deeds and bills of sale on major purchases, record of securities owned, guarantees and instruction books; inventory of your personal property, record of where you worked and when you worked there.

FOR A YEAR AFTER THEY ARE CLOSED OUT: Evidences of what you owe, evidences of what is owed to you, automobile maintenance record, home maintenance record.

FOR SIX YEARS: Check stubs, bank statements, evidences of business expenses and charitable contributions, payroll records and record of other income, record of securities, duplicate tax returns.

ONE YEAR: Receipts, receipted bills. Duplicate deposit slips.

SIXTY DAYS: Sales slips.

SAVINGS ACCOUNT LOANS: Your bank will usually make a loan on your bank book at about twice the interest paid by the bank. This is advisable only when the loan is for a short period, as just before the date when interest is paid. Otherwise, it is best to withdraw the money and "pay yourself back" by making regular deposits.

INSURANCE LOANS: Your insurance company will lend you up to the cash surrender value of your policy. The loan may be repaid at any time. If it is not repaid at the time of death, the amount is deducted from the sum paid to the beneficiary. It is often possible to obtain loans on life insurance policies from commercial banks at slightly lower interest rates than those charged by your insurance company.

BANK LOANS: Your local bank may give you a loan based on its estimate of your ability to pay. The bank may require co-signers of your note, who will guarantee payments if you fail to make them; or the bank may accept security in the form of stocks, bonds, life insurance policies, or a mortgage on your car or another valuable asset. Bank loans are usually repayable in monthly installments over a year's time or at a fixed date within 90 days.

CREDIT UNIONS: Associations are often formed for the purpose of lending money to members. These are usually sponsored by social or fraternal groups, or trade unions. You may join even at the time you require a loan. They are really cooperative lending organizations run by members without pay. Borrowers must usually be stockholders. Interest rates are usually the same as those charged by reputable banks. Such loans are usually repayable in monthly installments.

PERSONAL LOAN COMPANIES: Special companies are licensed to make small loans to individuals. They usually accept less security than a bank will require. They will accept the signature of co-makers or they may take a mortgage on your furniture, car, etc. Often they ask that you assign a portion of your wages, which they can attach if you fail to pay. These companies are permitted by law to charge 2 to 3 times as much interest as banks. Loans are repayable in weekly or monthly installments.

PAWNSHOPS: Loans may be made on valuable personal property by licensed pawnbrokers. The interest and the principal must be paid periodically and at the time set on the pawn ticket or the property may be sold to redeem the loan. Such loans are usually made up to half the value of the property pledged.

MORTGAGES: Banks, insurance companies, and building and loan companies specialize in lending money using your home or other real property as security. Such loans are usually for a long period, from 5 to 30 years. Repayment, with interest, may be made monthly, quarterly, semi-annually, or annually. It is sometimes necessary to engage a broker to negotiate such a loan if the property is of questionable value. Mortgages should be read carefully by someone familiar with them before the signing of any papers. Clauses giving the right to repayment before maturity, particularly in case the property is to be sold; minimum interest rates, etc., may be included if requested at the time of the negotiation. Some insurance companies provide for special low-interest rates if insurance is taken at the time the mortgage is placed.

ABOUT INTEREST RATES: Interest rates are often not what they seem to be. Six percent interest may be 6 percent, 6.38 percent, 12 percent or some other amount.

If the lender "discounts" your $100 note, you pay $6 on $94 or 6.38 percent interest.

If the lender charges $6 on a $100 loan repayable in monthly installments over one year, the average amount of the loan is only half the $100, and the real interest is 12 percent. A true 6 percent should be charged only on the unpaid balance for any period. Often service charges, life insurance, special charges for late payment, etc., may bring up the cost of the loan. Sometimes the loan is re-negotiated. Then the interest is added to the principal, and you pay "compound" interest.

Installment Buying: This should be avoided if possible, as it generally increases the cost of the purchase. Installment contracts may contain the following clauses of which the buyer should be aware: (1) Assignment of wages. This gives the seller the right to attach a part of your wages, for payment. (2) Chattel mortgage on all or part of your household goods.

This gives the seller the right to take certain of your household goods if you fail to pay. (3) Right to repossess both the article purchased and any other article not completely paid for at the time of purchase. (4) Deficiency judgment. If the article is repossessed and sold for less than the amount owed, the debtor is liable for any difference between the balance due and the price for which it was sold.

## LIFE INSURANCE

Insurance should be carried on the life of the person who supports the family, to protect the family in case of his death. It may also be used to protect a business, so that if a key man, a stockholder, or a partner dies the business may continue; to protect a loan or mortgage; to pay inheritance taxes; or to serve any emergency foreseen. More than 200 types of policies are available. It is wise to plan your insurance program with an expert, so as to provide properly for all contingencies. Changing from one policy to another usually is costly. In selecting a policy, consider the standing of the insurance company as well as the policy offered. The rates on these policies are not standardized and may vary as much as 20 percent. The basic types of policy are:

(1) TERM INSURANCE: You pay a flat sum for insurance only, just as you pay for fire insurance. You get no cash surrender value, no refund, no matter how long you pay. The cost is much lower than other types of insurance. Term insurance may be taken for periods up to 30 years, or may be renewable for a number of years. However, premiums increase as the age increases. It cannot usually be renewed at ages over 60 or 65. It gives you the greatest amount of insurance for the amount of money you lay out. Often these may be converted into a different type of policy during a period of time. If you cannot afford other types of insurance protection, term insurance may be the best buy.

(2) ORDINARY LIFE INSURANCE: The next least expensive policy provides that you pay a fixed premium all your life. The beneficiary receives a fixed sum at the time of your death. The cash value (against which you may borrow) increases from year to year.

(3) LIMITED PAYMENT LIFE INSURANCE: This form provides that you pay premiums for a specified period. There-

after you remain insured for the rest of your life. There is a cash value on the policy usually after the second year. This value, after some years, may exceed what you paid in premiums.

(4) ENDOWMENTS: This is a fund accumulation program and life insurance combined. Premiums are larger than simple insurance policies, but the company agrees to pay you a certain sum on maturity. This sum may be payable in bulk, or in an annuity, at once or at specified times.

(5) ANNUITIES: This is a fund to be paid to you or to your beneficiary at a certain date. It may be paid for in one sum at one time, or it may be paid for over a period of years. The company may return the money plus interest in one sum; or in annual payments for the rest of your life, or on some other basis. (See that the full amount is guaranteed.)

(6) GROUP INSURANCE: This is the cheapest type of insurance, usually term insurance for a group of persons related in certain specified ways—as, all the employees of a company. It can usually be obtained without a medical examination.

(7) INDUSTRIAL INSURANCE: This is similar to ordinary life insurance, but premiums are payable weekly or monthly. Because of the additional collection expense involved on the part of the company, this is expensive insurance.

(8) COMBINATIONS: Special policies are created including two or more characteristics of these policies to meet specific insurance needs. A common combination includes a minimum ordinary life policy combined with a larger term policy. This enables a young man to obtain maximum protection for growing children at a minimum premium. After some years, when protection of children is no longer imperative, the term policy expires and the ordinary life policy remains in effect.

Types of Insurers: You can buy life insurance from a savings bank in some states (up to $5000 for adults, $1000 for children), or from stock companies which are formed for the purpose of selling insurance, or from mutual companies which are owned by the policy holders. Mutual companies usually charge higher rates, but most profits of the company are distributed to policy holders as dividends. These dividends may bring the net cost of the insurance below that charged by stock companies. Dividends may be withdrawn, applied against premiums, or allowed to accumulate interest at rates usually higher than savings banks.

Special Clauses Available in an Insurance Policy: A provision may be inserted so that if you have an accident, and die, the amount paid by the insurance company is doubled. This is Double Indemnity, or Additional Death Benefit, and requires an extra premium.

DISABILITY: Policies that pay a specified sum if you are no longer able to work have been discontinued by life insurance companies. However, a clause under which your premiums are suspended if such circumstances prevail for 6 months, is available for an added fee. This is called Waiver of Premium.

TRUSTS: The money paid upon your death may be paid to a trust. The trust may pay certain sums to your wife till her death, then to your children. This may save inheritance taxes.

AUTOMATIC PREMIUM LOAN: A provision may be inserted without cost that automatically pays your premium on the due date with a loan against your policy, if you neglect to pay this premium. Otherwise, such an oversight gives the company the right to turn your policy into extended term insurance for a smaller amount. Usually under such circumstances, the company will not reinstate the policy unless you can pass another medical examination.

ANNUITY PAYMENTS: You may have the option of converting the cash surrender value into an annuity. This annuity may be payable to you for life, with a guaranteed minimum payment for 10, 15, or 20 years; or the annuity may be made payable so long as you or your wife live. But these options must be made available to you at the time you take out your policy or soon after. Annuity payments are largest if paid out annually. It may be wise to take out several (or twelve) policies at different periods of the year so that payments are made periodically and you get maximum benefits.

TYPE OF PREMIUM PAYMENTS: The cheapest way to pay your insurance premiums is annually. The most expensive way of paying is weekly. If you want to break up payments, take up two or four policies at various times of the year for smaller amounts, and thus spread payment dates.

## CHECK LIST OF COMMON INSURANCE POLICIES AVAILABLE

Personal:
  LIFE
> (1) Term insurance for business partnerships.
> (2) Other forms for permanent insurance.

(Buy only policies approved by State Insurance Department or other non-commercial organization.)

OLD AGE INCOME

EDUCATIONAL ENDOWMENT

PERSONAL EFFECTS FLOATER: Good for traveling people. Covers valuables at all times.

ALL RISKS FUR FLOATER

PERSONAL PROPERTY FLOATER: Covers personal property of the family against loss due to fire, theft, etc., but not against ordinary breakage, war, wear, and tear.

SCHEDULED PROPERTY FLOATER: Against fire, burglary; for fur, jewelry, etc.

ALL RISKS JEWELRY FLOATER

ALL RISKS FINE ARTS FLOATER

HOBBIES

PERSONAL HOLD-UP

SAFE DEPOSIT BOX BURGLARY AND ROBBERY

SPORTS AND PERSONAL ACTIVITIES: Comprehensive Liability covers this.

YACHTS; OUTBOARD MOTORS

CAMERAS AND PHOTOGRAPHIC SUPPLIES: Separate policy listing items.

ILLNESS, DISABILITY: This may cover possible wage losses, medical and hospital expenses for a limited period.

ACCIDENT: Coverage varies widely. Read the policy carefully. It may cover only rare accidents or common accidents under rare circumstances.

HOSPITALIZATION: Note that this does not cover all situations, allows only for semi-private room. Most policies have a minimum waiting period for maternity, hernia, etc.

SURGICAL: Pays all medical and surgery; also sold by Blue Cross as Blue Shield.

MEDICAL: Overall medical service.

**Automobile:**

BODILY INJURY LIABILITY: Covers your liability for hurting someone, due to owning, maintaining or driving a car. Should cover at least $10,000 per person, $20,000 per accident.

PROPERTY DAMAGE LIABILITY: Liability for property damage as above. Should cover at least $5,000.

MEDICAL PAYMENTS: Covers medical expenses up to $500 for anyone injured while in your car, in case of accident, regardless of legal liability.

FIRE: See comprehensive.

THEFT: See comprehensive.

WINDSTORM: See comprehensive.

COLLISION: Covers accident to your car. Usually covers only sums over $50 ($50 deductible). May be $25 to $100 deductible.

COMPREHENSIVE: Covering fire, theft, broken glass, damage from hail, earthquakes, flood, etc., but not collision, war damage, arson.

### Private Residence:

FIRE: On building and garage—on contents, covers loss due to fire, lightning, smoke or water incidental to putting out fire.

WINDSTORM

EXTENDED COVERAGE of fire policy, covers damage from storms, explosions, riot, motor vehicles, falling aircraft, for small additional fee.

RESIDENCE AND OUTSIDE THEFT: Can be included in Personal Property Floater.

PLATE GLASS

HEATING BOILER AND PRESSURE VESSELS

WORKMEN'S COMPENSATION: Necessary in some states if you have 1 or more employees working over 40 hours.

DISABILITY: Necessary in some states if you have 4 or more employees.

EMPLOYERS' LIABILITY

COMPREHENSIVE PERSONAL LIABILITY: Covers legal liability for injury, illness, death or property damage suffered by a non-member of your family while in your home or on your property. (Including extended coverage.)

RENTAL VALUE

EXPLOSION

AIRCRAFT PROPERTY DAMAGE

WATER DAMAGE AND REPAIR

VEHICLE DAMAGE

EARTHQUAKE

TITLE INSURANCE: Covers lawsuits or loss if someone proves you do not have proper title to your land.

**Insurance Pointers:** Cover yourself first against accidents which could result in substantial losses—as liability to others for injury or damage. Rates vary widely, so shop for your insurance. Cover current replacement values—don't underinsure or overinsure.

## SOCIAL SECURITY

You may be eligible for four types of payments under Social Security—old-age, survivors, disability and hospital coverage. Your account is credited in terms of "quarters of coverage." You earned credit for a quarter of coverage if you were paid $50 or more in a three-month period after 1936. If you were self-employed, you may have earned four quarters of coverage if you earned $400 or more in a calendar year after 1950. The number of credits you must have earned to be eligible for benefits depends on when you apply. Under a 1972 law men and women who are the same age and have equal earnings will receive the same benefits.

| Year you are 65 | Quarters of coverage needed for retirement benefits | | Quarters of coverage needed for hospital coverage | |
|---|---|---|---|---|
| | *Men* | *Women* | *Men* | *Women* |
| 1957 or earlier | 6 | 6 | 0 | 0 |
| 1958 | 7 | 6 | 0 | 0 |
| 1959 | 8 | 6 | 0 | 0 |
| 1960 | 9 | 6 | 0 | 0 |
| 1961 | 10 | 7 | 0 | 0 |
| 1962 | 11 | 8 | 0 | 0 |
| 1963 | 12 | 9 | 0 | 0 |
| 1964 | 13 | 10 | 0 | 0 |
| 1965 | 14 | 11 | 0 | 0 |
| 1966 | 15 | 12 | 0 | 0 |
| 1967 | 16 | 13 | 0 | 0 |
| 1968 | 17 | 14 | 3 | 3 |
| 1969 | 18 | 15 | 6 | 6 |
| 1970 | 19 | 16 | 9 | 9 |
| 1971 | 20 | 17 | 12 | 12 |
| 1972 | 21 | 18 | 15 | 15 |
| 1973 | 22 | 19 | 18 | 18 |
| 1974 | 23 | 20 | 21 | 20 |
| 1975 | 24 | 21 | 24 | 21 |
| 1976 | 24 | 22 | 25 | 22 |
| 1977 | 24 | 23 | 26 | 23 |
| 1978 | 24 | 24 | 27 | 24 |
| 1982 | 28 | 28 | 31 | 28 |
| 1986 | 32 | 32 | 35 | 32 |
| 1990 | 36 | 36 | 39 | 36 |
| 1994 or later | 40 | 40 | 40 | 40 |

EXAMPLES OF MONTHLY CASH PAYMENTS

| Average yearly earnings after 1950* | $923 or less | $1,800 | $3,000 | $4,200 | $5,400 | $6,600 | $7,800 | $9,000 |
|---|---|---|---|---|---|---|---|---|
| Retired Worker 65 or older Disabled Worker under 65 | $ 84.50 | $134.30 | $174.80 | $213.30 | $250.60 | $288.40 | $331.00 | $354.50 |
| Wife 65 or older | 42.30 | 67.20 | 87.40 | 106.70 | 125.30 | 144.20 | 165.50 | 177.30 |
| Retired worker at 62 | 67.60 | 107.50 | 139.90 | 170.70 | 200.50 | 230.80 | 264.80 | 283.60 |
| Wife at 62, no child | 31.80 | 50.40 | 65.60 | 80.10 | 94.00 | 108.20 | 124.20 | 133.00 |
| Widow at 60 | 73.30 | 96.10 | 125.10 | 152.60 | 179.30 | 206.30 | 236.70 | 253.50 |
| Widow or widower at 62 | 84.50 | 110.80 | 144.30 | 176.00 | 206.80 | 238.00 | 273.10 | 292.50 |
| Disabled widow at 50 | 51.30 | 67.30 | 87.50 | 106.80 | 125.50 | 144.30 | 165.60 | 177.30 |
| Wife under 65 and one child | 42.30 | 67.20 | 92.50 | 157.40 | 217.30 | 233.90 | 248.30 | 265.90 |
| Widowed mother and one child | 126.80 | 201.50 | 262.20 | 320.00 | 376.60 | 432.60 | 496.60 | 531.80 |
| Widowed mother and two children | 126.80 | 201.50 | 267.30 | 370.70 | 467.90 | 522.30 | 579.30 | 620.40 |
| One child of retired or disabled worker | 42.30 | 67.20 | 87.40 | 106.70 | 125.30 | 144.20 | 165.50 | 177.30 |
| One surviving child | 84.50 | 100.80 | 131.10 | 160.00 | 188.00 | 216.30 | 248.30 | 265.90 |
| Maximum family payment | 126.80 | 201.50 | 267.30 | 370.70 | 467.90 | 522.30 | 579.30 | 620.40 |

* Generally, average earnings are figured over the period from 1951 until the worker reaches retirement age, becomes disabled, or dies. Up to 5 years of low earnings or no earnings can be excluded. The maximum earnings creditable for social security are $3,600 for 1951-1954; $4,200 for 1955-1958; $4,800 for 1959-1965; $6,600 for 1966-1967; and $7,800 for 1968-1971. The maximum creditable for 1972 is $9,000. The maximum creditable for 1973 will be $10,800, and beginning in 1974, it will be $12,000. However, average earnings cannot reach these amounts until later. Because of this, the benefits shown in the last column on the right generally will not be payable until later. When a person is entitled to more than one benefit, the amount actually payable is limited to the larger of the benefits.

Certain workers who are 72 before 1969 and do not meet the above requirement may be insured with less work. This exception also applies to widows 72 or over before 1969.

If you become disabled or die before reaching 65 (62 if a woman) you are fully insured if you have credit for one-quarter year of work (earned at any time after 1936) for each year after 1950 and up to the year of your death or disability. In counting the number of years after 1950, omit the year in which you reached age 21 and all previous years.

How much you will receive depends on (1) your average earning in the best years since 1955 under a complicated formula and (2) whether you begin at age 62 or 65.

A. See attached table.
B. When a worker receives old-age, disability benefits, or dies, payments can also be made to certain of his dependents, including:
   • unmarried children under 18 years of age;
   • unmarried full time students up to age of 22;
   • unmarried children 18 or over who were severely disabled before they reach 22 and have remained so since;
   • a wife regardless of her age, if she is caring for a child under 18 who is getting payments based on the worker's social security account;
   • a wife 62 or older even if there are no children entitled to payments;
   • a dependent husband 62 or over;
   • a divorced wife at 62 if she has been married at least 20 years before the divorce.

Additional survivors' benefits may be paid to:

   • widow and dependent widower at age 60;
   • dependent parents at 62;
   • a divorced wife or surviving divorced wife, if married 20 years.

In addition, a lump-sum death benefit payment may be made to the widow or widower who was living in the same household with the worker at death; otherwise, it goes to whoever paid or pays the worker's burial expenses, but it cannot exceed $255.00

Monthly payments to the wife or dependent husband of a person entitled to old-age or disability insurance payments can be made after the marriage has been in effect at least 9 months. However, the marriage does not have to be in effect 9 months if the couple are parents of a child, or if the wife or dependent husband was eligible for social security payments on the account of another person at the time of the marriage.

If the wife of a living worker chooses to start getting payments before she reaches 65, she gets a reduced amount for as long as she receives a wife's benefits unless she is caring for a child who is getting payments on her husband's account. Full benefits to a widow, however, are payable at 65 provided her husband never filed for reduced benefits. Or she may elect reduced benefits at 60.

To receive benefits, apply at your local social security office. You will need proof of age, marriage certificate, children's birth certificate and social security card.

If you become disabled before age 65, you may qualify for monthly disability benefits, and certain members of your family may also be paid monthly benefits. The amount of your monthly disability insurance payment is the amount of the old-age insurance benefit you would get if you were 65.

If you work after you are 65, you may earn as much as $175 in any month or $2100 in a year without having any benefits withheld. Under no circumstances will more than one-half of your excess earnings be withheld in benefits.

A domestic worker's cash wages (including carfare if paid in cash) from an employer for work in a private household are covered by the law if they amount to $50.00 or more in a calendar quarter.

If you employ a household worker who will come under the law and you are not receiving the forms for making the tax reports, ask your social security office or your Internal Revenue Office for a copy of Leaflet SSI-21.

## MEDICARE AND HEALTH CARE FOR THE AGED

Medicare is a health-insurance program under social security in two parts—hospital insurance and medical insurance. Retirement is not necessary for eligibility.

Hospital insurance helps pay for care as a patient in a hospital and for certain follow-up care. Most people 65 and over are eligible for hospital insurance automatically.

Medical insurance under Medicare helps pay doctor bills and other medical items and services, including out-patient services, not paid under hospital insurance. Nearly everyone over 65 may sign up for this, but must do so at certain times and several months before they are covered. There is a premium payable on this policy.

Hospital insurance covers 90 days of hospital care in each benefit period at the rate of $68 for the first 60 days and $17 for the next 30 days. There is an additional lifetime allowance of 60 covered days at a $34 deductible basis. In addition, 100 days of care at an extended care facility (nursing care) are covered fully for 20 days, and with an $8.50 per day deductible thereafter. In addition, it covers 100 home health visits from a home health agency.

Medical insurance pays doctor bills in the United States and other medical items not covered under hospital insurance.

## THE LAW OF CONTRACTS

A contract is an agreement between two or more persons who are legally competent and who bind themselves, either in writing or orally, for a consideration, to perform certain acts, or refrain from doing certain things.

There are express and implied contracts.

An express contract is one in which the parties, orally or in writing, state to each other the provisions of the contract.

An implied contract is one which the law sees but where there is no express agreement. For instance: When one person lends money to another, the return of the money is implied, though not specifically promised. Where one person works for another by request, the law sees an agreement to pay a reasonable sum for the services, even though no promise to pay was given.

Certain contracts must be in writing:

(1) For the sale or creation of an estate in real property.

(2) Leases for more than one year.

(3) Contracts which, by their terms, cannot be performed within one year from the making.

(4) Contracts for the sale of personal property exceeding $50 in value.

(5) Contracts in contemplation of marriage or in consideration of marriage.

(6) Trust agreements.

(7) Promise to answer for the debt or default of another.

(8) Promise to pay a debt discharged in bankruptcy.

Parties to a contract must have capacity to contract. The following persons do not have such capacity in law:

(1) Persons mentally incompetent.

(2) Infants. A contract to which an infant is a party is voidable. The infant may at any time disaffirm any agreement to which he is a party, except an agreement to furnish him with necessities. This is so even if the other party did not know he was under 21, or was told he was over 21. Only the infant himself has the right to cancel his contract, but he must do so within a reasonable time after he becomes 21.

There must be mutual assent (an absolute and definite understanding between the contracting parties) as to the details of a contract. A contract not based on mutual assent is not valid as there is no "meeting of the minds." There must also be an intention to enter into a contract. If a mistake has been made in a contract and the mistake is a mutual one, or is made by one party with the knowledge of the other, the contract is considered voidable.

When one of the contracting parties has wilfully misrepresented the actual condition which induced the other party to enter into the contract, or if he has concealed some material fact which would cause the other party not to enter into the contract, the contract was obtained by fraud. Such a contract may be rescinded by the person who was defrauded and the parties returned to their previous condition, or the injured party may sue for damages for the fraud. If the contract has been obtained under threat (the legal term is, "under duress"), it is voidable.

Any agreement of which the subject matter is illegal cannot be enforced by either party. Contracts against public policy, such as betting contracts, are also invalid.

All contracts must contain the element of consideration. Consideration is the giving up of something, or some legal right, by the person to whom the promise runs. The promise of one party not to do a lawful act is consideration for the other party's promise. These are called mutual promises. When a contract has a seal next to the signature, no consideration is considered necessary.

No act performed in the past can be made the basis of a present contract. Any act or promise to do an act you are legally obligated to do, either by a former contract or by operation of law, cannot be the basis of consideration for another contract. Sometimes circumstances arise over which the contracting parties have no control, or situations are created which could not have been foreseen, and which prevent the performance of a contract. Only acts of God or war, however, excuse performance. Strikes are not considered sufficient cause to release a contracting party from fulfilling his contract unless special provision to that effect is contained in the contract.

**Repairs:** Any person who receives goods for repair, warrants that he is reasonably skilful in such work. If because of lack of skill the property is damaged, then he is liable for such damage.

**Sales of personal property:** A sale is a contract which transfers property from one person to another and which has money as its consideration. A contract to sell is one in which the transfer of title to the property is postponed for a future time.

**Warranties:** Goods sold are "warranted" to be as described. A warranty is expressed if it is made as a statement of fact or any oral promise, or made in writing by the seller, the natural tendency of which is to induce the buyer to buy. The seller's statement as to value or his opinion only as to any other matter is not a warranty.

An implied warranty is one the law reads into a contract of sale. The following warranties are implied: (1) That the seller has right to the goods or will have when the sale is to be completed. (2) That the buyer shall have the goods free from claims of others. (3) Where there is a sale by description or sample, the goods comply with the description or the sample. (4) Where the buyer tells the particular purpose for which the goods are to be used and relies on the seller's skill or judgment that they are reasonably fit for such purpose. (5) If the goods are sold for human consumption, it is implied that they are fit to be eaten; if for sale from a dealer that they are "merchantable."

There is no implied warranty of quality where: (1) The buyer has examined the goods as to any defects, which such examination ought to have revealed. (2) If the goods are sold by their patent or trade name there is no implied warranty of fitness for any particular purpose. (3) Goods sold "as is."

Unless there is an agreement to do so, acceptance of the goods does not discharge the seller from a claim for breach of any warranty. But the buyer must give notice of the breach to the seller within a reasonable time after he knows or should have known of it. Failure to give notice relieves the seller of liability. The time within which to give such notice may be specified.

The buyer has the following remedies for breach of warranty:

(1) Accept the goods and deduct the damages from the purchase price.

(2) Accept the goods and sue the seller for damages.

(3) Rescind the contract and refuse the goods, or if the goods have been received, return or offer to return them and recover the price or any part which has been paid.

(4) If title has not passed, reject the goods and sue for damages.

When the buyer elects one of the above remedies, he waives all others. Where the buyer is entitled to and elects to rescind, he is not liable for the purchase price if he returns or offers to return the goods.

The seller who has not been paid has the right to: (1) Retain goods if they are in his possession; (2) Rescind the sale and sue for damages; (3) Resell for the buyer's account and charge him for the difference in price received; (4) Stop the goods if in transit if buyer is insolvent; (5) If title has passed to the buyer sue for the price; (6) Where the contract specifies the payment of the price on a certain day irrespective of delivery or transfer of title and same is not paid, seller may sue for the price; (7) Where title has not passed and the goods cannot be sold at a reasonable price, the seller may offer to deliver to the buyer and if he refuses to accept and pay, sue for the price; (8) Sue for damages for non-acceptance.

When goods sold are to be delivered, the seller must follow the directions of the buyer in sending it, if they are given. If the seller disregards directions he becomes liable for damages that may result. When the seller delivers goods sold, in good condition, to a common carrier (railroad, express company, etc.) and he has complied with the instructions of the buyer as to shipping, his responsibility ends with delivery to the carrier. He is not liable for damages which may result to the goods while in transit.

## WILLS

Both husband and wife should make a will. The will should be made up by a lawyer, as it is an intricate technical document. Some of the points to remember:

A will must be made in writing by a competent person (of sound mind and full age). A child over 18 may make a will disposing of personal property only. The will should state that it is a last will and revokes previous wills, should provide for payment of debts and death expenses. It should unmistakably describe the persons to whom property is left. If wife or children are not to receive under a will, mention should be made of this fact so that it will be known that they were not overlooked. It should be signed in the presence of two witnesses (some states require three witnesses) who are not parties in interest, who know they are witnesses to a will. Their addresses should be shown.

Provision should be made for an administrator and executors (with bond or specifically stating none is necessary), guardians, alternate beneficiaries, administrators, etc.

## BURGLARIES

Burglars seldom enter a house which they believe to be occupied. They look for milk bottles, stuffed mailboxes, newspapers, a single light, or an open garage door. Alarm systems for homes utilize contact devices, vibrators, mats on floors, photoelectric cells, and ultrasonic filled areas which sound an alarm when a contact is broken.

When leaving for an evening, leave some lights burning, perhaps a radio playing. When leaving for an extended period, have mail and other deliveries held, lend out domestic animals, don't draw shades. Have phone disconnected so that an on the spot telephone check whether you are home can't be made. Avoid newspaper publicity on your projected vacation.

## HOUSEWIFE BEWARE—SOME SCHEMES AND RACKETS TO KNOW ABOUT

ABSENTEE FARMING: The offering of land in a distant state on a cooperative arrangement to raise fruits or nuts has its share of racketeers who sell land at exorbitant prices, minimize the hazards, and quote misleading figures which, if true, should make you comfortable for life.

ADVERTISING: Don't buy ads in unknown year books or directories, or other publications sponsored by unknown organizations, until you know the circulation and other pertinent facts.

BABY CONTESTS: Photograph salesmen trick proud mothers into ordering baby pictures by falsely representing that their studios are conducting baby contests.

BAIT ADVERTISING: Bait advertising of certain articles at bargain prices to entice the customer into the store with the idea of selling him a substitute at a higher price.

CEMETERY LOTS: Be wary of memorial park or cemetery lot salesmen who use a speculative or resale appeal, promising to resell your lots at a big profit for you.

COAL: Bootleg coal claimed to be "Direct from the mines" at "Bargain Prices" may be stolen from mining property, weighed by guess, improperly cleaned, and may contain considerable slate.

C.O.D.: You are asked to accept and pay for a C.O.D. package for your neighbor who is not at home. The package may contain crumpled newspapers, a bottle of water, or a brick. It is sometimes worked on business concerns when the employer is away.

CONTRACTS: Know what you sign. Tricksters have printed advertising contracts over signatures obtained in innocent appearing ways. Don't issue your signature promiscuously. It is also of paramount importance that you fully understand any paper you sign. Some contracts have vague or tricky terms that are entirely at variance with what the salesman represents.

COSMETIC AND HEALTH SCHEMES: Authorities declare that the difficulties of getting a proper fitting denture or glasses by mail are overwhelming. There is no known product that, in itself, constitutes a competent treatment for such conditions as diabetes, influenza, kidney disease, or tuberculosis. There is no drug or combination of drugs known to medical science which can "restore" the "original" color to hair, or grow hair once hair roots have died. There is nothing that, put in the bath water, will reduce weight. Reducing remedies that contain desiccated thyroid, laxatives, or dinitro-phenol are potentially dangerous.

COUNTRY CLUBS: Some country club memberships offered as "free" may carry an alleged "tax" sufficient to pay all ordinary expenses of membership and net the promoters a handsome profit as well.

COUPONS: Coupons allegedly worth money toward the purchase of fountain pens, perfume, photographs or other merchandise are distributed, but the claimed valuation is often fictitious and the goods misrepresented.

DEATH VULTURES: "Hearse Chasers" victimize the bereaved by selling them flowers, Bibles, land and other things, falsely claiming that they had been recently ordered by the deceased. Sometimes they render bills when nothing is owed. Sometimes they claim part payment has been made by the deceased and endeavor to collect the alleged balance.

DIAMOND APPRAISALS: Gyp diamond salesmen sometimes suggest that you obtain a "disinterested" appraisal from a nearby concern. A confederate arranges for a "fake" appraisal.

DISCOUNT CLUBS: Be sure that the value of the merchandise is as represented. Many of these schemes are lotteries.

ENDLESS CHAIN: The Post Office Department has declared many of them lotteries and, therefore, illegal. Many are outright frauds.

FICTITIOUS LIST PRICES: Often used as a basis of comparison with a sale price to misrepresent that the difference in the two prices is a "saving."

FORTUNE TELLING: Crystal gazing, astrology, palm reading, or phrenology, or any other form or manner of fortune telling is the "bunk."

FREE ENCYCLOPEDIAS: When a high-pressure salesman states that because of your position in the community, you have been selected to receive a "free" encyclopedia, his game may be to sell an extension service which includes the cost of the encyclopedia.

HEIRS: Articles represented as family heirlooms may have been recently manufactured. If someone informs you that you are the heir to an interest in an old and fabulous estate, investigate! Crooked promoters have fraudulently collected millions of dollars for faked legal and other expenses.

HONORARY MEMBERSHIP: Don't be duped by the award of honorary membership in a fake society with imposing name. You may later be billed $25 for a certificate.

HORSE RACE TIPS: Horse race tipsters sometimes split their recommendations with different clients so as to cover all horses in the race. Winning clients are thus ready suckers for expensive follow-ups.

JEWELRY AUCTIONS: By means of "cappers" and fake bids, junk is sometimes sold at exorbitant prices.

MATRIMONIAL: Persons who patronize agencies or correspondence clubs may expose themselves to manifold dangers. Some of these have been shakedown rackets, used by adventurers and swindlers of all kinds.

MEXICAN DIVORCES: Divorces obtained by mail through Mexican courts have been held invalid in the United States.

MODEL SCHOOLS: The mannequin school that offers attractive girls the chance to earn while they learn should be thoroughly investigated.

MONEY-BACK GUARANTEE: A money-back guarantee is only as good as the company that makes it. The promises of a swindler mean nothing.

NEWS PHOTOS: Gyp photo salesmen flatter businessmen and others by claiming their pictures are wanted for the press. Their idea is to sell photos at exorbitant prices.

OLD COINS: Frequently the appraisal fee is more than the value of the appraised coin.

OLD GOLD: Beware of gold buyers who call at your home and offer a price per "pennyweight," so you get about half the value of your gold. A pennyweight is about the weight of two U. S. cents.

FREE PERMANENT WAVES: The holder of the "free" certificate later learns that it refers to the "permanent waving" only, not the shampoo or setting, and that she is required to pay for the other essential operations—a price more than adequate to cover the complete process.

PONZI SCHEMES: If you are confidentially offered the opportunity to invest in a surefire proposition offering miraculous returns, look out! It is probably a Ponzi scheme that "robs Peter to pay Paul." Ponzi schemes are fraudulent and the majority must lose.

PUFF SHEETS: "Puff Sheets" are magazines filled with complimentary articles about companies and businessmen. Their sole circulation is the number of copies ordered by flattered subjects. "Mug Books" are similar but contain pictures.

RADIO AUDITIONS: Those who give legitimate radio auditions do not generally ask a fee.

RESIDENCE DEALERS: Dealers in furs, furniture, jewelry, etc., in private residences are called "residence dealers" and may operate "stuffed flats." They misrepresent and charge excessive prices.

SMUGGLED GOODS: All kinds of cheap merchandise, furs, lace, rugs, linens, suiting materials, etc., are sold by peddlers as "smuggled goods." These "phonies" affect foreign accents and frequently dress as seafaring men. Misrepresentation is their stock in trade.

SOLICITATIONS: Investigate all charitable solicitations before you give. Advertising projects, dances, and other benefits frequently net the charity little, but the promoter much. Telephone charitable solicitations by strangers are seldom worthy of donation. Many are conducted by professional solicitors who work on a high commission.

SPANISH PRISONER: Beware of intriguing letters from the Spanish or Mexican prisoner who offers you part of a secret fortune if you advance money to get him out of jail. This is probably the oldest international swindle known.

SWEEPSTAKES: Sweepstakes lotteries violate postal laws of the U. S. and Canada. Many are swindles that benefit only the promoters.

THEATRICAL: Crooked promoters who sell young dancing girls the idea of playing distant or foreign engagements may disappear after getting the girls to advance the cost of their transportation.

TRAVEL BUREAUS: Wildcat buses or share-expense travel agencies sometimes dump their customers at wayside points even though the fares are paid in full. Not only have customers lost their baggage but they have been insulted and suffered other indignities, inconvenience, and loss.

UNORDERED MERCHANDISE: Many schemers make a living by mailing unordered merchandise in hopes that you will pay for it. Sometimes they use a charity or sympathy appeal. Recipient is under no obligation to remit for it or return it.

# BOOK XII

## Household Almanac

| | |
|---|---|
| Jan. 1 | New Year's Day (Circumcision of Christ) and its eve. Watch-night services. Tin horns, confetti, domino masks. New Year's resolutions. Visiting. Eggnogs. Old Father Time with his scythe, and the infant representing the New Year. |
| Jan. 6 | Epiphany. Twelfth Night. Last day of the Feast of the Nativity. Commemorates manifestation of Christ to Gentiles by the visit of three wise men to Bethlehem. An old English festival marking 12 days between Christmas and Epiphany. Cake baked with bean and pea in it. The finder of the bean is the king and the finder of the pea, the queen. The end of Christmas decoration. Burning of the Christmas tree with a dash of bay, rosemary, and frankincese added. |
| Jan. 19 | Lee's Birthday. |
| Jan. 20 (every 4th year) | Inauguration Day in District of Columbia. President takes office. |
| Feb. | Ash Wednesday. Commemorates the custom of placing ashes on the head as a sign of penitence and a reminder that man is dust. Beginning of Lent, commemorating Christ's 40 Days of Suffering. (Lent.) Catholics attend no celebrations, eat no meat. |
| Feb. 12 | Lincoln's Birthday. Lincoln stories and the lesson of opportunity in America. The Gettysburg Address, Civil War songs. The birch log and hatchet representing the Rail Splitter. Log cabins. |

| | |
|---|---|
| Feb. | Shrove Tuesday. Mardi Gras in Louisiana. |
| Feb. 14 | Valentine's Day. Lacy cards "to my Valentine," Cupids. Red candles, red hearts. Homemade cards by the children. |
| Feb. 15 | Susan B. Anthony Day. Birthday of the crusader for women's rights. |
| Feb. (third Monday) | Washington's Birthday. Cherry pie. The story of the cherry tree. Tricorn hats with red, white, and blue cockades. Mt. Vernon. |
| Mar. 17 | St. Patrick's Day. Commemorates Ireland's patron saint, who freed the island of snakes and converted it to Christianity. Wearing-of-the-green. Three-leafed shamrock, shillelagh, stovepipe hats, clay pipes, rubber snakes. Parades. |
| Mar. | Jewish Festival of Purim. Commemorates deliverance in Persia. Three-cornered cakes. (Hammantashen.) Noisemakers. Masquerades. Reading the "Megilloth" or Scroll of Esther. Sending of gifts, especially to the poor. |
| Mar. or April | Holy Week: Palm Sunday. Commemorates Christ's triumphal entry into Jerusalem, the populace strewing palm branches before Him. Holy Monday. Maundy Thursday. Commemorates the betrayal and arrest of Christ, the agony of Christ in Gethsemane, the washing of the feet of the 12 apostles by Christ, and the institution of the Eucharist. Good Friday. Commemorates the crucifixion of Christ. Saddest day of the Christian year. Holy Saturday. Devoted to the contemplation of Christ under the power of death. Easter Sunday. Festival of Christ's resurrection. Most joyous day of the Christian year. Schools out for a week. Colored eggs in baskets, nests, or by themselves. Bunnies and chicks. Egg-rolling. Ham. Plants and flowers. Sweet peas, jonquils, lilies, tulips, hyacinths, orchids. |

| | |
|---|---|
| April 1 | All Fool's Day. Watch out for pranks, and surprises. Treasure hunts. |
| April 10 (and other dates in various States) | Arbor Day. Tree Planting Day. Bird Day. A legal holiday in Arizona and Nebraska. |
| Mar. or April | Jewish Festival of Passover (8 days). Commemorates the deliverance of the first-born during the 10th plague in Egypt. Circa 1300 B.C. Special food and dishes for the 8 days. "Seders" are held each night, particularly first two and last two days. |
| April 14 | Pan American Day. |
| May 1 | May Day. Maypoles. May baskets filled with flowers. Child Health Day. Labor celebrations. |
| May (40 days after Easter Sunday) | Ascension Day—Commemorates ascension of Christ into Heaven. |
| 10 days later, 50 days after Easter) | Whitsunday—Commemorates the descent of the Holy Spirit on the infant Christian Church in Jerusalem. |
| (7 days later) | Trinity Sunday. Commemorates the revelation of God's nature as Father, Son, and Holy Ghost. |
| May (second Sunday) | Mother's Day. Gifts, and cards for mother. Flowers. |
| May | Jewish Feast of Weeks. Shebuoth. Commemorates the giving of the law at Mount Sinai and the end of the wheat harvest. |
| May (third Saturday) | Armed Forces Day. |
| May (third Sunday) | I Am An American Day. Display the flag. Speeches. Parades. |
| May 30 | Decoration or Memorial Day. In honor of those who fell serving the nation. Display the flag. |

| June | Father's Day. Gifts and cards for father. |
|------|-------------------------------------------|
| June 14 | Flag Day. Betsy Ross. Display the flag. |
| July 4 | Independence Day. Display the flag. Be careful about fireworks. Watermelons. Picnics. Speeches. |
| Aug. | Jewish Fast of Tishah B'ov. Commemorates the destruction of Jerusalem by the Babylonians 586 B.C. and by Titus, 70 A.D. |
| Aug. 15 | Assumption of the Blessed Virgin Mary. |
| Sept. (first Monday) | Labor Day. Watch out for the traffic. Picnics. Closing the summer season. Select fruit and vegetables for canning. |
| Sept. or Oct. | Jewish New Year, Rosh Hashonah (2 days). Festival. |
| (8 days later) | Day of Atonement (Yom Kippur), a day of fasting. Services. |
| (5 days later) | Jewish Festival of Succoth (Harvest). Building of an arbor in the yard. |
| Oct. (second Monday) | Columbus Day. |
| Oct. 31 | Hallowe'en. The eve of All Saints' Day. Ghosts, goblins, witches, hollowed pumpkins. Painting up the town. Bobbing for apples. Biting the apple on a string. Fortune telling. Love charms. Trick or treat. |
| Nov. 1 | All Saints' Day. |
| Nov. (1st Tuesday after 1st Monday) | Election Day. Tin horns. Bonfires. Torchlight parades. Listening to returns. |
| Nov. (second Monday) | Veterans Day. Commemorating the end of World War. I. Display the flag. Two minutes of silence at 11 A.M. Prayers. |
| Nov. (next to last Thursday) | Thanksgiving. Family get-together. Prayer and charity. Turkey, golden squash, chestnut stuffing, cranberry jelly, nuts, apples, pumpkin pie, sweet cider, pompons, birch or oak leaves, gourds, ivy, zinnias. Pilgrim tradition. Lighting the fireplace. Masquerades. "Anything for Thanksgiving?" |

| Dec. 8 | Immaculate Conception. |
|--------|------------------------|
| Dec. 21 | Forefather's Day. Celebrates the landing at Plymouth Rock in 1620. Dinners by New England societies. |
| Dec. | Jewish Festival of Hanukah. Commemorates the recovery of the Temple by Judas Maccabeus in a rebellion against the Romans, 162 B.C. |
| Dec. 25 | Christmas. Family get-together. Services. Gifts. Santa Claus. The stocking in the fireplace. The tree and decorations. Cards to everyone. Holly, mistletoe, pine, spruce, and balsam. Christmas dinner. Turkey, mincemeat, plum pudding. Carols. The family together. Thank-you notes. |

## WHEN EASTER FALLS

Easter is the first Sunday following the Paschal full moon, which happens upon or next after the 21st of March. Easter thus may vary between March 22 and April 25, over a period of 35 days.

If Paschal full moon falls on Sunday, then Easter Day is the next Sunday. The Paschal full moon is the fourteenth day of a lunar month reckoned according to an ancient ecclesiastical computation and not the real or astronomical full moon.

Lent, the period of fasting in the Christian Church, begins on Ash Wednesday, which comes 40 days before Easter Sunday, not counting Sundays.

Lent comprises 30 days of fasting, omitting all the Sundays and also all the Saturdays except one. Pope Gregory added Ash Wednesday to the fast, together with the remainder of that week.

Passion Week precedes Holy Week. The last seven days of Lent constitute Holy Week, beginning with Palm Sunday.

Easter is the chief festival of the Christian year, commemorating the resurrection of Christ. In the second century A. D., Easter Day was, among Christians in Asia Minor, the 14th of Nisan, the seventh month of the Jewish calendar. The Christians in Europe observed the nearest Sunday.

### DATES ON WHICH ASH WEDNESDAY AND EASTER SUNDAY FALL

| Year | Ash Wed. | Easter Sun. | Year | Ash Wed. | Easter Sun. |
|------|----------|-------------|------|----------|-------------|
| 1951 | Feb. 7 | Mar. 25 | 1976 | Mar. 3 | April 18 |
| 1952 | Feb. 27 | April 13 | 1977 | Feb. 23 | April 10 |
| 1953 | Feb. 18 | April 5 | 1978 | Feb. 8 | Mar. 26 |
| 1954 | Mar. 3 | April 18 | 1979 | Feb. 28 | April 15 |
| 1955 | Feb. 23 | April 10 | 1980 | Feb. 20 | April 6 |
| 1956 | Feb. 15 | April 1 | 1981 | Mar. 4 | April 19 |
| 1957 | Mar. 6 | April 21 | 1982 | Feb. 24 | April 11 |
| 1958 | Feb. 19 | April 6 | 1983 | Feb. 16 | April 3 |
| 1959 | Feb. 11 | Mar. 29 | 1984 | Mar. 7 | April 22 |
| 1960 | Mar. 2 | April 17 | 1985 | Feb. 20 | April 7 |
| 1961 | Feb. 15 | April 2 | 1986 | Feb. 12 | Mar 30 |
| 1962 | Mar. 7 | April 22 | 1987 | Mar. 4 | April 19 |
| 1963 | Feb. 27 | April 14 | 1988 | Feb. 17 | April 3 |
| 1964 | Feb. 12 | Mar. 29 | 1989 | Feb. 8 | Mar. 26 |
| 1965 | Mar. 3 | April 18 | 1990 | Feb. 28 | April 15 |
| 1966 | Feb. 23 | April 10 | 1991 | Feb. 13 | Mar. 31 |
| 1967 | Feb. 8 | Mar. 26 | 1992 | Mar. 4 | April 19 |
| 1968 | Feb. 28 | April 14 | 1993 | Feb. 24 | April 11 |
| 1969 | Feb. 19 | April 6 | 1994 | Feb. 16 | April 3 |
| 1970 | Feb. 11 | Mar. 29 | 1995 | Mar. 1 | April 16 |
| 1971 | Feb. 24 | April 11 | 1996 | Feb. 21 | April 7 |
| 1972 | Feb. 16 | April 2 | 1997 | Feb. 12 | Mar. 30 |
| 1973 | Mar. 7 | April 22 | 1998 | Feb. 25 | April 12 |
| 1974 | Feb. 27 | April 14 | 1999 | Feb. 17 | April 4 |
| 1975 | Feb. 12 | Mar. 30 | 2000 | Mar. 8 | April 23 |

## CHURCH FASTS

The Roman Catholic days of obligation are: Jan. 1 (Circumcision of Christ); Ascension Day (40 days after Easter Sunday); Aug. 15 (Assumption of the Blessed Virgin); Nov. 1 (All Saints' Day); Dec. 8 (Immaculate Conception); Dec. 25 (Christmas), and all Sundays.

The Roman Catholic canon law prescribes abstinence for every Friday of the year. Abstinence and fast together are to be observed on Ash Wednesday, the Wednesdays and Fridays of Lent (in the United States), the Ember Days, the Vigils of Pentecost, the Assumption of the Blessed Virgin Mary, the Feast of All Saints, and the Nativity of Our Lord. The law of fast alone is prescribed for all the remaining days of Lent except Sundays.

In the American Episcopal Church, days of fasting or abstinence to be observed, according to the Book of Common Prayer, are the 40 days of Lent, the Ember Days, and all the

Fridays of the year except Christmas and the Epiphany. The three Rogation Days are days of solemn supplication.

In the Greek Church the four principal fasts are those in Lent, the week succeeding Whitsuntide, the fortnight before the Assumption, and forty days before Christmas.

Ember and Rogation Days are certain periods of the year

## EPISCOPAL HOLIDAYS

| Days | Approximate Month | Days | Approximate Month |
|---|---|---|---|
| Septuagesima | ..............Feb. | Easter Day | ................Apr. |
| Ash Wednesday | ....Feb or Mar. | Rogation Sunday | .........May |
| 1st Sunday in Lent | .Feb. or Mar. | Ascension Day | ............May |
| Passion Day | .......Mar. or Apr. | Whitsunday | .......May or June |
| Palm Sunday | ......Mar. or Apr. | Trinity Sunday | ...........June |
| Good Friday | ..............Apr. | 1st Sunday in Advent | Nov. or Dec. |

## MAJOR JEWISH HOLIDAYS, FESTIVALS AND FASTS

| Festivals and Fasts | Hebrew Date | | Usually Falls In |
|---|---|---|---|
| New Year (Rosh Hashonah) | Tishri | 1, 2 | Sept. or Oct. |
| Fast of Guedalia* | Tishri | 3 | Sept. or Oct. |
| Day of Atonement (Yom Kippur) | Tishri | 10 | Sept. or Oct. |
| Tabernacles, 1st and 2nd Days | Tishri | 15, 16 | Sept. or Oct. |
| Tabernacles, 8th Day | Tishri | 22 | Oct. |
| Rejoicing of the Law | Tishri | 23 | Oct. |
| Hanukah, begins, last 8 days | Kislev | 25 | Dec. |
| Fast of Tebet | Tebet | 10 | Dec. or Jan. |
| Purim | Adar | 14 | March |
| Purim (in Leap Year) | Adar Sheni | 14 | March |
| Passover, 1st and 2nd Days | Nisan | 15, 16 | April |
| Passover, 7th Day | Nisan | 21 | April |
| Passover, Last Day | Nisan | 22 | April |
| Shebuoth (Feast of Weeks) | Sivan | 6, 7 | May or June |
| Fast of Tammuz* | Tammuz | 17 | July |
| Fast of Abh* | Abh | 9 | July or Aug. |

* If Saturday, substitute Sunday immediately following. All Jewish holidays, etc., begin at sunset on the day previous to that given in the table. The months of the Jewish year are: 1. Tishri; 2. Heshvan (also Marcheshvan); 3. Kislev; 4. Tebet (also Tebeth); 5. Sebat (also Shebhat); 6. Adar; A month is added in leap years, Adar Sheni; 7. Nisan; 8. Iyar; 9. Sivan; 10. Tammuz; 11. Abh; 12. Elul.

devoted to prayer and fasting. Ember Days (twelve annually), about the beginning of the four seasons, are the Wednesday, Friday, and Saturday after the first Sunday in Lent, in Spring; after the feast of the Pentecost (Whitsunday), Summer; after the festival of the Holy Cross, Sept. 14 in Autumn, and after the festival of St. Lucia, Dec. 13 in Winter. Ember Weeks are weeks in which the Ember Days appear.

Rogation Days occur on Monday, Tuesday and Wednesday immediately preceding Ascension Day.

## SIGNS OF THE ZODIAC

| | | |
|---|---|---|
| Capricorn | The Goat | Dec. 23 to Jan. 20 |
| Aquarius | The Water Bearer | Jan. 21 to Feb. 18 |
| Pisces | The Fishes | Feb. 19 to Mar. 20 |
| Aries | The Ram | Mar. 21 to April 20 |
| Taurus | The Bull | Apr. 21 to May 20 |
| Gemini | The Twins | May 21 to June 20 |
| Cancer | The Crab | June 21 to July 22 |
| Leo | The Lion | July 23 to Aug. 22 |
| Virgo | The Virgin | Aug. 23 to Sept. 22 |
| Libra | The Balance | Sept. 23 to Oct. 23 |
| Scorpio | The Scorpion | Oct. 24 to Nov. 22 |
| Sagittarius | The Archer | Nov. 23 to Dec. 21 |

## DAYLIGHT SAVING TIME

Daylight Saving Time prolongs the hours of daylight during the spring and summer months by advancing the clocks one hour. It begins at 2 A.M., the last Sunday in April and ends at 2 A.M., the last Sunday in October.

## STANDARD TIME

Standard time is reckoned, like longitude, from Greenwich, England. The world is divided into 24 zones, each 15 degrees of an arc. New York City and Washington, D. C., are in the most easterly zone in the U. S. and have Eastern Standard Time.

For Central Standard Time deduct one hour.

For Mountain Time deduct two hours.

For Pacific Standard Time deduct three hours.

## THE SEASONS

| | | | |
|---|---|---|---|
| Winter begins | Dec. 22 | Summer begins | June 21 |
| Spring begins | Mar. 21 | Autumn begins | Sept. 23 |

## FORECASTING THE WEATHER

Local forecasts are available from the United States Weather Bureau for two days. In nine cities, this forecast may be obtained by merely dialing Weather 6-1212. Experimental 30-day "Long Range Weather Outlooks" are made on the 1st and 15th day of each month and are available from the Superintendent of Documents, Washington, D. C., at $4.80 per year.

Weather maps give an indication of local weather. The weather usually rides with the wind. Wind directions are indicated by arrows. Rain, snow and cloudiness are indicated by other symbols. Connecting lines indicate equal air pressure. In general, low pressure areas are cloudy and rainy; high pressure areas are clearer, cooler.

Other indications of weather conditions:

| Condition | Probable Forecast |
|---|---|
| Falling barometer (air pressure)<br>South or east wind<br>High humidity<br>Dark low clouds | Rain within 3 hours. |
| Sheet of thick, gray (alto-stratus) clouds thickening toward the west. These sometimes show bright patch in neighborhood of sun or moon. | 60 percent probability of rain within 8 hours. |
| High, small, globular masses or white flaked clouds (cirro-cumulus) or large globular white or grayish (alto-cumulus) clouds usually arranged in groups or lines. | 50 percent probability of rain within 16 hours. |

| Condition | Probable Forecast |
|---|---|
| Detached, delicate, fibrous looking, (cirrus) clouds, generally white. | No more than normal probability of rain. |
| Halos in advancing edge of cirro-stratus clouds. Coronas within a sheet of alto-cumulus cloud. Wind from the south. Rising temperature. | Added indications of probable rain. |
| Rosy sunset. | Fair weather. |
| Unusual transparency of the air. Pure twilight colors. | Cooler, fair weather for next day usually followed by rain within two days. |
| Hazy air. Sun setting as a fiery ball. | Droughty conditions, temperature above normal. |
| Rapid rise in temperature. | Rainfall and windy weather within a few hours. |

"Evening gray and morning red
'Twill pour down rain on traveler's head;
But evening red and morning gray
Will set a traveler on his way."

## WEDDING ANNIVERSARIES

The wedding anniversary lists are prepared by various associations in the jewelry industry. The original list was prepared in 1937 and by agreement revised in 1948.

| Number | 1937 Version | Current Version | Traditional Version |
|---|---|---|---|
| 1st | Paper | Clocks | Paper |
| 2nd | Cotton | China | Cotton |
| 3rd | Leather | Crystal, glass | Leather |
| 4th | Books | Electrical appliances | Fruit and flowers, silk |
| 5th | Wood, clocks | Silverware | Wooden |

| Number | 1937 Version | Current Version | Traditional Version |
|--------|--------------|-----------------|---------------------|
| 6th | Iron | Wood | Sugar and candy, iron |
| 7th | Copper, bronze or brass | Desk, pen and pencil sets | Woolen or copper |
| 8th | Electrical appliances | Linens, laces | Bronze or pottery |
| 9th | Pottery | Leather | Willow or pottery |
| 10th | Tin, aluminum | Diamond jewelry | Tin or aluminum |
| 11th | Steel | Fashion jewelry, accessories | Steel |
| 12th | Silk or linen | Pearls or colored gems | Silk or linen |
| 13th | Lace | Textiles, furs | Lace |
| 14th | Ivory | Gold jewelry | Ivory |
| 15th | Crystal | Watches | Crystal |
| 16th | | Silver hollow ware | |
| 17th | | Furniture | |
| 18th | | Porcelain | |
| 19th | | Bronze | |
| 20th | China | Platinum | China |
| 25th | Silver | Sterling silver | Silver |
| 30th | Pearl | Diamond | Pearl |
| 35th | Coral, jade | Jade | Coral |
| 40th | Ruby | Ruby | Ruby |
| 45th | Sapphire | Sapphire | Sapphire |
| 50th | Gold | Golden Jubilee | Golden |
| 55th | Emerald | Emerald | Emerald |
| 60th, 75th | Diamond | Diamond Jubilee | Diamond |

## BIRTH STONES AND LANGUAGE OF STONES

| Month | Ancient | Modern |
|-------|---------|--------|
| Jan. | Garnet | Garnet (faithfulness) |
| Feb. | Amethyst | Amethyst (peacemaking) |
| Mar. | Jasper | Bloodstone (courage and wisdom) or Aquamarine |

| Month | Ancient | Modern |
|-------|---------|--------|
| April | Sapphire | Diamond (innocence) |
| May | Agate (health and longevity) | Emerald (true love) |
| June | Emerald | Pearl or moonstone |
| July | Onyx | Ruby (true friendship) |
| Aug. | Carnelian (contentment) | Sardonyx (conjugal happiness) or peridot |
| Sept. | Chrysolite | Sapphire (repentance) |
| Oct. | Aquamarine | Opal (hope) or tourmaline |
| Nov. | Topaz | Topaz (friendship) |
| Dec. | Ruby | Turquoise (happiness in love) Lapis Lazuli |

## FLOWERS OF THE MONTH

| | | | |
|--|--|--|--|
| January | Carnation or snowdrop | July | Larkspur or water lily |
| February | Violet or primrose | August | Poppy or gladiolus |
| March | Jonquil or daffodil | Sept. | Aster or morning glory |
| April | Sweet pea or daisy | October | Calendula or cosmos |
| May | Lily of the valley or hawthorn | November | Chrysanthemum |
| | | December | Narcissus or holly |
| June | Rose or honeysuckle | | |

## LANGUAGE OF FLOWERS

ACACIA, friendship

ALMOND BLOSSOM, encouragement

ALOE, grief

ANEMONE, soul of goodness

APPLE BLOSSOM, you are preferred

ARBUTUS, I love but thee

ASTER, always gay

BALM, sympathy

BEGONIA, steadfast

BLACKTHORN, courage under trials

BLUEBELL, true and tender

BUTTERCUP, homeliness

CAMELLIA, beautiful but cold

CARNATION, (white), purity

CARNATION (deep red), my heart is broken

CHRYSANTHEMUM, hope springs eternal

CLEMATIS, poor but honest

CLOVER, (white), think of me

CLOVER, (red), sweetness

COLUMBINE, bound to win

CORNELIAN, May, content

CROCUS, ever glad

DAFFODIL, welcome

DAHLIA, gracious

DAISY, innocence

FERN, sincerity

FORGET-ME-NOT, forget me not

## LANGUAGE OF FLOWERS—Cont.

FOXGLOVE, deceitful

FUCHSIA, fickleness

GENTIAN, hope

GERANIUM, warm regard

HAWTHORN, courage in adversity

HEATHER, I am lonely

HOLLY, rejoice together

HONEYSUCKLE, devotion

HYACINTH, hard fate

IRIS, have faith in me

IVY, I cling

JASMINE, friends only

LAUREL, triumph

LAVENDER, sweets to the sweet

LILAC, unadorned beauty

LILY, austere purity

LILY OF THE VALLEY, doubly dear

MAGNOLIA, magnanimity

MARIGOLD, honesty

MIGNONETTE, undiluted pleasure

NASTURTIUM, optimism

OLIVE, peace

ORANGE BLOSSOM, happiness in marriage

PANSY, thoughts

PETUNIA, I believe in thee

PIMPERNEL, consolation

POPPY, forgetfulness

PRIMROSE, do not be bashful

ROSE (red), love

ROSE (white), worthy of love

ROSE (yellow), why waneth love?

ROSEMARY, remembrance

SNOWDROP, goodness unalloyed

SWEET PEA, I long for thee

SWEET WILLIAM, pleasant dreams

TULIP, unrequited love

VERBENA, you have my confidence

VIOLET, modesty

WHITE HEATHER, good luck

---

## TABLES OF WEIGHTS AND MEASURES

### Linear Measure

1 foot = 12 inches.

1 link = 7.92 inches.

1 yard = 3 feet or 36 inches.

1 rod = 5½ yards or 16½ feet.

1 mile = 320 rods.

1 mile = 5280 feet or 1760 yards.

1 mile = 8000 links or 320 rods or 80 chains.

1 nautical mile = 6080.2 feet or 1.15 mile.

1 knot = 1 nautical mile per hour.

1 furlong = ⅛ mile. (660 feet or 220 yards.)

1 league = 3 miles, or 24 furlongs.

1 fathom = 2 yards.

1 chain = 100 links, 22 yards.

1 hand = 4 inches.

1 span = 9 inches.

### Square Measure

1 sq. foot = 144 sq. inches.

1 sq. link = 0.4356 sq. feet.

1 sq. yard = 9 sq. feet.

1 sq. rod = 30¼ sq. yards.

1 acre = 160 sq. rods or 43,560 sq. feet or 100,000 sq. links, or 10 sq. chains.

1 sq. mile = 640 acres or 102,400 sq. rods.

1 sq. rod = 625 sq. links.

1 sq. chain = 16 sq. rods.

## Square Measure—Cont.

100 acres = 1 hectare.

1 sq. meter = 10.76 sq. feet or 1.2 sq. yds.

## Cubic Measure (Volume)

1 cubic inch = 16.4 cubic centimeters.

1 liter = 61.035 cubic inches or .035 cubic feet.

1 cubic meter = 35.3 cubic feet or 1.3 cubic yds.

1 cubic foot = 1728 cubic inches.

1 cubic yard = 27 cubic feet or 46656 cubic inches.

1 ton, shipping ms. = 100 cu. feet.

1 cord = 128 cubic feet, 8' long x 4' wide x 4' high.

1 board foot = 144 cubic inches, 12"x12"x1".

## Avoirdupois, Weight or Mass

$27\frac{11}{32}$ grains = 1 dram.

16 drams = 1 ounce.

16 ounces = 1 pound = 7000 grains = 256 drams.

2000 pounds = 1 short ton.

1 pound = 16 ounces or .454 kilograms.

1 hundredweight = 100 lbs.

1 ton = 20 hundredweight or 2000 lbs.

1 long ton = 2240 lbs.

1 metric ton = 2204.6 lbs.

1000 micrograms = 1 milligram.

1000 milligrams = 1 gram.

1000 grams = 1 kilogram or 2.2 lbs. or 35.3 ounces.

1000 kilograms = 1 metric ton.

1 kilogram = 2.204 lbs.

## Troy Weight

(Used in weighing gold, silver, and jewels.)

1 pennyweight = 24 grains.

1 ounce = 20 pennyweight.

1 pound = 12 ounces.

## Apothecaries' Measure

1 scruple = 20 grains.

1 fluid dram = 60 minims(m).

1 dram = 3 scruples.

8 fluid drams = 1 fluid ounce.

16 fluid oz. = 1 pint (o).

8 pints = 1 gallon (Cong.).

A minim is about 1 drop.

## Metric Linear

1 centimeter = 10 millimeters.

1 decimeter = 10 centimeters.

1 meter = 10 decimeters.

1 dekameter = 10 meters.

1 hektometer = 10 dekameters.

1 kilometer = 10 hektometers.

1 inch = 2.54 centimeters.

1 meter = 39.37 inches.

1 yard = 0.914 meters.

## Dry Measure—Capacity

1 dry quart = 2 dry pints or .125 pecks or 1.101 liters.

1 peck = 16 dry pints or 8 dry quarts.

1 bushel = 64 dry pints, or 32 dry quarts, or 4 pecks, or 35.2383 liters, or 2150.42 cubic inches.

1 liter = .908 dry quarts.

### Liquid Measure—Capacity

1 drop = 1 minim or .05cc.

1 teaspoon = 1½ fluid drams or 120 drops of water or 60 drops of thick fluid.

2 teaspoons = 1 dessert spoon.

1 tablespoon = 460 drops or 4 drams or 3 teaspoons or 15cc.

1 medical teaspoon = 1 fluid dram, ¼ tablespoon.

1 cup = 16 tablespoons; 8 fluid ounces or ½ pint.

3 teaspoons = 1 tablespoonful.

2 tablespoonfuls = 1 fluid ounce.

15 milliliters = 1 tablespoonful.

1 pint = 2 cups.

1 ounce = 30cc.

8 fluid drams (fl. dr.) = 1 fluid ounce.

4 fluid ounces = 1 gill.

1 tumbler = 8 ounces or 240cc.

1 pint = 16 ounces or 480cc or 4 gills.

1 quart = 2 pints or 32 ounces or 960cc or .946 liters.

1 gallon = 4 quarts or 231 cubic inches.

### Prefixes and Words in the Metric System

milli = 1/1000 = one thousandth.

centi = 1/100 = one hundredth.

deci = 1/10 = one tenth.

deka = 10 = ten.

hecto = 100 = one hundred.

kilo = 1000 = one thousand.

### Approximate Food Weights

1 pint (2 cups) measure of sugar = 1 pound.

1 pint (2 cups measure of butter = 1 pound.

1 pint (2 cups) measure of lard = 1 pound.

1 pint (2 cups) measure of flour = ¼ pound.

9 to 10 eggs = 1 pound.

1 pint milk = 1.075 pounds.

4 teaspoons baking powder = 1 ounce.

5⅛ cups coffee = 1 pound.

6½ cups tea = 1 pound.

Meter is used to measure length.

Gram is used to measure weight or mass.

Liter is used to measure capacity, dry or liquid.

## RULES FOR COMPUTATION

Circumference of a circle = diameter x 3.14159265.

Area of a circle = square of diameter x .785398.

Cubic content of a cylinder or pipe = area of bottom x height.

Area of a rectangle = side x side.

Area of a right triangle = ½ base x altitude.

Diameter of circle = circumference x .3183.

Area of an ellipse = long diameter x short diameter x .7854.
Area of a sector of a circle = length of arc x half radius.
Area of a triangle = ½ base x altitude.
Area of a parallelogram = base x height.

## TEMPERATURE

To convert Centigrade to Fahrenheit, multiply Centigrade degrees by 9, divide by 5, add 32. To convert Fahrenheit to Centigrade, subtract 32, and multiply by 5/9.

    32 degrees F = 0 C (freezing).
    70      "    F = 21.1 C (ordinary room).
    110     "    F = 43.3 C (bath).
    212     "    F = 100 C (boiling).

Milk, at 68° Fahrenheit, weighs 8.60 lbs. a gallon provided it contains 3 percent of butter fat; cream 8.37 lbs. a gallon, if it has in it 28 percent of butter fat. When cream contains 40 percent of fat it weighs 8.28 lbs. a gallon.

## HOME CALCULATORS

Electric pocket size and desk calculators costing between $60 and $200 depending on sophistication are a convenient aid in figuring such things as income taxes and the family budget, or to check bills. They operate on battery and/or AC current and generally do multiplication, division, addition and subtraction. Most allow you to chain arithmetic operations and to accumulate subtotals as you go along. The good ones have a floating decimal point, rounding in multiplication and division and set an overflow indicator when a number too large to be stored in the register is reached. (Machines without the overflow indicator just give a wrong number.) The number of digits generally varies between 8 and 12. This number determines the size of the registers, the magnitude of the numbers the machine can handle and the accuracy of the calculations, and is an important factor in determining the machine's usefulness as well as its cost. Some machines allow you to store a constant, which is helpful when you have to do a series of multiplications or divisions using the same base or rate as in determining sales tax. A few of the more sophisticated and expensive machines allow you to take square roots and compute special functions like exponentials and cosines automatically. Others have gimmicks like special buttons for quickly squaring numbers, raising to a power or taking percentages.

## CONSUMERS SERVICES

CONSUMERS UNION, 256 Washington Street, Mt. Vernon, N. Y.—a non-profit testing organization which buys, tests and analyzes the value of everything bought by consumers. Publications: Consumers Reports, monthly, $5 per year including a summary buyers guide issue.

CONSUMERS' RESEARCH, INC., Washington, N. J.—a non-profit organization which carries on tests and research on a wide variety of goods, materials and appliances. Publications: Consumers Research Bulletin, monthly, $3 per year.

UNDERWRITERS LABORATORIES, INC., 161 Avenue of the Americas, New York 13, N. Y.—a non-profit organization sponsored by the National Board of Fire Underwriters to test and approve products which might cause fires. Standards are set up for most products. Approved products are listed in a catalogue and booklets. Most approved products carry the U. L. label.

NATIONAL ASSOCIATION OF SECONDARY SCHOOL PRINCIPALS, 1201 Sixteenth Street, N.W., Washington 6, D.C.—a Consumer Education Study has produced text books on consumer problems.

CONSUMER EDUCATION LIBRARY OF HOUSEHOLD FINANCE CORPORATION, Prudential Plaza, Chicago 1, Ill., offers educational materials to help individuals and families to be more businesslike in management of money. Publications on 25 subjects are available at 5c each.

Literature on buymanship is also available from mail-order catalogues, private consumer services, business organizations in the trade, government bulletins and books. Your local librarian will help you locate this material. Much of it is available for the asking or for a small fee.

# BIBLIOGRAPHY

You will find the following booklets and pamphlets of particular help in giving you more information about the subjects in The Household Encyclopedia. For copies write to Consumer Product Information, Public Documents Distribution Center, Pueblo, Colorado 81009. Send cash, check, money order or coupons available or arrange for a deposit account.

## APPLIANCES

DISHWASHERS. 1972. 20pp. 001A. 70¢. Descriptions of various features, selection, and maintenance.

MICROWAVE OVEN RADIATION. 1971. 9pp. 002A. 15¢

ROOM AIR CONDITIONERS. 1972. 24pp. 003A. 45¢. How they work, selection, use, and maintenance.

SUNLAMPS. 1972. 2pp. 004A. Free. Precautions for safe use.

VACUUM CLEANERS: Their selection, Use and Care. 1972. 16pp. 005A. 60¢

WASHERS AND DRYERS. 1972. 24pp. 006A. 45¢. Selection and maintenance.

## BUDGET

BUDGETING FOR THE FAMILY. 1972. 16pp. Steps in developing a budget with charts for estimating income, planning family spending, and recording expenses.

HELPING FAMILIES MANAGE THEIR FINANCES. 1968. 51pp. 019A. 40¢. Guide to financial planning includes information on use of credit, savings accounts, investments and life insurance.

PLANNING FOR THE LATER YEARS. 1969. 51pp. 020A. 35¢. Comprehensive guide for retirement planning with discussions of income, health maintenance, housing, legal problems and use of leisure time.

## CHILD CARE

PRENATAL CARE. 1970. 92pp. 027A. 20¢. Preparing for the baby's arrival; medical care, nutrition, necessary clothing and equipment.

TIPS ON DRUG ABUSE PREVENTION FOR PARENTS OF A YOUNG CHILD. 1972. 13pp. 028A. 10¢

TOY SAFETY. 1972. 24pp. 029A. 45¢

TOYS BANNED BY THE FOOD AND DRUG ADMINISTRATION. 1972. 030A. Free.

INFANT CARE. 1970. 108pp. 033A. 20¢

YOUR CHILD FROM 1 TO 6. 1970. 98pp. 034A. 20¢

YOUR CHILD FROM 6 TO 12. 1970. 98pp. 035A. 55¢

## CLOTHING, FABRICS AND LAUNDERING

CLOTHING AND FABRIC CARE LABELING. 1972. 7pp. Free. Information that must appear on labels of clothing and fabrics and how to use this information.

CLOTHING REPAIRS. 1970. 30pp. 037A. 25¢. Twenty-five repairs to prolong the usefulness of garments.

FIBERS AND FABRICS. 1970. 28pp. 038A. 65¢. Basic information about the properties, uses and care of the principal natural and man-made fibers.

LOOK FOR THAT LABEL. 1971. 8pp. 039A. Free. Mandatory labeling requirements for fiber content of fabrics and furs.

REMOVING STAINS FROM FABRICS. 1968. 32pp. 040A. 20¢. Stain removers and instructions for removing 142 common stains.

SANITATION IN HOME LAUNDERING. 1970. 8pp. 041A. 10¢. Disinfectant in home or coin-operated washing machines; when to use, how to select and use properly.

SOAPS AND DETERGENTS FOR HOME LAUNDERING. 1971. 8pp. 042A. 10¢.

## CONSUMER PROTECTION

GUIDE TO FEDERAL CONSUMER SERVICES. 1971. 151pp. 049A. $1.00. A summary of the consumer related services, programs and consumer publications offered by 34 federal departments and agencies.

HOW TO BUY FOODS/COMO COMPRAR LOS COMESTIBLES. 1971. 31pp. 050A. 50¢. A bilingual teaching aid for use in family economics and consumer education courses in secondary schools and adult education programs.

MAIL ORDER INSURANCE. 1971. 8pp. 053A. 15¢. Four common insurance frauds; how to protect yourself; procedures for reporting to the Federal Trade Commission.

READ THE LABEL. 1972. 24pp. 056A. 40¢. Information that must appear on the labels of food, drugs, cosmetics, and household chemicals; how to use this information.

TENANT'S GUIDE TO RENT CONTROLS. 1972. 14pp. 058A. Free. What rents are controlled, computing base rents, allowable increases and procedures the landlord must follow in giving notice of a rent increase.

TRUTH IN LENDING. 1970. 6pp. 059A. Free. Consumer's rights under the Truth in Lending Law of 1969; includes right to discovery of terms of credit.

## FOOD

CARE OF PURCHASED FROZEN FOODS. 1971. 6pp. 071A. 10¢. Shopping pointers, storage periods; procedure to follow when the freezer stops operating.

FAMILY FOOD BUDGETING. 1969. 16pp. 072A. 15¢. Food plans for adequate diets at four income levels.

FEDERAL FOOD STANDARDS. 1972. 4pp. 073A. Free. Brief summary of voluntary and regulatory standards for quality, identification and wholesomeness.

FOOD AID FOR THE ELDERLY. 1972. 6pp. 074A. Free. Information on food stamps, meals-on-wheels, donated foods, etc.

KEEPING FOOD SAFE TO EAT. 1972. 075A. 10¢. Necessary sanitation and food handling techniques.

SEASONING WITH HERBS AND SPICES. 1972. 4pp. 078A. Free.

SOME QUESTIONS AND ANSWERS ABOUT CANNED FOODS. 1971. 2pp. 079A. Free.

STORING PERISHABLE FOODS. 1971. 12pp. 081A. 10¢. Storage methods, times, and temperatures for maintaining quality.

YOUR MONEY'S WORTH IN FOODS. 1970. 25pp. 083A. 25¢. Guides for budgeting, menu planning and shopping for best values.

## DIET AND NUTRITION

CALORIES AND WEIGHT. 1970. 76pp. 084A. 30¢. Pocket guide indicates calories per portion of common foods; information on planning weight reduction diets.

FOOD AND YOUR WEIGHT. 1969. 30pp. 089A. 15¢. Suggestions for controlling weight; plans for nutritious weight reduction diets; listing of calories per portion of common foods.

FOOD GUIDE FOR OLDER FOLKS. 1972. 24pp. 090A. 20¢. For persons over 60 years of age; information on meal planning, buying and preparing foods to assure adequate nutrition.

NUTRITIVE VALUE OF FOODS. 1970. 41pp. 092A. 30¢. Nutrient content, including saturated and unsaturated fat content of common foods; recommended dietary allowances.

### DAIRY AND EGGS

CHEESE IN FAMILY MEALS. 1972. 30pp. 093A. 20¢

EGGS IN FAMILY MEALS. 1970. 30pp. 094A. 20¢

MILK IN FAMILY MEALS. 1972. 24pp. 095A. 15¢

### FRUITS AND VEGETABLES

FRUITS IN FAMILY MEALS. 1970. 30pp. 096A. 20¢. Nutritional importance; buying, storing and using; includes recipes.

VEGETABLES IN FAMILY MEALS. 1971. 32pp. 097A. 20¢. Nutritional importance; buying, storing and using; includes recipes.

### MEAT, POULTRY, AND SEAFOOD

HOW TO BUY BEEF ROASTS. 1968. 16pp. 100A. 10¢

HOW TO BUY BEEF STEAKS. 1968. 16pp. 101A. 10¢

HOW TO BUY MEAT FOR YOUR FREEZER. 1969. 28pp. 102A. 20¢

STANDARDS FOR MEAT AND POULTRY PRODUCTS. 1972. 6pp. 104A. Free. Minimum meat and poultry content for approximately 200 food products (e.g., chili con carne, frozen dinners, frankfurters, etc.).

BEEF AND VEAL IN FAMILY MEALS. 1970. 30pp. 105A. 20¢

LAMB IN FAMILY MEALS. 1971. 32pp. 106A. 20¢

POULTRY IN FAMILY MEALS. 1971. 32pp. 20¢

### HEALTH

CANCER: WHAT TO KNOW, WHAT TO DO ABOUT IT. 1969. 8pp. 108A. 10¢

CAUSE OF HEART ATTACKS: HARDENING OF THE ARTERIES. 1972. 16pp. 109A. 25¢

EYE COSMETICS. 1972. 6pp. 110A. Free. Safety tips to avoid bacterial contamination.

NURSING HOME CARE. 1972. 32pp. 113A. 45¢

PLAQUE. 1969. 10pp. 114A. 25¢. Use of dental care products to combat tooth decay and gum diseases.

SICKLE CELL ANEMIA. 1971. 8pp. 115A. 10¢. Causes, symptoms, treatment and prevention through genetic counseling; pointers for the patient and his family.

### CIGARETTES AND ALCOHOL

IF YOU MUST SMOKE—FIVE WAYS TO REDUCE THE RISKS OF SMOKING. 1970. 5pp. 116A. 10¢

ALCOHOL: QUESTIONS AND ANSWERS. 1971. 16pp. 119A. 25¢

### HEARING AIDS

HEARING AIDS. 1971. 36pp. 120A. 60¢. Selection, maintenance and care; causes of hearing loss.

### MEDICINE AND DRUGS

ASPIRIN. 1972. 2pp. 123A. Free. Composition, quality controls and safe use.

FIRST FACTS ABOUT DRUGS. 1972. 16pp. 124A. 25¢. Information on over-the-counter drugs, prescriptions and drugs of abuse.

## HOUSING

BUYING AND FINANCING A MOBILE HOME. 1972. 12pp. 127A. Free.

HOUSE CONSTRUCTION: HOW TO REDUCE COSTS. 1970. 16pp. 134A. 10¢. Guidelines for savings in location, style, interior arrangements, selections of materials and utilities, and construction.

LOW COST WOOD HOMES. 1969. 112pp. 136A. $1.00. Do-it-yourself guide to selection of materials and construction.

MAKING BASEMENTS DRY. 1970. 10pp. 137A. 10¢. Selection of building site; selection and care of materials and dehumidifying equipment.

SELECTING AND FINANCING A HOME. 1970. 24pp. 139A. 15¢. Comprehensive guide; includes whether to buy or rent, budgeting for housing expenses, shopping for a house, and shopping for a mortgage.

WOOD-FRAME HOUSE CONSTRUCTION. 1970. 223pp. 141A. $2.25. Comprehensive guide to selecting materials and constructing wood-frame houses; includes instructions for laying foundations.

## HEATING AND COOLING SYSTEMS

7 WAYS TO REDUCE FUEL CONSUMPTION IN HOUSEHOLD HEATING. 1970. 10pp. 143A. 25¢

11 WAYS TO REDUCE ENERGY CONSUMPTION AND INCREASE COMFORT IN HOUSEHOLD COOLING. 1971. 19pp. 144A. 30¢

## HOME MAINTENANCE AND IMPROVEMENT

PAINT AND PAINTING. 1971. 32pp. 148A. 60¢. For both interior and exterior painting; selection of equipment, paint and finish; preparation of surface and application.

PLANNING YOUR HOME LIGHTING. 1968. 22pp. 150A. 20¢. Requirements for the selection and maintenance of lighting fixtures.

PROTECTING YOUR HOME AGAINST TERMITES. 1972. 2pp. 151A. Free.

PROTECTING YOUR HOME AGAINST THEFTS. 1972. 2pp. 152A. Free.

SIMPLE PLUMBING REPAIRS. 1970. 14pp. 153A. 10¢. Equipment and methods for repairing faucets, valves, leaks in pipes and tanks, frozen pipes, toilets and clogged drains.

## HOME SAFETY

A DESIGN GUIDE FOR HOME SAFETY. 1972. 180pp. 155A. $1.50. Guide to safer home environment; stairs, bathroom, windows, doors, kitchen, floors, electrical design, exteriors, etc.

FIRE EXTINGUISHERS: THE ABC'S AND THE ONE, TWO, THREE'S OF SELECTION. 1971. 16pp. 156A. 40¢

SAFETY OF COOKING UTENSILS. 1971. 2pp. 158A. Free. Safety of Teflon and aluminum cooking utensils.

## LANDSCAPING, GARDENING, AND PEST CONTROL

BETTER LAWNS. 1971. 32pp. 159A. 25¢. Preparations for planting, selection of grasses, planting and care.

CONTROLLING HOUSEHOLD PESTS. 1971. 32pp. 160A. 20¢. Procedures and proper pesticide for controlling rats, cockroaches, termites, clothes moths, carpet beetles, etc.

GROWING FLOWERING PERENNIALS. 1970. 32pp. 161A. 25¢

GROWING GROUND COVERS. 1970. 16pp. 162A. 15¢. Use of low-growing plants, varieties, selection, planting and care.

SAFE-USE OF PESTICIDES. 1972. 6pp. 166A. 10¢

SELECTING AND GROWING HOUSE PLANTS. 1968. 32pp. 167A. 15¢

SELECTING SHRUBS FOR SHADY AREAS. 1970. 16pp. 168A. 15¢

TREES FOR SHADE AND BEAUTY. 1970. 8pp. 170A. 10¢